Josephus, Judaism, and Christianity

JOSEPHUS, JUDAISM, AND CHRISTIANITY

Edited by Louis H. Feldman and Gohei Hata

WAYNE STATE UNIVERSITY PRESS, DETROIT, 1987

Library of Congress Cataloging-in-Publication Data

Josephus, Judaism, and Christianity.

  Includes bibliographies and index.
  1. Josephus, Flavius. 2. Jews—History—168 B.C.–
135 A.D.—Historiography. 3. Judaism—History—
Post-exilic period, 586 B.C.–210 A.D.—Historiography.
4. Bible. O.T.—Criticism, interpretation, etc., Jewish.
I. Feldman, Louis H. II. Hata, Gōhei, 1942–
DS115.9.J6J66 1987   933′.0072024   87-8270
ISBN 0-8143-1831-2
ISBN 0-8143-1832-0 (pbk.)

Louis H. Feldman received his B.A. and M. A. degrees from Trinity College and
his Ph.D. from Harvard University. A professor of classics at Yeshiva University, Dr.
Feldman has also taught at Trinity College and Hobart and William Smith Colleges.
    Gohei Hata received his B.A. at the International Christian University, his M.A. at
Kyoto University, and his Ph.D. at Dropsie University. A professor at Tama Bijutsu
University, he previously taught at Kyoto Sangyo University and the Graduate School
of Kyoto University.

The manuscript was edited by Anne M. G. Adamus. The book was designed by
Joanne E. Kinney. The typeface for the text and the display is Times Roman with
American Uncial used as an additional display face. The book is printed on 60-lb.
Arbor text paper. The cloth edition is bound in Holliston Mills' Roxite vellum over
binder's boards. The paper cover is 12 pt. Carolina C1S.
    Manufactured in the United States of America.

To the memories of Dr. Solomon Zeitlin and Dr. Morton S. Enslin
of Dropsie University

Contents

Contributors

Betsy Halpern Amaru, visiting associate professor of religion at Vassar College, has written several articles on "land theology" in Josephus and Philo and is currently completing a study of the concept of "land" in the Apocryphal and Jewish Pseudepigraphical literature.

James L. Bailey teaches New Testament studies at Wartburg Theological Seminary in Dubuque, Iowa. He has published several articles on various topics connected with the New Testament.

Zvi Baras, a research fellow at the Dinur Center Institute of the Hebrew University in Jerusalem, is the author of *The Twilight of the Byzantine Rule and the Persian Conquest of Palestine* (1982) and is the editor of two volumes in "The World History of the Jewish People" series—*The Herodian Period* (1975) and *Society and Religion in the Second Temple Period* (1977)—as well as of *Eretz Israel, from the Destruction of the Second Temple to the Muslim Conquest* (2 vols., 1982–1985).

Albert A. Bell, Jr. is associate professor of classics and history at Hope College in Holland, Michigan. He has published articles in *Classical World, Jewish Quarterly Review, Latomus, New Testament Studies*, and *Revue Benedictine*, among others.

Otto Betz has served as professor of New Testament studies at Tübingen University in West Germany and at the Chicago Theological Seminary. He is the author of *Offenbarung und Schriftforschung in der Qumransekte* (1960), *Der Paraklet* (1963), *Was wissen wir von Jesus?* (1963), and *Wie verstehen wir das Neue Testament?* (1981).

Steven Bowman, associate professor of Judaic studies at the University of Cincinnati, has written *The Jews of Byzantium, 1204–1453* (1985). He is currently preparing an annotated translation of the *Josippon*.

R. J. Coggins teaches Old Testament studies at Kings College in the University of London. His contributions to Samaritan studies include *Samaritans and Jews* (1975) and "The Samaritans and Acts" in *New Testament Studies* (1982).

Guy N. Deutsch, author of *Iconographie de l'illustration de Flavius Josèphe au temps de Jean Fouquet* (1986), teaches the history of Jewish art at Bar-Ilan University in Israel.

Louis H. Feldman, professor of classics at Yeshiva University, New York, is the editor of Books XVIII to XX of Josephus' *Antiquities* in the Loeb Classical Library (1965) and is the author of an extensive Prolegomenon to the reissue of M. R. James' version of *Pseudo-Philo's Biblical Antiquities* (1971) and of *Josephus and Modern Scholarship* (1984) and *Josephus: A Supplementary Bibliography* (1986).

David Flusser, professor of the history of religions at the Hebrew University, Jerusalem, has written numerous books and articles about Jewish and Christian antiquity. He has published a critical edition of the Hebrew *Josippon* (2 vols., 1978–1980) with a commentary.

David M. Goldenberg is associate professor of rabbinic literature at and president of Dropsie College in Merion, Pennsylvania. His doctoral dissertation was on *The Halakhah in Josephus and in Tannaitic Literature: A Comparative Study* (1978).

Gohei Hata is assistant professor at Tama Bijutsu University and lecturer at Tokyo Union Theological Seminary. He has completed the translation of Josephus into Japanese in sixteen volumes and has edited, together with Dr. Feldman, a four-volume collection of essays in Japanese on Josephus. He is now engaged in translating the Septuagint and the works of Eusebius into Japanese.

David J. Ladouceur is currently chairman of the Department of Modern and Classical Languages at the University of Notre Dame. A classical philologist and historian, he has published a number of studies on Josephus and on the New Testament in such journals as *Classical Philology, Harvard Theological Review,* and *Greek, Roman, and Byzantine Studies.*

Wataru Mizugaki is professor of Christian studies at Kyoto University, Japan. His latest book, in Japanese, is *Problem of Religious Quests in the Early Christian Thought* (1984).

Jacob Neusner, University Professor and Ungerleider Distinguished Scholar of Judaic Studies at Brown University, is the author of *A History of the Jews in Babylonia* (5 vols., 1965–1970), *The Rabbinic Traditions about the Pharisees before 70* (3 vols., 1971), *Eliezer ben Hyrcanus* (2 vols., 1973), *A History of the Mishnaic Law* (43 vols., 1974–1985), *The Tosefta* (6 vols., 1977–1985), *The Talmud of the Land of Israel* (15 vols., 1982–1986), *The Talmud of Babylonia* (6 vols., 1984–1985), *Genesis Rabbah* (3 vols., 1985), *The Foundations of Judaism* (3 vols., 1983–1985), plus numerous other books.

Tessa Rajak, lecturer in classics at the University of Reading, England, is the author of *Josephus: The Historian and His Society* (1983) and is at present writing a book about Jews and Christians in the cities of the Roman Empire.

Lawrence H. Schiffman is professor of Hebrew and Judaic studies at New York University. He has written *The Halakhah at Qumran* (1975), *Sectarian Law in the Dead Sea Scrolls* (1983), and *Who Was a Jew? Rabbinic and Halakhic Perspectives on the Jewish-Christian Schism* (1985).

Heinz Schreckenberg is the author of *Bibliographie zu Flavius Josephus* (1968), its supplement (1979), *Die Flavius-Josephus-Tradition in Antike und Mittelalter* (1972), *Rezeptionsgeschichtliche und textkritische Untersuchungen zu Flavius*

Josephus (1977), and *Die christlichen Adverusus-Judaeos-Texte und ihr literarisches und historisches Umfeld (1.-11. Jh.)* (1982). He belongs to the teaching staff of the University of Münster, West Germany.

E. Mary Smallwood held a chair in Romano-Jewish history at the Queen's University of Belfast until her retirement in 1983. She has edited Philo's *Legatio ad Gaium* (1961) and has written *The Jews under Roman Rule* (1976).

Morton Smith is professor emeritus of ancient history at Columbia University. He has written extensively on both classical and biblical topics; his best-known works on the latter are *Palestinian Parties and Politics that Shaped the Old Testament* (1971), *The Secret Gospel* (1973), and *Jesus the Magician* (1978).

Menahem Stern, professor of Jewish history at the Hebrew University, Jerusalem, is the author and editor of numerous books and articles on Jewish history in the Hellenistic and Roman periods, among them *Greek and Latin Authors on Jews and Judaism* (3 vols., 1974–1984).

Editors' Preface

LOUIS H. FELDMAN

*t*he importance of Josephus may be gauged by a comparison of what we know about the century before the end of the first Jewish insurrection against the Romans with what we know about the century thereafter. The difference is that Josephus has supplied us with a detailed account of the events leading to this war and to the destruction of the Second Temple; we have no such historian for the succeeding events. It is no exaggeration to say, for example, that we have more information about the infamous Herod than any other figure in Greek or Roman antiquity—even Alexander or Julius Caesar.

The significance of Josephus is particularly great in the following areas. (1) Inasmuch as he presents us with a paraphrase of the Bible, he is an important early witness to the biblical text whose paraphrase can be compared not only with the Hebrew and the Septuagint in its various versions but also with the Dead Sea fragments. (2) He represents one of the earliest extant stages in the history of midrashic tradition, in which his work can be compared with not only the later rabbinic Targumim and Midrashim but also with the writings of Philo, the Apocrypha, Pseudepigrapha, Pseudo-Philo's *Biblical Antiquities,* and such a work as the Dead Sea Genesis Apocryphon. (3) He is one of the earliest witnesses to the Jewish Halakhic (legal) tradition, earlier by a century than the rabbinic Mishnah and to be compared with Philo and with such works as the Dead Sea Temple Scroll. (4) He presents by far our fullest account of the momentous change—one may well call it a revolution—in the history of Judaism, including its enormously successful proselytizing activities, which led from its biblical phase to its rabbinic era. (5) His works, along with some Samaritan inscriptions and papyri and the Dead Sea Scrolls, are our fullest account of the development of sectarian movements in Judaism—Samaritanism, the Pharisees, the Sadducees, the Essenes, and the revolutionary Fourth Philosophy. (6) The period he covers in such detail is the era just before and during the emergence of Christianity and hence is crucial for an understanding of the infant years of the new religious group. (7) He is the chief guide for the archaeologist in the process of recreating the economic, social, political, and cultural life of Judea, particularly for the two centuries before the destruction of the Second Temple. (8) He occupies an important place in the history of Greek and Roman historiography, a link in the joining of the Isocratean and Aristotelian schools. (9) He is an important source for much of Greek, Roman, and Parthian political and military history (for example, he gives us a far fuller account of the assassination of the Emperor Caligula and the accession of Claudius than any other writer. (10) He is by far our most important source for the relations between Jews and non-Jews, including, in particular, the phenomenon of anti-Semitism, during the Hellenistic and Roman periods. (11) As the author of the first extant autobiography from antiquity, he is important for establishing the canons of this genre, which was to culminate in Augustine's *Confessions*. (12) He is an important source for Greek vocabulary and grammar of the Hellenistic period and sheds great light in both areas on an understanding of the writings of the period, notably those of Philo, the New Testament, and papyri.

In view of all this, it is not surprising that during the Middle Ages Josephus was regarded as an authority in such diverse fields as biblical exegesis, chronology, arithmetic (the so-called Josephus-spiel was a popular problem in arithmetic), astronomy, natural history, grammar, etymology, and Jewish theology; and, of course, through the *Testimonium Flavianum,* he was considered the most crucial non-Christian witness to the life, crucifixion, and resurrection of Jesus. Moreover, Josephus was the chief guide to the sites of the Holy Land for pilgrims and Crusaders; his works were even permitted to be read during Lent at the monastery of Cluny. In the period that followed, from 1450 to 1700, there were more editions printed of Josephus' *Antiquities* and *Jewish War* than of any other Greek work. Because of his data on the background of the birth of Christianity, he also played a key role in the controversies of the Reformation.

In more recent times, the translation of Josephus into English by Whiston in 1737 has been reprinted or reedited 217 times and in this version has very often occupied a place on the shelves of English-speaking persons between the Jewish Scriptures and the New Testament, since he spans particularly that period. Indeed, among strict English Protestants only the Bible and Josephus were permitted to be read on Sundays. In fact, the earliest book by a Jewish author (other than the Bible) printed in America was L'Estrange's translation of the *Jewish War* in 1719, and the second book of Jewish authorship to be issued in America was Morvvyn's translation of *Josippon,* the Hebrew paraphrase of the *Jewish War.*

Very great progress has been made in the study of Josephus during the past century: (1) the scientific establishment of his Greek text (which is often, particularly in the *Antiquities,* in poor condition) independently by Niese and by Naber, and more recent studies of the transmission of Josephus' text by Schreckenberg; (2) the establishment of definitive texts of the Slavonic version and of the Hebrew paraphrase (*Josippon*) of the *War;* (3) important studies of Josephus' biblical text by Mez, Thackeray, Rahlfs, and most recently by Ulrich (the last in view of important fragments of the Book of Samuel found in the Dead Sea caves); (4) studies of Josephus' modifications of the biblical narrative, especially as compared with Greek models and with rabbinic midrashim; (5) important studies, especially the most recent by Goldenberg, of Josephus' place in the history of the Jewish legal tradition; (6) the publication by Pines of an Arabic version of the *Testimonium Flavianum,* which sheds considerable light on the original version; (7) the findings by archaeology, notably in Jerusalem and at Masada, enabling us to check on the validity of Josephus' descriptions; (8) the completion of a concordance-lexicon to Josephus by Rengstorf and his colleagues; and (9) the compilation of annotated bibliographies to Josephus by Schreckenberg and myself.

The present collection of essays, all of them written expressly for this work, is an attempt to survey critically for the intelligent reader the present state of scholarship on the various topics where research on Josephus has been pursued—Josephus as a biblical interpreter; Josephus as a guide to Jewish religious beliefs, practices, and movements; his sources; his place in the history of historiography; his validity as historian of the Jewish War; his relation to archaeological discoveries; and his influence in the Middle Ages, in the Renaissance, and in the Reformation period. It differs from previous collections in that the topics were selected not by the contributors but by the editors, who are also responsible for the choice of authors, in order to achieve balanced and comprehensive coverage of various representative areas of research in Josephus. This book's companion volume, *Josephus, the Bible, and History,* containing fourteen essays and a lengthy critical bibliography of Josephus, continues the presentation of quality scholarship begun in this volume.

That the idea of these collections, published simultaneously in Japanese and in English, should have been conceived in Japan is truly a tribute to the tremendous surge of interest in that country in Judaism and in the origins of Christianity. It may now be confidently expected that, with the completion of the annotated translation of Josephus into Japanese by Gohei Hata, this interest will have still further impetus. The hope may here also be expressed that this work will contribute to the cooperation of Jewish and non-Jewish scholars in the study of Judaism during the period of the Second Temple and of its relationship to the birth of Christianity.

GOHEI HATA

*t*he book meets an unforeseeable destiny the moment it leaves the hands of the author. This is true of the books in our own times, but it was also true of the books in ancient times. Some books met with an even more favorable reception from readers than the authors had hoped for, and, as a result, the books were copied, paraphrased, and even translated into another language at an early time. On the other hand, some books were treated coldly by their expected readers and the relays of transcription soon stopped; when this happened, the books were immediately thrown into oblivion. How many books were lost in this way!

The works of Flavius Josephus, the Jewish historian of the first century A.D., can be said to have met a predictable destiny if their place is to be examined in Christian history. Although the works of Josephus were hesitantly read in the beginning by the Christian church because the author was a Jew, the Christians in time came to accept them gladly and even with enthusiasm because as they scrutinized them they found Josephus referring to Jesus (Christ), John the Baptist, James, "the brother of the Lord," the court of Herod, three religious sects (the Pharisees, Sadducees, and Essenes), the fall of Jerusalem, and the loss of the Temple in A.D. 70, which they firmly believed Jesus had predicted, and other information necessary to understand their own sacred text, the New Testament. As to the diffusion of the works of Josephus in ancient Christendom, Dr. Heinz Schreckenberg has rightly pointed out that Church officials placed the *Jewish War,* the first work of Josephus (written between A.D. 75 and 79), next to the *Jewish Antiquities* (written between A.D. 92 and 94) because they wanted their fellow Christians to conclude that the history of the Jewish people resulted in catastrophe in A.D. 70 as a result of their adamant refusal to accept Jesus as Christ. What Dr. Schreckenberg has pointed out is very important because this intentional steering of readers to a biased Christian interpretation was not rectified and is still accepted. For example, the work of William Whiston, one of the modern translations of Josephus that is still widely read even today (217 editions have been printed, according to Dr. Louis H. Feldman), follows the traditional arrangement of the four works of Josephus. Accordingly, in Whiston's edition, readers encounter *Life* first, then go on to the *Jewish Antiquities,* the *Jewish War,* and finally *Against Apion.* That this arrangement is very favorable to a Christian purpose can be seen from the fact that the last volume of the *Jewish Antiquities*, which contains the references to Jesus and John the Baptist in Book XVIII and the reference to James, the brother of Jesus, in Book XX, ends just before the outbreak of the Jewish War against the Romans in A.D. 66. In this way, readers can smoothly (or naturally) move onto the *Jewish War*. Thus, when they have read through the *Conquest of Jerusalem* (*Halosis*, one of the Greek titles applied to the *Jewish War*) with some preoccupation, they are easily led to think that because the Jewish people did not accept (=sin) Jesus as Christ, they lost both Jerusalem and the Temple (punishment). The fact that Josephus sometimes interpreted the fall of Jerusalem and the loss of the Temple theologically (see, for example, *BJ* V, 378–401, VI, 267–270) can also induce Christian readers to interpret the results of the Jewish War using their own theological perspective. This kind of Christian interpretation would not have been anticipated by Josephus. Josephus interpreted the fall of Jerusalem and the loss of the Temple theologically not because the Jewish people did not accept Jesus as Christ but because, in his opinion, those who instigated the war against the Romans were not faithful to the Law and thus unworthy of *eleutheria* (freedom).

In reading the works of Josephus we should be free from the traditional Christian interpretation and try to understand what Josephus really wanted to say or assert for his own people and for himself while he was leading a precarious life in the court of the Roman emperors. I do wish and believe that this collection of essays, which originated in Japan to commemorate the completion of the publication of the Japanese translation of the works of Josephus in sixteen volumes (1975–1984), will be helpful to the proper understanding of the works of Josephus, some of the most important and influential classics of the world.

Abbreviations

A	*Antiquitates Judaicae*
AHR	*American Historical Review*
AIPHOS	*Annuaire de l'Institut de Philologie et d'Histoire Orientales et Slaves* (Université libre de Bruxelles)
AJP	*American Journal of Philology*
AJSR	*Association for Jewish Studies Review*
ALL	*Archiv für lateinische Lexikographie*
ANET	*Ancient Near Eastern Texts,* 3rd ed., edited by James B. Pritchard (Princeton, 1969)
ANRW	*Aufstieg und Niedergang der römischen Welt*
AOAW	*Anzeiger der Oesterreichischen Akademie der Wissenschaften*
Ap	*Contra Apionem*
Arndt-Gingrich	W. F. Arndt, F. Wilbur Gingrich, W. Bauer, *A Greek-English Lexicon of the New Testament* (Cambridge, 1957)
⁼Arukh	*Sefer ⁼Arukh ha-Shalem,* by Nathan ben Jehiel of Rome, edited by Hanokh Jehudah (Alexander) Kohut, 8 vols. (Vienna, 1876–1892); *Musaf He-⁼Arukh* by Samuel Krauss (Vienna, 1937).
ARW	*Archiv für Religionswissenschaft*
ASTI	*Annual of the Swedish Theological Institute*
B.	Babylonian Talmud
BA	*Biblical Archaeologist*
BF	*Byzantinische Forschungen*
BICS	*Bulletin of the Institute of Classical Studies* (University of London)
BJ	*Bellum Judaicum*
BJRL	*Bulletin of the John Rylands Library*
BK	*Bibel und Kirche*
BO	*Bibliotheca Orïentalis*
BSEB	*Byzantine Studies/Etudes Byzantines*

BT	Babylonian Talmud
BTB	*Biblical Theology Bulletin*
CChr	*Corpus Christianorum*
CCL	*Corpus Christianorum Latinorum*
CFHB	*Corpus Fontium Historiae Byzantinae*
CO	*Classical Outlook*
CP	*Classical Philology*
CPJ	*Corpus Papyrorum Judaicarum,* edited by Victor Tcherikover, Alexander Fuks, and Menahem Stern, 3 vols. (Cambridge, Mass., 1957–1964)
CQ	*Classical Quarterly*
CS	*Cultura e Scuola*
CSEL	*Corpus Scriptorum Ecclesiasticorum Latinorum*
CSHB	*Corpus Scriptorum Historiae Byzantinae*
DOP	*Dumbarton Oaks Papers*
DTT	*Dansk Teologisk Tidsskrift*
EI	*Eretz Israel*
EJ	*Encyclopaedia Judaica,* 16 vols. (Jerusalem, 1971)
E & V	*Esprit et Vie*
FGrHist	*Die Fragmente der Griechischen Historiker,* edited by Felix Jacoby (Berlin and Leiden, 1923–1958)
GCS	*Die Griechischen Christlichen Schriftsteller der ersten drei Jahrhunderte*
GLAJJ	*Greek and Latin Authors on Jews and Judaism,* by Menahem Stern, 3 vols., (Jerusalem, 1974–1984)
GRBS	*Greek, Roman, and Byzantine Studies*
HR	*History of Religions*
H & T	*History and Theory*
HThR	*Harvard Theological Review*
HUCA	*Hebrew Union College Annual*
IDIBW	*Informationsdienst des deutschen Instituts für Bildung und Wissen* (Paderborn)
ISSQ	*Indiana Social Studies Quarterly*
JAOS	*Journal of the American Oriental Society*
JBL	*Journal of Biblical Literature*
JC	*Jerusalem Cathedra*
JE	*Jewish Encyclopedia,* 12 vols. (New York, 1901–1905)
JHI	*Journal of the History of Ideas*
JJA	*Journal of Jewish Art*
JJGL	*Jahrbücher für jüdische Geschichte und Literatur*
JJS	*Journal of Jewish Studies*
JNES	*Journal of Near Eastern Studies*
JQR	*Jewish Quarterly Review*
JRS	*Journal of Roman Studies*

J-S	*Josephus-Studien: Untersuchungen zu Josephus, dem antiken Judentum und dem Neuen Testament, Otto Michel zum 70. Geburtstag gewidmet,* edited by Otto Betz, Klaus Haacker, and Martin Hengel (Göttingen, 1974)
JSHRZ	*Jüdische Schriften aus hellenistisch-römischer Zeit*
JSJ	*Journal for the Study of Judaism*
JSNT	*Journal for the Study of the New Testament*
JSp	*Jewish Spectator*
JSS	*Jewish Social Studies*
JTS	*Journal of Theological Studies*
JWI	*Journal of the Warburg Institute*
Levy	Jacob Levy, *Neuhebräisches und chaldäisches Wörterbuch über die Talmudim,* 4 vols. (Leipzig, 1876–1889)
Lewis-Short	Charlton T. Lewis and Charles Short, *A Latin Dictionary* (Oxford, 1879, revised 1962)
Liddell-Scott	Henry G. Liddell and Robert Scott, *A Greek-English Lexicon,* 9th ed. (Oxford, 1940)
M.	Mishnah
MGWJ	*Monatsschrift für Geschichte und Wissenschaft des Judentums*
MS	*Medieval Studies*
NT	*Novum Testamentum*
NTS	*New Testament Studies*
PAAJR	*Proceedings of the American Academy for Jewish Research*
PEQ	*Palestine Exploration Quarterly*
PG	*Patrologia Graeca,* edited by Jacques Paul Migne, 165 vols. (Paris, 1857–1866)
PIASH	*Proceedings of the Israel Academy of Sciences and Humanities*
PL	*Patrologia Latina,* edited by Jacques Paul Migne, 221 vols. (Paris, 1844–1855)
PRIA	*Proceedings of the Royal Irish Academy*
P.T.	Palestinian (Jerusalem) Talmud
RB	*Revue Biblique*
RBén	*Revue Bénédictine*
RBPH	*Revue Belge de Philologie et d'Histoire*
RE	*Realencylopädie der klassischen Altertumswissenschaft,* edited by August Pauly and Georg Wissowa (Stuttgart, 1893–)
REG	*Revue des Études Grecques*
RGVV	*Religionsgeschichtliche Versuche und Vorarbeiten*
RhM	*Rheinisches Museum*
RiBi	*Rivista Biblica*
RIL	*Rendiconti dell' Istituto Lombardo, Classe di Lettere, Scienze morali e storiche*
RPARA	*Rendiconti della Pontificia Accademia romana di Archeologia*
RQ	*Revue de Qumran*

RSA	*Rivista storica dell' antichità*
RSC	*Rivista di Studi Classici*
RSI	*Rivista storica italiana*
SBLSP	*Society of Biblical Literature Seminar Papers*
SH	*Scripta Hierosolymitana*
SHR	*Studies in the History of Religions*
SIFC	*Studi Italiani di Filologia Classica*
SJLA	*Studies in Judaism in Late Antiquity*
SK	*Skrif en Kerk* (Pretoria)
T.	Tosefta
TAPA	*Transactions of the American Philological Association*
TDNT	*Theological Dictionary of the New Testament,* edited by Gerhard Kittel and Gerhard Friedrich, translated by Geoffrey W. Bromiley, 9 vols. (Grand Rapids, 1964–1974)
V	*Vita*
VC	*Vigiliae Christianae*
VT	*Vetus Testamentum*

Introduction

LOUIS H. FELDMAN

t he study of Josephus has made particular progress in two areas, which this collection of essays attempts to explore: what is the reliability of Josephus as a historian, and what is the secret of his tremendous influence, notably on the church fathers and on the writers of the Middle Ages, the Renaissance, and the Reformation?

As to the first, a number of questions are here addressed: does Josephus' reliability depend on how far removed he is from personal involvement? How precise is he in his terminology? Inasmuch as his works were composed over a period of perhaps thirty years, did he improve with time and experience? Does his reliability depend on that of his sources? How does his credibility compare with that of Philo, the other great Jewish writer of the period? How can we test him when most of his sources, most notably what is generally considered to be his chief source, the works of Nicolaus of Damascus, exist only in fragments? To what degree is he acquainted with rabbinic legal and homiletic discussions, and how can we explain his selectivity and modifications in his use of them? Can we discover his sources when he does not name them? To what degree does he contradict himself in the earlier *Jewish War* and the later *Antiquities,* especially when they cover the same ground, as they do for the period from Antiochus Epiphanes to the outbreak of the war against the Romans, and particularly in the attitude toward the Samaritans and the Pharisees? Is there a consistent pattern in the modifications he makes in his reworking of the biblical narrative? Why is his history so uneven, including extraordinarily detailed discussions of certain personalities and events (notably the reign of Herod), as well as numerous, often extensive, digressions, for example, the suicide at Masada (which militarily was of little importance), the summary of Jewish law, and the conversion of the royal family of Adiabene? To what degree are the speeches put into the mouths of his characters valid, and to what degree are they mere rhetorical exercises? To what degree does he consciously attempt to downgrade theological and miraculous elements? To what audiences were his works directed? How fair is he in his treatment of his opponents, whether individuals, such as Justus of Tiberias, or groups, such as the Samaritans? To what degree is he prejudiced because of the pension and many other gifts that he had received from the Romans? To what degree does misogyny influence his judgments? To what extent do apologetic motifs influence his portrayal of events, particularly in his paraphrase of the Bible? How far has he been influenced by motifs from Homer, Herodotus, Greek tragedy, and novels, with which he was apparently so well acquainted, in his version of history? To what degree does Josephus in his treatment in general reflect the events of the era in which he writes? Does he unduly emphasize political and military events, to the neglect of economic, religious, and cultural factors? To what degree has Josephus put his own personal imprint upon his treatment of events? To what extent has archaeology confirmed or refuted him?

As to the second area, is Josephus' influence due primarily to the passage about Jesus, the *Testimonium Flavianum,* the authenticity of which has been so much debated? Why has he survived in his entirety, whereas the works of his great rival, Justus of Tiberias, have utterly, or almost utterly, perished? How can we explain the fluctuations in Josephus' influence through the ages? What role did his works, particularly the *Jewish War,* as interpreted by the church, with its view that the destruction of the Temple was divine punishment for the crime of deicide, play in anti-Semitism? Why is Book VI of the *Jewish War* referred to so often and Book VII so seldom? To what degree was Josephus' moralistic philosophy of history directly influential? How can we explain his negligible influence upon Jewish writers and thinkers until the nineteenth century? Why was he not only merely translated but also very freely paraphrased, and why were these paraphrases so influential?

Professor Menahem Stern, in his essay on Josephus and the Roman Empire, raises the question of Josephus' reliability in his *Jewish War,* and notes that, despite the fact that Josephus does not mention, in his introduction, his use of Vespasian's and Titus' commentaries, he must have used them. We may comment that in antiquity it was very often true that an author would name the sources that he should have used, while omitting those he actually did employ. In view of the fact that Josephus was living in Vespasian's palace while he was writing the work and presumably had access to the Roman archives, it would appear likely that he used the notes of their campaigns in Judea.

As to Josephus' reliability in his account of the burning of the Temple, we may add that Josephus himself in the *Jewish War* VII, 1, states that Titus ordered the whole city of Jerusalem and the Temple to be razed. Likewise, in a remark (*A* XX, 250) made *en passant* (and, therefore, of greater value), he speaks of the day on which Titus captured and set fire to the Temple. We may note, moreover, that Valerius Flaccus, a contemporary of Josephus, contradicts Josephus' view that Titus opposed the burning of the Temple, since he speaks in his proem of Titus hurling brands and spreading havoc in every tower.

If, indeed, Josephus was so prejudiced in favor of the Romans we may wonder at Professor Stern's finding that there is only a single allusion in the *Jewish War* to the view that the Jews had benefited from Roman rule. This is especially remarkable, we may add, since there are a number of comments in the Talmud, some of them presumably reflecting an earlier era, praising Roman justice. Thus, for example, Resh Lakish (*Genesis Rabbah* 9.13) applied the verse (Gen. 1:31) "And behold it was very good" to the Roman Empire because "it exacts justice [the passage uses the Greek word *dikē*] for men." The rabbis are likewise impressed (*Leviticus Rabbah* 35.5) with the security which the empire had brought its inhabitants against robbers and notes (e.g. *Tanḥuma* B, *Yitro* 3, *Teẓe* 5) the benefits bestowed by emperors in distributing food during the frequent shortages of grain and the aid which they gave in rehabilitating desolated cities (*Midrash on Psalms* 90.7). We may further note that the rabbis' comments in appreciation of the benefits of the *Pax Romana* find parallels in the writings of a number of contemporary pagan provincials, notably Aelius Aristides, Plutarch, Dio Chrysostom, Pausanias, Lucian, Dio Cassius, and Menander of Laodicea, as well as in the works of such Christian writers as Athenagoras, Irenaeus, Theophilus, Tertullian, Hippolytus, Origen, Gregory Thaumaturgus of Neocaesarea, Eusebius, Ambrose, and Augustine. Why, then, is Josephus silent about the benefits of Roman rule? We may guess that he realized that such an appreciation would have alienated the masses even further from him and would have led to the accusation that he was an assimilationist (an accusation that could not be made against those rabbis who favored a rapprochement with the Romans); hence he preferred a more pragmatic tack and thus stressed the Roman invincibility in war. If, in the *Antiquities,* Josephus cites frequent instances of Roman benefactions toward the Jews, this may be because, in view of the lapse of so many years after the conclusion of the war, he could afford to display a pro-Roman stance, especially since, at almost the same time that he was issuing the *Antiquities,* Joshua ben Ḥananiah, the greatest sage of the time, stressed, in his fable of the lion and the crane, the importance of accepting the Roman yoke without complaint.

Josephus' reliability is again central in Dr. Tessa Rajak's discussion of his relation to Justus of Tiberias' work. Scholars generally assume, as does Dr. Rajak, that Josephus cannot be trusted when he charges (*V* 359) that Justus had delayed the publication of his work until after the deaths of Vespasian,

Titus, and Agrippa, so that they would not be able to challenge his accuracy. In the search for alternative explanations she suggests that the delay may perhaps be explained by the sheer strength and painstaking nature of Justus' work. We may here note Josephus' grudging reference (*V* 338) to Justus' eagerness to obtain a reputation as being a lover of toil (φιλόπονος). Or we may suggest that Justus was too busy as court secretary to Agrippa II to complete the work, though we may remark that Nicolaus of Damascus, despite the fact that he served a far more powerful and demanding king, Herod, managed to find time to compose a history of 144 books, the longest historical work known to us from antiquity. Alternatively we may suggest that Justus, as a moderate, may have aimed to avoid aggravating tensions that remained after the war through seeking a "cooling-off period" before presenting his appraisal

We may also wonder whether part of the animosity that Josephus felt toward Justus was due to his jealousy in that Justus, like himself, had written a work of Jewish history covering much of the same period that he had dealt with in his *Antiquities,* namely from the time of Moses to the death of Agrippa II. Indeed, to judge from a fragment (quoted by Diogenes Laertius, II, 41) in which Justus tells how Plato ascended the platform while Socrates was being tried, Justus' work may have included more than merely Jewish history and may, in truth, have been somewhat like the comprehensive world history of Nicolaus of Damascus. The fact that, despite the large number of histories of the war (*BJ* I, 1), Josephus sees fit to mention only Justus by name would seem to indicate that he was, indeed, a formidable rival.

As to why Justus' work has not survived, the usual answer is that it did not because it did not contain a notice of Jesus; but, if so, we may ask why an interpolator did not insert such a passage, just as he did, according to most scholars, into Josephus' work; and presumably there would have been an occasion for doing so, inasmuch as Justus' extensive history apparently included the period of the procurators, covering the period from Moses to the death of Agrippa II. The real reason may be simply that the scribes who made such decisions decided that Josephus' work was more comprehensive, more exciting, and more readable.

The irony of it all, as Dr. Rajak notes, is that Josephus and Justus seem so similar in their ability to write literary Greek and in their ambivalent attitudes toward the Romans and even in their charges against each other. In this respect there is also a resemblance between two ostensible opponents, Josephus and John of Gischala. We may, however, suggest that the fact that Justus fell out of favor with Agrippa II on several occasions, even being twice imprisoned, is a major difference between him and Josephus, who always managed to find a modus vivendi with every ruler, even the ever-suspicious Domitian.

A litmus paper test of the reliability of Josephus is to be seen in his handling of the Masada episode, since here we have the extremely thorough excavations by Yigael Yadin at Masada. We may, however, note that while, on the whole, Josephus' account is confirmed by the archaeological findings, there are a number of discrepancies. Professor David Ladouceur, in his essay "Josephus and Masada," is concerned with the question of why Josephus included it in his history—and, we may add, in such detail, especially when we consider that the capture of Masada was militarily of minor importance.

Though memories were cultivated in antiquity and though the acoustics in the underground cistern where the Romans' informant hid were excellent, the twin speeches put into the mouth of Eleazar ben Jair can hardly be historical and must have been penned in Josephus' scriptorium in Rome. We may remark that these speeches are reminiscent of those put into the mouths of Josephus' biblical characters in the first half of the *Antiquities*. Aside from the fact that there are at least five echoes from Plato's *Phaedo* in Eleazar's speeches, the extended parallel drawn with the Indians (*BJ* VII, 351–357) who pursue philosophy (σοφίαν) is a commonplace and could hardly have been spoken by a Jewish religious fanatic who almost surely had nothing but disdain for philosophy and for secular pursuits generally, as we see, for example, in Josephus' remark (*A* XX, 264) that pious Jews look down upon those who have mastered foreign languages or who cultivate refined diction. To speak of the Indians with such praise when they practice cremation (*BJ* VII, 355) seems highly unlikely. The two speeches, we may add, have an antiphonal rhetorical relationship to each other, with the second repeating motifs from the first but with additional rhetorical elements taken from Hellenistic diatribe. We may add that the fact, noted by Lindner,[1] that the three great speeches in the *War*, those of Agrippa II (II, 345–404), Josephus (V, 362–419), and Eleazar (VII, 323–388), all stress the same theme, that Roman rule exhibits God's judgment in a deterministic and apocalyptic sense, shows that they all bear the imprint of Josephus' own thinking. Moreover, the extended description of the suicide follows a pattern adopted elsewhere in Greek literature (Polybius), as well as in Josephus.

When we view Josephus against the backdrop of the period (the 70s) in which he wrote the *War*, we may see in Eleazar's speeches echoes of the sentiments being expressed at that time in Rome by fanatical opponents of the Flavian regime who looked upon Socrates as the model par excellence of the martyr and of the de facto suicide. That Josephus perceived contemporary implications in his review of past events can be seen also, we may add, in his autobiographically inspired portraits of Abraham, Joseph, Saul, and Mordecai, for example.

One of the problems in connection with the Masada episode is how to explain Josephus' apparent praise by the Romans of the "amazing fortitude"

(*BJ* VII, 405) of the defendants, the Sicarii, as well as "the nobility of their resolve and their contempt of death" (*BJ* VII, 406), whereas earlier in the same work (VII, 262) he condemns them in the blackest terms, remarking that they "were to set the example of this lawlessness and cruelty to their kinsmen, leaving no word unspoken to insult, no deed untried to ruin." It is Ladouceur's contention that the word (τόλμημα), which Thackeray in his Loeb translation renders "fortitude," actually means "boldness" or "audacity" and never elsewhere is used in the *War* with a positive connotation. We may comment that the word (γενναιότης) translated by Thackeray as "nobility" is in every other instance in Josephus (*A* XVII, 333; XIX, 122, 212, 251) a reference literally to noble birth. The positive, figurative meaning of "nobility" is nowhere to be found in Josephus; and, indeed, the corresponding adjective, γενναῖος, elsewhere in Greek literature often means "genuine," "intense," and even (in the description of an earthquake) has the negative meaning of "violent." Others[2] have asked why the Sicarii did not fight to the last man, as brave guerrillas do. The answer, we may reply, is that they were not brave guerrillas but rather fanatics who, as Professor Ladouceur contends, turned their destructive impulses against themselves rather than against the enemy. We may add that the Talmud's silence about the whole remarkable incident at Masada would seem to reinforce the view that the rabbis regarded it as ignominious rather than heroic.

As to the suicide itself, those who have cast doubt upon Josephus' narrative on the ground that the taking of one's life is a serious breach of Jewish law forget that the Sicarii at Masada were members of a deviant sect, and fanatics at that. Moreover, the fact that they conducted a raid at Engaddi (*BJ* IV, 402) on Passover would indicate that they had a different calendar (as did the Dead Sea Sect) and that their standard of law deviated from that of the Pharisaic rabbis. If, indeed, we may add, it were Josephus' purpose to build up the reputation of the Roman general at Masada, Flavius Silva, as a member of the family into which he had been adopted, he would have done better to have the Sicarii fight fiercely until the last man.

Cohen[3] rejects the idea that Josephus, in his account of Masada, was referring to the Cynic opposition to the Flavian regime and claims that there was no prominent Cynic philosopher at the time that Josephus wrote the *War*. Aside from the fact, noted by Professor Ladouceur, that Demetrius the Cynic was active precisely during this period, we may note the important conclusion of Morton and Michaelson[4] that the style of Book VII of the *War* differs significantly from that of the other books of the *War;* and, as Seth Schwartz[5] has most recently pointed out, there is good reason to believe that it (or parts of it) were composed as late as the reigns of Nerva and Trajan.

One of the few authors who at all parallels Josephus at any length and, hence, can be used as a check upon him is Philo. Professor E. Mary Smallwood, in her essay, "Philo and Josephus as Historians of the Same Events," concludes that Philo has greater historical credibility despite the fact that he is a philosopher and a theologian rather than a historian. We may suggest that Josephus' central focus is, after all, the land of Israel, though, we may note, he accompanied Vespasian to Alexandria (*V* 415) in 69, married a woman from that city, and remained there until the year 70, when he accompanied Titus to the siege of Jerusalem. During the period that he was in Alexandria he may well have gathered information about the Jewish community and its history; and, we may suggest, because of Josephus' close relationship with Titus, he may also have gathered information from Tiberius Julius Alexander, the nephew of Philo, who was a native of Alexandria, who had been appointed governor of Egypt in 66, and who was, indeed, second in command in Titus' army in Judea in 69 or 70. We may also suggest that Josephus not only mentions Philo (*A* XVIII, 259–260) as a philosopher and as the head of a delegation of Alexandrian Jews to the Emperor Gaius Caligula but also may have used him as a source for the early books of the *Antiquities,* especially in his allegorical interpretation of the Temple (*A* III, 181ff.) and in his summary of Jewish law in the treatise against Apion (II, 190–219), which bears (especially *Ap* II, 213) striking resemblances to Philo's *Hypothetica.*

One episode mentioned by Professor Smallwood that may give us a clue as to the relative reliability of the two authors is the one that describes Pilate's introduction of the emperor's standards into Jerusalem. Here, we may note, the differences are great: the episode of the standards, as described by Josephus (*BJ* II, 169–174; *A* XVIII, 55–59), occurred at the beginning of Pilate's administration, whereas the introduction of the shields, as delineated by Philo (*Legatio ad Gaium* 299–305), took place much later. Moreover, the standards bore images, while the shields did not. Finally, in Josephus the people appeal successfully to Pilate at Caesarea, whereas in Philo they appeal unsuccessfully to Pilate, apparently in Jerusalem. Daniel Schwartz[6] has argued that the descriptions represent a single event and that the discrepancies may be explained by the apologetic bias of Philo (or of Agrippa I, the hero of the episode), and that the account of Josephus is simpler and more convincing. We may comment that because Josephus, a native of Jerusalem, is describing an event in the land of Israel we would expect him to be more reliable than one who lived in Alexandria; but because Philo is describing an event that occurred during his own lifetime we would expect him to be more trustworthy than Josephus, who was not born until several years after the event. We may conclude that perhaps both are right, and that separate events are being described. If we ask how this is possible for two accounts which, after all, are very similar, we may suggest a parallel in the case of the edict of Claudius (*A* XIX, 280–281) and his letter in a papyrus (London Papyrus 1912) with regard to the rights of Jews in Alexandria, the latter of which Josephus neglects to mention but which does appear, to judge from details of language, to be a separate document. In both reports of our incident we have only the Jewish side of the story, but we may guess that Josephus, who is more often pro-Roman than pro-Jewish, would have tried to present the Roman case as favorably as possible, especially since he is, on the whole, well disposed toward the emperor Tiberius (*A* XVIII, 169–179), in whose reign the event occurred.

As to the plan of Emperor Gaius Caligula to introduce a statue of himself into the Temple, Philo, it would seem, is a more reliable source, particularly, we may suggest, since he could hardly have argued against it to the emperor unless he was fully acquainted with the details of the proposal. Josephus' account is particularly suspect because it highlights to such an extent the role of Agrippa I, who is also the hero in Josephus' unusually long excursus on the assassination of Caligula and the accession of Claudius (*A* XIX, 1–273). We may note that, remarkably, Josephus' parallel account in the *War* does not mention Agrippa at all, and that only the *Antiquities* does so. We may also express skepticism about Josephus' account, since he does not mention that the Jews took up arms, whereas Tacitus (*Histories* V, 9. 2) says specifically that they did.

In my essay on "Hellenization in Josephus' *Jewish Antiquities:* The Portrait of Abraham," I likewise raise the issue of the reliability of Josephus as seen in his reworking of the biblical narrative. Here, we may remark, Josephus had ample precedent for his additions and modifications, namely the Septuagint, which Josephus himself (*A* I, 10–12) regards as a forerunner of his work. Inasmuch as Josephus knew the Hebrew original of the Pentateuch well, he must have been aware of the fact that the translators had taken liberties, often of a very considerable nature; and yet, he clearly looks with favor upon the translation, as, incidentally, did the rabbis, who regarded the changes as having been instituted miraculously by all the translators, though they were in separate cubicles (*Megillah* 9a).

Are the changes introduced by Josephus haphazard? I have argued that there is an internal consistency and that one can see the same pattern in his treatment of such biblical figures as Abraham, Moses, Joseph, Saul, David, and Solomon. All represent the Hellenistic (especially Stoic) ideal of the sage; and Josephus is eager to show his audience, which consisted predominantly of non-Jews, as we can see from his apologetic nature, that Jews are in no way inferior to the philosophers and wise men produced by the pagans. If we compare Josephus' portrait of Abraham or, for that matter, of any of the other major biblical figures mentioned above, we shall see striking parallels with Plato's portrayal of the philosopher-king, with the traditional portrayal of the Stoic sage, and with the depiction of Thucydides' ideal statesman, Pericles. The recitation of Abraham's virtues, we may add, is a veritable aretalogy, such as was popular in Hellenistic times. Inasmuch as Stoicism was the favorite philosophy, at least among intellectuals, at the time when Josephus wrote his *Antiquities* in Rome, it is not surprising that he presents, for example, a proof for the existence of God that is couched in Stoic terminology. In view of the negative attitude of the rabbis toward Greek wisdom (*Baba Kamma* 82b, *Menaḥoth* 64b, *Sotah* 49b), Josephus is here seeking to accommodate Greek and Jewish wisdom, clearly departing from the tradition in which he had been trained.

We may here add that the very fact that Josephus centers his narrative around great heroes would defend the Jews against the charge (*Ap* II, 135) that they had failed to produce outstandingly wise men. Here Josephus follows the Peripatetic tradition (exemplified, incidentally, by Nicolaus of Damascus, his major source for much of the second half of the *Antiquities*), which presented history as the biography of great men. This is, moreover, in line with his downgrading of the role of God in directing human action. We may note a similar tendency to build up biblical heroes, notably Moses, in such Hellenistic Jewish writers as Aristeas (in his *Letter*), Artapanus, Ezekiel the tragedian, Philo the Elder, and Philo the philosopher.

In his portrayal of Abraham, as in his portraits of others, Josephus, no less than in his essay *Against Apion,* is seeking to refute the virulent anti-Semitism of his day. We may here note that among those living in Rome at the very time that Josephus was writing were such vicious anti-Semites as Quintilian, Martial, Tacitus, and Juvenal. Tacitus (*Histories* V, 1), for example, remarks that while the Jews are extremely loyal to one another and are always ready to show compassion to their compatriots, they feel only hate and enmity toward all other peoples. Hence, it is not surprising that Josephus adds to the biblical narrative by having Abraham show pity even for the wicked Sodomites.

Similarly, we may remark, after the advances in scientific geography that had been made in the Hellenistic period by such a giant as Eratosthenes and in view of the knowledge of descriptive geography manifested in the works of such historians as Polybius and Strabo, Josephus appeals to the interest in geography on the part of his readers. Thus, he expands very considerably (*A* I, 122–147) the biblical account of the table of nations descended from Noah's sons (Gen. 10), as well as from Abraham's sons by Keturah (*A* I, 238–241) and from the sons of Esau (*A* II, 4–6).

In particular, inasmuch as Stoicism was so popular among Hellenistic intellectuals, it is not surprising that Josephus should attempt to appeal especially to the Stoics in his recasting of the biblical narrative. Thus, we may remark, the term ἀπαθής, which is found in connection with Abraham's ironic hope (*A* I, 223) that he would leave his son Isaac unscathed when he dies, is a common Stoic term indicating freedom from emotion. That Stoic influence is at work here is indicated by the fact that Josephus does not employ the synonymous word ἀβλαβής, which also means "unharmed" and which he uses six times in the first half of the *Antiquities*. Likewise, we may add, the favorite Stoic word πρόνοια ("Providence"), which, as we have noted, Josephus uses in the Abraham pericope (*A* I, 225), where he states that it is divine providence that ordains everything for his favored ones, is found no fewer than seventy-four times in the first half of the *Antiquities,* where Josephus is paraphrasing the Bible.

Parallel to my study of Josephus' treatment of Abraham is Professor James Bailey's essay on "Josephus' Portrayal of the Matriarchs," in which he likewise concludes that Josephus has significantly Hellenized the matriarchs by, in effect, presenting idealized portraits of them. This would seem rather remarkable in view of his misogyny, as seen, for example, in his snide remark (*A* I, 49) that God punished Adam for yielding to a womanish counsel and in his condemnation (*BJ* I, 111–112) of Queen Salome Alexandra (whose piety, according to the rabbis in *Sifra Beḥuqotai* 1. 1, was so great that during her reign the grains of wheat grew to be as large as kidneys) for allowing the Pharisees (with whom, remarkably, Josephus identified himself) to take advantage of her naiveté, though, in the end, he grudgingly admits, in a half-baked compliment (*A* XIII, 430), that "she was a woman who showed none of the weakness of her sex."

As to Josephus' portrayal of the matriarchs, even the scene in Sarah's tent, as Professor Bailey has noted, has been changed to a Greek courtyard (αὐλή, *A* I, 196) rather than the Septuagint's tent (σκηνή, Gen. 18:2), which would indicate primitiveness, perhaps, we may suggest, under the influence of the similarly sounding word *'ohel* in the original Hebrew. Moreover, he has added a number of touches that would elevate her to the status of the Hasmonean and other Hellenistic queens so familiar in his own era.

We may also add that Josephus, in his paraphrase, caters to the political interests of his audience. Thus, according to Josephus' addition (*A* I, 164), God thwarted the pharaoh's unjust passion toward Sarah by bringing about an outbreak of disease and of political strife (στάσει). Indeed, we may comment, a goodly portion of Book IV (11–66, 141–155) of the *Antiquities* is devoted to accounts that illustrate the degree to which στάσις is the mortal enemy of political states. Thus, in his treatment of the rebellion of Korah, he states (*A* IV, 12) that it was a sedition (στάσις) "for which we know of no parallel, whether among Greeks or barbarians," clearly implying that information about seditions was familiar to his readers.

We may here also add that Josephus has recast his narrative in the form, so to speak, of a Greek tragedy. Thus, the reader will think of the opening of Sophocles' *Oedipus the King* when he reads (*A* I, 164) that God thwarted the pharaoh's criminal passion toward Sarah by causing an outbreak of disease. Indeed, in order to find a remedy for the plague, the pharaoh, like Oedipus, consults priests, who declare that the calamity is due to the wrath of God because the pharaoh had wished to outrage (ὑβρίσαι—a familiar word in tragedy) the stranger's wife. Similarly, we may add, the harsh behavior (Gen. 16:6) of Sarah toward her handmaid Hagar, who, according to the Bible (Gen. 16:4), despised Sarah after she (Hagar) had become pregnant through Abraham, is now clearly justified in Josephus' additional language, which has the ring of Greek tragedy, that Hagar's plight was due (A I, 189) to her arrogant (ἀγνώμονα) and presumptuous (αὐθάσῃ) behavior toward her mistress. The reader will inevitably be reminded of the harshness (αὐθαδίαν) of Kratos in Aeschylus' *Prometheus Bound* (79) and of the obstinacy (αὐθαδίαν) imputed to Oedipus (Sophocles, *Oedipus the King*, 549–555) by Creon, as well as of the arrogance (ἀγνωμοσύναν) decried by the Chorus in Euripides' *Bacchae* (883–884).

In his recasting of the portrait of Rebekah, Josephus, we may note, has given particular emphasis to her hospitality (especially A I, 246). We may suggest that this was in order to answer such anti-Semites as Lysimachus (*Ap* I, 309), who had charged that Moses had instructed the Israelites "to show good will to no man, to offer not the best but the worst advice."

In reply to such charges we may call attention to the fact that when Eliezer, Abraham's servant, arrives in Nachor in search for a wife for his master's son Isaac, the other maidens (A I, 245), just as in Homer's *Odyssey* (VI, 137–141), except for Rebekah, refuse to show him hospitality. Likewise, Rebekah rebukes the other maidens (A I, 246), in terms reminiscent of Nausicaa to her companions (*Odyssey* VI, 198–210). Thereupon, Eliezer (A I, 247), in a remark that reminds the reader of Odysseus' reaction to Nausicaa's hospitality, declares that the parents of such a child should be congratulated and that she deserves to be married to the son of his master.

We may also suggest that an apologetic motif is behind Josephus' remark (A I, 311) that the reason why Rachel stole her father Laban's *teraphim* was that in case they were pursued by Laban she might pacify her father by returning them to him. To a Jewish reader—and we can see from Josephus' highlighting of certain episodes, notably the incident of Israel's sin with the Midianite women (Num. 25:1–9; A IV, 131–155), which Josephus expands from nine biblical verses to twenty-five paragraphs, and Samson's relations with alien women (Judg. 14:1–16:3; A V, 286–317), that his work is also directed to those Hellenized Jews who sought assimilation with Gentiles—the idea that Rachel, one of the matriarchs, should have worshipped household gods very similar to the Lares and Penates of the Romans and should have acted deceptively toward her own father must have been utterly repugnant. Indeed, we may remark, the rabbis also seek various reasons for the theft, notably (*Genesis Rabbah* 74. 5) that she sought to remove idolatry from her father or (*Pirke de-Rabbi Eliezer* 36) that they should not tell Laban that she and Jacob had fled.

In connection with Rachel, we may call attention to the fact that Josephus here, as elsewhere, has diminished the divine role and elevated the human dimension. Thus, Josephus (*A* I, 305) omits Jacob's angry exchange with Rachel (Gen. 30:1–2) in which, in the biblical version, he says, "Am I in God's stead, Who hath withheld from thee the fruit of the womb?" Josephus omits the connection of her lack of fecundity with God and instead restricts himself to the human dimension, as he psychologizes in his statement that Rachel fears that her sister's fecundity will lessen her own share in her husband's affections. Again, when Rachel gives birth to Joseph, Josephus (*A* I, 308) does not repeat the reference to God found in both the Hebrew and the Septuagint versions (Gen. 30:23) that "God hath taken away my reproach."

We may also add that Josephus has recast his portraits so as to add romantic motifs reminiscent of Homer, Herodotus' account (I, 8–12) of Candaules' wife and Gyges, Xenophon's *Cyropaedia,* and Hellenistic novels. Thus, in an extrabiblical comment that has no rabbinic parallel, Josephus (*A* I, 162) mentions the Egyptians' frenzy for women and Abraham's fear that the pharaoh would put him to death so that he might have Sarah. The erotic motif is further developed in the pharaoh's meeting with Sarah (*A* I, 165), where, in terror, he asks who she is and who the man is who accompanied her. The Genesis Apocryphon (col. 20) of the Dead Sea Scrolls, on the other hand, we may note, emphasizes not the pharaoh's terror but Abraham's grief. Again, there is more romance in Josephus (*A* I, 165) than in the Bible (Gen. 12:19) in the pharaoh's statement that he had set his affections on Sarah because he had believed that she was Abraham's sister, and that he had hoped to marry her rather than to outrage her in a transport of passion.

Dr. Gohei Hata, in his essay on "The Story of Moses Interpreted within the Context of Anti-Semitism," focuses, in particular, on the apologetic element in Josephus. We may comment that while it is true that such an extrabiblical detail as the prediction (*A* II, 205) by one of the Egyptian sacred scribes that a child would be born to the Israelites who would humble the rule of the Egyptians and exalt the Israelites is paralleled in rabbinic tradition (e.g., *Pirke de-Rabbi Eliezer* 48), we may well ask why Josephus, who seems to be well acquainted with rabbinic tradition, omits the great majority of the rabbinic amplifications of Scripture and yet chooses to insert such an account as this. We may suggest that to a Jew defending Judaism, as was Josephus in the *Antiquities* and in *Against Apion,* it seemed necessary to match the greatest Jewish leader, namely Moses, with the great kings of other nations. A similar amplification of Scripture, we may note, is found in the fragments of Josephus' predecessor, the Egyptian Jew Artapanus, who, presumably like Josephus, answering an anti-Jewish Egyptian account, combines in the single personality of Moses the political, military, religious, philosophical, technical, and cultural achievements that are found separately in the Egyptian deities Isis, Osiris, Thoth-Hermes, and the Egyptian national hero Sesostris. We may also remark that, as seen in writers such as Manetho and Berossus, the Oriental peoples generally, in the Hellenistic and Roman times, and as a defensive measure developed the stories of their national heroes; and the Jews were no exceptions, especially in their zeal to counteract the anti-Semitic tales mentioned in *Against Apion* that were circulating about them. We may also suggest that Josephus, in inserting the story of the prediction that a child would be born who would win everlasting renown by abasing the sovereignty of the Egyptians, might well have had in mind the story of the birth of the mythical Perseus, who, like Moses, was exposed in a chest, or the birth of Cyrus, the great national hero of the Persians, after Astyages, king of the Medes, had dreamed that his daughter would bear a son who would conquer Asia.

We may also call attention to the obviously apologetic motif in Josephus' extrabiblical account of Amram's dream (*A* II, 216), which predicted that Moses would be remembered "so long as the universe shall endure, not by Hebrews alone but even by alien nations." We may suggest that this last phrase is Josephus' own addition, since it is absent from a very similar account found in a fourteenth-century Samaritan poem.[7]

We may also suggest that though Josephus' statement (*A* II, 224), that when the pharaoh's daughter beheld the infant Moses she was enchanted by his size and beauty, is paralleled by the midrashic tradition (*Tanḥuma* on Ex. 2:7), Josephus omits much else that is found in the midrashic tradition. His inclusion of this detail is probably to make Moses conform to the prototypes of the great hero and the philosopher-king (we may note, in particular, Plato's remark [*Republic* VII, 535A11–12] that the philosopher-king should, so far as possible, be extremely handsome). We may also add that in Josephus' statement (*A* II, 231) that persons meeting Moses as he was borne along the highway road were attracted by the child's beautiful appearance, he may have had in mind the beauty of Pythagoras (whose doctrines concerning God are said [*Ap* II, 168] to have been similar to those of Moses), whom, when he was a child, everyone turned to gaze at (Apollonius, *Iamblichus* 10 [p. 11, ll. 6–7]).

We may likewise suggest that the reason why Josephus gives the name of the pharaoh's daughter, which is not found in the account in Exodus, is that such information is designed to grant greater credibility to the author. Artapanus called her Merris; we may guess that Josephus preferred the name Thermutis (in Egyptian, Tuarmut), "great mother," because it was a surname of Isis and thus gave her more stature than in pagan circles.

Neither the Bible nor Philo mentions any attempt to have Egyptian women nurse Moses, let alone his rejection of their milk. Josephus (*A* II, 225–227), in common with the Talmudic tradition (*Sotah* 12b), adds such a detail, which would again enhance the legend of the wisdom that Moses possessed even as an infant.

We may call attention to another extrabiblical detail in Josephus' narrative, namely, his statement (*A* II, 230) that the young Moses' very games showed his maturity and gave promise for the future. This picture is paralleled in the description by one of Josephus' favorite authors, Herodotus (I, 114), of the ten-year-old Cyrus, whose parentage was discovered through an incident that occurred while he was playing with the village boys, during which he ordered one of them to be beaten because he had disobeyed his command.

It may be of interest here to comment on Josephus' remark (*A* II, 230), absent in Scripture, that at the age of three, Moses grew wondrously in stature. It would presumably have been grotesque for Josephus to repeat the rabbinic tradition (*Bekhoroth* 44a) that Moses grew to be ten ells (approximately thirty-seven and a half feet) high; the number, we may suggest, may be derived from the rabbinic tradition (*Genesis Rabbah* 38), which declares that it was at this age that Abraham showed unusual maturity by recognizing that the idols of his father, Terah, were naught and destroyed them all. But the theme of precocious growth also has a number of parallels in Hellenistic and later literature—Evangelos of Miletus (Conon, *Narratio,* 44), Amphoteros and Akarnan, the son of Callirhoe (Apollodorus III, 7.6), and the Aloades (Apollodorus I, 7.4).

We may add that the story, again without biblical foundation, told by Josephus (*A* II, 233) of how the pharaoh, to please his daughter, who had decided to adopt Moses as her child and heir to his kingdom, placed his crown upon Moses' head only to have Moses tear it off and trample it underfoot, has its rabbinic parallel (*Sotah* 57a). But we may also suggest that Josephus had in mind the story of Herodotus (I, 114), who, as we have noted, often parallels Josephus, in which Cyrus as a young boy already plays at being king. And, thus, we see the equation of Moses to other national heroes.

Finally, the most striking difference between the biblical narrative and Josephus' account of Moses is to be seen in Josephus' introduction of the episode of Moses' campaign against the Ethiopians (*A* II, 238–253). We may suggest that while Josephus may have derived some motifs from Artapanus, he may have conceived the general idea through his knowledge of the stories of the mythological Jason and Heracles, both of whom are given close to impossible tasks to perform. It is significant that when Josephus wishes to show how much regard Ptolemy Philometor and Cleopatra had for the Jews, he stresses that they placed their entire army under the command of Jewish generals, Onias and Dositheus (*Ap* II, 49). Just as Apion, according to Josephus, ridiculed these generals instead of showing gratitude to them for saving Alexandria, so, Josephus is saying, the Egyptians ought to admire and thank Moses for saving their land from the Ethiopians instead of calumniating him. It is interesting that when Josephus lists the main topics of the Bible (*A* I, 13), he emphasizes military matters, notably the heroic exploits of generals. Indeed, in summarizing the achievements of Moses (*Ap* II, 157–163), Josephus, perhaps reflecting his own role as a general in Galilee in the war against the Romans, stresses that Moses proved the best of generals when leading the Jews out of Egypt.

Professor David Goldenberg's essay, comparing two laws as stated in the *Antiquities* with early rabbinic law, concludes that there is agreement and that when there are disagreements they are due to the speculations of a following century. We may note that since our earliest codification of the oral law, the Mishnah, dates from approximately a century after the publication of the *Antiquities,* Josephus, because his summary of and allusions to Jewish law are so extensive, is a major source for our knowledge of Pharisaic interpretation, especially since he himself says that after he had experimented with the various sects he chose to ally himself with the Pharisees (*V* 12). We may add that the very fact, mentioned in several places, notably at the very end of the *Antiquities* (XX, 268), that he announces his plans to write a work on the laws, obviously more extensive than his summary treatment in Books III and IV of the *Antiquities* or his succinct résumé in *Against Apion* (II, 190–219), is a further indication that he regarded himself as eminently qualified to write such a work. Indeed, Josephus (*Ap* II, 178) would have us believe that every Jew was exceedingly well versed in the laws, so that he could "repeat them all more readily than his own name."

We may here add to the two examples cited by Professor Goldenberg a number of other instances where Josephus seems to be in accord with the oral tradition as we know it from the Talmudic corpus: (1) he notes (*A* III, 226) that a lamb that is offered for sacrifice is to be one year old, as specified also in the Mishnah (*Parah* 5. 3); (2) he declares (*A* III, 261) that a menstruating woman is removed from pure things and is separated from the public on account of uncleanness, just as the rabbinic tradition (*Tanna de-be Eliyahu,* M. Friedmann, ed. 16, 75–76) states; (3) Josephus (*A* IV, 202), like the Mishnah (*Sanhedrin* 6. 4), indicates that blasphemers are stoned and hanged, whereas the Torah (Lev. 24:14–16) specifies only stoning; (4) he, like the rabbis (*Berakhoth* 27b), speaks (*A* IV, 212) of two statutory prayers daily; (5) he mentions (*A* IV, 214), as does the Talmud (*Megillah* 26a), that civic bodies are to have seven members; (6) he states (*A* IV, 219), as do the rabbis (*Sifre* 109b), that the evidence of women is not acceptable; (7) he declares (*A* IV, 224), as does the Talmud (*Sanhedrin* 2a, 20b), that a king must consult the Sanhedrin of seventy-one before engaging in a voluntary war; (8) he reduces (*A* IV, 238), as do the rabbis (*Makkoth* 22a), the number of lashes inflicted in the penalty of scourging from forty to thirty-nine; (9) he (*A* IV, 253), like the school of

Hillel, which prevails in rabbinic law (*Gittin* 90a), permits divorce for any reason whatsoever; (10) the penalty of paying double in the case of theft, according to Josephus (*A* IV, 271), applies not only if one steals animals, as in the Bible (Ex. 22:3), but also if one steals money—a provision paralleled in the Talmud (*Baba Kamma* 64b); (11) he (*A* IV, 274), like the rabbinic tradition (Tosefta, *Baba Mezia* 2. 19), in discussing the law of the restitution of lost property, differentiates on the basis of where the object was found, whereas the Bible (Deut. 22:1–3) makes no such distinction, and likewise Josephus mentions (*A* IV, 274) public proclamation of the place where it was found, as does the oral tradition (Mishnah, *Baba Meẓia* 2. 1), though it is only in the fourth century that we hear of a rabbi (Rava, in *Baba Meẓia* 22b) who holds this view; (12) Josephus (*A* IV, 276), as pointed out by Goldenberg,[8] agrees with the oral tradition (Tosefta, *Baba Meẓia* 2. 29) in placing the law of pointing out the road to one who has lost his way immediately after the law of lost objects; (13) he (*A* IV, 277), like the rabbinic Tosefta (*Baba Kamma* 9. 5–6), declares that one is not punished if the person whom he has struck remains alive several days before dying; (14) in his interpretation of the *lex talionis* (Ex. 21:24), Josephus (*A* IV, 280) gives the victim the choice of accepting a monetary settlement, similar to the rabbis (*Baba Kamma* 83b), who, to be sure, prescribe a monetary penalty and declare that the amount is to be fixed by a court; (15) Josephus (*Ap* I, 31), in declaring that a priest must marry a woman of his own race, that is, not a proselyte, is in accord with the Mishnah (*Yevamoth* 6. 5), which equates a proselyte and a prostitute, whereas the Torah itself (Lev. 21:7) says merely that a priest may not marry a prostitute; (16) like the Talmud (*Moed Katan* 27b, *Kethuboth* 8b), he (*Ap* 2. 205) indicates opposition to costly shrouds; (17) in saying that Jews do not erect conspicuous monuments to the dead, Josephus (*Ap* II, 205) is in agreement with the Jerusalem Talmud (*Shekalim* 2. 7. 47a); and (18) if the reading of Eusebius (*Praeparatio Evangelica* VIII, 8. 36) is correct, Josephus (*Ap* II, 205) agrees with the rabbinic tradition (*Kethuboth* 17a, *Megillah* 29a) in declaring that all who pass by a funeral procession must join it.

And yet we may also cite a number of instances where Josephus does not agree with the Pharisaic interpretation, at least as codified in the Mishnah in the following century and as understood by the Amoraic rabbis who followed: (1) he identifies (*A* III, 245) "the fruit of goodly trees" (Lev. 23:40) as the persea, a fleshy one-seeded fruit of the laurel family, the most common member of which is the avocado, though elsewhere (*A* XIII, 372), to be sure, he refers to it as a citron, as do the rabbis (*Sukkah* 35a); (2) he declares (*A* III, 282) that debtors are absolved of their debts in the Jubilee year, whereas the biblical text (Deut. 15:1–11) speaks of the remission of debts in the seventh or sabbatical year, a provision about which Josephus, though he discusses the regulations of the sabbatical year in the passage just before this (*A* III, 280–

281), says nothing; (3) he understands (*A* IV, 175) the Bible (Num. 36:3) literally when it declares that if a daughter marries into another tribe the inheritance remains in her father's tribe, whereas the rabbis (*Baba Bathra* 112b) declare that the inheritance is transferred; (4) he says (*A* IV, 207), following the Septuagint's understanding of Exodus 22:27, that it is forbidden to blaspheme the gods that other people revere, whereas Deuteronomy 7:25 mandates the destruction by fire of the graven images of the heathen; (5) he declares (*A* IV, 209) that the high priest is to read the laws every seven years, whereas Scripture (Deut. 31:10–13) does not specify who is to read them, and the Mishnah (*Sotah* 7. 8) states that it is the king who reads the passage; (6) he speaks (*A* IV, 240) of a third tithe (Deut. 14:28–29) for the poor, whereas the rabbis understand this as taking the place of the second tithe in the third and sixth years of the sabbatical period; (7) he states (*A* IV, 248) that if a man betroths a bride in the belief that she is a virgin and it turns out that she is not, she is to be stoned if not of priestly parentage but burnt alive if she is of priestly stock, whereas the Bible (Deut. 22:21) prescribes stoning for all cases; (8) according to Josephus (*A* IV, 254), the child born of a levirate marriage (Deut. 25:5–10) is the heir to the estate, but the rabbis (Mishnah, *Yevamoth* 4. 7) declare that the levir himself is the heir; (9) he says (*A* IV, 263) that the law of the rebellious child applies to sons and daughters, and he does not mention the necessity of bringing the child to a court to be judged, as prescribed by Scripture (Deut. 21:9), while the Bible itself (Deut. 21:18) and the rabbis (Mishnah, *Sanhedrin* 8. 1) restrict the law to sons alone; (10) he likewise requires (*A* IV, 264) the condemned child to be exposed for a day after he has been stoned to death, whereas there is no such statement in the Bible (Deut. 21:21) or in the Talmud; (11) he declares (*A* IV, 273) that a slave woman and her children go free with her in the Jubilee year, but the rabbis affirm that the children of a Canaanite slave woman are like herself in all respects (*Kiddushin* 68b–69a) and that they are regarded as property (*Megillah* 23b); (12) Josephus says (*A* IV, 278) that if a man kicks a woman and causes her to have a miscarriage, he is to be fined by the judge and a further sum is to be given to her husband, whereas Scripture (Ex. 21:22) speaks of one fine alone to be determined by the judge; (13) he says (*Ap* II, 199) that the sole purpose of sexual relations in marriage is to have children, whereas the rabbis permit such relations during pregnancy, for example (*Yevamoth* 12b), and they permit (Mishnah, *Yevamoth* 6. 6) a man to marry a woman incapable of bearing children if he has already fulfilled the commandment "Be fruitful and multiply"; (14) he declares (*Ap* II, 202), without qualification, that a woman is forbidden to have an abortion, whereas the rabbis (*Sanhedrin* 72b) state that an abortion is permissible if the fetus is endangering the life of the mother; (15) he indicates (*Ap* II, 207) that for a judge to accept bribes is a capital crime, but there is no such law in the Talmud; (16) he declares (*Ap* II, 215) that violating an unmarried woman is a capital crime, without indicating (Deut. 22:23–24) the crucial proviso that this applies only to a betrothed woman; (17) he maintains (*Ap* II, 271) that maltreatment (presumably castration) of a brute beast is a crime punishable by death, but there is no such penalty specified in the Bible (Lev. 22:24) or in the Talmud (*Ḥagigah* 14b); and (18) he says (*V* 65) that representation of animals is forbidden by Jewish law and declares (*A* VIII, 195) that Solomon violated the law in making images of bulls under the sea, which he had set up as an offering, and of lions around his throne, but the Talmud (*Avodah Zarah* 43b) declares that only a human shape is halakhically forbidden.

How, we may ask, can we explain this checkered picture of Josephus' relationship to the rabbis? To answer this, perhaps we should first ask why Josephus includes a survey of the laws, while other historians, such as Dionysius of Halicarnassus and Livy, in their histories of Rome, do not. We may remark, in reply, that Josephus, indeed, realizes that a survey of laws does not really belong in a history. He is clearly self-conscious when introducing his survey of the regulations concerning purity laws. "I cease," he says (*A* III, 223), before giving a brief survey (*A* III, 224–286), "to speak about these [laws], having resolved to compose another treatise about the laws." Moreover, when he gives his more extensive survey of the laws, he is again self-conscious and offers (*A* IV, 196) two reasons for the digression. The first is that it is consonant with the reputation for virtue (ἀρετῆς) of Moses. Since Josephus is presenting an apologetic work and since Moses is *the* greatest Jewish hero, whatever redounds to Moses' credit will redound to the credit of the Jewish people. The second is that it will enable those who read (ἐντευ-ξομένοις, "chance upon") his book to learn of the nature of the laws from the beginning, thus directing the digression to his non-Jewish readers, presumably for apologetic reasons. Josephus (*A* IV, 198) says that he will restrict himself to those laws pertaining to the Jewish polity (πολιτείαν), reserving for his projected treatise those pertaining to the mutual (private) relations (πρὸς ἀλλήλους) between men, though he seems to include some of these in his survey as well.

A good example, we may note, of Josephus' recasting of biblical law for apologetic reasons is to be seen in his extension (*A* IV, 276) of the injunction against putting a stumbling block in front of the blind (Lev. 19:14, Deut. 27:18) into a law that one must point out the road to those who are ignorant of it. This would seem to be a direct refutation of the bitter anti-Semitic satirist Juvenal who declares (*Satires* 14. 103) that Jews do not point out the road except to those who practice the same rites. Josephus likewise declares (*A* IV, 283) that those who dig wells are required to keep them covered not in order to keep others from drawing water from them, but rather to protect passersby from falling into them. Here, too, he seems to be answering Juvenal's charge (14. 104) that Jews conduct "none but the circumcised to the desired fountain."

Sometimes Josephus seems to have reformulated the law in order to avoid embarrassment in comparison with non-Jewish law. Thus, in equating abortion with infanticide (*Ap* II, 202), Josephus, as Riskin[9] has remarked, did not want to have it appear that Jewish law was more lenient than the Noachian law that is applicable to non-Jews, inasmuch as, according to the Talmud (*Sanhedrin* 57b), Noachian law, on the basis of an interpretation of Genesis 9:6, forbids killing a fetus in the womb of its mother. Moreover, Josephus apparently felt uneasy that Jewish law on this topic was more lenient than that of Plato (*ap*. Plutarch, *De Placitis Philosophorum* 5. 15), who declares that a fetus is a living being.

Again, as Cohn[10] has pointed out, according to the earlier Roman law (*Lex Cornelia testamentaria* of 81 B.C.), the penalty inflicted upon a judge for accepting a bribe was exile, the death penalty not being imposed until A.D. 392. Josephus (*Ap* II, 207), eager that it should not appear that Jewish law was less stringent than that of the Gentiles in such a sensitive area, declares that a judge who accepts bribes suffers capital punishment. Here again, Noachian law did require a death penalty, and Josephus did not want it to appear that he was less severe.

Moreover, Josephus' omission of the prohibition of converting to Judaism the Ammonites and Moabites until the tenth generation (Deut. 23:4) and the Edomites and the Egyptians until the third generation (Deut. 23:9) seems to have been actuated by the eagerness to answer the charge that the Jews were exclusivistic and haters of mankind, as we have noted above. This apology was particularly important because the Jewish proselyting activities, so enormously successful during this period, depended upon making it clear that Jews welcome all those who come to them in true sincerity.

Professor Goldenberg[11] has systematically challenged the thesis that Josephus' goal in his formulation of Jewish law was apologetic by noting, for example, that his omission of child sacrifice to Molech (Lev. 18:21) was far from being due to apologetic purposes, since if Josephus was interested in showing the humanity of Judaism a prohibition against child sacrifice was certainly one law not to omit. He likewise notes[12] that if it were for apologetic reasons that Josephus omitted the prohibition of setting up an asherah tree or a pillar (Deut. 16:21–22), Josephus should also have omitted the prohibition against graven images, which he does mention (*A* III, 91; *Ap* II, 191) and even emphasizes, as we see. Likewise, if it is for apologetic reasons that Josephus omits the reference to sacrifices to foreign gods (Ex. 22:19), Josephus should not have expanded (*A* IV, 126–149) the incident of the fornication with the Midianite women.

Similarly, the omission of the prohibition (Deut. 18:10–11) against consulting a soothsayer, a sorcerer, or a necromancer is inconsistent with Josephus' anecdote (*Ap* I, 200–204) of the Jewish soldier Mosollamus, who shot and killed a bird that a seer was observing and who sneeringly asked how any sound information could come from a creature that could not provide for its own safety. Again, the mention of the prohibition of the use of non-Jewish oil (*V* 74) would seem to play into the hands of those who charged that Jews were haters of mankind. Likewise, Josephus (*A* IV, 266) has not omitted what would seem to be the embarrassing law (Deut. 23:21) that one may charge interest from a non-Jew but not from a Jew, to which Josephus adds as the reason, "for it is not just to draw a revenue from the misfortunes of a fellow-countryman." To these objections we may remark that the *argumentum ex silentio* is particularly dangerous, since Josephus is not presenting a systematic code of law, and that he is not merely seeking to defend Jews against the charges of anti-Semites but that he is also eager to attract non-Jews to Judaism, hence the statement about interest-free loans, which might well prove to be a major attraction in winning proselytes.

In response to the fact that Josephus does differ in some points from the rabbinic code, we could comment that Josephus, who was under constant attack from his fellow Jews, would hardly have dared to present such deviations unless he had solid ground for his interpretations. We may explain his deviations by stating either that he is merely paraphrasing biblical law or that he reflects the law in force in his own day (in which case Josephus, like Philo presumably, would be very important as a stage in halakhic development prior to the codification of halakhah by Rabbi Judah the Prince in the Mishnah at the end of the second century), in contrast to the law which prevailed at the time when the Mishnah was reduced to writing. Alternatively, perhaps he reflects sectarian law, or is influenced by Philo or by Roman law, or is more strict than the rabbinic law, or is presenting merely good advice rather than legal prescriptions, or reflects the law that he believes will take force in the messianic future. As to the possibility that Josephus is paraphrasing the Bible, the statement (*A* IV, 175) that the heritage of Zelophehad's daughters should remain in the tribe is merely a restatement of the Bible (Num. 36:8), whereas the rabbis (*Sifra Emor* on Lev. 22:3) declare that the law was in force only when the land was divided according to tribes.

In explaining these discrepancies, we may cite a parallel in the differences between Josephus' description (*A* XV, 410–411) of the Temple and that of the Mishnah in the tractate *Middoth*.[13] Perhaps the Mishnah represents the period before Herod, whereas Josephus depicts the period after him; or the Mishnah may be setting forth the ideal, if ever the Temple is to be rebuilt in the future. Surely Josephus, who himself was a priest and of the most eminent of all the priestly families (*V* 2), would have had an intimate acquaintance with the Temple's dimensions and description.

Dr. Otto Betz, in his essay on "Miracles in the Writings of Flavius Josephus," well illustrates the danger of blithe generalizations in connection with Josephus. Thus, while it is true that Josephus sometimes rationalizes or even omits miracles mentioned in the Bible, he often does report them, though at times he adds well-known comments from the writings of Herodotus (II, 123; V, 45), Thucydides (VI, 2. 1), Dionysius of Halicarnassus (I, 48. 1; I, 48. 4; II, 40. 3; II, 74. 5; III, 36. 5), Lucian (*Quomodo Historia Conscribenda Sit* 10), and Pliny (*Natural History* VIII, 18), leaving it to the reader to believe or not believe them, as an expression, presumably, of Josephus' courtesy and tolerance.

We may note, for example, that Josephus, as much as he might have liked to exaggerate Samson's exploits in order to build up his stature as a hero, is careful to omit miraculous and magical elements. Thus, whereas the Bible (Judg. 16:9) declares that Samson broke the bowstrings binding him "as a string of tow snaps when it touches the fire," Josephus omits the miraculous element, and we are left with the statement (*A* V, 310) that Samson burst the bowstrings (twigs) asunder. Again, the Bible (Judg. 16:1–2) remarks that Samson snapped the ropes off his arms as if they were a thread, but Josephus (*A* V, 311) states merely that Delilah's device met with no success. We may here suggest that perhaps Josephus' de-emphasis on miracles reflects the talmudic view, possibly in reaction to the early Christian emphasis on Jesus' alleged miracles. This is illustrated, for example, in the story (*Baba Meẓia* 59b) of Rabbi Eliezer's proofs from the carob tree torn from its place, from the stream of water flowing backwards, from the wall caving in, and from a voice from heaven indicating that he was right, the point being that such miraculous "proofs" do not establish the law, which is "not in heaven." A similar downgrading of miracles may be seen in the rabbinic emphasis (*Ex. Rabbah* 24:1) on the daily miracles of life that do not express themselves in violations of the laws of nature or in the statement (*Pesaḥim* 46b) that it is forbidden to rely upon miracles.

We may here suggest that Josephus' apparent inconsistency arises from the fact that in the *Antiquities* he has not thought through his theological position, as presumably he would have done if he had lived to write his projected work "On Customs and Causes" (*A* IV, 198). In point of fact, Josephus prefers to approach the Bible as history rather than as theology, as is clear from a number of references in the *Antiquities* indicating that he intends to discuss elsewhere such theological matters as the reasons for the commandments generally (*A* I, 25), the reasons for the practice of circumcision (*A* I, 192), the major portion of the laws (*A* III, 94), the reason for the shewbread (*A* III,

143), the laws concerning mutual relations (*A* IV, 198), and the Jewish belief concerning God and His essence and the reasons for the commandments (*A* XX, 268). We may note that a similar ambiguity is to be found in the Talmudic corpus, largely because theology was not of paramount concern to the Talmudic rabbis, in whose midst Josephus was raised.

We may also suggest that if, as Dr. Betz contends, Josephus has de-emphasized faith, this is in line with the tendency of the Pharisaic rabbis, who stressed the performance of *mitzvoth* rather than adherence to a creed. In fact, Jewish religious leaders saw no need to formulate a creed until the twelfth century, when Maimonides did so, in passing, in the course of his commentary on the Mishnah *Sanhedrin,* whereupon he was almost immediately challenged. One is reminded, in this connection, of the famous rabbinic Midrash (*Leviticus Rabbah,* introduction) that ascribes to God Himself the statement: "Would that they [the Jews] abandoned me, but observed My commandments."

If, indeed, as Dr. Betz notes, Josephus stresses the concept of Providence, we may suggest that he does so because this was such an important concept in Stoicism, which, as we have noted, was the favorite philosophy of intellectuals in Rome at the time that Josephus was living there. We may note that he uses the favorite word for providence, πρόνοια, no fewer than 121 times in the *Antiquities* and 39 times in his other works. Thus, in an extrabiblical comment describing the primeval Utopia, Josephus (*A* I, 46) remarks that all things that contributed to enjoyment and pleasure sprang up spontaneously through God's providence (πρόνοιαν). Moreover, as I have indicated elsewhere,[14] Josephus uses Stoic terminology in connection with his proof for the existence of God (*A* I, 156). Similarly, we may remark, in his encomium of Moses, Josephus (*A* IV, 328) stresses that Moses found favor chiefly through his thorough command of the passions (παθῶν αὐτοκράτωρ), another key Stoic phrase. Again, as I have also previously noted,[15] Josephus, in his portrait of Solomon, consciously colors his narrative with Stoic phraseology to make it more intelligible and attractive to his readers. Likewise, in his view of εἱμαρμένη ("fate"), as Martin[16] has shown, he is indebted to popular, nontechnical Stoicism.

We may well ask why Josephus generally de-emphasizes the role of God in his retelling of the Bible but does not do so in his account of Moses. Thus, in an extrabiblical addition (*A* II, 222–223), Josephus comments that the miraculous way in which Moses was saved after he had been placed in the ark after birth shows plainly that human intelligence is of no worth and that God accomplishes whatever He intends to do. At the burning bush (*A* II, 272), it is God who exhorts Moses to have confidence, and not, as in Artapanus (*ap.* Eusebius, *Praeparatio Evangelica* IX, 27. 22), Moses himself who takes courage. When Moses returns to Egypt from Midian, the Hebrews, we are told (*A* II, 280), were hopeful that all would be well, "since God was taking forethought [προνοουμένου] for their safety." Likewise, Josephus (A II, 293) declares that one of the reasons why he has chosen to mention all of the plagues inflicted upon the Egyptians is that one should learn the lesson that those who provoke God's wrath are punished. Again, at the Red Sea, where all hope seemed lost, Moses (A II, 332) encourages the Israelites by remarking that God helps people precisely at the time when He sees that they have lost all hope. Josephus similarly explains the sweetness of the waters of Marah (A III, 5–9), the miraculous gift of quails and manna (A III, 22–32), and the miracle of the water from the rock (A III, 33–38) as indications of God's providence. This emphasis, however, on God and on His providence is the exception in Josephus' history and may be explained by the fact that since the Greeks believed that great leaders, such as a Lycurgus, had to be divinely directed, so Josephus, for apologetic reasons—inasmuch as he knew that Moses would be compared with other lawgivers and formulators of constitutions actual or ideal [17]—similarly emphasized that Moses had been directed by God's providence (A II, 329, 331, 335). That, indeed, Josephus is actually de-emphasizing the role of God may be seen by the fact that the Dead Sea Temple Scroll excludes Moses entirely in its statement of the laws and instead ascribes them directly to God, while Josephus mentions Moses by name constantly as the author of these laws, identifies the virtue of his constitution with his own virtue (A I, 20), and nowhere quotes God directly in his citation of legal materials. [18]

As to Elijah, Josephus does not suppress his miraculous raising of the widow's son from the dead (A VIII, 325–327) and the miracles associated with his victory over the priests of Baal (A VIII, 336–342), but when it comes to Elijah's bodily ascent into heaven (II Kings 2:11), Josephus merely says that Elijah disappeared and "to this day no one knows his end." The reason for this may be that he did not want Elijah to seem more important than Moses, who, he wishes to stress (A IV, 326), in answer to those who spoke of Moses in divine terms, did die and did not "go back to the divinity."

Professor Morton Smith's pioneer study "The Occult in Josephus" notes Josephus' terminological muddle when it comes to theology, for example, in the notion of *daimones* and *daimonia*. This, too, would reflect Josephus' lack of interest, at least in the *Antiquities,* in theological matters. We may also suggest that apologetic motives are behind his vagueness in referring to divinity; indeed, we would call attention to the fact that Josephus, though he surely knew the Hebrew original of Exodus 22:27 ("Thou shalt not revile Elokim") and most probably the talmudic interpretation that it forbids cursing judges, nevertheless adopts the Septuagint's interpretation that understands it (A IV, 207) as a prohibition against blaspheming "gods" of other nations, presumably out of tolerance.

We may suggest that the view that Judaism contains secrets is reflected in the remark of Josephus' contemporary, the satirist Juvenal (14. 102), that Moses transmitted the law in an arcane book (*arcano . . . volumine*). Such a view, we may guess, may have arisen from the fact that it was prohibited to teach the Torah to Gentiles (*Ḥagigah* 13a) or from the fact that it was prohibited (*A* XV, 417) for outsiders to enter the precincts of the Temple. Hence, Philo (*De Vita Mosis* II, 15, 71) describes Moses as one who had been instructed in all the mysteries of his priestly duties and declares (*De Somniis* I, 26, 164) that God is a mystagogue who has the power to introduce man to "the fast-locked lovelinesses invisible to the uninitiated." Philo even goes so far as to distinguish the Greater Mysteries in Judaism (*Legum Allegoria* III, 37. 100; *De Cherubim* 44. 49; and *De Sacrificiis Abelis et Caini* 16. 62) from the Lesser Mysteries (*De Sacrificiis Abelis et Caini* 16. 62 and *De Abrahamo* 24. 122).

We may comment that Jews were particularly well known for their practice of magic, as may be seen in the statement of Pompeius Trogus (*ap.* Justin, *Historiae Philippicae* 36, Epitome 2. 7) at the end of the first century B.C. that the biblical Joseph won the favor of Pharaoh by his mastery in the arts of magic. There is a canard attributed to Posidonius (*ap.* Strabo XVI, 2. 43. 764) that the Jews are sorcerers and pretend to use incantations in cutting asphalt (presumably extracted from the Dead Sea). Moreover, Josephus' older contemporary Pliny the Elder (*Natural History* XXX, 11) declares that there is a branch of magic derived from Moses, Jannes, Lotapes, and the Jews. Likewise, Lucian (*Philopseudeis* 16) describes a Syrian from Palestine, presumably a Jew, who was able to exorcise spirits. We may add that the second-century Celsus (*ap.* Origen, *Contra Celsum* I, 26) had charged that the Jews are addicted to sorcery, of which Moses was their teacher.

We may also suggest that in his positive attitude toward the occult, Josephus, on the whole, parallels only one side of the talmudic debate. Thus we hear (*Sanhedrin* 68a) that the great Rabbi Eliezer, a younger contemporary of Josephus, enunciated a magic word and a whole field was covered with cucumbers; with the utterance of a second magic word, all of the cucumbers were collected. We also hear (*Gittin* 45a) that the daughters of Rabbi Naḥman (late third and early fourth centuries A.D.) were able to stir a pot of boiling water with their bare hands without being scalded, presumably because of their piety. On the other hand, Josephus does not reflect the opposition to magic seen in a number of mishnaic statements, denouncing magical remedies as being the customs of the Amorites (*Shabbath* 6. 15) and declaring (*Sanhedrin* 10. 1) that a person who pronounces a magic formula over a wound loses his share in the world to come, as well as in a number of later Amoraic statements that "he who acquires a single item of knowledge from a magician forfeits his life" (*Shabbath* 75a) and "harlotry and magic have caused the destruction of all" (*Sotah* 48a).

We may express surprise, as does Professor Smith, that there are no direct references in Josephus to astrology, though we may note that Josephus does mention (*BJ* VI, 289), as a portent of the forthcoming destruction of the Temple, a star resembling a sword, which stood over the city of Jerusalem, and a comet, which continued for a year. The lack of a direct reference to astrology is all the more surprising when we note that notwithstanding the statement of the third-century Rabbi Johanan (*Shabbath* 156a) that there is no planet (*mazal*) for Israel, we find the remarks of Rabbi Ḥanina bar Ḥama (early third century) (*Shabbath* 156a) that there are planets for Israel, as well as the formulation of rules of health and agriculture by the third-century Mar Samuel (*Shabbath* 129b, *Eruvin* 56a) based on astrology, and the refusal of the fourth-century Rabbi Joseph ben Ḥiyya (*Berakhoth* 64a) to accept an appointment as head of a yeshiva because of the warnings of Chaldean astrologers.

We must stress that in this realm of magic, as in that of miracles, Josephus is not utterly consistent. Just as he sometimes omits or rationalizes biblical miracles, while at other times insists upon taking them literally, so in the realm of magic, he insists (*A* II, 286) that the magic of the Egyptians is merely a human technique, whereas Moses' feats proceed from God's providence and power.

The most interesting episode in Josephus pertaining to magic, in which he seems to contradict his above-stated critique, is the story (*A* VIII, 46–48) of a certain Eleazar, who, in the presence of Vespasian, exorcised demons by using a ring that had under its seal one of the roots prescribed by Solomon. Such a story, we may suggest, is to be considered with the many Talmudic tales about King Solomon's occult powers and Ashmedai, where, indeed, a ring is mentioned (*Gittin* 68a). Josephus' attitude toward magic, we may comment, is reflected in the ambiguity among the Romans, where, on the one hand, it is forbidden, as we see in the case of Apuleius (*Apology*), who is charged with the practice of magic, which was prohibited as long before as the time of the Twelve Tables (*Apology* 47), while, on the other hand, magic was actually practiced by even the most enlightened people. A distinction is thus made between black and white magic.

A litmus test of Josephus' fairness may be seen in his treatment of the Samaritans. Fortunately, we have the Samaritans' own chronicles by which we can check him. In the first place, we may ask, as does Professor R. J. Coggins in his essay, whether Josephus had any personal knowledge of contemporary Samaritanism. The answer is likely to be negative, since, as we learn from the categorical statement in John 4:9, in the incident of Jesus' conversation with the Samaritan woman, that "Jews have no dealings with Samaritans." Again, we note, as Professor Coggins remarks, that Josephus' comments about the Samaritans are ambiguous; sometimes he regards them as part of the community of Judaism, and at other times he looks upon them as outsiders. In the second century B.C. Ben Sira speaks of them not as a separate people but as refusing reunion with their brethren by foolishly and stubbornly rejecting the oral law. Josephus reflects the difference of opinion among three of his younger contemporaries (*Kiddushin* 75b): Rabbi Ishmael declares that they are "proselytes through fear of lions" and hence are to be regarded as absolute Gentiles; Rabbi Akiva, generally the most influential rabbi of his era, states that they are true proselytes and hence that they are Israelites; and Rabbi Eliezer, generally the most logical of all, says that some of them are true proselytes, while others are not, and that even among those who are true proselytes, there are those who are not thoroughly versed in the minute details of the precepts, and hence resemble the *amei ha-aretz,* those who are ignorant of legal minutiae. Rabbi Simeon ben Gamaliel, another contemporary, remarks that the matzah of the Samaritans may be eaten on Passover, since they are careful in observing those commandments that are based on the written Torah. Indeed, the Mishnah rules (*Berakhoth* 7. 1) that a Samaritan may be counted as one of the three necessary for reciting the special formula in the grace after meals. An interesting comment is that of Rabbi Abbahu (ca. 300), who, when the Samaritans asked him why he regarded them as Gentiles in all ritual matters, whereas the previous generation of Jews had found their food and wine acceptable, replied (Jerusalem Talmud, *Avodah Zarah* 5. 4. 44d): "Your fathers did not corrupt their ways, but you have yours."

Professor Coggins raises the important point as to whether Josephus looked upon the Samaritans as a political or as a religious group. Josephus may have viewed them in religious terms because he thus defined Judaism, of which they were a branch, opposed as he was to those groups, notably the Zealots and the Sicarii, who looked upon Judaism as primarily a political entity. We may guess that this is a misreading of the Samaritans, who, as we can see from their several revolts to establish their independence, regarded themselves, as did the Jews, as a nation.

We may also conjecture that the Roman procurator Pontius Pilate's ruthless treatment of the multitude gathered round the Samaritan leader who promised to show his followers the sacred vessels allegedly deposited on Mount Gerizim by Moses (*A* XVIII, 85–87) indicates that Pilate regarded him as a messianic figure who would, in accordance with the prevalent view of the messiah at that time, lead a political movement for independence. The fact that the Samaritans appealed to Vitellius, the Roman governor of Syria, is not necessarily an indication that the Samaritan masses were not anti-Roman but rather that the Samaritan leaders had such an attitude.

We may here comment on Josephus' confusion in stating (*A* XI, 302–303) that a grandson of Jehoiada married the daughter of Sanballat, who had been named satrap by the last Darius, whereas Nehemiah 12:10–11:22 dates Jehoiada in the time of Darius a century earlier. Professor Frank Moore

Cross[19] notes that the newly discovered Wadi Daaliyeh papyri show that there was a Sanballat in the early fourth century, and hence we may assume that there was papponymy in the Samaritan ruling family. The stories are, however, so similar (aside from the fact that Josephus refers to Jehoiada's grandson, whereas Nehemiah refers to his son) that it seems more likely that Josephus has simply confused his facts. The confusion may have arisen because Josephus or his source, like the Book of Esther (which speaks of Mordecai as having been exiled by Nebuchadnezzar despite the fact that he was a contemporary of Xerxes a full century later), thought that the Persian period was shorter than it actually was.

Josephus may well have doctored his account of the Persian attitude toward the Samaritans in order to fit it into his thesis that the Persians' rule endured only so long as they behaved properly toward the Jews and persecuted the Samaritans. Josephus, as Shaye Cohen[20] has demonstrated, had little hard evidence for a reversal of policy on the part of the Persians and hence tried to fit what little evidence he had into a procrustean bed. Sanballat's attitude, as adopted by Darius, represents the new Persian approach; Alexander broke with that policy and reverted to the earlier policy of showing favor toward the Jews. For the period closer to Josephus' own day, Josephus appears to be much more antagonistic toward the Samaritans in the *Antiquities* than in the *War*. We may speculate that this is because Josephus' sources for the *Antiquities* were more hostile to the Samaritans or that the rift between the Jews and the Samaritans had increased in intensity during the period between the completion of the two works.

Professor Jacob Neusner, in his essay "Josephus' Pharisees: A Complete Repertoire," raises the question of Josephus' reliability as a historian of this group. We may remark that the very fact that Josephus does not even see fit to mention the Pharisees before the reign of Jonathan the Hasmonean (A XIII, 171–173), despite the fact that he himself admits (A XVIII, 11) that they had existed from the most ancient times, would indicate that they played little if any role in the political affairs of the Jews—the chief subject of Josephus' history. We may also express wonderment that when Josephus contrasts the views of the Pharisees and the Sadducees, as he does in several places, he only once, and very briefly (A XIII, 297), mentions what is surely the most basic difference between them, namely that the Pharisees accept the oral law and that the Sadducees do not.

Professor Neusner contends that the difference in portrayal of the Pharisees in the *Antiquities*, in contrast to that in the *War*, is due to Josephus' effort to show that Palestine is ungovernable without Pharisaic support. This shift is due presumably to his desire to win support from the Romans for the Pharisees against the Sadducees, though the Sadducees had, for practical purposes, lost power with the destruction of the Temple in 70, and hence the

Pharisees had already become the dominant party in Palestine. The differences between the works, we may suggest, are largely due to the different classes of readers for whom they are intended—the *War* for the Jews and the *Antiquities* for the Romans. Here, too, Josephus is hardly consistent, for though in the *Antiquities* he generally presents a more favorable picture of the Pharisees, and especially of their influence with the masses, a passage such as *Antiquities* XIII, 410–411, in which the Pharisees behind Queen Salome Alexandra are depicted as evil geniuses who are ruthless in cutting down their opponents, could hardly strike a reader as enhancing their cause.

We may well wonder at Josephus' statement (*A* XIII, 401; XVIII, 10) about the great influence of the Pharisees among the masses, in view of the fact that he himself (*A* XVII, 42) gives their number as merely "more than 6000" at the time of Herod, when the Jewish population of Palestine must have been at least one or two million. The fact that Josephus here contrasts the six thousand, who refused to take an oath of allegiance to the emperor and to Herod, with "all the Jewish people," who did swear allegiance, indicates that the Pharisees' influence, at least in Herod's time, was not great. If, indeed, the Pharisees were so influential, we may assume that the delegation of Jews, which went to Rome after Herod's death to urge Augustus to end the rule of his successor Archelaus, was headed by Pharisees; yet, Josephus, himself a Pharisee (*V* 12) and, as a descendant of the Hasmoneans, a bitter opponent of Herod, makes no mention of the Pharisees' role in this delegation. If it was Josephus' major aim to convince the Romans that they should rely upon the Pharisees for support in governing Judea, we may wonder why, in his overall presentation of the sects, he stresses (*A* XIII, 171–172; XVIII, 12–15) their theological views, particularly their attitude toward fate and free will, rather than their political reliability. Finally, in the *Life,* which was written after the *Antiquities,* we have the damning evidence against the Pharisees that Simeon ben Gamaliel (*V* 191), a Pharisee from a most illustrious family, highly gifted with intelligence and judgment, and an old and intimate friend of Josephus' arch-rival the revolutionary John of Gischala, succeeded in persuading the high priest to send a delegation, composed of Pharisees, to seek Josephus' removal from command.

Josephus is also inconsistent in his account of John Hyrcanus' relationship to the Pharisees in the *Antiquities.* Thus, we are told that the Pharisees were particularly hostile ($\kappa\alpha\kappa\hat{\omega}\varsigma \ldots \ \epsilon\hat{\iota}\chi\sigma\nu$) to him (*A* XIII, 288) and then, in the very next paragraph, that he was a disciple of theirs and was greatly loved ($\mathring{\eta}\gamma\alpha\pi\hat{\alpha}\tau\sigma$) by them (*A* XIII, 289). The fact that Josephus uses the imperfect tense for both verbs indicates, paradoxically, a continuing hostility and love. Indeed, we see the Pharisees entertained hospitably by him and very indignant when he is falsely accused (*A* XIII, 289–292). When later (*A* XIII, 296) he speaks of the hatred that arose toward him on the part of the masses, he follows this with the amazing statement that after he had suppressed the opposition of the Pharisees he lived happily thereafter. And, at the close of his account of Hyrcanus in the *Antiquities* (XIII, 299–300), when we would expect a bitter condemnation of him for his fierce opposition to the Pharisees, we are told that he died after administering the government in the best fashion (τὸν ἄριστον τρόπον) for thirty-one years, and that he was deemed by God worthy of three of the greatest privileges, the kingship, the high priesthood, and the status of prophet—attributes that would make him the ideal ruler according to the Stoics and to Philo. These are hardly the kinds of statements we would expect from one who is seeking to advance the cause of the Pharisees.

One may well wonder whether Josephus' inconsistent portrayal of the Pharisees largely reflects his sources, as Daniel Schwartz[21] has indicated. In particular, we may call attention to the passage (*A* XVII, 41) where we are introduced, as if it were for the first time, to "a group of Jews" who are "called Pharisees," language that seems to indicate a non-Jewish source, probably Nicolaus of Damascus. Moreover, in this latter passage the Pharisees are punished with a fine for refusing to take an oath, whereas earlier (*A* XV, 370) we are told explicitly that they were not rebuked for failing to do so.

Professor Lawrence Schiffman's essay on the conversion of the royal House of Adiabene raises the question of Josephus' reliability in his use of his sources. We may here suggest that Josephus (or his source) may have embellished his narrative in a way similar to that which he employs in his paraphrase of the Bible, especially since we find such themes as Izates' birth as a result of an incestuous relationship (*A* XX, 18), the prediction while he was still in his mother's womb that he would have a fortunate end (*A* XX, 18), the hatred of his brothers toward him (*A* XX, 22), which is so reminiscent of the story of Joseph, and the fact that he not only ruled for twenty-four years but left twenty-four sons and twenty-four daughters (*A* XX, 92), a motif reminiscent of the twenty-four descendants of Korah who were destined to prophesy under the influence of the Holy Spirit (*Numbers Rabbah* 18. 8) and the twenty-four days that Joseph is said to have spent in prison (*Testament of Joseph*, 15. 1).

We may well ask why Josephus inserted such a long digression into his history, especially since it appears in the midst of his account of the deterioration of relations between the Jews of Palestine and the procurators. We may guess that one major reason was to emphasize, as he had done in the *War,* the stupidity of going to war with the Romans, since Izates (*A* XX, 69–70), when the Parthians try to convince him to join in war against the Romans, argues that so great is the might and good fortune of the Romans that to hope to defeat them was to expect the impossible. It is significant, incidentally, that though Josephus in the *War* (II, 520; VI, 356) acknowledges that some kinsmen of the king of Adiabene joined the ranks of the revolutionaries, he says nothing in the *Antiquities* about this; nor, for that matter, does he indicate in the *War* that the Adiabenians were proselytes.

We may here note that in the *War,* in addition to his silence about the conversion of the Adiabenians who assisted the rebels (he even [*BJ* II, 388] refers to them as ὁμόφυλοι, "belonging to the same tribe"), Josephus omits reference to the conversion of the Idumaeans and the Ituraeans by the Hasmonaeans. Likewise, in the *Antiquities* the cases of conversion are all viewed negatively: thus those who become proselytes at the time of Esther (*A* XI, 285) or of John Hyrcanus (*A* XIII, 257–258) or of Aristobulus (*A* XIII, 318–319) do so because of their fear of the Jews. It is clear that Josephus is opposed to such forcible conversions, as we can see from his statement (*V* 112–113) opposing the forcible circumcision of refugees on the ground that "everyone should worship God in accordance with the dictates of his own conscience." Likewise, we see (*A* XVIII, 81–84) the unhappy result when the noble lady Fulvia is converted to Judaism, only to have her gifts to the Temple taken by Jewish embezzlers.

We may conjecture that the reason why Josephus ignores proselytism or views it negatively was because the Romans, as we see from the bitterness in such writers as Tacitus and Juvenal, resented the subversion of their way of life by a people who intolerantly found no place in their pantheon for the pagan gods and hence had been expelled in A.D. 19 (Dio Cassius, LVII, 18. 5a). Inasmuch as the *Antiquities,* as we can see from the proem (*A* I, 5), is directed to "the whole Greek-speaking world," it would have been impolitic to offend his readers so violently. This, however, raises the question of why Josephus should have chosen to present the Adiabenian episode, with its very positive attitude toward conversion, at such length. Here we may suggest that the key is that Adiabene lay outside the Roman Empire. Inasmuch as Adiabene, as Josephus (*A* XX, 72) stresses, opposed the Parthians, the great national enemy of the Romans, their abandonment of the Parthian gods could well be understood and applauded by the Romans, since a nation was generally identified with its gods. We may also suggest that the fear expressed by Izates' mother, Helena (*A* XX, 39), that the Adiabenians would not tolerate the rule of a Jew over themselves may reflect the view that Parthian subjects would look askance at a Jew because the Jewish people were subjects of the Romans—and, so far as Josephus was concerned, with the exception of some diehards, were loyal subjects.

The fact that the account of Josephus is paralleled by rabbinic versions enables us to see the different uses made of the same story by two sources. In the first place, however, we may note the remarkable similarity in both the rabbinic accounts (notably *Genesis Rabbah* 46. 11) and Josephus that the conversion takes place after Izates reads the biblical passage pertaining to circumcision. In both sources Izates' mother, Helena, plays a key role, and in both

Izates is rescued by divine intervention from an ambush that is set for him in war. But whereas the background and focus in the rabbinic versions are the religious aspects of the conversion, in Josephus the focus is the political and military side, and even, we may add, the economic aspect, since it is a merchant (*A* XX, 34) who plays the key role in interesting Izates in becoming a Jew. The fact that he converts the king's wives may indicate that he was really a missionary, who pointed out the economic advantage of becoming a Jew, perhaps in terms of the financial advantage of being able to borrow money without interest and having economic ties with Jewish merchants throughout the world.

Dr. Heinz Schreckenberg has highlighted the tremendous influence of Josephus on the early Christian church and, in particular, on the development of the Christian view that the destruction of the Temple in Jerusalem and the degradation of the Jews is God's belated punishment inflicted upon them for their terrible sins. We may here note, in this connection, that in the first three centuries of the Christian era, precisely the period when Josephus' influence was minimal, the church was far less virulent in its anti-Judaism. Thus, for example, in the second-century Justin Martyr's *Dialogue with Trypho,* the relationship between the Jewish and Christian disputants is represented as one of mutual courtesy. We may add that the earliest Christian canonical works are not nearly so hostile toward the Jews as the later works are, and, indeed, the extracanonical writings show no particular bitterness toward them. In fact, there is evidence that Jews and Christians in ordinary walks of life managed to live alongside one another in relative peace. It was only when the Christian polemic against the Jews became more and more strident in the fourth and fifth centuries, at the time when Christianity became the official religion of the empire, that the relationship between the two groups deteriorated into mutual hatred—an attitude that continued to be characteristic of Jewish-Christian relationships for many centuries and is only very recently beginning to be understood and to be overcome.

In this shift of attitude Josephus' works play a key role, particularly, as Dr. Schreckenberg notes, *The Jewish War,* with its poignant description of the destruction of the Temple, which was interpreted as divine punishment for the alleged role of the Jews in the death of Jesus. We may thus call attention to the coincidence of the following factors in the fourth century: Christianity became the official religion of the Roman Empire; the *Testimonium Flavianum,* stating that Jesus was accused before Pilate "by men of the highest standing amongst us" first appears in Eusebius; and the most vicious anti-Jewish diatribes by John Chrysostom and Gregory of Nyssa appear.

Dr. Schreckenberg has called our attention to the fact that the anti-Judaism of the Christian theologians was built, to a considerable degree, upon the foundation of Josephus' violent opposition to the Zealots (and, we may add, to the other four revolutionary groups he enumerates in *The Jewish War* VII, 262–274), whose point of view they equated with that of the Jews generally, though Josephus would have us believe that these revolutionaries were a minority who had browbeaten the rest of the Jews into supporting them. The fact that the Christians were eager to appear to be loyal to the Roman Empire and that they did not join the Jews in the revolutions against Rome in 66–74 or in 115–117 or in 132–135 probably contributed to their later effort to sharpen the contrast between themselves and the Jews. The Christians thus sought to ingratiate themselves with the Romans; it is no coincidence that the word "Romans" appears only once in the Gospels (John 11:48), thus downgrading their role in the story of the passion of Jesus. Of course, the Christians could not support the Bar Kochba rebellion (132–135), since it recognized a different messiah, Bar Kochba; and if, as seems likely, there were messianic movements behind the first two rebellions, we may well understand Christian opposition.

It is interesting that *The Jewish War,* as Dr. Schreckenberg remarks, became more influential than the *Antiquities* in Christian polemic; and we may consequently remark that it is surprising that the *Testimonium Flavianum* is interpolated into the *Antiquities* rather than into the corresponding passage about Pilate's procuratorship in *The Jewish War* (II, 169–177), as it is in the Slavonic version.

The picture of the Jew as a monster that we find in the works of such fourth century writers as John Chrysostom is inspired, it seems, by Josephus' portrait of the last desperate days of the Jews in Jerusalem as depicted in *The Jewish War,* Book VI, and, in particular, by the account of Maria, who actually devoured her own child. We may further note that it is precisely this sixth book of the *War* that was translated into Syriac and that became, in effect, an extracanonical book of the Syriac Bible.

Professor Wataru Mizugaki's essay, "Origen and Josephus," shows how important Josephus was for the church both in filling in the period between the Jewish Scriptures and the Gospels and in expounding the Bible. We may well ask why Josephus was virtually ignored before Origen; and the answer, we may suggest, is that the early writers of the church were not sufficiently learned, especially in exegesis, and insufficiently sophisticated in historical matters to appreciate him. A similar question may be asked as to why Philo was ignored prior to the third century; and we may similarly answer that the early fathers were insufficiently trained in philosophy to appreciate his biblical exegesis.

We may also ask why Origen refers to *The Jewish War* by the title Περὶ Ἁλώσεως (*On the Capture*), whereas Josephus himself on three occasions (*V* 412; *A* XVIII, 11, XX, 258) refers to his work as *The Jewish War.* The reason may be that Origen viewed the work from a Christian perspective as concerned primarily with the capture of Jerusalem and the destruction of the Temple, in fulfillment of Jesus' prophecy. Hence, we may note that the *War*, in effect, ends with Book VI; and, indeed, Origen never quotes from Book VII, which deals with events after the destruction of the Temple. Similarly, though Eusebius, Origen's great pupil, cites Josephus from the *War* 101 times, he cites nothing beyond Book VI, which, we may reiterate, actually became a canonized book in the Syriac church, presumably because it contained the actual description of the fall of Jerusalem and the destruction of the Temple.

Professor Mizugaki notes and seeks to explain discrepancies between Origen's and Josephus' texts. We may suggest that due to the unpopularity and even condemnation of Origen as heterodox by his contemporaries and successors in the church, only a small portion of his works (which have been estimated to number six thousand!) has survived in the original, and his text may well have been tampered with. Indeed, even in his own day, Origen had to complain of falsifications of his works and forgeries under his name. The modifications also suggest that Origen is either quoting from memory—and memories were much more cultivated in those days—or he is paraphrasing somewhat loosely, in accordance with the prevalent practice of the time, as we can see from the fact, for example, that when Eusebius quotes the *Testimonium Flavianum* he varies the wording each of the three times he does so.

Undoubtedly the most discussed passage in Josephus, and perhaps in all ancient literature, is Josephus' statement about Jesus, the *Testimonium Flavianum* (*A* XVIII, 63–64). I have noted more than a hundred discussions of this topic during the past fifty years. Dr. Zvi Baras presents the original suggestion that the interpolation may have taken place in the same way that Origen and Eusebius add to Josephus' notice (*A* XX, 200–203) concerning James the brother of Jesus the statement that the destruction of the Temple was divine punishment inflicted upon the Jews for their condemnation of James. Dr. Baras suggests that the passage in Josephus (*A* XI, 297–305) about the punishment inflicted by God upon the Jews for the terrible murder of a priest coincidentally named Jesus by his own brother during the Persian period may have influenced Origen. We may add that Origen's ascription of moralizing to Josephus in the case of James may have been influenced by Josephus' own statement, in the proem to his work (*A* I, 14), that the main lesson to be learned from his history by his readers is that those who obey God will prosper and that those who do not will suffer disaster in proportion to their sins. Thus, for example, Josephus expounds (*A* IV, 11–58, 131–155) on the terrible punishment that descended upon the Israelites for their participation in Korah's rebellion and for their consorting with the Midianite women. Likewise, in the very book in which the *Testimonium Flavianum* appears, in his introduction to the narrative of events leading to the destruction of the Temple, Josephus (*A* XVIII, 9) moralizes, declaring that "here is a lesson that an innovation and reform in ancestral traditions weighs heavily in the scale in leading to the destruction of the congregation of the people." Likewise, Josephus (*BJ* VII, 271) stresses that each of the five revolutionary groups that he enumerates suffered "a fitting end, God awarding due retribution to them all." In particular, we may suggest that the immediate model of Origen and Eusebius is Josephus' own comment (*A* XVIII, 119) that the verdict of the Jews was that the destruction visited upon the army of Herod Antipas was God's punishment for his execution of John.

As to the *Testimonium* itself, we may remark that it seems remarkable that this is the only passage in Josephus (with the possible exceptions of those about John and James) that has been suspected of interpolation, though the most recent commentator on the passage, J. Neville Birdsall,[22] has argued that it contains several words or meanings of words that are not customary in the rest of Josephus. One would have expected that an interpolator would have modified Josephus' passage about John the Baptist (*A* XVIII, 116–119) so as to make the occasion of John's death accord with the Gospels and to indicate that he was a forerunner of Jesus. That, indeed, Josephus did say something about Jesus is indicated, above all, by the passage—the authenticity of which has been almost universally acknowledged—about James, who is termed (*A* XX, 200) the brother of "the aforementioned Christ." To be sure, Per Bilde[23] has argued that the reference to James is intended merely to distinguish him from other persons named Jesus (there are twenty-one mentioned by Josephus alone) and does not presuppose a text about him. We may comment, however, that it is hardly in character for Josephus to mention someone, especially someone with such a curious surname as *Christos* (the only one with that title in all of Josephus), without describing the implications of this word or giving an anecdote to illustrate it. The fact that Josephus does not add any such explanation would seem to indicate that he had already informed the reader about him. We may further note that Justin Martyr, in his *Apology* (I, 30), written about half a century after the *Antiquities,* has almost exactly the same phrase employed by Josephus (*A* XX, 200)—τὸν παρ᾽ ἡμῖν λεγόμενον Χριστόν, "the so-called Christ among us." As to the recent suggestion by Tessa Rajak[24] that the passage about James is a Christian interpolation because it has such a derogatory view of Ananus the high priest (Josephus elsewhere [*BJ* IV, 319–321] praises him), we may remark that there are a number of instances in the *Antiquities* where Josephus contradicts what he says in the *War.* In any case, it would seem more likely that a forger would have been more careful than to contradict outright what Josephus says elsewhere. Moreover, it makes no sense for Origen to express wonder (*Commentary on Matthew* 10:17) that Josephus did not admit Jesus to be the messiah if Josephus did not even mention him.

That Josephus may have had some data that are not in our extant Greek text may be indicated by the fact that in the tenth-century history of the world by a Christian named Agapius we read that, according to Josephus, Herod burned the genealogies of the tribes so that it would not be known that he had an undistinguished ancestry—a fact that is not found in our extant Josephus but is stated in Eusebius (*Historia Ecclesiastica* I, 7. 13). Such a legend, however, might well have arisen because it is clear from both Josephus and the Talmud (*Baba Bathra* 3b–4a) that Herod was extremely sensitive about his ignoble origin.

That the passage is, indeed, interpolated seems indicated by the fact that in the statement in the *War* about the deeds of Pilate, which parallels this in the *Antiquities,* there is no mention of Jesus, despite the fact that the length of the account is almost as great as that in the *Antiquities*. In addition, Justus of Tiberias (*ap.* Photius, *Bibliotheca* 33), Josephus' great contemporary and rival, apparently made no mention at all of Jesus. The fact that an ancient table of contents, already referred to in the Latin version of the fifth or sixth century, omits mention of the *Testimonium* (though, admittedly, it is selective, one must find it hard to believe that such a remarkable passage would be omitted by anyone, let alone by a Christian, summarizing the work) is further indication that either there was no such notice or that it was much less remarkable than it reads at present. Furthermore, it is not cited until Eusebius does so in the fourth century, despite the fact that such a passage would have been extremely effective, to say the least, since it comes from a Jew who was born only a few years after Jesus' death, in the debates between Jews and Christians, especially since we know that Justin Martyr (*Dialogue with Trypho* 8) attempted to answer the charge that Jesus had never lived and that he was a mere figment of Christian imagination. And yet, I have counted[25] no fewer than eleven church fathers prior to or contemporary with Eusebius who cite various passages from Josephus (including the *Antiquities*) but who do not mention the *Testimonium*. Moreover, during the century after Eusebius there are five church fathers, including Augustine, who certainly had many occasions to find it useful and who cite passages from Josephus but not this one. It would also seem remarkable that Jerome, who does cite the passage (*De Viris Illustribus* 13. 14), says that Jesus *was believed* (*credebatur*) to be the messiah, and not, as Josephus has it in our text, that he *was* the messiah. Moreover, though Jerome knows Josephus so well that he cites him no fewer than ninety times and, indeed, refers to him as a second Livy (*Epistula ad Eustochium* 22), he cites the *Testimonium* only this one time. To be sure, all this is the *argumentum ex silentio,* but as a cumulative argument it has considerable force.

One of the problems, however, with regard to Eusebius' role in connection with our *Testimonium* is that he quotes it differently in the three places where he mentions it. The simple explanation for this would be scribal modification or error in the transmission of the text, though this must always be a last resort in textual criticism. More likely, the divergent versions are due to the difficulty that writers in antiquity had in consulting original texts and their consequent greater reliance upon memory. There are parallels to such variant quotations in the writings of Clement of Alexandria and Jerome.

As to Josephus' motive for inserting the *Testimonium,* the most famous theory is that of Richard Laqueur,[26] who asserts that Justus of Tiberias, in one of his lost works, had charged that Josephus had misinterpreted the Bible and had taken the Septuagint rather than the Hebrew text as his basis at a time when in rabbinic circles the movement against the Septuagint was becoming strong and was to lead to the sanctioning of a new and more faithful translation by Aquila. According to this theory, Josephus now turned to the Christians to gain their support, since they looked upon the Septuagint as divinely inspired. But such a theory rests on quicksand, for we have none of Justus' writings, and Josephus himself in his *Life* cites no such charge despite the fact that he cites several others. Moreover, Josephus very often does diverge from the Septuagint. As to seeking a market for his works among Christians, Josephus was well enough off with his royal pension, and while he might have gained a minuscule Christian audience he probably would have alienated a much larger Hellenistic Jewish audience.

Finally, the dramatic rediscovery by Shlomo Pines[27] of the tenth-century Agapius' version in Arabic of the *Testimonium* reveals that the order of the statements differs sharply from that in Josephus' Greek text and indicates that we are dealing here with a paraphrase, one that is based upon Eusebius' *Historia Ecclesiastica,* which was the chief source through which Josephus' work was known in the eastern Mediterranean during the Middle Ages. This, of course, still leaves the question as to how a believing Christian could quote Josephus as saying that Jesus "was perhaps the messiah." This may have been due to Agapius' realization that, as a Jew, Josephus could hardly have accepted Jesus as the messiah; and so, like Jerome, he qualifies Josephus' statement.

We may remark that no ancient author had an influence in the Latin West and in the Greek East as great as Josephus and from such an early period. By comparison only a few of Philo's works, for example, were translated into Latin. The influence of Josephus upon the Latin West is, to a considerable degree, filtered through the free paraphrase by Pseudo-Hegesippus. Professor Albert Bell's essay establishes the fact that the writing of Pseudo-Hegesippus is more than a paraphrase but is a historical work, with its own distinct Christian point of view, in its own right. In particular, it illustrates the concerns of the fourth century, during which it was composed, particularly the foiled attempt of Julian the Apostate to rebuild the Temple in Jerusalem. We may add that another event that may well have added to the bitterness between Jews and

Christians was the attempt shortly before this time of a converted Jew to construct churches in Palestine in towns where they had never been built before. Jews attacked the builders, most of whom were converts to Christianity, and were bloodily suppressed by Roman imperial legions, though only after a full-scale Jewish revolt.

The central focus of Pseudo-Hegesippus is, indeed, the destruction of the Temple as divine punishment for the sins of the Jews, notably that of deicide. As Professor Bell notes, it is precisely in the fourth century that the anti-Semitic venom of the church fathers reached its height. We may see it in the comments of Gregory of Nyssa and Jerome and, above all, in John Chrysostom. Part of the vehemence of this anti-Semitism is perhaps due to the desire of the Christians, in the face of countless heresies, to prove their orthodoxy. And what better way to prove one's orthodoxy than to lash out at the historic enemy of the Christians, the Jews? By comparison Pseudo-Hegesippus is mild indeed; but the work is important for the influence it had in spreading the view of the collective guilt of the Jews for the death of Jesus and of the justness of the suffering they endured, first at the hands of the Romans and later at the hands of the Christians. Ironically, the work is also important for its influence upon the tenth-century Hebrew paraphrase *Josippon,* whose dependence upon Pseudo-Hegesippus, is clear from the fact that the author never includes anything from Josephus that had been omitted by Pseudo-Hegesippus, whereas he omits much that Pseudo-Hegesippus had taken from Josephus.

We may also remark that Pseudo-Hegesippus, unlike Josephus, who stresses that it makes no sense to oppose the Romans, takes a positive attitude toward the achievements of the Romans, particularly peace. In this, too, he reflects the aim of the Christians to present themselves as loyal subjects of the Romans, unlike the Jews, who had revolted three times within two generations. Similarly, the role of the Romans in the crucifixion of Jesus is minimized in the New Testament, so that the very word "Roman" is found only once in the Gospels (John 11:48).

Professor Steven Bowman's essay, "Josephus in Byzantium," highlights the popularity of Josephus in the Byzantine Empire. Surely, aside from the Bible itself, there is no parallel to the works of an ancient author that survive in their entirety (or even more than in their entirety, since IV Maccabees was falsely ascribed to Josephus), except for a brief passage of *Against Apion,* for which we must depend upon the Latin translation, that are so widely copied (133 manuscripts are extant in Greek), that are epitomized, and that are very freely paraphrased in both Old Russian and Hebrew, as they had been previously translated into Latin and Syriac. Professor Bowman speculates that one reason for Josephus' popularity was that he could be used both by the entrenched Orthodox church against its opponents and by challengers to the status quo. The text of the Bible was frozen by the accuracy of Bible transmission and by the authority of the New Testament canonization backed by imperial edict, whereas Josephus was more flexible in his interpretation of the Bible. In a sense the flexibility inherent in the Talmudic and midrashic tradition, with which Josephus was so well acquainted, influenced such Christian exegesis, despite its Jewish origin, and initially because—or largely because—of the two small paragraphs in Josephus paying tribute to Jesus.

The key figures in the transmission of Josephus are, as Professor Bowman notes, the fourth-century Eusebius and the tenth-century Photius, the first sometimes suspected as the one who interpolated the *Testimonium Flavianum* and the second responsible for the decision to disregard the history by Justus of Tiberias. In addition to Professor Bowman's suggestion that Justus was disregarded because he failed to mention Jesus, we may add that Photius was very much influenced by Eusebius' very positive appraisal of Josephus and very negative view of Justus. We may also suggest that we have more of Justus than we think and that it is only anonymously that he is preserved by Eusebius because of Josephus' strictures against him and because of his omission of mention of Jesus.

We may also ask why Josephus' main source for so much of his work, Nicolaus of Damascus, whose history of the world in 144 books is the longest work known from antiquity, has been lost, except for excerpts and fragments. One answer may be the very length of the work, which made it so cumbersome to consult in an age in which there were no indexes; hence, mere excerpts were preserved of the portions deemed most interesting. Another reason could be that Nicolaus, after all, was a pagan and the right hand of Herod, an arch-villain to Christians because of the massacre of the innocents.

As to the freedom taken by the Slavonic and Hebrew paraphrases of the *War,* this is in line with the philosophy that we can see exemplified in Pseudo-Hegesippus. The paraphraser looks upon himself as a historian in his own right and, in effect, comments on the current scene through his reinterpretation of ancient events. Indeed, we may even have a paraphraser of a paraphraser, as we find in *Josippon*'s use of Pseudo-Hegesippus and in the twelfth-century Jerahmeel's use of *Josippon*.

Professor David Flusser's study of *Josippon* illuminates its author who, like Pseudo-Hegesippus, deserves to be called a historian in his own right. Like Pseudo-Hegesippus, he does not, despite what many of his readers (even to the present day)[28] thought, pretend to be Josephus, but rather cites him. We may remark that the author of *Josippon* shows an acquaintance with an impressive variety of sources in addition to Pseudo-Hegesippus—Josephus, the Bible, the Apocrypha, the Talmud, early medieval Latin works, and Jerome's *Chronicle.*

One may wonder why, if the author of *Josippon* had Josephus' works available, he read Pseudo-Hegesippus, especially since it contains several distinctly Christian passages. Professor Flusser suggests that the author wrongly believed that Pseudo-Hegesippus had also been written by Josephus but that the work had been interpolated. As an alternative, we may suggest that the author of *Josippon* thought that Josephus himself was a Christian and used him selectively in the same way, though, of course, to a much greater degree, than he used the work of Jerome, or, for that matter, the Latin translation of the Bible, with its Christological interpretations. The fact that *Josippon* cites the persecution of the Jews by Caligula, which is narrated at some length in Book XVIII of the *Antiquities,* the very book which, in the Latin version used by *Josippon,* did contain the *Testimonium Flavianum* about Jesus, may be an indication that the author of *Josippon* thought that the real Josephus was a Christian (as did William Whiston, the famous translator of Josephus, incidentally, as late as the eighteenth century). His preference for Pseudo-Hegesippus may be due to his attraction to an account that is considerably briefer and simpler than the original Josephus.

Professor Flusser makes the interesting suggestion that the author of the *Josippon* may have been a physician in southern Italy, possibly in Naples. We may remark that during the Middle Ages, Josephus himself, as Lewy[29] has shown, was regarded as an expert physician who had cured the Roman general (later emperor) Titus of a swollen leg. Moreover, Naples was near Salerno, where, in the century before the composition of *Josippon,* a medical school had been founded in which, we hear, there were Jewish instructors and where some have thought that Hebrew was one of the languages of instruction.

Professor Flusser calls our attention to two manuscripts of *Josippon* that contain interpolations about Jesus reminiscent of similar passages in the Slavonic version of the *Jewish War,* which apparently dates from the century after *Josippon.* Such passages might have been inserted into the work by an apostate who perhaps in debates with Jews thought that it would be useful to cite an apparently Jewish historian who acknowledged the messiahship of Jesus. If it is striking that the interpolator put Jesus in the time of the emperor Gaius Caligula, we might note that he found his reference to Jesus in the eighteenth book of Josephus' *Antiquities,* where it appears in close proximity to an extensive discussion of the persecution of the Jews by Caligula. Also, perhaps he placed Jesus in the time of Caligula in order to emphasize the value of the *Josippon's* notice about him, since Josephus (*V* 5) states that he himself was born in the year of the accession of that emperor. All in all, the author of *Josippon* emerges as a major figure in the renaissance of Hebrew literature in southern Italy at the time that the Golden Age was beginning in Spain. In both cases this renaissance was stimulated by a significant Jewish contact with non-Jewish languages and literatures, whether Latin, as in the case of *Josippon,* or Arabic in the case of Spain.

The popularity of *Josippon* quickly became so great that its study was specifically permitted on the ninth day of Av, a fast day in the Jewish calendar that commemorates the destruction of the two Temples and on which, because it is a day of mourning, the joy of normal study is prohibited. Because it was thought to be by Josephus and perhaps because of its brevity, *Josippon* was sometimes preferred by Christians, who knew of both authors, to the actual works written by Josephus. It has been suggested that *Josippon* played a role in the attempt of Oliver Cromwell to gain readmission of the Jews to England in the seventeenth century. It was, moreover, the second book of Jewish authorship to be published in colonial America (1722).

Josephus' vast influence in literature, art, and music remains to be studied systematically. Dr. Guy N. Deutsch's essay, which traces this influence in the illustration of manuscripts down to the sixteenth century, shows how Josephus was utilized in each period to reflect issues or teachings. Just as the art in cathedrals served to educate Christians during this period, so the choice of topics and the depictions themselves in the manuscripts educated many generations of Christian readers. Because Josephus included midrashic-like additions in his version of biblical history, his works became a source of Christian knowledge of such Jewish traditions; and the illustrations in the manuscripts served to etch these more definitely in the medieval consciousness.

In particular, as Dr. Deutsch notes, the depiction of Herod proved popular because of his role in the massacre of the innocents. Thus, Nordström[30] has called our attention to two manuscripts in Gerona, Spain, one from 975 and the other from about 1100. The earlier manuscript portrays a scene from the attempted suicide of Herod and the later one pictures him with his genitals exposed, illustrating his terrible suffering.

We may also here call attention to the influence of Josephus on the illustration of manuscripts of the Bible. Thus, as Weitzmann[31] has shown, the illustrations in the sixth-century Cotton Genesis, the twelfth-century Vatican Octateuch, and a twelfth-century English miniature in the Morgan Library in New York of Moses as a child running into the open arms of the pharaoh are taken from Josephus' addition (*A* II, 264). Likewise, the representation of Agag being executed, not by Samuel as in the Bible but by an executioner (presumably because Josephus felt that it was improper for Samuel, a Nazirite, to do so), in the ninth-century miniature of the *Sacra Parallela* of John of Damascus owes its origin to Josephus (*A* VI, 244), as does the depiction of the persecution of the priests of Baal by the Israelites (*A* VIII, 343) rather than by Elijah. It was largely through Josephus, moreover, that the Latin Middle Ages gained its knowledge of the Greek writers, such as Strabo, whom he so often cites. And the depiction of Babylon's position, its defenses, and its conquest by Cyrus in a miniature in the Ripoll Bible is due to Josephus, since Herodotus' data on this matter are mentioned by Josephus, whereas Herodotus himself was unknown in the Latin West during the Middle Ages.

Josephus was widely read for what he tells about the intertestamental period, for which he is our only systematic source. Likewise, he was quarried as a source for Roman history, especially for the period of the life of Jesus and of the early church. But, of course, Josephus' chief influence was due to the two short paragraphs constituting the *Testimonium Flavianum* and, in particular, for his testimony, as interpreted by Christian illustrators, to the punishment meted out to the Jews for their responsibility in connection with the death of Jesus. His popularity was greatly enhanced by the Crusades, since Josephus provided by far the most extensive guide to the Holy Land, and especially to Jerusalem and its remains. The illustration, we may suggest, of the struggle between Jacob and Esau for the birthright thus becomes indicative of the encounter between Christendom (which, ironically, appropriated the figure of Jacob) and Jewry (which is represented by Esau). The coordination between these pictorial representations of biblical scenes (and the theological import assigned to them) and the scenes in the mystery and passion plays alluded to by Dr. Deutsch remains to be traced in detail.

The surprising fact that we have almost no illustrated manuscripts from the thirteenth and fourteenth centuries may be explained by the fact that during these centuries Christendom was preoccupied with philosophical rather than historical questions and by the fact that the Crusades were, for practical purposes, over. If Josephus reemerges into public favor in the fifteenth century it is probably due to the interest in classical historians in the early Renaissance (note, for example, the excitement with which Boccaccio proclaims his rediscovery of the historian Tacitus, whose works had been lying "shamefully neglected" in the Benedictine abbey of Monte Cassino) and to the fact that Josephus so often provides a link between biblical events and occurrences in the histories of Greece, especially during the Hellenistic period, and Rome. In this connection, we may note that Burke[32] has found that for the period from 1450 to 1700 there were more editions of Josephus' *Antiquities* (seventy-three) and of his *War* (sixty-eight) than of the works of any other Greek historian. In an age of ecumenism, when, we may recall, a Pico della Mirandola hoped to synthesize Plato, Aristotle, Jewish Kabbalah, and Christian mysticism, Josephus appears as a Faustian polymath—historian, geographer, theologian, natural scientist, physician, mathematician, grammarian, and general; and in an age of Renaissance *condottieri* it is not surprising that the portrayal of Josephus the general is most popular.

Professor Betsy Halpern Amaru's essay, "Martin Luther and Flavius Josephus," calls attention to the influence that Josephus had upon the Reformation, especially in challenging the Roman Catholic interpretation of the Bible. It is significant that there were no fewer than four different translations of Josephus into German published in the sixteenth century.

In his philosophy of history, as in so much else, Luther seems to have had contradictory views. On the one hand, he declares[33] that "in the Scriptures no allegory, tropology, or anagoge is valid unless the same thing is expressly said *hystorice.*" Professor Amaru calls our attention to Luther's statement, particularly important for the Reformation, which objected to the church's "perverse" interpretation of history, that "histories are nothing else than a demonstration, recollection, and sign of divine action and judgment, how He upholds, rules, obstructs, prospers, punishes, and honors the world and especially men, each according to his just desert, evil or good." We may suggest that Luther is here closely paralleling Josephus' own statement (*A* I, 14) of the moral lesson to be learned from history: "Speaking generally, the main lesson to be learnt from this history by any who care to peruse it is that men who conform to the will of God, and do not venture to transgress laws that have been excellently laid down, prosper in all things beyond belief, and for their reward are offered by God felicity; whereas, in proportion as they depart from the strict observance of these things, things [else] practicable become impracticable, and whatever imaginary good thing they strive to do ends in irretrievable disasters."

And yet, on the other hand, Luther uses the term *historicus* as a synonym for "carnal" and "Jewish."[34] A similar ambivalence is to be seen in his attitude toward Josephus. Luther had a profound respect for the Jewish Scriptures, which he felt had not been properly appreciated by the Roman Catholic Church, and Josephus was a scholarly interpreter of the Jewish biblical tradition; but Josephus was, from Luther's point of view, profoundly wrong in not realizing the true significance of that tradition in presaging the mission of Jesus.

In addition to the places where Luther cites Josephus by name, Professor Amaru notes that there are other indications that he used Josephus. We may here cite one such example,[35] where Luther speaks of "Sadducean, that is Epicurean." This strange equation is readily intelligible if we note that Josephus (*V* 12) speaks of the Pharisees as "a sect having points of resemblance to that which the Greeks call the Stoic school." Inasmuch as the great opponents of the Pharisees were the Sadducees and inasmuch as the great opponents of the Stoics were the Epicureans, Luther makes the equation of Sadducees = Epicureans.

It is, we may suggest, in Luther's notorious essay "On the Jews and Their Lies" (which occasioned dismay from Melancthon, Andreas Osiander, and Henry Bullinger, the last of whom wrote to Martin Bucer that Luther's views on the Jews resembled those of the Inquisition) that the influence of Josephus is particularly strong. For Luther, Josephus is the chief source for his view that the suffering of the Jews was due to their role in the death of Jesus. Indeed, he cites Josephus:[36] "This delusion regarding their false Christ [that is, messianic pretender] and their persecution of the true Christ cost them eleven times one hundred thousand men, as Josephus [*BJ* VI, 420] reports, as well as the forfeiture of scepter, temple, priesthood, and all that they possessed." In view of the venom of this essay, we may remark that it is surprising that Luther does not cite what would surely have strengthened his argument, namely that the one Jew of antiquity who was scholarly and who had a sense of history did recognize Jesus as the messiah, as he does in all our texts (*A* XVIII, 63). We may suggest that Luther's silence about the *Testimonium* may be due to his own doubts as to its authenticity (although it was not until the end of the century that Lucas Osiander was to argue in print, for the first time, that it was a forgery) or due to his desire to denigrate Josephus simply because he was Jewish. Finally, we may ask why, as noted by Professor Amaru, Luther objects so vehemently to Josephus' idealized portrait of Saul. We may suggest that the idea of a brave and proud Jewish fighter was utterly repugnant to Luther, who harbored the medieval stereotype of the meek Jew who cringed before his master.

In summary, the essays included in this volume would give Josephus mixed grades so far as his reliability as a historian is concerned. On the whole, he seems to be well acquainted with the land of Israel, which is the central focus of his accounts; he is well versed not only in the Bible but also in the body of oral law, as later codified in the Talmud, though disagreeing in many respects with it; he is well read in a wide variety of authors and has direct access to the commentaries of Vespasian and of Titus, even when he does not explicitly mention them; and he is generally supported by archaeological excavations, notably at Masada. However, he seems to be mistaken in many details, such as those in connection with the episode describing Pilate's introduction of the emperor's standards into Jerusalem, where Philo serves as a corrective, and even those in his description of the buildings at Masada; he is guilty of promoting the cause of his Roman patrons, in claiming, for example, that Titus was opposed to setting fire to the Temple, whereas Sulpicius Severus shows that he favored it; he reflects sentiments being expressed at the time of his writing in Rome, as seen in the speeches he puts into the mouth of Eleazar ben Jair at Masada; he is guilty of misogyny, though perhaps it is no greater than it is in most other writers of the day and though he does present idealized portraits of the matriarchs; he unduly emphasizes political and military events and largely neglects economic, social, religious, and cultural factors, though in this he is certainly no worse than Thucydides; he is anything but careful in his terminology, especially in theological matters; he is guilty of viewing Judaism (and Samaritanism) as a religion rather than the Jews as a people or a nation; and he is inconsistent in his attitude toward the Pharisees, Samaritans, proselytism, miracles, and magic.

As to his influence, the two chief reasons for its magnitude are the *Testimonium Flavianum* about Jesus and the interpretation given by Christian writers to his *Jewish War* to reinforce their view that the sufferings of the

Jews, and in particular the destruction of the Temple, were due to alleged Jewish complicity in the condemnation of Jesus. Given this theological basis, Josephus' works were also widely read because he was viewed as an excellent guide to biblical exegesis who has, moreover, many tales to supplement the narrative, and who was the best guide for pilgrims traveling to the Holy Land, since he knew the country of his birth so intimately. Moreover, he gained a reputation as a polymath—expert in grammar, etymology, geography, mathematics, natural science, and the art of war. Finally, he makes for exciting reading, possessing a great flair for rhetoric in the speeches of his characters, and supplying an abundance of purple passages.

Notes

1. Helgo Lindner, *Die Geschichtsauffassung des Flavius Josephus im Bellum Judaicum. Gleichzeitig ein Beitrag zur Quellenfrage* (Leiden, 1972).

2. Trude Weiss-Rosmarin, "Masada, Josephus and Yadin," *JSp* 32, no. 8 (Oct., 1967) 2–8, 30–32; *idem,* "Masada Revisited," *JSp* 34 (Dec., 1969) 3–5, 29–32.

3. Shaye J. D. Cohen, "Masada, Literary Tradition, Archaeological Remains, and the Credibility of Josephus," *JJS* 33 (1982) 385–405.

4. Andrew Q. Morton and Sidney Michaelson, "Elision as an Indicator of Authorship in Greek Writers," *Revue de l'Organisation Internationale pour l'Étude des Langues Anciennes par Ordinateur* (1973, part 3) 33–56.

5. Seth Schwartz, *Josephus and Judaism from 70 to 100 of the Common Era* (diss., Ph.D., Columbia University, New York, 1985), appendix: "The Composition and Publication of BJ VII."

6. Daniel R. Schwartz, "Josephus and Philo on Pontius Pilate," *JC* 3 (1983) 26–45.

7. Moses Gaster, *The Asatir: The Samaritan Book of the "Secrets of Moses" Together with the Pitron or Samaritan Commentary and the Samaritan Story of the Death of Moses* (London, 1927) 73.

8. David Goldenberg, *The Halakhah in Josephus and in Tannaitic Literature: A Comparative Study* (diss., Ph.D., Dropsie College, Philadelphia, 1978) 118.

9. Steven Riskin, *The Halakhah in Josephus as Reflected in Against Apion and The Life* (diss., M.A., Yeshiva University, New York, 1970).

10. Haim Cohn, "Flavius Josephus as Historian of the Laws of Punishment" [Hebrew] (unpublished lecture, Hebrew University, Jerusalem, 27 March 1972).

11. Goldenberg (above, n. 8) 218–235.

12. Goldenberg (above, n. 8) 226.

13. See my discussion, *Josephus and Modern Scholarship (1937–1980)* (Berlin, 1984) 438–444.

14. Louis H. Feldman, "Abraham the Greek Philosopher in Josephus," *TAPA* 99 (1968) 146–149.

15. Louis H. Feldman, "Josephus as an Apologist to the Greco-Roman World: His Portrait of Solomon," in *Aspects of Religious Propaganda in Judaism and Early Christianity,* ed. by Elisabeth Schüssler Fiorenza (Notre Dame, 1976) 71.

16. Luther H. Martin, "Josephus' Use of *Heimarmene* in the Jewish Antiquities XIII, 171–173," *Numen* 28 (1981) 127–137.

17. Cf., e.g., Strabo (XVI, 2. 38–39, 762), who makes Moses parallel to the revered

Cretan king and lawgiver Lycurgus as a lawgiver who claimed divine sanction for his laws. Cf. also Numenius (*ap.* Clement of Alexandria, *Stromata* I, 22. 150. 4), who compares Moses with Plato: "For what is Plato but Moses speaking in Attic?"

18. See David Altshuler, "On the Classification of Judaic Laws in the *Antiquities* of Josephus and the Temple Scroll of Qumran," *AJSR* 7–8 (1982–1983) 11.

19. Frank M. Cross, "A Reconstruction of the Judean Restoration," *JBL* 94 (1975) 4–18.

20. Shaye J. D. Cohen, "Alexander the Great and Jaddus the High Priest According to Josephus," *AJSR* 7–8 (1982–1983) 41–68, especially 62.

21. Daniel R. Schwartz, "Josephus and Nicolaus on the Pharisees," *JSJ* 14 (1983) 157–171.

22. J. Neville Birdsall, "The Continuing Enigma of Josephus's Testimony about Jesus," *BJRL* 67 (1985) 609–622.

23. Per Bilde, "Josefus' beretning om Jesus" ("Josephus' Text about Jesus"), *DTT* 44 (1981) 99–135.

24. Tessa Rajak, *Josephus: The Historian and His Society* (London, 1983) 131.

25. Louis H. Feldman, "The Testimonium Flavianum: The State of the Question," in Robert F. Berkey and Sarah A. Edwards, edd., *Christological Perspectives: Essays in Honor of Harvey K. McArthur* (New York, 1982) 179–199, 288–293.

26. Richard Laqueur, *Der jüdische Historiker Flavius Josephus. Ein biographischer Versuch auf neuer quellenkritischer Grundlage* (Giessen, 1920) 274ff.

27. Shlomo Pines, *An Arabic Version of the Testimonium Flavianum and Its Implications* (Jerusalem, 1971).

28. E.g., Yeruham Lainer, "On Josephus and His Books in Rabbinic Literature" [Hebrew], in Samuel K. Mirsky, ed., *Sura* 1 (Jerusalem, 1953–1954) 428–438, identifies the author of *Josippon* with Josephus and does not realize that *Josippon* is a medieval work.

29. Hans Lewy, "Josephus the Physician: A Mediaeval Legend of the Destruction of Jerusalem," *JWI* 1 (1937–1938) 221–242.

30. Carl-Otto Nordström, "Herod the Great in Two Beatus Miniatures," in J. Bergman et al., edd., *SHR: Supplements to Numen* 21–22 (= *Ex Orbe Religionum: Studia Geo Widengren,* vol. 1 (Leiden, 1972) 245–253.

31. Kurt Weitzmann, "The Question of the Influence of Jewish Pictorial Sources on Old Testament Illustration," in Joseph Gutmann, ed., *No Graven Images: Studies in Art and the Hebrew Bible* (New York, 1971) 79–95.

32. Peter Burke, "A Survey of the Popularity of Ancient Historians 1450–1700," *H&T* 5 (1966) 135–152.

33. *D. Martin Luthers Werke Kritische Gesamtausgabe,* vol. 55, part 1 (Weimar, 1883ff.), p. 4, lines 20–23.

34. *Ibid.,* vol. 55, part 1, p. 2, lines 10–11.

35. Martin Luther, *Works,* ed. Franklin Sherman and Helmut T. Lehmann, vol. 47 (Philadelphia, 1971), p. 227.

36. *Ibid.,* vol. 47, p. 233.

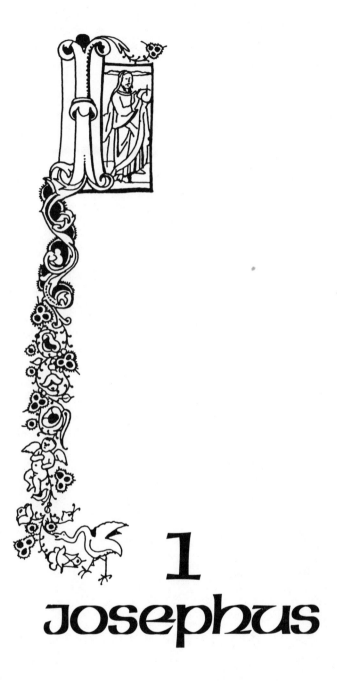

1
JOSEPHUS

1 Josephus and the Roman Empire as Reflected in The Jewish War

MENAHEM STERN

osephus states that *The Jewish War,* written in Greek, was preceded by an Aramaic version sent to the barbarians of the interior.[1] In this way, he hoped the Parthians, the remote Arab tribes, the Jews beyond the Euphrates, and the inhabitants of Adiabene might learn about the events of the war. The spread of Josephus' history, written in Aramaic and emphasizing the folly of rising against the Roman Empire, undoubtedly served the Roman aims of preventing Parthian intervention west of the Euphrates or any Jewish unrest that the Adiabene or Babylonian Jewry might foment. Its very title, *The Jewish War,* shows that it was written from the Roman standpoint, like the designations the Punic or Gallic Wars.[2]

Furthermore, an important and perhaps the main part of the written sources available to Josephus were official Roman sources which he expressly refers to in his *Autobiography* as the *Commentarii* of Vespasian and Titus. In his polemic against the rival historian, Justus of Tiberias, Josephus remarks that Justus' account contradicts that of Vespasian in the *Commentarii.*[3] Elsewhere in the same work, Josephus declares that Justus cannot be an authoritative historian of the siege of Jerusalem, since he was not on the spot at that time and had not read the *Commentarii* of Caesar (i.e. Titus).[4] From this remark we may conclude that Josephus had read them. Thus, the fact that he does not mention these sources in his introduction to *The Jewish War,* even though he criticizes the historical works already written about the war, does not necessarily mean that the *Commentarii* had not yet been composed. It is more reasonable to suppose that Josephus did not allude to them at that time because these *Commentarii,* like those written by Julius Caesar, were not a polished literary composition. Rather, the Flavian *Commentarii* were the raw material which an artistic historian could rework.[5] The excellent information about the Roman army and the details of individual acts of heroism characteristic of military *commentarii* may derive from this source.[6]

The Jewish War in the extant version is written in fine literary Greek and belongs to the great tradition of classical Greek historiography, which followed in the path of Thucydides.[7] It is commonly assumed that *The Jewish War* was published between the years A.D. 75 and 79,[8] though some scholars have expressed the view that it should be dated in the reign of Titus (A.D. 79–81) and that Book VII was published as late as the reign of Domitian (A.D. 81–96).[9]

Josephus' close ties with the Flavian dynasty were natural considering the historian's special relations with Titus[10] and the conditions in which he found himself in Rome. Josephus himself asserts that, because of his complete confidence in the veracity of his narrative in *The Jewish War,* he called upon Vespasian and Titus to witness this fact, and sent them copies.[11] In his *Life* he says that Titus even signed the books with his own hand and gave orders to publish them since he was interested that the public should learn the facts of the war only from this work.[12] Of course, Titus' special interest in his client's books derived less from the personal ties between the two men than from the fact that the emperor had been the central figure of the war and that his victory over the Jews constituted the greatest military achievement of Titus and, in fact, of the entire Flavian house.[13]

Indeed, throughout the main part of *The Jewish War* we feel the impact of Titus' personality. The historian continually magnifies his martial feats. However, he describes Titus not only as an excellent military commander but also as a very humane personage who shows mercy to the Jews and even endeavors to save Jerusalem from destruction. Certainly regarding the destruction of the Temple, which in Jewish eyes constituted the most tragically significant event in the history of the Jewish people and symbolized more than anything else the depth of the national disaster, Josephus does his best to clear his royal friend and benefactor of all guilt. Himself a priest, Josephus could hardly have been indifferent to the question of Titus' responsibility for the destruction of the Temple. Yet he felt that it was his duty to prove to his readers, even the Jewish ones, that Titus was not to be held responsible for this crime. In describing the burning of the Temple, he explicitly states that it was not Titus who gave the orders. In fact, he did all he could to prevent the fire from spreading. In Titus' address to the leaders of the revolt he says, "I will preserve the Temple for you even against your will." [14] According to Josephus, it was the Jews who started to burn parts of the western porch of the Temple in order to immolate the Roman soldiers.[15] Thus it was the Jews who, with their own hands, set fire to the Temple which Titus and the Roman army were protecting for them.[16] Or again, when Titus heard that a starving mother had eaten her own child during the siege, Josephus clears the Roman leader by observing that he had offered the Jews peace and amnesty for all past offenses.

Yet another incident in *The Jewish War* seems to reflect this tendency to whitewash Titus. To determine the fate of the Temple, Titus convened his council of officers. In the discussion, three opinions were expressed. Some held that the laws of war should be enforced, for the Jews would continue to revolt as long as the Temple stood. Others expressed the view that if the Jews abandoned the Temple, it should be spared, but if they made it a base for military operations, it should be burnt. Opposing both these views, Titus himself declared that under no circumstances would he burn such a magnificent building, for it would be a loss for the Romans too, as its existence redounded to the glory of the empire.[17] Three of the officers upheld Titus' view. Thus, the tragedy that occurred ran counter to the will of Titus. During the struggle between the Jewish defenders of the Temple and the Roman soldiers who attempted to put out the blaze already burning in the inner court, one of the Roman soldiers, moved by a demonic impulse, hurled a torch through the golden gate into the Temple. Titus tried to stop the fire by shouting commands and gesticulating, but failed. Hence, against the will of Caesar, the Temple was burnt.

Josephus' description of this event raises grave doubts about the accuracy of his account. These doubts are only increased by comparing it with that of the Christian chronicler Sulpicius Severus. Here a wholly different picture emerges. Sulpicius, who presumably draws on a lost part of the *Histories* of Tacitus,[18] also tells of a convocation of the council of Titus in order to determine the fate of the Temple. But, in contrast to Josephus, the Christian chronicler relates that some participants in the council maintained that the Temple should be permitted to stand whereas Titus was in favor of destroying it. Sulpicius Severus' version, dependent as it is on Tacitus, is probably closer to the truth, especially since we know that at Vespasian's behest, the Romans also destroyed the temple of Onias in Egypt.[19]

In a similar vein Josephus relates the story of Titus and Gischala (Gush-Ḥalav).[20] The emperor could easily have captured the township with an attack, but the knowledge that this would result in the indiscriminate slaughter of multitudes led him to abandon this plan. Furthermore, at the capture of the Second Wall of Jerusalem, he did not allow any of the captives to be killed. When Titus toured the walls of besieged Jerusalem and saw the ravines full of corpses, he groaned and, raising his hands, called on God to bear witness that he had not done this.[21]

By contrast, Josephus describes Vespasian as an experienced general of a moderate and authoritative character who nonetheless does not hesitate to treat the Jews harshly. Thus, at the capture of Gabara he mercilessly executed all the male inhabitants of the city.[22] After the indiscriminate slaughter of the inhabitants at the conquest of Tarichaeae, Titus endeavored to spare at least the permanent population of the town.[23] In contrast, Josephus emphasizes the vigor with which Vespasian killed the refugees. Vespasian even went back on his promises to these refugees after his friends persuaded him that nothing done to Jews was a crime, and that expediency was preferable to the creation of a favorable impression when it was impossible to achieve both.[24] This breach of promise by Vespasian was criticized even in late antiquity by the Antiochene rhetor Libanius (fourth century A.D.), who derived his information from Josephus.[25]

Of interest in this connection is Vespasian's behavior towards Antiochus, king of Commagene, whose son Epiphanes was the loyal ally of Titus during the siege of Jerusalem. It is difficult to explain why Josephus treated the overthrow of Antiochus at such length in a work on Jewish history. In any case, the facts relating to Antiochus of Commagene as recounted in *The Jewish War* do not add much luster to Vespasian's name. For the general was moved by the praetorian legate of Syria's groundless accusation that the king of Commagene was plotting with the Parthians to revolt against Rome. This same legate, at the head of one of the Syrian legions (the sixth), invaded Commagene. Antiochus and his men were taken by complete surprise and surrendered to the Romans without resistance. Two of Antiochus' sons, among them the aforementioned Epiphanes, escaped to the king of Parthia.[26] But after learning that Vespasian was treating him well, they rejoined their father.

Josephus does not expressly criticize Vespasian for permitting this injustice to the king of Commagene; yet from the narrative it clearly emerges that Vespasian did not subsequently reinstate the king or his sons in their ancestral kingdom, nor did he censure the legate of Syria for committing this grave injustice. Josephus' obvious sympathy for the dynasty of Commagene may be accounted for by its close ties with Agrippa II and the Herodian house. We should note in passing that members of the house of Commagene were to rise to great heights in Roman society. The grandson of Antiochus became consul in Rome and left his mark on the life of Athens.[27] To summarize, in *The Jewish War* Vespasian emerges as a great emperor and savior of Rome, but also as a general and statesman who occasionally treated his supposed enemies harshly. Titus, on the other hand, is depicted as a kind, humane ruler who could show mercy even to the most intransigent rebels and exert himself to help the Jews who, he assumes, were dragged by extremists into the conflict with Rome.

However, Josephus' warm, sympathetic attitude towards Titus is not always identical with that towards the Roman Empire. The introduction to *The Jewish War* includes traditional *topoi* of Greek historiography which appear in other ancient introductions to historical works.[28] Nonetheless, besides those traditional *topoi* we can discern some ideas specific to Josephus, such as his emphasis upon the Romans' desire to show mercy to the Jews and Titus' repeated efforts to save Jerusalem and the Temple through effecting some kind of reconciliation with the rebels.[29]

Even more than the introduction, the speeches of the historical figures reflect the historian's views. The most notable example is King Agrippa II's speech in which he attempts to persuade the excited crowd in Jerusalem not to rise against the Romans.[30] Agrippa first refutes the arguments of the would-be rebels by pointing out their inherent contradictions. On the one hand, they complain of the injustice inflicted on them by the procurators, and, on the other hand, they glorify liberty for its own sake. This means that subjection and slavery are a disgrace even if the rulers are honest men. But to criticize the procurators is an act of folly, for, in doing so, the rebels harm only themselves, since instead of covertly committing transgressions of which they were ashamed, the procurators now commit them openly. Even if one grants that the emissaries of Rome are harsh governors, this does not imply that all the Romans, particularly the emperor himself, are unjust to the Jews. In fact, the emperor does not endorse the evil deeds of the procurators, nor do the Romans residing in the West see what is happening in the East. News also travels so slowly. For these reasons, it is sheer folly to declare war on a whole nation because of the deeds of a single individual and to resort to arms against a powerful empire that does not even understand the nature of Jewish complaints. In any case, no procurator remains for long in his post, so it is reasonable to assume that his successor would act more benignly. As for the love of liberty, the Jews should have fought for it when Pompey invaded Judea. Now it is too late, for he who has once accepted slavery and then attempts to shake off the yoke will be considered an obstinate slave rather than a lover of liberty.

Above all, will the Jews who have inherited slavery be able to withstand the entire Roman Empire? Agrippa then lists all the peoples who have succumbed to the power of Rome: Athens, which once shattered the naval might of all Asia off the coast of Salamis and was the leading city of Greece, now receives its orders from Italy. The same holds true for the Lacedaemonians, Macedonians, and other peoples. Where are the armies, the fleets, the treasures on which the Jews can rely in time of war? Do they suppose that they will be fighting Egyptians or Arabs? Can they close their eyes to the power of the Roman Empire and their own weakness?

Moreover, the Jews have often been defeated by their neighbors while the Romans have never been beaten in all their wars throughout the whole inhabited world. All the great nations have been conquered by the Romans: the Greeks, the Macedonians, the five hundred cities of Asia (i.e. in the province of Asia in Asia Minor), as well as innumerable other peoples. Consider the Gauls, who could so readily defend themselves, yet who now obey a small Roman military unit. The Iberians, Germans, and Britons share a similar fate. Even the Parthians, a nation of splendid fighters, send hostages to Rome. Thus, nearly every nation under the sun is subject to the Romans. Only the Jews dare to oppose them. Apparently, they are blind to the fate of the Carthaginians and the fact that Africa (the province of Africa), which supplies

Rome with corn eight months a year, is held by a single Roman legion. But why look so far afield when there is the example of Egypt so close to home? Egypt, with its seven and a half million inhabitants and corn enough to supply Rome for four months out of every year, is surrounded on all sides by deserts, seas, and swamps. Yet all these advantages did not save her from the might of the Romans.

What emerges from the speech of the Roman citizen Julius Agrippa as composed by another Roman citizen Flavius Josephus is the conviction that Rome is invincible and that all opposition is futile. Conspicuously absent is any expression of appreciation of the civilizing achievements of Rome or some expression of goodwill and awareness of the aspirations and ideals common to provincials as well as rulers. The speech reflects no awareness of the benefits of the "Imperial Peace," the renowned *Pax Romana* which provided security for all the inhabitants of the empire in sharp contrast to earlier periods when a more or less permanent state of war prevailed all over the Mediterranean basin.

Here there are grounds for a comparison of the speech of Agrippa with one which appears in the *Histories* of Tacitus and which was delivered on a similar occasion.[31] I refer to the speech of the Roman general Cerialis in Gaul before a crowd of Treviri and Lingones in which he attempted to dissuade the people from joining the revolt against Rome. His arguments are as follows: the Romans arrived in Gaul at the invitation of the natives in order to save them from the Germanic invaders. The Romans occupied the banks of the Rhine not to defend Italy but to prevent Ariovistus from conquering Gaul. The same factors that in former times led to the Germanic invasions of Gaul exist at present. Moreover, wars were common in Gaul even before the advent of the Romans. And while it is true that the Romans imposed taxes on the Gauls, they were necessary to cover the expenses of maintaining peace in Gaul. Actually, Romans and Gauls have everything in common. The latter even act as commanders of legions and are appointed as provincial governors. Thus, they enjoy the benefits of good emperors no less than the people living near Rome while largely escaping the evil effects of bad and cruel rulers, who are mainly suffered by those nearest them. Should the Romans ever be expelled from Gaul, universal turmoil and destruction would result from the ensuing wars. The Gauls benefit greatly from the peace that Roman rule has brought to conquerors and conquered alike, and all enjoy equal rights.

Greek literature of the imperial age, from Strabo to the famous speech of Aelius Aristides, contains many expressions of the outlook and feelings of Greek cities towards Rome.[32] Even in Jewish literature we find acknowledgments of the praiseworthy aspects of the Roman Empire. Thus Philo pays tribute to the achievement of Augustus, the great benefactor of mankind who spread peace to the ends of the earth.[33] In the Talmud as well, we find expressions of admiration for Rome: Rabbi Judah commenced by observing: "How fine are the works of this people! They have made streets, they have built bridges, they have erected baths."[34]

Yet the speech of Agrippa in *The Jewish War* contains scarcely a hint of such a positive attitude. In other parts of *The Jewish War* as well, the chief emphasis is upon Roman military might. In Book III, Josephus states that meticulous preparations during peacetime make victory certain in war and that a close examination of the Roman military organization shows that the Romans acquired their empire as a result of their virtue and not as a gift from Tyche.[35] In his address to his soldiers before the conquest of Tarichaeae, Titus reminds them that they are men from whose hands no part of the civilized world has escaped. The emphasis throughout is on Roman discipline, which distinguishes them from their enemies who act on mere impulse.[36] The speech of Titus before the walls of Jerusalem contains echoes of the arguments presented by Agrippa on the subjugation of the Germans and Britons and the conquest of the Carthaginians.[37]

There seems to be only a single allusion in *The Jewish War* to the view that at least the Jews in the Diaspora benefited from Roman rule, and that within the Roman Empire the Jewish communities in the Hellenistic East were more secure than in the Hellenistic cities without Roman control and supervision. This would seem to be the implication of asserting that Titus categorically rejected the demand of the Antiochenes to expel the Jews from their city on the grounds that the Jews had lost their mother country and had no place else to go if they were expelled.[38] Here again this merciful attitude is attributed to Titus alone; it is not Josephus' opinion regarding the Roman Empire. In the *Antiquities,* however, Josephus adduces plenty of documents issued by Roman emperors and other personages which tended to secure and stabilize the status of the Jews in various countries under Roman rule.

In addition to his emphasis on military and political power in the long tradition of historical realism that began with Thucydides and Polybius, there is another facet to Josephus' representation of the Roman Empire. Its very attainment of world domination and political predominance could be the result only of divine will. Hence, the Jewish rebels can expect no help from God because He is on the side of the Roman Empire. From the speech of Josephus before the walls of Jerusalem, the idea emerges that God had gone from nation to nation, giving the scepter of empire to each in turn; now He has bestowed it upon Italy.[39]

The divine origin of Roman invincibility is reinforced by Josephus' interpretation of the messianic belief of the Jews, an interpretation which seemed justified by events and which is found both in Josephus and Tacitus.[40] Both relate that the Jews were inspired to hope for liberation on the strength of an ambiguous prophecy in the sacred writings of the Jews. It foretold that someone from their own country would become the ruler of the world. This prophecy, according to Josephus, referred to Vespasian and Titus.

To sum up, in *The Jewish War* Josephus' attitude towards the Roman Empire represents a combination of Thucydidean realism and traditional Jewish thought. There is a conspicuous lack of any expression of cultural or spiritual solidarity with the empire. All that we do find is a feeling of sympathy with and gratitude towards Titus and respect for the Flavian house.

Notes

1. See *BJ* I, 3.

2. See R. Laqueur, *Der jüdische Historiker Flavius Josephus*, Giessen 1920, 98; see now the reservations made by T. Rajak, *Josephus, the Historian and His Society*, London 1983, 201ff.

3. See *V* 342.

4. See *V* 358.

5. On *commentarii* in general see F. Bömer, "Der Commentarius," *Hermes* LXXXI (1953), 210–250; E. Noè, "La memorialistica imperiale del I secolo," *Atti della Accademia Nazionale dei Lincei, Rendiconti, Classe di Scienze morali, storiche e filologiche* XXXV (1980), 163–180. On the *commentarii* of Vespasian see Noè, *op. cit.*, 175–180; H. Peter, *Historicorum Romanorum Reliquiae* II, Leipzig 1906, cxxxxiiiff.; H. Bardon, *Les empereurs et les lettres latines d'Auguste à Hadrien*, Paris 1968, 271f. Bardon maintains that the *commentarii* were composed only at the end of Vespasian's reign.

6. This Roman element in *BJ* has been emphasized by W. Weber, *Josephus und Vespasian*, Berlin 1921. On Josephus' dependence upon the *commentarii* see also H. St. J. Thackeray, *Josephus, the Man and the Historian*, New York 1929, 38–40. It has been surmised that Josephus used also the *commentarii* of Silva. See L. H. Feldman, *Studies for Morton Smith at Sixty* III, Leiden 1975, 236.

7. On Thucydides' influence upon Josephus see H. Drüner, *Untersuchungen über Josephus*, Diss. Marburg 1896, 1–34. For more on the influence of classical authors see also the introduction of Thackeray to the Loeb translation of Josephus, *The Jewish War*, xv–xix. In general, see also A. Wolff, *De Flavii Iosephi Belli Iudaici Scriptoris Studiis Rhetoricis*, Halle 1908.

8. See H. Vincent, *RB* VIII (1911), 371; G. Hölscher, *RE* IX, s.v. Josephus, col. 1942; G. Ricciotti, *Flavio Giuseppe, lo storico giudeo-romano*, Torino 1937, 46; O. Michel and O. Bauernfeind, "Flavius Josephus, De Bello Judaico," *Griechisch und Deutsch* I², München 1962, xx; E. Schürer, *The History of the Jewish People in the Age of Jesus Christ (175 B.C.–A.D. 135)*, a new English version revised and edited by G. Vermes and F. Millar I, Edinburgh 1973, 47f. This dating is based mainly on two data: a) In *BJ* VII, 158, we read of the completion of the Temple of Peace, which was inaugurated in A.D. 75, according to Cassius Dio (LXVI, 15, 1); and b) in *Ap* I, 50, and in *V* 361, Josephus declares that he submitted his books for reading to both Vespasian and Titus, and Vespasian died in June 79.

9. See my study "The Date of Composition of *The Jewish War*" [in Hebrew], *Proceedings of the Sixth World Congress of Jewish Studies* II, Jerusalem 1976, 29–34, in which I argued that the work was published towards the end of Vespasian's life or even in the reign of Titus. However, I am now inclined to accept the first view. For the dating of the first six books of *The Jewish War* in the time of Titus and of the seventh in the time of Domitian see S. J. D. Cohen, *Josephus in Galilee and Rome*, Leiden 1979, 84–90. In *BJ* IV, 634–644, we detect a clearly negative attitude towards Caecina. This man, after betraying Vitellius, deserted to Vespasian, who honored him. However, we should note that Caecina's execution is dated in the time of Vespasian, though

at its very end (see H. Bengtson, *Die Flavier*, Munich 1979, 157), and hence Vespasian may have changed his mind about Caecina.

10. On the nature of these connections see Z. Yavetz, "Reflections on Titus and Josephus," *GRBS* XVI (1975), 431f.

11. See *Ap* I, 50–52.

12. See *V* 363.

13. The victory of Titus over the Jews is prominent in a famous inscription (*ILS* no. 264 = E. Gabba, *Iscrizioni greche e latine per lo studio della Bibbia*, Torino 1958, no. XXVII: "gentem Iudeorum domuit et urbem Hierusolymam omnibus ante se ducibus regibus gentibus aut frustra petitam aut omnino intemptatam delevit") as well as in the Latin poetry of that time. See M. Stern, *Greek and Latin Authors on Jews and Judaism* I, Jerusalem 1974, nos. 226–228.

14. See *BJ* VI, 128.

15. See *BJ* VI, 177–185.

16. See *BJ* VI, 214–216.

17. See *BJ* VI, 237–243.

18. See Stern, *op. cit.*, II, 1980, no. 282, 64–67, and the literature there cited. The first to prove the dependence of Sulpicius Severus on Tacitus for the account of the burning of the Temple was J. Bernays, *Gesammelte Schriften* II, Berlin 1885, 159–200. On Sulpicius Severus' dependence upon Tacitus see also T. D. Barnes, *CP* LXXII (1977), 225–228.

19. See *BJ* VII, 421.

20. See *BJ* IV, 92.

21. See *BJ* VI, 409–412.

22. See *BJ* III, 132f.

23. See *BJ* III, 501.

24. See *BJ* III, 532–542.

25. See Libanius, *Orationes* XX, 30, and Stern, *op. cit.* II, 1980, no. 495b.

26. See *BJ* VII, 219–243; D. Magie, *Roman Rule in Asia Minor* I, Princeton 1950, 573f., II, 1434, no. 19, and 1435, no. 20; R. D. Sullivan, *ANRW* II, 8 (1977), 785–796.

27. See H. Halfmann, *Die Senatoren aus dem östlichen Teil des Imperium Romanum bis zum Ende des 2 Jh.n. Chr.*, Göttingen 1979, 131–133.

28. See H. Lieberich, *Studien zu den Proömien in der griechischen und byzantinischen Geschichtsschreibung* I, Munich 1899; the introductions of the Greek historians in English translation are conveniently available in A. J. Toynbee, *Greek Historical Thought*, New York 1952, 29–97.

29. See *BJ* I, 27.

30. See *BJ* II, 345–401; on the speech of Agrippa see H. Lindner, *Die Geschichtsauffassung des Flavius Josephus in Bellum Judaicum*, Leiden 1972, 21–25; E. Gabba, "L'impero romano nel discorso di Agrippa II," *RSA* VI–VII (1976–1977), 189–194; on the military data in the speech see A. v. Domaszewski, "Die Dislocation des römischen Heeres im Jahre 66 n. Chr.," *RhM* XLVII 47 (1892), 207–218; Ritterling, *RE* XII, col. 1261–1263 (1924), s.v. Legio.

31. See Tacitus, *Historiae* IV, 73f.

32. See, e.g., the speech of Aelius Aristides to Rome, 29, 36, 60, 70, 99, and 104: "We have to pity all those who are beyond the bounds of the empire because of the good things which are not their lot." The speech of Aelius Aristides provides an example of the identification of the Greek world with the Roman Empire. An interesting picture emerges from the works of Plutarch. See now C. P. Jones, *Plutarch and Rome*, Oxford 1971, 122–130. In general see also G. (W.) Gernentz, *Laudes Romae*, Rostock 1918.

33. See Philo, *Legatio ad Gaium*, 143–158, 309–318; G. Delling, "Philons Enkomion auf Augustus," *Klio* 54 (1972), 171–192. See also F. F. Bruce, "The Romans through Jewish Eyes," *Mélanges offerts à Marcel Simon*, Paris 1978, 3–12.

34. See *Shabbat* 33b.

35. See the description of the Roman army in *BJ* III, 70–109; A. Schuh, *Römisches Kriegswesen nach dem Bellum Judaicum des Josephus Flavius,* Mähr-Weisskirchen 1902.

36. See *BJ* III, 475f.

37. See *BJ* VI, 331f.

38. See *BJ* VII, 100–111; G. Downey, *A History of Antioch in Syria,* Princeton 1961, 204–207.

39. See *BJ* V, 367.

40. See *BJ* VI, 312; Tacitus, *Historiae* V, 13; Stern, *op. cit.,* II, 61f.; P. Fornaro, *Flavio Giuseppe, Tacito e l'impero,* Torino 1980, 52–56; E. Norden, *Kleine Schriften zum klassischen Altertum,* Berlin 1966, 263–271. On eschatology in the works of Josephus see also U. Fischer, *Eschatologie und Jenseitserwartung im hellenistischen Diasporajudentum,* Berlin-New York 1978, 144–183; M. deJonge, "Josephus und die Zukunftserwartungen seines Volkes," *J-S,* 1974, 205–219; A. Momigliano, "Cio'che Flavio Giuseppe non vide," *RSI* XCI (1979), 564–574.

2 Josephus and Justus of Tiberias

TESSA RAJAK

J ustus of Tiberias, a Jewish councillor in a minor Greek city, was a figure
in the public eye during the early stages of the Jewish revolt in Galilee;
later he became the secretary of a Roman client king, Agrippa II, as
well as the author of a limited historical work or works, now lost. His interest
for us lies first in his being a representative of the partly Hellenized Palestinian elite of the first century A.D., which was caught short and largely destroyed by the revolt against Rome in A.D. 66; second, in the fact that for a
small part of his career a narrow beam of light is shed on his persona by Josephus in the *Vita*—and in studying the ancient world, we have to make the
most of what little we know; third, in that we can only understand what Josephus was doing as Galilee's commander only insofar as we can make sense of
Justus' role there, even if it be solely by sifting through the dubious evidence
of the antagonistic Josephus; and last, but not least important, in the various
points of similarity which Justus has with his greater contemporary, a comparison which lends perspective and refinement to our portrait of Josephus.[1] It
was with a novelist's eye for the possibilities inherent in the contrast that Lion
Feuchtwanger, in his remarkable trilogy about the historian, elevated Justus
into a lifelong rival and constant shadowing presence, dogging Josephus in
Palestine and in Rome.

I am happy to have this opportunity to reassess Justus. Since my article of
1973,[2] the subject has been further explored;[3] and I myself have independently
modified my views on some matters.[4] It is a good time to pull the threads
together. With a debate which, in its "modern" phase, has been going on for
seventy-five years,[5] we ought now to be able to distinguish such conclusions as
are, if not certain, at least probable, from that which remains and must remain
mere hypothesis. What can be known about Justus?

There are, it may be said, two major and related questions, concerning the rival writers, which remain unresolved. (1) How far was Josephus' *Vita* meant as a polemic against Justus? To what extent has this tainted what Josephus says? (2) How much of what Josephus tells us is it sensible to believe? How far are we able securely to reconstruct Justus' actions in Galilee? In presenting the evidence, I shall have these questions in mind.

The starting point must be the literary exchange, and, first of all, the writings of Justus, to which Josephus was, at least in part, replying. Here the testimony is not exclusively Josephan, though the caution has to be offered immediately that all other allusions are far from contemporary, dating in fact from considerably later periods; that the majority of them (which I shall not discuss here) presuppose knowledge of Justus derived only from Josephus;[6] and that it is Josephus' evidence which remains most useful for our purposes. It is best to begin by extracting whatever we can from Josephus.

According to Josephus, Justus had "even attempted to write the history of these matters with the aim of overcoming the truth by means of this account" (*V* 40). "These matters" might mean the detailed issues under immediate discussion: the pressure in Tiberias, in 66, to take up arms against Sepphoris, the resentment of Agrippa's control, the debates in Tiberias as to what to do about the revolt against Rome, and the armed attacks on neighboring Decapolis cities. Equally, however, "these matters" may refer to the war in its entirety. In any event, the question of the coverage of the work (though not its level of detail) is later settled for us, when Josephus chides Justus for writing of happenings that he had not himself witnessed nor learnt about from eyewitnesses— the Roman invasion of Galilee, the siege of Jotapata—and of happenings on the subject of which he had failed to read the imperial commentaries, that is, the siege of Jerusalem (*V* 357–358). We also learn that Justus had, following the fashion of classical historians, claimed his account as superior to any other, a claim which Josephus dismisses with scorn.

This contentious work of Justus, whatever exactly it consisted of, was made public in the nineties A.D., after the death of Agrippa II and, Josephus maintains, some twenty years after Justus had first written it (*V* 359).

Justus, then, wrote about the revolt either as a separate subject or as part of a wider work. He touched on a delicate area in Josephus' career, that is to say, the siege of Jotapata, perhaps merely in its place in the narrative, perhaps with extra emphasis, as a contrived attack on Josephus; Josephus certainly took exception to what Justus had written, but that fact does not tell us how deliberately or how virulently anti-Josephus Justus had really been. What is more, the literary weapons brandished by Josephus (and so much emphasized by some scholars) may give a somewhat exaggerated impression even of his own level of personal animosity. Then there is the long delay before publication: Josephus puts this down to what, for a historian, is the most disreputable of motives, saying that Justus had waited for the demise of the eyewitnesses, above all, King Agrippa, who might have discredited his account. But this polemical ascription of motive has, of course, no special claim to belief; indeed it appears to belong to a standard repertory of literary charges. Thus at Rome Pliny the Younger urged his friend Maximus to publish quickly certain pieces defending himself and criticizing the prefect of Egypt, Pompeius Planta; Pliny expressed the fear that the objectivity of the work would be discredited now that Planta had died if people imagined that Maximus had been cravenly waiting for just that event: "You must keep up your reputation for standing by your convictions, and can do so if it is known to your friends and enemies alike that you did not pluck up courage to write as a result of your enemy's death, but that your work was already finished for publication when his death intervened" (Pliny, *Ep.* 9, 1). Justus' much-maligned delay may, then, have had quite a different motive from that alleged by Josephus. I suggested before that Justus could not publish before Agrippa had gone, because Agrippa had endorsed the Josephan version.[7] But it must be admitted that extraneous factors of a more creditable kind could equally have been responsible. Cohen suggested that of local patriotism: it would have been natural for Justus' work to have a local bias, and the death of Agrippa would have been the right moment to claim autonomy for the city of Tiberias.[8] And we may even wish to go in a different direction and suggest that Agrippa's death might have been associated with the timing of the publication only by the critical Josephus. The long delay could be explained simply by the demands of the work, an explanation which will be even more attractive to those who suppose that the passages on the war were part of something bigger.

Yet here we merely touch upon another area of uncertainty. For our picture of Justus' output as a whole has its own limitations, so that we cannot be sure how the war story fitted into the wider framework. This is largely because the brief notice of Photius,[9] upon which we are dependent, does not state in clear fashion the scope and content of what he saw. The patriarch reports "a chronicle of which the superscription was 'Justus of Tiberias' [book] of the Jewish kings in the genealogies'" (ἐν τοῖς στέμμασιν); and goes on to make a few points about this Chronicle—its starting point (Moses), its end point (the death of Agrippa II, with a patently mistaken dating of that event[10]), its concision and (which may explain why the work is described as too concise) its omission of Jesus Christ and all that concerned him (since the author suffered from "the Jewish disease"). Our present difficulty stems from the final short section which is of a biographical nature. Having given us the name of Justus' father, it cites Josephus on Justus' character ("the worst of rogues") and speaks of the argument between the two men. Nothing in this section suggests direct knowledge of what Justus had written on the subject: the terms used are "it is said" (λέγεται) and "they say" (φασί). Nor, on the other hand, does it explicitly state that Photius was aware of the existence of another work by

Justus, a war history, which he did not see but knew merely by repute. All we can say is that Photius had not read any such work himself, for his practice where he really has read more than one work by a particular individual is to say quite clearly that there also exists a different book by the same author;[11] while it is evident that here he was relying upon his memory of Josephus' remarks on the subject. That Photius was fully acquainted with Josephus is perfectly well established.[12] Though there is one allusion to Justus' *writings* (as distinct from the actions) at this point, it takes a very vague form: "They say that the account (ἱστορίαν) which Justus wrote is fictitious for the most part and especially where he recounts the Roman war against the Jews and the capture of Jerusalem." The word ἱστορίαν means both a narrative or story and a written history; so its use here does not enable us to choose between the two possibilities: on the one hand, that there was a work called the "History" separate from the "Chronicle"; nor, on the other hand, that one and the same work had both appellations and contained the war story along with other things. The resulting ambiguity is most unfortunate. As Photius does not choose clearly to explain, and perhaps was himself ignorant, where the war history of Justus came in, it is hardly surprising that we too are unsure. There may have been a separate account of the war, which Photius did not have and which had perhaps been lost before his time.[13] Equally, Justus may have attached the war story to the chronicle, of which it could have formed the culmination and conclusion; it was possibly, then, a summary account, like the rest of the chronicle; or, again, the chronicle might have been a mere digression (like, say, Josephus' retrospective list of high priests at *Antiquities* XX, 224 ff.) in a mainly contemporary history.[14] On this hypothesis, either it was Photius' decision not to bother with that part of the work, which would not be uncharacteristic of his procedures,[15] or else the matter would have been decided for him by the prior extraction and separate publication of the genealogical section of the work.[16]

The crucial question, as to the scale and balance of the war history, thus, cannot be settled. An impression does, however, emerge that Justus did not compose on a broad canvass; neither Josephus, in relation to the war narrative, nor Photius, in the so-called "chronicle," in any way suggests that they were dealing with large-scale works. The name "chronicle"—whether it was Justus' original title or applied to his work later—implies a summary account.[17]

It is true that a more discursive approach might be suggested by an anecdote ascribed, unexpectedly, to Ἰοῦστος ὁ Τιβερεὺς ἐν τῷ Στέμματι by Diogenes Laertius in his third-century life of Socrates (41). Plato, at Socrates' trial, is said to have ascended the rostrum and professed his inexperience at public speaking, whereupon the judges shouted at him to come down. But this anecdote could perhaps have found a place in some kind of self-justifying preface or conclusion by Justus, where it might have formed a parallel to Josephus' famous protestations about his ignorance of Greek in the closing section of the *Antiquities* (XX, 263–265). This citation does not justify our enlarging our model of Justus' historical works,[18] or altering our conviction that he was no Josephus. If we regret the loss of his works, it is for the information they would have given us, not for literary reasons.

I shall have more to say later about the literary comparison with Josephus. Here we return to the controversy about the revolt. Whatever Justus' principal purpose, one effect of what he wrote was to challenge Josephus. This, in turn, casts some light on the composition and publication of the *Vita*, but without explaining everything; yet it was taken more or less unquestioningly as the work's sole cause by most scholars (including, initially, by myself).[19] Now I would suggest that it is well worth remembering Josephus' other critics, even if Justus is the only one addressed by name. Such people dogged his entire career;[20] but information contrived to do him damage may have begun to circulate with renewed intensity around the time when publication of the *Antiquities* was known to be imminent. All of them would have contributed to the decision of appending the *Vita*, with its detailed defense of Josephus' generalship, to the twenty books of the *Antiquities*, with their broad scope and large ambitions. Here, too, it is easy to credit Justus with too much simply because we know all too little about him. After all, in the *Bellum* he had not even merited a single mention.

The one clear fact is that Josephus accorded Justus the dubious honor of addressing certain direct remarks to him by name, in a passage inserted prominently into the body of his narrative and aptly called by Cohen "the great digression" (345–367). In it, Josephus rejects Justus' smear that he, Josephus (together with the "Galilaeans"), bore responsibility for making the city of Tiberias revolt against Rome. The charge is then flung back at its author: Justus and his party had taken up arms first, in marching out against the territories of nearby cities of the Syrian Decapolis—Gadara, Hippos, and Scythopolis (*V* 340–344).

The real issue is warmongering: who had been the more anti-Roman of the two? And the focus is narrow—just the locality of Tiberias. It is understandable that in the nineties A.D., and especially in the context of a Romano-Greek literary ambiance, a revolutionary past should have been deeply disgraceful. In 66–67, things may well have been somewhat different; and even in the seventies, when Josephus wrote the *Jewish War*, he could still afford to admit that he had at first prosecuted the campaign with vigor (albeit under compulsion). Now he had to emphasize his efforts to maintain peace.

Far from being confined to the digression against Justus, this important argument is, indeed, one of the leading strands in the *Vita*. It can be traced right through the work and while it is relevant to the quarrel with Justus, there may have been other targets as well, now nameless, but once to be found among Josephus' many enemies. Thus the "peace-loving argument" (as we may name it) lies behind the early emphasis in the *Vita* on the massacres of Jews in the Greek cities; for the conclusion drawn from those unhappy events is that the revolt was born of necessity not choice (27); and that, of course, implies that Josephus could not have been the man who made it take root in Galilee. Again, it is the "peace-loving argument" which lies behind Josephus' insistence that he did nothing but obey Jerusalem's instructions once he had taken up his post (28–29). After a period of waiting and equivocation, these instructions led to the struggle to subordinate and control the revolutionaries; to obstruct aggressive acts, such as the seizure of a supply of the emperor's corn by John of Gischala (70–76), which he claims his colleagues, and not he, had been responsible for allowing; and, in general, to suppress the unhealthy influence of John, a local leader who early on became, one way or another, committed to a largely pro-war stance.

The long, drawn-out explanation of the commander's dealings with the influential John of Gischala is the linchpin of the *Vita*. It links the one main theme, the "peace-loving argument," with the other prop of Josephus' self-defense, which revolves around his command. It may be noticed that a large part of the *Vita* is taken up with the question of Josephus' authority. His problem is to justify his hanging on to his position once the provisional government of Jerusalem had decided to replace him and to explain why he had dodged the four emissaries sent out to divest him of it. Here Josephus needed somehow to clear himself of the dishonor of being rejected by his own associates, who included, after all, such authoritative and scholarly figures as Simeon ben Gamaliel. Josephus rests his case upon the contention that John had instigated the dismissal and (according to the *Vita*, though not the *Bellum*) that he had employed bribery to bring it about. Thus, John's rascality becomes in its turn a central point, and it is in fact John, rather than Justus, who is the principal villain of the piece. By the date of publication John himself was long gone, for we may presume that he was not seen again after the Judean triumph, when the Romans consigned him to perpetual imprisonment (*BJ* VI, 433–434); anything could therefore be permitted as far as his reputation was concerned. This whole aspect of the *Vita* is not necessarily connected with the argument with Justus.

Again, we cannot judge to what extent the moral side of Josephus' defense, that is to say, those statements which are patently designed to clear his own besmirched character, are responses to matters raised by Justus. On the one hand, vituperation is likely to have had a place in Justus' history, given the predilection of ancient writers for colorful verbal assaults on their personal enemies; on the other hand, we may notice that there is relatively little mud slung in the other direction, that is to say at Justus by Josephus, apart from the accusation of irresponsible personal ambition (36) and general villainy (344,

393). The most bitter and wild invective is reserved for the more important (and perhaps more talented) John. The defenses, based on character and ably disentangled by Drexler and later by Schalit,[21] turn out to be, in part, refutations of the standard charges employed by Greek and Roman writers (and, indeed, by many others through the ages) and, in part, specifically Jewish in their orientation. In the first category we may put the charges of bribery and corruption, vindictiveness, aspirations to tyranny, and the fostering of *stasis* (79–83, 100, 260–261). Josephus' counter-assertions about his own public spirit, honesty, moderation, forbearance, clemency, and reticence are frequent (100, 102–103, 110–111, 265, 321, 329–330, 379–380, 385 ff.). In the second category come the charges surrounding observance of the Law: the other side insisted that Josephus had flouted it (135, 149), while he stressed his respect for the Sabbath (159). In just the same way, he in his turn had many times over in the *Jewish War* accused the revolutionaries of religious improprieties of every kind—culminating in the desecration of the sanctuary itself (*BJ* VII, 260–264, etc.).

Such a mix of Greek and Jewish patterns could well have featured in Justus' writings too, but we are not in a position to attribute these specific arguments to him, except in so far as the mild treatment of Tiberias or Tiberians is briefly in question (174–178).[22] Perhaps the answer would not very much affect our overall understanding of the situation, even if it would contribute in obvious ways to our picture of Justus.

So much for the literature. We know that Justus attacked Josephus in writing as a warmonger; presumably, therefore, he emphasized his own pacific role in the chain of events that preceded Vespasian's invasion of Galilee. But what had the Tiberian intriguer in fact been up to? In seeking an answer, we depend, naturally enough, upon the words of Josephus. In this there is nothing unusual; our position is the same for almost every aspect of the Jewish War, for, just as in the case of the Peloponnesian War half a millennium earlier, the vagaries of the survival and destruction of ancient texts have left the record of the Great Revolt of 66–73/74 in the hands of its one major historian, who is the only contemporary one extant. I have argued in my book on Josephus that in general the problems are superable; it is possible to extract some check on the historian from internal coherence and external plausibility. However, this method breaks down in one particular sphere, and that is where Josephus is writing about any personality with whom he was actively involved, be it friend (such as Titus) or foe (such as John of Gischala). The case of Justus falls under this head: we have to take great care in reading anything that Josephus says about him and be ever ready to suspend belief.

However, this does not mean that all of what Josephus offers on the subject falls under suspicion. His reader is protected by one consideration: that outright invention on the writer's part would have earned the scorn of surviving witnesses of the original events; it is a protection which holds good even in cases, such as this one, where personal attitudes come into play. What is more, while people with accurate memories of those times will have been rarer in the nineties than they had been when the *Bellum* was issued, there must still have been enough of them to occasion and to entertain such a debate and to attend both to Justus' writings on the war and to Josephus' *Vita*. Therefore, we must take it that the stories found in the *Vita* are not fabrications; we should direct our mistrust mainly towards explanations of motive and towards the author's distorting selectivity. It would be wrong to forget altogether that the *Vita* is meant as a polemic; it does not even claim the objectivity pretended to by the *Bellum*.

With these principles in mind, we may now consider the actions which Josephus ascribes to Justus and see if it is possible to reach a conclusion about Justus' true role in the events of 66–67. What happened—or rather what is said to have happened—can be easily summarized, and the circumstantial detail is such that the incidents must be deemed real. What is harder to gauge is the level and quality of Justus' involvement as an individual, especially as our impression of that depends often enough on alleged statements or even upon imputed desires or aspirations. Yet it is upon assessment of these that the verdict on his position over the question of war or peace will hang.

Josephus' charge against Justus is, as we have seen, a replica of Justus' objection against Josephus—that he had caused Tiberias to revolt from Rome. Even the most enthusiastic upholder of Josephus' veracity must admit that this charge is never adequately substantiated in the body of the narrative. Josephus' first visit to Tiberias reveals Justus as a waverer but nothing more extreme than that (32 ff.); he is the leader, together with his father, Pistus, of a middle party, lying between the prosperous pacifists with their Herodian names (33) and the ordinary people, a nameless group who wanted war. Even at this stage, then, Justus could not be presented as having sought revolt from Rome. The middle party is shown as pretending to hesitate, but being really bent on a revolutionary change which could enhance its own power. Such slurs are valueless as evidence; what is telling is that the speeches and actions here laid at Justus' door testify that he was militant to a degree, yet not quite enough for it to amount to definite disaffection from Rome. For the middle party was concerned with prosecuting local feuds, in particular with whipping up the Tiberians against the rival city of Sepphoris, which was now the Galilaean capital (Nero had added Tiberias to the territory of Agrippa II [37]). And Justus' activities resulted in the marauding raid by Tiberias against frontier villages belonging to three Decapolis places, where there had already been large-scale trouble between Jewish and Syrian Greek inhabitants (*V* 42; *BJ* II, 466–478).[23]

We do not need to follow Schalit and Cohen[24] in their dismissal of the very existence of a third party in Tiberias (it is never desirable to rewrite Josephus in such a thoroughgoing fashion) in order to accept that Justus was not in any real sense pro-war. Indeed, at this point in time, it was entirely unclear which way the war would go, and what happened in Galilee was something separate: everywhere, local tensions and feuds were unleashed, now that there was a license to take up arms. On the other hand, it should be noted that Justus' verbal assault on Sepphoris did entail rejection of the obedience owed to Agrippa, and we are told in addition that the king was much abused by Justus (39). If the latter is true, then so will be Josephus' assertion that Justus was at this stage poised to go either way, towards war or towards peace. For Agrippa, having failed to dissuade the Jerusalemites from provoking Rome, had been expelled from Jerusalem before the Roman sacrifices had been stopped in the Temple, had helped the procurator Florus to crush disturbance in the city in the summer of 66, and had himself led a military detachment that joined the invading legion of Cestius Gallus in the autumn (*BJ* II, 407, 417 ff., 500–503). To damage Agrippa could be a challenge also to Rome. So, neither doubting nor accepting every word in Josephus, we have to grant that in the early days Justus did indeed sit on the fence. His reason for doing so is another matter, be it prudence, politics, ambitions, or genuine perplexity. Either way, we cannot accept that he took Tiberias all the way to war, especially as the city was still to change sides four times in the course of the coming months (82).

Justus, then, emerges as an ambivalent character not unlike Josephus himself. To accept this requires not naive credulity but simply a straight reading of the *Vita*, and when such a reading has been rejected, it has been largely in the interests of proving an underlying point about Josephus.[25] The contrast with Josephus springs from the differing importance of the two men. Josephus, whatever doubts he personally felt about the revolt, had more than merely local significance; he was (at least until his rejection) part of a provisional government which had taken over the action in an attempt by its members to keep the lid on the ferment, to stall as long as possible and to save themselves from the class hatred of their more militant compatriots.[26] Once they had done this, they had to go through with at least the semblance of resistance to Rome. Justus was a simple local politician, and such associates as he had appear to have been drawn first and foremost from his family; not only were there his father and brother, but he included among his relatives by marriage a man known as Philip, son of Jacimus, who was a maverick agent of Agrippa II (177–178). Beyond this, Justus was to an extent in harmony with his fellow members of the town council of Tiberias, but we cannot suppose that they always constituted a united body. Justus thus had to reach his own decisions sooner than Josephus, and it no doubt became easier to make up his mind after his brother was mutilated by militant "Galilaeans" at Gamala (177).

So for Justus the period of uncertainty may have been rather shorter (although the chronological picture to be derived from Josephus is not at all clear). Josephus mentions him and his father in passing, as being eager to join John of Gischala's movement against Josephus' leadership (87). That happened when the Galilaean patriot first went to Tiberias; whether or not it implies hostility to Rome depends upon our assessment of John's position: some would see him as a moderate, though I have been inclined to interpret his position as a rebellious one throughout.[27] At any rate, nothing came of the attempted coup, since it was anticipated by Josephus; John ran away and there is no further mention of Justus' plans. No great weight should be put on so slight a statement (88) by Josephus that Justus and his father sought to join John. Though perhaps suspect, in that it contributes to Josephus' objective of pinning the blame for the Tiberian troubles on Justus, there is nothing inherently implausible about it, and it fits in well with the confusion and uncertainty of this early period, as well as with our impression that Justus and Josephus had already conceived an intense personal dislike of one another. Josephus felt that Justus had aspirations to power of his own in Galilee (37, 391).

On the other hand, Justus did not repeat his rash challenge to Agrippa. His change of heart did not come a moment too soon, for he was before long to depend upon Agrippa's favor for rescue from a death sentence imposed by Vespasian, at the prompting of indignant Greeks of the Decapolis (342–343). The change of heart is first revealed when Justus is found among those who resist official demands for Agrippa's Tiberian palace to be destroyed because it bore pictorial representations of animals unacceptable to some of the strictest Jews. In fact, the mob took the law into its own hands, before any formal action could be adopted. Here again, Justus' presence among the leading men of Tiberias (64) is given a brief mention; there is some slight room for doubt, but little is to be gained by treating the inclusion of Justus as a libellous fabrication by Josephus. The leader's action is, in any case, one of civilized moderation, not necessarily implying a particular stance towards the war.

As we have indicated, the city of Tiberias seesawed in its allegiance as different elements took control of its democratic organs or managed to gain an ascendancy over its mob. Josephus' displeasing task continued to be to prevent the city from declaring for Agrippa and to keep it within the revolt; this is what he did, however contrary it may have been to his deepest sympathies and instincts. Justus was, of course, playing a different game, and was, with his father, among the councillors and leading commoners arrested by Josephus after he had suppressed the city's disloyalty by means of a mock fleet and a trick (169, 174). An interesting episode is related in which Josephus, so he says, gave dinner to Justus and Pistus and advised them to accept his authority. "I remarked that I was well aware myself of the unrivalled might of the Roman arms, but, on account of the brigands, kept my knowledge to myself" (175). The little vignette would hardly have been worth inventing; its implication is that Justus and Pistus should have been well able to understand Josephus' predicament, and would have approached the war from a standpoint sufficiently similar, to enable them to grasp both its undesirability and the good sense there was in playing along with the rebels.

Caution, however, took Justus in a different direction, and his opportunity for desertion came before any fighting, during a second bid by his city to get Agrippa to come in and take over (381). There was a serious risk of violent reprisals by the Galilaean hordes, a risk from which Josephus, in boastful vein, claims to have saved the city through his influence with the rebels (389). In fact, Justus' decision to communicate with the client king through his agent Crispus, who was then present, and afterwards to make his escape, is quite understandable as a bid for safety; we may overlook the disappointed ambition and the fear of Josephus, which are named, somewhat absurdly, as the main motives (390–393). For Josephus' aim is to rob Justus of any credit he might acquire as a respectable pacifist: "but you, Justus, will urge that you at least were no enemy [of Rome] because in those early days you sought refuge with the king. I reply that it was fear of me which drove you to do so" (357). Nor is there anything surprising in Justus attaching himself to Agrippa: the association through members of Justus' family will have made up for early disloyalty to the king.

The "great digression" is not the place to look for accurate representations of Justus' position, and least of all in the case of so personal a statement as this one. It looks as though we should also treat with a pinch of salt a rather wild paragraph which precedes these accusations of fear and which has often gone unnoticed. In it Josephus claims a considerably greater and longer resistance on the part of Justus than is borne out by the rest of his narrative, allegations that it was in the later stages of revolt that Justus was active at Tiberias, that he was still anti-Roman after the fall of Jotapata (in the summer of 67), and that he laid down arms only when Vespasian was at the walls of Tiberias (349–352). Yet only a little later, we have Josephus insisting that Justus could not have understood the campaign in Galilee, let alone the events at Jotapata, because he was at Berytus with Agrippa during this whole period (357). We can suppose only that Josephus wrote the earlier paragraph before he had looked into the facts of Justus' flight and failed to alter it afterwards. Were the claims tenable, he would have had every reason to exploit them more fully, as they could have made a major contribution to his case that Justus had been the true warmonger.

The *Vita* exposes a number of loose ends and puzzling little problems. Nonetheless, we have been able to derive with a fair degree of certainty a sketch of Justus before the war as a pro-peace individual who had made some pro-war noises. In this he emerges as a pale shadow of Josephus, just as he does in his writing. It is remarkable that even the circumstances of their respective defections enhance this impression: in Justus' case, after rescue from Vespasian's death sentence, he returns to Agrippa and eventually to a secretaryship with the client king of a marginal kingdom, in Josephus' case, a defection to Vespasian and Titus, and, after imprisonment, to the friendship of emperors and to residence in an imperial property in Rome itself. The scope and talents of Josephus are highlighted through the comparison.

The later years of both men are shrouded in obscurity; with Josephus we have the writings, it is true, but regrettably little biographical background against which to set them. For Justus, we have Josephus' jaundiced statement that he fell out of favor several times with Agrippa, being twice imprisoned, twice exiled, once sentenced to death, and eventually banished after a fraud charge (355–357). Yet even the activities and powers of the client king are for this period unknown to us,[28] let alone the doings of his secretary.

What can, however, be divined is an interesting similarity of cultural attitudes and goals between the two writers—again, writ larger in the case of Josephus. In each case, political ambivalence has its cultural correlative: the indications are that, like Josephus, Justus tried to bridge Hellenism and Judaism through historiography. In his early days he had been something of an orator (V 40). The medium for this still may have been his native Aramaic or even Hebrew, rather than Greek.[29] But the techniques will have been sharpened by the Greek education of which, according to Josephus, Justus had had at least a smattering. And it is Josephus, a man who, after all, had every reason to understand the situation, who says that it was pride in this facility which later induced the Tiberian to set himself up as a historian. In what Justus wrote about the war he evidently treated Jewish politics in a Greek language narrative. In the text on the "Jewish kings" he presumably followed Hellenistic-Jewish precedent in working out a chronology for biblical antiquities: genealogical reconstruction made it possible to relate the Greek mythical past to the Jewish, and, if only by implication, to demonstrate the superior historicity and greater length of Jewish tradition. It is interesting that works to which the same title was at least sometimes applied had earlier been produced by two Hellenistic-Jewish writers, Demetrius, an Alexandrian, probably in the third century B.C.,[30] and Eupolemus, perhaps from Palestine and of the second century B.C.[31] The few fragments of Demetrius to survive are skeleton resumes of biblical stories; Eupolemus seems to have been more of a chronographer. Justus may well have taken such treatment down to the present, with the Herodian dynasty in whose pay and service he himself was placed.

The royal secretaryship, too, which will have offered some opportunity for political involvement as well as for writing, must have combined Justus' Jewish with his Greek interests. Agrippa, like his predecessors, had been granted a general tutelage over the Jewish people in addition to his kingdom around the margins of Palestine. But Agrippa's main sphere of operations—

again like his predecessor's—was on the larger stage of the Hellenized Greek East, a world of cities (to which Agrippa's great-grandfather Herod had made such notable benefactions), and, above all, of client kingdoms. Agrippa's secretary, too, would have had to appear on both the smaller stage and the larger. In this respect there is no exact parallel with Josephus so far as we know; but another prototype springs to mind, and he is Nicolaus of Damascus, who had been Herod's minister and a Greek historian, as well as being a staunch advocate of the Jewish cause (though he himself was in fact a pagan).[32] Again, Justus was by a long way the lesser in stature, both as writer and politician.

In general terms, then, Justus can become a comprehensible, even a predictable figure. Nor does further study and interpretation of the detail require any change in the overall assessment which I made on concluding my original study of Justus and Josephus: the modern historian's predicament can best be defined by saying that we have to learn from Josephus about Justus, and then, through observing Justus, we can come to improve upon our grasp of Josephus. In this way, the two men's disputes have turned, in the end, to a kind of mutual support.

Notes

1. That Josephus' works rather than Justus' have survived is unlikely to be a matter of accident: see T. Rajak, "Justus of Tiberias," *CQ* n.s. 23 (1973), p. 345 and n. 3.

2. See previous note.

3. Notably by S. J. D. Cohen, *Josephus in Galilee and Rome: His Life and Development as a Historian* (Leiden, 1979), especially Chapter V; by Y. Dan, "Josephus and Justus of Tiberias," in *Josephus Flavius: Historian of Eretz-Israel in the Hellenistic Roman Period,* ed. U. Rappaport (Yad Izhak ben Zvi, Jerusalem, 1982; Hebrew), pp. 57–78, and, so far as the writings go, in *Fragments from Hellenistic Jewish Authors,* Vol. I: *Historians,* ed. C. R. Holladay (Chico, California, 1983), pp. 371–389.

4. See my *Josephus: The Historian and His Society* (London, 1983; Philadelphia, 1984), p. 152 and n. 19. I shall not refer further in these notes to specific arguments in Chapter VI of the book.

5. Taking as a starting point H. Luther's *Josephus und Justus von Tiberias: Ein Beitrag zur Geschichte des jüdischen Aufstandes* (Halle, 1910).

6. Eusebius, *Historia Ecclesiastica* III, 10, 8; Jerome, *de Viris Illustribus* 14; Steph. Byz., s.v. "Tiberias"; Suda, s.v. "Justus" and s.v. "Tiberias."

7. Rajak, *op. cit.,* p. 355.

8. Cohen, *op. cit.,* pp. 138–139.

9. Photius, *Bibliotheca* 33 = Jacoby, *FGrHist* 734 T2.

10. The dating is to the third year of Trajan. Yet all other evidence points to Agrippa's being dead by the date of the composition of Josephus' *Antiquities,* A.D. 93–94. See Schürer-Vermes-Millar, *The History of the Jewish People in the Time of Jesus Christ,* Vol. I (Edinburgh, 1973), pp. 480–483. If the wrong date were inserted by Photius, such an error would be unsurprising. See now also D. A. Barish, "The Autobiography of Josephus and the Hypothesis of a Second Edition of His Antiquities," *HThR* 71 (1978), pp. 61–75.

11. As he did, for example, in the case of the historian Hesychius (cod. 69).

12. See T. Hägg, *Photios als Vermittler antiker Literatur* (Uppsala, 1973), p. 192. Photius claimed, in fact, to have worked from memory: see N. G. Wilson, "The Composition of Photius' *Bibliotheca,"* *GRBS* 9 (1968), pp. 451–455.

13. See Cohen, *op. cit.* (referring to earlier exponents).

14. So, notably, F. Ruhl, "Justus von Tiberias," *RhM* 71 (1916), pp. 289–308. Y. Dan, *op. cit.*, p. 60, suggests two works, put together at a date preceding Photius, who saw both bound together, but noticed mainly the chronicle.

15. Cf. Cohen, *op. cit.*, p. 143, n. 145, and Hägg, *op. cit.*, p. 199.

16. Rajak, *op. cit.*, pp. 360, 364.

17. On the nature of such a compressed work (for which the Latin would normally be *breviarium*) see A. J. Woodman, *CQ* 25 (1975), pp. 282–288 and especially p. 284, n. 4. This point refutes the view of the old source critics that Justus' lost history was the origin of various traditions about Jewish history that do not derive from Josephus: for an example see H. Gelzer in *Sextus Julius Africanus* (Leipzig, 1880–1898), pp. 225–226. Such theories can now be happily buried. For discussion, see Rajak, *op. cit.*, pp. 365–368.

18. To make it into a work of general rather than Jewish culture, as Otto does in *RE* suppl. ii (1913), p. 14. There is less justification in positing a third work, as in H. Luther, *op. cit.*, pp. 53–54.

19. The position was, however, correctly stated by Cohen, *op. cit.*, p. 144.

20. See *V* 424–425, 429; *Ap* I, 45–46. It is unreasonable to take Justus as the specific target of the *Contra Apionem* refutation, as proposed by M. Gelzer, "Die Vita des Josephus," *Hermes* 80 (1952), p. 67 = *Kleine Schriften* III (Wiesbaden, 1964), p. 299.

21. H. Drexler, "Untersuchungen zu Josephus und zur Geschichte des jüdischen Aufstandes 66–70," *Klio* 9 n.s. 1 (1925), pp. 277–312; A. Schalit, "Josephus und Justus: Studien zur Vita des Josephus," *Klio* 26 (1933), pp. 67–95.

22. Cohen, *op. cit.*, p. 135.

23. On the distinction between action against Gentile Greeks and action against Rome, see U. Rappaport, "John of Gischala: From Galilee to Jerusalem," *JJS* 33, nos. 1–2 (1982) = *Essays in Honour of Yigael Yadin*, p. 481 and n. 8.

24. Schalit, *op. cit.;* Cohen, *op. cit.*

25. Thus Cohen's purpose is to argue that Josephus in the *Vita* was bent on concealing his erstwhile militancy; for this the evidence had to be systematically distorted, which required denying Justus' true position as essentially a pacifist.

26. This is explained in the *Bellum;* see *BJ* II, 449, 562 ff.

27. See Schürer-Vermes-Millar, *op. cit.*, pp. 480–483.

28. See Dan, *op. cit.*, p. 61 and n. 12.

29. On Hebrew and Aramaic as Josephus' native languages, see Rajak, *op. cit.*, appendix 1.

30. For Demetrius' fragments, see F. Jacoby, *FGrHist* III C, 722, and now Holladay, *op. cit.*, pp. 51–91, or N. Walter, *Fragmente jüdisch-hellenistischer Exegeten, JSHRZ* III, 2 (Gütersloh, 1975), pp. 280–292.

31. For Eupolemus' fragments, see *FGrHist* III C, 723; Holladay, *op. cit.*, pp. 93–156; N. Walter, *Fragmente jüdisch-hellenistischer Historiker, JSHRZ* I, 2 (Gütersloh, 1976), pp. 93–108; and B. Z. Wacholder, *Eupolemus: A Study of Judaeo-Hellenistic Literature* (Cincinnati, 1974). It was Clement of Alexandria (*Strom.* I, 153.4) who gave this title to Eupolemus' book.

32. On Nicolaus, see B. Z. Wacholder, *Nicolaus of Damascus* (Berkeley, 1962).

3 Josephus and Masada

DAVID J. LADOUCEUR

The Problem

f ew problems in Josephan scholarship have generated so much controversy as the interpretation of the Masada narrative.[1] One elusive
question that has emerged from the polemics of the past fifteen years
is why Josephus, our only source for the actions of Masada's defenders, included this incident in his history. Usually regarded as an opportunistic
traitor, here he seems to present a detailed record of heroism on the part of the
very people whom he had allegedly betrayed. What was his purpose and motivation in composing this narrative?

Some Previous Solutions

Yigael Yadin, the excavator of Masada, has suggested that he was
conscience-stricken and simply overwhelmed by the heroism of the people he
had forsaken.[2] In his account, however, Josephus is alluding to the Sicarii, not
the Jewish people in general. The activities of that sect he explicitly and consistently condemns both before (*BJ* VII, 262) and after (*BJ* VII, 437) the Masada episode. A psychological explanation, therefore, is insufficient.

Even less convincing is the view that Josephus composed the suicide account as an apologetic cover-up for a Roman atrocity, specifically the massacre by Roman soldiers of all the men, women, and children.[3] From whom
was he hiding the truth? Romans of a liberal persuasion, who in the seventies
felt a special sympathy for Jews? "Parcere subiectis et debellare superbos"
was the Roman principle. Modern concepts of an atrocity, especially here in
an armed rebellion, punishable by crucifixion or the arena, would be irrelevant by Roman norms. Also, elsewhere in the *Bellum* Josephus recounts in
horrifying detail Roman brutalities, once even after a pledge of safety was
granted.[4] Since the *Bellum* was written partly to deter revolt (*BJ* III, 108), the

historian could allow himself on occasion to make the consequences of such revolt chillingly clear.

A third and equally unsatisfying solution is to refer the whole episode to the category of a literary commonplace, a *topos*. In both classical literature and art there often occurs a conventional presentation of the ends of one's enemies in heroic and melodramatic terms. To cite only a few examples: Aeschylus' Persians ennobled by their suffering, the heroic depiction of dying Gauls on the Great Altar at Pergamum, the noble barbarian confronting a choice of *servitus* or *libertas* in Caesar's *Commentarii*. This approach, however, does not really explain why Josephus included the Masada episode, but merely aspires to classify the story and cite supposed parallels in other works. But at Jotapata, Josephus as insurgent general chose life, Eleazar at Masada chose death. In portraying these diametrically opposed choices, surely Josephus had more in mind than literary conventions. As a man whose own war actions were subject to criticism and as a Jew, would he have wished to depict Eleazar as a noble and heroic "barbarian," a sort of Vercingetorix, particularly in the charged Roman atmosphere of the seventies after a protracted Jewish war? The answer is obvious, but curiously this third solution, with modifications, continues to attract followers.

Common to nearly all these solutions is the belief that Josephus meant his audience to interpret the deaths of the defenders and their families as heroic. One argument to substantiate this belief, at the risk of caricature, often reduces to these propositions: the Stoics approved of suicide. Romans were almost by nature inclined to Stoicism. Therefore, the Romans would have approved of the suicide of the defenders. As though to cut the Gordian knot, I have argued elsewhere that it was not Josephus' intention to portray unreservedly the defenders as heroes, and so there actually exists no inconsistency between his depiction of the Sicarii in the Masada episode and elsewhere in the *Bellum*.[5] Though difficulties do exist in Josephus' text, modern scholars, to a certain extent, have themselves created inconsistency in ways which it may be useful to enumerate. First, there has been a general failure to reconstruct the Graeco-Roman political environment in which the Masada account would have been read. Next, the thematic and formal relationship of the Masada episode to other parts of the *Bellum* has been overlooked. Also, in explicating the text, irrelevant literary parallels have been drawn. Scholars have, in addition, employed oversimplified notions of Stoicism and the limits it set on suicidal acts, and in citing secondary suicide literature, have sometimes relied on older, uncritical compilations rather than on contemporary work. In some presentations there occur errors of fact in Roman history, and, finally, arguments have at times been based on actual mistranslations.

Inasmuch as the literature on Masada published since 1980 has either confirmed or little affected my own analysis, I shall briefly restate my views, but where later scholars have at points added refinements, I have expanded my account. For the sake of comparison, I shall also show how in a few instances some current work, scarcely differing from the earlier, persists in the same methodological flaws as those listed above.

Analysis of the Suicide Speeches

Central to an understanding of the Masada episode are Eleazar's speech (actually two speeches) urging suicide and Josephus' speech at Jotapata against suicide.[6] Though separated from one another by three books, they are, in fact, designedly antithetical and in them specific arguments and counter-arguments are balanced against one another. Further linking the orations is common recourse to a Platonic dialogue, the *Phaedo,* as a sort of proof text.

The prefatory context of Josephus' speech is a prayer addressed to ὁ ϑεός (*BJ* III, 354), words and phrases of which H. Lindner tried to explicate through Septuagintal usage. For him Josephus' relationship to the divinity must be viewed in terms of Jewish sacerdotal cult.[7] Much of the religious terminology, however, I have shown, may be paralleled in the literature of later Stoicism, in Seneca and Epictetus for example.[8] Whatever the significance of these pagan parallels, it is questionable to explicate only through the Septuagint an Atticistic text directed to a Graeco-Roman audience—all the more so when a theme central to late Stoicism, suicide, immediately follows.

The oration itself is of the species *deliberativum* and conforms to rhetorical conventions. Greek philosophy more than Jewish teaching informs its argument against suicide. In the late first century A.D. the Platonic *Phaedo* became a proof text of sorts on the question of suicide. In particular, sections 61 b–62 d, in which Socrates states that it is unreasonable to kill oneself before a god sends some "compulsion" (ἀνάγκη), served as a *locus classicus* both as a justification for and a condemnation of suicide. The ambiguity lay in how one interpreted "compulsion." The nearly verbatim citation of the *Phaedo* in III, 372 suggests that the unnamed lawgiver in III, 376 may be Plato, or the reference may be purposely inclusive since both Jewish and Greek practices are set forth immediately afterward.[9] At any rate, in III, 372, Josephus invokes the dialogue in its second role. Also, both in Josephus' speech and in Eleazar's speeches there occurs the well-known ἐλευϑερία/δουλεία topos. Josephus, however, in his speech passes over the political aspects of "freedom." For him, to paraphrase *BJ* III, 366–368, it is slavery to inflict death unwillingly upon oneself simply in fear of death at the hands of one's enemies. As Seneca says, "stultitia est timore mortis mori. Venit qui occidat. Expecta" (*Ep.* 70.8).

To turn now to Eleazar's words, they, too, are infused with classical allusions.[10] Phrases from Euripides, possibly Posidonius, and Plato recur throughout his speeches. There are at least five references to the *Phaedo,* but Eleazar, unlike Josephus, appeals to the *locus classicus* to justify the act of suicide, God, in his opinion having brought on the ἀνάγκη (*BJ* VII, 330; cf. VII, 387). Unlike Josephus, Eleazar alludes to freedom in a religio-political sense; for him the concept entails "being a slave to neither the Romans nor any other except God" (VII, 323). This first speech, according to Josephus (VII, 337–340), failed to actuate his followers. In his second speech, Eleazar again invokes ἐλευθερία, but now in a more philosophical or spiritual sense: "Life, not death, is man's misfortune. For it is death which gives liberty to the soul" (VII, 343–344). An everlasting form of liberty is contrasted with a fleeting secular liberty: "And is it not foolish, while pursuing liberty in this life, to grudge ourselves that which is eternal?" (VII, 350). As he pursues his argument in these philosophical terms, he adduces such examples as Indian self-immolation, draws in the *Phaedo,* and as part of an *enumeratio malorum,* also delineates the hideous punishments that await them if they are captured alive. The defenders, in Josephus' description, are almost daimonically impelled to their final act by this second speech (VII, 389).

Although some scholars have tried to dehellenize these speeches and so discover a perceptible Jewish substratum,[11] more recent examinations have substantiated my own view that one must look to Greek models not only for the form of these speeches but also for their content. M. Luz, for example, has classified Eleazar's second speech as ostensibly a *parakeleusis,* a form of rhetorical exhortation.[12] Parallels to Eleazar's arguments, he convincingly and meticulously demonstrates, are to be found not in Jewish thought, but in stereotyped genres of Hellenistic literature, in suicide pieces and more so in *consolationes.* Even Eleazar's references to "ancestral and divine precepts" (*BJ* VII, 343) are shown to have their parallels in the *consolationes.* Thus, there is no need to seek Jewish sources for this theme.[13]

Whether Josephus himself directly drew upon Plato or simply took over certain Platonic *loci communes* already present in his Hellenistic models, the *Phaedo* clearly presents itself as a major influence. Eleazar's arguments on the immortality of the soul display an intimate relationship with Socrates' three *epicheiremata.*[14] Sources aside, however, several points are noteworthy in Josephus' presentation. Although the notion of "no master but God" was clearly fundamental to the Sicarii (*BJ* VII, 418), Josephus here in the Masada account portrays Eleazar's recourse to this principle as unpersuasive to his followers. Only when the Jewish "fanatic" essays the arguments of Greek philosophical oratory, embraces an alien and morbid tradition of the *symphora* of life, and enumerates what evils will befall his followers if they are captured alive, do his arguments incite his followers to suicide. Apart from distorting the actual absorptions of the Sicarii, Josephus through these fictitious speeches transforms Eleazar into a philosopher figure. The reasons for this transformation may be properly understood only after recalling certain political conditions of Flavian Rome.

The Flavian Political Environment

Despite the fragmentary nature of the evidence, primarily scattered citations from Suetonius, Tacitus, and Dio, a clear impression emerges that political conditions in Rome of the seventies were indeed tense.[15] The conspiracy of Caecina and Marcellus about 79, once viewed as a trumped-up case against the remnants of Mucianus' faction, has more recently been analyzed as an actual plot aimed at undermining the rule of Vespasian and Titus.[16] Such an analysis sheds new light on Suetonius' statement (*Vesp.* 25) that Vespasian's reign was plagued by "constant conspiracies." There were also those disturbed by Titus' actions before he actually came to the throne, who saw in him another Nero (*Tit.* 7.1). His activities as *praefectus praetorio,* in particular his summary execution of Caecina and his liaison with Berenice, Mommsen's miniature Cleopatra and a Jewess, which played upon Roman fears of orientalizing tendencies, scarcely endeared him in some quarters.

Furthermore, from nearly the beginning of his reign, Vespasian and his supporter Mucianus had encountered resistance from a so-called "philosophic opposition."[17] The leaders of this resistance were in part the survivors of the so-called Stoic opposition that had been directed against Nero. A principal figure was Helvidius Priscus, who married the daughter of Thrasea Paetus, an arch-martyr who had been forced to commit suicide under Nero. Vespasian hated him, according to Dio LXV, 12.2, "because he was a turbulent fellow who cultivated the mob and was forever praising democracy and denouncing the monarchy." In addition, however, as Dio also makes clear (LXVI, 13.1–2), Cynic philosophers, actuated by Stoic principles—men like Demetrius—played a part in this opposition too. Sometime between 71 and 75 Vespasian's patience wore thin. At the instigation of Mucianus he banished and later executed Helvidius and expelled Stoic and Cynic philosophers from Rome. In 75 two expelled Cynics, Diogenes and Heras, slipped back into Rome to inspire opposition to Titus' marriage to Berenice. The first was flogged, the other beheaded, a punishment which suggests he directly attacked Vespasian himself (*Dio Cassius* LXV, 15). In this period Vespasian was enthusiastically creating chairs of rhetoric at Rome, while philosophy fell into disfavor. It was at this time that Dio Chrysostom was insinuating himself into the Flavian court. His anti-philosophical works, curious given his own later proclivities, according to Synesius, attacked Socrates, Zeno, and his followers, and perhaps must be seen against this background hostile to certain philosophers.

After all, Socrates and Zeno, in Cynic estimation, were veritable paragons of virtue.[18]

Against this background, too, Josephus' apparently incongruous transformation of Eleazar into a sort of philosopher who spouts Socratic arguments at critical moments takes on meaning. In a stimulating article, Zvi Yavetz has suggested that the picture of Titus presented in the *Bellum* as a man imbued with *clementia* "reflects more prevalent attitudes in the society in which Josephus moved when writing than any real historical person acting in Judea."[19] Titus might have welcomed any effort to change his unpopular image. The historian, a Flavian client and friend of sorts, perhaps understood the situation; and his portrait of Titus, endowed with *clementia,* a virtue "maxime . . . decora imperatoribus" (Sen. *De clem.* 1.5.1), soon followed.[20] If the interests of Roman politics have colored the portrait of Titus, so also, I would argue, may they have influenced the characterization of Eleazar. It is perhaps more than coincidence that the form and content of his speech have much in common with the so-called Stoic-Cynic diatribe,[21] and also that like some Cato he goes to his suicide only after reciting the required lines from Euripides and Plato's *Phaedo.*

Throughout the first century, as MacMullen has shown,[22] the cult of the Republican Stoic martyr and suicide, Cato, was repeatedly turned politically against the Roman emperors. In the hagiographic tradition of Cato enshrined in Plutarch, the martyr is portrayed as spending his final hours in reading the *Phaedo.*[23] The guardian philosopher of Cato was none other than Thrasea Paetus, who under Nero wrote a *Cato,* apparently modelled on the *Phaedo,* and shortly thereafter was forced to commit suicide. By marriage Thrasea was related to Caecina Paetus, who with his wife was one of the more memorable Claudian suicides. And, again, the man who was drawn into Thrasea's family traditions by marriage was Vespasian's chief opponent, Helvidius Priscus. Very near the period when Josephus was composing the *Bellum,* between July 74 and July 75, Curiatius Maternus delivered his praetexta, *Cato,* too enthusiastically. Vespasian and Titus were offended, and there was much talk about the matter throughout the city (Tac. *Dial.* 2.1). Around this time, too, Helvidius was executed and Demetrius the Cynic exiled.

Within this charged atmosphere, it is not implausible to sense political overtones in Josephus' suicide speeches. In his own speech, he reverses the opposition's interpretation of the *Phaedo.* Eleazar, in citing the required lines of the group's stock dialogue before enjoining suicide, is made to echo the sentiments of opponents of the Flavian regime, men who venerated their models of suicide. Admittedly the *Phaedo* was conventionally associated with suicide in the literature of the period, but such an association does not preclude the possibility of a relationship between these speeches and the actual circumstances in which Josephus was writing. In the same way the freedom/slavery debates in the speeches might be dismissed as mere *topoi* were the *libertas* motif not so recurrent a theme in Flavian coinage, one of antiquity's most efficacious devices for imperial propaganda.[24]

This is not to say that Josephus, the parvenu from the provinces, was deliberately opposing himself to the urban aristocracy or parodying in the figure of Eleazar some specific member of the resistance, such as Helvidius. The limits of our evidence do not warrant so precise a formulation. The spectrum of political disaffection in the Neronian and Flavian periods passed by nearly imperceptible gradations from simple discontent to conspiracy; even to locate the opposition on this spectrum is no easy task. Stoicism itself in this period ranged from certain purer and more traditional forms (note how some of Josephus' own arguments in his speech have Stoic parallels) to radical manifestations, which blended indistinguishably into the libertarian and subversive views of the Cynics.[25] Hence, it is a fallacy in modern discussions of Masada to speak of Stoicism in this period as though it were a single body of doctrine that contained well-defined and approbatory teachings on suicide. Anyone who entertains such a simplistic view would do well to ponder the problematic ending of Seneca's *Hercules Furens*. Not every Stoic hero chooses suicide.[26]

Rather, in portraying Eleazar, Josephus invested the figure with certain philosophical characteristics, the political significance of which would not have been lost on a Graeco-Roman audience of the seventies. In an opportunistic way he may have drawn upon actual tensions within his Roman environment that had literary counterparts in genres such as suicide pieces. The portrait of Eleazar as a subversive both renders him intelligible and distorts his central tenets. Distinctions are blurred as a Jewish fanatic takes on the outlines of a home-grown opponent of Vespasian's rule. The audience's attention is drawn away from Josephus' own acts as insurgent general to the interest of Roman politics. The historian's own speech becomes not only a moral rejection of suicide but also a pledge of allegiance to the new rulers; opponents of the regime, on the other hand, find their sentiments echoed by a Jewish fanatic. Yet, in fashioning his suicide narratives, Josephus, as we shall shortly see, both adheres to and departs from convention in a number of ways.

The Masada Narrative within the *Bellum*

Circumstances in Josephus' Roman environment may help to explain why he presents Eleazar, the Jewish "fanatic," in the seemingly incongruous role of a philosopher. They little resolve the question why the historian included the Masada account in his narrative. Rather than pursuing elusive intent, the question might better be posed how, in a unitarian sense, does the narrative fit within and relate to the rest of the *Bellum*.

From a form-critical perspective the Masada account is but one example of a type of suicide narrative found elsewhere in Josephus. In both the *Antiquities* and the *Bellum,* as Newell has convincingly demonstrated,[27] there occur two patterns of reporting suicide: a shorter form, the suicide episode, in which (1) the reason for the suicide is given, and (2) the act is described (e.g., *BJ* VI, 186–187, on the death of the Roman soldier Longus); and a longer form, the suicide narrative, in which (1) a desperate situation is described, (2) a direct or indirect speech urging suicide is delivered, and (3) the act is related (e.g., the Masada account). As a form, the suicide episode occurs as early as Herodotus (1.82, on the death of Othryadas). Though Newell dates the first appearance of the more elaborate form to the first century B.C. in Roman military commentaries,[28] in fact it may be found earlier in Greek sources, in the writing of Polybius (e.g., XVI, 31–34, on the description of the fall of Abydos to Philip in 200 B.C.). Be that as it may, Josephus himself was not the originator of these forms nor would he have found fully articulated examples in earlier Jewish literature, Saul's death offering only an imperfect parallel. Indeed, what examples exist in Hellenistic Jewish literature all seem to have been influenced by classical prototypes.

The entire Masada account, therefore, may be regarded as a literary unit which is exemplified elsewhere in the *Bellum.* In the Jotapata account Josephus employs precisely the same conventional form, but there changes its purpose so as to oppose the act of suicide. As Josephus' and Eleazar's speeches present balanced arguments and counterarguments, so, too, the longer narratives in which they are embedded are related formally as antithetical units. Apart from a formal relationship, however, the Masada account, after close philological examination, reveals thematic links to the rest of the *Bellum.* These links, in turn, present parallels and contrasts to certain *topoi* of Silver Age literature. Those who have appealed to a vague Stoicism, such as might be deduced from scattered citations of Seneca, have found passages there to justify the suicides of the defenders. In this same author, however, there occurs a notion fundamental to this Stoicism, an antipathy to the baser influences of the emotions in place of rational judgment. Even in the matter of death, *libido moriendi,* like other passions, must be avoided: "A man who is brave and wise should not flee from life, but take his leave" (*Ep.* 24.25). In describing what motivated the defenders to their final act, Josephus is ambiguous. On the one hand, he suggests it was calculation, ὁ λογισμός (VII, 390), though by inserting the particle ὡς he conceals his own opinion. Yet he also portrays (VII, 389) the defenders as filled with some uncontrollable passion, ἀνεπισχέτου τινὸς ὁρμῆς πεπληρωμένοι, in a state of frenzy, δαιμονῶντες, and seized by a passionate desire, ἔρως, to kill their wives, their children, and themselves. Though ὁρμή in a Stoic text might refer neutrally to "appetition," in this context, juxtaposed to words expressing lack of control, frenzy, and lust, it probably should be taken in a negative sense, and so Josephus' description of the defenders' motivation here hardly fits the model of the Stoic sage calmly and deliberately electing the time and manner of his death. Indeed, more than once Josephus emphasizes the haste with which the defenders pursue their deaths. The defenders, moreover, after they have killed their families, are depicted as unable to bear the emotion of grief at their actions (VII, 397), a natural but not Stoic reaction. What parallels may exist to the conventional Stoic *exitus illustrium virorum* are there, it would seem, in part to heighten a contrast.[29]

The reference to ἔρως that impels the defenders to suicide and murder does suggest a well-known theme in violent Silver Age literature: *amor mortis*.[30] Josephus' Eleazar is a preacher of death who will not himself contemplate flight nor allow any of his followers to escape (VII, 320). God, to him, has sentenced the whole Jewish race (VII, 327). Embracing an alien philosophy of the *symphora* of life, he believes it is death that gives true liberty to the soul (VII, 344). In his grim and single-minded determination on death, Eleazar resembles Lucan's Vulteius in the *Pharsalia,* who, in urging his men to commit mutual suicide, utters the lines "Proieci vitam, comites, totusque futurae / Mortis agor stimulis: furor est" (IV, 516–517). Vulteius' suicide pact, as one man kills the other, becomes for Lucan a miniature enactment of civil *nefas* ("Concurrunt alii totumque in partibus unis / Bellorum fecere nefas" IV, 548–549) and so calls to the poet's mind the Theban brothers Eteocles and Polynices as well as the Cadmean *spartoi* who "filled the vast furrows with kindred blood."[31]

Perhaps in a similar way for Josephus the Masada account with its graphic description of Jew murdering Jew, serves as a sort of concentrated scene that dramatizes vividly one of his most persistent themes in the *Bellum.* From the days when the internal struggles of the Hasmonean brothers brought on Roman intervention down to this final disaster (πάθος), it has been the Jews themselves who have worked their own destruction. "στάσις οἰκεία," he writes in his prologue, destroyed the country, and it was the Jewish tyrants who drew down upon the Temple the unwilling hands of the Romans (I, 10). Perhaps this theme was calculated to strike a responsive and sympathetic chord in a Roman audience, which itself had recently been subjected to civil disorder. In his speech condemning the Zealots, at any rate, Josephus' Ananus explicitly rejects ἐλευθερία as the Zealot pretext for war and argues that the real enemies of Jewish freedom and law are the Jewish tyrants within the walls (IV, 177–185). Famine and other horrors of the siege, so minutely recounted in the fifth book, were, in the historian's opinion, provoked by the Jews themselves (V, 25). The Masada account, however, inculcates an even more specific application of this general theme, for the Sicarii, after all, according to Josephus (VII, 262), were the first to set the example of lawlessness and cruelty towards their kinsmen. In the end it is again the Sicarii, who, as "wretched victims of necessity" (VII, 393), are compelled to kill those closest to them, their families and themselves. A classical audience, accustomed to the methods of so-called "tragic" history, would look upon the Masada account as an attempt to thrill (ἐκπλήττειν) readers by invoking feelings of pity and fear and to dramatize the vicissitudes of fortune (τύχης μεταβολαί), since civil murderers, by a proper retributive logic, are now forced to turn their destructive impulses inward.[32] Indeed, in the words of Eleazar himself, the act of self-destruction will be a penalty the defenders will pay to God for their injustices against their own countrymen (VII, 332–333). This special notion of precisely fitting retribution, a commonplace of Greek historiography from the classical period onwards, pervades the writings of Josephus' contemporaries, Luke and Plutarch.[33] At times Plutarch seems so preoccupied with this notion of retribution that he distorts well-known historical facts to illustrate what he believes is an exemplum. In the *Erotikos,* for example, Vespasian's execution of the Gallic chieftain Sabinus and his wife, who had just borne him a son, brings upon the emperor divine retribution, which destroys his whole line in a short time (770 d–771 d). That Vespasian died in peace and Domitian survived some twenty years afterwards, Plutarch fails to note.

Whether Josephus distorted any facts in portraying the deaths of the defenders must remain unknown since he is our only source for the Masada incident. What is clear is that in the seventh book Josephus is preoccupied with the principle of divine retribution. The capture of Simon ben Giora inspires remarks (*BJ* VII, 32–34) that call to mind Plutarch's essay "On the Delay of the Divine Justice." The rebels, he generalizes (*BJ* VII, 271), "each found a fitting end, God awarding due retribution to them all." Indeed, the book itself ends with the story of the divine retribution visited on Catullus (*BJ* VII, 451–453).[34] Through Eleazar's own witness Josephus "sets up" the defenders' suicide as an act of retribution. Even without that explicit testimony, a classical audience, used to such endings, would probably have felt the working out of a divine, logical punishment. According to Plutarch, Vespasian's extirpation of the family line of Sabinus led, in turn, to the extirpation of his own family line. In Josephus, as the Sicarii have over and over again murdered their own countrymen, so in their final moments they are forced to murder those closest to them, their own families, and at last themselves.

Questions of Translation

It is time now, to turn to problems of translation. Although generally regarded as the standard rendition of the *Bellum.* Thackeray's elegant version, in fact, contains a number of mistranslations. These, in turn, have been responsible for certain misunderstandings of the narrative. As though he himself had begun with certain preconceptions, Thackeray renders Josephus' difficult narrative as if it were an unequivocally laudatory presentation of the defenders. ἀλκή at VII, 321 may mean no more than "defense," but Thackeray renders it "gallant endeavor." After Eleazar's first speech, some defenders are described as "filled with delight at the thought of a death so noble" (VII, 337); but more literally the phrase runs "filled with pleasure supposing such a death to be noble." At VII, 393 τόλμημα is rendered "daring deed" to describe the suicide act itself, but at VII, 405 it is inconsistently translated "fortitude." In fact, here and elsewhere in the *Bellum,* Josephus commonly describes Jewish actions as motivated by "audacity" or "boldness," while ἀρετή attended by λόγος is, with few exceptions, reserved for descriptions of Roman military actions. In his speech commending the troops after the destruction of Jerusalem, Titus himself is made to point out this same contrast between the valor of the Romans (ἀρετή) and the reckless daring (ἀλόγιστοι τολμαί) and bestial savagery of the Jews (VII, 7). Against Thackeray's translation, however, is the simple fact that elsewhere in the *Bellum* τόλμημα is never used with positive connotations.[35] Also, at VII, 406, the Romans coming upon the scene are portrayed as "encountering the mass of the slain." The phrase translated as "the slain" is more properly rendered "the murdered" or "the massacred" since the verb is φονεύω, precisely the same verb used by Ananus to describe the victims of Zealots (IV, 165, 170, 181). Curiously in Ananus' speech Thackeray translates the verb correctly, but here in the Masada account, he drains it of its proper force. So also, the last survivor of the suicide pact is described as surveying the fallen multitude to see if anyone was left alive "amid the shambles" (VII, 397). The last phrase trivializes Josephus' ἐν πολλῷ φόνῳ, "amid much murder [or slaughter]." In this context even the seemingly positive reaction of the Roman soldiers that "they admired the nobility of their resolve" might better be translated as "they were astonished at the high spirit of their resolve" (VII, 406). But there is no need to force the Greek. Under desperate military circumstances, a Roman soldier himself might resort to suicide and so the act in itself would not be regarded as cowardly.[36] One must remember, however, that Josephus is carefully controlling his presentation and thus manipulating his audience's response. The suicide he portrays is retributive, both atonement for and acknowledgment of crimes against the rebels' own countrymen. In Eleazar's *enumeratio malorum,* the suicide becomes a means of escaping brutal Roman punishment. The irony lies in the fact that the defenders display resolution not in fighting the Romans but in murder and suicide. Also, the report of the Romans' reaction may serve at least in part to emphasize Roman magnanimity after a long siege.

Finally, in stark contrast to the *topos* of the heroic barbarian or acts of military suicide, Josephus nowhere portrays the defenders as soldiers actively fighting against the Romans. The reasons for his failure to include a single battle scene may only be surmised. To be positivistic, perhaps quite simply none occurred. Better, however, the omission is consistent with his portrayal of the Sicarii not as patriotic soldiers but as killers of their own kind. The single foray which he attributes to them is the attack on Engaddi during the feast of unleavened bread. There they massacre seven hundred Jewish women and children (IV, 398–405). In his depiction, then, they do not assist their fellow rebels at Jerusalem; and when they themselves are cornered at Masada, they turn their destructive impulses inwards rather than against the external enemy. Josephus' portrayal of the Sicarii in the Masada account is not, then, as inconsistent as some have maintained, if one studies it within its proper literary and historical context.

Other Approaches

In some quarters the view persists that Josephus, for some reason or other, wished without reservation to portray the Sicarii in the Masada account as heroic freedom fighters. For the sake of comparison this conception must be critically analyzed. An article by S. Cohen most recently exemplifies this approach.[37]

Cohen's thesis is little more than a variant of Yadin's. Like his predecessor, he admits to being "swept away" by Eleazar's rhetoric (p. 405). Though, admittedly, the totally dispassionate and objective historian was always the figment of someone's imagination, Cohen's feelings in this matter would seem to have too much affected his approach to the problem. Josephus, in his opinion, quite simply "forgot that he wished to heap opprobrium, not approbation, on them" (p. 405). To Yadin, Josephus was "conscience-stricken"; to Cohen, apparently, he was merely stricken. Obviously, however, a man who not only survived the Jewish War but also turned up in Rome in the Flavian entourage may scarcely be dismissed as a forgetful fool. Even a superficial reading of the Josephan corpus, moreover, makes plain of the historian that "quem amat, amat, quem non amat, non amat."

Firmly convinced of his thesis, Cohen does not carefully reexamine the Greek text and thus overlooks ambiguities and difficulties which Thackeray's translation obscures. To prove, for example, that the tone of the Masada story is favorable, he notes (p. 393) how Eleazar tells his men that their suicide will be a deed of "prowess and courage," $\dot{\alpha}\rho\epsilon\tau\dot{\eta}$ and $\epsilon\dot{\upsilon}\tau o\lambda\mu\dot{\iota}\alpha$ (VII, 342). Cohen then instructs his reader to compare $\tau\dot{o}\lambda\mu\eta\mu\alpha$ at 393 and 405, which he translates "act of daring," thus uncritically following Thackeray. But $\tau\dot{o}\lambda\mu\eta\mu\alpha$ to describe Jewish military action in the *Bellum,* as we have just seen, has negative connotations, and $\dot{\alpha}\rho\epsilon\tau\dot{\eta}$ is practically never used of Jewish military action during the war.[38] The point is obvious. Though Josephus allows Eleazar to describe the act as $\dot{\alpha}\rho\epsilon\tau\dot{\eta}$ in a speech to his followers, the historian's own narration undercuts that description. Apart from particular usages, then, Cohen fails to distinguish between the use of words in dramatizing speeches and their use in supposedly "objective" narrative sections.

Though Cohen himself makes little attempt to reconstruct the Graeco-Roman background against which Josephus was writing, he rejects the idea of any reference to the philosophic opposition on the grounds that there were no prominent Cynic philosophers in the early eighties and that it was only under Domitian that the opposition came to include Cynic philosophers. So transparent a historical error scarcely deserves comment. One need only point out that the most famous Cynic philosopher of the first century A.D. was born about A.D. 10, came to attention under Caligula, attended Thrasea Paetus, the arch-martyr of the opposition under Nero, in his final hours, and was, together with Helvidius Priscus, involved in the philosophic expulsion under Vespasian.[39] If one has not heard of Demetrius the Cynic, there is little point in mentioning Isidorus, Diogenes, and Heras.

Historical errors aside, to prove his central thesis, he assembles from Graeco-Roman literature a corpus of sixteen cases of collective suicide which he believes closely parallel the Masada account. Herodotus, Xenophon, Polybius, Livy, Appian, Plutarch, Pausanias, Florus, Justinus, and Orosius are among the authors cited. From this corpus he concludes first that the defenders of Masada were not the only ones in the ancient world who practiced collective suicide; second, that ancient writers sometimes embellished the truth in narrating such suicide, and, for some, the descriptions become virtual *topoi;* and, third, that ancient writers, with the sole exception of Livy, generally approve of collective suicide (pp. 389–392). For some reason or other (forgetfulness, p. 405), in drawing upon this tradition for the Masada story, Josephus failed to reconcile this usual approbatory attitude with his condemnation of the Sicarii (p. 404).

Though Cohen consults Livy, he is apparently unaware that his first conclusion was anticipated more than ten years ago in the standard commentary on that author by J. Briscoe, who used some of the very same evidence.[40] His second conclusion is correct, as he himself convincingly shows, in dealing with the Xanthian and Saguntine suicides. His third conclusion is questionable, which is unfortunate, since it is essential to his theory. A historian of antiquity must react with skepticism to a methodology which polls for a generalization writers as distinct in attitudes, circumstances, subjects, and audiences as Herodotus, Polybius, Livy, and Justinus, all the more so when one is dealing with an issue as complex and fraught with taboos as suicide. After all, more than centuries separate these authors. Further, a cursory examination of his corpus discloses that more than half of his examples involve barbarians, while Greeks and Romans are cited only once each. The Roman example, moreover, occurs during the special circumstances of a civil war. If, as Cohen believes (p. 386), his examples "fairly represent all the available material," one expects some explanation for the skewed distribution. He furnishes none, but merely concludes that collective suicide was generally practiced throughout the ancient world. Obviously, given his own evidence, such a conclusion is unwarranted.[41]

Even if, however, one suppresses these initial misgivings, a detailed examination of the corpus reveals that in places the evidence has been forced or misinterpreted. Herodotus at 1.176, for example, mentions but neither approves nor disapproves of the collective suicide of the Xanthians. Instead, his positive remarks are focused on the Xanthians fighting and dying in battle against overwhelming odds. Xenophon (*Anabasis* IV, 7.13–14), rather than approving of the mass suicide of the Toachians, describes the whole scene as a "dreadful spectacle" ($\delta \varepsilon \iota \nu \grave{o} \nu \ \vartheta \acute{\varepsilon} \alpha \mu \alpha$) and then relates how a Greek lost his life in trying to prevent a man from leaping over a precipice. Thus, although Cohen tells us that all the writers, with the sole exception of Livy, approve of collective suicide, his own third citation clearly contradicts his statement. Like the Herodotus passage, the citations from Justinus, *Philippic Histories* XIII, 6.1–3, Orosius V, 14.5–6, and the summary of Book LVII of Livy do not clearly reveal the historians' own opinions on mass suicide. Similarly, both Appian (*Illyrian War* 21) and Dio Cassius (XLIX, 35.4) describe but neither admire nor condemn the suicide of the Metulians in 35 B.C.

Even Florus (I, 34.15–17), who most explicitly eulogizes Numantia, describes the suicide of its citizens as the act of men "in ultimam rabiem furoremque conversi," a description which Cohen fails to reconcile with the eulogy. The Phocian incident, mentioned by Polybius XVI, 32.1–2, does not present an exact parallel to Masada since the women and children were to be killed only if the Phocians were worsted in battle. Also, though Cohen tells us that "Polybius and his followers clearly admire the desperate resolution of the Phocians," one of his followers presents a more neutral account. More than that, however, Pausanias (X, 1.7) provides us with the interesting information that in his time, $\dot{\alpha} \pi \acute{o} \nu o \iota \alpha \ \Phi \omega \kappa \iota \kappa \acute{\eta}$ was proverbially synonymous with "callous plans." In other words, the Phocian incident was still remembered six centuries afterwards, not, however, as an example of glorious death but rather as an exemplification of desperate ruthlessness.

Livy's description of the falls of Astaspa and Abydos, as Cohen himself realizes (p. 392), poses problems for his thesis since the historian sees no virtue and no nobility but condemns the citizens of both towns, especially for the murder of women and children. His attitude is in sharp contrast to his source, Polybius. And yet, it is precisely differences such as these between two such closely related authors that should have given Cohen pause in generalizing. On the Abydenian affair Polybius writes as a ruthless, pragmatic historian whose criteria in judging an action are success and consistency. To Livy's Augustan sensibility the whole story is one of unrelieved horror. To ask vaguely which of the two is more "representative" of ancient attitudes is quite simply pointless.[42]

Similarly, Appian's laudatory account of the suicide of Xanthians (*Civil Wars* IV, 80) contrasts sharply with that found in Plutarch, *Brutus* 31. Rather than depicting the Xanthians as heroes, the biographer portrays them as men "suddenly possessed by a dreadful and indescribable impulse [ὁρμή] to madness which can be likened best to a passion for death [ἔρωτι θανάτου]." Interestingly, then, Josephus' contemporary Plutarch, in motivating the Xanthians, resorts to *amor mortis,* precisely the same theme which we have independently derived from Josephus' own text and a comparison with Lucan. Though Plutarch's witness does not confirm our reading of Josephus, it certainly establishes it as a possible one by a contemporary audience—all the more so when Josephus' text itself, through Eleazar's speeches, creates the portrait of a veritable preacher of death.

Rather than proving his thesis, Cohen's corpus at points fails to substantiate or actually contradicts his major conclusions. The evidence itself, as one would expect, is complex. Even if one allows that some ancient historians under certain circumstances glorified collective suicide, Cohen himself is forced to admit that he is amazed that Josephus suppresses all references to Jewish military action (pp. 400–401). Given such a *topos,* one might expect a description of heroic defense. It is, however, precisely this omission which furnishes us with an insight into Josephus' intent. The omission is "amazing" only if we begin with the presupposition that Josephus meant to portray the Sicarii, at least in the Masada account, as heroic freedom fighters. What is, however, most troubling in Cohen's approach is that he ventures on a hunting expedition through so many other writers without first trying to understand the Masada narrative within the context of the *Bellum* itself.

Concluding Observations

However frustrating the observation may prove to certain neo-Rankians, we shall probably never know exactly what happened at Masada on the fifteenth of Xanthicus. Josephus remains our only literary source, and he writes "ad probandum non ad narrandum." The archaeological excavations of the site, as one might have expected, have served neither to sustain nor discredit the central suicide story. Perhaps some of the defenders did in fact commit suicide, and around this historical kernel Josephus shaped an elaborate narrative influenced by literary models and political conditions of his Roman environment. Eleazar's speeches, though obviously fictitious, merely fit the rhetorical patterns of ancient historiography and thus in themselves prove nothing. Other Jews during the war, moreover, did apparently commit suicide; and so in itself the story is not implausible.

Still, we have resisted the temptation here to engage in endless conjectures. Rather, we have focused narrowly on the interpretation of the Masada narrative within both its historical and literary context. It is a mistake and a reflection of modern preoccupations to assume that Josephus inconsistently, for certain ill-defined psychological reasons, wished to portray the Sicarii in the Masada account as heroic freedom fighters. Though he does describe the Romans' amazement at the defenders' resolve and contempt of death, he so structures his narrative as to impress upon his audience that the suicide was both a penalty paid by the Sicarii for crimes against their own countrymen and an acknowledgment of their guilt. Indeed, he uses Eleazar's own speech to enforce that view of the suicide. In a way, their punishment exactly fits their crime. As they have habitually engaged in the murder of their own people, so in their final hours they are forced to kill those closest to themselves. Even without Eleazar's own explicit testimony, to a classical audience such an ending would have appeared retributive. This sort of "proper ending" was a commonplace of the classical literary tradition, and not only in historiography. Josephus' contemporary Plutarch furnishes in his *Lives* numerous examples of an almost obsessive working out of this principle of divine retribution. As for alleged parallels to the deaths of Stoic martyrs, Josephus presents the deaths of the defenders as in part daimonically impelled. This causality, rather than the *topos* of Stoic wise men who dispassionately choose the time and manner of their deaths, accords better with the notion of some divine intervention. What parallels do exist to the *exitus illustrium virorum,* particularly in the speeches, must be read historically against the background of Flavian political conditions and attitudes toward philosophers.

In a more general way, the Masada narrative serves to dramatize vividly the historian's recurrent themes of οἰκεία στάσις and ὁμόφυλος φόνος, which helped to work the destruction of the Jews. Though Thackeray's translation has obscured the exact meaning of Josephus' language, words and phrases in this narrative find their echoes in Ananus' speech condemning the Zealots. In this respect, the Sicarii, though historically a distinct group, exemplify all the rebel groups. The frustration of their hopes, in turn, represents the inevitable frustration of all the rebels' hopes. Inevitable, since in Josephus' view God had ordained that the Jews be subject to Rome and that Rome serve as a protectress to the Jews not only in Judea but in the hostile environment of the Diaspora as well. It is no coincidence that Josephus inserts the Masada narrative between the Antiochene incident and the description of the retributive death of Catullus. In granting Rome and her agents power, God also assigned responsibilities. Those who discharge their responsibilities, like Titus, prosper; those who do not, like Catullus, are punished, in this case by the time-honored method of an incurable bowel disease.

On the Jewish side, it was not a matter of rendering unto Caesar what was

Caesar's and rendering unto God what was God's. In Josephus' mind the two activities were indistinguishable, for in rendering unto Caesar one was also rendering unto God—hence, what in his opinion must have been the internal contradiction of the Sicarii's central tenet of no master but God. They, he thought, had simply failed to read God's purpose. On this political-theological synthesis, he probably sincerely believed, rested the continued survival of his people and their faith. If we consider the precarious state of existence of his fellow Jews in the Diaspora, however mistrustful we may be of his narrative, we may scarcely dismiss him as an unprincipled traitor.

Notes

1. In addition to the standard Josephan bibliographies, for an invaluable critical bibliography on Masada from 1943 to 1973, see L. H. Feldman, "Masada: A Critique of Recent Scholarship," in J. Neusner, ed., *Christianity, Judaism and Other Graeco-Roman Cults* (Leiden 1975) 218–248. This paper was completed for translation into Japanese in 1983, and only a few minor additions have been possible here.

2. *Masada: Herod's Fortress and the Zealots' Land Stand,* trans. M. Pearlman (New York 1966) 15.

3. T. Weiss-Rosmarin, "Masada Revisited," *JSp* 34 (1969) 29–32. More recently T. Weiss-Rosmarin, *JSp* 46 (1981) 3–9.

4. E.g., the fate of the rebels who had congregated at Tarichaeae (*BJ* III, 532–542).

5. D. J. Ladouceur, "Masada: A Consideration of the Literary Evidence," *GRBS* 21 (1980) 245–260.

6. For citation and discussion of earlier analyses, see Ladouceur (*supra* n. 5) 248–253.

7. H. Lindner, *Die Geschichtsauffassung des Flavius Josephus im Bellum Judaicum* (Leiden 1972) 60.

8. Ladouceur (*supra* n. 5) 248–249.

9. For suicide and the role of the *Phaedo* in philosophic discussions, see R. Hirzel, "Der Selbstmord," *ARW* 11 (1908) 74–104, 234–282, 417–476. See especially 451 ff. Also, in general for a more modern approach, see Y. Grisé, *Le suicide dans la Rome antique* (Paris 1982). Recently T. Rajak has argued that Josephus' argument is cast in Jewish not Greek terms and that the legislator at III, 376 must therefore be Moses: T. Rajak, *Josephus, the Historian and His Society* (Philadelphia 1983) 169. Here, as elsewhere, however, she underestimates the Greek elements in Josephus. In proving her argument, she curiously passes over the near verbatim citations of the *Phaedo* in Josephus' speech and resorts to some hypothetical proscription of Jewish oral law, for which, of course, there is absolutely no hard evidence until the post-Talmudic tractate *Semahot (Evel Rabbati)*. See below, note 11. To prove that the legislator must be Moses, she asserts that Josephus invokes Jewish practice at III, 377 and simply ignores 378, the second half of his statement which refers to the Athenian practice of severance of the corpse's hand (Aeschines, *Against Ctesiphon* 244). 377 and 378 are linked by μέν . . . δέ, which suggests that the article before "legislator" is generic and that 376 is generalizing.

10. Ladouceur (*supra* n. 5) 251–252.

11. See, for example, I. Jacobs, "Eleazar Ben Yair's Sanction for Martyrdom," *JSJ* 13 (1982) 183–186. Jacobs makes the interesting suggestion that Eleazar is referring to Deut. 6.5 when he invokes the sanction of the "laws" in urging his followers to die (*BJ* VII, 387). The early Tannaim did interpret this verse as scriptural sanction for martyrdom; but as Jacobs himself fairly

points out, there is no hard evidence for this interpretation before R. Akiba, two generations after Masada. Also see below n. 13.

12. M. Luz, "Eleazar's Second Speech on Masada and Its Literary Precedents," *RhM* 126 (1983) 25–43.

13. Luz (*supra* n. 12) 36.

14. Luz (*supra* n. 12) 28.

15. J. Crook, "Titus and Berenice," *AJP* 72 (1951) 162–175. More recently, Z. Yavetz, "Reflections on Titus and Josephus," *GRBS* 16 (1975) 411–432, especially 427 ff., and P. M. Rogers, "Titus, Berenice and Mucianus," *Historia* 29 (1980) 86–95.

16. Rogers (*supra* n. 15) 93–95.

17. G. Boissier, *L'Opposition sous les Césars*[5] (Paris 1905; first ed. 1875), presents a dated view of the opposition as harmless literati. For a more modern approach, see C. Wirszubski, *Libertas as a Political Idea at Rome during the Late Republic and Early Principate* (Cambridge 1950) 129 ff., and R. MacMullen, *Enemies of the Roman Order* (Cambridge 1966) 1–94.

18. For Dio's early works in a Flavian context, see C. P. Jones, *The Roman World of Dio Chrysostom* (Cambridge 1978) 15–16.

19. Yavetz (*supra* n. 15) 430.

20. Yavetz (*supra* n. 15) 424.

21. Ladouceur (*supra* n. 5) 256 n. 38.

22. For the cult of Cato and also of Brutus, see R. MacMullen (*supra* n. 17) 1–45, and P. Oecchiura, *La figura di Catone Uticense nella letteratura latina* (Turin 1969). For philosophers as subversives, see MacMullen 46–94.

23. Plut. *Cato Minor* 68.2.

24. E. Ramage, "Denigration of Predecessor under Claudius, Galba, and Vespasian," *Historia* 32 (1983) 201–214.

25. Cf. MacMullen (*supra* n. 17) 59: "Cynicism has been well described as 'a kind of radical Stoicism.'"

26. For a discussion of the problematic ending, see Amy Rose, "Seneca and Suicide: The End of the Hercules Furens," *CO* 60 (1983) 109–111.

27. R. Newell, "The Suicide Accounts in Josephus: A Form Critical Study," *SBL SP* (1982) 351–369.

28. Newell (*supra* n. 27) 359.

29. On the origin and structure of this *topos*, see A. Ronconi, "Exitus illustrium virorum," *SIFC* 17 (1940) 332 ff.

30. On this theme, see W. Rutz, "Amor Mortis bei Lucan," *Hermes* 88 (1960) 462–475.

31. For an analysis of this episode, see F. M. Ahl, *Lucan, An Introduction* (Cornell 1976) 119–121.

32. On so-called "tragic history" see F. W. Walbank, "Tragic History—A Reconsideration," *BICS* 2 (1955) 4 ff.

33. On Luke, see D. J. Ladouceur, "Hellenistic Preconceptions of Shipwreck and Pollution as a Context for Acts 27–28," *HThR* 73 (1980) 435–449; for Plutarch, see F. E. Brenk, *In Mist Apparelled* (Leiden 1977) 256–275.

34. See D. J. Ladouceur, "The Death of Herod the Great," *CP* 76 (1981) 25–34, for other examples of this *topos*.

35. Aside from VII, 393 and VII, 405, the Masada passages, τόλμημα occurs eight times in the *Bellum*, six times in Book IV and twice in Book VII, in every case with negative connotations: IV, 146, to describe the heinous acts of the Zealots; with precisely the same reference in Ananus' speech, IV, 171, and in John's speech, IV, 221; again with hostile and negative connotations in the chief priest Jesus' speech against the Idumaeans IV, 245, IV, 257; in IV, 401 to refer to the Sicarii massacre at Engaddi; VII, 89, to refer to a Scythian revolt; VII, 257 to describe what

people suffered at the hands of the Sicarii. Thackeray's translations include "atrocity, tale of crime, audacity," hardly consistent with "fortitude" in the Masada account. Cf. *BJ* VII, 419, which Cohen (393), following Thackeray, regards as a positive description. ἰσχὺς τόλμης is not far from *contumacia*. With few exceptions (e.g. VI, 82) τόλμα is used again and again in Books IV, V, VI, and VII to refer to the undisciplined impetuosity of Jewish fighters in battle or the simple audacity of rebels.

36. Cf. here the suicide of Longinus, *BJ* VI, 187. Newell (*supra* n. 27) 363 has also cited the mass suicide of Roman soldiers defeated during the Gallic War (*Commentarii* 5.37). There, however, Caesar's attitude is not quite obvious. He singles out L. Cotta as dying while fighting "cum maxima parte militum," mentions also by name L. Petrosidius who died fighting "fortissime," then merely reports that the rest, "desperata salute," killed one another that night. In citing the Vulteius episode from the *Pharsalia,* Newell overlooks Lucan's profound irony and the theme of *amor mortis* (363–364). In reading Lucan's military descriptions, the fundamental irony posed by the figure of Scaeva must be kept in mind: "pronus ad omne nefas et qui nesciret in armis / quam magnum virtus crimen civilibus esset" (VI, 147–148). All this is not to deny that Romans in some desperate circumstances might see suicide as a fitting way out of a dilemma. Cf. J. Bayet, *Croyances et rites dans la Rome antique* (Paris 1971) 130–176. The trend of modern scholarship, however, is to circumscribe more strictly the allowable situations in contrast to the older views of Hirzel (*supra* n. 9), who believed in the existence of a suicide mania among the Romans. For the new approach, see Y. Grisé, "De la fréquence du suicide chez les Romains," *Latomus* 39 (1980) 17–46, also not cited by Newell, especially "il n'existait pas de courant suicidogène chez les Romains" (18) and that suicide was an exceptional act practiced in exceptional circumstances (46). In the light of this new research some of Newell's conclusions, based on the older and uncritical studies of H. Fedden and A. Alvarez, require modification, e.g., justification of defenders' suicide by recourse to monolithic Stoicism. Also, the Spartan law that no soldier should turn his back on the enemy is seen as the institutionalization of the belief that a man should commit suicide to avoid capture by the enemy and is related to the suicide of Demosthenes. Plutarch, however, with his principle of divine retribution, is almost embarrassed to explain why his hero died by suicide (*Demosthenes* 30.4). The Spartan law, moreover, concerns the typical Greek ethos of glorious death in battle, not anticipatory suicide. Newell's form analysis, however, and use of Jewish evidence is both stimulating and valuable.

37. S. J. D. Cohen, "Masada: Literary Tradition, Archaeological Remains, and the Credibility of Josephus," *JJS* 33 (1982) 385–405.

38. Not surprisingly, the few other instances in which ἀρετή is applied to Jewish military action in the course of the war are when Josephus himself is involved (*BJ* III, 347, III, 380).

39. For a recent study of Demetrius with detailed citation and analysis of the ancient evidence, see M. Billerbeck, *Der Kyniker Demetrius* (Leiden 1979). Needless to say, Cohen's later chronology for Book VII against the *communis opinio* only makes his case worse.

40. J. Briscoe, *A Commentary on Livy Books XXXI–XXXIII* (Oxford 1973) 103.

41. In the "noble savage" *topos* suicide often plays a part. More than a literary commonplace, however, among some barbarians the practice in a military context was institutionalized, e.g. the Gallic *soldurii* devoted to die with their leader. It is quite wrong of Cohen to use the exceptional Phocian incident as proof that collective suicide as an alternative to glorious death in battle was common among Greeks. Cf. Bayet (*supra* n. 36) 132. If the Spartans at Thermopylae, in despair at the overwhelming odds, had cut their own throats before the Persians reached them, the world would be poorer by a few lines of Simonides.

42. For analysis of the different approaches of these two historians, see A. H. McDonald, "The Style of Livy," *JRS* 47 (1957) 155–172, especially 168–170, and F. W. Walbank, "Political Morality and the Friends of Scipio," *JRS* 55 (1965) 1–16, especially 11.

4 Philo and Josephus as Historians of the Same Events

E. MARY SMALLWOOD

P hilo was a prominent member of the Greek-speaking Jewish community in Alexandria and died in the early forties A.D. He was primarily
a philosopher and religious thinker, and over 90 percent of his considerable literary output, most of which is extant, consists of works on Jewish
law, legend, early history, and customs. In these works he sets out to make
Jewish thought and literature accessible and intelligible to educated Gentiles
by expounding it in terms of Greek philosophy and thought and by using allegorical and symbolic explanations to surmount difficulties of interpretation.
In only two of his treatises does he write directly about historical events of his
own day (and the very rare historical allusions in his other works are too vague
to be of much significance), but neither of these treatises is a straight historical work comparable with Josephus' *Bellum Judaicum* or *Antiquitates Judaicae.* Both are polemics against individuals, and the long narrative passages
in them deal with events for which the objects of the attacks were, in Philo's
eyes, responsible. The main aim of the works is not to give to the world accounts of those events but to show up the malice which he believed that his
two bêtes noires felt towards the Jews and the ways in which they gave expression to it.

Philo's first bête noire was Aulus Avillius Flaccus, prefect (governor) of
the Roman province of Egypt from A.D. 32 until late in 38. Alexandria, a
Greek city, had been the capital of Egypt since its foundation by Alexander
the Great in the late fourth century B.C., and it naturally became the Roman
administrative capital when Egypt was annexed in 30 B.C. This earlier of
Philo's two historical treatises is entitled *In Flaccum* (*Against Flaccus*),[1] and
its main subject is the vicious attack made in the summer of A.D. 38 by the
Greek citizens of Alexandria on the resident Jewish community, which com-
prised perhaps 30 percent of the city's population and was the largest of all
Diaspora communities in the Roman Empire, and the part played in that at-

tack by Flaccus. In the course of the riots, which were to some extent the result of an attempt to undermine the Jews' civic rights, many Jewish lives were lost, much of their property was destroyed, and most of the synagogues were desecrated or burnt in defiance of the Roman protection of Jewish religious liberty. Philo lays the maximum possible blame for the trouble on Flaccus (who, indeed, cannot be exonerated of responsibility), and he devotes the last quarter of the treatise to describing, with considerable satisfaction, the retribution which immediately befell him: he was arrested, taken to Rome for trial, exiled, and finally executed.

Philo's other bête noire was the Roman emperor Gaius (often miscalled by the nickname "Caligula," or "Little Boots," which had been his as a small boy), who reigned from the spring of A.D. 37 until he was assassinated in January 41. Philo's slightly later treatise is always known now as *Legatio ad Gaium (The Embassy to Gaius)*[2] from its concluding pages, which contain a graphic and memorable picture of the extraordinary hearing given by Gaius to a delegation of Alexandrian Jews, headed by Philo himself, which had been sent to Italy after the riots of 38 in the hope of getting redress for the wrongs suffered by their community. But the fortunes of that embassy occupy less than 10 percent of the whole treatise, which is, in fact, an invective against Gaius illustrated by various examples of his irresponsible, savage, or megalomaniac behavior. Philo begins with three political murders perpetrated early in Gaius' reign, then discusses his demand for divine honors in his lifetime, and goes on from that to retell the central part of the story of the Alexandrian riots, supplementing but in some particulars diverging from his earlier account.[3] He continues with the sequel to the riots, recounting briefly the reception of his delegation in Italy, and from that makes an easy transition to what is really the main item in his case against Gaius—the emperor's attempt to convert the Temple in Jerusalem into a shrine of the imperial cult—when messengers from Palestine bring the news of the proposed outrage to Philo and his fellow envoys. The narrative of this episode, begun by the messengers and completed by Philo writing in his own person, occupies nearly half the treatise.

Gaius' attack on the Temple is the only event related by Josephus in sufficient detail to allow of any worthwhile comparison between his account and Philo's, and it must therefore form the main subject of this essay. But in the case of the Alexandrian riots, Josephus virtually takes over where Philo leaves off, and the two writers thus supplement each other so usefully that it does not seem inappropriate to include some discussion of that topic, even though hardly any direct comparison is possible. Josephus' reference to the riots is negligible and his account of the embassy adds nothing of significance to Philo's. His value lies in his quotation of the edict by which Claudius sought to restore the *status quo ante* almost immediately after he had succeeded Gaius as emperor and which Philo may well not have lived to see issued.[4] (And even if he did, he would have had no reason even to mention legislation which had no connection with either of the individuals he was attacking in his two treatises.) The Alexandrian riots and their sequel also need to be outlined because of chronological links between the movements of Philo's embassy and the train of events in Palestine.

Other overlaps between Philo and Josephus are slight, though worth a brief mention. In the *Legatio* Philo incidentally provides a number of isolated scraps of information about the fortunes of the Jews both of Judea and of the Diaspora under Augustus and Tiberius, information which in almost every case supplements rather than complements Josephus. But it will be convenient to leave them for consideration at the end of this essay, in defiance of chronology, since the context in which most of them occur is Philo's account of Gaius' attack on the Temple.

Josephus, hardly surprisingly, does not mention the events of A.D. 38 in Alexandria at all in *Bellum Judaicum* II, where his sole concern is to show how Roman misrule in Judea led inexorably to war. But in the *Antiquitates Judaicae,* where his horizon is wider and he has quite a lot to say about the Diaspora, he devotes one page to the Alexandrian embassies.[5] On their raison d'être and mission, however, he is less than helpful: "After an outbreak of civil strife in Alexandria between the Jewish residents and the Greeks, three delegates were chosen by each side and appeared before Gaius." That is all— and it can be noted straightaway that the number three is certainly an error. Philo must be right when he says that the embassy which he headed numbered five, and it is unlikely that the Greeks sent a weaker delegation. The reader of Josephus gets the impression from the account which follows of Gaius' hearing of the envoys that the bone of contention in Alexandria had been simply the Jews' refusal to participate in the imperial cult—although their privilege of religious liberty carried with it automatic exemption from such participation. It is only through his later quotation of Claudius' edict that Josephus incidentally reveals that the Jews' civic rights had also been a point at issue.[6] But his failure even to attempt to explain there what had been in dispute and why, and in what ways Jewish rights had been infringed, leaves the reader completely in the dark. Philo comes to the rescue.

Philo's account of the "civil strife" in the *In Flaccum* is exceedingly long and detailed, and the central episodes in it are also related in the *Legatio.* The Greek attack on the synagogues, a gross violation of the religious liberty granted to the Jews by Roman legislation, is fairly straightforward. But for an understanding of the attack on the Jews' civic rights it is necessary to supplement and elucidate Philo's narrative, which was written for people who were familiar with the situation and could, therefore, plunge in medias res, by giving a brief analysis of the civic status of the Jewish community in Alexandria vis-à-vis the Greeks.[7] This analysis is reached by combining what may be read between the lines in Philo with scattered and often merely inferential evidence from Josephus, papyri, and other sources.

Jews had had the right of residence in Alexandria almost from the city's foundation. The community had grown so rapidly that at an early date one of the five districts into which the city was divided was allocated to them, and by the Roman period a second was mainly occupied by Jews, though neither formed a ghetto to which they were compulsorily confined; some Gentiles lived in the "Jewish" districts and some Jews elsewhere. The Alexandrian Jews, like a number of other large Diaspora communities in cities around the eastern Mediterranean, acquired in the course of time a form of political organization as a quasi-autonomous civic unit known as a *politeuma,* a word denoting a formally constituted corporation of aliens with the right of domicile and with independent control over their own affairs, a kind of city within a city. (Organized ethnic groups of this kind were a common feature of Hellenistic cities.) The Alexandrian Jewish *politeuma* had a council of elders under the presidency of an ethnarch, an assembly, a record office, and a law court for cases involving Jewish law.

There is incontrovertible evidence that a few prominent and wealthy Jews became members of the Greek citizen body in addition to being members of their *politeuma.* The question which was long and hotly debated early in this century on confused and contradictory evidence, drawn mainly from Josephus, Philo, and papyri, was whether the whole Jewish community enjoyed double citizenship, both Jewish and Greek. It was settled, in the eyes of almost all scholars, with a firm negative some sixty years ago by the publication of Claudius' *Letter to Alexandria;*[8] and logically this was no surprise, since Greek citizenship, with its corollary of pagan associations, would surely have presented serious problems to an orthodox Jew. But it appears that by the thirties A.D. there was a sizable minority of Alexandrian Jews agitating for admission to Greek citizenship—presumably liberal and unorthodox Jews who were prepared to compromise their religion for the sake of the social prestige attendant on Greek citizenship—and that this was the root cause of the violence which flared up in the summer of A.D. 38. The aspirations of these Jews, some of whom were actually acquiring Greek citizenship by irregular, if not illegal, means, were opposed by a belligerent party among the Greeks. These Greeks were, at the same time, nationalists, objecting to Roman rule; and their hostility toward the prefect Flaccus, the visible embodiment of what they regarded as foreign domination, was closely connected with their anti-Semitism; for the Jews had enjoyed the favor and protection of Rome ever since Julius Caesar and Augustus had guaranteed the religious liberty of the Diaspora by legislation, and the Greeks were jealous of this favor.

Philo opens the *In Flaccum* with a brief account of the efficiency and general excellence of Flaccus' administration of Egypt until Gaius' accession in March 37, of the deterioration which then set in as a result of his pre-occupation with personal anxieties about his relationship with Gaius, and of the hold which the Greek nationalists began to establish over him as a result.[9] He then goes straight into a vivid description of the nationalists' reaction to an ostentatious visit made to Alexandria in the summer of 38 by a grandson of Herod the Great, Agrippa I, when en route from Rome to the territories in northern Transjordan, of which he had just been appointed king: they parodied the Jewish parade with the local lunatic, known as "Cabbage," dressed up to play the part of the king.[10] This studied insult, which Flaccus neither attempted to check nor punished, was the prelude to fierce anti-Semitic riots, described also in the *Legatio,* in which the Greek mob got completely out of hand, evicting Jews from their homes and massacring them, burning and looting houses and shops, and destroying or desecrating synagogues.[11] In view of the space which Josephus devotes to the much less serious afflictions of the Jews in Rome in A.D. 19,[12] his unsatisfying half dozen words about the situation in Alexandria in 38, which, even when allowance is made for some exaggeration in Philo's emotional and colorful narrative, must be admitted to have been very grave, would appear to be clear evidence that he was not acquainted with Philo's writings.

The riots were more than the wanton attack on the Jews' lives, property, and religion that the *Legatio* represents them as being. In the *In Flaccum* Philo explains that they were given a semblance of legality by an edict extorted by the Greek nationalist leaders from Flaccus declaring the Jews "aliens," [13] i.e., people without the legal right of domicile in Alexandria on which the existence of their *politeuma* was based. The mob interpreted this edict as meaning that the Jews had the right to reside only in the section of the city originally allocated to them, and proceeded to hound them into it and convert it into a ghetto regardless of its inadequate size. It was this wrongful action by Flaccus which Claudius was to reverse in his edict.

The details which Philo gives of the later stages of the anti-Jewish movement need not detain us here. By October 38 passions had cooled, the violence had lost its momentum, and an uneasy peace had returned. But the Jews' civic status in Alexandria and their right of religious liberty were both now in a precarious position and open to further attack. Hence, the embassies sent by both sides, though apparently not till over a year later,[14] the Jewish one to appeal for the restitution of their former rights and the Greek one, presumably, to argue against it and exculpate their people for the recent disturbances.

To the list of the members of the Greek embassy Josephus usefully contributes the name of Apion, the writer whom he took as the "type" of the anti-Semite in his *Contra Apionem,* making him the spokesman in place of the nationalist leader Isidorus, who has that function in Philo's account. But he knows nothing of the preliminary hearing which Philo describes Gaius as giving to the delegations soon after their arrival in Italy in the spring of A.D. 40—only a brief hearing, but one in which Philo represents the emperor's attitude toward them as reasonable.[15] The only hearing of which Josephus knows is clearly the second one, held a few months before the assassination of Gaius, of which Philo's vivid and entertaining picture is justly famous.[16] According to Philo, two matters were under discussion: first, the Jews' exemption from participation in the imperial cult, which had been outraged during the riots, when the Greeks had desecrated synagogues which they could not destroy by placing statues of the emperor in them, thus in effect converting them into shrines of the imperial cult; and second, the Jews' political status, which Flaccus' edict had undermined. Josephus mentions only the former issue, but he agrees with Philo that the complaint against Philo's delegation concerned the Jews' refusal to join in the imperial cult, which by that time meant acknowledging Gaius as already divine in his lifetime. Josephus' account ends in much the same way as Philo's, with Gaius giving no decision but dismissing the envoys ungraciously. But it is not a summary of Philo, and indeed it contains one significant difference—a private interview between Philo and Gaius—which suggests that it is based on an independent (and erroneous?) tradition.

Civil strife of unspecified cause and nature leading to an argument about the imperial cult would be a baffling story without Philo to elucidate it. But it appears from the various passages in which Josephus has clouded the issue of Jewish civic status in Alexandria for scholars that he did not understand its intricacies. If so, the grounds for the quarrel in the thirties A.D. and the points at stake in 38 will have been beyond his comprehension, and we should perhaps be grateful to him for not making confusion worse confounded by attempting to explain them or even setting them down according to his lights.

Josephus briefly continues the story but without taking it to its conclusion. According to him, the news of Gaius' assassination on 24 January 41, news which is unlikely to have reached Alexandria before March, was greeted by a Jewish attack on the Greeks, which Flaccus' successor put down. Meanwhile, the new emperor, Claudius, had begun to consider the problems of Alexandria, and by March at the latest, in ignorance of the renewed wave of violence, had issued an edict, which Josephus quotes, restoring to the Jews the rights which they had enjoyed in Alexandria before the riots of 38 and specifically that of religious liberty. That for Josephus was the end of the story.[17] But Claudius' *Letter to Alexandria,* written some six months later after further delegations from both sides had come to Rome, gives the emperor's final and considered answer, confirming the Jews' existing rights both civic and religious but refusing to allow any extension of the former by opening avenues to Greek citizenship to them as a body. The chance survival of a papyrus both winds up the tale left unfinished by Philo when Flaccus' personal involvement ended with his recall to Rome in disgrace, and helps to elucidate some details in it.

We turn now to the comparison of Philo's and Josephus' accounts of Gaius' attack on the Jewish Temple in A.D. 40. This episode was central to Josephus' theme in both *Bellum Judaicum* II and *Antiquitates Judaicae* XVIII–XX, that of Roman misrule in the province of Judea, and it naturally gets full coverage in both. The differences between his two accounts are few and insignificant, but there are many wide divergences both in details and in indications of chronology between his versions of the story and that of Philo in the *Legatio*. In some places the two authors contradict rather than supplement each other. Let it be said straightaway that where they appear to conflict irreconcilably, Philo's version may be accepted as preferable on general grounds: first, though not a Palestinian, Philo was a contemporary of the events, and he had a chronological connection with them in that his delegation heard of Gaius' proposal while in Italy and was probably involved in Agrippa I's intervention; second, his account is free from such fairy-tale elements as rain from a cloudless sky, a banquet leading to the offer of a boon, and the providential escape of a hero from death, all of which reduce the credibility of Josephus' version;[18] and third, Josephus' muddled chronology and causation for the opening of the episode cast some doubt on the reliability of the rest of his story.

Basically the episode is simple and straightforward, and the two authors agree on its essentials. Gaius decided to have a statue of himself installed in the Jewish Temple; the Jews protested vehemently and won the sympathy of the Roman official in charge of the operation. The official appealed to Gaius on their behalf, but to little effect; however, shortly afterwards Gaius abandoned his scheme at the request of his friend Agrippa I. We shall now attempt to reconstruct the sequence of events in detail, dovetailing Philo's and Josephus' accounts whenever possible and discussing the apparent contradictions.

Only Philo gives the prelude to the episode and the reason for Gaius' shattering decision to appropriate the Temple as a shrine of the imperial cult. During the winter of A.D. 39–40 the Jews of the coastal city of Jamnia destroyed an altar built in Gaius' honor by the Greek minority resident there. When this piece of admittedly provocative behavior reached Gaius' ears in the spring, he decided to punish the Jews' outrage by having a statue of himself in the guise of Zeus erected in the Temple.[19] According to Josephus, Gaius' only motive was annoyance at the attitude taken up by Philo and his embassy towards the imperial cult,[20] but that is chronologically impossible, since the Alexandrian embassies were not given a full hearing by Gaius until the autumn of 40, and, as will be shown below, operations to install the statue were well under way by the early summer of that year.

Philo and Josephus agree that Gaius put the execution of his scheme into the capable hands of Publius Petronius, the legate (governor) of the large adjacent province of Syria, and instructed him to take two of his garrison of four legions with him when he went to Judea.[21] Gaius clearly knew that there was bound to be opposition much too serious for the procurator of Judea with his half dozen small auxiliary units to cope with; and the province of Judea with its junior, inexperienced governor and inadequate garrison had in any case been under the supervision of the legate of Syria since its formation in A.D. 6.

Philo alone gives the next stage of the story. Petronius, realizing the folly of Gaius' plan and fearing that the eastern Diaspora might come to the support of the Palestinian Jews in their inevitable opposition, played for time by arranging for the statue to be made at a distance in Sidon and by summoning the Jewish leaders, probably to his headquarters in Antioch, in order to break the news and urge them to use their influence to get the desecration accepted quietly. Their horror and their flat refusal to comply can hardly have come as a surprise to him.[22]

The stories then begin to converge again. As stiff opposition was certain, Petronius and his legions marched south, Philo says vaguely "to Phoenicia," while Josephus usefully gives the precise place where they halted—Ptolemais, just north of the frontier of Galilee, which was then still a client kingdom and had recently come under the rule of Agrippa I—and adds that from there Petronius notified Gaius of his plan of campaign. By this time news of the proposed sacrilege had spread throughout Galilee, and vast crowds of Jews streamed out to demonstrate against it in front of Petronius. Their repeated protestations that they would rather die than suffer the defilement of the Temple made Petronius realize that, if he persisted, there would be armed resistance.[23]

At this point the stories differ but can be woven together neatly as complementary rather than contradictory. Philo says that the Jews asked permission to send an embassy to plead their case before Gaius and that Petronius refused.[24] Josephus then contributes a more important piece of information: Petronius left his troops at Ptolemais and took his personal staff to Tiberias, the capital of Galilee. There he faced further appeals and lengthy demonstrations, during the course of which he conferred with a number of the Jewish leaders, who begged him to write to Gaius on their behalf.[25] Philo agrees that it was the Jews' earnestness and obvious distress which induced Petronius to write to Gaius, even at the risk of bringing the imperial wrath down on his own head, and to urge him to abandon his scheme, though Philo connects this with the only demonstrations known to him, those at Ptolemais. In Philo's version of the letter Petronius apologized for his delay in erecting the statue, which he blamed on the time taken by the artists as well as on Jewish opposition, explained that the Jews' conscientious objections were so strong that they were neglecting the agricultural operations of the season and that he feared that they might go to the length of destroying the corn then ripe or the autumn fruit crop, and pointed out that food shortages would be inconvenient for the voyage which Gaius intended to make in the near future to Alexandria via the Syrian-Palestinian coast.[26]

It is here that we encounter the most serious chronological problem in the conflation of Philo's and Josephus' accounts. Philo says that the grain harvest was ripe, which gives a date between April and June. Josephus, however, says that because of the demonstrations the fields were not being sown, which gives an autumn date, when the first rains make plowing and sowing possible. This contradiction cannot satisfactorily be resolved by dating the demonstrations at Ptolemais to about May and those at Tiberias to the autumn, since the two places are only about thirty miles apart and Josephus says that Petronius "hurried" from Ptolemais to Tiberias. A choice must be made, and Philo's date is preferable for reasons other than the general grounds adduced above: first, since navigation in the ancient world was restricted, except in cases of extreme urgency, to the period between mid-March to mid-November, Gaius' projected eastern voyage could have been imminent in May or thereabouts but not in the late autumn; second, there is a possible synchronization of seedtime and harvest in the early summer, since sowing for a second grain crop in the late summer can be done up to the end of the rains, but no such synchronization is possible between the second harvest in about August and the sowing for the main crop in October or later.

Josephus and Philo, hardly surprisingly, agree that Gaius was greatly annoyed by Petronius' letter, but they are totally at variance over his reaction. Josephus' version is melodramatic: Gaius was furious that a mere legate had presumed to offer him advice, accused him of taking bribes from the Jews, and wrote telling him to commit suicide. Mercifully for Petronius this missive took three months to reach him by sea and arrived after the news of Gaius' death, which automatically invalidated its contents.[27] Philo, however, says that Gaius curbed his irritation with Petronius because he realized that a provincial governor with legions behind him was a dangerous person to provoke and simply told him to proceed with the erection of the statue at once, since the harvest would be gathered by the time his letter arrived.[28] According to Philo's chronology (allowing a month or so each way during the summer sailing season for the letters), it must have been about August when Petronius received Gaius' reply. Philo does not say what excuse the legate then found for continued inaction, but it seems that no decisive step had yet been taken when toward the end of the year another letter, wholly unexpected, arrived from Gaius with the welcome news that his order was rescinded.[29] (The divergent accounts of the remarkable achievement of Agrippa I in persuading the emperor to give up his scheme will be discussed below.) Josephus' chronology is quite different, and is self-consistent: a letter dispatched from Palestine in about October, late in the sailing season, would probably not have arrived until toward the end of the year, so that Gaius' reply would have been sent off not long before his assassination in January 41; and Josephus explicitly places Gaius' receipt of Petronius' letter after his cancellation of his order for the erection of the statue. But it has already been argued that Philo's date for the demonstrations is preferable to that of Josephus, and history and legend is too full of tales of the last-minute escape of good men from death at the hands of tyrants for much weight to be put on that feature of the story, although it is not in itself impossible or incredible.

Philo and Josephus agree that Agrippa I intervened successfully with Gaius and saved the Temple—or prevented a Jewish revolt in its defense. They profoundly disagree, however, about his method of tackling the problem. According to Philo, Agrippa came to visit Gaius, a friend of his since the latter years of Tiberius' reign,[30] almost immediately after the emperor had received and answered Petronius' letter and before his indignation against the legate had cooled, in complete ignorance of Gaius' scheme for the Temple. (This ignorance, incidentally, means that Agrippa must have left his kingdom before Petronius disclosed Gaius' scheme to the Jewish leaders and must have spent some three months traveling to Italy. This is surprisingly slow for a summer journey, but he may have chosen to travel by easy stages, and it presents no serious chronological problem.[31]) One day in September 40,[32] realizing that Agrippa had noticed his agitation, Gaius told him about his order for the desecration of the Temple and the Jews' reaction. The shock of this caused Agrippa to collapse with what was probably a stroke. On his recovery he wrote Gaius a long, well-argued, and well-documented letter, begging him to follow the example which Augustus and Tiberius and their subordinates had set in showing toleration and even favor toward the Jews and not to violate the Temple. Gaius was not pleased, but he did accept the logic of Agrippa's arguments and agreed to his request, sending Petronius instructions to abandon the whole project and take his legions back to Syria, but at the same time warning the Jews to show reciprocal toleration toward any future Gentile attempts to introduce the imperial cult outside Jerusalem—a perfectly reasonable stipulation on which Philo puts the malicious interpretation that it was an open invitation to Jew-baiting, though he has to admit that no instances actually occurred.[33]

Josephus introduces Agrippa as "staying in Rome," says nothing about how he learned of Gaius' scheme for the Temple, and knows nothing of any illness. His version of Agrippa's appeal is another typical "tyrant tale." Agrippa invited Gaius to a banquet of unparalleled sumptuousness, and the emperor, when mellow with wine, felt moved to offer him fuller recompense than he had so far given him for his loyalty during the last year of Tiberius' life.[34] He expected a request for further territorial aggrandizement,[35] but to his utter amazement the boon for which Agrippa asked was merely the abandonment of Gaius's scheme to erect his statue in the Temple. Gaius granted the request, partly because he admired Agrippa's disinterested concern for the Jewish law and religion and partly because he dared not go back on a promise made in front of witnesses. His letter to Petronius, however, had a twist in it: the scheme was to be abandoned only if the statue had not yet been erected; if already in place, it was to stand. Gaius could argue sophistically that this met Agrippa's request, which was not for the removal of a statue already in position but for the abandonment of "further thought" of having it erected![36]

The literary picture of Gaius given by Suetonius in particular suggests that a banquet would have been more to Gaius' taste than a twenty-five-hundred-word memorandum, and it is, of course, not impossible to combine the two versions and suppose that Agrippa attempted to soften Gaius up with a banquet before presenting him with the cold facts in writing. But if a choice must be made, the superficial improbability of Philo's version is, in fact, a reason for accepting it in preference to that of Josephus, even if the latter did not smack of the fairy tale. The hostility of the literary tradition about the Julio-Claudians increases with time. Philo is writing what is avowedly an invective against Gaius, and yet he admits that when Gaius received the long letter in which Agrippa confronted him with argument, precedent, and documentation, he did not toss it aside but read it carefully point by point, and that, far from being impervious to reason, he was impressed by Agrippa's presentation of the case for the Jews. This very fact supports Philo. Moreover, Philo and his embassy were in Italy at the time, waiting patiently (or impatiently) for a second hearing before Gaius, and although Philo gives no hint of it, he would surely have got into touch with Agrippa, with whom he had family connections,[37] and he may well even have helped Agrippa to draft his memorandum. Agrippa, leaving his kingdom in ignorance of Gaius' scheme, would hardly have come armed with detailed evidence about earlier emperors' treatment of the Jews, whereas Philo and his fellow envoys had already submitted to Gaius memoranda which could well have incorporated such evidence.[38]

Philo alone adds a coda to the episode: Gaius soon regretted his generosity to Agrippa and revived his scheme, but with the difference that the second statue was to be made in Rome so that he could take it with him on his forthcoming eastern tour (now postponed till the following year) and supervise its installation in person. Since his assassination prevented the tour from taking place, we cannot assess the truth or falsity of what Philo says. But it is possible that it is a smear, of unknown provenance, designed to deny Gaius the credit of having admitted that he had made a mistake.[39]

Here, then, are the two versions of Gaius' attack on the Temple. As in the case of the Alexandrian riots, it is abundantly clear that Josephus did not know Philo's account and based his on a wholly independent tradition. We now turn to a by-product of Philo's version, the evidence provided by the long section of the *Legatio* in which he purports to give a verbatim transcript of Agrippa I's memorandum to Gaius.[40]

Whether this is, in fact, exactly what Agrippa presented to Gaius is open to considerable doubt, given the conventions of ancient historiography and the historian's license to put words into other people's mouths. But be that as it may, in this composition Philo has preserved for us a great deal of invaluable material about relations between the emperors Augustus and Tiberius and the Jews, especially those of the Diaspora, material which in some places complements and in others supplements Josephus.

Josephus devotes much space to the question of the civic and religious rights of Jewish minorities resident in the Greek cities of Cyrenaica and Asia Minor, which became a burning one during the time of Augustus and led to quarrels, appeals, and legislation. In Roman law the synagogues[41] into which Diaspora communities were divided were equated with *collegia*[42] because of superficial resemblances, but when a ban was placed on *collegia* by late republican and Augustan legislation because they were being misused for subversive political purposes, the synagogues, as patently innocuous associations, were exempted and allowed to continue in existence. The ban remained in force throughout the period of the empire as a precautionary measure against possible further misuse, and with it the exemption of the synagogues. Like *collegia,* the synagogues had common funds, since they were responsible for the collection of the Temple tax, a small annual tax levied by the Jewish authorities on all male Jews, slave or free, over the age of twenty wherever they lived for the upkeep of the Temple and its liturgy. From the time of the late republic it had been established that Diaspora communities had the right to collect this tax and transmit it to Jerusalem, but in Augustus' time it became a bone of contention in a number of cities with large Jewish minorities.

Josephus tells how the Jews of Cyrenaica and Asia Minor once sent a joint deputation to Augustus complaining that their civic rights were being infringed and their Temple tax confiscated by the Greek authorities of the cities in which they lived. The emperor reaffirmed their rights and sent letters to that effect to the relevant officials. Josephus gives no precise date for this episode, but its position in his narrative suggests a date soon after 12 B.C. He then quotes six documents which he apparently believes were issued in response to this appeal, two of which are in fact earlier and two much later! The other two are a letter from Augustus to a certain Gaius Norbanus Flaccus, proconsul (governor) of the province of Asia, dealing only with the Temple tax, and a letter from Flaccus to the city of Sardis, passing on the emperor's ruling.[43] Here Josephus links up with Philo, who, without even the vaguest indication of date, includes in Agrippa I's memorandum a passage on Augustus and the question of the Diaspora Jews' right of assembly and right to collect the Temple tax. He mentions no appeal by the maltreated Jews but merely says that Augustus "discovered" that trouble had occurred and therefore reaffirmed with letters to provincial governors the two rights that were in dispute. He then quotes a letter from the same Flaccus, this time to Ephesus, passing on Augustus' ruling.[44] It is by no means word for word the same as Josephus' alleged transcript of Flaccus' letter to Sardis, even on the matter of the Temple tax, and it covers the right of assembly also. Of course, it cannot be taken for granted that Flaccus' two letters to two cities on the identical subject were couched in identical terms; but the differences enhance the serious doubts felt by scholars about the reliability of what Josephus purports to be verbatim transcripts in his works (and indeed in those of other ancient writers). As regards date, a C. Norbanus Flaccus was consul in 38 B.C. and another, probably his son, in 24 B.C. There is no evidence to show which of them later became proconsul of Asia, but if any reliance can be placed on Josephus' indication of date, the younger seems the more probable.

More interesting, in that it concerns one of the most notorious (and yet politically negligible) Romans of all time, is the overlap between Philo and Josephus on Pontius Pilate's governorship of Judea (A.D. 26–36). Josephus has three stories about Pilate, the first two portraying him as deliberately provoking his subjects by riding roughshod over their religious susceptibilities and the last showing him taking such severe measures against what appeared to be an incipient rising that his subjects succeeded in securing his dismissal.[45] Philo has one story, related in Agrippa's memorandum to Gaius, as evidence that the emperor Tiberius had followed Augustus' example in championing Jewish religious liberty.

Josephus' first story about Pilate is that, with deliberate intent to annoy, Pilate went to Jerusalem (presumably for one of the major festivals, at which the governor's presence was desirable in case religious fervor led to civil disorder), taking with him a military unit whose standards bore portraits of the emperor, i.e., objects of pagan cult. The Jewish reaction was demonstrations of protest, which continued unabated even when the demonstrators were surrounded by troops and threatened with a massacre, and Pilate was sufficiently impressed by the Jews' readiness to die in defense of their law to capitulate and withdraw the offending unit. The point behind this story is that, while the bulk of the Roman garrison of Judea was normally stationed in the administrative capital, the basically Greco-Syrian city of Caesarea, a small force was always maintained in Jerusalem; but out of respect for the Jewish law against "graven images" that were objects of worship, the unit stationed there had always previously been one with aniconic standards.

Philo's story is that, again with deliberate intent to annoy, Pilate set up votive shields bearing inscriptions in honor of Tiberius on the walls of his own residence in Jerusalem. This also aroused protest, but in the form of a deputation of high-ranking Jews who requested Pilate to remove the shields. In what way they "violated native customs," as the Jews complained that they did, is hard to see, since Philo explicitly says that they "bore no figure and nothing else that was forbidden"; but a possible interpretation is that the inscriptions appeared to imply some connection with the imperial cult. Pilate was too proud to comply voluntarily, but he refused the Jews' request for leave to send an embassy to Tiberius, fearing that they might use the opportunity to present the emperor with a catalogue of his crimes, specified by Philo as "his venality, his violence, his thefts, his assaults, his abusive behavior, his endless executions of untried prisoners, and his endless savage ferocity." The Jews, however, appealed to Tiberius by letter, and this elicited a very strong missive from the emperor to Pilate with instructions, which he dared not disregard, to remove the shields to Caesarea.[46]

The differences between these two stories are so obvious that they cannot be treated as variants of a single story. Philo's value here lies in the way in which he supplements Josephus by providing an extra episode in Pilate's career of tactlessness in Judea. But perhaps the most interesting point in it is the fact that the Jews appealed to Tiberius, which they had never done before and which they would not have done then unless they had had reasonable confidence of success. Philo gives no indication of date. But earlier in the *Legatio* he attributes to Tiberius' all-powerful minister Sejanus a policy of violent anti-Semitism, and indeed a scheme for the organized extermination of the Jews throughout the empire, which Tiberius countermanded immediately after Sejanus' fall in A.D. 31.[47] Even if Philo has grossly exaggerated the threat which Sejanus posed to the Jews at large (and Josephus' complete silence about it suggests that it was, in fact, far less serious than Philo believed), the appeal to Tiberius and his favorable response would seem to place the episode after 31 and to reflect an improvement in the Jews' position consequent to the removal of Sejanus' influence. Pilate's fear of impeachment if the Jews reported on his misdeeds also points to a time when they had endured many years of his harsh and unsympathetic administration.

There is much that can be culled from the pages of Philo's *Legatio* about the fortunes of the Jews, mainly those of the Diaspora and in particular the community in Rome, from the late republic to his own day; but this is information which has no parallel in Josephus, and as such it is not for discussion here. Philo's narratives have a greater sense of immediacy than those of Josephus, but in the critical comparison attempted here of the two authors' versions of the only story given by both in full it has been argued that, despite all the passion and resentment which blaze through Philo's invective against Gaius, he emerges as the writer with the greater historical credibility. If that conclusion is correct, we can accept his evidence on matters for which Josephus provides no parallel with a fair degree of confidence. But if we have to thank Philo for hard facts, we must not omit to thank him also for the liveliness of his pen, which has left us one of the most vivid word-pictures to survive from the first century A.D.—the farcical interview between Gaius and the Jewish envoys from Alexandria.

Notes

1. Many works written in Greek are known now by Latin translations of their titles; cf., e.g., the titles of Josephus' works. Editions of *In Flaccum* are H. Box (Oxford, 1938), with introduction, English translation, and commentary; F. H. Colson (Loeb Classical Library: Philo vol. IX, 1960); and A. Pelletier (Paris, 1967), with introduction, French translation, and notes. The treatise is believed to have been written immediately after the events related in it, since it contains no reference to anything later than the end of A.D. 38 or early 39.

2. Editions are E. M. Smallwood (Leiden, 1961; 2nd ed., 1970), with introduction, English translation, and commentary; and F. H. Colson (Loeb Classical Library: Philo vol. X, 1962). For discussion of the alternative title of the work, *On Virtues,* see Smallwood, *op. cit.,* pp. 39–41.

3. By distorting chronology and dating Gaius' self-deification to his first regnal year, Philo can represent the Greek attack on the synagogues as compliance with the imperial demand for worship and thus pin indirect responsibility for it on to Gaius.

4. A passing reference in *Leg.* 206 to Claudius' execution of one of Gaius' most obnoxious courtiers, probably soon after his accession as part of his reaction against his predecessor, is evidence that Philo lived into Claudius' reign and gives the *terminus ante quem* for the composition of that treatise.

5. *A* XVIII, 257–260.

6. *A* XIX, 278–285.

7. For much fuller discussion of this complicated and hotly disputed subject, with documentation and bibliography of earlier works on it, see *Legatio,* ed. Smallwood (above, note 2), pp. 3–11, and E. M. Smallwood, *The Jews under Roman Rule* (Leiden, 1976; 2nd ed., 1981), pp. 225–230.

8. Papyrus London 1912, first published by H. I. Bell, *Jews and Christians in Egypt* (London, 1924). Its contents are discussed later in the essay.

9. *In Fl.* 1–24.

10. *In Fl.* 25–40. Josephus, despite his extensive knowledge both of Agrippa I's life from A.D. 23 to 37 (*A* XVIII, 143–237) and of his career as king (*ibid.,* 238–252; XIX, 236–353; and the discussion later in the essay), does not mention this visit to Alexandria.

11. *In Fl.* 41–72; *Leg.* 120–137 reverses the order of events as given in *In Fl.* and puts the attack on the synagogues, here described more fully, after that on the Jews' persons and property. For discussion, see *Legatio,* ed. Smallwood (above, note 2), pp. 45–47.

12. *A* XVIII, 65, 80–84.

13. *In Fl.* 54.

14. For discussion of the date see *Legatio,* ed. Smallwood (above, note 2), pp. 47–50. The actual dispatch of the embassies is nowhere related; they just appear in Italy in the *Legatio.*

15. *Leg.* 172–183.

16. *Leg.* 349–367.

17. *A* XIX, 278–292, giving also a precautionary edict issued immediately afterwards confirming Jewish rights throughout the empire.

18. *A* XVIII, 285, 289–300, 303–309, with *BJ* II, 203.

19. *Leg.* 199–203, with 346 for the identification with Zeus.

20. *A* XVIII, 261; *BJ* II, 184–185.

21. *Leg.* 207. Petronius was probably appointed to Syria in A.D. 39, and Josephus' implication in *A* XVIII, 261 that he received Gaius' orders with his appointment is incompatible with his own causation and with Philo's date.

22. *Leg.* 213–224.

23. *Leg.* 225–242; *A* XVIII, 262–268; *BJ* II, 186–187, 192.

24. *Leg.* 239–247.

25. *A* XVIII, 269–276; *BJ* II, 193–199. The leaders included several Herodian princes but not Agrippa I, who was in Rome (see discussion later in essay).

26. *Leg.* 248–253; *A* XVIII, 277–288; *BJ* II, 202.

27. *A* XVIII, 302–305; *BJ* II, 203.

28. *Leg.* 254–260.

29. *Leg.* 333.

30. *A* XVIII, 161–237.

31. Cf. Agrippa's absence from Galilee at the time of the demonstrations (note 25).

32. Gaius had spent the summer in Campania, waiting to enter Rome in an "ovation" (a kind of minor triumph) on his birthday, 31 August. Josephus provides a date by noting that Agrippa made his appeal "in Rome," whereas Philo gives no precise location.

33. *Leg.* 261–337.

34. An unwary remark (Josephus, *A* XVIII, 187) that he hoped that Tiberius would soon die and leave the throne to Gaius had landed Agrippa in prison.

35. On his accession Gaius had made Agrippa king of a large area in northeast Transjordan, and earlier in 40 had deposed Antipas from Galilee and added his territory to Agrippa's.

36. *A* XVIII, 289–301. The *BJ* account omits all reference to Agrippa.

37. His brother had lent Agrippa money, and his nephew was shortly to marry one of Agrippa's daughters (*A* XVIII, 159–160, XIX, 276).

38. *Leg.* 178–179.

39. *Leg.* 337–339. J. P. V. D. Balsdon (*The Emperor Gaius* [Oxford, 1934], p. 139) suggests this charitable interpretation.

40. *Leg.* 276–329.

41. Literally "synagogue" means a "meeting," and the word, like "church," denotes primarily a worshiping group and only secondarily a building set aside for worship. The commoner Greek term for the building was a (place of) "prayer."

42. Workmen's clubs and mutual benefit societies which, *inter alia*, held funds with which to defray members' funeral expenses.

43. *A* XVI, 160–173, with the letter from Augustus to Flaccus in section 166 and Flaccus' letter in section 171.

44. *Leg.* 311–315.

45. *A* XVIII, 55–62, 85–89; *BJ* II, 169–177.

46. *Leg.* 299–305.

47. *Leg.* 159–161.

2
JUDAISM

5 Hellenizations in Josephus' Jewish Antiquities: The Portrait of Abraham

LOUIS H. FELDMAN

General Considerations

𝖂 hen setting forth his program in the proem of the *Antiquities,* Josephus (I, 17) declares quite clearly that he will present precise details (τὰ ἀκριβῆ) of what is written in the Scriptures (ἐν ταῖς ἀναγραφαῖς), each in its proper place (κατὰ τὴν οἰκείαν τάξιν), neither adding nor omitting anything (οὐδὲν προσθεὶς οὐδ᾽ αὖ παραλιπών). The very fact that Josephus, who in real life had been a general in Galilee during the war against the Romans, uses the term τάξις, which in the first instance has the connotation of the order or disposition of an army, would seem to imply that Josephus has carefully marshaled his data. In fact, he says (*A* I, 5) that his work has been translated (μεθηρμηνευμένην) from the Hebrew records. And yet, even a glance at Josephus' narrative will show how false Josephus has been to his own program.

The phrase "neither adding nor omitting anything," of course, as several scholars[1] have noted, may simply be a traditional and polite way of affirming one's accuracy, as we see, for example, in Dionysius of Halicarnassus (*Thucydides* 5 and 8) and Lucian (*Quomodo historia conscribenda sit* 47). Perhaps it should not be taken too literally, any more than Jesus' statement (Matt. 5:18) that he has come not to destroy but to fulfill and that not one iota will pass from the law until all is accomplished, a passage which is paraphrased in the Talmud (*Shabbath* 116b).

Inasmuch as Josephus himself (*A* I, 10) here cites the Septuagint as a precedent for presenting the scriptural narrative to a non-Jewish audience, we may note that the very same verb, μεθερμηνεύω, is used in the *Letter of Aristeas* (38) with reference to the translation of the Torah into Greek so that it may appear in Ptolemy Philadelphus' royal library. Elsewhere (*Ap* I, 167), Josephus definitely uses the verb in the sense of "to translate" when he says that the word "korban," translated (μεθερμηνευόμενος) from the dialect of the Hebrews, means "God's gift." It is in this strict sense of "to translate" that we find it used by Polybius (VI, 26.6), who says that *extraordinarii, ὅ μεθερμηνευόμενον,* is "select"; and Dionysius of Halicarnassus, who, to some degree, was Josephus' model, at least so far as the title *Antiquities* and the number of books in his work were concerned, likewise uses the term in the sense of "to translate" (II, 7.3), when he says that *tribus,* "translated" (μεθερμηνευόμενος), is φυλή and that *consules,* when translated, is συμβουλοί (4.76).

One possible answer to this apparent inconsistency on the part of Josephus is that Josephus understands the word "translate" to mean loose translation, just as Josephus' model, the Septuagint, though it had been done with piety (ὁσίως, *Letter of Aristeas* 306), as if the translators were divinely inspired (καθάπερ ἐνθουσιῶντες, Philo, *Life of Moses* 2.37), and though it had presumably been done with the greatest of accuracy, since a curse was pronounced upon anyone who would add or subtract or transpose anything (*Letter of Aristeas* 311), yet contains numerous changes from the original— modifications which were approved by the rabbis (*Megillah* 9 a), who likewise referred to the miraculous fashion in which the translators had arrived at identical versions despite the fact that they had been placed in isolation from one another. The very fact that Josephus, in his treatise *Against Apion* (I, 54), says that in his *Antiquities* he has translated (μεθηρμήνευκα) from the sacred writings (ἐκ τῶν ἱερῶν γραμμάτων), and then in the next breath adds that, as a priest, he had acquired a knowledge (μετεσχηκώς) of the philosophy (φιλοσοφίας) in those writings, is an indication that he regarded the task of translation as more than a mechanical one and that it involved interpretation, amplification, and explanation in the broadest sense.[2] The additional fact that the rabbis themselves (*Megillah* 25 a) justify omitting the translation in the synagogue of certain passages from Scripture is further evidence that they regarded it as permissible and even necessary to take such liberties. Moreover, the curse imposed upon those who modified the Septuagint was apparently not taken too seriously, as we may see from the fact that by the time of Jerome in the fourth century so many alternate readings had appeared that Jerome (preface to the Book of Chronicles; Migne, *Patrologia Latina* XXVIII, 1324–1325) speaks of three major recensions.

One would expect Josephus to have made major revisions in the biblical narrative not only because he was writing history (the Bible consists of many genres of writing) but also because he was addressing two classes of readers, as we may see from his proem. In the first place, as we have indicated, he is writing, at least in large part, for pagan Greeks, as he makes clear when he cites (*A* I, 5) as a precedent the translation of the Torah into Greek at the request of Ptolemy Philadelphus. This aim is also clear from the end of the work (*A* XX, 262), when Josephus boasts that no one else, Jew or Gentile, would have composed so accurate a treatise for the Greeks (εἰς Ἕλληνας). The fact that Josephus (*A* XX, 263) boasts of his knowledge of Greek prose and poetry and of Greek grammar and the further fact that, according to Josephus (*A* XX, 265), only two or three Jews have achieved the mastery of Greek which he claims to have achieved are additional indications that he is aiming chiefly at a non-Jewish audience. That he employed assistants (*Ap* I, 50) for the sake of polishing his Greek in composing the *Jewish War* is evidence of his eagerness to reach a more sophisticated Greek audience. By the time that he wrote the *Antiquities* a dozen years later, he apparently no longer had need of such assistants.[3] It is clear that in the *Antiquities* he had achieved not only a considerable mastery of the Greek language but also such a sophistication of vocabulary, syntax, and style that only someone well versed in the intricacies of Greek literature would have been able to appreciate his work.

That, however, Josephus is also directing his work to Jews seems clear from his statement (*A* I, 14) that "the main lesson to be learnt from this history by those who care to peruse it" is that God rewards those who obey His laws and punishes those who do not. Josephus, of course, realized that Gentiles are obligated to obey only the seven Noachian commandments, whereas Jews are required to observe 613 commandments; his statement here appears to be directed to his fellow Jews, since he gives no indication that when he speaks of "laws" he is distinguishing between Noachian and other commandments. Moreover, his emphasis on certain episodes, such as the incident of Israel's sin with the Midianite women (Num. 25:1–9; *A* IV, 131–155), which Josephus expands from a mere nine verses to twenty-five paragraphs, and the account of Samson's relations with alien women (Judg. 14:1–16:31; *A* V, 286–317), is intended for those Jews who sought assimilation with Gentiles. Likewise, Josephus seems to be addressing assimilationists among his fellow countrymen when he stresses that the fortunes of Anilaeus and Asinaeus, the Jewish robber-barons who had established an independent state in Mesopotamia, began to deteriorate as soon as Anilaeus had an affair with the wife of a Parthian general "in violation of the Jewish code at the bidding of lust and self-indulgence" (*A* XVIII, 340). That, however, Jews were not his main audience seems to be manifest from his statement (*A* IV, 197) that he deems it necessary to note that he has merely reclassified the laws without actually modifying them at all, "lest perchance any of my countrymen who chance upon (ἐντυγχανόντων) this work should reproach me at all for having gone astray." Evidently, therefore, he expected that his fellow Jews would read his book only by chance.

In the course of his works Josephus mentions by name, as Niese[4] has noted, no fewer than fifty-five authors whose writings he had consulted. Even if we cynically suppose that many of these names were simply copied from his sources, we must note that there are numerous reminiscences of the major Greek authors. For example, not only is Homer mentioned several times by Josephus (*Ap* I, 12; II, 14, 155, 256; *A* VII, 67), but he even knows that Homer nowhere uses the word νόμος and, moreover, actually quotes from him (*A* XIX, 92; *Iliad* 14. 90–91). There are also Sophoclean and Thucydidean traces throughout the *War* and the *Antiquities*, as Stein and Ladouceur have shown.[5] There are likewise several allusions to Euripides, as Thackeray has remarked.[6] In addition, Ek[7] finds Herodotean phrases throughout the *Antiquities*.[8] Furthermore, Josephus shows an acquaintance with Plato by mentioning him in three different passages (*Ap* II, 168, 223–225, 256–261). Finally, Josephus is clearly acquainted with the historians Hecataeus and Pseudo-Hecataeus, Berossus, Alexander Polyhistor, Nicolaus of Damascus (who had himself read very widely, particularly in the Peripatetic philosophers, and who was probably Josephus' main source for his history of the Hasmoneans, Herod, and much else), Strabo, who was himself the author of a scholarly history and geography, Dionysius of Halicarnassus, Polybius, and (in all probability) Philo.[9]

I have remarked[10] on the fact that Josephus spent at least a dozen years (79/81–93/94) writing the *Antiquities*, living on an imperial pension and apparently without any additional duties. In view of the fact that there are approximately 44,250 lines of Greek in the *Antiquities*, this would average out to about ten lines of Greek per day. Josephus, moreover, had already completed (79/81) a masterly historical work, the *Jewish War*, and hence was well acquainted with the historian's craft. Finally, inasmuch as Josephus was so strongly hated by his fellow Jews, his only major audience would have consisted of non-Jews, and the sole way to reach them was through a work that met the highest standards of historiography, especially in view of the fact that so many histories were being written during this period.

Josephus' method as a historian, and particularly his Hellenizations, have only recently begun to be studied, despite the obvious interest and importance of such scholarship. The only book of the Bible which has been systematically compared with Josephus' version is Genesis. Franxman, who has made this study, has, however, omitted much, as I have noted.[11] Nonetheless, Franxman's conclusions are of value, namely that Josephus has, for the book of Genesis, expanded the text considerably in ten pericopes, that he has considerably abridged it in twelve passages, and has stayed close to the original in twelve other instances. In answer to the question as to whether these changes are haphazard, he concludes[12] that beneath the surface of Josephus' style is to be found a careful author whose alterations may represent exegetical traditions much better thought out than has been heretofore supposed. Similarly, Holladay,[13] after cursorily examining Josephus' portrayal of five major biblical figures—Moses, Abraham, Joseph, David, and Solomon—concludes that the most striking feature of these portraits is their generally uniform mold, all of them having been transformed into "images reflecting the Hellenistic ideal of the virtuous (wise) man,"[14] particularly as seen in popular, semi-philosophical ethics characteristic of the atmosphere of the first-century Mediterranean world. Similarly, Attridge has stressed Josephus' internal consistency in his basic theological outlook and in his terminology, which, he concludes, is not simply window dressing designed to add a superficial Hellenistic coloration.[15]

Inasmuch as I have already done a number of studies of Josephus' treatment of biblical episodes and personalities,[16] what I propose to do here is to examine at some length, and much more systematically than did Holladay,[17] the key biblical figure of Abraham to see whether there is, indeed, a consistent picture, particularly when it comes to Hellenization, and to consider the reasons for and the sources of Josephus' treatment.

Abraham

In his portrait of Abraham, Josephus has a striking, unified, and coherent conception. The patriarch emerges as the typical national hero, such as was popular in Hellenistic times, with emphasis on his noble genealogy, his qualities as a convincing speaker, a logician, a philosopher, a scientist, a general, and the supremely good host to strangers. Moreover, Josephus diminishes the role of God and of miracles and heightens the portrait of Abraham as a Stoic philosopher and man of faith who follows God as he accepts divine providence. Finally, to appeal to the Hellenistic readers of the novels that were becoming popular at this time, Josephus presents Abraham as a romantic hero. In his depiction Josephus is quite clearly answering the charges of the anti-Semites, such as Apion (*Ap* II, 135–136), that the Jews had not produced "any geniuses, for example, inventors in arts and crafts or eminent sages," or such as Apollonius Molon (in *Ap* II, 148), that the Jews were the only people who had contributed no useful invention to civilization, and that the Jews were haters of mankind, arousers of political dissension, and dissemblers.

In the first place, the typical national hero must have a long and noble genealogy, connecting him with remote antiquity. Indeed, the first of the thirty-six stages, according to the Greek rhetorician Theon,[18] who was probably a contemporary of Josephus, in eulogizing a person, whether living or dead, real or mythical, was to praise his noble birth ($\varepsilon \dot{\upsilon} \gamma \acute{\varepsilon} \nu \varepsilon \iota \alpha$). Thus, when Abraham is first mentioned by Josephus (*A* I, 148), he tells us, following the Bible (Gen. 11:10–27), that he was tenth in descent from Noah and adds that he was born 992 years after the flood. Josephus has thus increased by 701 years the interval (as found in our Hebrew text) between the flood and the birth of Abraham. Moreover, Josephus may be answering those anti-Semites, such as Apollonius Molon (in Eusebius, *Praeparatio Evangelica* 9. 19. 2–3), who had asserted that Abraham was born only three generations after Noah. In addition, inasmuch as he is writing primarily for a pagan Greek audience who would be conscious of the fact, as the Egyptian priests had pointed out to Solon (Plato, *Timaeus* 22 B), that "you Greeks are never anything but children," Josephus was particularly eager to stress the antiquity of his people.

In the second place, Josephus wishes to portray Abraham as possessing the qualities of the ideal statesman, as delineated by Thucydides in his account of Pericles (2. 60–65), who, as we have noted above, was one of Josephus' favorite sources for style. One of those qualities (Thucydides 2. 60) is the ability to persuade; and, indeed, Josephus (*A* I, 154), in an extrabiblical detail, describes Abraham as persuasive (πιθανός) with his listeners (τοῖς ἀκροωμένοις). Abraham's power of persuasion is seen particularly in his ability to convince the Egyptians (*A* I, 167) on any subject on which he undertook to speak. The ideal statesman is also a philosopher-king; and the portrait of Abraham as a philosopher is conveyed by the fact that his hearers are termed ἀκροωμένοις, a word used especially for students who listen to lectures in the philosophical schools, as we see in Xenophon's *Symposium* (3. 6). Moreover, skill in logic is imputed to Abraham in that he is described (*A* I, 154) as not mistaken in his inferences (περί τε ὦν εἰκάσειεν οὐ διαμαρτάνων). His cleverness in understanding (δεινὸς ὢν συνιέναι) is reminiscent of Oedipus (φρονεῖν . . . δεινόν, in Sophocles, *Oedipus Tyrannus* 316); and indeed, it is because of these gifts that Abraham is said to have arrived at more lofty conceptions (φρονεῖν μεῖζον, in *A* I, 155) of virtue than the rest of mankind and to have determined to reform current theological ideas. This power of logic is seen particularly in the proof for the existence of God, which Josephus (*A* I, 156) has ascribed to Abraham.[19] The fact that this proof is in the form of the arguments promulgated by the Greek philosophical schools, notably the Stoics, and that Josephus uses several favorite Stoic words (προνοῆσαι, εὐταξία, and τοῦ κελεύοντος) in presenting it would make a particular appeal to his audience, inasmuch as Stoicism was the favorite philosophy of the Hellenistic world.[20] The Stoics, however, as seen in Cleanthes' argument (Cicero, *De Natura Deorum* II, 14–15) for the existence of God as based upon the regularity of celestial phenomena, are clearly challenged by Josephus, who offers an argument based upon certain irregularities observed in these phenomena. That Josephus is here answering the Stoics may be inferred from the fact that in the very next sentence after the one giving Abraham's proof, Josephus refers to the Chaldaeans, to whom Philo (*De Migratione Abrahami*

32. 179) imputes certain conceptions of God which are definitely Stoic. More-over, to be a true philosopher one had to be open-minded; therefore, in the account of Abraham's journey to Egypt Josephus describes the entrance of one who intended to be a disciple (ἀκροάτης, like ἀκρωμένοις, as noted above) of a Greek-like philosophical school.[21]

To be appealing to his Hellenistic audience Abraham had to be more than a rhetorician, a logician, and a philosopher. Since this was the age in which science came into its own,[22] Josephus felt it advantageous to stress that Abraham was the one who taught the Egyptians the very sciences for which they later became so famous. He cheerfully gives (χαρίζεται) them his knowl-edge of mathematics, the study of which had been stressed by both Plato and Isocrates, the founders of the two leading schools of education in the fourth century B.C., and transmits to them his lore about astronomy, a science of which the Egyptians had been previously ignorant and which was to become the most popular of the four branches of mathematics in Hellenistic times.[23] It is significant that although, according to the Hellenistic Jewish historian Artapanus (ca. 100 B.C.), Abraham had taught the pharaoh astrology, Josephus has elevated Abraham's stature by having him teach the Egyptian philoso-phers and scientists. Again, whereas the rabbis (*Sanhedrin* 91a) declare that Abraham bequeathed to the sons of his concubines his knowledge of sorcery and black magic, Josephus has Abraham converse with philosophers and scientists.

Along with possessing these traits, the founder of a nation would have been expected by Josephus' Hellenistic audience to be a great general as well. Josephus does not disappoint them, presenting Abraham as a kind of fore-runner of Josephus himself, as Josephus was later to do with Moses. It is im-portant for Josephus to stress the military excellence of his biblical heroes, since the Jews had been reproached with cowardice by such anti-Semites as Apollonius Molon (in *Ap* II, 148). Josephus quotes Nicolaus of Damascus as stating that Abraham was an invader who had come from Chaldaea with an army and who had reigned in Damascus (*A* I, 159), where his fame was still celebrated (*A* I, 160) in Nicolaus' own day. In several instances Josephus adds details to the biblical picture to enhance Abraham's military prowess. Thus we read (*A* I, 172) that the battle between the Assyrians and the Sodomites was a stubborn contest, that (*A* I, 177) Abraham determined to help the Sodomites without delay, that he set out in haste, that he fell upon the Assyrians in an attack in which he caught the enemy by surprise, and that he slew some while they were still asleep and put to flight others who were drunk. In contrast, we may note, the rabbis stress the miraculous side of this episode by remark-ing that an angel named Night attacked the enemy (*Sanhedrin* 96a), that Abraham himself was actually a giant (*Midrash Tanḥuma* B. 1, pp. 73–74, ed. Buber), that the victorious battle with the kings took place on the fifteenth of Nisan (the night reserved for such miracles, since the great miracle of the Exodus occurred on this night) (*Pirke d'Rabbi Eliezer* 17), that all the weapons thrown at Abraham miraculously proved fruitless (*Genesis Rabbah* 42. 3), that the planet Jupiter made the night bright for him (*ibid.*), and that the 318 men who, according to the Bible (Gen. 14:14), assisted him really consisted of his servant Eliezer alone, the numerical value of the letters of whose name adds up to 318 (*Midrash Tanḥuma* B. 1, p. 73, ed. Buber).

This stress on Abraham the general is continued in a remarkable addition to the biblical narrative (*A* I, 234), where we are informed that Abraham's tradition of generalship was continued by his grandson by Keturah, Eophren, who conquered Libya. Josephus then (*A* I, 240–241) quotes the non-Jewish writer Alexander Polyhistor, who reports that, according to Cleodemus the prophet, also called Malchus, two of Abraham's sons by Keturah joined the legendary Heracles in his campaign against Libya and Antaeus, the giant son of Earth, and that Heracles actually married the daughter of one of them. This would serve to elevate the Jews, since it would connect them with the Spartans, who likewise claimed descent from Heracles.

Among the qualities prized by the ancients there is almost none more important than to be a good host and to be a good guest. It is thus not surprising that a major epithet of Zeus is Ξένιος, implying that he is the protector of the right of hospitality. It is this aspect of Zeus of which Odysseus (*Odyssey* 9. 271) reminds Polyphemus the Cyclops and which the latter flagrantly disregards. Similarly, the gravest charge against Heracles (*Odyssey* 21. 11–41) is that he slew Iphitus in his own house, although he was Iphitus' host.

Josephus' stress on Abraham's hospitality is intended to rebut the charge, so often directed against the Jews in those days, that the Jews hated other peoples. Haman, according to Josephus' version (*A* XI, 212), held that the Jews were unsociable (ἄμικτον, "refusing to mingle") and incompatible (ἀσύμφυλον, "not of the same race," "unsuitable") and hostile to all mankind. Even Hecataeus of Abdera (*ap.* Diodorus XL, 3. 5), who is otherwise favorably disposed toward the Jews, says that Moses, as a consequence of the expulsion of his people, established a way of life which is termed ἀπάνθρωπόν τινα ("somewhat unsocial") and μισόξενον ("hostile to strangers"). One clear sign, to the Greeks and Romans, of pre-civilization was the practice of human sacrifice. This charge was made against the Carthaginians (Virgil, *Aeneid* I, 525), the Gauls (Strabo IV, 198), and the Thracians (Strabo VII, 300). The historian Damocritus (*ap.* Suidas, s.v. Δαμόκριτος), who lived in approximately the first century A.D., had carried this charge to the point of reporting a blood libel to the effect that the Jews captured and sacrificed a stranger every seven years; and his presumed contemporary Apion (*ap. Ap* II, 91–96) reports that the Jews annually fattened up and sacrificed a Greek and swore an oath of hostility to the Greeks. Juvenal (14. 103) remarks, in noting the Jews' dislike of strangers, that the Jew is commanded by the law of Moses to point out the road to none save his own co-religionists. As Radin[24] has noted, to the Greeks a major test of civilization was the manner in which a ξένος was dealt with; and since in the Graeco-Roman world the Stoics, in particular, stressed the brotherhood of mankind, this charge against the Jews was especially serious.

We first see Abraham graciously reciprocating (I, 181) Melchizedek's lavish hospitality with a most gracious offer of a tithe of all the spoil he had taken in the campaign against the Assyrians. It is not clear from the Hebrew Bible (Gen. 14:20) whether Abraham gave a tenth or received it from Melchizedek; and Josephus is here in line with the Septuagint, the Genesis Apocryphon (col. 22, line 17), Jubilees (13:25–27), and the rabbis[25] in interpreting this passage to mean that Abraham gave a tenth to Melchizedek. Josephus (A I, 200) notes that Abraham's nephew Lot had learned the lesson of hospitality to strangers from Abraham. It is true that the rabbis (*Pirke de-Rabbi Eliezer* 25) similarly state that Lot learned from Abraham; but they speak in general terms of hospitality, whereas Josephus specifies that Lot learned to be φιλάνθρωπος, presumably in answer to those critics who called the Jews misanthropic. Moreover, in the later episode of Abimelech and Isaac (A I, 259), Josephus recalls Abraham's hospitality by adding to the biblical narrative (Gen. 26:1) that Abimelech welcomed Isaac in virtue of the former hospitality (ξενίαν) and friendship of Abraham and consequently showed him the utmost goodwill. Again, from the virtues which Eliezer, Abraham's servant, praises in others, we can surmise what he learned from his master Abraham. He particularly admires kindliness (φιλανθρωπίαν, "love of mankind") (A I, 250), a quality which we have seen exemplified by Abraham. And, like a good guest, he does not wish to be burdensome to his hosts and offers to pay for their gracious hospitality (φιλοξενίας) and to live at his own expense.

Josephus was particularly sensitive to the charge that Abraham was illiberal. Indeed, both the Book of Jubilees (11:16–12:21), which Josephus appears to have used elsewhere, and the rabbinic midrashim (*Genesis Rabbah* 31. 13 and parallels) have accounts of Abraham smashing and burning the idols of Nimrod and of his father Terah; but Josephus, presumaby because such tales would be offensive to his Greek audience, omits them. Indeed, we may comment that elsewhere (A IV, 207 and Ap II, 237) Josephus, like Philo (*De Specialibus Legibus* I, 9. 53), goes so far as to follow the Septuagint rather than the Hebrew text in interpreting Exodus 22:28 to mean "Thou shalt not revile gods," rather than "Thou shalt not revile God," and infers from this that one is expressly forbidden to deride or blaspheme the gods recognized by others, out of respect, he adds (Ap II, 237), for the very word "God."

Abraham's treatment of the pharaoh and his readiness to sacrifice his son Isaac might well have been regarded as instances of misanthropy and barbarism; Josephus, therefore, takes pains to defend him and the Jews against these charges. Thus, the pharaoh, for his part, is excused, in connection with Sarah, as having acted under the impulse of passion. He is portrayed as generous toward Abraham not, as in the Bible (Gen. 12:16), before the discovery that Sarah is his wife, where he obviously had ulterior motives, but as a good Greek or Roman host who sends his guest away with abundant gifts (A I, 165) *after* he learns that he cannot keep Sarah. As to the charge of misanthropy against the Jews, Josephus' answer is to show (A I, 166) that it is more properly brought against the Egyptians, who had the reputation of possessing the greatest wisdom in antiquity, and who, being addicted to a variety of different customs (ἔθεσι), disparaged (ἐκφαυλιζόντων, "belittled," "depreciated") one another's practices (νόμιμα, "usages," "customs") and were constantly hostile (δυσμενῶς) to one another. Abraham, on the other hand, is a kind of mediator, patiently conferring (συμβαλών) with each group and pointing out their errors. One is reminded of the passage in Herodotus (III, 38) in which the Greeks and Indians appear before the Persian king Darius and are horrified by one another's customs with regard to the disposal of the dead, whereupon Herodotus concludes, in the words of Pindar, that custom (νόμος) is king of all. The Jews were accused (cf., e.g., Tacitus, *Histories* V, 4) of having instituted new rites, opposed to those of all the rest of mankind, of regarding as profane all that was sacred among other peoples, and of permitting that which was prohibited by others (probably an allusion to the prohibition of imitating the ways of idolators in Leviticus 20:23). Josephus is in effect saying in this passage (A I, 166) that it is the Egyptians who had peculiar customs, as Herodotus (II, 35) also notes, since they "seem to have reversed the ordinary practices of mankind"—the very charge made against the Jews.

The contention that the Jews had an implacable hatred of all other peoples (Tacitus, *Histories* V, 5) and were devoid of pity for anyone who was not of their religion is refuted by Josephus in several extrabiblical details in his account of Abraham. We learn (A I, 176), for example, that he was moved, upon hearing of the Sodomites' disaster, not only by fear for his kinsman Lot, who had been captured, but also by pity for his friends (φίλων) and neighbors (γειτνιώντων), the Sodomites. In the Bible (Gen. 14:14) it is clear that Abraham undertook his expedition against the Assyrians in order to rescue his nephew Lot; and in the Genesis Apocryphon (col. 22, line 5), Abraham weeps for his nephew. In the rabbinic literature (*Sanhedrin* 109 a–b) much is said about the misanthropy of the Sodomites, but it is only in the much-later Zohar (1. 112 b) that we read, as we do in Josephus, of Abraham's friendship with the Sodomites. On the other hand, Josephus (A I, 194) attacks the Sodomites as hating foreigners (μισόξενοι) and as declining all association (ὁμιλίας) with others, thus emphasizing that such an attitude is incompatible with Judaism. To be sure, this picture of the Sodomites' misanthropy is also found in the Book of Wisdom (19:13–14) and in rabbinic literature (*Pirke de-Rabbi Eliezer* 25); but the fact that Josephus uses the word against them that anti-Semites had directed against the Jews emphasizes Judaism's opposition to misanthropy. Likewise, Josephus (*A* I, 200) adds to the biblical account in stating that Abraham's nephew Lot had learned from Abraham to be very kindly to strangers; the word that Josephus uses, φιλάνθρωπος, is the very opposite of the misanthropy of which Abraham's descendants were accused by the anti-Semites. Moreover, the fact that the Sodomites are depicted in even blacker colors in Josephus than they are in the Bible glorifies still more the figure of Abraham for showing pity toward them and for praying to God in their behalf (*A* I, 199).

Again, we are impressed with the pity that Abraham shows for Abimelech. In the Bible (Gen. 20:7) God orders Abimelech to restore Sarah to Abraham and promises that Abraham will pray in his behalf. In Josephus the figure of Abraham the merciful looms larger: Abimelech begs Abraham directly to act indulgently (πράως, "mildly," "gently") toward him and to conciliate God's favor. Abraham then shows his devotion and kindness to Abimelech. According to Josephus' version (*A* I, 210), in contrast to the biblical version (Gen. 20:14–15) in which Abimelech invites Abraham to stay, Abimelech gives him a choice of leaving or staying, and Abraham chooses to stay, "to show that he was in no way responsible for the king's illness but anxious for his recovery" (*A* I, 211).

According to the rabbis (*Pirke de-Rabbi Eliezer* 30), Abraham's most severe trial up to that point was whether he should send away his own son Ishmael. The Bible (Gen. 21:11) reports that Sarah's proposal to have Abraham send away Hagar and Ishmael was very grievous in Abraham's sight on account of his son. The Abraham of Josephus (*A* I, 216), however, takes a stronger stand and, showing pity, refuses at first to agree to Sarah's proposal, though Josephus has made it more reasonable, thinking that it was most savage (ὠμότατον, "most brutal," "most fierce," "most cruel," "most harsh") to send off an infant (νήπιον, *A* I, 216)—actually he is at least an adolescent at this point—with a woman lacking the necessities of life. When Abraham finally yields to Sarah's behests, he again shows compassion for Ishmael (*A* I, 217) by committing him to his mother, Hagar, since he is "not yet of age to go alone." Abraham's seeming cruelty toward Hagar is further softened by omitting (*A* I, 218) the biblical statement (Gen. 21:14) that she lost her way in the wilderness of Beer-sheba, a scene which Targum Jonathan presents with even more vividness than does the biblical text. And finally, that pathetic scene

(Gen. 21:16) in which Hagar lifts up her voice and weeps is completely omitted by Josephus (*A* I, 218), since it would apparently cast an unfavorable reflection on Abraham as pitiless.

The charge that the Jews practiced human sacrifice was a particularly serious one. Josephus goes to great lengths to point out, in a speech (*A* I, 233–236) put into the mouth of God rather than of an angel as in Genesis 22:11, that the God of the Jews does not crave human blood and that he is not capricious in taking away what He has given and that He had given His command to Abraham only "to test his soul and see whether such orders would find him obedient." This would seem to be in direct contrast to Artemis, who, according to the chorus in Euripides' *Iphigenia in Aulis* (1524–1525), "rejoices in human sacrifices." [26] That Josephus may well have had Euripides in mind may be seen not only from the similarity of theme between the sacrifice of Iphigenia and the proposed sacrifice of Isaac but also from the pathetic irony of the fact that Abraham seeks happiness only through his son, whereas his son is about to be sacrificed. This irony is matched by that in Euripides' play, where the chorus, catching sight of Queen Clytemnestra and her daughter as they approach in a chariot, start to chant ironically, ἰώ, ἰώ, μεγάλαι μεγάλων εὐδαιμονίαι ("Oh! oh! great happinesses of the great!"). We may cite as further evidence that Josephus was aware of Euripides in this part of his work the fact that just before his summary of the Aqedah passage, he imitates Euripides (*Hercules Furens* 323–324) when he describes (*A* I, 218) how Hagar lay her child Ishmael at his last gasp under a tree and wandered away so that he might not die in her presence. [27]

Josephus also sought to protect Abraham—and the Jewish people—from other charges of defects in character. Thus, telling the truth, which the Greeks so admired in the Persians (Herodotus I, 136, 139), is a virtue which Josephus felt he had to preserve for his biblical heroes. Hence, the pains Josephus (*A* I, 162) took to explain why Abraham had to lie when he came to the pharaoh with Sarah. Likewise, Josephus (*A* I, 207) attempts to justify Abraham's lie to Abimelech (Gen. 20:2–7), corresponding to that which he told the pharaoh, that Sarah was his sister, by explaining that he acted from fear, for he dreaded Abimelech, who was prepared to seduce Sarah. Moreover, Josephus omits the biblical passage (Gen. 20:9) in which Abimelech bitterly remonstrates to Abraham for deceiving him; instead, we are told (*A* I, 209) that Abimelech sent for Abraham and bade him have no further fear of any indignity to his wife. Again, in the Bible (Gen. 22:5) Abraham appears to be disingenuous in telling the young men who accompany him to the scene of the sacrifice of Isaac that he and Isaac will worship and return to them; the rabbis explain this lack of truth by saying that Abraham is here prophesying unconsciously that they will return. Josephus characteristically, for apologetic reasons, omits this statement altogether. Likewise, to present a picture of Abraham bargaining with God was apparently degrading both to the lofty character of God and to the noble character of Abraham. Hence, Josephus (*A* I, 199) omits the anthropomorphic details of the bargaining (Gen. 18:23–32) and instead says merely that Abraham, in sympathy with the Sodomites, implored God not to destroy the good along with the wicked. Similarly, the Bible (Gen. 25:5–6) ascribes to Abraham an apparently unequal treatment of his sons, for he is said to have bequeathed all that he had to Isaac and to have given only gifts to his sons by Keturah. Josephus, for apologetic reasons, omits Abraham's distribution of his property altogether.

Not only does Josephus stress the aggrandizement of Abraham, but he achieves a similar end by diminishing the role of God in the narrative, as we have already seen in the case of Josephus' depiction of Abraham's qualities as a general. There is less emphasis [28] placed on God's promise of Palestine to Abraham; and, in fact, this promise is omitted in the passage (*A* I, 157) which parallels Genesis 12:7, as well as in the passage (*A* I, 170) which parallels Genesis 13:14–17, in that (*A* I, 184) which parallels Genesis 15:18, and in that (*A* I, 193) paralleling Genesis 17:19–21. On the other hand, Josephus, seeking to build up a picture of Abraham and of his descendants as fighters rather than as mere heirs, has God add (*A* I, 185) in his promise to Abraham (Gen. 15:13–16) that his posterity will vanquish the Canaanites in battle and will take possession of their land and cities. Similarly, Josephus' version of God's covenant with Abraham in Genesis 17:1ff. is much briefer, with God hardly being mentioned, and with the additional statement that the Israelites will win possession of Canaan by war (*A* I, 191). Significantly, the fullest statement (*A* I, 235–236) of God's promise of the supremacy which Abraham's descendants will exercise is found in God's statement to Abraham before the appearance of the ram at the climax of the Aqedah, when Abraham had shown supreme faith and had proven himself worthy of God's blessings. There, too, we find the statement (*A* I, 235) that they will subdue Canaan by force of arms and thus be envied by all men. Likewise, in speaking of circumcision (*A* I, 192), Josephus omits its connection with the covenant between God and Abraham as stated in the Bible (Gen. 17:10–11) and instead gives a purely practical reason for this practice, namely, to prevent assimilation.

Not only is the role of God diminished in Josephus' narrative but the miracles of Scripture are often toned down. Thus, according to the Bible (Gen. 18:10), God promises that He will return and that Sarah will have a son "according to this season of life," that is, a year from that time. The rabbis (*Tanḥuma, Wa-yera* 13) heighten the miracle by having one of the angels visiting Abraham draw a line on the wall and declare that Isaac will be born when the sun returns to that line. But in Josephus (*A* I, 197) the angels leave the time of their return indefinite, stating merely that one of them would return some day in the future (εἰς τὸ μέλλον) and find that Sarah had given birth to a son.

Then, when the birth itself occurs (*A* I, 214), Josephus says merely that it occurred during the following year.

And yet, side by side with de-emphasizing the role of God in the Abraham story, Josephus endeavors to increase Abraham's stature as a man of faith. Josephus must have deemed this particularly necessary because, as we can see from Philo's comment (*De Abrahamo* 33. 178), there were "quarrelsome critics" who did not regard Abraham's behavior in connection with the Aqedah to be great or wonderful. In fact, as Josephus stresses in the opening of his work (*A* I, 14), the main lesson of his history is that men who obey God "prosper in all things beyond belief and for their reward are offered by God felicity." The greatest indication of Abraham's faith in God is, of course, seen in his willingness to sacrifice Isaac at the command of God. Here, with several deft touches, Josephus heightens Abraham's faith. What Josephus presents is, in effect, a drama, reminiscent, as we have indicated above, in theme and occasionally even in language, of Euripides' *Iphigenia in Aulis,* commencing with a prologue in which God appears to Abraham; moving to the play proper, so to speak, which contains a dialogue between Abraham and Isaac; and ending with an epilogue, in which God commends Abraham and predicts the glorious future of his descendants. First of all, this is done through noting (*A* I, 222) that Abraham passionately loved (ὑπερηγάπα) Isaac, whereas Genesis 22:2 says merely "whom thou lovest." This exceedingly great love is due to the fact that Isaac was born (*A* I, 222) "on the threshold of old age" (ἐπὶ γήρως οὐδῷ), and this added detail, which is a phrase from Homer (ἐπὶ γήραος οὐδῷ, *Iliad* XXII, 60), evokes a picture of Abraham as a Homeric hero recalling Priam. The amplified virtues of the child Isaac—his practice of every virtue, his devoted filial obedience, and his zeal for the worship of God—call forth still more the affection of his parents and indicate how great Abraham's faith is that he is willing to sacrifice such a child. Josephus (*A* I, 224) further stresses Abraham's faith by noting that God required him to offer up Isaac by his own hand. His zeal is so overwhelming that, according to an added detail in Josephus, he tells no one in his household, not even his wife, Sarah, about his resolve to sacrifice Isaac, lest they should attempt to hinder him from attending to God's service. It would appear natural that Abraham should have some doubts about the sacrifice; and, indeed, the rabbis (*Tanḥuma, Shelaḥ* 27, ed. Buber) declare this openly; but Josephus, in his effort to build up Abraham as a knight of faith, declares bluntly (*A* I, 225) that Abraham believed that nothing would justify disobeying God.

The actual binding of Isaac (Gen. 22:9), which would probably be too much for a Greek audience and would be incriminating toward Abraham, is omitted by Josephus (*A* I, 228). But, whereas Abraham in the Bible starts to perform the sacrifice in silence (Gen. 22:10), in Josephus the description of Abraham's faith reaches its climax in a speech full of pathos made by

Abraham to Isaac. In the speech, which was invented by Josephus (*A* I, 228–231), Abraham first recalls his prayer for Isaac's birth, then his care for Isaac's upbringing and his hope to bequeath his dominion to him. Abraham then finishes with a statement of his supreme faith that it is to God, whose gift Isaac was in the first place (in a manner transcending nature) that he is yielding his son and that Isaac will be the protector of his old age (γηροκόμον)[29] by giving him God instead of himself. The pathos of this scene, and consequently the degree of Abraham's faith, is all the greater, since the whole purpose of marriage, as Josephus informs us (*A* IV, 261) in an extrabiblical addition, is to produce children who will tend their parents in their old age. The fact that Josephus in this brief pericope (*A* I, 222–236) on five occasions uses a form of the word for happiness emphasizes how important happiness was to Abraham; and yet, his readiness to forego this shows how great was his faithfulness to God. The rabbinic accounts (*Yashar Wa-yera* 44b–45a) are likewise full of embellishments at this point, but they stress the role of Satan in trying to deter Abraham, whereas Josephus omits this supernatural element and focuses instead on Abraham himself.

Yet, to present Abraham as having mere blind faith would be unsatisfactory to Josephus' cultured Greek readers; and so Abraham appears in the guise of a kind of Stoic philosopher who believes, as did the Stoics, that it is divine providence (προνοίας) that ordains everything (*A* I, 225) for God's favored ones. This picture is continued in the answer given by Abraham to Isaac when the latter asks what sacrifice they are about to offer. The Bible (Gen. 22:8), at this point, has Abraham's simple and direct statement that God would Himself provide the lamb. Josephus' Abraham explains the nature of God's providence to Isaac. The end of Josephus' romanticized account (*A* I, 236) of the Aqedah is reminiscent of Hellenistic novels,[30] for after the appearance of the ram, which restores them to each other beyond all hope, and after hearing God's promises of great plenty, father and son embrace each other, return home together, and live happily ever after, with God assisting them in all that they desired.

Since the ancients believed that children reflected the virtues or the vices of their parents, the fact that Isaac's qualities (*A* I, 222) are greatly amplified and that he is spoken of as practicing every virtue and as showing devoted piety toward his parents and toward God adds luster to the portrait of his father. Thus, in a glorious scene wholly invented by Josephus (*A* I, 232), Isaac, when told of his father's intention to sacrifice him, matches the supreme faith of his father by receiving his words with noble spirit (γενναῖον . . . τὸ φρόνημα) and joyfully. Were this the resolution of his father alone he would not hesitate to obey; now that he realizes that it is the will of God he dramatically rushes (ὥρμησεν) to the altar and to his death. Likewise, Abraham's sons by Keturah clearly reflect their grandfather's qualities; and in an expansion of the biblical material (Gen. 25:1–6) we are told (*A* I, 238) that these sons were strong to labor and quick of understanding (πρός τε πόνους καρτεροὶ καὶ δεινοὶ συνιέναι). The most striking new features of Abraham's descendants by Keturah are that his grandson Eophren, in a portrait reminiscent of Abraham himself, is depicted as a great general, who is said (*A* I, 239) to have led a successful expedition against Libya, and whose grandsons settled there and named the land Africa after their grandfather. Josephus (*A* I, 240–241) cites the external witness of the non-Jewish writer Alexander Polyhistor, who quotes Cleodemus the prophet, also known as Malchus, to the effect that one of Abraham's sons by Keturah, Sures, gave his name to Assyria, and that two others, Japhras and Apheras (i.e. Eophren), gave their names to the city of Aphra and the country of Africa. Finally, the fact that (*A* I, 241), according to Cleodemus or Malchus, two of Abraham's sons by Keturah joined Heracles in his successful expedition against Libya and Antaeus and that Heracles married the daughter of one of them is cited with obvious pride by Josephus as proof of the military prowess and prestige of Abraham's descendants. By stressing that Abraham's descendants played such a key role in establishing colonies in distant lands, Josephus was seeking to answer the charge that the Jews were provincial and had had little impact upon the history of the world (*Ap* II, 148).

Another characteristic of Josephus' narrative of Abraham, to which there are many parallels elsewhere in his work, is the introduction of erotic elements reminiscent of Hellenistic novels. Thus, in an extrabiblical comment which has no rabbinic parallel for this passage, Josephus (*A* I, 162) speaks of the Egyptians' frenzy (ἐπιμανές) for women and of Abraham's consequent fear that the Egyptian pharaoh would slay him because of his wife's beauty. Josephus thus presents a better case in defense of the deceit practiced by Abraham than that found in the Bible (Gen. 12:11–13). To create the romantic interest that his Hellenistic readers craved, Josephus speaks in terms of the fulfillment of Abraham's suspicions, whereas the Bible (Gen. 12:14) merely says: "And it came to pass." In Josephus the erotic interest is further aroused by a face-to-face meeting of the pharaoh with Sarah (*A* I, 165) at which, in terror, he asks her who she is and who this man is whom she has brought with her. In contrast, the Genesis Apocryphon (col. 20), in narrating the tale of the restoration of Sarah to Abraham, puts the emphasis not on the pharaoh in his terror but on Abraham in his grief, who "prayed and supplicated and entreated God," complaining with flowing tears. Again, Josephus has the dramatic impact of the direct confrontation of the pharaoh and Sarah, whereas the Apocryphon (col. 20) has Lot as the intermediary between Abraham and the pharaoh's prince, Hyrcanus, informing the pharaoh why Abraham cannot pray to have the plague alleviated. There is no meeting between the pharaoh and Sarah in the Bible; there (Gen. 12:18), the pharaoh summons Abraham and complains about the deceit that he has practiced. Again, in the Bible (Gen. 12:19), in the confrontation between the pharaoh and Abraham, the pharaoh upbraids Abraham for deceiving him, "so that I took her to be my wife." Josephus (A I, 165) phrases the pharaoh's charge and his excuse in more romantic terms: it was in the belief that Sarah was Abraham's sister that he had set his affections (σπουδάσαι, "make haste," "be eager," "be serious or earnest") on her, that he had aimed to contract a marriage alliance (συγγένειαν) with her rather than to outrage (ἐξυβρίσαι, "to break out into insolence") her in a transport of passion (κατ᾽ ἐπιθυμίαν ὡρμημένος, i.e. "having rushed headlong into passion"). Furthermore, Josephus (A I, 212) introduces a romantic element into the covenant between Abimelech and Abraham by having it entered into after the episode of Abimelech and Sarah rather than after the dispute concerning the well (Gen. 21:22–34).

The Bible (Gen. 12:17), moreover, says nothing of what the pharaoh does or attempts to do with Sarah, and we are left to draw our inferences from the statement that "the Lord plagued Pharaoh and his house with great plagues because of Sarai." Josephus (A I, 163), as might be expected, is more direct in supplying erotic details to his readers: he arouses suspense by saying that the pharaoh was at the point of laying hands on her. Because Josephus feels the need to defend Abraham's deceit in connection with this episode, he paints the pharaoh in blacker colors, and hence we read of the pharaoh's unjust passion, which God thwarts with an outbreak of disease and of political disturbance (στάσει τῶν πραγμάτων). The former trouble is reminiscent of the terrible punishment inflicted upon Oedipus for his incest;[31] indeed, in typical Greek fashion reminiscent of Sophocles' *Oedipus the King,* in order to discover a remedy (ἀπαλλαγῆς) for the plague, the pharaoh, like Oedipus, consults the priests (ἱερεῖς), who reply that the calamity (τὸ δεινόν) is due to the wrath (μῆνιν) of God because the pharaoh had sought to outrage (ὑβρίσαι) the stranger's wife. As to the political disturbance, the phrase is strikingly similar to Thucydides' description (3. 82–84) of revolution at Corcyra.[32] We may also note that one of the charges of the anti-Semite Apion that Josephus takes great pains to answer is that the Jews are guilty of fomenting sedition in Alexandria (Ap II, 68). Josephus is here implicitly declaring that it is not the Jews who are responsible for this sedition, but rather the enemies of the Jews, as he there states (Ap II, 68–70) when he remarks that the real promoters of sedition are Egyptians such as Apion and that the Jews are noted for their concord.

A similar romantic flavor is given by Josephus to the episode of Eliezer's search for a wife for Abraham's son Isaac. Thus, in a passage (A I, 244) which has no parallel in Scripture (Gen. 24:10), the difficulty of Eliezer's journey is stressed; he goes through a land which is muddy in winter and drought-stricken in summer, a country infested with bands of robbers—details which are reminiscent of Hellenistic novels. Then Josephus (A I, 245) adds a romantic scene in which the other maidens refuse to show hospitality to Eliezer and only Rebecca agrees, just as in Homer's *Odyssey* (VI, 137–141), when Nausicaa's companions shrink in fear of Odysseus and only she herself stands her ground and shows him hospitality. Rebecca's rebuking words to the other maidens (*A* I, 246) are also similar to Nausicaa's rebuke of her companions (*Odyssey* VI, 198–210). In an addition to the biblical narrative (Gen. 24:23), which is reminiscent of Odysseus' reaction to Nausicaa's hospitality in Book VI of the *Odyssey*, Eliezer (*A* I, 247) says that the parents of such a child are to be congratulated, and he expresses the wish that they may arrange a marriage for her into the house of a good man to whom she may bear children. She has won a contest in courtesy and hospitality, and so (*A* I, 249) he offers her a prize.

Conclusion

A comparison of Josephus' treatment of Abraham with his recasting of other biblical characters, as indicated by this author's other studies of Saul, Solomon, and Esther, will show that Josephus follows a consistent pattern. He stresses, on the one hand, the hero's genealogy, his qualities as the ideal statesman (so reminiscent of the portrait of Pericles in Josephus' favorite Thucydides), including his ability to persuade and his ability as a general, as well as his qualities as a good host, and his erotic appeal, while, on the other hand, he diminishes the role of God and of miracles. The figure that emerges is the prototype of the Platonic philosopher-king and the Stoic sage. While it is true that some of Josephus' changes are paralleled in rabbinic and other sources, the majority are not; and the very fact that he selects some and not others is itself significant. While the uniqueness of some of the Hellenizations in Josephus' revisions may be questioned, the *cumulative* effect, especially in view of Josephus' acknowledged wide reading of classical and Hellenistic Greek literature, is decisive.

We may now ask basically the same question about Josephus that scholars have been asking about Philo: is he more a Greek in Jewish clothing or a Jew in Greek clothing? Inasmuch as scholarship has blurred the distinctions between Palestine and the Diaspora and has noted a bewildering variety of Judaisms for this period, the question becomes much more complex: which variety of Judaism does Josephus represent? Despite his profession of allegiance to Pharisaism, his birth in Jerusalem, and his claim to an excellent Jewish education, the question remains. What complicates it is that Josephus chose to write his work as an extended apologetic, a genre for which we do not have other extant examples. What complicates it still further is the question of Josephus' own personal contribution to his synthesis. We can here suggest merely that Josephus could have written a midrashic-like sermon in Aramaic like any of the rabbis of his day; instead, he chose to write a history, with all that it connoted in his era, and in a language, Greek, intended for a wider audience. In this essay I have attempted to show how he followed the patterns and rhetorical guidelines of his craft.

Notes

1. See most recently Shaye J. D. Cohen, *Josephus in Galilee and Rome: His Vita and Development as a Historian* (Leiden, 1979) 27–29. The fullest discussion of this formula is by Willem C. van Unnik, "De la règle Μήτε προσθεῖναι μήτε ἀφελεῖν dans l'histoire du canon," *VC* 3 (1949) 1–36; see also the critical review of van Unnik's *Flavius Josephus als historischer Schriftsteller* (Heidelberg, 1978) by David Goldenberg in "Josephus Flavius or Joseph ben Mattithiah," *JQR* 70 (1979–1980) 180, n. 4.

2. In "Hellenizations in Josephus' Portrayal of Man's Decline," *Studies in the History of Religions* 14 = *Religions in Antiquity: Essays in Memory of Erwin Ramsdell Goodenough*, ed. Jacob Neusner (Leiden, 1968) 336–337, I suggest that the γραμμάτων (A I, 5) and the ἀναγραφαῖς (A I, 17), which Josephus promises not to modify and which must, as the words themselves indicate, refer to written works, allude not to the Bible alone but to the Jewish tradition generally. This tradition, including materials later incorporated into Midrashim, had already been reduced to writing in part, as we may see, for example, from the Genesis Apocryphon, which dates from somewhere between the end of the first century B.C. and the middle of the first century A.D., and from the *Liber Antiquitatum Biblicarum*, falsely ascribed to Philo and dating from the end of the first century A.D. Both works either antedate or are approximately contemporaneous with Josephus. Another possibility is that Josephus' phrase "neither adding nor omitting anything" is derived from Deuteronomy 4:2 and 12:32, where it is stated that "thou shalt not add nor subtract," and that Josephus understood the phrase, as did the rabbis, in the sense that one was not permitted to alter the *law*, but that presumably one might take liberties with the narrative portions of the Bible.

3. The theory of Henry St. John Thackeray in *Josephus, the Man and the Historian* (New York, 1929; reprinted, 1967) 107–118, that Josephus, in Books XV and XVI of the *Antiquities* utilized an assistant who had a particular love of Greek poetry, especially Sophocles, and that in Books XVII–XIX he had the help of an assistant who was especially fond of Thucydides can be questioned, since there are Sophoclean and Thucydidean traces throughout the *Antiquities*. Furthermore, the presence of many of the Sophoclean and Thucydidean phrases in the other Greek writers of the period, notably Dionysius of Halicarnassus, shows that they are characteristic of first-century Greek rather than that they are the work of a special assistant. Moreover, the Sophoclean element in Books XV and XVI may be due to Herod's secretary Nicolaus of Damascus, who was steeped in Sophocles and who was Josephus' chief source for Herod in Books XIV– XVII. Finally, Schreckenberg (*per litt.*) has criticized Thackeray's theory, noting that he has observed, in connection with his work on the concordance to Josephus, more stylistic unity on the part of Josephus than is generally granted. As an alternative to this theory, Robert J. H. Shutt in *Studies in Josephus* (London, 1961) 85–92, argues that Josephus follows Nicolaus of Damascus in those places where stylistic peculiarities are discernible.

4. Benedictus Niese, ed., *Flavii Josephi Opera*, Vol. 7 (Berlin, 1895) 87.

5. Elchanan Stein, *De Woordenkeuze in het Bellum Judaicum van Flavius Josephus* (Amsterdam, 1937); David J. Ladouceur, "Studies in the Language and Historiography of Flavius Josephus" (Diss., Brown University, Providence, 1977).

6. Thackeray (above, note 3) 117–118.

7. Sven Ek, "Herodotismen in der jüdischen Archäologie des Josephus und ihre textkritische Bedeutung," *Skrifter utgivna av Kungl. Humantistiska Ventenskapssam fundet i Lund: Acta Regiae Societatis Humaniorum Litterarum Lundensis* 2 (Lund, 1945–1946) 27–62, 213.

8. See now also Eckhard Plümacher, *Lukas als hellenistischer Schriftsteller. Studien zur Apostelgeschichte* (Göttingen, 1972) 62–63.

9. For Hecataeus and Pseudo-Hecataeus, see Franz Dornseiff, *Echtheitsfragen antikgriechischen Literatur: Rettungen des Theognis, Phokylides, Hekataios, Choirilos* (Berlin, 1939); for Berossus, see James T. Shotwell, *The History of History*, Vol. 1, rev. ed. (New York, 1939) 102–103. Alexander Polyhistor is discussed by Nikolaus Walter in "Zur Überlieferung einiger Reste früher jüdisch-hellenistischer Literatur bei Josephus, Clemens und Euseb," *SP* 7 (1966) 314–320. For Nicolaus of Damascus, see Ben Zion Wacholder, *Nicolaus of Damascus* (Berkeley, 1962). On Strabo see Robert J. H. Shutt (above, note 3) 106–109, and Menahem Stern, "Strabo's Remarks on the Jews" (in Hebrew), in M. Dorman, Shmuel Safrai, and Menahem Stern, edd., *In Memory of Gedaliahu Alon, Essays in Jewish History and Philology* (Tel Aviv, 1970) 169–191. For Dionysius of Halicarnassus, see Shutt, 92–101; Harold W. Attridge, *The Interpretation of Biblical History in the Antiquitates Judaicae of Flavius Josephus* (Missoula, Montana, 1976); and David Altshuler, "Descriptions in Josephus' Antiquities of the Mosaic Constitution" (Diss., Hebrew Union College, Cincinnati, 1976). On Polybius, see Shutt, 102–106, and on Philo, see especially Salomo Rappaport, *Agada und Exegese bei Flavius Josephus* (Vienna, 1930).

10. Louis H. Feldman, "Josephus' Portrait of Saul," *HUCA* 53 (1982) 97.

11. See Thomas W. Franxman, *Genesis and the "Jewish Antiquities" of Flavius Josephus* (Rome, 1979); and Louis H. Feldman, "Josephus' Commentary on Genesis," *JQR* 72 (1981–1982) 121–131.

12. Franxman (above, note 11) 289.

13. Carl H. Holladay, *Theios Aner in Hellenistic-Judaism: A Critique of the Use of This Category in New Testament Christology* (Missoula, Montana, 1977) 67–79.

14. *Ibid.*, 78.

15. Attridge (above, note 9) 182, 289.

16. "Josephus' Commentary on Genesis," *Jewish Quarterly Review* 72 (1981–1982) 121–131: "Hellenizations in Josephus' Account of Man's Decline," *E. R. Goodenough Memorial Volume* (*Studies in the History of Religions* 14, ed. by Jacob Neusner [Leiden, 1968]) 336–353; "Abraham the Greek Philosopher in Josephus," *TAPA* 99 (1968) 143–156; "Josephus' Version of the Binding of Isaac," *SBL: 1982 Seminar Papers* (ed. by Kent H. Richards) 21 (1982) 113–128; "Josephus' Portrait of Saul," *HUCA* 53 (1982) 45–99; "Josephus as an Apologist to the Greco-Roman World: His Portrait of Solomon," *Aspects of Religious Propaganda in Judaism and Early Christianity*, ed. E. S. Fiorenza (Notre Dame, 1976) 69–98; and "Hellenizations in Josephus' Version of Esther," *TAPA* 101 (1970) 143–170.

17. Holladay (above, note 13).

18. See Leonardus Spengel, ed., *Rhetores Graeci*, Vol. 2 (Leipzig, 1854) 109ff.

19. Louis H. Feldman, "Abraham the Greek Philosopher in Josephus," *TAPA* 99 (1968) 143–156.

20. So William Tarn and G. T. Griffith, *Hellenistic Civilisation*, 3rd ed. (London, 1952) 325. See Luther Martin, "Josephus' Use of *Heimarmene* in the *Jewish Antiquities* XIII, 171–3," *Numen* 28 (1981) 127–137. D. L. Tiede, in *The Charismatic Figure as Miracle Worker* (Missoula, Montana, 1972) 207–224, emphasizes the influence of the motif of the Stoic sage upon Josephus.

21. Cf., e.g., Aristotle, *Politics* 1274a 29; *Nicomachean Ethics* 1095a 2.

22. See H. I. Marrou, *A History of Education in Antiquity*, trans. G. Lamb (New York, 1956) 176–185.

23. *Ibid.*, 182.

24. Max Radin, *The Jews among the Greeks and Romans* (Philadelphia, 1915) 183.

25. See Ben Zion Wacholder, *Eupolemus: A Study of Judaeo-Greek Literature* (Cincinnati, 1974) 106.

26. The fact, well supported, that Josephus knew the tragedy entitled *Exagoge* of the second century B.C. Hellenistic Jewish writer Ezekiel, at least in Alexander Polyhistor's excerpts, makes it more likely that Josephus was influenced by Euripides, at least indirectly, since J. Wieneke (*Ezechielis Judaei Poetae Alexandrini Fabulae Quae Inscribitur Fragmenta* [Diss., Münster, 1931]) and now Howard Jacobson (*The Exagoge of Ezekiel* [Cambridge, 1983]) establish it without any reasonable doubt that Ezekiel's *Exagoge* in phraseology, style, dramatic technique (e.g. of the major tragedians only Euripides seems to have introduced quotations into speeches in his prologues—*Ion, Phoenissae, Iphigenia among the Taurians,* and *Stheneboia*—as does Ezekiel [24–25, 28–29]), meter and prosody (especially in the frequency and patterns of resolution), and structure was much influenced by Euripides.

27. Elsewhere, as Thackeray (above, note 3) 118, notes, we even have in Josephus (*A* XIV, 96) an allusion to a lost play of Euripides, the *Ino.* Moreover, Martin Braun (*History and Romance in Graeco-Oriental Literature* [Oxford, 1938] 44–93) has indicated how much Josephus is indebted to Euripides' *Hippolytus* in his great expansion of the incident of Joseph and Potiphar's wife (*A* II, 41–59). On Josephus' imitation of Euripides' rhetorical excesses, see Samuel J. Pease, *The Technique of Battle Descriptions in the Greek Historians* (Diss., University of Chicago, 1932).

28. Cf. Betsy H. Amaru, "Land Theology in Josephus' *Jewish Antiquities,*" *JQR* 71 (1980–1981) 201–229.

29. Cf. Hesiod, *Theogony* 605, who speaks of the curse of not having anyone to tend one in one's old age (γηροκόμοιο).

30. Abraham Schalit, trans., Josephus, *Antiquitates Judaicae* [Hebrew] (Jerusalem, 1944–1963), *A* I, 236 (notes, p. 40, n. 265), compares Xenophon's *Ephesiaka* V, 15 and the anonymous tale of *Apollonius of Tyre* 43.

31. On Josephus' indebtedness to Sophocles for his portrait of Solomon, see my "Josephus as an Apologist to the Greco-Roman World: His Portrait of Solomon" (above, note 16) 82–89.

32. On Josephus' indebtedness to Thucydides throughout his works see my discussion of the literature in my *Josephus and Modern Scholarship (1937–1980)* (Berlin, 1984) 827–830.

6 *Josephus' Portrayal of the Matriarchs*

JAMES L. BAILEY

Introduction

S tudies about women in antiquity generate much interest today. These studies normally focus on ancient literature which was written by and for men and thus reflects male attitudes toward subjects discussed, including that of women. Though the writings of most key figures from the Graeco-Roman world have been quarried for their yield on this topic, little has been published on the view of women presented in the writings of Flavius Josephus, Jewish historian of the first century A.D. whose works comprise ten volumes in the Loeb Classical Library.[1] A careful examination of Josephus' writings could yield important results for the study of women in antiquity since these works offer depictions of Hasmonaean and Herodian women of the postbiblical period and Josephus' own reworked portrayals of women from the biblical tradition. Further, as is obvious from what we know about Josephus' biography, he was a Jew who became thoroughly acquainted with Hellenism, residing as he did (for the last thirty years or so of his life) under imperial auspices in Rome.[2] Since it is impossible in this paper to examine carefully all major Josephan depictions of women, a far more modest project is proposed: the investigation of Josephus' handling of the Genesis narratives that describe the matriarchs.

Professor Feldman has already shown how Josephus significantly Hellenized the biblical portrait of Abraham, presenting the patriarch "as a typical national hero, . . . with emphasis on his qualities as a philosopher and scientist."[3] But no comparable study has been done on one or all of his portrayals

---

My research and preparation of this article were largely completed during the summer of 1983 as a participant in the seminar "The Greek Encounter with Judaism in the Hellenistic Period" sponsored by the National Endowment for the Humanities. I am grateful to the NEH Committee and especially to Professor Louis H. Feldman, leader of the seminar, who expertly and graciously guided my work on this project.

of the matriarchs—Sarah, Rebekah, Rachel, and Leah. Franxman, in his detailed study of Josephus' treatment of the Book of Genesis, has considered the passages depicting the matriarchs, yet his purpose was to characterize in general terms Josephus' handling of the entire narrative of Genesis.[4] He was not concerned with drawing any composite picture of Josephus' treatment of the matriarchal stories.

In what follows I have drawn attention to the Josephan modifications of the Genesis stories involving the matriarchs. My comparative analysis supports the thesis that Josephus has significantly Hellenized these stories and in the process offered idealized portraits of Sarah, Rebekah, Rachel, and Leah for his Roman readers. Undoubtedly influenced by Hellenistic literary models which exalted the beautiful and exemplary aristocratic woman, Josephus chose to present the matriarchs in a similar light to win admiration for these Jewish heroines and thus the Jewish people, despite his sharing commonly held attitudes which were condescending toward women in general, attitudes current both in Jewish circles and the larger Graeco-Roman world.

Background on Josephus' View of Women

Near the close of his autobiography, Josephus discloses something about his domestic history.[5] Evidently in the late sixties A.D., he married a native of Caesarea who had been taken captive by Vespasian's army. Josephus specifically mentions that she was a virgin (*parthenos*), perhaps to fend off any criticism contending that a member of a priestly family should not marry a captive, since such a woman was likely violated by her captors.[6] This first wife separated from him when he accompanied Vespasian to Alexandria. It was there that Josephus married again, a woman he later divorced in Rome, offering as a reason "being displeased at her behavior."[7] His third wife, and presumably his last, he married thereafter, and this woman he describes in laudatory terms: being of a Jewish family that had settled in Crete, she came from "very distinguished parents, indeed the most notable people in that country. In character (*ēthei*) she surpassed many of her sex, as her subsequent life showed." He ends this section by naming his two sons by this third wife, having already named the one surviving son by his second marriage. However, Josephus does not give the names of any of these women in his personal life, not even the third wife for whom he has words of praise. In recounting his family history, he thus reveals that the male members carry more importance than do the females.

Further, we note that by Josephus' own admission at least two royal women were helpful to him. In the Hellenistic world, royal women often acted in the role of intercessor. When Josephus visited Rome in the early sixties A.D., he informs us that he received aid from Poppaea, Nero's consort, in securing freedom for certain Jewish priests. This same woman, later as Nero's wife, pleaded the cause of Jews in another situation.[8] We learn also that (during his latter years in Rome) Josephus knew Domitia, the wife of Emperor Domitian. At the end of his autobiography, he comments, "Moreover, Domitia, Caesar's wife, never ceased conferring favors upon me."[9] Though likely an exaggeration, Josephus probably knew Domitia and counted his friendship with this influential woman crucial for his career in Rome. Thus, we can conclude that although he was part of a male-dominated society, Josephus understood the advantage of knowing women who had access to powerful men.

There are other passages in Josephus' writings which clearly reflect the male prejudice against women. For example, Josephus extols one woman survivor at Masada with the following words: "but an old woman and another, a relative of Eleazar, superior in sagacity (*phronēsis*) and training (*paideia*) *to most of her sex.*"[10] Such an evaluation suggests that women are in a category apart from men, although this does not necessarily imply a negative attitude toward females.

More blatant is Josephus' comment in his depiction of the people in the wilderness after escaping from Pharaoh. Explaining why the "army" of people was not moving well in the desert, he declares: "for this was no sound army, capable of meeting the stress of necessity with manly fortitude, but one whose nobler instincts were vitiated by a rabble of women and children (*alla diephtheire to kat' ekeinous gennaion paidōn te kai gynaikōn ochlos*) too feeble to respond to oral admonition."[11]

Further, there seems to be a direct attack on women in Josephus' quotation of a proverb in the story of Samson: "Nor is ought more deceitful than a woman who betrays our speech to you." This saying does not appear in the biblical account (see Judges 14:18).[12] Elsewhere Josephus has reported the Essenes' low esteem for women.[13] This does not necessarily imply that he shared their opinion, although it is evident that he greatly admired the Essenes. Finally, Josephus' basic attitude toward women seems evident in his elaboration of two biblical commandments. In *Antiquities* IV, 219, he writes: "From women let no evidence be accepted, because of the levity and temerity of their sex." The opening clause, though not in the Bible, represents a rabbinic ruling.[14] However, the final clause about women's levity (*kouphotēs*) and temerity (*thrasos*) seems to represent Josephus' own expansion.[15] As well, we note *Against Apion* II, 201, where among the commandments regarding marriage, Josephus includes the statement that "the woman, says the Law, is in all things inferior to the man. Let her accordingly be submissive, not for her humiliation, but that she may be directed; for the authority has been given by God to the man." It is striking that Josephus includes this traditional teaching based on Genesis 3:16 while having omitted mention of that very passage when recounting the creation and fall stories in Genesis (see *A* I, 48–49).[16]

With the above as evidence, it would appear that there are ample reasons to suggest that Josephus clearly shared pervasive attitudes of his time, both Jewish and Graeco-Roman, which viewed women as indisputably inferior to men and often weak in mind and character.[17]

Josephus' Reworking of the Matriarchal Stories

Turning our attention to Josephus' treatment of the episodes in his *Antiquities* that involved the matriarchs, we assume, with others,[18] that he had available both a Hebrew and a Greek text of the Bible, not at all unlike our present Masoretic and Septuagint versions, for composing his Jewish history. Every major difference in the Josephan retelling, as compared with the content and style of the biblical account, has been checked against a number of midrashic-type writings that chronologically precede or are roughly contemporary with Josephus' work: *The Book of Jubilees, The Genesis Apocryphon, The Book of Biblical Antiquities* of Pseudo-Philo, and the writings of Philo.[19]

Pseudo-Philo essentially offers no parallels to Josephan elaborations since it includes only a compressed summary of the patriarchal stories (section VIII). As we shall see, a few Philonic passages will be noted, but generally Philo's penchant for allegorical interpretations has precluded his dealing with details of the narrative as such; rather, wherever one of the matriarchs is mentioned she is portrayed as representing certain virtues or characteristics. Sarah stands for "virtue" or "wisdom"; Rebekah is the symbol of "patience" or "steadfastness in excellence"; Rachel typifies "sense-perception"; and Leah, in contrast to Rachel, is described as above passion and "beautiful in soul."[20]

For a collection of the rabbinic traditions, I have consulted the work of Ginzberg, and have noted also the judgments of Franxman and Rappaport.[21]

Portrayal of Sarah

Turning our attention directly to Josephus' treatment of the episodes involving the matriarchs, we consider first his portrayal of Sarah. The first major episode involving Sarah is Genesis 12:10–20, a story which has received elaborate attention in the tradition. This biblical story depicting Abraham's sojourn in Egypt during a famine and his claiming Sarah as a sister in order to save his life exhibits similarities to Genesis 20:1–18 and 26:1–16. As Franxman demonstrates, there is evidence that Josephus has borrowed some motifs of the second story for his telling of this first one.[22]

Josephus has narrated Genesis 12:10–20 with numerous alterations but with little change in its picture of Sarah. As in the Bible, he emphasizes her beauty. In fact, the entire incident is predicated on her extreme attractiveness: otherwise, Abraham would not have to worry when entering Egypt. In Josephus' description, Sarah's "beauty was noised abroad," thus presenting the picture of a town crier making it known (I, 163, *ekboaō*). While the Septuagint speaks of her "fairness of face" (*euprosōpos* in Gen. 12:11) and as "very beautiful" (*kalē . . . sphodra* in Gen. 12:14), Josephus describes her beauty by the Greek words *eumorphia* (I, 162) and *kallos* (I, 163), the former term undoubtedly intended to emphasize the beauty and elegance of Sarah's entire person, not just her face. In the tradition, Sarah's beauty became legendary, even being compared with that of Eve.[23]

Unlike the biblical account, Josephus casts the Egyptians in a negative light and stresses their passionate nature: this implies that Sarah is in even greater danger from the king. This, in turn, makes God's intervention more crucial in reversing the situation of Abraham and Sarah. Josephus speaks of the Egyptians' "frenzy for women" (I, 162) and subsequently describes the king's uncontrollable desire to get his hands on Sarah (I, 163). Then, at the end of the story, where Josephus presents the chastised king profusely apologizing to Abraham for taking his wife, he has the king explain that "it was . . . in the belief that she was his sister, not his wife, that he had set his affections on her; he had wished to contract a marriage alliance and not to outrage her in a transport of passion" (I, 165, *epithumia*). The Egyptians' reputation as licentious people, or at least that their rulers exhibited this inclination, was certainly current in Josephus' time, as Philo's account of this biblical incident suggests.[24] Josephus later depicts Potiphar's wife, an Egyptian woman, as love-crazed (*A* II, 41–59) and the Egyptian ruler Cleopatra, of his own times, as intent upon seducing Herod (*A* XV, 96–103).

Both the biblical account and Josephus' rendition focus primarily on the figure of Abraham.[25] In contrast, Sarah remains less prominent in the story. In the biblical version, Abraham addresses Sarah (Gen. 12:11–13), the king has her brought to his house (Gen. 12:15), and in the end the king releases her along with her husband (Gen. 12:20); throughout, she plays a passive role, although her beauty prompts the story's action. Josephus' retelling depicts Sarah in a similar manner, except, we are told, the Egyptian king in his terrified state inquires of Sarah regarding her identity and that of Abraham after he has learned from the priests the reason for the disease and political disturbance (I, 164–165).[26] Presumably, it is from Sarah that he learns the truth.[27]

Josephus' use of this story in his earlier *Jewish War* (V, 379–381) suggests its significance for him. In the passage, Josephus describes himself employing this story to urge his countrymen to surrender to the Romans, on whose side God was. For him the story demonstrated how God's power won out over that of the Pharaoh so that Sarah—designated "a princess" (from the meaning of her name) and "the mother of our race"—was returned "immaculate" to Abraham. Although his use of the story in that setting seems somewhat forced, it is obvious that Josephus counted Sarah's deliverance as a prime example of God's surprising and powerful activity.

Next we consider Josephus' retelling of Genesis 16:1–16, the story of Sarah and Hagar (see *A* I, 186–190). At the outset of this episode, he makes Abraham, not Sarah, the one impatient with her sterility (I, 186). Josephus describes Abraham beseeching God for a male heir, and in response the patriarch is reassured by God that he would have children in the future (*paidōn esomenōn*). At this point, Josephus makes another alteration. In Genesis 16:1–2, it is Sarah herself who instructs her husband to have a child by her servant girl Hagar; in Josephus' version this happens by divine command. In this way, the somewhat impatient action of Sarah is given over to God's initiative. She simply does as commanded.[28]

The subsequent scene involving the pregnant Hagar is also considerably altered by Josephus. While Genesis simply reports that "when she saw that she had conceived, she looked with contempt on her mistress" (Gen. 16:4), Josephus has emphasized Hagar's insolence in the following manner: "Becoming pregnant, this servant had the insolence to abuse Sarra, assuming queenly airs, as though the dominion were to pass to her unborn son" (I, 188). Next, the biblical account states, "Then Sarai dealt harshly with her [Septuagint, *kakoō*], and she fled from her" (Gen. 16:6b). Interestingly, at this point Josephus makes it less obvious that Sarah actually treated Hagar harshly (see I, 188).[29]

Finally, Josephus' modification of the scene depicting Hagar in the wilderness is noteworthy (Gen. 16:7–14). In the biblical story, the angel instructs Hagar to return to her mistress, promises her descendants, and names her yet unborn son. In Josephus, the divine messenger makes it quite clear that Hagar's plight is of her own making and that she has sinned against Sarah and should seek pardon when she returns home. We are then told that, obedient to the angel, Hagar did return to her master and mistress and did receive pardon. Thereafter, she gave birth to Ishmael.

Thus, by slight yet significant alterations, Josephus casts a favorable light on Sarah, the mother of the Jewish race, who still remains childless. Though she is clearly pictured as the victim of severe abuse from her own maidservant, Sarah does not deal harshly with her but extends a pardon to her.

Sarah next appears in the scene involving the angelic visitors at Mamre (see Gen. 18:1–15). In the Josephan retelling, Abraham does not specifically instruct Sarah to prepare meal cakes for the visitors as in the biblical account (Gen. 18:6). Hellenizing the scene, Josephus describes the action as taking place at the entrance to the courtyard of a Greek house (I, 196, *aulē*), rather than before a tent (Gen. 18:2), and depicts Abraham acting as the master of the house commanding assistants to prepare food for the visitors (I, 197).

Further, Josephus has abridged Sarah's part in the story, omitting apparently negative references to her. We hear nothing about her listening at the door and about her denial, prompted by fear, that she has laughed at the announcement of the approaching birth of her child (see Gen. 18:9–15).[30] Rather, she is shown "smiling" (I, 198, *meidiaō*), because she knows that childbearing is impossible at her age. Josephus closes this account with the divine messengers revealing their identity.

In *Antiquities* I, 207–212, Josephus recounts Genesis 20:1–18, the incident involving Abraham and Sarah in Gerar and the encounter with Abimelech. Little new information is added in Josephus' depiction of the matriarch. Once again, presumably due to her great beauty, Sarah becomes the intended victim of the lustful desires of a foreign king. Once again, her husband Abraham is not blamed for his apparent deception but is accorded great deference and honor. Once again, it is God's intervention which punishes an evil king and brings him and others to a recognition of the importance of Abraham and Sarah. It is indeed significant that Josephus has chosen to include this story, which is so similar to the previous one. He has evidently considered their themes worthy of reemphasis.

Genesis 21:1–7, which relates the birth of Isaac, is recounted by Josephus in *Antiquities* I, 213–214. Here he links "laughter" as the meaning of Isaac's name (I, 213, *gelōta*) with his earlier reference to Sarah's "smiling" (*meidiasai*), which is less logical than the biblical account's description. Consistently avoiding direct speech, Josephus also here omits Sarah's own words, "God has made laughter for me; every one who hears will laugh over me. . . . Who would have said to Abraham that Sarah would suckle children? Yet I have borne him a son in his old age" (Gen. 21:6f.).

In the final major scene involving Sarah and Hagar (Gen. 21:8–21), Josephus offers some modifications of the story in his retelling. Right at the outset, he comments that Sarah had held an affection for Ishmael as though he were her own son until she gave birth to Isaac (I, 215). Then, as in the biblical account (Gen. 21:10), she wants Ishmael sent away. In Josephus, her motive seems more reasonable since she fears for Isaac's life, thinking that once Abraham is dead Ishmael will do him harm.[31] In the Bible, we are told only that Sarah does not want Ishmael, the slave, to be an heir with her son. In dealing with his wife's request, Abraham is pictured by Josephus as a noble humanitarian who resists her suggestion out of sympathy for Ishmael and Hagar, but he finally submits to it when he learns of its divine approval.

A few other isolated passages must be cited to fill out Josephus' portrait of Sarah. It is striking that Josephus inserts in the narrative of the Aqedah (Gen. 22:1ff.) the following explanation: "Abraham . . . concealed from his wife God's commandment and his own resolve concerning the immolation of the child; nay, revealing it not even to any of his household, lest haply he should have been hindered from doing God's service" (I, 225). Although the implied motive is noted, thus stressing Abraham's determination to be obedient to God's plan, it is noteworthy that Sarah is here brought into the story at a place where she is not mentioned in the Bible.[32]

Then in *Antiquities* I, 236, after the sacrifice of Isaac has turned out favorably, Josephus writes an ending not in the biblical account (cf. Gen. 22:19): "And they [Abraham and Isaac], restored to each other beyond all hope and having heard promises of such great felicity, embraced one another and, the sacrifice ended, returned home to Sarra and lived in bliss, God assisting them in all that they desired." In this way, Josephus brings the Sarah story to a happy conclusion. Immediately hereafter he mentions her death, following Genesis 23:1–2, and states that she was buried in Hebron, where the local residents "offered burial-ground for her at the public expense" (I, 237).[33] Although Abraham does not accept their offer, Josephus' little addition makes it clear that even the people outside Sarah's family recognize her grandeur as the wife of Abraham and the mother of the Jewish race (see again *BJ* V, 380). All in all, Josephus has painted a rather positive portrait of this first matriarch.

Portrayal of Rebekah

Next we consider Josephus' portrayal of Rebekah. His retelling of Genesis 24:1–67, the story describing the search for a wife for Isaac, holds primary importance for his depiction of Rebekah. Here, he has altered more than details; he has changed the overall thrust of the story (see *A* I, 242–255).

In the biblical narrative, Genesis 24 provides another step toward God's fulfilling the promise reiterated in 24:7: "To you I will give this land and to your seed" (my translation of the Septuagint). The focus is on Abraham and how, in particular, securing a wife for Isaac is essential to the divine promise to him. Before Abraham dies, the readers know that Isaac is to marry and will thereupon continue the lineage of his father.

In contrast, Josephus' retelling of the first verse already reveals a rather different purpose. Drawing on Genesis 25:20, Josephus begins by explaining that Isaac is forty years old, a sufficient age for marriage.[34] Eliminating the suspense of the biblical account, where it is not yet known who will be the bride, Josephus states that Abraham has decided to arrange for Isaac a marriage with Rebekah, the granddaughter of his brother Nahor (I, 242). In other words, the Josephan account begins as though it is describing a marriage alliance being prearranged by the head of the family, Abraham himself. Like the biblical account the focus is on Abraham, but it is for different reasons.

This change in emphasis is further seen in Josephus' retelling of Genesis 24:2–9. Though Josephus does mention, and even explains for his Gentile readers, the Oriental manner of taking an oath (I, 243), he omits Abraham's reason for administering it—to insure that his servant does not seek a wife for Isaac from the daughters of the Canaanites (see Gen. 24:3). He can even subsequently have Abraham's envoy boast of the marriage which could have been arranged in Canaan with "the wealthiest of the women yonder" (I, 253). Perhaps Josephus made these modifications for apologetic reasons, wishing to portray Jewish openness to the non-Jewish world.

Further, Josephus omits reference to the "divine messenger," [35] describing instead Abraham's sending rare and priceless gifts to the ones in Mesopotamia (I, 243), a theme not mentioned in the biblical account until Genesis 24:10, where there is no emphasis on the rare and priceless quality of the gifts. He also has changed the thrust of the servant's conversation with Laban and Rebekah's mother, which in the biblical account demonstrates God's guiding purpose for Abraham through the events which have transpired (see Gen. 24:34–49). Though in *Antiquities* I, 254, he does mention that all on the servant's journey was according to God's will, Josephus uses the servant's speech to highlight the following themes: the authority and prestige of Abraham, Isaac as the legitimate and sole heir to Abraham's estate, and the importance of the marriage proposal to Rebekah's family (see I, 253–255).

In summary, then, though mention is still made of God's will, the weight of Josephus' account is on the significance of the man Abraham and on the importance of Rebekah's family accepting his marriage proposal for his legitimate heir. Josephus seems more interested in portraying the marriage alliance arranged by Abraham than the biblical theme of God's fulfilling the promise about Abraham's descendants inheriting the land. Writing from Rome after the fiasco of A.D. 70, Josephus would have seen little reason to highlight the bibli-´ cal promise about the land, a theme which could have appeared treasonous to the Romans.[36]

Before we conclude our analysis of Josephus' rendition of Genesis 24, we need to note how he portrays Rebekah in contrast to the Bible's depiction. When Rebekah first appears in the biblical narrative (Gen. 24:15f.), she is immediately described in the following manner: "The maiden [Septuagint, *parthenos*] was very fair to look upon [Septuagint, *kalē tēi opsei sphodra*], a virgin [*parthenos*], whom no man had known." Both her physical attractiveness and virginity are emphasized, making her an appropriate wife for Isaac. Further, fulfilling the sign established by the servant's prayer, Rebekah eagerly gives him a drink of water when requested and gladly waters the camels as well (Gen. 24:17–20).

Josephus makes some significant changes in this scene. He omits the reference to her physical beauty and virginity,[37] and has Rebekah rebuke the other women for refusing to give the servant water (I, 246). To quote Franxman, "The form of Rebekah's rebuke is moralizing and somewhat sophisticated: 'What will you ever share with anyone, who refuse even a drop of water?' "[38] Thus, Rebekah is here portrayed as one who knows the demands of hospitality and exhorts her peers who ignore them. In turn, she offers water to the stranger "hospitably" (*philophronōs*).

Only at this juncture in the story does Josephus include descriptive words for Rebekah. They are not of her external appearance but of her moral and mental qualities: the servant commends her for her "nobility" (*eugeneia*) and "kindness" (*chrēstotēs*), the former term pointing to noble ancestry and aristocratic mentality (I, 247). According to Josephus, these descriptions are appropriate because she did not hesitate "to minister to another's need at the cost of her own toil" (I, 247). Further, Josephus notes that the jewelry is specifically given to Rebekah as a reward for her graciousness (I, 249). Then, in superlative fashion, she is commended as one "having outstripped so many maidens in charity" (*agathēn*). Finally, we are told that the servant deduces the qualities that Rebekah's mother and brother must possess from observation of her virtue (I, 250, *aretē*).

All in all, Rebekah is portrayed as a worthy match for Isaac. She is a young woman of noble ancestry and exhibits praiseworthy qualities. Her moral excellence takes precedence over her physical beauty. Abraham's marriage proposal is gladly accepted by her family not only because it is divinely blessed, but also because it honors Abraham and unites two outstanding families (see the words of the servant in I, 247). Since we have discovered few parallels between the biblical narrative and Josephus' account, it appears that he has freely retold this story to make it more attractive to his Hellenistic audience.

Having considered the longest segment in which Rebekah is a central figure, we must still briefly examine Josephus' recasting of other biblical sections mentioning her. First, we consider I, 257–258, which offers Josephus' account of Genesis 25:20–26. Following Genesis 25:1–18, which traces Abraham's progeny through his other wife Keturah and notes the patriarch's death, Genesis 25:20–26 shifts the focus to Isaac and Rebekah. Emphasis here is on the delay in the promise that Abraham will have descendants via Isaac, this point being made by the bracketing notations of Isaac's age: he was forty when he married Rebekah and sixty years old after the birth of the twins. Thus, for twenty years Rebekah remained barren, and this provided the motive for Isaac's prayer to God. God answered his prayer and Rebekah conceived.

According to the Josephan account, Isaac's "young wife" (the diminutive form *gynaion*) conceives immediately following Abraham's death. In this case, Isaac consults God because he sees his wife "inordinately big with child" (I, 257). In the biblical narrative it is Rebekah who inquires of God about the twins struggling within her (see Gen. 25:22f.), while in Josephus the Lord informs Isaac about the twins, including the fact that the younger would excel the older one. Josephus ends this section by combining information about the twins' names with the mention of the parents' preferences (mentioned in Gen. 25:28): "The father loved the elder son . . . , but Jacob the younger was the darling (*prosphilēs*) of his mother." [39]

Second, Josephus has omitted the incident involving Isaac's concealing that Rebekah was his wife while dwelling in Gerar among the Philistines (Gen. 26:6–11). Although Josephus has related the two similar stories about Sarah, he makes no mention of this episode in I, 259–262. Perhaps he has done so since he has avoided mentioning Rebekah's physical beauty, a feature crucial to this incident (Gen. 26:7), and wants to portray her as an exemplar unworthy of such treatment.[40]

Third, the reference to Esau's two Hittite wives making "life bitter for Isaac and Rebekah" (Gen. 26:35) is omitted by Josephus in I, 265–266. We are told rather that Esau contracted his marriages on his own without consulting his father. Though not approving these marriages, Isaac "resolved to hold his peace."

Fourth, as in the biblical account of Jacob's securing his father's blessing ahead of Esau (Gen. 27:5–17), Rebekah plays a role in the Josephan version, though somewhat reduced and nuanced differently (see I, 269–270). In Genesis 27:5ff., Rebekah overhears her husband instructing Esau to secure savory food prior to his blessing him, and she then devises the plot which allows Jacob to win that blessing. When Jacob is fearful of detection and being cursed, Rebekah bluntly states, "Upon me be your curse, my son; only obey my word" (Gen. 27:13). This statement of Rebekah is not repeated in Josephus' account; rather, he portrays her as a strong woman who helps to work God's purpose in the situation: "But Rebekah, being determined to invoke God's favor (*eunoia*) upon Jacob, even in defiance of Isaac's intent, bade him kill some kids and prepare a meal. And Jacob obeyed his mother, taking all his instructions from her." Rebekah is here portrayed as the dominant force who seeks to win God's approval for her beloved son.[41]

Fifth, Genesis 27:42–46, wherein Rebekah hears of Esau's plan to kill his younger brother and gets Jacob to flee to Laban, is summarized by Josephus I, 276 with the words, "Jacob being now in terror of his brother . . . was rescued by his mother, who persuaded her husband to take a wife for him from his kinsfolk in Mesopotamia." Rebekah here becomes the rescuer and the "source of the idea of a marriage with a Mesopotamian relative."[42] Further, in I, 278, we are told that Isaac consented to the marriage "in compliance with his wife's wishes."

Finally, later in the narrative when Jacob relates his story to Laban and family, Josephus has him speak of his mother's role in securing the blessing for him as issuing from her "wisdom" (I, 295, *sophia*). He also indicates that his coming to them was in compliance with his mother's command (I, 296, "kata tēn tēs mētros entolēn").

In conclusion, we have seen that Josephus' retelling of the episodes involving the matriarch Rebekah adds up to a rather consistent and positive portrayal of her. She is a woman of noble background who exemplifies virtuous characteristics; thus, she is a good match for Isaac, the son of Abraham. In the episodes involving Rebekah and Isaac, Josephus presents her as a strong woman, who, in favoring Jacob, acts decisively and prudently to assist in determining God's favor for him. He thus has presented a more positive evaluation of Rebekah than does the biblical narrative.[43]

Portrayal of Rachel and Leah

Given Josephus' penchant for abridging much of the biblical narrative, it is noteworthy that he retells the meeting of Jacob and Rachel at the well with considerable elaboration (compare Gen. 29:1–29 with *A* I, 285–302).[44] Josephus' reworking of the opening scene of this story has assigned more action to Rachel than is the case in the biblical account. In addition to noting that young maidens[45] as well as young men are at the well to welcome Jacob (I, 285) and that all view Laban as a prominent man in the community (I, 286), Josephus depicts Rachel's reaction to meeting Jacob as youthful exuberance. Unlike Genesis 29:13, where Laban greets Jacob with a kiss, in the Josephan version Rachel is the one to welcome Jacob affectionately upon hearing of the close relationship between their families. Recalling the story her father told about Jacob's mother, Rebekah, Rachel breaks into tears and flings her arms about Jacob. After this tender embrace, she declares that Jacob's arrival will bring the greatest pleasure to her father (I, 292).

Although he omits Jacob's kiss of Rachel (see Gen. 29:11), Josephus emphasizes Jacob's erotic love for her. Josephus declares that Jacob is strongly attracted to Rachel, not merely due to the affection of kinship but because of passionate feelings (I, 288, *erōs*). Jacob is deeply stirred by her beauty, Josephus noting that Rachel possessed a beauty "such as few women of those days could show" (I, 288). Perhaps Josephus considered a kiss by Jacob inappropriate since in his depiction it would be prompted by more than the affection of a relative.[46]

The next part of the story, Jacob's conversation and agreement with Laban, also exhibits different accents in Josephus' retelling. The biblical account straightway describes Jacob's agreement with Laban, committing Jacob to work for seven years in exchange for Rachel. Here Leah is introduced and described with the phrase "[her] eyes were weak" (Septuagint Gen. 29:17, *astheneis*), while for the first time we are told that Rachel was beautiful and lovely ("kalē tōi eidei kai hōraia tēi opsei"). Further, we are informed that the seven years "seemed to him but a few days because of the love he had for her" (Septuagint Gen. 29:20, *agapan*). Then Laban's deception on Jacob's wedding night is described, when he substitutes Leah for Rachel. In response to Jacob's angry questions, Laban explains his motive for doing so and then promises to give Rachel as a second wife after the nuptial week with Leah is completed. Thus, after one week Jacob is given Rachel as well, for whom he will work another seven years (Gen. 29:21–30).

Josephus considerably expands the conversation between Laban and Jacob, having it occur some days after Jacob's arrival (I, 294). Expressing great joy at his presence, Laban inquires about Jacob's reason for coming. In response, Jacob recounts all that has happened, rehearsing the trouble between him and his brother and crediting Rebekah's wise action in securing him the blessing. Further, he cites Esau's threat on his life and notes how in compliance with his mother's order he came to Laban's family (I, 295–296). Strikingly, Josephus has Jacob describe Esau's anger at being deprived of "God's destined gift of the kingdom [basileia] and of the benefits invoked by his father," as though he were reporting a struggle between two claimants to a throne in the Hellenistic world.

At this juncture in the conversation, Laban promises to shower every kindness on Jacob because of their kinship and particularly because of his devotion to his sister Rebekah. He plans to make Jacob overseer of his flocks and further indicates that Jacob may return to his home whenever he pleases, laden with gifts and honors as a relative (I, 297). Jacob agrees to remain with Laban for some time and requests that he be given Rachel as wife in payment for his work. According to Josephus, Jacob stresses how worthy Rachel is of his esteem because of her service to him when he arrived, but again Jacob's passionate love for her is noted (I, 298). Agreeing to seven years of service, Jacob wants this time to prove his worth to Laban (I, 300). When the wedding night arrives, Josephus first mentions Leah and describes her as "devoid of beauty" (I, 301, "tēn opsin ouk euprepē").[47] Further, he attempts to explain how Jacob could have been deceived by Laban; Jacob was "deluded by wine and the dark" (I, 301). At daylight, when the deceit is discovered, Laban asks for Jacob's pardon and indicates that if he still loves (erōnti) Rachel, he may have her as wife after another seven years of service (I, 302). Jacob, we are told, submits to this because of his love (I, 302, erōs) for the maiden. Unlike the biblical account, in which Jacob is given Rachel as wife and then works an additional seven years, Josephus suggests a seven year lapse of time before Jacob takes Rachel as wife.[48]

Though like the biblical account Josephus portrays Jacob and Laban as the prominent figures in this section, both Rachel and Leah are important to the action. Josephus depicts Leah as physically unattractive, evidently interpreting the biblical phrase to mean this; otherwise, he in no way adds to her part in the story. Having already described the beauty of Rachel, in this portion Josephus repeatedly draws attention to Jacob's love for her, each time employing Greek words which connote passionate and erotic love, a theme which is prominent in his writings.[49]

We must analyze a few more segments of the narrative to complete Josephus' portrayal of Rachel and Leah. First of all, Josephus' account of Genesis 29:31–30:24, relating the domestic struggle between Jacob's two wives, begins by his noting that the two handmaids were "in no way slaves but subordinates" (I, 303). Thereupon, he explains Leah's fecundity as a result of her continual supplication to God. Her prayers for children had been prompted, we are told, by her being negatively affected by Jacob's passion for Rachel. Leah was hoping to win her husband's esteem and affection by giving him male heirs. Unlike the silence of the Bible at this point, Josephus informs us that Jacob was indeed drawn to Leah after the birth of the first son (I, 304). According to Josephus, Rachel's motive for offering her maid to Jacob was her fear that Leah's "fecundity would lessen her own share in her husband's affection" (I, 305). Nothing is mentioned of Rachel's angry exchange with Jacob, wherein her barrenness is linked with God (Gen. 30:1–2). After the two sons were born to Rachel's maid, Josephus indicates that Leah "responded to her sister's action by the same strategem: she too gave her own handmaid as concubine" (I, 306). The closing episode involving the mandrake roots is re- told quite in accord with the content of the biblical account except in two re- spects. Josephus notes that Jacob slept with Leah "to please Rachel," [50] and he neglects to include the reference in Genesis 30:22f. that when God remem- bered Rachel, her response was "God has taken away my reproach."

In summary, Josephus' treatment of this segment involving the competi- tion between Jacob's two wives emphasizes the struggle between Rachel and Leah more so than does the Bible. Rachel is portrayed as the favorite wife, but Leah's desperate efforts to win her husband's affection are at least temporarily successful. This success, in turn, causes Rachel to worry about her place with Jacob. This emotional tug of war for Jacob's affection and the struggle to pro- vide him male heirs seem to be of keen interest to Josephus by the way he retells the stories. His retelling, with its accent on erotic romance and domes- tic intrigue, is reminiscent of some of his other stories recounting Hasmonaean and Herodian families.

Finally, with little comment we note a few remaining references to Rachel and Leah in the Josephan narrative. Once Jacob is prepared to leave Laban, he tests his wives' feelings about this, and we learn that they are willing to mi- grate (I, 310). We are then told, as in the Bible, that Rachel took Laban's household gods. However, Josephus makes clear that she does so not because she worships them but because they will serve as a bargaining tool with Laban, for Rachel has been taught to "despise such worship" by Jacob (I, 311). As in the biblical account (Gen. 31:34f.), Rachel does not rise from the camel due to her womanly condition when Laban comes searching for the images (I, 322). In Jacob's long exchange with Laban, he indicates that his wives follow him because of their own affection, particularly for their children (I, 318), and subsequently he swears to love these two daughters of Laban.

As in Genesis 35:16–20, Rachel dies while giving birth to Benjamin (I, 343). Josephus emphasizes that she is deeply mourned and mentions that only she was not honored with a burial at Hebron. As in the Bible, Josephus never tells us about Leah's death. He does mention, however, that Rebekah was not alive when Jacob returned to Hebron (I, 345). The matriarchs are gone from the scene, but not forgotten.

Josephus has generally portrayed Rachel and Leah in terms similar to the biblical narrative, making occasional modifications to emphasize certain themes. Josephus highlights Rachel's beauty and Jacob's deep affection for her, but her position as the favored wife was threatened by her failure to bear children. Though not given much action in most of the stories, Rachel is depicted by Josephus as enthusiastic and delightfully affectionate in her opening scene of meeting Jacob. In her struggle with her sister, Rachel could act out of desperation, and in stealing the images she could act deceptively. Leah, on the other hand, is given even less action. Josephus makes clear that she is "devoid of beauty" and thus at a disadvantage in regard to Rachel. But Leah is the one who is extremely successful in childbearing, and this wins at least temporary affection for her from Jacob. Both wives return with Jacob to Canaan and are loved by him. Tragically, Rachel dies in childbirth and is deeply mourned. The Bible, and Josephus, say nothing about Leah's death. She fades from the scene but remains known through her sons.

Conclusion

Our study has demonstrated just how freely Josephus has rendered the episodes involving the matriarchs, so that when compared to the biblical accounts many striking differences appear. He has done so despite his claim that he neither added nor omitted anything from the biblical narrative (A I, 17). As my endnotes reveal, a number of these Josephan alterations have some parallel, though most often not close, in the Jewish midrashic tradition. On the whole, it would appear that Josephus has been influenced by Hellenistic literary conventions (certainly also influential in other parts of the midrashic tradition) and has sought to provide positive portrayals of the matriarchs so that they would be viewed as exemplary representatives of the Jewish people. His Hellenizing idealization of these women accords with his expressed motive for writing the history of his people, directing it primarily to non-Jewish readers: "And now I have undertaken this present work in the belief that the whole Greek-speaking world will find it worthy of attention; for it will embrace our entire ancient history and political constitution, translated from the Hebrew records" (I, 5).

Josephus is writing apologetically; he wants his history to demonstrate the superiority of the Jewish religion in its witness to the one God and in its moral excellence. The Josephan versions of the matriarchal stories, as is indeed the case in his retelling of the Abrahamic stories, seem to serve this overarching apologetic. The women are portrayed in ways to make them understandable, attractive, and even exemplary to Hellenistic readers.

Josephus has portrayed the matriarchs as strong figures and good matches for their husbands. Bearing some likeness to prominent mothers in the Hellenistic history later narrated by Josephus, the matriarchs are concerned with the affection of their husbands and the fortune of their children: Sarah protects the welfare of Isaac in the face of Ishmael; Rebekah invites divine blessing on her favorite son, Jacob, rather than Esau; and Rachel and Leah contend for Jacob's love primarily by producing sons as heirs for him. It seems unlikely that Josephus could have told these stories without recalling the exploits of Hasmonaean and Herodian women and others closer to his day who were engaged in similar domestic struggles. In contrast to some of these later stories, the matriarchs are generally pictured in a positive light and are undoubtedly intended as examples of moral excellence to be admired by Greek readers.

In particular, Rebekah stands out as the wise woman of noble upbringing who exhibits exemplary moral qualities. By the early Roman imperial period, an idealized picture of the noble matron has developed in literature; she is praised for her noble traits as well as her fecundity.[51] In his *Jewish War,* Josephus more than once accents this motif when describing female figures, one example being his depiction of Herod's favorite wife, Mariamme (she was of Hasmonean descent), not only as beautiful but also as "most sagacious of women" (I, 262). Readers were probably being invited to view Rebekah and the other matriarchs as exemplifying this kind of woman. Further, in the spirit of the Hellenistic romances, the beauty of Sarah and Rachel is especially highlighted, though he has avoided mentioning Rebekah's physical attributes. Rachel had beauty surpassing many of her day, while Sarah was so attractive that foreign kings desired her.

Throughout his writings, Josephus has revealed much interest in the theme of erotic love, which was given increasing emphasis during the Hellenistic time.[52] In the stories examined, he seems to depict passionate love both positively and negatively. On the positive side, he stresses that erotic feelings attract Jacob to Rachel and prompt him to labor another seven years to win her as his second wife. Josephus leaves the impression that Rachel remains Jacob's favorite wife to the end of her life (he spends a night with Leah only to please Rachel).

On the other side, Josephus presents the two episodes involving Sarah as the object of a foreigner's lustful intent to demonstrate the negative force of unchecked passion. Two later biblical stories, as revised by Josephus, make this lesson even more explicit. In his version of the incident between Joseph and Potiphar's wife (an Egyptian woman), he pictures Joseph as a righteous follower of God, resisting temptation and lecturing her on the folly of passion (*A* II, 51–52). Josephus has undoubtedly reworked this biblical story with full awareness of his post-biblical accounts, in which prominent and influential men were wasted by their passion for beautiful women (e.g., *BJ* I, 243, where he depicts "Antony, now a slave to his passion for Cleopatra"). With a somewhat different twist, this theme regarding the danger of erotic love permeates Josephus' retelling of the story of the Midianite daughters who lead the Hebrew males to idolatry (*A* IV, 126–151). Also, in his final description of the lawgiver Moses, he suggests his ideal for a man controlling his passions, and in doing so he comes close to the Philonic depiction of the patriarchs who strive for the higher life of reason over passion: "In speech and in addresses to a crowd he found favor in every way, but chiefly through his thorough command of his passion (*tōn pathōn*), which was such that he seemed to have no place for them at all in his soul, and only knew their names through seeing them in others rather than in himself" (*A* IV, 328–329).

Though the erotic theme plays a role in Josephus' rendering of the matriarchal stories, it is clear that such feelings are to be confined to marriage, as this later speech of Joseph teaches. Both Sarah and Rachel are beautiful, yet portrayed as faithful to their husbands.

In summary, we have seen that Josephus has not only Hellenized the stories of the matriarchs but also altered the biblical narrative toward an idealization of these women from Jewish history, in particular Sarah, Rebekah, and Rachel. At a number of points, he has clearly enhanced the portrayals of the matriarchs, but by no means going so far as to allegorize them into virtues as did Philo. In the Josephan depiction, the matriarchs still come across as realistic figures, who, like their patriarchal counterparts, are exemplary in most of their actions and thoughts.

Below I list the biblical details altered or excised by Josephus. Most of these modifications seem to enhance the portraits of the matriarchs:

Sarah's Portrait
Her impatient action of giving Hagar to Abraham is by divine command (I, 187)
Her complaint to Abraham about Hagar is omitted (cf. Gen. 16:5)
Her dealing with Hagar harshly is omitted (cf. Gen. 16:6)
Her servant role of making meal cakes for visitors is omitted (cf. Gen. 18:6)

Her listening behind the tent door is omitted (cf. Gen. 18:10)

Her laughter and apparent disbelief are changed to a "smile" (I, 198)

Her denial that she laughed, prompted by fear, is omitted (cf. Gen. 18:15)

Her positive words are omitted (cf. Gen. 21:6f.; Josephus generally eliminates dialogue)

Her jealous motive is altered (cf. Gen. 21:10)

Rebekah's Portrait

Mention of her beauty is omitted (cf. Gen. 24:16)

Her barrenness is not emphasized (cf. Gen. 25:21)

Her inquiry about the twins within (to God) is replaced by Isaac's prayer (cf. Gen. 25:22f.)

The Gerar scene, where Rebekah is the object of passion, is omitted (cf. Gen. 26:6ff.)

Mention of Esau making life bitter for her and Jacob is omitted (cf. Gen. 26:35)

Her overhearing Isaac's instructions to Esau is omitted (cf. Gen. 27:5)

Her devising and executing the scheme to get a blessing for Jacob is omitted (cf. Gen. 27:6–10)

Her inviting the curse upon herself is omitted (cf. Gen. 27:11–13)

Her hearing of Esau's intent to kill Jacob and causing Jacob to flee is omitted (cf. Gen. 27:42–46)

Rachel's Portrait

Her being kissed by Jacob at their meeting is omitted (cf. Gen. 29:10f.)

Her envy and angry exchange with Jacob, implying that her barrenness is divinely caused, are omitted (cf. Gen. 30:1–2)

Her statement that God has taken away her reproach is omitted (cf. Gen. 30:22f.)

Her stealing the household images is given a more honorable motive (I, 311)

Her deception of her father is lightened by a statement that he did not suspect her (I, 323)

Leah's Portrait

Reference to her "weak eyes" is omitted but later replaced with another statement about her lack of beauty (cf. Gen. 29:17)

The statement "When the Lord saw that Leah was hated" is omitted (cf. Gen. 29:31)

Keeping in view this sizable list of Josephan omissions and alterations of apparently negative aspects of the biblical accounts, we now offer a composite picture for each matriarch of the favorable features and depictions that might invoke the reader's sympathy. Whenever there is an asterisk preceding the entry, that particular description is also in the biblical account though in a different form.

Sarah's Portrait

Text	Favorable Features	Other Features
Gen. 12: 10–20	*beauty of body (*eumorphia*) (I, 162–163) tells the truth to king (I, 165) *chastity preserved by God (I, 164–165)	*Object of foreigner's passion (I, 161–165)
Gen. 16: 1–16	Not impatient with herself for her sterility (I, 186) Hagar reminded by angel of the good life with her mistress (I, 189f.) Sarah and Abraham grant pardon to the returning Hagar (I, 190)	*Object of Hagar's abuse (I, 188) *Sarah still without child (I, 186)
Gen. 18: 1–15	Sarah "smiles" (I, 198)	
Gen. 20: 1–18	*beauty not explicitly mentioned *Sarah not violated (I, 209)	*Object of foreigner's passion (I, 207–208)
Gen. 21: 8–21	Deep affection for Ishmael (I, 215) Reasonable motive for expelling Ishmael (I, 215)	*Abraham's initial refusal to comply altered by seeing that Sarah's wish is sanctioned by God (I, 217)
Gen. 22: 1ff.		Abraham conceals plan for sacrifice of Isaac from Sarah (I, 225)
Gen. 22: 19	Final bliss for Sarah and Abraham (I, 236)	
Gen. 23: 1–2	People offer burial place to honor Sarah at her death (I, 237)	

Rebekah's Portrait

Text	Favorable Features	Other Features
Gen. 24: 1–67	Marriage proposal heightens Rebekah's importance —she is given rare and priceless gifts (I, 243) —the envoy endures difficult trip (I, 244) —she is to marry the legitimate and sole heir of the wealthy Abraham (I, 253) —marriage could have been arranged with a wealthy Canaanite family (I, 253) —marriage is to honor her and her family (I, 253–254) She is shown as morally exhorting other women (I, 246) She possesses characteristics of nobility and kindness (I, 247) Jewelry rewards her goodness (I, 249) Her virtue is apparent (I, 251) Her family is noble, humanitarian, and generous (I, 251) Her virginity is under the guardianship of Laban (I, 248)	
Gen. 25: 20–26	As young wife, she conceives (I, 257)	Isaac prays over Rebekah's condition (I, 257) *Jacob is her "darling" (I, 258)
Gen. 26: 6–11	(the entire episode omitted)	
Gen. 27: 5–17	She invokes God's favor on Jacob (I, 269) *Jacob obeys Rebekah's command (I, 269)	
Gen. 27: 42–46	She rescues terrified Jacob (I, 276) She initiates the idea to send	

Jacob for a Mesopotamian
marriage (I, 276)
*Isaac complies with her wishes
(I, 278)

Gen. 29:   Jacob refers to Rebekah's
1ff.   wisdom (I, 295)
         Jacob obeys his mother's order
         (I, 296)

Rachel's Portrait

Text	Favorable Features	Other Features
Gen. 29: 1–29	Rachel's father is well known (I, 286) She reacts youthfully and openly to Jacob (I, 287) *She possesses beauty ("such as few women of those days could show," I, 288) Rachel warmly embraces Jacob (I, 292) Rachel is worthy of Jacob's esteem (I, 298) *Leah is devoid of beauty in comparison with Rachel (I, 301) *Jacob's love causes him to work for seven more years (I, 302)	*Jacob's passion for Rachel is stressed (I, 288, I, 298, I, 302)
Gen. 29: 31–30: 24	Jacob spends a night with Leah to please Rachel (I, 307)	*Handmaids are not slaves but subordinates (I, 303) Rachel fears losing Jacob's affection (I, 305)
Gen. 31: 1ff.	*Rachel (and Leah) are consulted by Jacob about leaving (I, 310) Rachel is said to follow Jacob because of her affection for husband and child (I, 318) Jacob swears to love her (and Leah) (I, 327)	
		*At death, Rachel is deeply mourned and is the only one not honored by burial at Hebron (I, 343)

Leah's Portrait

Text	Favorable Features	Other Features
Gen. 29: 1–29	*Leah as older daughter is substituted for Rachel (I, 301)	She is devoid of beauty (I, 301)
Gen. 29: 31–30: 24		*Handmaids are not slaves but subordinates (I, 303) Leah's fecundity results from prayers prompted by her jealousy of Jacob's passion for Rachel (I, 303) Leah wins Jacob's affection for a while (I, 305)
Gen. 29: 31	*Leah has many sons (I, 304–308) She bargains mandrake root for a night with Jacob since Rachel robbed her of husband's esteem (I, 307)	*She has Jacob for another night, though not as his favorite wife (I, 307) *She gives her handmaid to Jacob in a counter strategy (I, 306)
Gen. 31: 1ff.	*Leah (and Rachel) are consulted about leaving (I, 310) Leah (and Rachel) accompany Jacob because of wifely and motherly affection (I, 318) Jacob swears to love her (and Rachel) (I, 323) She is known for her six sons (I, 344)	*Dinah, Leah's daughter, is raped (I, 337–340) Leah's death or burial place are not noted

Though using another literary form, Ben Sira saw fit to praise only the famous men of Israel's history, including Abraham, Isaac, and Jacob (see Ben Sira 44:1–50:24). In contrast, Josephus has reworked the biblical history so as to offer praise to some women as well. Recently Feldman has further shown that Josephus has clearly aggrandized the major male biblical heroes, such as Abraham, Joseph, Moses, and even Saul.[53] We have seen that Josephus has not left untouched the portraits of the matriarchs. They, too, have been recolored in favorable tones, if ever so subtly at points, undoubtedly to commend them as strong and attractive heroines out of the Jewish tradition. Thus, Josephus has enhanced the portraits of the matriarchs, but he has done so without any apparent change in his own misogynistic attitudes toward most women. For him, this would present no contradiction, since he likely assigned the matriarchs to the aristocratic class, as understood in terms of his day, and not to be compared with common women.[54] Thus, Josephus could hold vastly divergent attitudes toward these two categories of women.

Notes

1. I know of three studies that investigate Josephus' treatment of specific biblical stories involving women. Martin Braun, *Griechischer Roman und hellenistische Geschichtsschreibung* (Frankfurt, 1934) analyzes Josephus' version of the story of Joseph and Potiphar's wife and concludes that Josephus has refashioned it along the lines of a Hellenistic romance. W. C. van Unnik, "Josephus' Account of the Story of Israel's Sin with Alien Women in the Country of Midian (Num. 25:1ff.)," *Travels in the World of the Old Testament: Studies Presented to Prof. M. A. Beek* (Assen, 1974), 241–261, demonstrates that Josephus' elaboration of this biblical incident highlights how the Midianite women sexually entice the Hebrew young men into the sin of idolatry, and thus his reworked version becomes a warning to Jews in Hellenistic times not to apostatize. Only Louis H. Feldman in his article "Hellenizations in Josephus' Version of Esther," *TAPA* 101 (1970), 143–170, focuses on a biblical story of a Jewish heroine. Feldman concludes that Josephus' Hellenizing alterations of the Esther story were designed to make it more appealing to Gentile readers of the first century A.D., and in various ways to combat anti-Semitic propaganda. As far as I can determine, no scholar has undertaken a study which attempts to treat systematically Josephus' portrayal of women in the *Antiquities* or in all his writings.

2. In *V*, 362–364, Josephus' comments suggest that *The Jewish War* was completed during the reign of Titus (A.D. 79–81), and in *A* XX, 267, he states that *The Jewish Antiquities* were finished in the "thirteenth year of the reign of Domitian Caesar," or A.D. 93/94. His two minor works, *Life* and *Against Apion*, were composed later than A.D. 94. For treatments of the scant biographical data about Josephus, read H. St. John Thackeray, *Josephus: The Man and the Historian* (New York, 1929; reprint, Ktav, 1967), 15f., and Thomas W. Franxman, *Genesis and the "Jewish Antiquities" of Flavius Josephus* (Biblica et Orientalia 35) (Rome, 1979), 1–5.

3. Louis H. Feldman, "Abraham the Greek Philosopher in Josephus," *TAPA* 99 (1968), 143–156, especially 156.

4. Franxman (above, note 2), 285–289, concludes his investigation by noting the sections of the Genesis narrative either expanded or abridged by Josephus, or those accorded a balance between the original material in Genesis and Josephan modifications. Thus, in conclusion, Franxman offers rather broad generalizations as to how Josephus has overall reshaped Genesis.

5. *V*, 414–415.

6. *Ap* I, 35, Josephus himself notes this prohibition based on the rabbinic understanding of Lev. 21:7. See *Yebamoth* 61a and especially *Kethuboth*, 36b.

7. Cf. *V*, 426–428.

8. See *V*, 16 and *A* XX, 195. In the latter passage, Poppaea is described as a "worshiper of God" (*theosebēs*).

9. *V*, 429.

10. *BJ* VII, 399. I have underlined for emphasis.

11. *A* III, 5.

12. See Louis H. Feldman, "Hellenizations in Josephus' Portrayal of Man's Decline," *Religions in Antiquity*, ed. J. Neusner, (*SHR* 14) (Leiden, 1968), 345. The proverb appears in *A* V, 294, but it is not clear precisely which words were proverbial. I have been unable to locate any parallel in Hellenistic literature.

13. *BJ* II, 120–121 reads, "Marriage they disdain, but they adopt other men's children. . . . They do not, indeed, on principle, condemn wedlock and the propagation thereby of the race, but they wish to protect themselves against women's wantonness (*aselgeia*), being persuaded that none of the sex keeps her plighted troth to one man."

14. *Rosh Hashanah* 22a makes clear that the evidence of a woman was legally accepted only in a limited number of circumstances (e.g., to testify to the death of her husband).

15. A similar comment is noted in the Gemara of *Shabbat* 33b, where a rabbi speaks to his son regarding his wife (on the fear that the Romans will discover them in hiding): "Women are of unstable temperament: she may be put to the torture and expose us." As the footnote suggests, "The context shows that he was not censuring women for constitutional instability, but feared their weakness."

16. Feldman (above, note 12), 345, comments, "During the Hellenistic period the status of women was greatly ameliorated; and presumably to avoid the accusation that Judaism places the woman in an inferior position, Josephus (I, 49) completely omits this statement." If this was his motive for the omission in *A* I, 49, then at a later time Josephus was not consistent or felt no need to be apologetic on this score. Perhaps, the explanation is in the different type of work, one historical and the other apologetic.

17. See Wayne A. Meeks, "The Image of the Androgyne: Some Uses of a Symbol in Earliest Christianity," *HR* 13:3 (February 1974), 167–180, who surveys the pertinent sources for assessing the place of women both in Judaism and in the Gentile world during the Hellenistic period. I quote part of Meeks's summary: "While the general status of women had vastly and steadily improved over several centuries, the change brought in some circles a bitter reaction in the form of misogyny. The groups that made possible full participation of women with men on an equal basis were few and isolated; the Epicurean school is the only important example. Among those who advocated preservation of the status quo, the constantly salient concern is a sense of order: everything must be in its place, and the differentiation and ranking of women and men became a potent symbol for the stability of the world order" (179f.)

18. For example, see Shaye J. D. Cohen, *Josephus in Galilee and Rome* (Leiden, 1979), 35f. Thackeray (above, note 2), 80–89, argues that Josephus is more dependent on a Hebrew text until the Book of Samuel and thereafter is more dependent on a Greek text. On this matter there appears to be considerable debate among Josephus scholars.

19. *The Book of Jubilees* presents a major elaboration of Genesis 1 to Exodus 12 and is to be dated in the second century B.C.; *The Genesis Apocryphon*, discovered at Qumran in fragmentary condition, contains an interpretive expansion at many points of early chapters in Genesis, including the episode involving Abraham and Sarah in Genesis 12:10–20, and is generally dated late first century B.C. or early first century A.D.; and Pseudo-Philo, dated the latter half of the first century A.D., offers a retelling of the biblical narrative from Genesis to the death of Saul. Since Philo died approximately A.D. 50, his writings date during the first half of the first century A.D. In regard to these suggested dates, cf. George W. E. Nickelsburg, *Jewish Literature between the Bible and the Mishnah* (Philadelphia, 1981), 78f., 265, and 267f. For the debate on dating Pseudo-Philo, see as well the revised Prolegomenon by Louis H. Feldman in M. R. James, *The Biblical Antiquities of Philo* (New York, 1971), xxviii–xxxi.

20. Cf. the "Index of Names" in Philo's writings (Loeb Classical Library, Vol. X) for the many references which so characterize the matriarchs.

21. Louis Ginzberg, *Legends of the Jews*, 7 vols. (Philadelphia, 1909–1938); Salomo Rappaport, *Agada und Exegese bei Flavius Josephus* (Wien, 1930).

22. See Franxman (above, note 2), 127–132, for a detailed comparison of the three biblical accounts and Josephus' use of them in his version in *A* I, 161–165.

23. See Ginzberg (above, note 21), 1:222 with note 68 in 5:220f. Further, Philo "On

Abraham," 93, describes Abraham as having "a wife distinguished greatly for her goodness of soul and beauty of body, in which she surpassed all the women of her time."

24. Philo, "On Abraham," 94–95, describes the Egyptian king as follows: "He sent for the woman [Sarah], and, marking her surpassing comeliness, paid little regard to decency or the laws enacted to show respect to strangers, but gave rein to his license and determined nominally to take her in marriage, but in reality to bring her to shame. She who in a foreign country was at the mercy of a licentious and cruel-hearted despot and had no one to protect her."

25. See Feldman's article on Abraham (above, note 3) to understand how the Josephan changes of Genesis 12:10–20 fit with his overall portrayal of the patriarch.

26. Franxman (above, note 2), 130, note 3, traces the tradition of the Pharaoh's consulting the priests to Pseudo-Eupolemus (cf. Eusebius, *Praep. Evan.*, 9.17).

27. In *Genesis Apocryphon* 20 (see English translation by G. Vermes, *The Dead Sea Scrolls in English* [New York, 2nd ed., 1975], 219), Lot informs Harkenosh that Sarah is Abraham's wife, and this messenger in turn tells the king.

28. Rappaport (above, note 21), 17, points to haggadic materials that speak of a divine command behind Sarah's offering Hagar to her husband. *Megillah* 14a describes Sarah as a prophetess.

29. Ginzberg (above, note 21), 1.238, describes some traditional elaborations of the story in the following manner: "No sooner had Hagar's union with Abraham been consummated, and she felt that she was with child, than she began to treat her former mistress contemptuously, though *Sarah was particularly tender toward her in the state in which she was*" (my underlining). Note also that Josephus omits Sarah's indignant remark to Abraham that prompted him to assign Hagar to her power (Gen. 16:5).

30. Ginzberg (above, note 21), 1.244, reports haggadic elaborations that consider Sarah's laughter as a sign of little faith, a theme already implicit in the biblical narrative.

31. Ginzberg (above, note 21), 1.263–264, refers to haggadic tradition which speaks about quarrels regarding Isaac and Ishmael over the rights of the first born and Ishmael's custom of shooting arrows at Isaac in jest. Given such explanations, Josephus' comment about Sarah's motive for sending Ishmael away would make sense. Franxman (above, note 2), 154, note 2, calls attention to a tradition in the Tosefta (*Sota,* 6.6) "where Isaac's mother witnesses external signs of Ishmael's ill-will for her son."

32. Ginzberg (above, note 21), 1.286–287, speaks of a tradition which depicts Satan in the form of a man informing Sarah of Abraham's sacrifice of Isaac, but he later returns to indicate that Isaac was not killed. See Franxman (above, note 2), 158, note 9, for similar traditions. Josephus' addition, however, functions somewhat differently from all these.

33. Ginzberg (above, note 21), 1.287–288, refers to the impact of Sarah's death on the whole country.

34. Josephus has drastically abridged the material in Genesis 25:1–18 and has employed the phrase "Now after Abraham's death," not the reference to Abraham's descendants (Gen. 25:19) and Isaac's age at marriage (Gen. 25:20), to introduce the account of Rebekah's giving birth to twins. Cf. Ginzberg (above, note 21), 1.311, who notes haggadic tradition which explains why Isaac married late in life. Isaac, we are told, was thirty-seven years old at the time of *Aqedah* and immediately thereafter had to mourn the death of his mother for three years. Of course, Josephus is simply dependent on the reference in Genesis 25:20.

35. In contrast, Ginzberg (above, note 21), 1.294, notes haggadic elaborations which depict a "convoy of two angels, the one appointed to keep guard over Eliezer, the other over Rebekah." In passing, we should also note that Josephus does not identify Abraham's servant with Eliezer (see Gen. 15:2) as does much of the later tradition.

36. Cf. Betsy Amaru, "Land Theology in Josephus' 'Jewish Antiquities,'" *JQR* 71 (April 1981), 201–229.

37. Josephus' omission is contrary to much of the tradition, which highlights Rebekah's beauty. For example, she was said to have surpassed Abishag in beauty (so Ginzberg [above, note 21], 5.261, note 290). It should be noted that Josephus later mentions Laban as guardian of Rebekah's virginity (I, 248).

38. Franxman (above, note 2), 166.

39. Although *Genesis Rabbah* 63.10 (so Ginzberg, [above, note 21], 1.316 and note) gives the reason for Rebekah's favoring Jacob (she "was more clear-sighted. She knew her sons as they really were"), Josephus offers no motives for the parental preferences, not even the one mentioned in Genesis 25:28.

40. Franxman (above, note 2), 177f., suggests motives for this Josephan omission, including the judgment that Josephus would consider it unlikely that both Abraham and Isaac would practice this deception on the same man (see Gen. 20:1ff.). *Jubilees* 24 also omits the deception incident.

41. Franxman (above, note 2), 182.

42. Franxman (above, note 2), 182, notes this.

43. Legends developed regarding Rebekah as a prophetess, but Josephus nowhere describes her in such terms. See Ginzberg (above, note 21), 1.341. In *Jubilees* 25:1–23 Rebekah blesses Jacob.

44. Franxman (above, note 2), 188, wonders if Josephus had a different version of this biblical story from the one preserved in the Masoretic and Septuagint texts. Although this question cannot be decided with certainty, it appears that Genesis 29 is not told any more freely than was Genesis 24.

45. Ginzberg (above, note 21), 1.355, mentions haggadic tradition which emphasizes that good fortune comes to a person when he meets young maidens on first entering a town.

46. Did Josephus eliminate Jacob's kissing Rachel because such action was not deemed appropriate in public? Ginzberg (above, note 21), 1.355, includes haggadic tradition which understands the kiss as between cousins; but even so bystanders began whispering, and it was this censure which caused Jacob's tears of repentance. See Louis M. Epstein, *Sex Laws and Customs in Judaism* (New York, 1948), 109.

47. *Jubilees* 28:5 states that Leah's eyes were weak but her form was very handsome. Josephus' phrase is evidently his interpretation of the biblical description.

48. Ginzberg (above, note 21), 5.295, note 166, thinks that Josephus' statement that the second marriage occurred after seven years "is due to a misunderstanding of the Hebrew *šābûaʿ* (Gen. 29:27), which means 'septinate' and 'week.'"

49. See Harold W. Attridge, *The Interpretation of Biblical History in the Antiquitates Judaicae of Flavius Josephus* (Missoula, 1976), 126–140, who discusses the themes of "passion" and "erotic love" in Josephus.

50. This addition by Josephus is quite different from the tradition that Jacob refused to go to Leah until compelled by God, who knew that Leah "acted from pure, disinterested motives" (Ginzberg [above, note 21], 1.367).

51. See Sarah B. Pomeroy, *Goddesses, Whores, Wives, and Slaves: Women in Classical Antiquity* (New York, 1975), 169f., 183–185, 188f.

52. Pomperoy, 142–146, talks about the new interest in eroticism in the Hellenistic period.

53. Louis H. Feldman, "Josephus' Portrait of Saul," *HUCA* 53 (1982), 45–99.

54. I owe this suggestion for making sense of the apparent contradiction between Josephus' idealization of the matriarchs and his general misogyny to Professor Bruce Malina. See John H. Kautsky, *The Politics of Aristocratic Empires* (Chapel Hill, N.C., 1982).

7 The Story of Moses Interpreted within the Context of Anti-Semitism

GOHEI HATA

*t*his essay is an attempt at reading, or reading into, the story of Moses (*A* II, 101–IV, 331) according to Josephus and within the context of anti-Semitism in the Mediterranean region, especially in Alexandria, where there lived a large Jewish population from the third century B.C. to the first century A.D.

A mere glance at *Greek and Latin Authors on Jews and Judaism,*[1] edited by M. Stern, shows that there were few non-Jewish authors who wrote books dealing conclusively with the religion, customs, and history of the Jews or the Jewish people, while there were numerous authors who did allude to them. In fact, Stern chronologically introduces the works or fragments of 160 authors, starting with Herodotus in the fifth century B.C. and ending with Simplicius in the first half of the sixth century A.D. Of these authors, 96 belong chronologically to the group from Herodotus to Herennius Philo of Byblus, who may be considered a contemporary of Josephus. Since we have so many authors whose works or fragments are extant, thanks to the mercy of history, we can assume that there should have been a far greater number of writers working in this field if we take into account the works that must have been scattered and thereby lost.[2]

Out of these 96 authors, several, either directly or indirectly, mentioned Moses or the Exodus. Listed in chronological order, they are: Hellanicus (fifth century B.C.), Philochorus (between the fourth and third centuries B.C.), Hecataeus of Abdera (ca. third century B.C.), Manetho (third century B.C.), Mnaseas of Patara (ca. second century B.C.), Castor (ca. second century B.C.), Thallus (ca. second century B.C.), Polemo of Ilium (first half of the second century B.C.), Posidonius (135–51 B.C.), Alexander Polyhistor (first century B.C.), Apollonius Molon (first century B.C.), Diodorus the Sicilian (first century B.C.), Strabo of Amaseia (64 B.C. to A.D. 20), Pompeius Trogus (toward the end of the first century B.C. to the beginning of the first century A.D.), Ptolemy the Historian (dates unknown), Lysimachus (first century B.C.), Apion (first half of the first century A.D.), Chaeremon (first century A.D.), "Longinus" (first century A.D.), Pliny the Elder (A.D. 23–79), Quintilian (A.D. 35–95), Nicarchus (first century A.D.), Tacitus (A.D. 56–120), and Juvenal (ca. A.D. 60–130). Of this group, Manetho, Lysimachus, Chaeremon, Apion, Posidonius, and Apollonius Molon (the last two are providers of material for Apion) are severely criticized in Josephus' *Against Apion* because they slandered and attacked Moses and the Jews by asserting that

1) the ancestors of the Jews were Egyptians (Apion);[3]
2) the ancestors of the Jews were lepers and cripples who lived among the Egyptians and who were banished from Egypt for that reason (Manetho, Lysimachus, Chaeremon, Apion);[4]
3) Moses was an Egyptian priest or a temple scribe (Manetho, Chaeremon, Apion);[5]
4) Moses was himself a leper (Manetho);[6]
5) Moses had a different original name (Manetho, Chaeremon);[7]
6) Moses preached atheism to the Egyptians (Lysimachus);
7) the Jews are atheists who do not worship the gods (Manetho, Lysimachus, Apion, Posidonius, Apollonius Molon);
8) the Jews worship the head of an ass placed in the Temple in Jerusalem (Mnaseas, Apion);[8]
9) the Jews offer men as sacrifices to the gods (Apion);[9]
10) Moses was a fraud and a charlatan whose commandments teach only evil, no virtue (Apollonius Molon, Lysimachus).

To be sure, slanders of this order were hurled not only by the anti-Semites around Alexandria, to whom Josephus addresses his *Against Apion*. As a matter of fact, Tacitus, who is a contemporary of Josephus and a typical Roman intellectual, records that the Jews practice animal worship in the temples and that their ancestors were *psora* (psoriasis) patients who had been exiled from Egypt because of their physical deformities.[10]

It is incontestable that Josephus had these slanderers, especially the anti-Semites, on his mind when he was conceiving the outlines of *Jewish Antiquities*. Manetho, Lysimachus, Chaeremon, and Apion all wrote their versions of Egyptian history in which the Jewish history was evidently, and necessarily, treated as something worthless. This was due in part to the histories' nature as official documents. Consequently, Josephus proclaimed that "the Jewish history embraced the history of five thousand years" (*A* I, 13; cf. *Ap* I, 1); that the Jews' fathers were not common people whose honor and titles were dubious; that the Exodus of the Jews was an honorable leave; that Moses, who commanded it, was a peerless leader; that Moses was a person who taught his people the way to virtuous life by "imitating so far as possible that best of all models" (*A* I, 19); and that the Jewish history had continued to that time without a break. By these assertions, Josephus made an apology for his fellow Jews who lived in the Diaspora, having lost their own country.

Josephus, however, thought this defense insufficient and, after completion of *Jewish Antiquities,* soon published *Against Apion* as a separate work. In the first book of *Against Apion,* which emphasizes the long history of the Jewish people, he introduces the evidence concerning the origin of the Jews as it is recorded in the chronicles of Egyptians, Chaldaeans, and Phoenicians, refuting the argument that assigned to them a shallow history. He then points out the contradictions in the assertions of Manetho, Lysimachus, and Chaeremon, who issued books providing false information about the origin of the Jews. In the second book he refutes, in particular, the assertions of Apion (Apion's name is used in the very title of the book). As a rebuttal to the slander that the ancestors of the Jews were Egyptians, he shows that the Jews came to Egypt from a different area. Likewise, he argues against the claim that the Jews' ancestors were banished from Egypt because of their physical handicaps by stating that they returned to their homeland after making a careful decision and that the departure itself was possible only because of their physical perseverance. He then lays out the main points of Moses' commandments and the many rewards they offered the people. He further portrays the stupidity and the ambiguity of the religious beliefs of the Greeks as an antithesis to those of the Jews.

The story of Moses by Josephus, therefore, is not really complete in *Jewish Antiquities;* but, when it is complemented by *Against Apion,* its significance is fully appreciated. In other words, Josephus' story of Moses in *Jewish Antiquities,* which gives an account of the life and achievements of Moses, reveals the intention of its author and the hidden current running under its narrative only when it is read within the context of the anti-Semitism that is attacked in *Against Apion.*

I

Exodus 2:1–10 relates that Moses' mother hides for three months the goodly child to whom she has given birth, and when she can no longer conceal him, she leaves him among the reeds by the bank of the Nile in an ark of bulrushes. Fortunately, he is discovered and saved by the daughter of the pharaoh. Moses' sister, who was watching, says that she will call a nurse for the child and brings the mother of Moses. His mother takes care of him while receiving wages from the pharaoh. When Moses comes of age, she gives him to the daughter of the pharaoh, who names him Moses. According to a priestly source, the name of Moses' father is Amram, that of his mother, Jochebed, and that of his brother, who is three years his senior, Aaron. As is seen, this well-known narrative of Moses' birth in Exodus is quite simple.

How does Josephus, then, treat Moses' nativity? Even before starting the story, he mentions the prediction of Moses' birth made by an Egyptian "temple scribe" and a revelation by God to his father, Amram. It is noteworthy that Josephus has a "temple scribe" (ἱερογραμματεύς), not a "diviner" (μάντις), for example, predict Moses' birth. According to Josephus, "they [temple scribes], as is said, originally received two commissions from royalty: divine worship and the supervision of learning" (Ap II, 141).[11] Of course, he does this in order to authorize the birth of Moses, utilizing the Egyptian authority, but this statement is not totally unrelated to the fact that Josephus' opponents, such as Manetho and Apion, were saying that Moses was a priest of Heliopolis (Ap I, 238, 250, 261, 265, 279; II, 10, 11, 13), and that Chaeremon called him a scribe of the temple of Isis (Ap I, 290).

The prediction of Moses' birth by a temple scribe is described by Josephus thus: "One of the sacred scribes—persons with considerable skill in accurately predicting the future—announced to the king that there would be born to the Israelites at that time one who would abase the sovereignty of the Egyptians and exalt the Israelites, were he reared to manhood, and would surpass all men in virtue and win everlasting renown" (A II, 205). This account elucidates, on one hand, the motive of the pharaoh in ordering the massacre of male infants. He fears the increasing number of Israelites and one young Israelite in particular. On the other hand, it stresses that the boy who is going to be born is not just another baby, but one chosen before birth, as was revealed to Amram by God (A II, 215). What, however, is remarkable here to us is that Josephus accentuates the virtuous nature of Moses at the very beginning of the narrative. This is a response to the distortions by Apollonius Molon, Lysimachus, and others, who called Moses a "charlatan" (γόης) or a "fraud" (ἀπατεών) who taught nothing but evil and did not encourage virtue (Ap II, 145, cf. II, 161). These accusations must have been occupying Josephus' mind, for the virtuous nature of Moses is repeatedly mentioned as the story proceeds.

Josephus' general plot, in which the infant is left in the Nile and saved by the daughter of the pharaoh, follows that of the Book of Exodus. The pharaoh's daughter, however, is given a name, Thermuthis,[12] no doubt to give the story a touch of historic reality. According to Exodus 2:6, the daughter of the pharaoh saves the child in the floating ark because it is crying. Josephus, on the other hand, alters her motive—she saves the infant because she is "enchanted at its size and beauty" (A II, 224).

In the next chapter, Josephus highlights the superior appearance of Moses when he narrates Moses' childhood and wanderings in the wilderness. This may be explained by the fact that he is consciously refuting Manetho's statement that Moses was a leper and Manetho's, Lysimachus', Chaeremon's, and others' contentions that the ancestors of the Jews were lepers and cripples who were banished from Egypt for that reason and that, therefore, Moses, who led them, was naturally a leper. Josephus' emphasis on Moses' beauty negates his image as a cripple or an ungainly leper.[13]

Exodus 2:10 records that the pharaoh's daughter names the infant "Moses" and explains the origin of that name. Josephus also elucidates the meaning of the name, writing, "The Egyptians call water *môu* and those who are saved *esês;* so they conferred on him this name compounded of both words" (*A* II, 228).[14] Josephus' reiteration of this explanation in *Against Apion* I, 286 is of significance because Manetho states that Moses was "a native of Heliopolis named Osarsiph after the Heliopolitan god Osiris, and that when he went over to this people he changed his name and was called Moses" (*Ap* I, 250, cf. I, 265, 286). This explanation Josephus found "extremely unconvincing" (*Ap* I, 286). Chaeremon, on the other hand, claimed that Moses' Egyptian name was "Tisithen" (*Ap* I, 290).

II

The Book of Exodus gives no account of the childhood days of Moses. Josephus, however, fills that gap in this way:

> His growth in understanding (σύνεσις) was not in line with his growth in stature, but far outran the measure of his years: its maturer excellence was displayed in his very games, and his actions then gave promise of the greater deeds to be wrought by him on reaching manhood. When he was three years old, God gave wondrous increase to his stature; and none was so indifferent to beauty as not, on seeing Moses, to be amazed at his comeliness. And it often happened that persons meeting him as he was borne along the highway turned, attracted by the child's appearance, and neglected their serious affairs to gaze at leisure upon him: indeed childish charm so perfect and pure as his held the beholders spellbound. (*A* II, 230–231)[15]

The superior appearance of Moses is dramatized here to its utmost. Further on, Josephus describes a scene where the pharaoh's daughter takes Moses to her father to report that she has adopted him. Josephus has her say that she "brought up a boy of divine beauty [μορφῇ . . . θεῖον] and generous spirit" (*A* II, 232). The stress on understanding (σύνεσις) is redoubled, along with the repetition of Moses' physical beauty, which is all part of the "whitewash" to enhance the image of Moses as a hero.

III

According to Exodus 2:11–15, the first remarkable incident in Moses' adult life is when he, seeing an Egyptian abusing one of his fellowmen, murders him and buries the body in the sand. In modern as well as in ancient times, this act would unequivocally be called murder and abandonment of a corpse. Josephus does not even mention this incident. For him, being acutely aware of the anti-Moses and anti-Jewish sentiments harbored by the anti-Semites in Alexandria at this time, this incident must have been too problematic to record.

According to Exodus 2:15ff., Moses escapes from Egypt in order to save himself from the pharaoh, who attempts to kill him for the murder of the Egyptian, and seeks shelter from a priest in Midian. The escape sequence from Egypt ends with his marriage to one of the seven daughters of the priest.

Josephus tries to evade this undesirable murder-and-escape sequence with an outflanking action. He fills the sizable gap created by the omission of the incident by inserting a story that is believed to have developed in the Jewish community in Alexandria—the legend about the Ethiopian expedition led by Moses (as the Egyptian commander) against the Ethiopians who invaded Egypt[16]—and by winding up with Moses' marriage.

Although this camouflage of exploiting a legend renders his honesty as a historian questionable, it proves his ingenuity as an extraordinary strategist. Inspired by this legend about Moses the hero, he skillfully fabricates a tale in which Moses, who is appointed by the pharaoh (how daring!) to counterattack the Ethiopians invading Egypt, makes an expedition to Ethiopia; drives them back to Saba (the capital of the Ethiopian realm), marries Tharbis, daughter of the Ethiopian king, on the condition that the Ethiopians yield their capital; castigates the Ethiopians; and finally makes a triumphal return to Egypt. As a result, Josephus simultaneously establishes a heroic image for Moses and provides a motive for his escape to Midian.

Josephus explains the motive thus:

> But the Egyptians, thus saved by Moses, conceived from their very deliverance a hatred for him and thought good to pursue with greater ardor their plots upon his life, suspecting that he would take advantage of his success to revolutionize Egypt, and suggesting to the king that he should be put to death.
>
> He, on his own part, was harboring thoughts of so doing, alike from envy of Moses' generalship and from fear of seeing himself abased, and so, when instigated by the hierarchy, was prepared to lend a hand in the murder of Moses. (A II, 254–255).

In this way, Josephus illustrates the hatred ($\mu\hat{\iota}\sigma\sigma$) and envy ($\phi\theta\acute{o}\nu\sigma$), which are, according to Josephus, the two basic feelings of anti-Semites (Ap I, 224) and those which the Egyptians bore against Moses the triumphant general. Now, Moses can do nothing but flee. He, confident of his perseverance, traverses the desert without carrying water and provisions with him (A II, 256) and escapes to the land of Midian. This successful adventure through the desert, equipped only with his endurance, revises the image of Moses; a body of steel and a will of iron are no possessions of lepers or of the crippled. Later on, Moses will ask the pharaoh for permission to let the Israelites leave Egypt as a reward for this marvelous feat (A II, 282).

IV

A voice emanating from a burning shrub on Mount Sinai gives Moses the vocation of emancipating the Israelites from the Egyptians. The strange voice first rebukes him "to be content with what he, as a man of virtue sprung from illustrious ancestors, had seen, but to pry no further" (A II, 267). Then it predicts that God will always be with him so that the Hebrews will "win glory and honor from men" (A II, 268) and orders him to return to Egypt to be a "leader" or a "general" of his fellow Hebrews. The voice further explains that there is no one but Moses, especially with his "understanding," who can lead his people to the promised land where Abraham used to live and bring happiness to them (A II, 269).

Moses had already been a general when he commanded the Egyptian army on the Ethiopian expedition. As is suggested by the Greek words στρατηγός (general) and ἡγεμών (sovereign commander), Moses acted as the general and the sovereign commander of a troop. The requirements for a person to lead people across the desert are not only understanding, judgment (both σύνεσις in Greek), virtue and boldness (both ἀρετή in Greek) but also an extraordinary physical strength. Moses had already proved that he possessed all of these traits in his expedition to Ethiopia and his escape to Midian. It is evident that Josephus' own experience as an army general in Galilee and his experience crossing the desert from Alexandria to Jerusalem with the Roman troops (BJ IV, 658–663, Ap I, 48) are incorporated in his description of Moses escorting the Jews across the desert (A II, 321; Ap I, 277, II, 24).

Moses at first hesitates to carry out his call, but God convinces him of the divine nature of his mission by showing him signs. According to the Hebrew version of Exodus 4:6, God shows Moses two signs, the first of which concerns us here. For this sign, God orders Moses to reach his hand inside the robe and "when he did, and took it out again, it was white with leprosy." The Septuagint translates this passage, "His hand turned white like snow" (ἐγενήθη ἡ χεὶρ αὐτοῦ ὡσεὶ χιών). The Alexandrian philosopher Philo, a predecessor of Josephus, writes, "His hand was suddenly seen whiter than snow" (ἡ χεὶρ λευκοτέρα χιόνος ἐξαπιναίως ἀναφαίνεται) [17] and thus leaves the cause (leprosy) unmentioned. Much in the same way, Josephus simply states that Moses' hand turned "white, of a color resembling chalk" (λευκὴν καὶ τιτάνῳ τὴν χρόαν ὁμοίαν) (A II, 273). It is obvious why Josephus discreetly alters this passage found in the Hebrew Exodus. After the signs, Moses believes God is his protector and accepts his vocation.

Moses petitions the pharaoh to free the Jews, but the pharaoh is hardened against them and refuses to let them leave. As a result, Egypt suffers ten calamities, and Josephus covers nine of them. The plagues sweep across Egypt one after another, and the pharaoh finally allows the Israelites to leave. According to Exodus 12:35–36, upon departure, the Israelites "asked the Egyptians for silver and gold jewelry and clothing . . . and thus stripped the Egyptians of these things." Josephus renders his ancestors' evacuation into a more honorable occasion by cautiously omitting references to the beggarly mentality manifest in Exodus. Josephus writes, "Among the Egyptians, there were ones who praised the Israelites by giving them farewell presents. There were ones who gave presents just to make them leave at once, others did so in expression of their neighborly love" (A II, 314). Josephus must have made such a modification in response to "the school of Lysimachus, Molon, and other authors of the like—pernicious Sophists who were attempting to misguide the youths" (Ap II, 236)—who denounced the Jewish people, calling them "the lowest of all the humanity" (πάνυ . . . φαυλοτάτους ἀνθρώπων).

Moses and his people thus leave behind the Egyptians who repent that they have abused the Israelites (A II, 315). Those Israelites "who were old enough to enroll in the army were numbered 600 thousand" (A II, 317). Moses, their general, was then eighty years old.

According to Exodus 14:7, the Egyptian army that followed after Moses and his people were "the pick of Egypt's 600 chariots and all other horses and charioteers." Josephus, on the other hand, relates that the pharaoh's cavalry consisted of "600 chariots, 50 thousand horsemen, and 200 thousand fully armed infantry" (A II, 324). The figures he mentions here, such as "50 thousand" or "200 thousand," may be simply groundless fabrications aimed at giving historical credibility to the story; but the latter number, "200 thousand," may be related to the figure that Josephus refers to in *Against Apion* from time to time—the fictitious figure Manetho gives when claiming that there were "200 thousand" (Ap I, 243, 263) shepherds who were banished to Jerusalem and "200 thousand" Israelites who were banished to Syria by Rameses (Ap I, 292, 300). The figure "200 thousand" when combined with the former "50 thousand" may be connected with the imaginary figure "250 thousand" (Ap I, 290, 295), the number of crippled Israelites, claimed by Chaeremon, who were supposedly exiled from Egypt by Amenophis.

After Moses and the Israelites cross the Red Sea, they march toward Mount Sinai. Josephus depicts Moses, who leads the caravan crossing the desert, as a superbly "virtuous [or courageous]" commander. For example, when the people's frustrations mount to an eruption, Moses, with his uniquely convincing speech, forces them to recall the grace of God and admonishes them to continue believing in providence. He appeases their anger, saves them from despair, and thus guides their way through the impossible. The many speeches inserted on such occasions are Josephus' creations based on Moses' utterances scattered throughout Exodus. According to Josephus, God encourages Moses on Mount Sinai, saying, "Words shall be given when you have to speak" (A II, 272)—and here we indeed see words given to Moses, by Josephus, in place of God.

In order to resolve the conflict at Mount Sinai, Moses, following the advice of Reuel, his father-in-law, divides his army and invests the respective captains with his command. The name of Reuel (Jethro), who counsels Moses to divide the troops, is found in Exodus 18:1ff. Here, Josephus finds an occasion to emphasize the "honesty" (ἀρετή) of Moses, who, instead of claiming it as his own idea, gives due credit to Reuel (A III, 73–74). The reinforcement of Moses' "honesty" is evident in his recording of the prophecy of Balaam, the diviner (A IV, 157), and further negates the image of him as a charlatan or a fraud. In any case, Moses succeeds "in making the whole people dependent upon himself, and, having secured their obedience in all things, he does not use his influence for any personal aggrandizement" (Ap II, 158).

At Mount Sinai, the commandments are issued, the altar in the tabernacle-tent is built, the high priest is elected, and the Law is given. The second of the Ten Commandments in the Hebrew Exodus 20:4 is the prohibition against carving images and reads, "You shall not make yourselves a graven image." The Septuagint translates this "graven image" as "idol" (εἴδωλον). Josephus, however, alters it to "image of living creature" (εἰκόνα ζῴου) and states that "the second commands us to make no image of any living creature" (A III, 91). This commandment is mentioned again in Against Apion II, 75 in the argument against Apion's accusation that the Jews do not build statues of the Roman emperor. Josephus argues, "Our legislator, not in order to put, as it were, a prophetic veto upon honors paid to the Roman authority, but out of contempt for a practice profitable to neither God nor man, forbade the making of images, alike of any living creature, and much more of God, who . . . is not a creature."

Much in line with this, an elaborate counter-argument is devoted to another of Apion's slanders, that "the Jews kept an ass's head in the shrine, worshipping that animal and deeming it worthy of deepest reverence" (Ap II, 80ff.). What must have been in Josephus' mind when he presents the second commandment was, of course, the attack on the Jewish refusal to erect the Roman emperor's statue, but more so the slanderous belief of the Jew's ass worship. In fact, this belief, of unknown origin, which is found in quite a number of variations, kept bothering the Jews of the Diaspora. That Josephus was acutely aware of this is seen in his total omissions of the biblical description in Exodus 4:20 that when Moses returned to the land of Egypt, he put his wife and his sons on an ass, of the calf-worshiping incident at Mount Sinai found in Exodus 32:1ff., and also in his careful description of the interior of the tabernacle where the ass's head was allegedly placed. For example, according to Exodus 26:31 (1 Kings 6:23–35, 7:29), there were embroidered images of "cherubim" on the curtain in the holy shrine, but Josephus ignores this and replaces them with flower patterns, descriptions of which are not found in Exodus nor in any other sources (A III, 126). Even when Josephus is forced to mention the "cherubim" in the necessary course of the narrative (about the ark and the Covenant of God), he cautiously adds that they were "in form unlike to any that man's eyes have seen, and Moses says that he saw them sculptured upon the throne of God" (A III, 137).[18] Then, after a long and detailed description of the sanctuary in the tabernacle and the vestments of the priests (A III, 102ff.), he concludes, "For if one reflects on the construction of the tabernacle and looks at the vestments of the priest and the vessels which we use for the sacred ministry, he will discover that our lawgiver was a man of God and that these blasphemous charges brought against us by the rest of men are idle" (A III, 180).

Throughout the forty years of his ordeal in the wilderness after leaving Mount Sinai and finally viewing Jericho, Moses is seen as an honorable commander who invariably devotes his heroic passion to his supreme God-given purpose. For example, when the people arrive at Hazeroth in the wilderness of Sinai, they grumble to him of the hardships they have had to bear during their previous wanderings (A III, 296–297). When they are informed of the difficulty of conquering the land of Canaan, they revolt against Moses (A III, 306–307). After the battle with the Canaanites, the Israelites, abandoning their discipline and obedience, move against him (A IV, 11–12). Later, a mutiny breaks out in the army due to the licentious acts of the youths, who are dominated by the Midianite women (A IV, 139–141). But on each of these occasions, Moses proves himself to be an extremely competent commander who, speaking directly to the hearts of his fellow men who have lost their discretion and purpose, helps them to regain their control and autonomy.

Moses, prior to his death, bequeaths to his people a book containing the commandments and the covenant, and blesses the people upon their expedition to the Canaanites. This being done, Josephus makes Moses confess thus: "Nay rather it was He who both gave the lead in those endeavors and granted the gracious issues, employing me but as His subaltern (ὑποστρατήγῳ) and subordinate minister (ὑπηρέτῃ) of the benefactions which He was fain to confer upon our people" (A IV, 317; cf. Ap II, 160). Here is a Moses who knows what is due him and what is due God. With such a characterization of Moses, no longer can one possibly view Moses as a fraud or a charlatan; one can only regard him with the greatest praise, for he is "the best of generals, the sagest of counsellors, and the most conscientious of guardians" (*Ap* II, 158).

V

In the passage from III, 224 through 286 of his *Jewish Antiquities,* Josephus introduces the ordinances concerning purification and sacrifice, mainly following Leviticus and Deuteronomy. What is of interest to us in this passage is Josephus' treatment of leprosy (*A* III, 261–268) and of food (*A* III, 259–260). The laws concerning leprosy are taken from Leviticus, chapters 13–14. Here Josephus does not provide any detailed description of its symptoms, nor does he elaborate on the details concerning the treatment of its victims and the rites of purification in case one is cured of it. He neglects these topics on purpose—a discreet decision, for it would have been a confirmation of the slander that Moses and the ancestors of the Jews were lepers.

Josephus begins by declaring that "He [Moses] banished from the city alike those whose bodies were afflicted with leprosy and those with contagious disease" (*A* III, 261). According to Leviticus 13:46, 14:3, the lepers were banished "outside the camp," but Josephus changes this to "from the city." This is a significant change that suggests to the reader that there were no lepers in Jerusalem, not only in the time of Moses but also after that. This impression is confirmed when Josephus stresses that "lepers, on the other hand, he banished outright from the city to have intercourse with no man and as in no way differing from a corpse" (*A* III, 264). After briefly mentioning the customary sacrifice made to God in gratitude for being cured of leprosy, Josephus refutes the assertion that Moses was a leper. This counter-argument may throw readers off because the actual theory equating Moses with leprosy is not mentioned at all. This may be regarded as quite natural, however, when it is read within the context of anti-Semitism, which is amply felt in *Against Apion.*

Josephus explains it thus:

> From all this one can but regard as ridiculous those who assert that Moses, being struck with leprosy, was himself forced to flee from Egypt and, taking command of all who had been expelled for the same reason, conducted them to Canaan.
> For, were this true, Moses would never have issued to his own humiliation statutes such as these, against which in all likelihood he would have himself protested had others introduced them, more especially since among many nations there are lepers in the enjoyment of honors, who far from undergoing contumely and exile, conduct the most brilliant campaigns, are entrusted with offices of state, and have the right of entry to sacred courts and temples.
> Consequently there was nothing to prevent Moses, had he or the host that

accompanied him been marred by any such accident to the skin, from laying down laws concerning lepers of the most favorable character, instead of imposing any penalty of this nature. No; it is clear that in making these statements about us they are instigated by jealousy, and that Moses was immune from all that, and, living among countrymen equally immune, that he legislated concerning those so diseased, and that it was in God's honor that he thus acted. (A III, 265–268)

Although there were numerous anti-Semites who claimed that the ancestors of the Jews were lepers,[19] as far as we know there was only one who actually insisted that Moses himself was a leper—Manetho (Ap I, 279), whom Josephus must have had in mind when he was writing this passage. This is evident in the following citation from *Against Apion:*

And that he suffered from no physical affliction of this nature is clear from his own statements.

In fact, he forbids lepers either to stay in a town or to reside in a village; they must be solitary vagrants, with their clothes rent; anyone who touches or lives under the same roof with them he considers unclean.

Moreover, even if the malady is cured and the victim returns to his normal condition, Moses prescribes certain rites of purification—to cleanse himself in a bath of spring-water and to cut off all his hair—and requires him to offer a numerous variety of sacrifices before entering the holy city.

Yet one would have expected, on the contrary, a victim of this calamity to have shown some consideration and fellow-feeling for others equally unfortunate. (Ap I, 281–283)

While a very detailed prescription of the food laws is found in Leviticus 11:1ff. and Deuteronomy 14:3ff., Josephus proclaims that Moses "distinguished in detail those which might be eaten and those, on the contrary, from which one must perpetually abstain. On these, whenever the occasion may come for treating of them, we shall discourse at length, supplying the reasons which influenced him in ruling that some of them were eatable and in enjoining us to abstain from others" (A III, 259). Josephus then only adds that blood, the flesh of an animal dying a natural death, the caul, and the fat of goats, sheep, and oxen should not be eaten.

Much merriment had been made of the Jewish abstinence from pork. Petronius, the Roman satirist, ridiculed the Jews, saying that they do not eat pork because they worship a pig,[20] and Tacitus claimed that the reason is because pork reminded the Jews of their former sufferings from psora.[21] But there were many others who also made fun of this Jewish dietary custom.[22] Is it not, then, unnatural that Josephus, who is so conscious of such vituperations, does not include pork in the list of food to be abstained from (Leviticus 11:7, Deuteronomy14:8)? Nonetheless, a sure proof of his acute sensitivity to such slanders may be found in his promise to discuss them "whenever the occasion may come [for dealing with them]." As a matter of fact, not only does

Josephus launch a counterattack against Apion, who denounced the Jews for not eating pork, by mentioning that the Egyptian priests also abstain from eating it (*Ap* II, 141), but he also points out that "even among the rest of the Egyptians, there is not a man who sacrifices a pig to the gods" (*Ap* II, 141), thus refuting such slanders as those hurled by a Petronius.

VI

From the passage in *Jewish Antiquities* IV, 196–301, we shall analyze the two laws concerning blasphemy (*A* IV, 202, 207) and those laws based on Deuteronomy 27:18 and Leviticus 19:14. One law regarding blasphemy is found in Leviticus 24:15b–16 and notes that "anyone who curses his God must pay the penalty: he must die. All the congregation shall stone him; this law applies to the foreigner as well as to the Israelite who blasphemes the name of Jehovah. He must die." In Deuteronomy 21:22–23a we read that "if a man has committed a crime worthy of death, and is executed and then hanged on a tree, his body shall not remain on the tree overnight. You must bury him on the same day." Josephus, on the other hand, writes thus: "Let him that blasphemeth God be stoned, then hung for a day, and buried ignominiously and in obscurity" (*A* IV, 202).

According to Josephus, one who blasphemes God is susceptible to a double punishment—he is to be stoned and hanged from a tree. M. Weil, one of the editors of the French translation of the *Collected Works of Josephus*, articulates in his commentary that although Josephus seems to be consistent with the customs of his time (*Siphre* 114b, Mishnah *Sanhedrin* 6.6), he actually deviates from them in his addition of "for a day."

What is of interest to us here is that while Josephus did follow the custom of his time, he also rendered the punishment for blasphemy unparalleledly severe, while ignoring the passage in Leviticus 24:16b, which states that this penalty is also applicable to "those of foreign origin." Without doubt, Josephus was aware of those, such as Manetho, Lysimachus, Apion, Posidonius, and Apollonius Molon, who accused the Jews of being atheists. Proof of this reaction by Josephus may be seen in his alteration of the object of blasphemy from the "Lord's name" (in the Septuagint τὸ ὄνομα κυρίου) to "God" and in his making the punishment so severe. The use of "God" here does not give the impression to pagan and Gentile readers that it merely refers to the "God" of the Jews. In short, the purport of Josephus in presenting this law is to confirm that the Jews do not dare to blaspheme any god, be it their own god or the gods of any other religion: the Jews are not "atheists," as it was being rumored. In fact, Josephus clearly sets forth in *Against Apion* II, 237 that "our legislator [Moses] has expressly forbidden us to deride or blaspheme the gods recognized by others, out of respect for the very word 'God.'" The reason why

Josephus does not mention "those from foreign lands" must have been due to his consideration for the Jewish Diaspora, lest the Jews be further attacked.

It is patent that Josephus was acutely sensitive to the calumny that the Jews were atheists or he would not have reiterated and reconfirmed the laws concerning blasphemy.

The Hebrew Exodus 22:27 reads, "You shall not curse your god." It is well known that the Septuagint Exodus 22:28 interprets this word "God" (*Elohim* in Hebrew) as "gods" and translates the passage, "You shall not blaspheme gods" (θεοὺς οὐ κακολογήσεις). Philo also remarks that this word "does not designate the primary God the Creator, but the gods of the cities" (οὐχὶ τοῦ πρώτου καὶ γεννητοῦ τῶν ὅλων ἀλλὰ τῶν ἐν ταῖς πόλεσι).[23] Josephus writes thus: "Let none blaspheme the gods which other cities revere [βλασφημείτω δὲ μηδεὶς θεοὺς οὓς πόλεις ἄλλαι νομίζουσι], nor rob foreign temples, nor take treasure that has been dedicated in the name of any god" (*A* IV, 207).

Here Josephus has Moses prohibit the ravaging of the temples and the pillaging of holy articles because Manetho claimed that Moses during the Exodus ordered his people to "overthrow any temples and altars which they found" (*Ap* I, 309) and that the ancestors of the Jews "not only . . . set cities and villages on fire, but also . . . pillage the temples [ἱεροσυλοῦντες] and mutilate the images of the gods" (*Ap* I, 249). They also "overran the country, destroyed the cities, burnt down the temples, massacred the priests, and in short indulged in every kind of crime and brutality" (*Ap* I, 264). Manetho finally hurled words, charged with hatred and malice, stating that the Jews themselves called their town "Hierosyla [meaning plunderer of temples] because of their sacrilegious propensities. At a later date, . . . they altered the name" (*Ap* I, 318).

Other biblical passages that Josephus modified with these anti-Semitic criticisms in mind are Deuteronomy 27:18 and Leviticus 19:14. Deuteronomy reads, " 'Cursed is he who misleads a blind man on the road.' And all the people shall reply, 'Amen.' " Leviticus reads, "You must not curse the deaf nor trip up a blind man as he walks." Josephus puts the same commandment thus: "One must point out the road to those who are ignorant of it, and not, for the pleasure of laughing oneself, impede another's business by misleading him. Similarly, let none revile the sightless or the dumb" (*A* IV, 276).

Juvenal, a contemporary of Josephus and a Roman intellectual, declared in accusation that the Jews "learn and practice the teachings of Moses," stating that even when asked, "they do not tell one the way unless the person observes the same rites as they, and they guide one who is thirsty to the fountain only if the person is circumcised" (14.101–104). He moreover slandered the Jews as being mean and narrow-minded "misanthropists." It is evident that Josephus was conscious of these and similar slanders. For example, Manetho stated that people were instructed by Moses "to have no connexion with any save members of their own confederacy" (*Ap* I, 261) and "to show goodwill to no man, to offer not the best but the worst advice" (*Ap* I, 309). Apion accused the Jews of swearing "by God who made heaven and earth and sea to show no goodwill to a single alien, above all to Greeks" (*Ap* II, 121). Apollonius Molon condemned the Jews "for declining to associate with those who have chosen to adopt a different mode of life" (*Ap* II, 258). Surely Josephus must have been thinking of these critics, for he emphasizes in *Against Apion* that the code of Moses was "designed to promote piety, friendly relations with each other, and humanity towards the world at large" (*Ap* II, 146). He mentions also the duty to share with foreigners and specifically enlists the articles of "humanity" (φιλανθρωπίαν), saying, "We must furnish fire, water, food to all who ask for them, point out the road, not leave a corpse unburied, show consideration even to declared enemies" (*Ap* II, 211). Moreover, when Josephus discusses the foreigners' rights to share in the harvest, based on the passages in Deuteronomy 24:19ff. and Leviticus 19:9ff. (*A* IV, 231ff.), he emphasizes, in more than one way, their rights, calling them "the others" (τῶν ἄλλων, τοῖς ἄλλοις), "wayfarers" (τοὺς ὁδῷ βαδίζοντας), "foreigners" (ξένοι), "ones met fortuitously" (τοὺς ὑπαντιάζοντας), and "strangers" (ἀφιγμένους δ' ἀλλαχόθεν ἀνθρώπους). Josephus is acutely conscious of the accusation that the Jews were "misanthropists" lacking humanity.

Conclusion

We have read the story of Moses by Josephus within the context of the anti-Semitic climate around Alexandria and have discovered that Moses is idealized as a hero of the Jewish race. His nativity is announced by a prediction and a divine revelation, which, in a way, raises him to the level of "the son of God"; his previously unknown youth is filled with descriptions of his superior understanding (intelligence) and beauty; the murder that he commits when he comes of age is completely omitted and substituted with his triumphal achievement on the Ethiopian expedition; and he is presented as a peerless commander of the Exodus in deliverance of his people of six hundred thousand.

The question raised by this is "Why must Moses be so dramatically idealized?" This is, indeed, problematic when those authors Josephus takes into account in his life of Moses, who haunt his *Jewish Antiquities,* and are actually referred to by their names and criticized in *Against Apion,* are writers who were not of Josephus' time. For example, Manetho lived in the third century B.C., Apollonius Molon and Lysimachus in the first century B.C., Apion, in the first half of first century A.D., and Chaeremon, in the first century A.D. Setting aside Chaeremon, whose date of death is not clear, the rest were personages of the past whom Josephus could have easily brushed aside. But this mystery is no longer a mystery when one is informed by implication, for example, by Tacitus' *History,* that the literature of the anti-Semites around Alexandria was widely read by the Roman intellectual class at the time of Josephus (A.D. 70–100) and that the slanders and vituperations against the Jews were continually repeated and reinforced.

Even if there may not be solid proof that these books were circulated in Rome, there were authors such as Seneca (4 B.C.–A.D. 65) and the satirical poet Persius (A.D. 34–62), who studied the customs of the Jews and concluded that their observance of the Sabbath was indeed a reflection of their lethargy, and the satirist Petronius (?–A.D. 66), who claimed that the Jews do not eat pork because they worship the pig. Consequently, it is only natural that Josephus devotes a considerable portion of his *Jewish Antiquities* to the story of Moses. Moses is, after all, the very person who is responsible for the religion, customs, and ethics of the Jews—he is the very embodiment of their nationality.

Did Josephus succeed in his attempt in *Jewish Antiquities* to idealize Moses? Josephus laments in the dedication to Epaphroditus in *Against Apion* that

> since, however, I observe that a considerable number of persons, influenced by the malicious calumnies of certain individuals, discredit the statements in my history concerning our antiquity, and adduce as proof of the comparative modernity of our race the fact that it has not been thought worthy of mention by the best known Greek historians, I consider it my duty to devote a brief treatise to all these points; in order at once to convict our detractors of malignity and deliberate falsehood, to correct the ignorance of others, and to instruct all who desire to know the truth concerning the antiquity of our race. (*Ap* I, 2–3)

The major point bothering Josephus is that his assertion concerning the antiquity of his race was not accepted. His story of Moses must have been equally unpersuasive. In the first half of *Against Apion,* Josephus devotes himself to the proof of the antiquity of the Jewish race, but in the second half, he concentrates on the rebuttal of the anti-Semitic slanders and on the commandments and political institutions ordained by Moses. Josephus believes that it is his "duty" (δεῖν) to defend his people, but his persistence is nothing other than a confession that he has failed in his attempt, and it confirms the vigor of the anti-Semitism existing in Rome. After completion of *Jewish Antiquities,* his masterpiece in twenty books, which took him about twelve years to write, Josephus felt he still had to employ the remainder of his life to compose, for the sake of the people of which he was a part, this apologia.

Translated by Katsutoshi Tsurumatsu

Notes

1. Three volumes (Jerusalem 1976, 1980, 1984); the first two volumes of this work will be abbreviated *GLAJJ* I or II. For further references to the secondary literature on ancient views concerning Moses in particular, see L. H. Feldman, *Josephus and Modern Scholarship* (Berlin, 1984) 149–163, and, in particular, John G. Gager, *Moses in Greco-Roman Paganism* (Nashville, 1972).

2. After having argued about the antiquity of the Jewish people, citing a Greek historian as a witness in *Against Apion* I, 216, Josephus continues, "In addition to those already cited, Theophilus, Theodotus, Mnaseas, Aristophanes, Hermogenes, Euhemerus, Conon, Zopyrion, and, may be, many more—for my reading has not been exhaustive—have made more than a passing allusion to us."

3. Posidonius states that it is "a most widely accepted opinion" that "the ancestors of the so-called modern Jews are the Egyptians" (a fragment preserved in Strabo's *Geography* 16.2.34 = cf. *GLAJJ* I, F 115). Strabo also attests that "the Jews also originated from the Egyptians" (cf. *GLAJJ* I, F 124, and the quotation from Strabo that is preserved in *A* XIV, 118 = *GLAJJ* I, F 105). Strabo does not mention Posidonius by name, though a number of scholars (see *GLAJJ* I, pp. 264–265) have assumed that Strabo's source is Posidonius. Diodorus also adopts the Egyptian origin theory (cf. *World History* 1.55.1 = *GLAJJ* I, F 57, *World History* 34.1.1.1 = *GLAJJ* I, F 63).

4. Hecataeus of Abdera (ca. 300 B.C.) claims that the Jews were aliens residing in Egypt who were banished when an epidemic broke out (cf. a fragment preserved in Diodorus' *World History* = *GLAJJ* I, F 11). Pompeius Trogus maintained that the ancestors of the Jews were *psora* patients and lepers (cf. *Fragments* by Justin 36.2.12 = *GLAJJ* I, F 137). Tacitus claims that the ancestors of the Jews were *psora* patients (cf. *Histories* 5.4.2 = *GLAJJ* II, F 281).

5. Posidonius also thinks that Moses was one of the Egyptian priests (cf. Strabo's *Geography* 16.2.35 = *GLAJJ* I, F 115).

6. Nicarchus also believes that Moses was a leper (cf. *GLAJJ* I, F 248).

7. Nicarchus records that Moses was called "Alpha" (cf. *GLAJJ* I, F 248).

8. Mnaseas is the first to mention the ass worship of the Jews; but Diodorus records that when Antiochus Epiphanes entered the sanctuary of the Temple in Jerusalem, he saw a "stone statue of a man with a long beard on the back of an ass and imagined that it was the statue of Moses who founded Hierosolyma, established the Jewish race, and gave the misanthropistic, unreasonable customs to the Jews" (cf. *World History* 34.1.3 = *GLAJJ* I, F 63). Damocritus (first century A.D.) recalls in his book *On Jews* that the Jews used to hold "a golden head of an ass" as the object of their worship (cf. *GLAJJ* I, F 247). Tacitus records that "a herd of wild asses led the Jews through the wilderness to a water place (cf. *Histories* 5.3.2 = *GLAJJ* II, F 281). Refer to *GLAJJ* I, pp. 97–98, for an explanation of ass worship.

9. Damocritus asserts that the Jews "captured a foreigner every seven years to use him as a sacrifice" (cf. *GLAJJ* I, F 247).

10. See notes 7 and 8.

11. All citations of Josephus are from the Loeb edition.

12. The Latin version reads Telmus. The Book of Jubilees 47.5, which is part of the Old Testament Pseudepigrapha, gives Tharmuth; the Babylonian Talmud, *Megillah* 13a, based on 1 Chronicles 3:17, Bithiah; Artapanus gives Merris. (Cf. Eusebius, *Preparation for the Gospel* 9.27.)

13. The only non-Jewish author who refers to the comeliness of Moses is Pompeius Trogus. He mentions "his [Joseph's] son who, besides the inheritance of his father's knowledge, was recommended also for the comeliness of his person" (cf. *Fragments* 36.2.11 = *GLAJJ* I, F 137).

14. Philo provides a similar explanation in *Life of Moses* 1.17 that reads, "He was drawn from water so that the princess called him Moses after it; the Egyptians call water '*môu.*'"

15. *Midrash Rabbah,* Exodus 2:10 reads, "The daughter of Pharaoh . . . no longer made him leave the king's palace. For he was handsome, and everyone wanted to lay his sight on him. [In fact,] those who saw him did forget themselves."

16. The latter half of this legend, that is to say, the episode of Ethiopians invading Egypt, is also recorded by Artapanus (Eusebius, *Preparation for the Gospel* 9.27).

17. Philo *De Vita Mosis* 1.79.

18. After describing the sanctuary and the cherubim in the Temple of Solomon (*A* VIII, 73), Josephus explains that "no one can explain or imagine what manner of being these *cherubeis* [cherubim] were."

19. See note 4.

20. Cf. *GLAJJ* I, F 195.

21. Cf. Tacitus *Histories* 5.4.2 = *GLAJJ* II, F 281.

22. Cf. Plutarch, *Quaestiones Convivales* 4.5 = *GLAJJ* I, F 258; Juvenal, *Satires* 14.96–100 = *GLAJJ* II, F 301. Also, see Macrobius, *Saturnalia* 2.4.11 = *GLAJJ* II, F 543.

23. Philo *De Vita Mosis* 2.205.

8 Antiquities *IV, 277 and 288,*
Compared with Early Rabbinic Law

DAVID M. GOLDENBERG

n his *Antiquities,* Josephus claims to set forth "the precise details of what
is written in the Scriptures [ἀναγραφαῖς] . . . , neither adding nor omitting anything" (*A* I, 17). Throughout his works he repeats this claim: "I
have recounted each detail here told just as I found it in the sacred books" (ταῖς
ἱεραῖς βίβλοις; *A* II, 347). He has recorded each event "as I have found them
in the ancient books [ἀρχαίοις . . . βιβλίοις]. . . . I was only translating
[μεταφράζειν] the books [βίβλους] of the Hebrews . . . promising to report
their contents without adding anything of my own to the narrative or omitting
anything therefrom" (*A* X, 218). Immediately before transmitting the biblical
laws, he again repeats his claim: "All is here written as he [Moses] left
it: nothing have we added . . . , nothing which has not been bequeathed
by Moses" (*A* IV, 196). He repeats twice more that his work consisted of
mere "translating": the *Antiquities* "will embrace our entire ancient history
and political constitution, translated from the Hebrew records" (τὴν παρ'
ἡμῖν ἀρχαιολογίαν καὶ [τὴν] διάταξιν τοῦ πολιτεύματος ἐκ τῶν Ἑβραϊκῶν
μεθηρμηνευμένην γραμμάτων; *A* I, 5, cf. XX, 261); and "in my *Antiquities,*
as I said, I have given a translation of our sacred books" (ἐκ τῶν ἱερῶν
γραμμάτων μεθηρμήνευκα; *Ap* I, 54).

Scholarly opinion ascribes Josephus' deviations from the biblical legal
material as due to one or more of the following factors: his knowledge of the
Jewish postbiblical legal traditions (oral law); his reliance on a written source
of Jewish legal matter, or on a Targum, or on Philo, or on Roman law; his
reporting of contemporaneous Jewish law as practiced in Palestine and ob-

---

I am grateful to Professors William Adler and Shaye Cohen for reading this article
and offering their comments. I am also thankful to Professor Louis Feldman for his remarks
below in n. 16.

served by him; his apologetic tendency to present Judaism in a favorable light to a non-Jewish audience; his own ignorance of the biblical source or his own interpretation of it; his intention to write a separate treatise on the laws which would have therefore influenced his presentation of the laws in the biblical paraphrase.[1]

Josephus says of his training, "I made great progress in my education [παιδείας], gaining a reputation for an excellent memory and understanding. While still a mere boy, about fourteen years old, I won universal applause for my love of letters [φιλογράμματον]; insomuch that the chief priests and the leading men of the city [τῶν τῆς πόλεως πρώτων = זקני העיר] used constantly to come to me for precise information on some particular in our ordinances" (νομίμων; V, 8–9). Josephus had an "expert knowledge of their [Pharisees'] laws" (τῶν νόμων paralleling ἔθη τὰ πάτρια; V, 198). He is "well versed in the study [φιλοσοφίας] of those writings [γράμμασι]," that is, the holy writings (ἱερῶν γραμμάτων), which he had translated (μεθηρμήνευκα) in the Antiquities (Ap I, 54).[2] "My compatriots [ὁμοεθνῶν] admit that in our Jewish learning [τὴν ἐπιχώριον . . . παιδείαν] I far excel them" (A XX, 263).

It would not appear unusual if Josephus, a Pharisee educated in Pharisaic tradition, would reflect this tradition in his works. As Rappaport says, "[Josephus] ist also ein Kind des Rabbinismus; er hat in seiner Jugend die Sagen und Auslegungen der Rabbinen gehört, hat die Bibel mit den Erweiterungen, wie sie in Palästina gelehrt wurden, gekannt; diese rabbinischen Kenntnisse durchziehen seine Werke, und so erklären sich die verschiedenen Zeugen mündlicher Überlieferung bei Josephus. Josephus ist Träger lebendiger rabbinisch-palästinensischer Tradition."[3] Whether this conclusion about nonlegal matter is valid as well for the legal material in Josephus remains to be seen.

In a previous article,[4] I compared legal matter found in Antiquities IV, 274–276 with rabbinic legal material of the tannaitic period (i.e., of the first two centuries A.D.). Josephus' description there of four laws—regarding lost objects, providing assistance to animals, giving directions to one lost, and reviling the deaf—was found to agree with tannaitic law in several particulars. In this article, I shall extend this comparison to Antiquities IV, 277 and 288, which respectively covers the law of quarrels with resulting injuries and the law of withholding wages.

It is not my intention here to draw conclusions about Josephus' sources for the sections under discussion. Any such conclusions would have to be based, optimally, upon the entire relevant block of legal material in Josephus, in this case Antiquities IV, 199–301.[5] For the same reason, at this stage nothing can be said about using Josephus as a reference in time for dating tannaitic halakhah and discerning its development. As David Daube pointed out in his review of Belkin's *Philo and the Oral Law*,[6] parallelism does not necessarily show dependency. Points held in common may be due to other factors.

Nevertheless, the first step toward showing dependency is showing parallelism. After Daube's "other causes" are ruled out and after the nature of the parallelism is fully explored (literary as well as thematic parallelism?) we may say something about dependence. This article is meant as a contribution to the first step.

The Law of Quarrels with Resulting Injuries

Antiquities IV, 277

Ἐν μάχῃ τις, ὅπου μὴ σίδηρος, πληγεὶς παραχρῆμα μὲν ἀποθανὼν ἐκδικείσθω ταὐτὸν παθόντος τοῦ πεπληχότος. ἂν δὲ κομισθεὶς παρ' ἑαυτὸν καὶ νοσήσας ἐπὶ πλείονας ἡμέρας ἔπειτ' ἀποθάνῃ, ἀθῷος ἔστω ὁ πλήξας, σωθέντος δὲ καὶ πολλὰ δαπανήσαντος εἰς τὴν νοσηλείαν ἀποτινέτω πάνθ' ὅσα παρὰ τὸν χρόνον τῆς κατακλίσεως ἀνάλωσε καὶ ὅσα τοῖς ἰατροῖς ἔδωκεν.

In a fight without use of the blade, if one be stricken and die on the spot, he shall be avenged by a like fate for him that struck him. But if he be carried home and lie sick for several days before he dies, that struck him shall go unpunished; howbeit, if he recover and hath spent much on his doctoring, the other shall pay all that he hath expended during the time of his confinement to his couch and all that he hath given to the physicians. (Thackeray)

Exodus 21:12
Whosoever strikes a man so that he dies shall be put to death.

Exodus 21:18–19
When men quarrel and one strikes the other with a stone or with his fist and the man does not die but keeps his bed, then if the man rises again and walks abroad with his staff, he that struck him shall be clean; only he shall pay for the loss of his time, and shall have him thoroughly healed.

Leviticus 24:17, 21
He who kills a man shall be put to death. . . . He who kills a man shall be put to death.

There is no biblical parallel to Josephus' statement that one goes unpunished if the person whom he struck remains alive several days before dying. Weyl thinks that Josephus has mistakenly combined two biblical laws: the killing of a freeman and the killing of a slave.[7] Exodus 21:20–21 speaks of a slave: "When a man strikes his slave, male or female, with a rod and the slave dies under his hand, he shall be punished. But if the slave survives a day or two, he is not to be punished." This Josephus paraphrases with the sentence "in a fight . . . shall go unpunished." The second part of *Antiquities* IV, 277, "howbeit . . . to the physicians," corresponds to Exodus 21:18–19, which speaks of a freeman. Thus far Weyl (followed by Reinach, Thackeray, and Schalit)[8], who bases his conjecture on two points. First, the distinction which Josephus makes between immediate death (=guilty) and delayed death (=innocent) is found only in the law regarding the slave. Secondly, Josephus' ἐκδικείσθω, "he shall be avenged," is not found in the law of the freeman but is found in the law of the slave (Ex. 21:20, נקם ינקם [Septuagint, δίκη ἐκδικηθήτω]).

However, this theory raises more questions than it answers. Most important, of course, is that Josephus is not talking here of slaves. Besides that, ἐν μάχῃ clearly corresponds to וכי יריבון אנשים in the law of the freeman (Ex. 21:18); ὅπου μὴ σίδηρος is probably a paraphrase for באבן או באגרוף (*ibid.*), as Thackeray has noted, and as Weyl himself states, it is meant to clarify the later recuperation of the *freeman* spoken of by Josephus;[9] and κομισθεὶς παρ᾽ ἑαυτὸν καὶ νοσήσας is clearly a paraphrase of ונפל למשכב, said of the freeman, and not of יעמד (Septuagint, διαβιώσῃ), said of the slave. Therefore, ἐπὶ πλείονας ἡμέρας is probably Josephus' own addition rather than a rendering of יום או יומים (Septuagint, ἡμέραν μίαν ἢ δύο) said of the slave—for which it would, anyway, be a faulty translation.

Lest undue emphasis be given to Josephus' use of ἐκδικείσθω, as Weyl would have it, the following are noted: ἀθῷος ἔστω ὁ πλήξας is patently a translation of ונקה המכה (Septuagint, ἀθῷος ἔσται ὁ πατάξας) said of the freeman; in fact, were Josephus paraphrasing the slave law we should expect an antithetical οὐκ ἐκδικηθήσεται, as the Septuagint translates לא יוקם; Josephus' explanation that the killer "suffer a like fate," that is, death, as punishment, is not mentioned in the slave law.[10]

Weyl seems to be aware of all these problems, for in his last footnote dealing with this part of Josephus he says, "daraus wird uns aber erstens klar, dass Josephus die Gesetze, zum Teil wenigstens, aus dem Gedächtnisse dargestellt hat." The scholar, with this statement, is apparently glossing over the fact that Josephus, throughout *Antiquities* IV, 277, has many parallels to the biblical law of the freeman but not to that of the slave. However, with this statement Weyl has destroyed his entire argument, for if Josephus is writing from memory, ἐκδικείσθω need not parallel the biblical נקם ינקם of the slave.

Finally, we note that Philo, too, when discussing the murder of a freeman, divides the law into the same three possibilities as Josephus (although

Philo claims payment for delayed death while Josephus does not and Philo's order differs): "He smites the other with his clenched fist or takes up a stone and throws it . . . [1] if his opponent dies at once the striker too must die . . . but if that other is not killed on the spot by the blow, but is laid up with sickness and after keeping his bed and receiving the proper care [3] gets up again and goes abroad . . . the striker must be fined twice over, first to make good the other's enforced idleness and secondly to compensate for the cost of his cure. This payment will release him from the death penalty [2] *even if the sufferer from the blow subsequently dies."* [11]

That Josephus in *Antiquities* IV, 277 is speaking only of the freeman is beyond doubt. The problem raised by the scholars—that Josephus differentiates between an immediate death and a delayed death—may be answered by pointing to tannaitic halakhah, which shares this differentiation. According to the Tosefta, "if one smites his fellow . . . and it was determined that the injured party would live but he, nevertheless, died, his heirs receive monetary compensation," [12] but he who smote is not put to death. This is also seen in another clause of the Tosefta: "If one smites his fellow . . . and it was determined that the injured party would live, a second determination for death is not made." [13] This means that if, after the determination of life, the injured nevertheless dies, the injurer is not liable to the death penalty. The amoraim, as well, understood this to be the tannaitic law, probably having in mind this last cited clause of the Tosefta. [14]

This is the meaning of Josephus' "if he be carried home and lie sick," i.e., if it appeared that he would live. [15] That this is the meaning connoted by Josephus is seen by his usage of ἔπειτα with a finite verb after a participle, a construction that "is often used to make an opposition between the participle and the verb, marking surprise or the like." [16] ἔπειτα, then, does not have merely a sequential force, as Thackeray had given it. Josephus' passage is to be translated thus: "If he be carried home and lie sick for several days but [surprisingly] nevertheless dies, he that struck him shall go unpunished."

The first statement in *A* IV, 277, that the penalty is death if the one smitten dies immediately, is not found in Exodus 21:18–19. It is possible that Josephus had in mind Exodus 21:12 (or Leviticus 24:17, 21). [17] It is more likely, however, that Josephus in all of *Antiquities* IV, 277 was dealing only with Exodus 21:18–19 and that this law was deduced (either by himself or by a source before him) from those very verses which declare that if the victim does not die "he that struck him shall be clear; only he shall pay." That is, if the victim does die, then he that smote him shall not be clear but shall die. This same deduction was made by the tannaim, although it is not as clearly enunciated as Josephus' statement until the amoraic period. [18]

In summary, Josephus (and Philo), in discussing injuries resulting from quarrels (Exodus 21:18–19), divides the possible results into three cases:

(1) death is immediate; the penalty to the striker is death; (2) death is delayed, the striker is not punished by death (Philo and the tannaim demand compensation; Josephus does not); and (3) there is no death but only injuries, the striker makes compensation. The entire three-part section in both Josephus and Philo parallels Exodus 21:18–19 and tannaitic halakhah (and perhaps Exodus 21:12).

The Law of Withholding Wages

Antiquities IV, 288

ὁμοίως δὲ τῷ περὶ παρακαταθηκῶν κἂν μισθόν τις ἀποστερήσῃ τῶν ἐπὶ σώμασι τοῖς αὐτῶν ἐργαζομένων, μεμισήσθω· ὅθεν οὐκ ἀποστερητέον ἀνδρὸς πένητος μισθόν, εἰδότας ὡς ἀντὶ γῆς καὶ τῶν ἄλλων κτημάτων ὁ θεὸς αὐτῷ τοῦτον εἴη παρεσχηκώς· ἀλλὰ μηδὲ ἀναβάλλεσθαι τὴν ἀπόδοσιν, ἀλλ᾽ αὐθημερὸν ἐκτίνειν ὡς οὐ βουλομένου τοῦ θεοῦ τῆς ἐξ ὧν πεπόνηκε χρήσεως ὑστερεῖν τὸν εἰργασμένον.

And as with deposits, so if anyone withhold the wages of those who labor with their bodies, let him be execrated; since one must not deprive a poor man of his wages, knowing that this, instead of land and other possessions, is the portion which God has granted him. Nay, one must not even defer payment, but discharge it the selfsame day, for God would not have the laborer kept waiting for the enjoyment of the fruits of his toil.

Antiquities XX, 220

(Shortly before the war with Rome broke out, the work on the Temple was completed, idling thousands. Public works projects, therefore, were found for them. Josephus then adds this parenthetic remark.)

εἰ μίαν τις ὥραν τῆς ἡμέρας ἐργάσαιτο, τὸν μισθὸν ὑπὲρ ταύτης εὐθέως ἐλάμβανεν.

If anyone worked for but one hour of the day, he at once received his pay for this.

Leviticus 19:13

You shall not oppress your neighbor or rob him. The wages of a hired servant shall not remain with you all night until the morning.

Deuteronomy 24:14–15

You shall not oppress a hired servant who is poor and needy, whether he is one of your brethren or one of the sojourners who are in your land within your towns; you shall give him his hire on the day he earns it, before the sun goes down (for he is poor, and sets his heart upon it); lest he cry against you to the Lord, and it be sin in you.

Josephus restricts this law to one who works with his body.[19] This point is interesting inasmuch as it conflicts with the tannaitic statement that the rent for one's animal or one's utensils must also be paid promptly.[20] This statement of the tannaim, given anonymously, cannot be dated. We can, however, give it a *terminus ante quem*. That animals and utensils were subject to this law was deduced exegetically from the verse in Deuteronomy (or Leviticus following Sifra). The exact nature of the biblical admonition regarding animals and utensils was then debated by R. Jose ben Judah and his contemporaries. In other words, the extension of the law to include property was accomplished no later than the time of R. Jose ben Judah (the end of the second and beginning of the third centuries). At any rate, we have no clear proof of a conflict here between Josephus and contemporaneous halakhah.

Josephus may simply be paraphrasing the verse in Deuteronomy under-standing ואליו הוא נושא את נפשו to mean "those who labor with their bodies." Such understanding, indeed, underlies the tannaitic exegeses of these words.[21] In fact, there is a *baraitha* which clearly restricts the law to work done by the laborer himself: "R. Hanania learned: The verse says 'Before the sun goes down, for he is poor,' i.e., only that which is subject to poverty and wealth, therefore excluding animals and utensils, which are not subject to poverty and wealth."[22]

To be sure, the editors of the Talmud understood this *baraitha* differently. R. Jose ben Judah is of the opinion that animals and utensils are subject only to the prohibition stated in Deuteronomy 24:14 but not to the commandment in the next verse. The above cited *baraitha* is adduced to support R. Jose ben Judah's view.[23] However, this support is unsatisfactory, as already noted by Yom Tob Isbili of the fourteenth century. For if the *baraitha* excludes animals and utensils from ניומו תתן שכרו it should exclude them from לא תעשוק שכיר עני too; for the basis of the exegesis, the word עני, is applicable in both verses.[24]

The editors of the Talmud, then, understood the *baraitha* to include prop-erty in the law of prompt payment but to restrict the Pentateuchal admonition concerning it to the words לא תעשוק שכיר עני. There is nothing, however, in the *baraitha* itself that demands such an interpretation; and, as we have seen, adducing this *baraitha* to support R. Jose ben Judah is problematical. I believe, therefore, that the *baraitha* is not concerned with which Pentateuchal words apply to animals and utensils but with whether the law of prompt pay-ment is applicable at all to them. In stating that it is not, the *baraitha* is ex-pressing the early halakhah mentioned by Josephus.

As to the next part of the law, Thackeray's rendering of μεμισήσθω with "let him be execrated" is ambiguous due to the double meaning of execrate in English: (1) to curse and (2) to hate. μεμισήσθω, however, means one thing only: "let him be hated." Similarly, the Latin *habeatur odibilis* means "let him be deserving of hate." A more felicitous rendering, therefore, would prefer this translation to that of Thackeray.[25]

That one ought to hate evil is a concept found—in a variety of literary forms—in the Old Testament, Qumran material, the New Testament and other early Christian literature, and a third-century rabbinic source. The following list compares the undeclined verb and its object in the various expressions of this concept as they appear in the sources:[26]

	verb	object	verb	object
Am 5:15	שנא	רע	אהב	טוב
Ps 97:10	שנא	רע		
Prov 8:3	שנא	רע		
IQS 1.3–4	שנא	כל אשר מאס	אהב	כל אשר בהר
IQS 4.24–25	שנא	עולה		
IQH 14.10	תעב	כל אשר [. . .]	[. . .]	כל אשר אהב
IQH 17.24	מאס	בכל אשר שנא	התהלך	בכל אשר אהב
CD 2.15	מאס	אשר שנא	בחר	אשר רצה
Rom 12.9	hate	evil	hold fast	good
Rev 2.6	hate	evil (works of Nicolaitans)		
Barnabas 19.2	hate	all not pleasing to God		
Barnabas 19.11	hate	evil		

E. F. Sutcliffe has shown that "hatred" in these sources means "to abhor," "to stay away from the evil object" (see also Learey, p. 121).[27] That this is so may be seen by the interchange of מאס, תעב and שנא as the verb in the formula (in particular compare שנא כל אשר מאס with מאס בכל אשר שנא with the antithesis in Romans "hate/hold fast," and with the full text of IQS 1.3–5, טוב כל אשר בחר ולשטא את כל אשר מאס לרחוק מכול רע ולרבוק בכל מעשי, which by chiastic parallelism would equate אהב with דבק and שנא with רחק. With these equations established, we may add to our list the following:[28]

	verb	object	verb	object
I Thess. 5.21–22	abstain	appearance of evil	hold fast	good
Polycarp 2.2	abstain	unrighteousness	love	what he loved
PT Berakhon 4.2, 7d	רחק	מכל מה ששנאת	קרב	לכל מה שאהבת
IQH 15.18–19	לא בחר	כאשר שנאת	רצה	בכל אשר צויתה
IQ22 1.5–7	לא בחר	[בשקועי ה]גו[י]ס ותו[עבותיהם	אהב	כאשר צויתי

The transition from act to actor, that is, from hating evil to hating the evil-doer, as in Josephus, *Antiquities* IV, 288, is made in the following sources:[29]

	verb	object	verb	object
IQS 1.9–11	שנא	כל בני חושך	אהב	כל בני אור
IQS 9.22–23	שנא	אנשי שחת		
IQS 9.15–16	שנא	איש כבור כפיו ולפי שכלו	אהב	איש כבור כפיו ולפי שכלו
Targum Ecclesiastes 3:8	סני	גבר חייבא	רחם	חד לחבריה
BJ 2.139	hate	the unjust	fight the battle	the just
Titus 3:3	hate	sinners		

Sutcliffe shows that the concept of hating evil and the evildoer is *imitatio dei,* derived from God's character as expressed in the Old Testament. It is "hateful to God and therefore to those who love God." [30] The lists above certainly show that this concept was a firmly established ethical principle in Judaism of Josephus' time, and we should not, therefore, be surprised to see an echo of it in Josephus' writings. [31] It cannot be ruled out, however, that $\mu\varepsilon$-$\mu\iota\sigma\dot{\eta}\sigma\theta\omega$ (if, indeed, it is the correct reading) grew out of faulty reading by Josephus (or Josephus' Bible) of שנא for נשא in Deuteronomy 24:15.

After introducing the subject of paying wages, Josephus then divides the law into two parts: (1) total denial of wages ($\dot{\alpha}\pi o\sigma\tau\varepsilon\rho\dot{\varepsilon}\omega$) and (2) deferment of wages ($\dot{\alpha}\nu\alpha\beta\dot{\alpha}\lambda\lambda o\mu\alpha\iota$). This structure is apparently based on Deuteronomy 24:14–15: "You shall not oppress a hired servant. . . . You shall give him his hire on the day he earns it, before the sun goes down." [32]

Josephus supplies a reason for the prohibition of withholding wages: "This, instead of land and other possessions, is the portion which God has granted him." His wages are his portion and denial of them would be theft, as would be the removal of one's possessions. Tannaitic literature also views the withholding of wages as theft. [33] Josephus, however, may not have relied on tannaitic statements but may have based the law on the same source as the tannaim, Leviticus 19:13: "You shall not oppress your neighbor or rob him. The wages of a hired servant shall not remain with you all night until the morning." [34] The reason given by Josephus for the prohibition of the deferment of wages ("for God would not have the laborer kept waiting") is simply a paraphrase of Deuteronomy 24:15.

Biblical law also states that the wages of the laborer must be paid on the same day of his work. Tannaitic law further discusses the time when payment is due for the different types of laborers. [35] One type of worker so discussed is the laborer who works by the hour. When he must be paid depends upon whether he is employed by day or by night. [36] The tannaitic law as we have it is somewhat muddled due to conflicting opinions, differing interpretations of a mishnaic text, and variant readings. [37] Nowhere, however, is there a tannaitic halakhah that the hourly worker is to be paid immediately upon completion of his work, as Josephus seems to intimate (*A* XX, 220).

Josephus' statement is, of course, a reflection of historical events and not a paraphrase of any law, tannaitic or otherwise. The halakhah, in determining the latest time of payment, does not preclude immediate payment. The point to be emphasized here, however, is the agreement between the historical reality as recorded by Josephus and the spirit of these halakhot, biblical and tannaitic: the laborer was to be paid with as little delay as possible.[38]

Notes

1. For a review and critique of the scholarly works on this issue, see my dissertation, "Halakhah in Josephus" (Dropsie College, 1978).

Two recent attempts have been made to explain the apparently blatant disagreement between Josephus' statements and his actions. Louis H. Feldman ("Hellenizations in Josephus' Portrayal of Man's Decline," *Religions in Antiquity: Essays in Memory of Erwin Ramsdell Goodenough*, ed. J. Neusner [Leiden, 1968], pp. 336–339) notes that (a) the word $\mu\epsilon\theta\epsilon\rho\mu\eta\nu\epsilon\acute{u}\omega$ may mean either translated verbatim or interpreted with some freedom, and (b) the writings ($\gamma\rho\alpha\mu$-$\mu\acute{\alpha}\tau\omega\nu$ $\grave{\alpha}\nu\alpha\gamma\rho\alpha\phi\alpha\hat{\imath}\varsigma$) which Josephus refers to are "not merely what is written in the Bible but also that which was included in the Jewish tradition of interpretation and which was regarded as an integral part of that tradition." (This point was already made by Gustav Tachauer, *Das Verhältniss von Flavius Josephus zur Bibel und Tradition* [Erlangen, 1871], pp. 45–46. Cf. also Marcus Olitzki, *Flavius Josephus und die Halacha. Erster Teil: Einleitung, die Opfer* [Berlin, 1885], p. 27, n. 36.) Feldman is referring specifically to nonlegal interpretation, but what he says may apply as well to legal matter.

Secondly, W. C. van Unnik (*Flavius Josephus als historischer Schriftsteller* [Heidelberg, 1978]) argues that the expression "neither adding nor omitting anything" merely means that nothing has been changed for the sake of adulation or enmity. This conclusion is based also on the author's earlier work, "De la règle Μήτε προσθεῖναι μήτε ἀφελεῖν dans l'histoire du canon," *VC* 3 (1949): 1–36.

2. The translation of $\phi\iota\lambda o\sigma o\phi\acute{\imath}\alpha$ as "study" is Thackeray's. Cf., however, *Ap* II, 47: τοὺς νόμους καὶ τὴν πάτριον ἡμῶν φιλοσοφίαν.

3. Salomo Rappaport, *Agada und Exegese bei Flavius Josephus* (Frankfurt am Main, 1930), p. xiv.

4. "The Halakhah in Josephus and in Tannaitic Literature," *JQR* 67 (1976): 30–43. See also עַל הִתְפַּתְּחוּתָהּ שֶׁל הֲלָכָה אַחַת, *Biẓaron*, Shevat-Adar 5737, pp. 111ff. where I deal with the development of the laws of assistance to animals.

5. Other legal material is found in: *A* III, 224–286, IV, 67–75; *Ap* II, 103–109, 190–219; and scattered throughout Josephus' works as incidental remarks to his narrative.

6. *BO* 5 (March 1948): 64–65. See also V. Tcherikover in the Prolegomenon to *CPJ*, pp. 32–33, n. 84, and the literature cited there.

7. Heinrich Weyl, *Die jüdischen Strafgesetze bei Flavius Josephus in ihrem Verhältnis zu Schrift und Halacha* (Berlin, 1900), pp. 54–57.

8. All in their respective editions of Josephus. So also Belkin, *Philo and the Oral Law* (Cambridge, 1940), p. 99 (where Ex. 21:26 is mistakenly written for Ex. 21:20). Schalit refers to the wrong page in Weyl.

9. Weyl, *op.· cit.*, p. 54. Josephus' paraphrase, according to Weyl, is also meant to clarify the fact that the injured lingered on for a while before succumbing; with a sword death would be immediate. (Cf. PT San 9.2, 27a: כשהוא בא אצל הברזל . . . אפילו צינורא קטנה דהיא יכלה .(מקים גו וושטא ומיקטליניה

10. Weyl (p. 56, n. 16) is aware of this problem and claims that Josephus was following the halakhic interpretation of the avenging found in Mekhilta Rabbi Ishmael *Nezikin*, 7 (p. 273; נקם ינקם מיתה); Philo, *De Specialibus Legibus* 3.141; and Targum Ps.-Jonathan. However, if we assume that Josephus is speaking of the death of a freeman, Josephus' statement is simply a paraphrase of the Bible; see below.

11. *De Specialibus Legibus* 3.105–107. Philo follows this last law with its reason: "For as he got better and walked abroad, his death may be due not to the blow but to other causes." Cf. M. Sanhedrin 9.1, רבי המכה את חברו . . . ואמדוהו למיתה והקל ממה שהיה ולאחר מכאן הכביד ומת חייב. נחמיה אומר פטור שרגלים לדבר, and see Albeck's notes to M. Nazir 9.4 in his edition of the Mishnah.

12. T. Baba Kamma 9.5–6: צער המכה את חבירו אמדוהו לחיים ומת משלם נזק ריפוי שבת ובושת ליורשיו.

13. T. Baba Kamma 9.5: המכה את חבירו אמדוהו . . . לחיים אין אומדין אותו למיה.

14. BT Sanhedrin 78b: ימות ונפל .אלא לרבנן תרי אומדני למה לי (רש״י: לכתוב ולא למשכב ונקה המכה שבתו יתן) חד אמדוהו למיתה וחיה וחד אמדוהו לחיים ומת (רש״י: ולא ימות, אם אמדוהו תחלה שלא ימות אפי' מת לאחר (מכאן שבתו יתן ורפא ירפא. Cf. Midrash Haggadol, ad loc.: ולא ימות שבתו יתן הא אם מת פטור מכאן אמרו . . . אם אמדוהו לחיים נותן and PT Nazir 9.5, 58a (PT Sanhedrin 9.3, חמשה דברים ונפטר ואפילו חלה חלה המוכה והכביד ומת 27a): . . . . מתניתא מסייעא ליה לרשב״ל אמדוהו לחיים ומת מאימתי נותנין לו

15. And not that it was clear from the outset that he would die but that he lingered on for a while, which is the meaning given by the tannaim to יום או יומים in regard to the slave law as opposed to the freeman law. Cf. Mekhilta Rabbi Ishmael, ad loc. (p. 272): ישראל שהחמיר בו שאינו ביום או יומים . . . כנעני שהקל בו שהוא ביום או יומים with M. Sanhedrin 9.1 (freeman): ואמדוהו למיתה והקל ממה שהיה ולאחר מכאן הכביד ומת חייב.

16. Liddell-Scott, s.v. ἔπειτα I, 3. Professor Louis Feldman points out to me that the examples of this usage given in Liddell-Scott, i.e., in Aeschylus (twice), Sophocles (twice), Aristophanes (twice), and Plato (twice), lend indirect support to the adversative force of ἔπειτα in *Antiquities* IV, 277, "since Josephus is stylistically fond of the tragedians, especially Sophocles, and he certainly knew Plato. (On Josephus' knowledge of Plato see *Ap* I, 7, where he borrows from *Timaeus* 22 B-C, without specifically mentioning it, the notion that 'in the Greek world everything will be found to be modern, and dating, so to speak, from yesterday or the day before.' Moreover, Josephus correctly remarks (*Ap* II, 168–169) that the philosophy of Plato is addressed only to the few, whereas the Torah's teachings are intended for the many. Again (*Ap* II, 192) he deliberately combats the idea that God had collaborators in the work of creation, though he mentions the names of neither Plato nor Philo, who held such views. Furthermore, Josephus cites Plato by name (*Ap* II, 223) as one admired by the Greeks for his dignity of character and persuasive eloquence but who is ridiculed by so-called experts. That he is acquainted with Plato's *Republic* is clear from his remark (*Ap* II, 224) that if one examines his laws, they will be found frequently easier than the Jewish code and more closely approximating the practice of the masses. He knows, moreover, that (*Ap* II, 224) Plato himself (*Timaeus* 28C) has admitted that it is not safe to express the true opinion about God to the masses. He cites the opinion (*Ap* II, 225) of those who regard Plato's discourses as brilliant but empty. He likewise is aware (*Ap* II, 256) that Plato banishes the poets, including Homer, from his ideal state in order to prevent them from obscuring with their fables the correct doctrine about God. Finally, Josephus declares (*Ap* II, 257) that Plato followed Moses in prescribing that all citizens must study the laws and memorize them verbatim, and that foreigners must not be permitted to mix at random with the citizens. As to

Josephus' possible knowledge of Aristophanes, see Yitzhak F. Baer, "Jerusalem in the Times of the Great Revolt: Based on the Source Criticism of Josephus and Talmudic-Midrashic Legends of the Temple's Destruction," (Hebrew) *Zion* 36 (1971): 127–190, who suggests that the source of Josephus' portrait of John of Gischala is the figure of Cleon in Thucydides and in Aristophanes. I admit that I do not have any specific proof that Josephus knew Aeschylus, unless Hildebrecht Hommel, "Das Wort Karban und seine Verwandten," *Philologus* 98 (1954): 132–149, is correct in connecting the word *korban* in Josephus with Aeschylus' Agamemnon (1061), καρβάνῳ)."

Professor Feldman also points to *Antiquities* IV, 246 and IV, 258 (both of which, like IV, 277, are legal passages) where ἔπειτα and the finite verb after a participle indicate a contrast. In addition to these instances, Feldman checked the instances of ἔπειτα occurring in Josephus and found that thirty-one cases have the participle followed by ἔπειτα and a finite verb. Of these, ten seem to have adversative force (*A* IV, 148; *BJ* I, 101, I, 256, I, 471, V, 548, VI, 7, VI, 165[?], VII, 98; and *A* IV, 246 and IV, 258 mentioned above).

17. Cf. Mekhilta Rabbi Ishmael, ad loc. 4 (p. 261): למה נאמר מכה איש ומת מות יומת לפי שנאמר ואיש כי יכה כל נפש אדם שומעני אפילו סטרו סטירה ת"ל מכה איש ומת מגיד שאינו חייב עד שתצא נפשו.

18. Mekhilta Rabbi Ishmael, ad loc. 6 (p. 270): ונקה המכה, שומע אני יתן ערבים BT Kethuboth 33b: ויטייל בשוק ת"ל אם יקום והתהלך בחוץ מגיד שחובשין אותו עד שמרפא אמר רב יעקב מנהר פקוד משמיה דרבא מלמד שחובשין אותו ואי מית קטלינן ליה ואי לא מית שבתו יתן ורפא ירפא. Cf. Midrash Haggadol ad loc. (p. 476): ואם אמדוהו למיתה אומרין את המכה בבית הסהר מיד ממתינין לזה אם מת יהרג המכה.

19. Cf. also Philo, *De Virt*. 88: "The wages of the poor man are to be paid on the same day . . . because the manual worker or load carrier who toils painfully *with his whole body* like a beast of burden, 'lives from day to day,' as the phrase goes, and his hopes rest upon his payment" (μισθὸν πένητος αὐθημερὸν ἀποδιδόναι . . . ὅτι . . . ὡς εἰπόν τινες, ἐφημερόβιος ὢν ὁ χειροτέχνης ἢ ἀχθοφόρος, ὅλῳ τῷ σώματι κακοπαθῶν ὑποζυγίου τρόπον, ἐπὶ τῷ μισθῷ τέθειται τὴν ἐλπίδα). Incidentally, note here Philo's agreement with the Septuagint interpretation of ואליו הוא נושא את נפשו in Deut. 24:15: καὶ ἐν αὐτῷ ἔχει τὴν ἐλπίδα, and with Targum Ps.-Jonathan: ומטולתיה הוא סבר לקיימא ית נפשיה.

20. Sifre Deut. 278 (p. 296): אין לי אלא שכר אדם שכר בהמה שכר כלים מנין תלמוד לומר אשר בארצך כל שבארצך (see Finkelstein's note *ibid.*, see also Midrash Tannaim to Deut. 24:15 (p. 159). M. Baba Meẓia 9.12: אחד שכר האדם ואחד שכר הבהמה ואחד שכר הכלים יש בו T. Baba Meẓia 10.3–4: משום ביומו תתן שכרו ויש בו משום לא תלין פעולת שכיר אתך עד בקר הכובש שכר שכיר עובר משום חמשה משום בל תעשוק ומשום בל תגזול ומשום בל תלין פעולת שכיר אתך עד בקר ביומו תתן שכרו ולא תבא עליו השמש כי עני הוא אחד שכיר אדם ואחד שכיר בהמה ואחד שכיר כלים משום שמות הללו ר' יוסי בר' יהודה אום' שכר אדם עובר משום הללו שמות שכר בהמה ושכר כלים עובר משום בל תעשוק BT Baba Meẓia דתניא . . . . אין לי אלא שכר אדם מניין לרבות בהמה וכולן וכלים ת"ל בארצך כל 111a–b: שבארצך עוברין בכל השמות הללו מכאן אמרו אחד שכר אדם ואחד שכר בהמה ואחד שבר כלים יש בו משום ביומו תתן שכרו ויש בהן פעולת שכיר רבי יוסי ברבי יהודה אומר . . . בהמה ובלים אין בהן אלא משום בל תעשוק בלבד . . . . דתנא דבי ר' ישמעאל אחד שכר PT Baba אדם ואחד שבר משום ביומו תתן שכרו ומשום לא תלין בהמה ואחד שכר כלים שי בו Meẓia 9.13, 12b: בארצך לרבות ההוהה והבהמה והעבדים בשעריך לרבות המטלטלין. Sifra Qedoshim 2.9 (p. 88b): לא תלין פעולת שכיר אתך עד בקר אין לי אלא שכר האדם שכר הבהמה מנין תלמוד לומר והכלים מנין שכר הקרקעות מנין תלמוד לומר לא תלין פעולת כל דבר.

21. Sifre Deut. 279 (p. 297): ואליו הוא נושא את נפשו למה עלה זה בכבש ומטר לך BT BM 112a: ואליו הוא נושא את נפשו מפני מה עלה זה בכבש ונתלה באילן ומסר; את נפשו מכלל שנאמר ואליו הוא נושא את נפשו אין לי Cf. Sifre Deut. 278 (p. 296): את עצמו למיתה אלא מלאכה שהוא עושה בנפשו מלאכה שאין עושה בנפשו מנין גרדי וסורק מנין תלמוד (= Midrash Tannaim Deut. 24:14, p. 158). Cf. Targum Onkelos: הוא לומר לא תעשוק מכל מקום

וְלֶה מסר ית נפשיה Targum Neofiti: ולאגר פעליה הוא מסר קדמך ית נפשיה, and Ben Sira 7:20: שכיר נותן נפשו (Septuagint: μίσθιον διδόντα τὴν ψυχὴν αὐτοῦ; Syriac: ܐܓܝܪܐ, ܕܝܗܒ ܠܗ ܢܦܫܗ).

22. BT Baba Meẓia 111b: תני רבי חנניא אמר קרא (לא תבא עליו השמש) כי עני הוא מי שהן באין לידי עניות ועשירות יצאו בהמה וכלים שאינן באין לידי עניות ועשירות. The words enclosed in parentheses are found in the printed editions but excluded in every extant manuscript. Variant readings for the name are: ר' חנין', רב חנניא, רב חנניה, רב חמנא.

23. Ibid.

24. Novellae ad loc., s.v. וקשיא לן א''כ: כי עני הוא דהכי הוא דריש [רבי יוטי בר יהודה] אמאי מרבינן להו ללא תעשוק דהא כתב לא תעשוק עני ואביון ונידוק מינה מי שבאין לידי אניות ועשירות יצאו בהמה וכלים ואפילו לאו דלא תעשוק ליכא.

25. The variant reading μημνήσθω ὅτι, rejected by Thackeray, Weill, and Schalit, was accepted by Whiston who translates thus: "After the same manner, as in these trusts [i.e., repayment], it is to be, if any one defraud those that undergo bodily labour for him. And let it always be remembered, that. . . ."

Incidentally, we can catch a glimpse here into the evolution of modern translations. Thackeray's translation was apparently based upon Weill's "qu'il soit exécré." While the French word may also allow both meanings, its primary meaning is "to hate"; the primary meaning of the English word, on the other hand, is "to curse." Hence, Schalit's translation החרם יחרימוהו, which means only "let him be banned [i.e., cursed]," and is therefore wrong, was apparently based upon Thackeray.

26. Barnabas will be found in Kirsopp Lake, trans., The Apostolic Fathers I:403, 405, of the Loeb Classical Library. The word "hate" in the Christian sources listed above translates μισέω or ἀποστυγέω. The objects of the verbs are always impersonal, referring to things, not people; see on IQS 1.3–4 P. Wernberg-Møller, The Manual of Discipline (Leiden, 1957), p. 45, and A. R. C. Learey, The Rule of Qumran and Its Meaning (Philadelphia, 1966), p. 199. On IQH 17.24, M. Mansoor, The Thanksgiving Hymns (Leiden, 1961), p. 190, understands the objects as personal. However, ב- התהלך always occurs in Qumran to denote the thing in which one walks (e.g., a field, CD 10.20; usually, the laws, the correct way, etc.). To express "going with someone," Qumran Hebrew always has עם אלה החוקים למשכיל להתהלך בם עם; IQS 9.12, התהלך עם; כל חי CD 12.21, 13.23, [laws] עם כל חי להתהלך בם. Thus, Ch. Rabin's equivocation in his translation to CD 2.15 may also be dismissed.

27. Sutcliffe, "Hatred at Qumran," RQ 7 (June, 1960), pp. 345–356.

28. Polycarp is to be found in The Apostolic Fathers I:285. The two Qumran sources are reconstructed from actual statements of how sinners behave: ולא רצו בכל אשר צויתה ויבחרו לוא [יא]הבו כאשר צויתי . . . [ויב]חר[ו בשקוצי and . . . , באשר שנאתה (reconstruction following DJD I, p. 92). PT Berakhoth is a prayer ותרחקינו . . . ותקרבינו by R. Ḥiyya bar Abba of the first half of the third century. In this group, too, we see the equation "hatred = abstain" by means of the antitheses in Polycarp (abstain/love) and IQ22 (אהבו/לא בחר).

29. IQS 9.15–16 concerns instructions to the maśkil vis-à-vis members of the sect. The text reads ואיש כבור כפיו לקרבו ולפי שכלו להגישו וכן אהבתו עם שנאתו. Targum Ecclesiastes on 3:8 ("A time to love and a time to hate") has "a proper time to love one another, and a proper time to hate the sinner"—so I translate גבר חייבא, a meaning חוב often has in the Targum. Cf. also Targum Ecclesiastes 7:4 in ed. Sperber, where כסילים is translated שנואין. BJ 2.139: μιμή- σειν δ' ἀεὶ τοὺς ἀδίκους, is said of the Essenes. Titus: "For we ourselves were once [sinners] and hateful," i.e., deserving to be hated, στυγητοί, odibiles.

30. See Sutcliffe, esp. pp. 347 and 349. While Sutcliffe finds the admonition to hate sinners in the Old Testament and Qumran literature, he does not find it in the New Testament. The doctrine at Qumran was the same as that of the Old Testament: sin and sinners were to be hated (p. 352). But in the New Testament, "Though the wicked may merit hatred [Titus 3:3], it is no-

where enjoined that we should actually hate them. There is a great difference in emphasis between this attitude and that considered proper at Qumran" (p. 353).

Sutcliffe must be read with caution. His proofs from the Psalmist's personal attitudes toward hating sinners (139:21–22, 26:5, 31:7) become an Old Testament injunction, which was then followed at Qumran. The Qumran view may indeed have derived from the Old Testament, but as with the New Testament, in the Old Testament "it is nowhere enjoined that we should actually hate [sinners]." Sutcliffe's real purpose is to show Christianity's *superiority* to Qumran morality (p. 353), the "imperfectly developed morality of the times" (p. 352), and to the Jewish conception of Old Testament morality which "Christ corrected" (p. 354), for after all, where rabbinic literature (ben Azzai, second century) shares New Testament ethical dicta it is only because the rabbis "were familiar with Christian teaching and would naturally and rightly take over any noble sentiments compatible with their own system" (p. 355). Naturally.

31. The concept of hating evil/evildoers and loving good/good-doers was of special significance at Qumran with its dualistic ideology; see D. Flusser, "The Dead Sea Sect and Pre-Pauline Christianity," *SH* 4 (1958), pp. 217–220.

32. Cf. Targum Ps.-Jonathan to Deuteronomy 24:14: לא תסלומון חבריכון ולא תשגון טוטריה דאגירא.

33. T. Baba Meẓia 10.3 (Sifre Deut. 278, pp. 295–296; BT Baba Meẓia 111a; Midrash Tannaim ad loc., p. 158): הכובש שכר שכיר עובר משום חמשה לאוין משום בל תעשוק ומשום בל תגזול.

34. Cf. Philo, *Spec. Leg.* 4.196: "He who having appointed the evening as the time in which a laborer would receive his recompense . . . and does not permit the wage . . . to be delayed . . . how much more does he forbid robbery and theft and repudiation of debts and other things of the same kind." Cf. also Lev. 5:21–22: נפש כי תחטא ומעלה מעל בה' וכחש בעמיתו בפיקדון או בתשומת יד או בגזל או עשק את עמיתו או מצא אבידה וכחש בו . . . . Note that the law of paying wages follows that of deposits in Josephus.

35. M. Baba Meẓia 9.11 and parallels.

36. T. Baba Meẓia 10.2: שכיר שעות ביום גובה כל היום שכיר שעות בלילה גובה כל הלילה.

37. Conflicting opinions, BT Baba Meẓia: תנאי היא דתניא שכיר שעות דיום גובה כל היום שכיר שעות דלילה גובה כל הלילה דברי רבי יהודה ר"ש אומר שכיר שעות דיום גובה כל היום שכיר שעות דלילה גובה כל הלילה וכל היום. Differing interpretations, BT Baba Meẓia 111a: אמר רב שכיר שעות דיום גובה כל היום שכיר שעות דלילה גובה כל הלילה ושמואל אמר שכיר שעות דיום גובה כל היום ושכיר שעות דלילה גובה כל הלילה וכל היום תנן שכיר שעות גובה כל הלילה וכל היום תיובתא דרב אמר לך רב לצדדין קתני שכיר שעות דיום גובה כל היום שכיר שעות דלילה גובה כל הלילה. Variant readings, T. Baba Meẓia 10.2: כל הלילה וכל היום. Both manuscripts have this reading (also the Mishnah Baba Meẓia 9.11). The printed editions, however, do not have this clause (cf. Moses Margalit, מראה הפנים on PT) and PT Baba Meẓia 9.11, 12a, quoting the Tosefta, has: שכיר שעות ביום ובלילה גובה כל הלילה וכל היום.

38. Similarly, Jesus' parable about the laborers in the vineyard (Matt. 20:8) undoubtedly reflects actual practice: "And when even was come, the lord of the vineyard saith unto his steward, Call the laborers, and pay them their hire." See J. Duncan M. Derrett, "Workers in the Vineyard: A Parable of Jesus," *JJS* 25 (1974): 71–73.

9 Miracles in the Writings of Flavius Josephus

OTTO BETZ

The Attitude of Josephus toward the Miracles in the Bible

t he history of Israel as reported in the sacred books of Moses and the prophets was full of miraculous events. God revealed his power and glory in epiphanies, saving deeds, and acts of punishment, and His prophets proved the reality of God and the truth of their mission through signs and wonders. Flavius Josephus used the narrative parts of the Old Testament as the main source of his work *Antiquitates Judaicae,* the "History of the Jews," but he seems to have had an ambiguous attitude toward the miracles. On the one hand, he wanted to be faithful to the biblical tradition and therefore had to retell the miracles reported in the Bible.[1] On the other hand, he sometimes added to his report on a miraculous fact or feature a concluding noncommital remark, such as, "On these things let everyone decide as he wants" (I, 108).[2] Even the great event of Israel's miraculous salvation at the Red Sea, which Josephus retold at full length and with some additional details,[3] ends with such noncommitment (II, 348), and the same holds true for the coming of God to Mount Sinai (III, 81). Moreover, this attitude can be found with regard to the story of the prophet Balaam (IV, 158), the origin of circumcision (VIII, 262), and Jonah's salvation through a whale and his preaching repentance at Nineveh (IX, 214). Josephus thereby followed the example of the historians of his time, especially of Dionysius of Halicarnassus, whose twenty books of *Roman Antiquities* may have served as the model for Josephus' twenty books of *Jewish Antiquities.* Dionysius, too, could remark in doubtful cases that each may make his judgment as he likes.[4] Furthermore, Josephus occasionally explained the working of a miracle in a rationalizing way, for example the changing of the bitter water at Marah (Ex. 15:25): it happened through incessant blows, which sifted and purified the well (*A* III, 8). The appearance of an angel is sometimes omitted[5] or played down. Hagar met an angel of God (*A* I, 189, and see Gen. 16:7ff.), but Josephus added shepherds who helped her (*A* I, 219). The divine beings who visited Abraham at

Mamre merely pretended to eat (*A* I, 197; cf. Gen. 18:8), and Gideon saw an apparition (φάντασμα) that looked like a young man (*A* V, 213).

However, Josephus really believed in miracles and tried to convince his readers of their truth. This he sometimes did by inserting a list of historians of antiquity, both Greeks and barbarians, who had reported on similar events or facts (*A* I, 107; see also II, 348). But his main witness was Moses himself. He "deigned to perpetuate the memory of Balaam," the awkward prophet, who "was prevented by divine providence" from cursing the Hebrews (*A* IV, 157f.).[6] To Josephus, belief in divine miracles is bound up with the true understanding of God; Moses has shown that God embodies perfect virtue, and man must strive to participate in it (*A* I, 23). For this, faith is required. Josephus invited his readers to accept the doctrine of God, presented by Moses, and to read his work with eyes illuminated by faith. For the believer nothing will be unreasonable (παράδοξον), "nothing incongruous with the majesty of God and his love for man" (*A* I, 24). In the *Antiquities,* the description of the creation of the world (*A* I, 27–39, according to Gen. 1–2) together with the story of Adam's fall (*A* I, 40–51, according to Gen. 3) serves as a kind of theological overture and lesson of faith in the marvelous power of God. The universe is created and directed by Him, so that it may endure (*A* X, 278). Both prophecy and miracles witness to the reality of God, to His guidance and care for human affairs, and to His providence (*A* X, 280); they disprove the Epicurean and Sadducean skepticism. Because of his admiration of God's majesty and power, Josephus elaborated the miracles sometimes in agreement with the rabbinic Midrash haggadah, taking over some of the legends about the birth and education of Moses[7] and adding other haggadic details.[8] For apologetic reasons Josephus has omitted embarrassing events in Israel's history, such as the Judah-Tamar story (Gen. 38) and the building of the golden calf (Ex. 32). Among them are some miracles, such as the healing of Miriam's leprosy (Num. 12), the story of the rock bringing forth water in violation of God's command (Num. 10:10–12), and the story of the brass serpent (Num. 21:4–9) with which Moses cured those who had been bitten by the fiery serpents.[9]

Divine Miracles in the Past History of Israel

Epiphanies as Manifestations of the Power of God
The miracles told in the Bible are manifestations of the reality and might of the one true God in whom Josephus believed. These miraculous actions, which reveal the nature of God, can serve as demonstrative lessons in theology.[10] Josephus presupposes monotheism without saying this explicitly or attacking pagan idolatry directly (but see *A* VIII, 343). He reports on the objectivity of the divine miracles and the epiphanies of God and remains faithful to

the fact that the decisive events in Jewish history which constitute the Jewish nation and make the Jews the people of God were due to the miraculous support of God, such as the exodus from Egypt, the wandering through the desert, the taking of the promised land, or the giving of the law at Mount Sinai. The great themes of the Pentateuch, which were recited in the Jewish cult as the great deeds of God ($sid^eqôth\ J.$), are reported by Josephus at full length and with all miraculous details, Moses being the great instrument of God. With regard to the Egyptian plagues, Josephus remarks that he will recount them all, first, because "no such plagues . . . ever befell any nation before," second, in order to show that all the predictions of Moses came true, and third, because mankind shall learn from this not to offend the deity, for they will be punished for their iniquities (II, 293). Israel's crossing of the Red Sea is called a "miraculous deliverance" ($\pi\alpha\rho\acute{\alpha}\delta o\xi os\ \sigma\omega\tau\eta\rho\acute{\iota}\alpha$; A II, 345), and the giving of the law at Mount Sinai culminated in "the coming of God" ($\dot{\eta}\ \pi\alpha\rho o\nu\sigma\acute{\iota}\alpha\ \tau o\hat{\nu}\ \vartheta\varepsilon o\hat{\nu}$; III, 80). There is no exact Greek equivalent for the Hebrew term $sid^eqôth\ J.$, the helping actions of righteousness, done by the Lord, His "mighty deeds." Therefore, Josephus has no word for summing up these marvelous decisive events in Israel's history, despite the fact that Moses recited these deeds of righteousness in a long speech, composed by Josephus himself (A III, 84–88). Josephus sometimes used the term $\dot{\varepsilon}\pi\iota\varphi\acute{\alpha}\nu\varepsilon\iota\alpha$, the glorious appearance of God, in the sense of a visible manifestation of divine guidance in history.[11] This is new and characteristic for the biblical miracles: they are actions related to the history of a nation and lessons in theology. The appearance of God is visible, insofar as it is indicated by the accompanying cloud (A III, 310). But God Himself remains invisible; He manifests His power by delivering His people through a "divine and marvelous event" (A IX, 58). The classic "epiphany," therefore, is the salvation of Israel at the Red Sea, which "was smitten by the staff of Moses and retreating into itself, withdrawing from its own bed" (A II, 338f.), opened a path through the sea (III, 86).

The coming of God to Mount Sinai is not termed an "epiphany"; Josephus calls it the "parousia of God" (A III, 80). It was accompanied not only by thunder and lightning but also by a heavy rainstorm (ibid.). Josephus has inserted these elements into the report of the destruction of the Egyptian army at the Red Sea (Ex. 14): "Rain fell in torrents from heaven, crashing thunder accompanied the flash of lightning, thunderbolts were hurled" (A II, 343). Josephus wanted to describe the two great events at the Red Sea and at Mount Sinai in a similar way; therefore, he reports for both the same characteristic signs of a theophany. But, strangely enough, he did not use the term "epiphany" for the coming of God to Mount Sinai, which, according to modern understanding, is the classic model of a "theophany," the manifestation of the divine. The term "epiphany" does not appear in the story of Elijah's encounter with God at Mount Sinai (I Kings 19) either, but characterizes the "divine and marvelous" deliverance of the prophet Elisha from the army of the Syrians: even the king of the Syrians was amazed at the marvel and the epiphany of the God of the Israelites (*A* IX, 60). Josephus understands the sacrifice of Elijah on Mount Carmel to be a "test" (διάπειρα), disdaining the strength of the foreign gods (VIII, 338) and making manifest the power of the one, almighty, and true God (VIII, 338, 343), who Himself taught a lesson about His true nature (VIII, 338). But there again the word "epiphany" is missing. This may be due to the fact that an epiphany of God should contain the essential elements of the *ṣid*ʿ*qôth J.*, of "the saving deeds of God," performed at turning points in Israel's history.

How does man react properly to an epiphany? It is not faith that is required. Josephus has omitted the biblical statement that Israel believed in God and in Moses after the saving epiphany at the Red Sea (Ex. 14:31). Rather, he reports that Israel passed the whole night in singing hymns of praise; Moses had composed a song of thanksgiving in hexameter verse (*A* II, 346). Besides that, in his report on the giving of the law at Mount Sinai, Josephus does not mention the remark (Ex. 19:9) that Israel believed in Moses; he speaks of joyful expectation and the festal mood instead (*A* III, 76–78).

The visible manifestations of God's might are marvelous, insofar as they transcend human understanding, causing amazement even among Gentiles (*A* IX, 60).[12] Therefore, Josephus often characterizes them by the adjective "incredible" (παράδοξος or παράλογος).[13] There are no equivalents to these Greek words in Hebrew. Josephus may have had the root *pälä'* (*niphla'ôth*) in his mind; he means something which goes beyond man's reason without being unreasonable or *contra rationem*. According to the famous and much debated *Testimonium Flavianum* (the testimony of Josephus about Jesus), the so-called Christ was "a performer of marvelous deeds" (παραδόξων ἔργων ποιητής; *A* XVIII, 63). This must refer to the miracles of Jesus and certainly does not betray the language of Christian tradition. Josephus never calls miracles "δυνάμεις" or "mighty deeds," a term used in the Synoptic Gospels for the healing miracles of Jesus.

Miracles and Prayer

In helping Israel in an unexpected way, God has answered the prayer of His beloved, such as Moses and the prophets. He thereby made them instruments of His salvation. According to Josephus, God hears prayers; He has "answered the prayers of the fathers . . . and brought deliverance to the multitude from their distress" (*A* VI, 89). Josephus says this in agreement with his biblical source (*A* III, 6f., 22, 26; IV, 40–50; VI, 25). But he emphasizes the importance of prayer (in *A* V, 201): he mentions a prayer of supplication made by the prophetess Deborah. This is not given in the Bible; it replaces the Song of Deborah in Judges 5.[14] Josephus has inserted prayers of thanksgiving (*A* III,

25; IV, 40–50) and enlarged a supplication given in the Bible (see A IV, 40–50 and Num. 16:28–30). This is in agreement with the miracles told about some charismatic rabbis: God has heard their powerful prayers and answered them.[15]

In those prayers composed by Josephus, quite often the great wonders and saving deeds of God are mentioned in order to support the supplication and to encourage the people in distress (A III, 17, 46; IV, 44–46; V, 73f.; VI, 89f., 93). It is an important task to remember the lessons of history (V, 115), and Moses himself becomes the great example to those who enumerate all the wondrous saving deeds of God in their prayers of supplication (A III, 17–20). Several facts are remarkable in God's wondrous ways of helping: (1) He brings deliverance in an unexpected and surprising fashion (ἐκ παραλόγου), when His people are on the verge of destruction (A III, 18). (2) He sometimes seems to tarry, because He wants to test the bravery of the people of Israel, their enjoyment in living, and their spirit of endurance (III, 19–20). (3) Hardships, such as starvation and pressures from enemies, as well as times of freedom and happiness, are foreseen and ordered by God through His providence. Therefore, no one should despair, because God can turn distress into salvation in an astonishing way. Faith in the saving acts and miraculous help of God can be easily acquired by those who trust in His providence (πρόνοια).

Miracles and the Providence of God

The providence of God is perhaps the most characteristic notion in the theology of Josephus. It explains the historical role of the divine miracles and justifies the duty of the historian to report them faithfully. Josephus does not apply providence to the realm of nature or to God's care for his creation, but to history. Providence (πρόνοια) is a Greek idea.[16] The Hebrew terms da'at and mah°shabah, when used for the knowledge and plan of God, can perhaps explain why Josephus could speak of the providence of God. But these terms must be related to history, to the fates of the individual and of the nations, which are determined by God from the very beginning. In the Bible, the plan of God and His marvelous deeds of salvation are not tied together explicitly. For Josephus, however, God and His providence are almost identical (A II, 24, 60), and the miracles reveal this identity. All that occurs to those who are favored by God is ordained by His providence (A I, 225); nothing done can be hidden from it (II, 24). That is why even those events which seem to be deplorable "turn to the very best for us" (II, 8). For providence is the protecting presence and guidance of God, who may save the righteous in a marvelous way (A II, 60–63). It has saved the life of Moses from the very beginning (II, 236); Moses, therefore, became its preacher by promising salvation when Israel was in a deplorable situation (II, 330–333). It is precisely in hopeless cases that God may display His strength and His providential care for the beloved. For He makes the little great and sentences the mighty oppressors (II, 332).

As the marvelous saving deeds point to the providence, power, and amazing leadership of God, so the prophets are witnesses to providence, proving its reality and faithfulness. The fact that a prophet such as Daniel had predicted the conquest of Jerusalem by the Romans and the destruction of the Temple speaks clearly against the Epicureans who want to deny providence and exclude the leadership of God from human life (A X, 277–281). True prophecy has a role quite similar to that of the miracles. They both disclose that certain men are greatly honored by God and become His chosen instruments, proving the existence of God's providential guidance not only for individuals but also for the nations and the whole world (A X, 278).

Josephus mentions "Fate" (τὸ χρεών). He also reflects on the "power of Fate" (ἡ τοῦ χρεὼν ἰσχύς; A VIII, 419) and notes that it gives to false prophets more credit than to the true ones (VIII, 409). "Fate" takes the place of an evil spirit, while "providence" obscures the fact that the true prophets are guided by the spirit of God. Josephus does not speak about the "Spirit of God" or "Holy Spirit" in connection with miracles.

Miracles of Punishment

The Red Sea event disclosed that God through His providence not only saves His people but also punishes their oppressors in unexpected ways. There are miracles of punishment, catastrophes falling upon the sinners, such as the generation of the Flood (A I, 72ff.). The emphasis on Noah's preaching repentance (A I, 74, cf. II Peter 2:5) is important, because punishment should not be applied without a warning first being uttered. The Egyptian plagues were caused by the stubbornness of the Pharaoh. They were disastrous catastrophes (δεινά) that never befell a nation before (A II, 293), for the Diety "lacked not the means to pursue and torment the sinner with diverse chastisements" (II, 304). Josephus gives an elaborate report on the rebellion and punishment of Korah and his fellow Levites together with Dathan and Abiram (A IV, 14ff., cf. Num. 16) in which Moses made a long speech with strong admonitions and explicit warnings (IV, 33f.; see also 37f.). The destruction of the rebels, who were suddenly swallowed by Sheol, the realm of death, was a demonstration of God's power (IV, 52), just as God's power is demonstrated in His saving deeds. Josephus even increases the disaster by adding nonscriptural details (IV, 53). On the other hand, he omits Miriam's punishment by leprosy and her miraculous restitution (Num. 12) and the incident of Elisha and the boys of Jericho who were devoured by bears (II Kings 2:23–25). But Josephus does report (A VIII, 240–245) the strange story of the disobedient prophet (I Kings

13), the story of the prophet rebuking king Ahab (I Kings 20; *A* VIII, 389–392), and the story of the punishment of King Uzziah by leprosy (II Chron. 26; *A* IX, 222–227).

The faith of Josephus in the saving and punishing providence of God is in full agreement with the historical theory of the Deuteronomist, according to whom the Israelites "by piety alone will retain the friendship of the Deity" (*A* V, 116), while disobedience and idolatry are punished immediately by disease, death, and destruction of the people (*A* IX, 99–101), and the warning of a prophet is important (*A* IX, 99). Josephus in his *Antiquities* has combined the report on Israel's history in the two books of Kings with that given in the work of the Chronist (*A* IX–X). The result is a rather painful picture of wars, miraculous victories, and disastrous defeats with exaggerated numbers of the losses on both sides.

Miracles in the Present Age

Josephus had to report on the great deeds of God, on His marvelous interventions on behalf of Israel in the past. But no such marvelous events occurred in the present age, in which the Jewish nation was occupied and humiliated by the Romans. How could catastrophes such as the defeat of Israel through Vespasian and Titus, the fall of Jerusalem, the destruction of the Temple, and the death or slavery of so many thousands of Jewish people happen? Why did God not make manifest His power and save the brave warriors who fought for the honor and the kingship of their God? In his *Bellum Judaicum* or *The War of the Jews,* Josephus says that he had tried in vain to tell his countrymen in the beleaguered city of Jerusalem that the power of Rome was irresistible in the present (*BJ* V, 364). He explained that God lets political leadership shift from one nation to another, and in the present He stands on the side of the Romans (*BJ* V, 367). This may explain the fact that saving deeds of God and epiphanies, which the Zealots or Essenes had hoped for, did not happen in Israel during the first century A.D. The evaluation of history given by Josephus and revealed in his work *The War of the Jews* did not allow for mighty acts of God in his own time. This is somewhat different in the *Antiquities.* There, Josephus followed the biblical view on God's leadership in the history of Israel and His chosen people. Even so, he says that Daniel had foretold the Roman occupation of Israel and the destruction of Jerusalem (*A* X, 277–281).

There are, however, miracles in early Judaism that show the influence of those done in the Bible. There arose men from among the Jews who claimed to be chosen instruments of God and prophets like Moses and who expected a marvelous intervention from heaven, leading to the liberation of Israel. Josephus knew them and mentions them in both of his great works, in the *War* and in the *Antiquities.*

Elijah and Elisha as Examples for Miracles of Healing

In the New Testament and among some charismatic rabbis, Elijah served as the great example of a man sent by God; he was able to heal seriously ill people by prayer[17] and to ask God for rain.[18] From this prophet, those rabbis learned the lesson that a miracle must be done for the honor of God, not for the glory of oneself and one's house.[19] For Elijah had prayed on Mount Carmel: "O Lord, God of Abraham, Isaac, and Jacob, let it be known this day that Thou art God in Israel, and that I am Thy servant, and that I have done all these things at Thy word!" (I Kings 18:36). However, the rabbis were always afraid that a miracle might be the work of sorcery or witchcraft and that someone might cast out Satan through Beelzebul; besides that, a true miracle could become misunderstood by the people as a demonic act. The prayer of Elijah (I Kings 18:37): "Answer me, O Lord, answer me!" they understood in the following way: "Answer me, that fire may fall from heaven; answer me, that people may not say: This is a work of witchcraft!"[20] Josephus did not concern himself with this problem. He lets Elijah ask that God "make His power manifest to the people which had now for so long a time been in error" (A VIII, 342). The reaction of the Israelites when they saw fire fall from heaven, consuming the altar and evaporating the water (I Kings 18:38), is rendered by Josephus in this way: "They fell upon the earth and worshiped the one God, whom they acknowledged as the almighty and only true God, while the others were mere names invented by unworthy and senseless opinions" (A VIII, 343). With such a confession of monotheism, Josephus interpreted the call of the people, "The Lord is God! The Lord is God!" (I Kings 18:39), while he omitted the double call of Elijah, "Answer me!," interpreted by the rabbis. However, Josephus and the rabbis decided an important issue of their own time by pointing to Elijah's example.

The same holds true for the consequences, drawn from the miracles of Elijah by Josephus. After the revelation of the power of God through fire from heaven and the confession of the Israelites, the prophets of Baal were seized by the people and killed at Elijah's behest (A VIII, 343). According to I Kings 18:40, however, the prophet himself had slaughtered them at the brook Kishon. Because of his religious zeal, the prophet Elijah had become the great hero for the Maccabees and the Zealots, who wanted to defend the honor of God in Israel by any means. Josephus in his War had deplored the disastrous role the Zealots had played and blamed them for the fall of Jerusalem and the destruction of the Temple (BJ I, 9–12, 27–29). In the Antiquities, therefore, he tries to draw a picture of Elijah that is free from any Zealot features. That is why he has changed the prophet's role in the killing of the worshipers of Baal. Moreover, the confession of Elijah, "I have been full of zeal for the Lord" (I Kings 19:10), is missing in the Antiquities, and the same is true for the prediction that Elisha will slay those that escape the sword of Jehu (I Kings 19:17; see A

VIII, 352). In the report on the call of Elisha, the slaughtering of the oxen is not mentioned (A VIII, 354, see I Kings 19:21); Elisha instead begins to prophesy.[21]

Furthermore, Elijah is not called "Man of God" in the *Antiquities*. According to A VIII, 327, the widow at Zarpath simply confessed that "now she clearly realized that the Deity spoke with him" (but see I Kings 17:18 and 24). This agrees with the beginning of the whole cycle of Elijah stories, in which Josephus introduces him as "a prophet of the most high God" (A VIII, 319). This negative attitude of Josephus toward the designation "Man of God" does not support the argument that Josephus knew of the "Theios Aner," the Hellenistic type of a "Divine Man" with supernatural abilities and the power to perform miracles. If this were true, Josephus would have used this title for Elijah, especially in rendering the passages I Kings 17:18 and 24. In my opinion, such a type of "Theios Aner," a wise man and miracle worker, never existed in Hellenism during the New Testament age; it is a product of the *Religionsgeschichtliche Schule*.[22]

Honi, the earliest of the charismatic rabbis, who became famous for having brought on rain through prayer, imitating Elijah,[23] is mentioned by Josephus also. He calls him "Onias," who had "once in a rainless season prayed to God to end the drought, and God had heard him and sent rain" (A XIV, 22). But Onias, "a righteous man, beloved by God" (*ibid.*), is introduced by Josephus at a very critical moment of Jewish history, during the civil war between the Hasmonean brothers Hyrcanus II and Aristobulos II (65 B.C.). Onias was asked by the party of Hyrcanus, which besieged Jerusalem where Aristobulos defended himself, to curse the enemies. He refused to do this, because he did not want to curse any one of his fellow Jews. Therefore, he was stoned to death (A XIV, 24).

King Solomon as the Great Master of Magic and Exorcism

Interest in the historical setting of a miracle or a miracle worker is quite characteristic for Josephus. This is even the case when he tells of a miracle that has nothing in common with the saving deeds of God, but is strongly reminiscent of the art of magic, which was widespread in the Gentile world of the Roman Empire, especially in Egypt. Josephus praises King Solomon as a man unsurpassed in wisdom and a master of the technique used "against demons for the benefit and healing of men" (A VIII, 45). The king, "whose knowledge was granted by God, had composed incantations by which illnesses are relieved, and left behind forms of exorcistic rites with which those possessed by evil spirits drive them out, never to return. And this kind of cure until now is of very great power among us to this day" (A VIII, 45f.). As an example of the lasting value of Solomon's wisdom and art of healing, Josephus refers to the Jewish exorcist and a contemporary of his, Eleazar, and to the way he healed persons possessed by evil spirits. Josephus says that he himself was present as an eyewitness when Eleazar in the presence of the emperor Vespasian, his sons, and his tribunes cast out an evil spirit from a sick man. Josephus describes every detail of the cure: Eleazar used a ring, under the seal of which was contained a root, prescribed by Solomon, and incantations composed by the king. He put this ring to the nose of the possessed man and drew out the demon through his nostrils. Objective proof of the successful and miraculous cure was given by the demon, who overturned a cup of water after he was driven out (A VIII, 46–48). Philostratus tells of a similar sign (τεκμήριον) of a successful act of exorcism by the Pythagorean philosopher and teacher Apollonius of Tyana (IV, 20),[24] and Lucian mentions a well-known Palestinian exorcist.[25] Josephus, however, wanted to reveal the understanding and wisdom of Solomon in order that "all men may know the greatness of his nature and how God favored him" (A VIII, 49).

Elisha and the Healing of the Well at Jericho

As we have already indicated, Josephus has omitted several miracles of the Elijah–Elisha cycle in I and II Kings, especially those done by Elisha. The assumption of Elijah to heaven is but briefly mentioned and is explained as a disappearance from among men (IX, 28; see II Kings 2:1ff.): like Enoch, he became invisible and no one knew of his death.[26] The two stories in II Kings 2:19–25, the four miracles in II Kings 4:8–48, and the healing of Naaman of Syria from leprosy (II Kings 5 and 6:1–7) are missing in the *Antiquities*. But Elisha's purification of the well at Jericho (II Kings 2:19–22) is told in *BJ* IV, 459–464. There, Josephus gives an explicit description of the fertility of the region around Jericho, and especially of the well near the city that contributed to the bliss. In this context, he retells the miracle done by Elisha (II Kings 2:19–22), through which the prophet actually became the benefactor of Jericho and its famous environment. Through this act he had purified and healed the water of this well, which had previously been unhealthy, causing death and miscarriages.

According to the Bible, Elisha had cleansed the water by throwing some salt into the well and by saying a brief word of healing. Josephus amplifies the story considerably with regard to both of these actions and with descriptions of the well and the practices of the prophet. Elisha changed (ἔτρεψεν) the well that had caused sterility and hunger so that it acquired an astonishing power, creating an increase in fertility and food (*BJ* IV, 464). According to Josephus, offerings, prayers to heaven and earth, and other actions were performed by the prophet, who now appears as an expert in natural science, magic, and prayer.

The Signs and Wonders (σημεῖα καὶ τέρατα):
Moses and the Messianic Prophets

Josephus knew very well that only a few people in Israel held his view of history, according to which God was on the side of the Romans. In the eyes of his countrymen, the current age of poverty and political humilation could very well be the time of God's testing His people, the birth pangs of the new age, preceding the glorious liberation of Israel through the messiah. He will "stand up" soon, as a redeemer like Moses, being the chosen instrument of God's mighty deeds. Moses had promised that God would raise a prophet like him to whom Israel would listen (Deut. 18:15–21). This promise was only partially fulfilled with his successor, Joshua. It remained a source of hope for liberation and became very real in early Judaism, when the Qumran Community was awaiting its fulfillment (4 Q Testimonia) and the Christians related it to Jesus Christ (Acts 3:22f.; 7:37). Josephus was aware of this state of expectance. He tells about prophets who believed that the salvation of Israel was at hand. According to the rabbis, prophecy in Israel had come to an end with Haggai, Zechariah, and Malachi. But under the oppressive administration of the Romans in Palestine, with procurators such as Pilate, Cuspius Fadus, Gessius Florus, and Albinus, during the decades preceding the First Jewish Revolt, there appeared prophets, charismatic leaders, and popular figures who called upon the masses to follow them. Some of them led the people into the wilderness, where they would "show them unmistakable marvels and signs [ἐναργῆ τέρατα καὶ σημεῖα] that would be wrought in harmony with God's design" (*A* XX, 168; cf. *BJ* II, 259). According to Josephus, they claimed to be prophets, but he calls them impostors (γόητες) and deceivers (ἀπατεῶντες; *ibid.;* see *BJ* VI, 288).

At this point the problem of finding the truth arises. The epiphanies and mighty deeds of God made His power manifest in an objective and irresistible way. The Jewish "prophets" of the first century A.D. expected such a marvelous liberating act from God for His people, and they wanted to be the messengers and instruments of salvation. But how could the people know whether the hope and the claims of these men were true, whether such "prophets" were really sent by God and proclaimed His will? Moses had promised that God would raise a prophet like him (Deut. 18:15), but he had also spoken of dreamers and seducers, who would try to lead the people of God astray, talking them into idolatry (Deut. 13). That is why the Jewish "prophets" promised a sign to prove their truth and commission by God. But a false prophet, too, could perform signs and wonders and test the faithfulness of Israel (Deut. 13:2). The question whether a miracle was a "sign" (*sēmeion*), pointing to God and revealing His will, or whether it was an act of magic, worked by the power of the Satan, had to be answered. The Old Testament conflict between true and false prophets thus reappeared on the scene of Jewish history during the first century A.D. Josephus does not speak in the dualistic terminology of apocalyptic Judaism where God and Satan, Light and Darkness, Truth and Falsehood, the Holy Spirit and evil spirits, the Children of Light and the Children of Darkness are opposed to each other in two different realms.[27] He could find meaningful and true "signs" (*sēmeia,* "prodigies") among the Gentiles also.[28] Egypt, being to the rabbis a place of magic and witchcraft, to Josephus became a field on which God's power battled Egyptian wisdom (*A* II, 285).

In this battle the term "sign" (σημεῖον, in Hebrew ʾōth) has its origin. Josephus could use it in the nonbiblical sense to mean "portent," "prodigy" (*A* VIII, 232, 236, 244 and XIX, 9), or "password" (XIX, 29ff.), or in the biblical sense as a miraculous deed[29] that verifies the claim of a messenger sent by God, as is the case in the biblical Moses-tradition (*A* II, 274ff.). Josephus used this word for retelling the commission of Moses and for reporting on the Jewish prophets of his own time. The word σημεῖον (-α), often connected with τέρας (-ατα in the plural, in Hebrew ʾōthōth umōphᵉtīm), does not have the meaning "miracle" in classical Greek. Josephus followed the usage of the Septuagint, which had rendered the Hebrew ʾōth with σημεῖον. It occurs especially in the Book of Exodus, in the dramatic report of Israel's liberation from the slavery in Egypt. From this context, Josephus and the Jewish prophets of his time knew the word *sēmeion* in the sense of a "miracle" pointing to God and confirming the mission that originated with Him.

I think it is important to see the difference between an epiphany on the one hand and a sign on the other.[30] The epiphany is a marvelous intervention of God which brings liberation to His people in a desperate situation. The sign identifies the liberator and man of God to whom authority has been given as the chosen instrument of God. It lends credit to his commission and creates faith in God, who has sent and authorized him. In the case of Moses, the epiphany of God took place at the Red Sea; the *sēmeia* happened before that, at his call by God and during the first encounter with the pharaoh. King Hezekiah, who was very ill, asked for a "sign" from the prophet Isaiah so that he might believe in Isaiah as a man coming from God and having the power to heal him (*A* X, 28). The epiphany as an act of liberation done by God is evident in an objective, overwhelming way through its great power and effect. The sign (*sēmeion*) takes place on a more modest level and can be met with unbelief. Its truth can be contested; it is open to criticism. The epiphany should be followed by hymns of praise and thanksgiving, sung by those who were saved by it (*A* II, 346). The adequate response to a *sēmeion* is faith and hope (see *A* II, 274, 276, 280, 283; X, 28f.).

The call of Moses through God and his first appearance before Israel and the pharaoh reveal best how Josephus understood such a "sign." After his vision at the burning bush (Ex. 3:1ff.) and his commission to lead the Israelites out of Egypt to Mount Sinai (*A* II, 264–269), Moses asked God how he could persuade his people to follow him and how he could force the pharaoh to permit the exodus (A II, 270f.). God promised to be with him and showed him the miracles of changing his rod into a snake, altering the color of his hand to a white color "resembling chalk"[31] and changing water into blood (A II, 272f.). He exhorted Moses to use those signs (σημεῖα) in order to be believed by all men (πρὸς τὸ πιστεύεσθαι) "that you are sent by Me and do everything according to My commandments" (A II, 274). The marvelous signs given by God and "seen by Moses" helped to overcome the doubts concerning his commission. Signs can create and demand faith in the man who performs them and in God, who is with him. The biblical passage (Ex. 4:8f.) contains the decisive terms "signs" (ʾ̄othōth) and "to believe" and even speaks of the "voice" (qôl) of a sign: "If they do not believe thee and if they do not listen to the voice of the first sign they will believe the voice of the last [i.e., second] sign." The third sign will bring the change of the water of the Nile into blood (Ex. 4:9). This means that the failure of the first two signs, which do no harm, will necessarily lead to a sign causing severe punishment among the Egyptians. That is why the Egyptian plagues sometimes could be called "signs" (Ex. 10:2; Ps. 78:43; A II, 327).

From this, several characteristics of a sign emerge: (1) The sign (sēmeion) is visible (A II, 280, 284); it also "speaks" with a voice, since it should be heard and obeyed just as though it were the voice of a prophet. To Josephus, the sēmeion has to be performed and to be seen. The countrymen of Moses did not believe him when Moses gave them a description[32] of the signs that God had shown him at the burning bush. They did become fully convinced, however, after Moses had performed the signs before their eyes: "Amazed at this astonishing spectacle, they took courage and were of good hope, since God did care for their safety" (A II, 280). (2) The sign has a discerning effect, dividing people into two groups: believers and unbelievers. It forces men who see it to make a decision of existential importance. The epiphany presupposes faith; the sign should be followed by it.[33] The sign can create faith. King Hezekiah, when Isaiah promised to get rid of his severe illness, asked the prophet "to perform some sign or miracle [σημεῖόν τι καὶ τεράστιον] in order that he might believe in him when he said these things, as in one who came from God" (A X, 28). (3) Through an epiphany of God a severe crisis of the people normally comes to an end, after great men of God have asked for help through prayers of supplication. The signs, however, were granted to Moses unexpectedly, and God had even commanded him to perform them. This Moses did against the will of the Gentile king. The epiphany is wholly the action of God. The signs given by God became a powerful weapon in the hand of Moses; they were "at his service at all times whenever he was in need of them" (A II, 276). (4) Whilst the epiphany is in itself an act of salvation or punishment, the sign normally does not function this way. It points to the coming liberation and reveals the human instrument of God. The passage at *Antiquities* II, 327, seems to contradict this definition, for it mentions "*sēmeia* wrought by God toward their liberation." The signs are recalled in the desperate situation of Israel arriving at the Red Sea (see Ex. 14:10) and may include the Egyptian plagues. But the saving of God has not yet come; the signs are remembered to create faith and confidence.

Faith in the signs means to trust and be obedient to the man appointed by God as a leader and savior. The pharaoh, however, reacted quite differently. His unbelief had disastrous consequences for his people and actually meant a kind of self-condemnation. The apostle Paul attributed the stubbornness of the Egyptian king to the predetermination of God, who wanted to reveal His power through the Egyptians (Rom. 9:17; see also Ex. 7:3, 9:16). Josephus does not say that, but retells the meeting between Moses and the pharaoh vividly and with additional details (*A* II, 281–292; see Ex. 5:1ff.; 7:1–13). Moses, who had just previously been hesitant and shrank from his commission (*A* II, 270f.), appeared before the pharaoh as a powerful hero.[34] He once had rendered important services to the Egyptians, especially in their battle against the Ethiopians (*A* II, 282), and is now in the service of the God of Mount Sinai, having received the "voices" of God, i.e., the revelation of His name for calling to Him in prayer (II, 275) and the power of the signs (*sēmeia*) to inspire faith in His orders (II, 283). Here again, the mere report of those miracles was of no avail and led to the mockery by the Egyptian king; Moses had to let him see the signs (βλέπειν τὰ σημεῖα) of Mount Sinai (II, 284), to perform them as he had done before the Israelites. Even then the pharaoh did not believe him and called Moses an evil fellow who wanted to deceive him by magic practices. The king did not doubt the magic abilities of Moses, since he had priests who could do miracles similar to those of Moses (II, 285). But he denied that they were signs of divine origin. Moses, therefore, had to prove that they were done "according to the providence and power of God," and not according to witchcraft and deception (II, 286). This demonstration was a failure, too; the king even doubled the affliction of the Hebrews. But Moses "steeled his soul" and devoted all his efforts to preparing for the people's liberty (II, 289f.). The plagues[35] upon the Egyptians now seemed to be unavoidable; they were, however, preceded by strong warnings, made by Moses to the king (II, 291–293).

This shows us that the sign participates in the providence and power of God, despite its preliminary character.[36] But the truth and validity of the sign is not free from ambiguity for those who see it. The signs of Moses were more powerful than those of the Egyptian priests, but there was no essential difference, nor a new quality such as unworldly otherness. Therefore, faith is required, which will be rewarded by salvation, whilst unbelief is followed by punishment (*A* II, 293).

The *Sēmeia* Promised by Jewish Prophets of
the First Century A.D.

Moses served as a norm and an example for some prophets of the first century A.D. That is why Josephus was so interested in the signs pointing to the coming liberation. Moses was the first redeemer of Israel; the messianic redeemer at the end of history was expected to act like him. The coming of God to Mount Sinai became the great model of hope for His coming at the end of history, visiting all the nations as the judge and king of kings. The biblical fundament for this analogy between Moses and messiah, deliverance from the slavery in Egypt and freedom from Rome, the coming of God to Mount Sinai and the parousia for the Last Judgment had been laid by the promise of a prophet like Moses (Deut. 18:15–22) and by the announcement of Second Isaiah that there would be a second exodus, led by God, which would be much greater than the first (Isa. 43:16ff.; 40:3ff.). Since eschatology in early Judaism was modeled after the Mosaic age, prophets who were believed to be instruments of salvation promised to perform "signs" (*sēmeia*), i.e., miraculous deeds, in order to prove their divine commission. We may assume that these signs had to be similar to those reported of Moses and Joshua in order to be "significant" in the light of Deuteronomy 18:15–22 and to reveal the new man as a prophet like Moses.

These assumptions are confirmed by the report of Josephus on prophecy in Israel during the first century A.D. He comments on it in both of his major works, *The War of the Jews* (*Bellum Judaicum*) and the *Antiquities*. According to him, however, these men were seducers and impostors, and we may ask for the criteria by which he reached such a judgment. His reports are twofold in nature and form: (1) There are brief stories about various "prophets," mentioned by their names, in which Josephus relates when they appeared, what promises they made, the way they gathered crowds that followed them, and finally their failure, with their dramatic ends caused through the intervention and sudden attack of Roman troops. Josephus says that these men claimed to be prophets and that they promised a miraculous deed, but he does not use the term "sign" for it. (2) This term "sign" appears only in its plural form, "signs" (*sēmeia*), mainly in the second type of reports on these prophets, in which Josephus speaks about impostors and seducers in a general way, without mentioning specific persons and their names (*BJ* II, 258–260; *A* XX, 167–168). There are two exceptions: first, a prophet who promised "signs of salvation" in the Jerusalem Temple, just before the very end (*BJ* VI, 285b); and second, a man called Jonathan, who after the Jewish War in Palestine rose in Cyrenaica and promised to show "signs and wonders" in the wilderness (*BJ* VII, 437f.). Josephus, however, does not report on any prophetic claim of Jonathan. He tells similar things of the "seducers" at the beginning of the Jewish revolt, who caused unrest and rebellion by pretending to be inspired by

God, created excitement among the masses in a demonic way, and led them into the wilderness. There, they said, God would show them "signs of freedom" (σημεῖα τῆς ἐλευθερίας), meaning miracles indicating the liberation and even bringing it about (BJ II, 259). According to the parallel passage (A XX, 168), the prophets themselves wanted to show "unmistakable wonders and signs" of what would happen according to the providential plan of God. These prophetic movements took place under the Roman governor Felix, who believed that they might be the beginning of a revolt and therefore attacked them with his troops and killed many (BJ II, 260; A XX, 168). This report may be compared with the revolt of Jonathan in Cyrenaica (BJ VII, 437–441) and with the warning prediction of Jesus, according to which false messiahs and false prophets will arise and give great signs (sēmeia) and marvels in order to seduce, if possible, even the chosen ones (Matt. 24:24; see 5:11). In War VI, 286, Josephus reports that the "tyrants" of the Jewish revolt used many prophets who admonished the people of Israel to wait for the help of God, especially during the siege of Jerusalem (BJ VI, 288).

The "Signs of Freedom"

The expression "signs of freedom" (BJ II, 259) was new. The word "freedom" (ḥerūth) did not yet occur in the Hebrew Old Testament; it was created by the revolutionary movement in early Judaism. Josephus himself may have coined the expression "signs of freedom" in order to explain the character of these miracles to his Gentile readers. The enthusiasts themselves most probably used the language of the Bible (ʾôth; in Aramaic, ʾāthā-) and announced "signs of salvation" (τὰ σημεῖα τῆς σωτηρίας) as did the false prophet in Jerusalem (BJ VI, 285). But "signs of freedom" and "signs of salvation" express quite well the historical and political purposes of such miracles that were hoped for by the Jews in the time of Moses and in the Roman age. The marvelous deeds point to the salvation of God's people, which is at hand. To the Jewish prophets of the first century A.D., they were even more than signs. We have to ask whether they understood them to be the first step toward a revolutionary event and freedom. In the parallel passage (A XX, 168) the biblical hendiadys (τέρατα καὶ σημεῖα, "wonders and signs") is chosen instead. It designates the great deeds of God for Israel under Moses but is also used for the miracles of the false prophets and seducers mentioned in Deuteronomy 13:2. It is precisely because those signs can be done by wicked people that Josephus lets his "prophets" declare that their wonders and signs will be "unmistakable" (A XX, 168). This means that they will be done in the name and by the power of God, not by the dark forces of magic and sorcery or with the intention to lead Israel astray. In the terminology of Josephus, they will "happen according to the providence of God," in harmony with His historical plan (ibid.). The Jewish prophets believed that Israel had suffered enough and that the slavery under Roman rule would soon come to an end, at the time appointed by God. They must have linked the biblical tradition of Moses and its signs and wonders with that of Daniel, to whom the timetable of the eschatological events had been disclosed in a vision (Dan. 9:20–27). The prophets' claims of being inspired by God (*BJ* II, 259) certainly included the conviction that they knew the mysteries of God, especially the future events and the time of their coming. Their message of the *kairos* of salvation must have created a "demonic excitement" in the crowds following them (*BJ* II, 259).

In my view, there is no difference between the promise that God will show those signs (*BJ* II, 259) and that the prophets themselves will perform them (*A* XX, 168). The prophets wanted to serve as the instruments of God for the work of Israel's salvation, just as Moses had understood himself to do.

Apart from this generalizing note on the Jewish enthusiasts, Josephus gives in both of his major works brief accounts about the appearance of individual prophets, their ascents, their claims and the miracles promised by them, their movements, and their sudden ends. Josephus does not give a special designation to the miracle each of these men wanted to show; rather, he describes the concrete nature of each. On the other hand, he explicitly says that each of them declared openly that he was a prophet.[37] According to Josephus, this claim proved to be false in all cases; they were impostors, false prophets (see *BJ* VI, 287f.).

Theudas,[38] the first among these Jewish prophets, appeared under the procurator Cuspius Fadus (about A.D. 45–46). He persuaded a large crowd of people to follow him to the Jordan River, promising them that the river would be divided and provide an easy passage to them (*A* XX, 97). In the terminology of Josephus, this miracle must have been understood as a "sign of freedom" (*BJ* II, 267), indicating and perhaps introducing the saving intervention of God. It would be a significant sign because Moses himself had parted the sea and provided a passage for Israel (Ex. 14). Moreover, his successor, Joshua, had led the Jews through the Jordan River in a miraculous way (Josh. 3:17ff.), and Elijah had parted this river, too (II Kings 2:8). In the light of Deuteronomy 18:15–22, the miracle of parting the water and bringing Israel safely to the other shore must have been quite convincing and effective in accrediting a man who was believed to be a prophet like Moses. Moreover, such a deed had more historical value for some time than the "signs" performed by Moses for the Israelites and the king of Egypt, such as changing his staff to a snake or altering the color of his hand. For parting the Jordan River and leading the people to the other side was in itself an act of liberation, a sign heralding the freedom of God and assuring Israel of His glorious presence. However, the activities of Theudas were crushed by Roman troops. Many of his followers lost their lives; Theudas was caught and his head cut off (*A* XX, 98).

According to the Book of Acts, Gamaliel, a teacher belonging to the

Pharisees, mentioned briefly Theudas's movement in his speech before the Jerusalem Synhedrion, comparing it with Judas and his disciples (Acts 5:36). The miracle that was promised by Theudas is omitted in this speech. But Gamaliel referred to the claim of Theudas. According to him, Theudas had declared himself to the people "to be someone," to be a somebody (εἶναί τινα ἑαυτόν). I believe that this vague and veiled version of Theudas' claim may be more correct than that given by Josephus, according to whom Theudas declared himself "to be a prophet" (A XX, 97). Theudas probably assumed that God, according to his will and plan, would determine the role that he should play, whether it be that of a prophet like Moses or of the messiah and redeemer of Israel. The successful performance of the "sign of liberation" might have been expected to become the occasion when this divine definition of the role of Theudas would be revealed. Until that moment Theudas was "someone," a man chosen by God. Speaking Aramaic, Theudas may have used the term *bar nash,* the "Son of Man," or "someone." This self-designation was vague to the outsider, but significant for those who lived and thought according to the promises of the Bible.

After his report on the enthusiasts promising "signs of freedom" in the desert, Josephus tells about the evil caused by the Egyptian Jew (*BJ* II, 261–263; *A* XX, 169–172). Here, too, he ascribes to this Jew the claim of being a prophet, but calls him a false prophet (*BJ* II, 261). This man came from Egypt and went to Jerusalem out of the desert, where he had gathered large crowds of followers whom he led to the Mount of Olives, which lies opposite Jerusalem. From there he wanted to show that at his command the walls of the holy city would fall down; in this way he promised to provide an entrance for his followers (*A* XX, 170). According to the parallel report in *War* II, 262, this Jew intended to enter Jerusalem by force, to imprison the Roman garrison stationed there, and to establish an autocratic rule of the Jewish people (*BJ* II, 262). I think that here, too, the miracle should serve as a "sign of freedom." The analogy with the fall of the walls of Jericho and the city's conquest through Joshua, the follower of Moses (Josh. 6), was intended to demonstrate to the Jews that God was with this man and that the hour of deliverance from the yoke of the Romans had come. Such a "sign" was already part of the work of liberation, transcending the original purpose of simply pointing to it. As in the case of Theudas, the significance of it originated from its similarity to the divine actions of help and deliverance in the time of Moses and Joshua. The Jews could have seen that the oracle in Deuteronomy 18:15–22 actually was fulfilled, that the time of Israel's redemption had come.

The connection with the time of Moses becomes even more evident in the activities of a Samaritan who caused disturbances in the Samaritan nation during the government of Pilate (*A* XVIII, 85–87). In this case, Josephus does not mention either his claim to being a prophet or his promise of a sign. But the conduct of this Samaritan reveals clearly that he must have attributed the prophetic passage (Deut. 18:15ff.) to himself and wanted to be the instrument of a liberating miracle of God. He commanded the people to follow him to Mount Gerizim, where he wanted to show them the sacred vessels deposited there by Moses and buried. Before they could go up to Mount Gerizim, the Roman prefect Pilate appeared with a detachment of cavalry and heavily armed infantry, which attacked the crowds, crushing the whole movement. In this case, the discovery of the buried vessels may have been the "sign of liberation," assuring the people of God's presence and help in a marvelous way.

According to *War* VI, 283–287, almost six thousand inhabitants of Jerusalem lost their lives in the Temple area, to which they had fled, because a "false prophet" had told them to do so, as it was a commandment of God; for there they should receive the signs of salvation (*BJ* VI, 285f.). Josephus explains the impact of this false prophet in a psychological and proverbial way: man easily complies with promises when faced with adversity (*BJ* VI, 287). The Jewish prophet may have pointed to a word such as that in Isaiah 28:16f., which played an important role in early Judaism (see 1QS VIII:7f.; 1QH VI:21ff.). Zion is God's foundation; he who believes will not be shaken.

Josephus does not declare explicitly whether the promised "signs" had been performed or not. But the way he reports about these movements, and his negative judgment of their leaders, whom he calls impostors and false prophets, suggest that their hopes were never fulfilled. Moreover, the disastrous end of these prophets and their followers, who had come together without arms (ἄνοπλοι; *BJ* VII, 440), reveals the failure. These people, who believed fully in the great hour of marvelous deliverance, became an easy prey for the Roman soldiers (*BJ* VII, 440). For Josephus, success or failure of such a prophet was the criterion by which to judge whether he told the truth and had the support of God or whether he had a false imagination and a self-made claim of commission[39] (*BJ* IV, 626). The passage in Deuteronomy 18:15–22 necessarily leads to such a conclusion: "If the word of such a prophet does not come to pass or come true, that is a word which the Lord has not spoken; the prophet has spoken it presumptuously." And Josephus may have taken the vocabulary used in his criticism against these men from Deuteronomy 13:1–11, in which severe measures against false prophets and seducers teaching rebellion against God are prescribed for Israel. The verbs *hēsīt* ("to deceive") and *hiddīah* ("to lead astray") designate the false prophets' dangerous activities and goals. In the Mishnah *Sanhedrin* VII: 4.11, these verbs are used as participles (*mēsīt, maddīah*) in a more technical way.

Josephus believed himself to be "a servant of the voice of God," whose predictions were fulfilled; even the Gentile general Titus had to admit this (*BJ*

IV, 626). God had told him in dreams about the coming calamities of the Jews and the glorious future of the Roman emperors (*BJ* III, 351). The prophets of doom were right (*A* VIII, 403–410; *BJ* VI, 300–309), not the self-made messengers of a miraculous liberation.

Signs as Portents

In some passages, Josephus uses the term "signs" (σημεῖα, τέρατα) in the sense of portents or prodigies (*prodigia*), meaning strange and marvelous events that predict the future.[40] According to I Kings 13:1–6, King Jeroboam was rebuked by a prophet for having built an altar and made himself high priest (*A* VIII, 230ff.). The announcement of the future destruction of the illegal altar was verified by as "sign" (σημεῖον; in Hebrew *mōphēt*): the altar was broken and the king's hand was paralyzed; from this he had to learn that the prophet "was telling the truth and possessed divine foreknowledge" (*A* VIII, 232–234). King Herod, too, understood certain events as prodigies (*BJ* I, 332, 377).

But most important for Josephus were the signs pointing to the destruction of the Jerusalem Temple. In the introduction to his work on *The War of the Jews* he mentions these "signs and wonders" (σημεῖα καὶ τέρατα; *BJ* I, 28), which later on are described in detail (*BJ* VI, 220ff.), just before the report on the greatest catastrophe, the conflagration of the Temple. The rabbis, too, mention portents happening in the Temple and pointing to its destruction (Babylonian Talmud, *Yoma* 39b). Josephus sees them in contrast to false prophecies which led so many people to their deaths. The signs did foretell the coming desolation of Jerusalem, but the Jews disregarded them and met them with unbelief (*BJ* VI, 288). Their attitude was incomprehensible to Josephus: for men can lie against God and, by pretending to be prophets, deceive people, but the portents occur with strong evidence, coming directly from God. They strike the senses, and only men who have no eyes to see and no minds to consider can overlook and disobey them (*BJ* VI, 288). Josephus may have thought of Isaiah 6:9f. when writing about the blindness and stubbornness of the Jews.[41] In his *Histories,* Tacitus speaks about these portents and the strange attitude of the Jews in a similar way.[42] For Josephus, these portents seem to replace prophecy during the time in which the spirit of God and true prophets were missing. They have the function of warning God's people and opening their eyes for the coming judgment; that is why they have such a strong evidence. On the other hand, these signs were understood differently. They seemed to be ambiguous, good or bad, prodigies or portents. Josephus himself admits that they need to be interpreted by experts: only scribes, well versed in the Holy Scriptures, recognized their true meaning (*BJ*

VI, 291). Therefore, one has to link these prodigies with Scriptural passages. Josephus has failed to do this. We, however, must try to understand them in this way.

Among the seven signs told by Josephus in connection with the conflagration of the Jerusalem Temple, four occurred in the Temple area, indicating that the holiness of this place and its order had been lost, so that the sacrifices and the prayers in this house were done in vain. First, Josephus tells that a star, resembling a sword, appeared and stood over the city and that a comet continued to flare for a year (*BJ* VI, 289). To Josephus, this must have been a bad sign. However, he does not try to explain this phenomenon, because a good messianic interpretation could be given to it, according to the oracle of Balaam: "A star shall come forth out of Jacob and a scepter [comet?] shall rise out of Israel" (Num. 24:17). For the next sign an exact date is given. It happened at the Feast of Unleavened Bread in the year A.D. 66: a great light shone around the altar and the Temple house, and for half an hour it appeared to be bright daytime (*BJ* VI, 290). Many Jews at the time may have thought of such passages as that in Isaiah 9:1–3 and of the tradition of the Passover night, which promises the final salvation and glorification of Jerusalem. According to Josephus and to the scribes, however, the opposite was meant (VI, 291). It is quite difficult to see how the latter could have reached their interpretation of doom, condemning the first and favorable one as an opinion of naive people (*ibid.*).

The four signs that follow are less ambiguous, their gloomy message quite evident; in them, Josephus finds correspondence between the content of the signal and the events meant by them (*BJ* VI, 297). The miscarriage of a sacrificial animal occurred in the Temple area, and a heavy Temple gate automatically opened during the night (VI, 292–293). Then, throughout the whole country, chariots and entire armies were seen in the heavens before sunset, dashing about in the clouds and surrounding cities (VI, 298–299).[43] At Pentecost, the priests serving in the Temple heard in the night noise and voices saying: "Let us depart from here!" (VI, 299–300). Because of the defilement of the Temple, the holy angels accompanying the divine Shekhinah, the manifestation of God dwelling in the Holy of Holies, decided to leave Jerusalem. This meant that the people of Israel, Jerusalem, and the Temple had lost their divine protection and had been delivered into the hands of their enemies. Pentecost was celebrated as the festival of the covenant, commemorating when God had come to Mount Sinai with His angels (see Ex. 19; Deut. 33:2–5). Now God had indicated that He would leave His people, just as the prophet Ezekiel had seen how the glory of God was leaving the holy city (Ezek. 11:23). As the Temple of Solomon was destroyed because of the sins of Israel (4Q Flor), so the Second Temple would be lost.

This series of portents was concluded by the appearance of Jesus, son of

Ananus, who became the voice of doom during the last seven years before the fall of Jerusalem. He had heard a voice from heaven, uttering woes against Israel, Jerusalem, and the Temple. Jesus proclaimed the message of this voice continuously and with the same words, despite severe punishment inflicted upon him by both Jewish and Roman authorities (*BJ* VI, 300–306). He was killed when his prophecy had come true, during the siege of Jerusalem, by a stone from a Roman engine (VI, 309). Josephus wanted to emphasize that genuine prodigies and true prophecy confirm each other and that history, guided by God's providence, provides the judgment of truth.

Notes

1. "I have recounted each detail here told just as I found it in the sacred books" (*A* II, 347); see also "I am constrained to relate them [i.e. the miraculous events] as they are recorded in the sacred books" (III, 81), and IX, 214. He also claims to have merely translated the books of the Hebrews into the Greek language (X, 218).

2. He says this in regard to the age of Noah, who lived 950 years. But Josephus gives several explanations for the truth of the biblical report (*A* I, 105–107).

3. *A* II, 320–349. Additions are found in II, 324, 333, 334, 343, 349. Josephus gives enormous figures about the Egyptian army and exaggerates the desperate situation of the Israelites (324f.). The name of the place is missing.

4. κρινέτω δὲ ὡς ἕκαστος τῶν ἀκουόντων βούλεται (I, 48, 1). See the general advice of Lucian ("Quomodo historia conscribenda sit," p. 60): "And should any myth come into question, it should be related but not wholly credited; rather it should be left open for readers to conjecture about it as they will; but do you take no risks and incline neither to one opinion nor to the other." (See also H. St. John Thackeray on *A* I, 108, in *Josephus the Man and the Historian*, [New York 1929], pp. 56–58.) L. H. Feldman (*Josephus and Modern Scholarship* [Berlin 1984], pp. 407f.) shows in his survey that the question of how much Josephus really depends on Dionysius is disputed, and G. Avenarius holds that the formula of noncommitment was a common motif (*Lukians Schrift zur Geschichtsschreibung*, Meisenheim-Glan 1956).

5. *A* VIII, 349: The angel who helped Elijah (I Kings 19:5) was merely "someone"; see *A* IX, 20, X, 259.

6. For the integrity (ἀρετή) of Moses as historian of Israel, see *A* III, 74.

7. *A* II, 205–223.

8. *A* III, 11; IX, 47f.; X, 27.

9. L. H. Feldman, "Josephus' Portrait of Saul," *HUCA* LIII (1982), pp. 45–99.

10. They are actions "as befit His power" and the reader may "test whether our Lawgiver has had a worthy conception of God" (*A* I, 15).

11. θεία ἐπιφάνεια (*A* I, 255) and ἡ ἐπιφάνεια τοῦ θεοῦ (*A* II, 339; III, 310; IX, 60). See *A* VIII, 119; XVIII, 75. However, the term "epiphany" is not always related to God, and not all the miraculous revelations of God are called epiphanies. There is no plural used for the term ἐπιφάνεια, as is the case for the Hebrew word ṣedaqah (ṣidᵉqôth, "[acts of] righteousness").

12. The amazement of the Syrian King Benhadad about God's epiphany in *A* IX, 60 is added by Josephus to the biblical report.

13. See *A* II, 223; IX, 14, 58; X, 214; and XII, 63. The Wisdom of Solomon, too, mentions the "incredible journey" of God's people when describing the miracle (παράδοξος ὁδοιπορία) of crossing the Red Sea (19:5).

14. Such a free rendering of Judges V is evident from *A* V, 205, where Josephus has used a statement of the Song of Deborah for his report on the battle.

15. See P. Fiebig, "Rabbinische Wundergeschichten," in H. Lietzmann, *Kleine Texte*, Nr. 78 (Berlin 1933).

16. For πρόνοια, see especially *A* I, 225; II, 8, 24, 174, 236, 331f., 349; IV, 47f., 117, 128, 184; X, 214, 279–281; XIII, 163; XIV, 462.

17. See Babylonian Talmud, *Berakhoth* 34b: R. Ḥanina ben Dosa healed the son of Rabban Gamaliel by prayer in the upper room, holding his head between the knees (see I Kings 17:19f. and 18:42).

18. Ḥoni (Onias), who became famous for his power to pray successfully for rain, used to draw a circle for his place of prayer (Mishnah, *Taʿanith* 3,8; Babylonian Talmud, *Taʿanith* 23a; see the trench which Elijah made on Mount Carmel around the altar). According to Babylonian Talmud, *Taʿanith*, 19b, Rabbi Naqdimon ben Gorion was able to procure rain by asking for twelve wells. They are reminiscent of the twelve jars of water, poured out by Elijah on Mount Carmel (I Kings 18).

19. Babylonian Talmud, *Taʿanith* 19b; *Baba Meẓiʿa* 59b.

20. Babylonian Talmud, *Barakhoth* 6b. See E. E. Urbach, *Chazʾal* (*The Wise Men* = "Rabbinic Teachers"), 2nd ed. (Jerusalem 1971), p. 86; O. Betz, "Das Problem des Wunders bei Flavius Josephus im Vergleich zum Wunderproblem bei den Rabbinen und im Johannesevangelium," in *Josephus-Studien . . . Otto Michel zum 70. Geburtstag gewidmet*, ed. Otto Betz, et al. (Göttingen 1974), pp. 23–44.

21. Anti-Zealot criticism of Elijah can be found in some rabbinic statements; see M. Hengel, *Die Zeloten, AGSU* I (Leiden 1961), pp. 127f.

22. See my article "The Concept of the So-called Divine Man in Mark's Christology," in *Studies in the New Testament and Early Christian Literature* (Jubilee volume for A. Wikgren) Supplement to *NT* XXXIII (Leiden 1972), pp. 229–240.

23. Mishnah, *Taʿanith* 3, 8; Babylonian Talmud, *Taʿanith* 23a.

24. See G. Delling, "Antike Wundertexte," in H. Lietzmann, *Kleine Texte*, Nr. 79 (Berlin 1960), pp. 11f.

25. "Philopseudes" 16: see Delling, *op. cit.*, pp. 13f.

26. Josephus, however, indicates that Moses may have been led to heaven in a bodily assumption, without having tasted death: a cloud came down upon him and he became invisible (*A* IV, 326). Josephus says that Moses wrote about his death because of his modesty—that no one should say that he was brought to God because of his unsurpassed virtues (*ibid.*).

27. This dualism appears in the writings of the Qumran Community and in the Gospel of John.

28. The signs were too great to believe that they might be false and unreliable (*A* XIX, 9).

29. In rabbinic literature, the term *nissīm* is used for the miracles done by God for the liberation of Israel from Egypt (see Mekhilta, Tractate *Shirata*). *Nes* means sign or signal in the Hebrew Bible, not miracle. It may be that the usage of *sēmeion* as "miracle" in Hellenistic Judaism has influenced this development.

30. G. Delling, "Josephus und das Wunderbare," *NT* II (1958), pp. 291–309, now in his *Studien zum Neuen Testament und zum hellenistischen Judentum* (Göttingen 1970), pp. 130–145 (see especially p. 143), holds that sometimes Josephus uses epiphany in the same sense as *sēmeion*. But this is not true. In the passage mentioned by him (*A* VIII, 119), δήλωσις and δείγματα are mentioned, not σημεῖον.

31. Josephus omits the biblical phrase of Moses' hand being white as snow (Ex. 4:6) because he wants to detach Moses from leprosy (see my forthcoming article on leprosy in the Bible).

32. This description is an addition to the biblical text.

33. Josephus is more conscious of the basic differences between these two categories of miracles. He has omitted Ex. 14:31b, the concluding statement of the crossing of the Red Sea: "And they [i.e. Israel] believed in the Lord and in His servant Moses" (see A II, 344). He says that they "believed themselves assuredly at liberty" (A II, 345) and that they "passed the whole night in melody and mirth." He mentions the song of praise and thankfulness, composed by Moses (A II, 346), and his intention to render to God "the offerings of thanks of the people for their deliverance" at Mount Sinai (A II, 349). The genuine answer to an epiphany is the song of praise and thanksgiving.

34. Having the miraculous signs at his disposal he has power (δύναμις) in Egypt (A II, 270).

35. The Egyptian plagues can be called ʾōthōth = sēmeia in the Bible (Ex. 10:1f.; Jer. 32:20; Ps. 78:43; Ps. 105:27). Josephus calls them "plagues" (πληγαί) (A II, 296, 305) or sufferings (πάθη) (A II, 293, 299), happenings of evil (προσβολαὶ κακοῦ) (A II, 300) or "evil" (κακά) (A II, 304). The fifth plague is omitted (see A II, 303f.).

36. In the writings of the Qumran Community we find a similar usage of the term ʾōth, however pointing to the end of history and the coming of the final catastrophe (1Q XXVII:1; I:1,5). God's plan and knowledge are directed toward this end also (1QS III:15f.).

37. προφήτου πίστιν ἐπιθεὶς ἑαυτῷ (BJ II, 261); προφήτης εἶναι λέγων (A XX, 169).

38. According to P. Winter, "Theudas" may have been a nickname, derived from the Hebrew word tᵉʿûdah or "sign." ("Miszellen zur Apostelgeschichte, 1: Acta 5,36: Theudas," Evangelische Theologie 17 (1957), 398f.)

39. This holds true for all the predictions of the future. Even a Gentile such as Titus admitted that the words of Josephus told to Vespasian came from God, because "time and the historical facts" had agreed with them (BJ IV, 629).

40. See S. V. McCasland, "Portents in Josephus and in the Gospels," JBL LI (1932), pp. 323–335; O. Michel and O. Bauernfeind, eds., Flavius Josephus, De Bello Judaico, Vol. I (Darmstadt 1959), p. 415, n. 148; G. Delling, "Josephus und das Wunderbare," NT II (1958), pp. 291–309.

41. Michel and Bauernfeind, op. cit., Vol. II, p. 179.

42. Histories V:13. Tacitus knows four portents related to the destruction of Jerusalem and seems to draw from Josephus or from the source used by Josephus. He complains about the superstition of the Jews, who are against true religions. The church father Eusebius has quoted in his Historia ecclesiastica III:8, 1–9 the passage from War VI, 288–304, in which Josephus tells of these prodigies.

43. It is precisely this sign that is confirmed most clearly by Tacitus (Histories V:13). For the biblical background of such a vision see II Kings 7:6, where God lets the Syrian army hear "the sound of chariots and of horses, the sound of a great army." According to II Samuel 5:24, the heavenly army can be heard in the tops of the balsam trees.

10 The Occult in Josephus

MORTON SMITH

I think that hitherto there has been no scholarly study of the occult in Josephus. First, the occult, although popular, is not fashionable in academic, rationalistic circles. Second, it is not prominent in Josephus' work, where military and political history and court intrigue hold the center of the stage, while religion, in the background, figures mainly as a cause and condition of actions and as a matter of legal observances and historical claims, anything but occult. Moreover, "the occult" is a vague concept—literally "the hidden," but now, in common usage, something mysterious, usually thought supernatural, something not a matter of socially accepted teaching or practice, a shadowy entity in the twilight zone of popular beliefs, where no precise line can be drawn around the shadow.

The ancient world, even more than the modern, lies mostly in that twilight. The intellectuals, the authors and readers of literary and scientific texts, are a tiny upper class, the thin, brilliant skin of a soap bubble filled with smoke. Flavius Josephus, Roman citizen, member of the hereditary priesthood of Jerusalem (a considerable civic honor), a well-known *sophistes* ("literary man"), who distinguished himself in imperial service, appears as a representative of that upper class. Though his native language is Aramaic, he writes in Greek for Romans and wealthy pagan provincials, in defense of his own people, and for wealthy Greek-speaking Jews, in defense of his own position: that cooperation with the Romans is necessary for Jewish survival. The surface of the soap bubble reflects the brilliant scene of the Roman Empire—consuls, armies and client kings, cities, temples, and theaters. Through these reflections we catch only glimpses of the dark cloud behind them. What is there?

To daimonion, "the demonic," a complex of supernatural powers.

Greatest among these powers is "the god," i.e., the god of the Jews. Josephus' Judaism and several schools of Greek philosophy had in common the teaching that the cosmos had only one cause, a god. Many Jews and a few pagans maintained that this god was the only—that is, the only "true"—one, and that all others were either inferior or totally false. Part of Josephus' religious tradition was an aggressive, monotheistic rhetoric, mainly derived from Isaiah 40–55, which declared all gods of all other peoples (sc. "the Gentiles") mere sticks and stones; more important were the Ten Commandments and other legal passages, which prohibited Israelites to worship any image at all, or any god but their own. Because of these, many Jews had made themselves conspicuous by refusing to join in Gentiles' worship, but others had proved more adjustable, some of them merely in order to get on with their neighbors, others in recognition of the many elements in the world which seem to have supernatural powers.

One common form of adjustment was to take advantage of the pagan and Old Testament practice of speaking of "god" without indicating which god was meant, as we say "God willing," in which the original (pagan) reference was to any god concerned. Since Hebrew, Aramaic, Greek, and Latin all lack an indefinite article, Jews and Christians found this anarthrous use of "god" a convenient way of referring to their god without making the reference explicit. Josephus' works are full of such references, which pagans would read as referring to "a god," but which Josephus expected his Jewish readers to understand as references to the Jewish god. For such references we shall use "a god," to indicate the absence of the definite article, sometimes important.

Almost equally convenient for Jewish adjustment to life in the pagan world was the belief then spreading among Jews that the true, personal name of their god should not be mentioned. It had not yet become unknown (as it since has—the form Yahweh, usually employed, is only a learned guess). Common people still knew it (*BJ* V, 438)[1] and used it in times of stress, but the upper class held to a (nonbiblical) law by which its use was, with rare exceptions, prohibited. When speaking Greek, they commonly referred to Yahweh as "the god"; pagans could take the reference as one to any god they chose. We shall try to preserve the effect by translating exactly, "the god."

Josephus was acutely aware of the necessity of getting on with the Romans—attempts to resist them had brought his city to ruin and him to the verge of death. However, he held to the traditional Jewish laws and monotheistic rhetoric. However, again, he was not a philosophic thinker, but shared the common notion of the world as full of supernatural beings. Consequently, he both repeated the rhetoric of monotheism and peopled his histories with a multitude of angels, spirits, *daimones,* and unspecified powers—an omnipresent, but usually inconspicuous, overworld of the occult. Here are some of the denizens:[2]

Gods: Though Josephus usually reserves the Greek word *theos,* "god," for the Jewish god, he occasionally uses it for others. Vespasian, on first arriving as emperor at the imperial palace in Rome, sacrificed to "the gods within" (*BJ* VII, 72); "the god" of the people of Akkaron was called *Myia* (A IX, 19). These are mere concessions to popular usage, but Josephus' own usage sometimes approached the popular. Retelling the story of David and Jonathan, instead of having Jonathan swear, as in I Samuel 20:12,[3] by "Yahweh, the god of Israel," he made him take David outdoors and swear by "this god whom you see to be immense and extended everywhere," i.e., the sky (*A* VI, 229f.). Did he identify Yahweh with "the god of the heavens" (Neh. 1:4, etc.) and so with Zeus? (Prof. Feldman has indicated further evidence that he may have done so—*A* XII, 22.) In spite of the Old Testament's prohibition of images and its occasional insistence that Yahweh never appeared in any form (Deut. 4:12–24, etc.), it contained a lot of reports of his appearance in various forms to various individuals; most of these Josephus took over with unabashed literalism. Worse, when he had no Old Testament model, he continued to write stories of "the god" and "the deity" appearing to men (*A* X, 194 end; XIII, 322). Which god? We should suppose Yahweh, of course. But other gods were being worshiped. The Essenes evidently thought the sun a subordinate deity; Josephus says they prayed to it before sunrise (*BJ* II, 128) and covered themselves when excreting "so as not to offend the rays of the god" (*BJ* II, 148; this must be the sun god).[4]

Josephus himself, indeed, went further than the Essenes. In describing their teaching about immortality he says they think souls are "composed of the finest ether" and "pulled down into bodies, as if into prisons, by some physical magic" (*BJ* II, 154). He emphasizes the similarity of their teachings to those of the Greeks (*BJ* II, 155f.). Therefore, we should probably understand "ether" in the Stoic sense, as the material of the highest god. This understanding is confirmed by Josephus' repetition of the theme, both in a speech he attributes to Titus (*BJ* VI, 47) and in the final speech that he puts into the mouth of Eleazar ben Jair in Masada. Urging the Sicarii to commit suicide, Eleazar tells them that life, not death, is man's misfortune, for the "connection between the divine (soul) and the dying (body) is unseemly" and death frees the soul to return to its natural purity (*BJ* VII, 344). Here the soul is unmistakably "divine." This cannot be thought of as a theory repudiated by Josephus. As a good *sophistes*, he uses the same argument for the opposite purpose in his own equally imaginary speech to his companions in the cave of Jotapata, urging them not to commit suicide, but to surrender. There he says flatly that the soul "is a part of a god housed in our bodies" (*BJ* III, 372).

This recognition of divinity in men opens the door for all sorts of occult developments, not only efforts to recognize, reverence, and exploit the present god, but also cults of the souls of the dead and necromancy. Josephus makes both Eleazar and Titus point out that after death the souls have "divine strength and wholly unlimited power, although they remain invisible to human eyes as is the god himself" (*BJ* VII, 346; cf. VI, 47). Nevertheless (though he does not point this out), it would seem that if they can be "pulled down into bodies . . . by some physical magic" (*BJ* II, 154), they might also be compelled or persuaded by magic or worship to use their power as the magician or worshiper wished. Living in ancient society, where necromancy was common, Josephus presumably thought of this possibility. He certainly knew of necromancy from I Samuel 28:11ff., which he retells, without changing the basic events, in *A* VI, 332–336.

The belief that souls are parts of a god has taken us from "the (Jewish) god" (*ho theos*) to "the deity" or "the divine" (*to theion* means both). Josephus himself makes the transition often, and often without seeming to notice the difference; on many occasions he uses first one term, then the other, obviously with the same reference, to avoid monotony (e.g., *BJ* III, 351f.; IV, 190f.). On the other hand, the adjective *theios* ("divine") has a much wider field of reference than the noun *theos* ("god"). Josephus uses "divine" to describe the god's nature, spirit, power, voice, anger, help, gifts—whether in man (understanding, strength, etc.) or in the external world (rain, the manna, and the like)—will, providence, appearances, miracles, laws, angels, prophets, scriptures, Temple, territory, and so on and on. The way in which each of these things was thought to participate in divinity, or belong to the sphere of the divine, has to be decided separately for each case.

An especially important class of cases is that of certain men with whom "the divine" or "the divine spirit" consorts in such a way that they become "divine men" in contrast to the rest of mankind. Moses is the outstanding example; anyone who considers his legislation "will find him a divine man" (*A* III, 180). Even the Egyptians recognized this (*Ap* I, 279). Isaiah, too, was "admittedly divine" (*A* X, 35) and Daniel, to whom "the deity became visible" (*A* X, 194), enjoyed "a reputation of divinity" among the people (*A* X, 268). Such "divine men" were prominent in contemporary paganism,[5] and Josephus seems a bit uneasy about the possibility of their being worshiped. This is understandable, since Christianity was growing up around him. He therefore insists that Moses "in the holy books declared himself mortal, fearing lest someone, because of his virtue's excess [of human limits?], might dare to say that he had gone to the divine" (*A* IV, 326). Yet of Enoch, on scriptural authority, Josephus himself said just that (*A* I, 85).

This notion of the special divinity of a few individuals does not contradict that of the divinity of all human souls. The difference may have been conceived as one of the adequacy and obedience of the different bodies. However he reconciled them, Josephus held both beliefs, and they alike proved that, for him, the deity was not wholly separate from the world; divine power penetrated creation and was manifest in many of its elements.

Some of these elements, however, had minds of their own and might, or might not, do as the god wished. His "messengers" (*angeloi,* "angels") appear mainly in Josephus' retellings of biblical stories and, as in the biblical texts, are sometimes called "gods" (*A* V, 213ff., 284; X, 271f., etc.), but Josephus, departing from his sources, also calls them *phantasmata,* "visionary beings." His references to angels, outside the biblical passages, are rare, but the angels were not. The Essenes knew (and kept secret?) their names (*BJ* II, 142); and Herod Agrippa II, when trying his utmost to persuade the people of Jerusalem not to revolt, called on "the Temple cult, and the holy angels of the god, and our native land" as witnesses that he had done all he could to save them (*BJ* II, 401). Herod's speech was, of course, written by Josephus long after the event, but it shows what Josephus thought would have been effective in the situation. Consequently, when he speaks of Israel's receiving the holiest laws "from the god, through *angelōn*" (*A* XV, 136) it is hard to tell whether he thought these "messengers" were the angels or the prophets. The distinction may not have been sharp to him because, as already shown, he thought the prophets, filled with the divine spirit, were themselves divine beings. He himself, when he had become "full of god" (*enthous*) and had, like Jacob, "laid hold of the dreadful *phantasmata*" of his prophetic dreams (*BJ* III, 353; cf. Gen. 32:25–29 and *A* I, 333), went to Vespasian and declared himself "an *angelos* . . . sent forth by a god" (*BJ* III, 400).

Whether gods or mere messengers, angels belong to the larger class of "spirits" (*pneumata*), which are likewise inconspicuous but important in Josephus' works. He once uses "the divine spirit" to translate "the angel of Yahweh" (*A* IV, 108 for Num. 22:27) and twice to translate "the spirit of *ᵓElohim*" or "of Yahweh" (*A* VI, 222f.; X, 239).[6] Three times, to fill out biblical narratives, he makes up passages in Old Testament style, using "the divine spirit" or "the spirit of the god," in Old Testament fashion, for the power that enters men and causes prophecy (*A* IV, 118f., VI, 166; VIII, 408). Similarly, he explains the vehemence of the Roman soldiers declaring themselves ready for war by saying that they are filled with some spirit like that of (the god) Ares (*BJ* III, 92). In man the spirit and the psyche cause life (*A* XI, 240), because "a part of" a god's spirit was put into man, just as (Josephus suggests) it was into the Temple (*A* I, 34; VIII, 114, 119; *BJ* III, 372). As cause of life, spirit and psyche are somehow identified with the blood (*A* III, 260), but the identification must be only temporary because "the spirits of evil men," presumably after death, become "the so-called *daimonia*" and get into the living and kill them (*BJ* VII, 185). The *daimonia* are distinguished from "the evil spirit" (both possessed Saul) in *Antiquities* VI, 211, another passage Josephus made up. Perhaps the distinction was dictated by I Samuel 19:9, which refers to Saul's tormenter as "the evil spirit of Yahweh," not to be explained as that of a dead man. In *Antiquities* VI, 214 it becomes simply the "demonic pneuma."

This terminological muddle reflects the fact that Josephus' thoughts about *daimones* (and *daimonia,* a diminutive, but commonly equivalent) were, like those of most men of his time and ours, confused. He was clearer as to what could be done about them. Solomon had left directions for driving them out, and these directions were still effective. Josephus himself had seen an exorcist display his skill before Vespasian, using Solomon's method (*technē*), a ring with Solomon's seal, and a plant Solomon had prescribed (*A* VIII, 45ff; the plant was probably *baaras,* which was said to have many magical properties [*BJ* VII, 180ff.]). The witch of Endor's ability to call up souls (*psychas,* not *daimonia* nor *pneumata*) of the dead was also described as a *technē* (*A* VI, 340). Josephus thinks well of such skills; Solomon's method, in particular, commonly practiced by Jews, is part of the heritage of the Jewish people, and Josephus is proud of it (*A* VIII, 46, 49), but he is little concerned about such matters. The wider range of his thought about the demonic appears more clearly when he uses the term for good powers. Even spirits of the dead might be beneficent. In Titus' account of immortality, the souls of brave men fallen in battle are said to become "good *daimones* and beneficent heroes" helpful to their people (*BJ* VI, 47). Josephus wrote the speech, but its pagan terminology is not used in the parallels he also wrote (*BJ* III, 372, 374; VII, 346ff.). However, he told many stories of the demonic powers of the dead working on the side of justice (*BJ* I, 82, 84b, contrast 84a!; *A* XIII, 314, 317, 416, etc.). He even says that the *daimones* of the sons Herod had executed went through all the palace, searching out and exposing those who had participated in the plot against them (*BJ* I, 599), and silencing those who would have warned their enemy, Antipater, that his guilt was being exposed (*BJ* I, 607). Seth Schwartz remarks that the explicit demonology of these last two passages was not copied into *Antiquities.* Perhaps Josephus came to disapprove of it.

Securing justice is a rather grim beneficence, but Josephus often credits *daimones/daimonia* with more amiable activities. When the unfortunate Alexander did something right, his father, Herod, thought he must have fallen in with good *daimones* (*A* XVI, 210). The *daimonion* used to talk with John Hyrcanus and told him everything that was going to happen; thus he enjoyed one of the three greatest gifts that are given to men: prophecy (*BJ* I, 69; cf. *A* XIII, 300). By contrast, Socrates' claim to have been advised by a *daimonion* cannot be taken seriously; he was just joking (*Ap* II, 263).

These examples have taken us from *daimon* to the cognate adjective, *daimonios.* This adjective covers the whole range of the supernatural, including both "the divine" and what we should call "the Satanic," [7] as well as the morally indefinite powers. Consequently, there is no adequate English translation for it, and I must use the term "demonic" with this explanation. Sometimes it seems to be trivialized: it can be used to describe an amazing escape, a devastating earthquake, or a violent wind (*BJ* I, 331, 370; IV, 76), but even in such contexts we must hesitate before dismissing it as merely rhetorical.

The escape in question was, for Josephus, a *teras,* a prodigy which made people think Herod "a man peculiarly dear to the gods" and so hastened his victory. When the earthquake came Herod argued that it was a natural event, not a sign of divine displeasure—but Josephus' summary of his argument is probably ironical (*BJ* I, 373–377). Josephus himself says that the demonic wind "arose for the destruction of" the defenders of Gamala (*BJ* IV, 76); and when describing the capture of Masada he also uses a wind, this time reversed, "as if by demonic providence," to give the Romans the victory (*BJ* VII, 318). To prove his point he makes Eleazar, the leader of the Sicarii, drive it home: "Clearly our hope of escape has been taken away by the god himself; for the fire [blown by the wind] . . . did not turn back naturally against the wall we built, but these things show (the god's) anger" (VII, 331f.).

This expresses what was, in *Bellum,* Josephus' major theme: it was not the Romans who conquered the Jews and destroyed Jerusalem, but the god himself who used them as his agents for his own purposes and repeatedly intervened to make sure that these purposes were carried through (*BJ* V, 376–419, and often). Most adjectival uses of *daimonios* in *Bellum* can and should be taken as expressive of this theme and therefore equivalent to "divine"/ "godsent," while the noun, *to daimonion* ("the demonic"), is often equivalent to "the god." *Daimonios* appears repeatedly in descriptions of critical elements in the course of events: the means by which Josephus' life was saved at Jotapata (*BJ* III, 341), Vespasian's courage and his decision to seize the throne (*BJ* IV, 34, 622), and so on. The climax comes with the burning of the Temple, when a Roman soldier, "not waiting for an order, . . . moved by some demonic impulse, snatches up some of the burning wood and . . . hurls the fire inside a golden door" (*BJ* VI, 252).

The god of the Temple was not there to put it out. Months (or years)[8] before, the priests, entering the Temple for their nightly service, had heard the sounds of movement "and then of (many) speaking in unison, 'We are departing hence'" (*BJ* VI, 299f.). Josephus reported the plural. He also referred indirectly to this omen in the speech he claims to have delivered to the defenders of Jerusalem (*BJ* V, 376–419). In this he reviews Jewish history and comes to the conclusion, "I think the divine has fled from the holy things" (i.e., from the sanctuary and the cult, [*BJ* V, 412]). One copyist changed "the divine" to "the god," but "the divine," with its range of meaning, probably reflects not only the plural in the reported omen, but also the plurality in Josephus' mind. He was thinking, probably, of the account in Ezekiel 11:22f., which described the departure from the Temple of the throne of Yahweh with its entourage of lightning and beasts and wheels and cherubim and all the multiplicity of the divine.[9]

Yet even if this be granted, the story of the omen is not wholly explained. For Josephus also knows and accepts the belief that *the Place* of the Jerusalem

Temple had or was a supernatural power. (Not the Temple itself, though Josephus thought the Herodian one the most marvelous building in the world and accordingly lamented its loss [*BJ* VI, 267]). His belief in the supernatural power of the Place appears most clearly in the historical section of his speech to the rebels (*BJ* V, 376–419), from which we quoted the climax. The speech is placed just before the final stage of the Roman attack; it urges the defenders to spare the Place from capture, by timely surrender. Addressed to Jewish nationalists, it appropriately appeals to the history of the people. Consequently, it is the fullest treatment in *Bellum* of subjects from Old Testament times. Unlike the Old Testament, however, its central power is not Yahweh, but "this holy Place" (*BJ* V, 377 end, the subject appropriate to the dramatic situation). It is from this Place that the rebels are fighting; this is the great ally, which they have polluted (Yahweh they could not). When Sarah was carried off by Pharaoh, Abraham, "raising his hands (in prayer) to the Place which you have now polluted, brought into battle on his side its invincible power" (*BJ* V, 380). After one night, Sarah was restored and Pharaoh, "worshiping the Place now polluted by you," fled (381). God brought our fathers out of Egypt to be guardians of this shrine (383; not "this temple"; though the word is *neōkoros*, there was no temple and would be none for four hundred years). After the ark was stolen, the Philistines, smitten with plagues, restored it, propitiating "the holy" (Place, understand *chōrion*, 385). Sennacherib was killed when he besieged this city (387). When the people were released from the Babylonian captivity they again became shrine guardians of their ally (389; the Temple had not yet been rebuilt). The Hasmonaeans brought down on us the Romans by sinning against "the holy things [the Place, Temple, and cult] and the laws" (397). Therefore, "those who inhabit a holy Place should leave everything to the god" (of the Place; 400). But under you "the Temple has become a receptacle of all [sins] and the divine Place has been polluted. . . . After these things do you look for the dishonored [Place] as an ally?" (402–403). On the contrary, the Place has made its springs flow more freely for Titus, as it did of old for the Babylonians (409ff.). From all this we come to the amazing conclusion quoted above: "Therefore, I think the divine has fled from the holy things [the Place, the sanctuary, and the cult] and is now with those you are fighting" (412).

The one sort of god who cannot leave his sanctuary is a holy Place, and the preceding speech has shown that Josephus thought the Place a supernatural power. This notion is not likely to have come from his supposed Greek secretaries. The speaker is Joseph ben Matityahu, the priest of Jerusalem, who traced the sanctity of the site back to Melchizedek (*BJ* VI, 438) and for whom it was "the Place worshiped by the whole civilized world" (*BJ* IV, 262; spoken by a chief priest). But Josephus also claimed to be a prophet (*BJ* III, 351–354, 400). In this same speech he compared himself to Jeremiah (*BJ* V,

392–393), and in claiming that the divine had departed he followed Ezekiel 11:22f. The god of the prophets, the god of Israel who could take the country or leave it, was not committed to its holy sites. Josephus was a divided man. The fission in his sacred books between the prophetic and the priestly traditions, the fission in his own and his people's life between the demands of religion and the requirements for survival, emerge in this contradictory conclusion that the divine has fled from itself. And this split in his world will be perpetuated by the split in Judaism between the worship of a universal god and the devotion to a holy place.[10]

A surprising proof of Josephus' occasional independence from his environment is the fact that among these supernatural powers there are no stars, except the sun, and no planets. Cosmic speculation had been active in the Jerusalem of his youth; it is clearly reflected in his accounts of the tabernacle and the Temple (BJ V, 214–217; A III, 144–146, 181–187), but the only trace of an astral cult is the Essenes' sun worship (BJ II, 128, 148). When the day destined for the destruction of the Temple came, it was determined not by astral configurations, but by its historical relation to the date of the burning by the Babylonians (BJ VI, 250, 268). The role of the luminaries is merely that of a cosmic clock—unless the practices that went with the Jerusalem speculation were part of what Josephus chose not to tell.

Since the demonic is multiplex, it deals with men and material objects in many ways. Josephus' favorite word for "providence," whether human, demonic, or divine, "of a god," or "of the god"[11] is the strictly descriptive one, "forethought" (pronoia). Mythological terms—"fate," "the lot," "the given," etc.,—he almost never uses, but he is fond of impersonal expressions meaning "it was/is necessary," some of which have strong moral overtones ("it is right"), but none of which, by itself, indicates a personal agent. Nemesis ("envy," "grudge," "anger") is occasionally attributed to a daimon (A XIII, 415) or to the god (A X, 12; it can be induced in him by prayer and sacrifice), or to Tyche ("chance" personified; BJ I, 431; cf. VI, 63), and sometimes it is an impersonal power (BJ VI, 37, 176; A XV, 241); but it rarely figures in Josephus' accounts and is more likely a literary reminiscence and dramatic device than one of the supernatural powers he commonly reckoned with.

Tyche, by contrast, was not only a popular pagan goddess, but also, in Josephus' mind, a complex of powers, everywhere active, and especially complex because every individual had his own set, what we should call his "luck" or "fortune." So does every people. The Tyche of the Romans was famous, and Josephus, like everybody else, believed in her (BJ III, 354, 359; VI, 399; her power and that of "the god" act together [BJ VII, 203; A XX, 70]). Josephus was aware of, but rejected, the theory that identified a man's Tyche with his fate ("the allotted"; A XVI, 397). Tyche was more personal than fate, therefore more capricious, and more likely to be affected by men's actions, literally a supernatural femme fatale. Like women, Tyche was jealous, particularly of human virtues, and was apt to destroy those who excelled in them (*BJ* VI, 63). She belongs in the world of the demonic, but her status there is never defined.

Besides the indirect governance of providence and the eccentric interference of Tyche, the various demonic beings intervened in human affairs in various ways, and men had been given or found out ways of foretelling and influencing the course of future events. The books of the Old Testament are mostly concerned with accounts of divine intervention in the past, prophecies of the future, and directions for observances—ritual, legal, and moral—said to please Yahweh and get desired results, while their neglect angers him and leads to predicted punishments. Implementation of these teachings and the observance of additional customs—the elements of an "unwritten law"—made up the recognized, legally authorized practice of Judaism and, therefore, do not belong to "the occult." Josephus was capable, when writing against Apion, of claiming that the mysteries of Judaism—which he defines as the teachings that the creator god is clearly known from his works and is to be served by moral behavior, but cannot be represented by any image—were well known and had been taught by Moses, not to a small circle of initiates, but to his many companions and all their descendants (*Ap* II, 168f., 188–192). Van Unnik was capable of taking this at face value and deriving from it the conclusion "that revelation in Moses' law had no hidden truth and was open to all." [12]

Nonsense. Josephus himself mentions a few secrets not to be written—Yahweh's true name, the ten words on the tablets written on Sinai, the locations of the graves of the kings (*A* II, 276; III, 90; VII, 394)—and he says that he prefers to keep secret Daniel's explanation of the stone destined to fill the world (*A* X, 210), and that nobody can declare or even conceive what the cherubim of Solomon's Temple looked like (*A* VIII, 73). But these are trivia. Except for Daniel, Josephus says almost nothing of the apocalyptic literature flourishing in his time; he refers to the traditions about ascent to the heavens and the divine throne, but only with remarks (in *A* XVIII, 18) so cryptic that their meaning has rarely been recognized. He never faces the extent to which Judaism seemed to outsiders a mystery religion, as Plutarch described it in *Quaestiones Conviviales* 4.6.1, where Jewish doctrines and ceremonies are described as "things not to be declared," and the question discussed is the identity of the unknown Jewish god. What actually did go on in that great Temple in Jerusalem, of which only the outermost court was open to Gentiles? Even ordinary Jews could not enter the innermost court, and the adyton was closed to all but the high priest. Speculations were widespread and wild (*Ap* II, 77–124). And what of their holy books? Legends told of divine punishments of men who had even thought of revealing their content (*A* XII, 111ff.;

BJ V, 378 is mere rhetoric). Where could one get copies? We do not know. The usual ignorance of ancient authors, down to the third century A.D., about the content of the Old Testament is puzzling. Were its texts commonly kept secret? From the pagan point of view, Judaism itself might be described as an occult religion. Philo did so describe it.[13] Josephus, however, tried to refute this notion, and we are concerned with what is represented in his work as occult.

First, Josephus regards knowledge of the future as occult. The various demonic beings reveal their intentions by signs and portents, which can be understood by those skilled in interpreting them, but not by common people or the wicked. These warnings occur, like the Northern Lights, from time to time throughout the course of history. The greatest display was that which preceded the destruction of the Temple (*BJ* VI, 288–310): a stationary comet; an abnormal light; a cow that gave birth to a lamb; a Temple gate that opened automatically; chariots and armed men flying through the sky; the *daimones'* departure, which the priests heard. In addition, a peasant for some years prophesied disaster, yet people did not understand. This collection is remarkably close to those found in the works of pagan authors. Josephus' beliefs about these matters seem to be those of the surrounding world.[14] But he also quotes a patently Jewish story to prove that birds are worthless for divining the future (*Ap* I, 201–204).

Besides omens, signs, and portents, the demonic communicated with men through dreams and prophecy.[15] These are closely related in Josephus' thought, as they were in that of the ancients generally. Pagan prophets (*manteis*, as opposed to Jewish *prophētai*) and *soi disant* "Chaldeans," were supposed to be expert in interpreting dreams, and were consulted even by Jewish kings, but in vain (*BJ* II, 112; *A* XVII, 345). Jewish prophets were of course better, and among them Josephus himself was outstanding. The god chose him to foretell the future and revealed to him the course of the war. The revelations were given in dreams, which, although obscure, he was able to understand because of his knowledge of the sacred books and his priestly background. The god also entered him, so that he prayed and prophesied (*BJ* III, 351–354; cf. *V,* 208f.). His most famous prophecy was that Vespasian would become emperor (*BJ* III, 400–402), but he also prophesied the exact length of the siege of Jotapata and his own imprisonment (*BJ* III, 406f.), and when these prophesies came true he continued to be consulted about the future (*BJ* IV, 629).

Besides himself, Josephus mentions a good number of prophets from postbiblical times, but only one other whose prophecy explicitly involved dreams. The god appeared to John Hyrcanus in a dream, and John took the opportunity to ask which of his sons would succeed him. (When told, he did what he could to make the god a false prophet, but, of course, failed; *A* XIII, 321f.). The Pharisees were also believed to prophesy, "because the god frequented" them (*A* XVII, 43), but of their three reported prophecies, two were disastrously wrong (*A* XVII, 43, 45), while the third was perhaps no more than a shrewd, albeit moral, prediction (*A* XIV, 174; no cause is named). Perhaps the Pharisees are also meant by "those who prophesy" or those "who refer things to divine causes" and who said (truly) that Herod's colitis was a god-sent punishment (*BJ* I, 656). Prophets were expected to declare past causes as well as future results; the verb used in the passage just cited means "to prophesy" as well as "to ascribe things to the gods," and the Pharisees were said to do both (*BJ* II, 162; *A* XVII, 43). However, the reference is uncertain. John Hyrcanus not only saw the god in dreams, but "the daimonion"/"the divine" talked with him so that he foreknew everything (*BJ* I, 69; *A* XIII, 282). The peasant who prophesied "Woe to Jerusalem" is said to have suffered from "somewhat demonic" inspiration (*BJ* VI, 303). Antipater had forebodings that dissuaded him from coming home "because his soul was already prophesying about its [fate]" (*BJ* I, 610).

Apart from these we find a surprisingly mixed lot. The pagan *manteis* and necromancers have their peculiar techniques, which sometimes work (*A* IV, 104ff.; VI, 327, 330, 340). The witch of Endor, incidentally, was a model of morality, and Balaam was the best *mantis* of his time (*A* IV, 104). Israelite prophets are also said to have had a *technē* (*A* VIII, 334), and the Essene prophet Judas is called a *mantis* (*BJ* I, 80; *A* XIII, 313). King Aretas of the Nabateans learned, from omens given by birds, that an impending Roman attack would fail (*A* XVIII, 125). A German prisoner, knowing the significance of birds, prophesied accurately the fate of Agrippa I (*A* XVIII, 195–202). The emperor Tiberius had great skill in divining from omens and birth dates (*A* XVIII, 211–223). Such examples are just what we should expect to find in any pagan historian's work of Josephus' time.

Besides these individuals, a good many anonymous authors had launched prophecies that circulated among the credulous. Josephus, though usually incredulous, thought some of these ambiguous and commonly misunderstood, but essentially true, for example: *Bellum* IV, 388 and its variant VI, 109, when factionalism arises, the Temple will be destroyed; *Bellum* IV, 311, the Temple will be destroyed when it becomes a square; and *Bellum* VI, 312, a world ruler will arise from Judea (this Josephus thought fulfilled by Vespasian). The last two, Josephus says, were "written in the [sacred] scriptures/sayings." If so, they were all he was willing to publish, besides Daniel, of the enormous eschatological literature of his time, some of which he evidently accepted as inspired and, perhaps for that reason, thought should not be revealed. He says that most of these prophecies were either disbelieved (*BJ* VI, 386) or misinterpreted (*BJ* IV, 312f.), and not only by his opponents, for "many of the wise erred" (*ibid.*). This is partly apologetic; he had been one of the errant. However, it expresses also a conclusion to which he had been brought by his error: "The god's nature . . . is complex and works in many ways" (*A* X, 142). Therefore, although his prophecies will come true, men, because of their ignorance and disbelief, are unable to profit from his ambiguous utterances (*BJ* VI, 314f.). Such prophecies must be interpreted by exegesis both learned and inspired, like his own (*BJ* III, 352). Thus the root of occultism is the nature of the god.

In the material Josephus did choose to publish, the true prophets most prominent during his own time are the Essenes. We are not here concerned with the actual Dead Sea sect or sects, but with what Josephus says of the groups for which this peculiar name was used. He represents them as an occult sect within Judaism, closed by its special purity laws not only to Gentiles but also to all Jews except its own initiates. The initiates had to undergo probation (*BJ* II, 129–133), requiring years of candidacy before full initiation (137–138), and take "frightful" oaths (139) not only to maintain good behavior, but also "to conceal nothing from fellow members, nor betray anything of theirs to others," to hand over the teachings and rules (*dogmata*) exactly, and to preserve the books of the sect and the names of the angels (as secrets? 141–142). This basic structure is supported by many traits common in occult groups: asceticism, communal economy (120–127), nocturnal silence, prayers at dawn to a special deity (here the sun; 128), peculiar ablutions, linen ritual garments, ritualized meals with common prayers (in ritual garments, to be put away afterwards), taciturnity, sobriety, subjection to superiors (129–134), and the study of ancient writings and the secret medical properties of plants and stones (136). Disputes and discipline are handled within this sect by its own courts (145), and the ultimate punishment is expulsion (143). Their doctrine of the natural immortality of the soul as an ethereal being magically imprisoned in the body (154–155) is to be reconciled with the report in *Antiquities* XVIII, 18, that they "immortalize" the soul, by supposing the immortalization to be a restoration of the soul's original condition, freeing it from carnal corruption; compare this with the famous rite for "immortalization" in the Paris Magical Papyrus.[16] "The access of the righteous man [to the heavens] is contested on all sides" (by demons, jealous angels, and heavenly guards; *A* XVIII, 18); therefore, this secret rite is needed.[17] Hence, too, their need to preserve the names of the angels, whom they would meet on the way—angels, like watchdogs, are quieted when called by their proper names.

Stories of ascents to the heavens pullulated in Palestine at this time; the Pseudepigrapha are full of them. The notion seems to have been a common dream which impressive, hypnotic ceremonies or powerful individual suggestion could transform into experiences the initiates would believe actual. Such experiences probably led to prophecies, hence Josephus' reports of Essenes "who profess to foresee the future, having been brought up from childhood on holy books and extraordinary purifications and pronouncements of prophets"

(*BJ* II, 159; notice that these pronouncements are distinguished from the holy books). Nor is it surprising that with all this sanctimonious secrecy the Essenes were widely revered and credited. Herod honored them as supernatural beings. (Had they not been immortalized and gone up to heaven?) One of them declared that Herod was chosen by a god for a happy reign of at least thirty years (*A* XV, 371–374, 377–379, and 375–376 are a correction by some enemy of Herod, probably Josephus).[18]

Magically induced prophecies are also said to have been mentioned by Nicholas of Damascus in his speech against Antipater; he satirized the "female foolishness" of Antipater's harem allies, "prophecies and sacrifices to harm the king," and assorted scandals that helped enliven his deadly denunciation (*A* XVII, 121). These goings on, however, are less likely to have been connected with the Essenes, most of whom avoided women,[19] than with the Pharisees, whom we have already seen practicing prophecy (*A* XIV, 174; XVII, 43, 45), and who also were protégés of the wife of Herod's brother, Pheroras (*A* XVII, 42). She was a leading lady in Antipater's circle.

The Essenes' study of the medicinal properties of plants and stones (*BJ* II, 136) would make them a likely source for some of the philtres and poisons that turned up so often in Herod's court, were it not that other sources seem even more likely. Poisoning is usually secret; the Greek word *pharmakon* means "drug, medicine, poison, magical material, spell" and, in the plural, "magic." Medicine and occultism were so closely connected that there is no telling how much of the latter was involved in the poison plots; some pretty certainly was (*BJ* I, 571, 582f.; *A* XVII, 62; cf. XIX, 193). But many circles had some knowledge of such drugs, so we must look at the persons directly implicated, and these again belong mainly to the circle of Pheroras and his womenfolk, whose connections were with the Pharisees rather than the Essenes. (To judge from the Dead Sea documents, the two sects were not friendly.) Josephus himself shows a little knowledge of magical pharmacology (*A* I, 93: tar from Noah's ark is an apotropaic; *A* VIII, 47 and *BJ* VII, 180ff.: the herb *baaras* has many magical properties and is sovereign for exorcism; *BJ* IV, 465, 476–481: the powers of Jericho spring water and of Lake Asphaltitis bitumen). He probably knew more.

The Essenes may have been the cause of many, and the source of some, of the traditions linking Judaism with other occult societies and mysterious peoples. Josephus states as a fact that they "use the way of life taught among the Greeks by Pythagoras" (*A* XV, 371; cf. *Ap* II, 168). In *Ap* I, 163–165 Hermippus is said to have remarked that Pythagoras borrowed from Judaism several observances; but these were mostly ones that the Jews never observed. By contrast, Josephus' statement is almost plausible, if reversed. Essene practices do resemble Pythagorean teachings so often and so closely that some Pythagorean influence (indirectly, through Egypt?) seems likely. Elsewhere in *Against Apion* (I, 179) Josephus quotes from "Clearchus" a report that Aristotle said the Jews are descended from some Indian philosophers called "Calani." No such Indian philosophers are known,[20] but an Indian named Calanus greatly impressed Alexander's companions by burning himself alive. Josephus' report shows how the story had ramified in the intervening four hundred years. The cornered Eleazar's appeal to his men in Masada to "imitate the Indian philosophers" (*BJ* VII, 351–357), though in a composition surely by Josephus, may possibly, if Josephus observed dramatic propriety, be evidence for occultism among the Sicarii, and this might show Essene influence, since it is coupled with the Platonic account of the afterlife, which Josephus attributes to the Essenes (*BJ* II, 154f.). By contrast, the Cypriot Jew who claimed to be a *magos* and was used by the procurator Felix to seduce Queen Drusilla (*A* XX, 142) is completely credible as a historical figure, but quite inadequate as evidence either of Persian or of Essene connections. *Magos,* in the usage of the time, was often merely a polite term for *goēs,* "magician." Elsewhere in Josephus *magoi* appear only in the Daniel stories, as Babylonian court magicians, to be disgraced, and in the story of Darius' accession, to be massacred (*A* X, 195–236, XI, 31).

Although Josephus says that an Essene (perhaps an ex-Essene?) was appointed to one of the six military commands set up at the beginning of the official Jewish revolt (*BJ* I, 567), the course of events indicates that the most influential prophets of antebellum Palestine were neither the Essenes, nor the Pharisees, nor any of the upper class and their hangers-on whom we have thus far reviewed, but the many popular prophets, who talked mostly of political deliverance by supernatural aid and who constantly encouraged the revolutionists (*BJ* I, 347, II, 650—cf. Dover on Thuc. 7.5a, VI, 285f.; *A* XX, 169ff.). Josephus is consistently hostile to them. They were lower-class, possessed by demons, and made up at will all sorts of bogus oracles; many were hired by the revolutionary leaders (i.e. "tyrants") to keep the people from surrendering; the one who told the people to go to the Temple "to receive the signs of salvation" became thus responsible for the great slaughter of civilians that occurred when the Temple was captured (loc. cit., esp. *BJ* VI, 285). In a word, they were the opponents' forecasters.

Except for the claims—doubtless often sincere—to divine possession and inspiration, there was nothing occult about such prophecies; they were produced for, and often during, public proclamation. However, by their general theme, and especially, in this last instance, by the teaching that the people must all go to some place where the divine power will be revealed, they are allied to the utterances of a class of false prophets, most of whom Josephus calls *goētes* (singular *goēs*), a term of which the meanings range from "magician" to "fraud." Basic is "magician" or, at least, "wonder worker," so

Josephus' frequent choice of the term, with its occult connotation, when he might have used something merely descriptive, e.g., "false prophet," suggests that there was more in their teaching than appears in his accounts. Here is a list of incidents involving these "false prophets":

In Pilate's time (ca. 26–36) the Samaritans were persuaded, by a lying demagogue (*not* called a *goēs*), to assemble on Mount Gerizim where he would reveal the vessels hidden by Moses (*A* XVIII, 85).

Under Fadus (ca. 44–46) one Theudas, a *goēs* who claimed to be a prophet, called the masses to the Jordan, which he said he would divide (*A* XX, 97).

Under Felix (ca. 52–60) appeared a swarm of "*goētes* and deceivers" who, pretending to prophesy, set the crowd mad and persuaded them to take to the desert where the god would show them signs of freedom. Josephus specifically distinguished these from the Sicarii, a terrorist organization (*BJ* II, 258ff.; *A* XX, 167f.).

Worse was an Egyptian *goēs* and prophet who led thirty thousand to the Mount of Olives, promising to take Jerusalem (by making the walls fall) (*BJ* 261ff.; *A* XX, 169ff.).

Goētes and bandits joined forces and pillaged the countryside (*BJ* II, 264f.; the parallel in *Antiquities* does not mention the *goētes*).

Under Festus (ca. 60–62) a *goēs* promised salvation and an end of evils to those who would follow him to the desert (*A* XX, 188).

Just before the capture of the Temple (August 70) a false prophet urged the people of Jerusalem to go to the Temple, where the god would show them signs of salvation (*BJ* VI, 285).

After the fall of Jerusalem, in Cyrene, ca. 72, a "most wicked man" led many of the poor into the wilderness, promising to show them signs and apparitions (*BJ* VII, 437f.; *V* 424).

All these gatherings the Romans put down by military force, but this tells us nothing of the teachings involved; it was merely the Roman method of discouraging illegal assembly. That Josephus does not call all these men *goētes*, and does use the term occasionally for mere deceivers (*BJ* IV, 85; V, 317), should not conceal the pattern common to this group. All these men promised miracles; the use of *goēs* to differentiate them from the rest of the revolutionists suggests that they were thought to do miracles. It may also reflect claims they made to be Moses *redivivus*, who was expected by many. Moses had often been described as a *goēs* because of his miracles, a description Josephus vigorously combats (*Ap* II, 145, 161). Besides rebutting the charge, he tried to suppress the evidence for it; he made God, not Moses, bring the plagues, and he removed the magical details—smiting with the rod, scattering ashes in the air, invocations, etc. (*A* II, 293–310; cf. *A* II, 284ff., 320). To justify Josephus' use of *goēs* for his contemporaries, we should like some such details about the methods they used; but for these, in Josephus' brief references, there was no space.

Consequently, such evidence is available only for Jesus,[21] and Josephus' mention of Jesus (*A* XVIII, 63f.) has been so much corrupted that no attempted reconstruction of the original can be relied on. At most the description, "a doer of amazing works," can be salvaged—it means "wonder worker"—and it not only accords with the gospel accounts of Jesus' public appearances, but also, in Josephus' work, connects him with the other *goētes*, although some differences deserve notice: he came a little before the others; the first of the above list, the Samaritan (who is not called a *goēs*) came at the end of Pilate's governorship, while Jesus was executed about the middle of it. Although crowds are said to have followed Jesus into the wilderness (Mk. 6:32ff., 8:1ff.), he is not said to have called them out, or promised signs of salvation if they would come. Of course, Christian tradition would have forgotten, not to say suppressed, evidence of illegal activity and failed promises. The crowds following him were not broken up by military force because he was not in Roman territory but in that of Herod Antipas, and the Roman government frowned on the use of violence by its subordinate rulers against their subjects; Antipas' younger brother had been deposed for that, and the lesson had not been lost. If only we knew a little more about Josephus' original notice, we could probably argue with more confidence from his silence. As things stand, we can only say that Josephus seems to have mentioned Jesus partly because of his miracles (he liked wonder stories) and partly because he had been the founder of a sect which, by the time Josephus wrote, was probably becoming important, though Josephus hoped it would not last: "The tribe of the 'Christians,' named for him, has not yet died out" (*A* XVIII, 64). With these words Josephus dismissed the most important occult movement of his time.

In a society on the verge of revolution, as Palestine was throughout Josephus' youth, prophecies are important. The concentration of Josephus' narrative on political events further exaggerated their importance. In everyday life, most people were often more concerned about their health, their jobs, and their families than about revolution. So if we had a social history of the time, we should probably find the Essenes most prominent for their magical cures, and the importance of other groups explained by other functions. As it is, we find in Josephus a mixed bag of different sorts of details reported in different connections. Most of these details have already been mentioned or belong to types of which examples have been given. To review them under the different headings by which they might be classed seems needless, but a few concluding notes are called for.

Josephus seems to share the common belief of his time in the efficacy of oaths, prayers, and curses, particularly dying men's curses, and adjurations using the secret name of the god (*BJ* II, 143; IV, 362; *A* II, 275; XIV, 28; XVII, 58; XVIII, 346; *V* 101, 275). In spite of the secrecy of the name, it was still used. Foragers who sneaked out by night from Jerusalem during its last weeks to find a little food, and were caught by the revolutionists, begged in the name of the god to be allowed to keep a part of what they had found, and were refused (*BJ* V, 438); propaganda, of course, but certainly intended for his Jewish readers, and therefore an indication of what they would find credible.

Of other magical means to ends, Josephus believed in the power of the spells left by Solomon to alleviate diseases (*A* VIII, 45ff.). His belief in demonic avengers has already been mentioned; his statement that Antipater used the demonic vengeance for his brothers to destroy his father (*A* XVII, 1) may refer to some sort of black magic, of which the women of his circle were often accused (*BJ* I, 571; *A* XVII, 62f., 121, etc.; we are not told what these women said about Salome!). Accusations of magic were evidently common in the society. When a couple of Agrippa's Gentile officers deserted to Josephus in Caesarea the opposition accused them of being magicians, and the charge found much acceptance (*V* 149ff.). Nevertheless, Simon's attempt to escape from the ruins of Jerusalem by passing himself off as a demon (*BJ* VII, 29ff.) succeeded only for a moment.

Similar notions of the world are introduced by Josephus in a few passages of his retelling of biblical stories. Sinai was haunted by the god (*A* II, 265). The god, by giving his true name to Moses, gave him the power to invoke him effectively; consequently, the god came to meet the Israelites "in response to Moses' wishes" (*A* III, 80) and came to the tent and the Temple "in response to our prayers" (*A* III, 100, end). The gems of the high priest's garments lit up to signal the god's presence and also to foretell victory in war (*A* III, 215f.).

In II Kings 2:19–21 Josephus found a brief biblical report that Elisha "healed" a spring at Jericho, which had formerly blighted crops and caused miscarriages, by throwing into it salt from a new pot and saying, "Thus saith Yahweh, I have healed these waters; there will be no more death and miscarriage from that place"—a nice little miracle, but too simple for the Roman carriage trade. Therefore, Josephus retold it, or preferred a source which had retold it, as follows:

> Elisha, . . . having been hospitably received by the people at Jericho, since they treated him with particular kindness, rewarded them and the whole district with an eternal favor. Going out to the [pestilential] spring and throwing into the stream a pottery vessel full of salt, then raising his righteous right hand to Heaven and pouring out on Earth propitiatory libations, he besought Earth to soften the stream and open sweeter veins [of waters], Heaven to mix with the stream more fertile airs and to grant the people of the land both proper production of crops and children to succeed them, and [he asked that] the waters which would cause these [blessings] should never fail so long as the people remained just. With these prayers, and with the performance of many additional rites

[known to him] from his art, he changed the spring, and the water which had formerly been a cause of their childlessness and famine was thenceforth made a source of healthy children and plentiful food. (*BJ* IV, 461–464)

Here is a Palestinian example of the Graeco-Roman "divine man" in action, his right hand raised to heaven, like that of a Hellenistic statue, pouring out his libations and prayers, not to Yahweh, but to Earth and Heaven, and uttering, not Yahweh's commands, but moralizing Hellenistic rhetoric, backed up by rituals from his (secret) knowledge. Josephus may have found all this in some source, but he found the source congenial to his taste and useful for his purpose, to re-do Judaism in Roman imperial style, of which an important decorative element was the occult.

For him, however, the occult was more than a decorative element. It was a constituent part of the Graeco-Roman world, a part made particularly important by the conflict between that world and his inherited Israelite monotheism. For the multifarious Graeco-Roman religious life, that monotheism, to which he was loyal, left no place. But that life was present and triumphant. Some place had to be found for it. If it was somehow to be made compatible with the henotheism of biblical law and the monotheism of Isaiah, their relationship could only be occult. He had to adopt the Septuagint's solution of the problem: "All the gods of the Gentiles are *daimonia*" (like Yahweh), "but the Lord" (Yahweh, as distinct from the others) "made the heavens." (Ps. 96:5, Septuagint 95:5).

Notes

1. This paper has been read by Professors Shaye Cohen, Louis Feldman, and Dr. Seth Schwartz. I acknowledge with thanks their numerous corrections and suggestions, but claim as my own the remaining mistakes. In citations of Josephus, *BJ, A,* and *Ap* are cited by two numbers, indicating book and section of the Naber and later editions, *V* is cited by section number only.

2. What follows may be compared with the standard account based on A. Schlatter, *Wie sprach Josephus von Gott?,* Gütersloh, 1910 (*Beiträge zur Förderung christlicher Theologie* 14.1). A recent reconsideration of the topic, to which Professor Cohen referred me, is R. Shutt's "The Concept of God in the Works of Flavius Josephus," *JJS* 31 (1980) 171ff.

3. I Samuel 20:12 is I Kingdoms/Kings 20:12 of the Septuagint and Vulgate. I shall follow the Hebrew book names, divisions, and verse numbers throughout.

4. They also seem to have planned to worship it on the roof of their projected temple; see M. Smith, "Helios in Palestine," *EI* (Orlinsky volume) 16 (1982) 199*ff.

5. See M. Hadas and M. Smith, *Heroes and Gods,* New York, 1965 (*Religious Perspectives* 13).

6. Yahweh and 'El were two gods worshiped by the early Israelites. In the Old Testament they are commonly identified. 'Elohim is a plural formed from the 'El root, probably to denote the society of gods, but commonly used in the Old Testament as equivalent to 'El and, like 'El, identified with Yahweh.

7. Satan does not appear in Josephus, though by Josephus' time he had long figured in Jewish thought. Nor does Josephus speak of any supreme power of evil. The evil he is concerned with results mainly from the wickedness of men (which forced the god to punish his people), and the wickedness of men results from the fact that some men are wicked.

8. The chronological reference of *Bellum* VI, 299f., is not clear. In VI, 288–309 Josephus has collected a number of omens evidently reported from or invented for a number of years prior to the revolt, but some of them should perhaps be located in the course of it. The reference to "four years before the war" in VI, 300 dates only the beginning of the prophecies of Jesus ben Ananos.

9. Between completing *Bellum* (about 80?) and beginning *Antiquities* (about 85?), Josephus seems to have turned away from *daimonion* and toward *theion. Daimonion* is relatively common in *Bellum*, but quite rare in *Antiquities; theion*, though not rare in *Bellum*, is much more frequent in *Antiquities*. The change may reflect either Josephus' movement toward Pharisaism (whence the unwillingness to class Yahweh with other *daimonia*) or a decline of his reliance on secretaries (whether pagans or Jews of the Diaspora).

10. The rabbinic use of "the Place" as a designation for Yahweh, and the rabbis' explanation of it as meaning "the Place of the world," may possibly result from an attempt to reconcile the traditions by giving "the Place" a new significance, after the Temple hill had been discredited and practically abandoned. Professor Cohen, however, reminds me that the rabbinic use was anticipated by Philo, *Somn.*1.63; *Fuga* 75; etc., and must therefore have originated long before A.D. 70.

11. "Of the god" is comparatively rare in *Bellum*, "of a god" (*theou*, without an article) in *Antiquities*. The difference is interesting because it parallels the change from *demonic* to *divine* (see above, n. 9). With what follows on *Tyche* cf. S. Cohen, "Josephus, Jeremiah, and Polybius," *H&T* 21 (1982) 373, whose equation of *Tyche* with the favor of Yahweh neglects its personal aspects. In all systems that make a single god the source of all being and power, everything that is or happens must be an aspect or action of the god. Nevertheless, monotheists do not commonly think of their neighbors as acts of god. The ancients attributed similar personal independence to their invisible neighbors, the supernatural powers.

12. W. van Unnik, "Flavius Josephus and the Mysteries," in *Studies in Hellenistic Religions*, ed. M. Vermaseren, Leiden, 1979 (*Etudes préliminaires* 78) 277.

13. E. R. Goodenough, *Jewish Symbols in the Greco-Roman Period*, New York, 1953–1968 (*Bollingen Series* 37) vol. 6, 206ff.; H. A. Wolfson, *Philo*, Cambridge, Mass., 1947, vol. 1, 43ff. The rabbis continued Philo's claims; see M. Smith, *Clement of Alexandria and a Secret Gospel of Mark*, Cambridge, Mass., 1973, 180ff., 197ff. Professor Feldman concurs, citing Philo's *Leg. Al.* 3.33.100, *Cherubim* 14.49, *Sac. Abel et Cain* 16.62, and *Abr.* 24.122.

14. See *BJ* I, 23, 28, 45; IV, 287, 623; *A* III, 215–217; XVII, 167; XVIII, 125, 195–202, 211–223, 284–286; XIX, 9, 87; XX, 19. I omit examples taken from the Old Testament, which therefore exemplify "religion," not "occultism." Professor Feldman cites as similar Tacitus, *Histories*, 5.13.1, and refers to G. Delling, "Josephus und das Wunderbare," *NT* 2 (1958) 291ff.; and to S. McCasland, "Portents in Josephus and in the Gospels," *JBL* 51 (1932) 323ff. for more evidence.

15. Prophetic dreams: *BJ* II, 112, 116; III, 351–354; *A* XI, 327; XII, 112; XIII, 322; XIV, 451; XVII, 345, 351ff.; V, 208f.; *Ap* I, 207. This list of examples does not pretend to completeness.

16. Bibliothèque Nationale, suppl. gr. 574, lines 475–820 = K. Preisendanz and A. Henrichs, edd., *Papyri graecae magicae²*, Stuttgart, 1973–1975, vol. 1, 88–100.

17. For the evidence for this interpretation see, besides the text of the Paris papyrus, the discussion in M. Smith, *Clement* (above, n. 13), 238–240.

18. Other Essene prophecies: *BJ* I, 78–80 = *A* XIII, 311–313; *BJ* II, 113 = *A* XVII, 348.

19. Admittedly, Josephus reports the existence of a (seemingly minor) branch of the Essenes who did marry—after putting their fiancées through three years' probation (*BJ* II, 160f.). It seems unlikely that ladies so conditioned, dressed in clothes that had to be worn till they fell apart (126) and prohibited from eating any food save their own (143), moved in the upper circles of the Herodian court.

20. On the *Suda*, s.v. "Kalanos," see M. Stern, *Greek and Latin Authors on Jews and Judaism*, Jerusalem, 1974–1984, vol. 1, 51.

21. It is presented in M. Smith, *Jesus the Magician*[2], San Francisco, 1981.

11 The Samaritans in Josephus

R. J. COGGINS

a ny treatment of the theme "the Samaritans in Josephus" must acknowledge from the outset two basic ambiguities. One of these ambiguities may to some extent be due simply to the paucity of our knowledge of the Samaritans just before and after the beginning of the Christian Era, but it is likely that its causes run deeper. It may be most patently stated by the fact that it is never fully clear to what extent the Samaritans regarded themselves, or were regarded by their neighbors, as a *political* grouping, inheriting some of the distinctive traditions of the old northern kingdom. Or was the raison d'être of Samaritanism a purely *religious* one, emerging from disputes with the Jerusalem community over the priesthood, the place of sacrifice, the status and extent of Scripture and other traditions handed down from earlier times? The available evidence suggests to us that the latter understanding is closer to the truth; but virtually all that evidence is, in fact, in the form of religious literature, for which religious differences would be of primary importance, and so we cannot be sure that we have anything approaching a balanced picture. As Judaism moved toward a more precise self-definition, its relation with Samaritanism would inevitably be seen in relation to religious issues.

The second ambiguity relates to Josephus himself. As we shall see when we look in more detail at the references to Samaritanism in his writings, he several times makes the point that the Samaritans varied in their attitude toward Judaism, sometimes distancing themselves from it, sometimes claiming to be an integral part of it. The point can easily be stood on its head, as an illustration of Josephus' own attitude toward the Samaritans. Sometimes he regards them as rivals to the Jerusalem community and essentially external to it; sometimes he regards them as part of the larger community of Judaism and true inheritors of the traditions of old. We shall need to bear these ambiguities in mind throughout our treatment, for they affect not only the historical presentation of Josephus but also his geographical presuppositions. Thus, in the account of the extent of Jewish territory with which he prefaces his description of Vespasian's first attack (*BJ* III, 35ff.), Samaria is included along with Galilee, Perea, and Judea. Here as elsewhere, of course, we must note the possibility that he was simply incorporating existing material into his final version without any specific debating point in view; and, in particular, on this point of the extent of the "promised land," it may well be that any Jewish writer trying to be loyal to the biblical tradition would feel obliged to include in his own description the whole area once occupied by the kingdoms of Israel and Judah. Nevertheless, it is certainly possible that we should also see the inclusion of Samaria as a pointer to the fact that Josephus "regarded the Samaritans as being essentially Jews, although heterodox."[1]

References to the Samaritans and Samaritanism of a specific kind in *The Jewish War* are, however, relatively infrequent; it is to the *Antiquities* that we must turn to obtain a fuller appreciation of Josephus' viewpoint. The first matter to be noted is that there are difficulties of terminology that still bedevil modern scholarly work on the subject. These relate to the fact that "Samaritans" is a term most appropriately limited to the description of members of a particular religious group, whereas it is also often used in practice for "dwellers in Samaria." This ambiguity results in confusion both at the geographical and at the religiopolitical level. As is well-known, the holy place of the Samaritans is Shechem, with the holy mountain the nearby Mount Gerizim; to associate the Samaritans with Samaria, which was a city of major political significance throughout the Second Temple period and was alleged to have a pagan background, may itself have been an example of Judahite polemic. One has nevertheless to recognize that the term "Samarians," which would be the obvious designation of the inhabitants of Samaria, has never come into general usage.[2] As for Josephus' own terminology, we note that in his account of the seizure of power by Jehu (*A* IX, 125ff.) he uses the term *Samareis* rather than *Samareitai,* that is, in effect, "Samarians" as against "Samaritans" (and this is the rendering found in the Loeb edition of Josephus). This is consistent with the fact that for Josephus it is only after the fall of the northern kingdom to the Assyrians in the eighth century B.C. that it is proper to speak of Samaritanism. He refers to it as the rites which "have continued in use even to this day among those who are called Chuthaioi [Cuthim] in the Hebrew tongue and Samareitai [Samaritans] by the Greeks" (*A* IX, 290). A little earlier (IX, 288) this religious practice, which is clearly condemned for its foreign and pagan origin, is described as Persian; whether this point is also intended polemically is less clear, for Josephus' other references to the Persians are not normally hostile.

Various basic points arise from this description. First, the religious rather than the political character of Samaritanism appears to be emphasized; no attempt is made to link the Samaritans with the wickedness of the rulers of the northern kingdom, which Josephus, following his biblical sources, frequently alludes to. Second, the nature of Josephus' description makes it clear that he regards Samaritanism as a new development on the Palestinian scene in the Assyrian period; there is no allusion, either at this point in his narrative, or at the relevant point in *Antiquities,* Book V, to what came to be the Samaritans' own view of their original breach with the Judahites, associating it with the time of Eli; such a tradition seems to be quite unknown to Josephus. Third, as has already been implied, the designations of the Samaritans in the *Antiquities* vary considerably. Sometimes this may simply be a matter of literary effect; at other times it may well betray the use of different sources, but there seems to be no ground for supposing that such sources betray a significantly different attitude to the Samaritans, which is still traceable in the final form of Josephus' work. Even if, as has been argued, Josephus occasionally had access to a source which originated with the Samaritans themselves, such material has been developed into a basically consistent picture in the present form of the work.

It is, therefore, with II Kings 17 that the biblical basis of Josephus' Samaritan material begins. It is now widely agreed that the present form of that chapter represents a later elaboration of the original account of the last days of the northern kingdom and their sequel,[3] but by the time of Josephus the chapter clearly existed in substantially its present form, and up to a point he could draw upon it as an account of Samaritan origins that tied in well with his own polemical inclinations. The limitation, "up to a point," is necessary, for, as F. Dexinger has clearly illustrated, there is a basic ambiguity in this chapter if it is to be used for anti-Samaritan polemic, an ambiguity which Josephus has not avoided, for "on the one hand he has to prove the inadequacy of their religious worship, while on the other he can make the averting of the 'lion plague' intelligible only by admitting that 'they worshiped him [God] in a respectful manner.' "[4]

An additional ambiguity arises from the fact that much of the material in II Kings 17 used in *Antiquities* IX, 288–291, has an underlying political dimension, concerned as it is with the origins and organization of those who came to settle in the territory of the old northern kingdom, yet it is used as a basis for religious polemic. This is also the first usage of the recurring theme in Josephus' treatment of the Samaritans: his charge that they claim to be Jews when they see the Jews prospering, but reject any ties of kinship in times of adversity for the Jews. This feature will recur; here we may note simply that it must surely be seen as reflecting the ambiguity of the situation in Josephus' own day. It is also noteworthy that it forms the climax to Book IX of the *Antiquities* and is thereby given special prominence.

It is from accounts of this kind that the standard textbook view of a Samaritan "schism" has been derived; the unsatisfactory nature of such a description has long been recognized and need not be discussed further here.[5] We need note only that, though Josephus is the first extant example of the specifically "anti-Samaritan" interpretation of the events described in II Kings 17, it is in general more likely that he is drawing upon an already existing tradition than that he is specifically engaged in his own mythmaking, for there is little in his account which goes beyond the biblical material.[6] It is the use he makes of that material which is striking, and even here he is well in line with much other anti-Samaritan polemic from his era.

When we come to consider the later references to the Samaritans in the *Antiquities,* it becomes much more problematic how far Josephus is drawing upon established tradition, for in these cases there is usually either no biblical parallel, or any such account has been warped almost beyond recognition. The expression "mythmaking" has already been used, and this is especially appropriate for the only reference to the Samaritans in *Antiquities,* Book X, for it provides the basis for a myth that has flourished down to our own day. Book X, 184, stresses the difference between the consequences of the northern and the southern exiles. The circumstances in each case were comparable, but whereas when the ten northern tribes were exiled the Assyrian king (whose identity is unclear) "settled in their place the nation of Chuthaeans, . . . who were then called Samaritans because they assumed the name of the country in which they were settled," in the south "the king of Babylonia, when he carried off the two tribes, did not settle any nation in their place." Such a view of the differing fates of the two areas, though based on late and polemical literary evidence, has come to be very widely regarded as factual and still plays a part in many serious accounts of the history of Israel. For Josephus it was only those who had gone through the experience of the Babylonian exile who were the true heirs of the promises to the forefathers.

It is, however, with the Persian period that the Samaritans once more come into prominence in Josephus' account, and here we are surely justified in supposing that his account of past events was intended to be construed as reflecting the situation of his own day. In his description of the reestablishment of the Jerusalem community (*A* XI, 84), Josephus elaborates on the biblical account to make it clear that the "adversaries of Judah and Benjamin" (Ezra 4:1), whose identity is not made specific in the biblical text, were Samaritans. (Some modern scholars also hold this view, but the historical question need not here detain us; the significant point is that Josephus made a specific identification where his underlying tradition was much less precise.)

The elaboration of the biblical text in *Antiquities* XI, 85–88, is particularly instructive. The Samaritans claim the right to share in the rebuilding of the Temple and in its worship; the Jewish leaders reject the request concerning the rebuilding on the grounds that they alone had received authorization from the Persian authorities to carry out this project. However, they did offer the Samaritans the right to worship ($\pi\rho\sigma\kappa\upsilon\nu\varepsilon\hat{\iota}\nu$) in the Temple when it was completed—but such an opportunity would be available for all who might wish "to come to the sanctuary and revere God." This reply, presented by Josephus as a generous offer, is interpreted by the Samaritans as a rebuff, and in their indignation they attempt to prevent the rebuilding of the Temple by making alliance with "the nations in Syria." That is to say, they are presented as associating with the heathen rather than acknowledging God's true community. They attempt also to persuade the Persian authorities to withdraw the permission given to the Jerusalem community to rebuild the Temple (XI, 97). But all these schemes are in vain, and the Temple is duly rebuilt with rejoicing in the Jerusalem community (XI, 106–108).

Two additional comments seem appropriate. First, it seems plausible to suggest that Josephus' favorable picture of the Persian rulers is intended as a hint to the Roman rulers of his own day how a distant and potentially hostile people should be governed, when their claims to political independence had ceased. The Persians are consistently presented in favorable terms, and one characteristic feature of this presentation is the emphasis on their ability to distinguish the acceptable elements among their subject peoples. This point, already implicit in the account of the rebuilding of the Temple, is made twice more in *Antiquities* XI. In one passage (XI, 61) we read that Darius "commanded the Samaritans and the Idumaeans and those in Coele-Syria to give up the villages which they had taken from the Jews and now held" (here it is noteworthy that Josephus himself appears to have added the reference to the Samaritans to an original text, reflected in I Esdras 4:50, which made no mention of them). In the other (XI, 114ff.), an attempt by the Samaritans to ingratiate themselves with the Persian rulers is firmly rebuffed.

Second, this text, like so many from the early part of the Common Era, illustrates the ambiguous position of the Samaritans vis-à-vis the Jewish community.[7] In this connection it is important to bear in mind that Josephus was writing at a time and in circumstances where the identification of the true Jewish community was inevitably to be a matter of prime concern. We lack any direct evidence bearing unequivocally on this matter from, say, the late first century A.D., and so the indirect evidence supplied by Josephus becomes all the more important.

Before leaving the account of the rebuilding of the Temple, it is worth noting that the substance of it had already been given in *Antiquities* XI, 19ff. It is not clear whether this repetition is simply the result of confusion concerning the proper historical sequence of events, evidence for such confusion being traceable as far back as the present form of Ezra 4, or whether it is a deliberate device to emphasize the importance of the events. While the former may seem to be the more probable hypothesis, the latter is not excluded. To the best of my knowledge no detailed study has been undertaken of the use by Josephus of repetition as a literary device for emphasis.

The other main section which concerns us in *Antiquities* XI, relates to the description of the events which led to the founding of the Samaritan temple on Mount Gerizim. It is a long and, in part, very involved account which occupies more than fifty sections of the book; it is also one of the first substantial sections of the whole work to be without any significant biblical basis, though individual episodes clearly relate to biblical material. In particular, the expulsion of a relation of the Jerusalem high priest for his marriage to a daughter of Sanballat, the governor of Samaria, shows a remarkable similarity between *Antiquities* XI, 302f., and Nehemiah 13:28, though the ostensible dating of the events as described in the two sources would differ by more than a century, since Nehemiah's activity is usually dated in the fifth century B.C., whereas Josephus links his story with the time of Alexander the Great, ca. 330 B.C.

The network of related historical problems in this account has been dealt with frequently by scholars, and it is not possible here to go into detail with regard to this aspect.[8] More helpful for our immediate purpose is some consideration of Josephus' likely method and intention. Here, as so often in Josephus, we need to recall that, like other ancient historians, he was not relating events for their own sake or for the purpose of presenting a dispassionate record; his account had an apologetic intention. Here it is not difficult to see, at least in general terms, some part of that purpose: the discrediting of one of the most distinctive and treasured features of Samaritanism: its holy place and temple. This is done in particular by emphasizing the way in which all those concerned with its foundation were apostates and renegades from the true Jewish community. The high priest was the son of a murderer, and so a sad falling away from the usual standard characteristic of the servants of the Jerusalem Temple; those involved in the building of the Gerizim temple were those guilty of mixed marriage, as Josephus would have regarded it; the Samaritans attempted to deceive their political master by a misleading pretense of loyalty; the only way in which Samaritanism could prosper was by its appeal to the basest elements among the Jews.

This last point is particularly emphasized by the conclusion of *Antiquities,* Book XI, where once again Josephus' hostility to the Samaritans is shown by the way in which their wickedness is made the subject of the final climactic section of the book. "Whenever anyone was accused by the people of Jerusalem of eating unclean food or violating the Sabbath or committing any other such sin, he would flee to the Shechemites, saying that he had been unjustly expelled" (*A* XI, 346f.; the last word varies between different versions, ἐκβεβλῆσθαι or ἐκκεκλῆσθαι, "expelled" or "accused"). Only those who had fallen away from the true community and its God-given practices and way of life could find refuge among the Samaritans.

It is noteworthy that the Samaritans are here, and in a number of other passages, called "Shechemites," and this usage has often been regarded as pointing to the availability to Josephus of different sources. It is of course well known that he freely acknowledged his dependence on a variety of sources.[9] Nevertheless, this fact does not of itself lead to any natural association between particular sources and particular attitudes to the Samaritans; all the material has been worked into the overwhelmingly hostile pattern of the whole, and detailed differences of names do not imply a different underlying attitude.

The beginning of *Antiquities* XII provides the first opportunity for Josephus to introduce the Jews of the Diaspora into his account, and it is with the community in Egypt that he is primarily concerned. He emphasizes that migration to Egypt was by no means necessarily a matter of enforced exile; it could not be compared with the Babylonian exile as a necessary stage in the development of the community. Rather, many "came to Egypt of their own accord, for they were attracted by the excellence of the country and Ptolemy's generosity" (*A* XII, 9). However, even in Egypt Jewish-Samaritan rivalry continued, for there was also a Samaritan diaspora community which looked to Mount Gerizim as its religious home, just as the Jews looked to Jerusalem.

In XII, 10, this point is made without further elaboration, but at XIII, 74ff., it becomes the occasion for a more elaborate account of a quarrel between the two communities. The quarrel as to the identity of the true temple is to be resolved by the verdict of the king of Egypt sitting in council with his friends (φίλοι). Andronicus, who engaged in debate on behalf of the Jews, was successful by virtue of his persuasive eloquence, and Sabbaeus and Theodosius, the Samaritan advocates, were killed, along with their supporters.

There are a number of curious aspects of this story. For the modern reader it is scarcely to be disputed that it is the Samaritans who will capture sympathy. They permit Andronicus to speak first; no indication is given whether or not they were even allowed to put their arguments to the king and his council, who had been carried away by Andronicus' eloquence; no previous suggestion has been made that the party unsuccessful in the debate was at risk of being put to death. Because of these apparent internal inconsistencies, it has often been argued that more than one source has been incorporated into this account, and this may indeed be the case. It is, for example, striking that there is no reference here to the pagan and foreign origins of the Samaritans, which Josephus so freely stresses elsewhere; the difference between Jews and Samaritans here is presented simply in terms of the correct place of worship.

Here as elsewhere, however, it is instructive to take the episode in its final form and see what we learn from it regarding Josephus' attitude to the Samaritans. Three points seem to emerge. First, we should be wise to set aside our modern assumptions concerning the likely impact of the story; there is no suggestion that the Samaritans' discomfiture was intended to be seen, or would in fact have been seen, as anything other than fully deserved. Second, the importance of the proper place of worship is stressed. Josephus was writing at a time when both the Jerusalem Temple and that on Mount Gerizim had been destroyed. The importance of the place of worship was, therefore, in a sense symbolic, yet should certainly not be underestimated on that account; the elaborate requirements of the Mishnah concerning the conduct of Temple worship might provide an appropriate comparison, for they, too, were promulgated at a time when nothing of the worship they describe was in fact practicable.

The third point that we should note concerns the existence of a Samaritan diaspora alongside the Jewish communities of the Mediterranean world. The nature and extent of such Samaritan groups remain almost totally unknown. The suggestion has been made that a building excavated at Delos in the Aegean Sea might have been a Samaritan synagogue, and though this is unlikely,[10] it is certainly probable from inscriptional evidence that a Samaritan group did exist on the island, perhaps around 100 B.C. A stele from that date refers to "The Israelites on Delos who make offerings to hallowed Argarizein."[11] There can be no serious question that the last word quoted is a Greek transliteration of *har g^{e}rizim*, the form in which Mount Gerizim is always found in the Old Testament (Deut. 11:29 and elsewhere); this or a closely comparable form appears to have been the usual Greek transliteration.[12] Unfortunately, for the moment at least, this discovery remains unique, the first piece of evidence of its kind. It is very difficult to assess its real significance until it can be placed in a larger context. At present, we have to accept the fact that our other knowledge of a Samaritan diaspora comes from a period later than the evidence provided by Josephus.

Arguments from silence are dangerous, but it is tempting to speculate whether the lack of any reference to a Samaritan diaspora in earlier sources may in part be due to the fact that the clear-cut division between Samaritans and Jews, which Josephus takes for granted and indeed emphasizes, was not so obvious at an earlier period. It is well known that the community at Elephantine in the fifth century B.C. made appeal equally to Samaria and Jerusalem,[13] and though this concerned the political rather than the religious authorities, the two cannot wholly be separated. Unfortunately, the date and place of provenance of other texts which appear to allude to the Samaritans in the intervening period are in almost every case uncertain; even the well-known reference in Ecclesiasticus 50:26, though it can be dated with fair confidence in the second century B.C., lacks any meaningful context which would enable us to place it in an appropriate typology of the development of Samaritanism.[14]

On this whole issue, then, we have to admit to uncertainty whether Josephus' references to the Samaritan diaspora should be seen as simply his recording of the known state of affairs or as a part of a considered presentation of Samaritanism as a deliberate inferior imitation of Judaism.

When we revert now to a consideration of the treatment of Samaritans in the *Antiquities*, it is necessary to examine Josephus' account of the Samaritans' role in the rebellion against Antiochus Epiphanes. To a considerable extent Josephus follows I Maccabees, both in the details recorded and in the overall view of the causes and progress of the revolt. There is, however, an important section, XII, 257–264, which is not paralleled in I Maccabees, and is largely concerned with the Samaritans. They are presented as approaching Antiochus Epiphanes, repudiating any links with the Jews but emphasizing their different origin and religious practice; their pleas are accepted, persecution ceases, and the Samaritan temple on Mount Gerizim is henceforth to be known as that of Zeus Hellenios.

The view of the Maccabean uprising presented by I Maccabees is that it was the only way in which Jewish political and religious freedom could be maintained against a ruthless and evil aggressor who was attempting to impose practices which would be rejected by all right-thinking Jews; in I Maccabees, any who were not fanatically opposed to Antiochus are branded as traitors, and this line is, in general terms, followed by Josephus. Recent study has, however, placed the whole conflict in a broader context and has, in particular, had the effect of suggesting that the supposed conflict between traditional Judaism and Hellenism was not so sharp as has conventionally been supposed.[15]

Part of the episode in Josephus is simply a reuse of themes with which we have already become familiar. It begins, for example, with the Samaritan repudiation of any links with Judaism, which Josephus asserts was regularly their reaction when they saw the Jerusalem Jews in trouble. Other aspects of the correspondence between the king and the Samaritans can, however, be explained in terms of differing views of Hellenism within Judaism. Thus, when Josephus describes the Samaritans' request that their temple might "be known as that of Zeus Hellenios" (*A* XII, 261), he can present that in terms of the presuppositions of his own day as something totally unacceptable to any true Jew. But there is clear evidence that designations of this kind were not so alien to the Judaism of the second century B.C.[16] It is also possible that Josephus, or the source on which he drew, has modified the tradition to make it more hostile to the Samaritans, since according to II Maccabees 6:2 the dedication of the Gerizim temple was to Zeus Xenios, which, it has been argued, would have been less offensive, since the title stressed the divine protection of strangers.[17] It is noteworthy also that the Samaritans make it clear that they maintain such Jewish observances as the Sabbath, even if Josephus glosses this claim with the comment that this is a mere superstitious imitation of Jewish practice. In short, while it is not easy to be certain how much, if any, of this material goes back to the purported time of its origin, it is certainly possible to see how Josephus has altered its thrust so as to discredit the Samaritans.

One particular characteristic of this section remains to be noted: the designation of the Samaritans as "Sidonians." This is not the first occasion on which it is found in Josephus; in *Antiquities* XI, 344, in the context of the rival bids for the favor of Alexander the Great already discussed, the Samaritans "said that they were Hebrews but were called the Sidonians of Shechem" and then went on to deny their identity with the Jews. There are a number of points in common between the confrontation with Alexander in *Antiquities* XI and that with Antiochus in *Antiquities* XII, so that both may be variants of the same original, but in any case the designation as Sidonians remains unexplained. It may be that a basically historical explanation should be sought and that there were, in fact, colonies of Sidonians in different Palestinian cities whose words are quoted in Josephus' source.[18] But in view of the strongly polemical tendencies of so much of the material in Josephus dealing with the Samaritans, it is more likely that a literary explanation should be sought and that "Sidonians" had come to be a derogatory term. Links have, for example, been seen with the traditions in Isaiah 23, where, in what is ostensibly an oracle concerning Tyre, some of the harshest condemnations are addressed to Sidonians (verses 2, 4).[19]

One of the emphases in the account of the Samaritan correspondence with Antiochus was on the importance of their temple, which had already been a prominent point in the encounter with Alexander the Great. All this being so, it is perhaps a little surprising that Josephus' reference to the destruction of that temple by John Hyrcanus is so brief and allusive. The account in *Antiquities* XIII, 255f., occurs in the context of a summary of Hyrcanus' campaigns and is not elaborated upon in any way save simply to note that it had been built with Alexander's permission, briefly sketching the circumstances and observing that it had survived for two hundred years. The explanation for this unusual brevity on Josephus' part may, of course, lie in the lack of more extensive source material available to him, but it may also be that this was not a subject upon which Josephus would have wished to expatiate, with the destruction of the Jerusalem Temple so recent a memory and with the constant ambiguity of the Samaritans' own position. If they were to be trusted as Jews, then it could not have been proper to take pleasure in the destruction of their temple, even if it were only an imitation of that at Jerusalem. And Josephus could never assert categorically that the Samaritans were quite separate from the Jews.

By comparison with the laconic and allusive description of the destruction of the temple on Mount Gerizim, Josephus has a much fuller description of Hyrcanus' later siege of Samaria, which should probably be dated between 111 and 107 B.C.[20] Here again a number of interrelated difficulties confront us. First, there is the possibility that what are described by Josephus as two campaigns are really variants of the same action; and a number of modern scholars have supposed that the destruction of the Gerizim temple actually took place in 108 B.C.[21] Second, and a more fundamental historical problem, is the question whether the Samaritans were, in fact, involved when Hyrcanus besieged Samaria. The Loeb edition of Josephus translates the relevant passage (*A*, XIII, 275) thus: "[Hyrcanus] attacked and besieged it [i.e. Samaria] vigorously; for he hated the Samaritans as scoundrels because of the injuries which, in obedience to the kings of Syria, they had done to the people of Marisa, who were colonists and allies of the Jews." But is the translation "Samaritans" justified? The word is Σαμαρεῦσιν, and this appears to imply the inhabitants of Samaria ("Samarians") rather than the Samaritans with whom we are concerned. Nor is it obvious that the particular charge which Josephus brings as supporting Hyrcanus' action could legitimately have been leveled against the Samaritans either in fact or in terms of the condemnations set out by Josephus himself. It may well be, therefore, that, important as this episode was for the way it illustrates Hyrcanus' capacity to take on the waning power of the Syrians and attack their allies with impunity, it is not immediately relevant to our present purpose.

From this point on, the references to Samaritans in the *Antiquities* become fewer, and they no longer have a political significance. As far as our evidence goes, the different patterns of rule imposed upon Palestine by the Romans took no account of the Samaritans as a significant political grouping, and all the allusions to them in the period of Roman rule that have survived imply that they were a religious group within the broader spectrum of Judaism. This shift of emphasis is to some extent, of course, characteristic of Judaism as a whole, as its political aspirations were denied it; but whereas there were Jewish groups in the form of Zealots and Sicarii who maintained resistance to Roman rule, there is no evidence of any such political motivation among the Samaritans. The nature of this shift to an increasingly religious emphasis accounts for some of the ambiguity in Josephus' presentation, which we noted at the outset of this essay.

Two episodes from the period of Roman rule are worth more detailed consideration in this light, the first from the time of Pontius Pilate, the second from that of Cumanus. In *Antiquities* XVIII, 85–89 there is an account of a disturbance within the Samaritan ἔθνος. (The Loeb translation here is "Samaritan nation," but this seems too limiting and precise; "people" would probably convey the sense more satisfactorily.) Disaffection was aroused on what seem to be incontrovertibly religious grounds, that is, a claim that the hidden vessels of the temple (which had, of course, been destroyed more than a century earlier) were to be revealed at Mount Gerizim. This disturbance alarmed Pilate, who seems to have regarded it as being, potentially, at least, a political revolt, and put it down with loss of life. The Samaritans appealed to Vitellius, the governor of Syria, and this in itself seems to be a strong indication that their aims were not anti-Roman. As a result Pilate was forced to return to Rome.

A noteworthy feature of this episode is that it is told by Josephus with almost no sign of anti-Samaritan feeling. The Samaritans are presented as being somewhat gullible in believing that the claim being made was true, but none of the characteristic polemic against the Samaritans is here found. The point of the story seems rather to have been to demonstrate that at its best Roman justice was capable of dealing fairly with offenses committed by its own officials and was not merely an instrument of oppression; to that extent the fact that it was Samaritans who were the occasion of the episode is merely incidental.

These events took place around A.D. 36; the second episode occurred some fifteen years later, under the rule of Cumanus, when the situation in Palestine had in many ways deteriorated sharply.[22] A number of complicating factors are bound to influence the assessment of the events. In particular, we have two distinct accounts of what must surely be the same conflict from Josephus himself, one in *Antiquities* XX, 118–136, the other in *The Jewish War* II, 233– 246 (pp. 132–134 of the Penguin Classics edition), as well as possible allusions in other sources that are not of immediate concern to us. Second, the interests and rivalries of four different parties in the conflict need to be borne in mind: the Samaritans, the Galilaean Jews, the Jerusalem Jews, and the Romans. As told in the *Antiquities,* the particular episode involving the Samaritans is placed in the context of a series of disturbances under the rule of Cumanus, and this impression is also given by the account in *The Jewish War,* even though the description there is much briefer. To that extent, therefore, as with the Pilate episode, Josephus' antipathy toward the Samaritans is subsumed in the larger concern of the injustice which had marred some aspects of Roman rule in Palestine.

In brief outline, the story in *Antiquities* XX tells of a quarrel between Jewish and Samaritan groups which originated when pilgrims from Galilee were passing through Samaritan territory on their way to Jerusalem for a festival. Cumanus took the part of the Samaritans (having been bribed to do so, according to Josephus) and had many of the Jews killed. There are discrepancies at this point between the version of the story in the *Antiquities* and that in *The Jewish War,* but they need not concern us here.[23] Two apparently incompatible consequences are said to have followed; on the one hand, Josephus asserts that the Jewish leaders persuaded those who had been fighting to lay down their arms; on the other hand, Josephus states that the country became "infested with bands of brigands" (XX, 124). Meanwhile, as in the case involving Pilate, the Roman governor of Syria, who at this time was Quadratus, was called in. He restored order, punishing the ringleaders on both sides. Cumanus, like Pilate before him, was ordered to return to Rome, and the province was restored to an uneasy peace. The account in *Antiquities* emphasizes the Jewish hostility to Roman rule, while that in the *War* gives rather greater prominence to Jewish-Samaritan antagonism, but there are no intolerable discrepancies between the two accounts.

Two comments may briefly be made. First, the similarities between this story and that involving Pontius Pilate are striking. There can be no serious doubt that two separate episodes are involved, but it is certainly possible that a common pattern has influenced the two presentations. If this were so, we might have a pointer toward an explanation of the minor inconsistencies in the present form of the narrative. Second, this story, like that relating to Pilate, is in both its forms (*Antiquities* and *War*) essentially concerned with Jewish grievances under Roman rule; the disputes with the Samaritans are almost incidental.

This characteristic feature is taken a stage further in the last episode that will directly concern us: the account in *War* III, 307ff. of Vespasian's attack upon the Samaritans at Mount Gerizim. One of Josephus' techniques for emphasizing the protracted gallantry of the Jewish resistance at Jotapata, in which he himself was involved, is to intersperse within the account descriptions of victories won by the Romans elsewhere; the reader is then, as it were, astonished when the spotlight returns to Jotapata and its continuing heroic defense. One of these interspersed accounts describes the Samaritans assembling on Mount Gerizim. It is stressed that they had no warlike intention, but the gathering together of so many in one area was regarded by the Romans as a potential threat. Encircled and without an adequate water supply in the heat of summer, some of the Samaritans died of thirst and some deserted to the Romans, but the great majority (Josephus speaks of 11,600) were massacred by the Romans.

The account is interesting, not least for what is omitted. There are here none of the slighting references to the Samaritans' alien origin and religious inadequacy, which were characteristic of the first mentions of them in the *Antiquities*. Indeed, the only hint of criticism of the Samaritans in this account is that they took "pride in their own weakness," which might be regarded as a very proper attitude for a religious group. Overall, the presentation is a sympathetic one, and, in particular, no attempt is here made to regard the Samaritans as basically different from Jews. Insofar, therefore, as the *War* is taken as a source that stands alone, without reference to the *Antiquities,* the picture of the Samaritans is from Josephus' point of view. The various allusions in the *War* all make it clear that they continued to worship on their own holy mountain even though the temple had been destroyed. Whereas in *Antiquities* this had been pictured in terms of a falling away from true worship, which was possible only at Jerusalem, here it is simply a characteristic practice of the Samaritans which does not involve any form of condemnation.

It is now appropriate, after this rapid sketch of some of the main passages in the two historical works of Josephus in which he tells us something of relations between the two communities (or, as it sometimes seems more appropriate to put it, of the place of Samaritanism within the larger spectrum of Judaism) at an earlier stage in their history, to attempt to bring together some kind of assessment. It should first be remarked that the limitation of the above discussion to those passages where Josephus makes clear reference to the Samaritans is quite deliberate. The attempts that have been made[24] to argue from Josephus' silence concerning patriarchal links with Shechem, that he thereby intended a deliberate anti-Samaritan polemic, seem to argue for too great a degree of subtlety, both in Josephus and his readers. Furthermore, it is not possible within the confines of a short article to give any consideration to possible Samaritan references in Josephus' other works; in any case, there seem to be no grounds for inferring that they would in any significant way affect our overall picture.

An appropriate frame for such a picture may be provided by the theme of self-definition, which has generated a good deal of scholarly interest in recent years. An obvious and relevant starting point can be the volumes entitled *Jewish and Christian Self-Definition,* edited by E. P. Sanders.[25] Both the overall title of the work and that of the most directly relevant article, to which reference has already been made, "Limits of Tolerance in Judaism: The Samaritan Example," by F. Dexinger, provide helpful and instructive clues to our understanding of the attitude of Josephus toward the Samaritans. The overall title first: it seems clear that an important, if secondary, purpose of Josephus in his writings, exemplified by his concern to spell out the different constituent elements of Judaism, was this concern for self-definition. Who might legitimately be regarded as Jews? Not only the circumstances of Judaism at the time when Josephus was writing, but also clear indications within his own output, reflect this concern. Thus, both in *Antiquities* XVIII, 11ff., and in *War* II, 119ff., there is an extended description of the three "philosophies," Pharisee, Sadducee, and Essene, which exemplify the particular religious emphases of the community. It is, indeed, true that this presentation (and especially the choice of the word φιλοσοφίαι) may have been intended to make his explanations intelligible to the thought-world of his readers;[26] it remains the case that a satisfactory definition of Judaism seems to have been an important part of Josephus' purpose.

But that brings us to the second point. What were to be the limits of tolerance in Judaism? Here the Samaritans were, as far as Josephus was concerned, in an ambiguous position. As we have already seen, this is well illustrated by his frequent claim that they wished to be regarded as Jews in times of prosperity and repudiated a Jewish connection in times of adversity. A major problem in assessing the significance of these statements is that we do not know whether Josephus had any direct links with, or personal knowledge of, contemporary Samaritanism, or whether he is entirely dependent upon traditions from the past that had come down to him. What is, in any case, clear is that, just as the divisions between Jews and Christians were much less precise than later writers on each side of the divide would wish their readers to believe, so a consciousness of unity between Jews and Samaritans continued in certain areas of life until well after the time of Josephus.[27]

The emphasis in all this is strongly upon religious concerns, yet there are also certain points, even if they are of a rather negative kind, which we should more naturally regard as "political," that emerge from Josephus' treatment. (It is perhaps relevant to comment that it would be very difficult to gain any undisputed *sociological* insights from the relevant material in Josephus. Never is there any indication of divisions within Samaritanism,[28] or of the Judeo-Samaritan tension reflecting identifiable class structures.) The first political point is that Josephus seems to provide no evidence that would suggest that the different ruling powers treated the Samaritans as a distinct political group. At times, the polemic which we have considered in this article may seem to imply a particular political standpoint, but it always appears as if this is simply the condemnation in which Josephus or his sources engage, without objective basis in the political realities of the period being described.

The lack of reference to a datable "schism" may also have a political dimension. "Schism" is a term with a religious frame of reference, but it is difficult to imagine that religious division could have taken place in the ancient, near-eastern world without political causes or consequences. Of such evidence there seems to be none. Even in the time of the Maccabean rebellion it is now possible to see the Samaritan attitude as one that takes a natural place within the spectrum of Jewish reactions to Hellenism.

In the end, therefore, it appears that Josephus bears witness, perhaps unconsciously and in spite of himself, to the fact that Samaritanism was essentially one variant within Judaism. There is ample evidence to illustrate the hostility toward Samaritanism of what was to become the normative Judaism of Mishnah and Talmud,[29] and Josephus was not exempt from the forces which brought about that hostility. His treatment at some points seems to betray ignorance or at least a lack of immediate knowledge; on other occasions he is clearly only too willing to adopt the viewpoint, probably already present in his sources, of Samaritanism as having a dangerously compromised past. All of this bears out to a remarkable extent the judgment first expressed by Montgomery nearly eighty years ago in his still valuable work on the Samaritans.

"Josephus," he wrote, "has abundant opportunity to refer to the Samaritans. . . . Unfortunately he no more than reflects the current Jewish prejudices of his day, and allows us to perceive some of the truth only through the contradictions in which he involves himself. . . . The worthy historian is a good example of the ambiguity which affects the whole Jewish attitude toward the sect." [30]

Notes

1. E. Schürer, *The History of the Jewish People in the Age of Jesus Christ*, II, rev. ed., Edinburgh, 1979, p. 7, n. 11.
2. For a discussion of this usage, cf. R. J. Coggins, *Samaritans and Jews*, Oxford, 1975, pp. 8–12.
3. Coggins, "The Old Testament and Samaritan Origins," *ASTI* 6, 1968, pp. 35–41.
4. F. Dexinger, "Limits of Tolerance in Judaism: The Samaritan Example," in E. P. Sanders ed., *Jewish and Christian Self-Definition* II, Philadelphia, 1981, p. 106.
5. See H. H. Rowley, "The Samaritan Schism in Legend and History," in B. W. Anderson and W. Harrelson, eds., *Israel's Prophetic Heritage*, London, 1962, pp. 208–222. (This article is one of the very few significant omissions from the Josephus bibliography compiled by Dr. L. H. Feldman, *Josephus and Modern Scholarship*, Berlin, 1984, pp. 528–541, 946.)
6. Coggins, *Samaritans and Jews*, p. 16.
7. The point is further discussed in Coggins, "The Samaritans and Acts," *NTS* 28, 1982, pp. 432f.
8. I have already discussed this point in *Samaritans and Jews*, pp. 94–97; see also Feldman, *op. cit.*, pp. 532–536, for a survey of other views.
9. Josephus, *Antiquities*, Preface, provides one such statement.
10. A. T. Kraabel, "New Evidence of the Samaritan Diaspora Has Been Found on Delos," *BA* 47, 1984, pp. 44–46. I am grateful to Dr. Kraabel for sending me a copy of his article and for valuable additional comments.
11. P. Bruneau, "Les Israélites de Délos et la juiverie délienne," *Bulletin de Correspondance Hellénistique* 106, 1982, pp. 465ff.
12. The various forms found are set out and discussed in H. G. Kippenberg, *Garizim und Synagoge* (*RGVV* 30), Berlin, 1971, pp. 53–55.
13. *ANET*, 492.
14. See the discussion by J. D. Purvis, "Ben Sira" and the Foolish People of Shechem," *JNES* 24, 1965, pp. 88–94, reprinted in his *The Samaritan Pentateuch and the Origin of the Samaritan Sect*, Cambridge, Mass., 1968, pp. 119–129.
15. The basic general study here is M. Hengel, *Judaism and Hellenism*, 2 vols., Philadelphia, 1974; the work of T. Fischer, *Seleukiden und Makkabäer*, Bochum, 1980, is valuable in applying these insights to the Maccabean revolt.
16. See J. A. Goldstein, *I Maccabees* (Anchor Bible), Garden City, 1976, p. 137.
17. Kippenberg, *op. cit.*, pp. 79f.; Goldstein, *II Maccabees* (Anchor Bible), Garden City, 1983, pp. 272f.
18. This is the view toward which R. Marcus inclines in the Loeb edition of Josephus, *Antiquities*, VI, pp. 480f.; see also the discussion in Kippenberg, *op. cit.*, pp. 73–80, which sets out a survey of scholarly views.
19. So most recently T. Fischer and U. Rütersworden, "Aufruf zur Volksklage in Kanaan (Jesaja 23)," *Welt des Orients* 13, 1982, pp. 45f.

20. Schürer, *op. cit.*, I, 1973, p. 210, and n. 22.

21. So D. S. Russell, *The Jews from Alexander to Herod,* London, 1967, p. 63.

22. D. M. Rhoads, *Israel in Revolution: 6–74 C.E.*, Philadelphia, 1976, is useful not only as a clear general survey of the period but also for its particular attention to the relevant material in Josephus. The book's subtitle is *A Political History Based on the Writings of Josephus.*

23. Rhoads, *op. cit.*, pp. 70–73, E. Haenchen, *The Acts of the Apostles,* Oxford, 1971, pp. 68f.

24. See notably A. Spiro, "Samaritans, Tobiads and Judahites in Pseudo-Philo," in *PAAJR* 20, 1951, esp. pp. 323–328.

25. Two volumes so far published, Philadelphia, 1980–81. Dexinger's article is in Vol. 2, pp. 88–114.

26. This point is made by the successive editors of the Loeb edition of the *Antiquities:* Marcus, in Vol. 7, p. 311; Feldman, in Vol. 9, p. 10.

27. Most recent discussions of Samaritan history have given some consideration to this question; see also J. Bowman, *Samaritan Problems,* Pittsburgh, 1975.

28. The possibility that such inner-Samaritan divisions can be traced behind the present form of the account of the quarrel between Jews and Samaritans in Egypt (*A* XIII, 74ff.) is discussed, with negative conclusions by S. J. Isser, *The Dositheans (SJLA* 17), Leiden, 1976.

29. The topic has been widely discussed; cf. e.g. Kippenberg, *op. cit.*, esp. pp. 87ff.

30. J. A. Montgomery, *The Samaritans,* Philadelphia, 1907 (reissued 1968). The quotations are from pp. 156f.

12 Josephus' Pharisees: A Complete Repertoire

JACOB NEUSNER

I n 1956 Morton Smith published a landmark study of Josephus' pictures of the Pharisees, "Palestinian Judaism in the First Century," in Moshe Davis, ed., *Israel: Its Role in Civilization* (New York, 1956), pp. 67–81. In the thirty years since then, Smith's discoveries have not made a perceptible impact on the historical understanding of the pre-A.D. 70 Pharisaism. Indeed, Heinz Schreckenberg, *Bibliographie zu Flavius Josephus* (Leiden, 1968), between 1956 and 1968 (pp. 263–312), lists no studies at all of Josephus' Pharisees, excluding the extensive citations in my *Life of Rabban Yohanan ben Zakkai* (Leiden, 1962, 1970², pp. 2, 166–171).

Furthermore, when Smith's article is alluded to, it is not accurately summarized. Louis H. Feldman (*Scholarship on Philo and Josephus [1937–1962] Studies in Judaica* [New York, 1963], p. 41b) states,

> Smith . . . notes that the Pharisees hardly figure in J[osephus'] account in *BJ* (2:162–63), but that in *AJ* [*Antiquities*], written some twenty years later, the Pharisees take first place in the discussion of the Jewish sects; this shift is due, he says, to a desire to win support from the Romans for the Pharisees against the Sadducees; but the picture of the Pharisees in *BJ*, we may note, is fully as favorable as and not much shorter than that in *AJ*.

Smith's point, however, is *not* that the picture in *The Jewish War* merely is shorter, but that it omits the most important claim made first in *Antiquities,* namely, that Palestine is ungovernable without Pharisaic support. Length does not figure in Smith's case. But, as a matter of fact, *Antiquities* does contain substantial materials not present in *War.* Apart from Feldman, who is presently revising *Scholarship* and may be relied upon for a more judicious account of Smith's article, I know of no significant effort to confront, let alone make use of, Smith's discoveries.

Here I wish to review the several references to Pharisees in Josephus' writings[1] and to spell out the sources in such a way that Smith's study will both receive the attention it deserves and be shown to be wholly correct, and therefore to necessitate the revision of our picture of pre–70 Pharisaism.

Four of Josephus' works, written in Rome, have come down from ancient times: *The Jewish War, Antiquities, Life,* and a treatise, *Against Apion.* The *War* was first written in Aramaic as an appeal to the Jews of the Parthian Empire not to blame Rome for the destruction of the Temple, which, Josephus argues, had been caused by the Jews' own misdeeds, and as a defense of the Romans' administration of Palestine and conduct of the war. This was then translated into Greek, in a second edition, and published sometime between A.D. 75 and 79. Sixteen years later, in A.D. 93–94, he issued his *Antiquities,* a history of ancient Israel up to A.D. 70. The *Life* came still later, sometime after A.D. 100, and *Against Apion* came last.[2]

Life

Josephus claims, in *Life,* that he himself was a Pharisee:

> At about the age of sixteen I determined to gain personal experience of the several sects into which our nation is divided. These, as I have frequently mentioned, are three in number—the first that of the Pharisees, the second that of the Sadducees, and the third that of the Essenes. I thought that, after a thorough investigation, I should be in a position to select the best. So I submitted myself to hard training and laborious exercises and passed through the three courses. Not content, however, with the experience thus gained, on hearing of one named Bannus, who dwelt in the wilderness, wearing only such clothing as trees provided, feeding on such things as grew of themselves, and using frequent ablutions of cold water, by day and night, for purity's sake, I became his devoted disciple. With him I lived for three years and, having accomplished my purpose, returned to the city. Being now in my nineteenth year I began to govern my life by the rules of the Pharisees, a sect having points of resemblance to that which the Greeks call the Stoic school. (*V* 10–12)

At the end of his life, Josephus thus claims he was a Pharisee. He repeatedly tells us that ancient Judaism was divided into three sects—though we know of others—and here he alleges that he underwent the training imposed by each of them.

If so, the whole process of entering the three sects seems to have been compressed into a very brief period. He says he began to study the several sects at the age of sixteen. He then lived with Bannus for three years. Now he is nineteen. He next declares he chose to follow the Pharisaic rules. So the three years of apprenticeship with Bannus consumed the whole time devoted to the study of all the sects. And Bannus himself is not represented as one of those sects. In all, Josephus does not suggest he studied Pharisaism, Essenism, and Sadduceism for a considerable period. Indeed, he could not have devoted much time to the several sects if he actually spent the whole three years in the wilderness. Pharisees generally required a training period of twelve months; as to the Sadducees, we have no information; and the Essenes likewise imposed a long novitiate. So Josephus' evidence about the sects and his story of what he himself did do not seem to correlate. What he wants the reader to know is that he knew what he was talking about—that, and one further fact: he himself was a Pharisee. But nothing else in the story of his *Life* tells us what being a Pharisee meant to Josephus. Like Luke's similar allegation about Paul (Acts 22:3), it is part of his credentials.

We do, however, gain a picture of how the Pharisees functioned, from Josephus' story of his doings during the revolutionary period of his life. On the eve of the war, Josephus says, he opposed sedition and, therefore, feared for his life. He sought asylum in the Temple court. "When . . . the chieftains of the . . . brigands had been put to death, I ventured out of the Temple and once more consorted with the chief priests and the leading Pharisees." [3]

Later, during Josephus' time as commander of Galilee, his enemies in Galilee sent a mission to Jerusalem to seek his removal as commander. The emissaries went to Simeon ben Gamaliel: "This Simeon was a native of Jerusalem, of a very illustrious family, and of the sect of the Pharisees, who have the reputation of being unrivalled experts in their country's laws. A man highly gifted with intelligence and judgment, he could by sheer genius retrieve an unfortunate situation in affairs of state" (*V*, 191–192). Simeon received the embassy and agreed to remove Josephus from office. The administration then sent a deputation "comprising persons of different classes of society but of equal standing in education. Two of them . . . were from the lower ranks and adherents of the Pharisees; the third, . . . also a Pharisee, came from a priestly family; the youngest . . . was descended from high priests":

> Their instructions were to approach the Galilaeans and ascertain the reason for their devotion to me. If they attributed it to my being a native of Jerusalem, they were to reply that so were all four of them; if to my expert knowledge of their laws, they should retort that neither were they ignorant of the customs of their fathers; if again they asserted that their affection was due to my priestly office, they should answer that two of them were likewise priests. (*V*, 198)

The Pharisees invariably are represented as experts in the law. Of greater importance, some Pharisees come before us as important politicians, in charge of the conduct of the war, able to make or break commanders in the field. In Jerusalem they enjoy the highest offices. Their leaders are men of political experience and great power. So much for the Pharisees of Josephus' *Life*.

The Pharisees of *War*

Josephus' first work, *The Jewish War*, presents an entirely consistent picture: the Pharisees were active in the court affairs of the Maccabean state. They constituted a political party, which sought, and for a time evidently won, domination of the political institutions of the Maccabean kingdom. In other words, however they might hope to teach people to conform to the Torah, they were prepared to coerce them to conform through the instruments of government. As E. J. Bickerman says, "Early Pharisaism was a belligerent movement that knew how to hate." [4]

When Alexander Jannaeus died, his wife, Alexandra Salome, succeeded him. This is the point at which Josephus' Pharisees first enter the picture. Alexandra Salome put the government in their hands. They thereupon executed Jannaeus' counselors, who had been their enemies, and exercised power with a high hand. The anti-Pharisaic opposition was now led by the queen's second son, Aristobulus. When the queen died in 67 B.C., Aristobulus won the throne. His brother, Hyrcanus, allied to Antipater the Idumaean, father of Herod, besieged Aristobulus in the Temple of Jerusalem. The Roman general in the Near East, Pompey, intervened and supported Aristobulus. But he found reason to change his mind and preferred Hyrcanus. The Romans then took Jerusalem, in the fall of 63 B.C., and the independent government of the Maccabean dynasty came to an end. A few years later, Herod was entrusted with the rule of Judea.

The Pharisees occur in three important passages of *War*. First, the Pharisees—not introduced, or extensively described, but standing without a history—suddenly make an appearance as the dominant power in the reign of Alexandra Salome. They later are alluded to in connection with the court affairs of Herod. And finally, in Josephus' long account of Jewish sectarianism, the Pharisees receive requisite attention.

The Pharisees and Alexandra Salome

Josephus describes the relationship between the Pharisees and Alexandra Salome thus:

> Alexander bequeathed the kingdom to his wife Alexandra, being convinced that the Jews would bow to her authority as they would to no other, because by her utter lack of brutality and her opposition to his crimes she had won the affections of the populace. Nor was he mistaken in these expectations; for this frail woman firmly held the reins of government, thanks to her reputation for piety. She was, indeed, the very strictest observer of the national traditions and would deprive of office any offenders against the sacred laws. Of the two sons whom she had by Alexander, she appointed the elder, Hyrcanus, high

priest, out of consideration alike for his age and his disposition, which was too lethargic to be troubled about public affairs; the younger, Aristobulus, as a hothead, she confined to a private life.

Besides Alexandra, and growing as she grew, arose the Pharisees, a body of Jews with the reputation of excelling the rest of the their nation in the observances of religion, and as exact exponents of the laws. To them, being herself intensely religious, she listened with too great deference; while they, gradually taking advantage of an ingenuous woman, became at length the real administrators of the state, at liberty to banish and to recall, to loose and to bind, whom they would. In short, the enjoyments of royal authority were theirs; its expenses and burdens fell to Alexandra. She proved, however, to be a wonderful administrator in larger affairs, and, by continued recruiting, doubled her army, besides collecting a considerable body of foreign troops; so that she not only strengthened her own nation, but became a formidable foe to foreign potentates. But if she ruled the nation, the Pharisees ruled her.

Thus, they put to death Diogenes, a distinguished man who had been a friend of Alexander, accusing him of having advised the king to crucify his eight hundred victims. They further urged Alexandra to make away with the others who had instigated Alexander to punish those men; and as she from superstitious motives always gave way, they proceeded to kill whomsoever they would. The most eminent of the citizens thus imperilled sought refuge with Aristobulus, who persuaded his mother to spare their lives in consideration of their rank, but, if she was not satisfied of their innocence, to expel them from the city. Their security being thus guaranteed, they dispersed about the country. (*BJ* I, 107–114)

The Pharisees are repeatedly represented by Josephus as "excelling" in religion and in teaching the laws. But the substance of their religion and of the laws they taught is not described. The party has no history; Josephus does not take for granted that we know who they are, for he tells us they are "a body of Jews with the reputation of excelling the rest." But their beliefs, doctrines, religious and social goals—these are ignored. They come to the fore as a "body of Jews" (*suntagma ti Ioudaiōn*). They play upon the queen's religiosity, take advantage of her credulity, and gradually assume real power. They, moreover, exercise that power to their own advantage. They murder their enemies—which tells us they have a sorry past to avenge in Maccabean politics. The allusion to their enemies prompts one to recall that under Alexander Jannaeus a rebellion took place, which led to the crucifixion of eight hundred of the king's enemies. In addition, "Eight thousand of the hostile faction fled beyond the borders of Judea" (*BJ* I, 97). But Josephus does not name the "hostile faction." Only now do we find reason to suppose the armed rebels of Alexander Jannaeus' time were, in fact, Pharisees. Thus, under Alexandra Salome, the Pharisees killed anyone they wanted, and eminent citizens took refuge with Aristobulus, the heir apparent.

In Herod's Court

Josephus discloses about the Pharisees that "the king was furiously indignant, particularly at the wife of Pheroras, the principal object of Salome's charges. He, accordingly, assembled a council of his friends and relations and accused the wretched woman of numerous misdeeds, among others of insulting his own daughters, of subsidizing the Pharisees to oppose him, and of alienating his brother, after bewitching him with drugs" (*BJ* I, 571). What is interesting in this reference is the view that the Pharisees, like any other political party, might be "subsidized" to support one party and oppose another.

A Philosophical School

Josephus summarizes the doctrines and the behavior of the Pharisees and the Sadducees thus:

> Of the first-named schools, the Pharisees, who are considered the most accurate interpreters of the laws, and hold the position of the leading sect, attribute everything to Fate and to God; they hold that to act rightly or otherwise rests, indeed, for the most part with men, but that in each action Fate cooperates. Every soul, they maintain, is imperishable, but the soul of the good alone passes into another body, while the souls of the wicked suffer eternal punishment.
>
> The Sadducees, the second of the orders, do away with Fate altogether, and remove God beyond, not merely the commission, but the very sight, of evil. They maintain that man has the free choice of good or evil, and that it rests with each man's will whether he follows the one or the other. As for the persistence of the soul after death, penalties in the underworld, and rewards, they will have none of them.
>
> The Pharisees are affectionate to each other and cultivate harmonious relations with the community. The Sadducees, on the contrary, are, even among themselves, rather boorish in their behavior, and in their intercourse with their peers are as rude as to aliens. Such is what I have to say on the Jewish philosophical schools. (*BJ* II, 162–166)

The foregoing account represents Josephus' Pharisees as of A.D. 75. We find no claim that the Pharisees are the most popular sect and have a massive public following, or that no one can effectively govern Palestine without their support. All we hear is their opinion on two issues, Fate and the punishment of the soul after death. The Sadducees are matched opposites: they do not believe in Fate or in life after death. The Essenes, who are described at far greater length (*BJ* II, 119–161), believe that the soul is immortal and that reward and punishment follow after death, and they can foretell the future. Josephus (*BJ* II, 158) adds, "Such are the theological views of the Essenes concerning the soul, whereby they irresistibly attract all who have once tasted their philosophy." Later on, as we have already seen, he would claim he himself had been able to resist their philosophy and so had joined the Pharisees.

The whole passage about the Jewish sects is introduced after an account of Judea as a Roman province under the procurator Coponius in A.D. 6–9. It is an entirely separate unit. Afterward, the sects are ignored; Josephus then turns to another subject entirely. The section is complete as it stands and could have been placed just as well in any other part of the narrative. It neither illuminates, nor is illuminated by, its setting.

Here the Sadducees and Pharisees address themselves to identical issues and take the two possible, extreme positions. In context, the two parties are not very important. Neither one receives a significant description. The Pharisees occur not as a political party, but as a philosophical school. The phrase about their being "the most accurate interpreters of the laws" and "the leading sect" are all that link the Pharisees of the sectarian passage to the Pharisees of the history of Queen Alexandra Salome.

The Pharisees of *Antiquities*

Twenty years later, Josephus greatly expanded his picture, adding both important details to familiar accounts and entirely new material as well. To understand the additions, we must recall that at the same time he wrote *Antiquities,* Josephus was claiming he himself was a Pharisee.

In Palestine in the twenty years from A.D. 70 to 90, the Pharisees, who had survived the destruction of Jerusalem in 70, had established themselves as the dominant group. Led by Yohanan ben Zakkai, they had created a Jewish administration at the coastal town of Yavneh. This administration had assumed those powers of self-government left in Jewish hands by the Roman regime. By A.D. 90, the head of the Yavnean government, Gamaliel II, grandson of the Gamaliel mentioned as the Pharisee in the Temple council in Acts 5:34 and son of Simeon ben Gamaliel, who was alluded to in Josephus' *Life* as a leader of the Jerusalem government in A.D. 66, had negotiated with the Roman government for recognition as head of the Palestinian Jewry. The basis for settlement was the Yavneans' agreement to oppose subversion of Roman rule in exchange for Roman support of the Yavneans' control over the Jews— that is, the same agreement offered to Pompey in 63 B.C. The Yavnean authorities, called rabbis—whence "rabbinic Judaism"—thus continued the Pharisaic political and foreign policies initiated at the end of Maccabean times. Now, however, the Pharisees met with no competition. The Herodian dynasty had long since passed from the scene. The Essenes were wiped out in the war. The Sadducees, who had controlled the country through their power in the Temple government, had lost their power base with the destruction of the Temple and evidently ceased to constitute an important political force.[5]

Without knowledge of the *Life* and reading only the *War,* one might have supposed that Josephus took a most keen interest in the Essenes and certainly sympathized with their ascetic way of life. That surmise would have received further support had we known that he spent three years of his adolescence with Bannus, whose way of living corresponded in important ways to that of the Essenes, though Josephus does not call Bannus an Essene. So one might have expected that the great historian would regard the Essenes as the leading Jewish "philosophical school." But he does not. The Essenes of *War* are cut down to size; the Pharisees of *Antiquities* predominate. And what Josephus now says about them is that the country cannot be governed without their cooperation, and he himself is one of them. Josephus, in fact, was part of the pro-Roman priestly aristocracy before the war of A.D. 66–73. Nothing in his account suggests he was a Pharisee, as he later claimed in his autobiography.

A Philosophical School

Antiquities has two "philosophical school" passages. The first is brief. It comes in the middle of Josephus' account of Jonathan Maccabee's agreement with Rome of about 140 B.C. and interrupts the narrative. The second coincides, as in *War,* with the beginning of procuratorial government, at the beginning of the first century A.D. Josephus here alludes to a rebellion led by Judas, a Gaulanite, and Saddok, a Pharisee, who together started a "fourth school of philosophy," in addition to the three already known, namely, of people who sought the destruction of Roman rule. The passage thus corresponds in position and function to *War* II, 162–166, discussed above.

The first account is as follows:

> Now at this time there were three schools of thought among the Jews, which held different opinions concerning human affairs; the first being that of the Pharisees, the second that of the Sadducees, and the third that of the Essenes. As for the Pharisees, they say that certain events are the work of Fate, but not all; as to other events, it depends upon ourselves whether they shall take place or not. The sect of Essenes, however, declares that Fate is mistress of all things, and that nothing befalls men unless it be in accordance with her decree. But the Sadducees do away with Fate, holding that there is no such thing and that human actions are not achieved in accordance with her decree, but that all things lie within our own power, so that we ourselves are responsible for our well-being. . . . Of these matters, however, I have given a more detailed account in the second book of the *Jewish History*. (A XIII, 171–173)

Fate, or providence, thus, is the primary issue. The three "schools" take all possible positions: fate governs all, fate governs nothing, fate governs some things but not everything. The Pharisees enjoy the golden middle. In the *War* the Pharisees are given the same position, but there the issue of the immortality of the soul is also introduced. The second philosophical account is as follows:

The Jews, from the most ancient times, had three philosophies pertaining to their traditions, that of the Essenes, that of the Sadducees, and, thirdly, that of the group called the Pharisees. To be sure, I have spoken about them in the second book of the *Jewish War,* but nevertheless I shall here too dwell on them for a moment.

The Pharisees simplify their standard of living, making no concession to luxury. They follow the guidance of that which their doctrine has selected and transmitted as good, attaching the chief importance to the observance of those commandments which it has seen fit to dictate to them. They show respect and deference to their elders, nor do they rashly presume to contradict their proposals. Though they postulate that everything is brought about by fate, they still do not deprive the human will of the pursuit of what is in man's power, since it was God's good pleasure that there should be a fusion and that the will of man with his virtue and vice should be admitted to the council-chamber of fate. They believe that souls have power to survive death and that there are rewards and punishments under the earth for those who have led lives of virtue or vice: eternal imprisonment is the lot of evil souls, while the good souls receive an easy passage to a new life. Because of these views they are, as a matter of fact, extremely influential among the townsfolk; and all prayers and sacred rites of divine worship are performed according to their exposition. This is the great tribute that the inhabitants of the cities, by practising the highest ideals both in their way of living and in their discourse, have paid to the excellence of the Pharisees.

The Sadducees hold that the soul perishes along with the body. They own no observance of any sort apart from the laws; in fact, they reckon it a virtue to dispute with the teachers of the path of wisdom that they pursue. There are but few men to whom this doctrine has been made known, but these are men of the highest standing. They accomplish practically nothing, however. For whenever they assume some office, though they submit unwillingly and perforce, yet submit they do to the formulas of the Pharisees, since otherwise the masses would not tolerate them (*A* XVIII, 11–17)

This considerable account adds to the Pharisees' virtues their simple style of living—the asceticism Josephus later admires in *Life*—and their deference to the elders. Earlier, Josephus had said the Sadducees were boorish. The issues of providence and life after death, last judgment, and reward and punishment for deeds done in this life are alluded to.

What is entirely new is the allegation that the townspeople follow only the Pharisees. The Temple and synagogues are conducted according to their law. Of this we have formerly heard nothing. With the Temple in ruins for a quarter of a century and the old priesthood decimated and scattered, it now is possible to place the Pharisees in a position of power of which, in Temple times, they had scarcely dreamed. The Sadducees, moreover, are forced to do whatever the Pharisees tell them, for otherwise the people would ignore them—an even more extreme allegation. Later on, it is alleged that the followers of Shammai, the rival in Pharisaic politics to the predominant leader, Hillel, know that the law really follows Hillel, and therefore in all their decisions, they rule in accord with Hillelite doctrine. The allegation of Josephus is of the same order, and equally incredible.

The Pharisees and John Hyrcanus

While in *War,* Josephus makes no reference to relationships between the Pharisees and the Maccabean monarchs before Alexandra Salome, in *Antiquities* he introduces a story, unrelated to the narrative in which it occurs, about a break between John Hyrcanus and the Pharisees. This same story, now told about Alexander Jannaeus (Yannai), furthermore occurs in the Babylonian Talmud, first attested by a reference to the narrative of a fourth-century Babylonian master, Abbaye (died approximately A.D. 340). Josephus' story is as follows:

> As for Hyrcanus, the envy of the Jews was aroused against him by his own successes and those of his sons; particularly hostile to him were the Pharisees, who are one of the Jewish schools, as we have related above. And so great is their influence with the masses that even when they speak against a king or high priest, they immediately gain credence. Hyrcanus too was a disciple of theirs, and was greatly loved by them. And once he invited them to a feast and entertained them hospitably, and when he saw that they were having a very good time, he began by saying that they knew he wished to be righteous and in everything he did tried to please God and them—for the Pharisees profess such beliefs; at the same time he begged them, if they observed him doing anything wrong or straying from the right path, to lead him back to it and correct him. But they testified to his being altogether virtuous, and he was delighted with their praise. However, one of the guests, named Eleazar, who had an evil nature and took pleasure in dissension, said, "Since you have asked to be told the truth, if you wish to be righteous, give up the high priesthood and be content with governing the people." And when Hyrcanus asked him for what reason he should give up the high priesthood, he replied, "Because we have heard from our elders that your mother was a captive in the reign of Antiochus Epiphanes." But the story was false, and Hyrcanus was furious with the man, while all the Pharisees were very indignant.
>
> Then a certain Jonathan, one of Hyrcanus' close friends, belonging to the school of Sadducees, who hold opinions opposed to those of the Pharisees, said that it had been with general approval of all the Pharisees that Eleazar had made his slanderous statement; and this, he added, would be clear to Hyrcanus if he inquired of them what punishment Eleazar deserved for what he had said. And so Hyrcanus asked the Pharisees what penalty they thought he deserved—for, he said, he would be convinced that the slanderous statement had not been made with their approval if they fixed a penalty commensurate with the crime—and they replied that Eleazar deserved stripes and chains; for they did not think it right to sentence a man to death for calumny, and anyway the Pharisees are naturally lenient in the matter of punishments. At this Hyrcanus became very angry and began to believe that the fellow had slandered him with their approval. And Jonathan in particular inflamed his anger, and so worked upon him that he brought him to join the Sadducaean party and desert the Pharisees, and to abro-

gate the regulations which they had established for the people, and punish those who observed them. Out of this, of course, grew the hatred of the masses for him and his sons, but of this we shall speak hereafter. For the present I wish merely to explain that the Pharisees had passed on to the people certain regulations handed down by former generations and not recorded in the Laws of Moses, for which reason they are rejected by the Sadducaean group, who hold that only those regulations should be considered valid which were written down [in Scripture], and that those which had been handed down by former generations need not be observed. And concerning these matters the two parties came to have controversies and serious differences, the Sadducees having the confidence of the wealthy alone but no following among the populace, while the Pharisees have the support of the masses. But of these two schools and of the Essenes a detailed account has been given in the second book of my *Judaica*.

And so Hyrcanus quieted the outbreak, and lived happily thereafter; and when he died after administering the government excellently for thirty-one years, he left five sons. (*A* XIII, 288–299)

The story in the Babylonian Talmud reads thus:

Abbaye said, "How do I know it [that the husband must divorce the wife if he remains silent in a case in which the wife is charged with committing adultery by one witness only]?"

As it is taught, the story is told (M'SH H):

Yannai the King went to Koḥalit in the wilderness and conquered there sixty towns. When he returned, he rejoiced greatly, and invited (QR') all the sages of Israel.

He said to them, "Our forefathers would eat salt fish when they were engaged in the building of the Holy House. Let us also eat salt fish as a memorial to our forefathers."

So they brought up salt fish on golden tables, and they ate.

There was there a certain scoffer, evil-hearted and empty-headed, and Eleazar b. Po'irah was his name.

Eleazar b. Po'irah said to Yannai the king, "O king Yannai, the hearts of the Pharisees are [set] against you."

"What shall I do?"

"Test (HQM) them by the plate (ṢYṢ) that is between your eyes."

He tested them by the plate that was between his eyes.

There was there a certain sage, and Judah b. Gedidiah was his name. Judah b. Gedidiah said to Yannai the King, "O King Yannai, let suffice for you the crown of sovereignty [kingship]. Leave the crown of the [high] priesthood for the seed of Aaron."

For people said that his [Yannai's] mother had been taken captive in Modi'im. The charge was investigated and not found [sustained]. The sages of Israel departed in anger.

Eleazar b. Po'irah then said to Yannai the king, "O King Yannai, That is the law [not here specified as the punishment to be inflicted on Judah] even for the ordinary folk in Israel. But you are king and high priest—should that be your law too?"

"What should I do?"

"If you take my advice, you will trample them down."

"But what will become of the Torah?"

"Lo, it is rolled up and lying in the corner. Whoever wants to learn, let him come and learn."

(R. Nahman b. Isaac [ca. A.D. 375] said, *"Forthwith heresy [Epicurean-ism ('PYQWRSWT)] was instilled in him [Yannai], for he should have said, 'That is well and good for the Written Torah, but what will become of the Oral Torah?'"*)

Immediately the evil blossomed through Eleazar b. Po'irah. All the sages of Israel were killed.

The world was desolate until Simeon b. Shetah came and restored the Torah to its former place. (b. Qid. 66a)

The italicized words are in Aramaic, the rest in Hebrew. It is as if a well-known event is referred to at the end: Simeon ben Shetah made peace between the Pharisees and Yannai (or he overcame Yannai). But we do not know what actually is attributable to Simeon, for what he said or did is left unexplained.

A persistent tradition on a falling out between the Pharisees and Alexander Jannaeus evidently circulated in later times. One form of the tradition placed the origin of the whole difficulty at the feet of Simeon ben Shetah himself, holding that the king believed he had been cheated by Simeon (Y. Berakhot 7:2); therefore, Simeon fled for a time, but later returned. A second, and different, set of traditions, of which the above is one exemplum, held that difficulties between Yannai and the Pharisees ("rabbis") as a group led to the flight of many of them to Alexandra. Simeon managed to patch things up—we do not know how—and, therefore, summoned the refugees to return. But the two traditions cannot be reconciled or translated into historical language, nor can we profitably speculate on what kernel of historical truth underlay either or both of them. All we do know is that Simeon ben Shetah was believed to have played a role in either the difficulty, or the reconciliation, or both.

The talmudic story is written in biblical, not mishnaic or rabbinic, Hebrew. In this respect one recalls the anachronistic, pseudo-archaic language of the Dead Sea Scrolls. It makes use of the conversive *waw,* which no longer occurs later on, the only such usage in all of talmudic literature. Solomon Zeitlin holds that the talmudic story is older than the version of Josephus: it could have been written "only at a time when the kings were not high priests, which was from the time of Herod onwards."[6] At any rate, there is an important lacuna in the talmudic version, for "that is the punishment" takes for granted the details available only in Josephus' account. It would seem to me that the talmudic narrator could not have had access to the Aramaic first edition of Josephus' *War,* since the story does not occur at all in *War.* So the relationship between the two versions is not clear. Either Josephus copied from a Hebrew source, or the talmudic narrator copied from Josephus, or both have relied on a third authority. At any rate, the story interrupts Josephus' narrative and contradicts it, for, after the disgrace, Hyrcanus lived happily ever afterward. One should have expected some more appropriate heavenly recompense.

Again we observe in *Antiquities* the stress put upon the Pharisees' enjoying mass support, while only the rich listen to the Sadducees. The difference between the two parties is, as was common in Hellenistic politics, between the wealthy few and the (virtuous) many. Whoever hopes to govern Palestine had best rely upon the leaders of the latter.

The Pharisees and Alexandra Salome

The new version of the Pharisees-in-power story in *Antiquities* is strikingly revised in favor of the Pharisees:

> And when the queen saw that he was on the point of death and no longer held to any hope of recovery, she wept and beat her breast, lamenting the bereavement that was about to befall her and her children, and said to him, "To whom are you thus leaving me and your children, who are in need of help from others, especially when you know how hostile the nation feels toward you!" Thereupon he advised her to follow his suggestions for keeping the throne secure for herself and her children and to conceal his death from the soldiers until she had captured the fortress. And then, he said, on her return to Jerusalem as from a splendid victory, she should yield a certain amount of power to the Pharisees, for if they praised her in return for this sign of regard, they would dispose the nation favorably toward her. These men, he assured her, had so much influence with their fellow Jews that they could injure those whom they hated and help those to whom they were friendly; for they had the complete confidence of the masses when they spoke harshly of any person, even when they did so out of envy; and he himself, he added, had come into conflict with the nation because these men had been badly treated by him. "And so," he said, "when you come to Jerusalem, send for their partisans, and showing them my dead body, permit them, with every sign of sincerity, to treat me as they please, whether they wish to dishonor my corpse by leaving it unburied because of the many injuries they have suffered at my hands, or in their anger wish to offer my dead body any other form of indignity. Promise them also that you will not take any action, while you are on the throne, without their consent. If you speak to them in this manner, I shall receive from them a more splendid burial than I should from you; for once they have the power to do so, they will not choose to treat my corpse badly, and at the same time you will reign securely." With this exhortation to his wife he died, after reigning twenty-seven years, at the age of forty-nine.
>
> Thereupon Alexandra, after capturing the fortress, conferred with the Pharisees as her husband had suggested, and by placing in their hands all that concerned his corpse and the royal power, stilled their anger against Alexander, and made them her well-wishers and friends. And they in turn went to the people and made public speeches in which they recounted the deeds of Alexander, and said that in him they had lost a just king, and by their eulogies they so greatly moved the people to mourn and lament that they gave him a more splen-

did burial than had been given any of the kings before him. Now although Alexander had left two sons, Hyrcanus and Aristobulus, he had bequeathed the royal power to Alexandra. Of these sons the one, Hyrcanus, was incompetent to govern and in addition much preferred a quiet life, while the younger, Aristobulus, was a man of action and high spirit. As for the queen herself, she was loved by the masses because she was thought to disapprove of the crimes committed by her husband.

Alexandra then appointed Hyrcanus as high priest because of his greater age but more especially because of his lack of energy; and she permitted the Pharisees to do as they liked in all matters, and also commanded the people to obey them; and whatever regulations, introduced by the Pharisees in accordance with the tradition of their fathers, had been abolished by her father-in-law Hyrcanus, these she again restored. And so, while she had the title of sovereign, the Pharisees had the power. For example, they recalled exiles, and freed prisoners, and, in a word, in no way differed from absolute rulers. Nevertheless the queen took thought for the welfare of the kingdom and recruited a large force of mercenaries and also made her own force twice as large, with the result that she struck terror into the local rulers round her and received hostages from them. And throughout the entire country there was quiet except for the Pharisees; for they worked upon the feelings of the queen and tried to persuade her to kill those who had urged Alexander to put the eight hundred to death. Later they themselves cut down one of them, named Diogenes, and his death was followed by that of one after the other, until the leading citizens came to the palace, Aristobulus among them—for he was obviously resentful of what was taking place, and let it be plainly seen that if only he should get the opportunity, he would not leave his mother any power at all—, and they reminded her of all that they had achieved in the face of danger, whereby they had shown their unwavering loyalty to their master and had therefore been judged worthy by him of the greatest honors. And they begged her not to crush their hopes completely, for, they said, after escaping the dangers of war, they were now being slaughtered at home like cattle by their foes, and there was no one to avenge them. They also said that if their adversaries were to be contented with those already slain, they would bear with equanimity what had taken place, out of genuine devotion to their masters; but if, on the other hand, these men were to continue in the same course, let them, they begged, at least be given their freedom; for they would never bring themselves to seek any means of safety but what should come from her, and would welcome death in her palace so long as they might not have disloyalty on their conscience. It would be disgraceful both for them and for her who ruled as queen, they added, if, being abandoned by her, they should be given shelter by the enemies of her husband; for Aretas the Arab and the other princes would consider it of the utmost value to enlist such men as mercenaries, whose very name, they might say, had caused these princes to shudder before they had heard it (spoken aloud). But if this could not be, and she had determined to favor the Pharisees above all others, let her, as the next best thing, station each of them in one of the garrisons, for, if some evil genius were thus wroth with the house of Alexander, they at least would show themselves (loyal) even though living in humble circumstances.

Speaking in this vein at great length, they called upon the shades of Alexander to take pity on those who had been killed and those who were in danger, whereupon all the bystanders burst into tears. And Aristobulus in particular made plain his sentiments by denouncing his mother bitterly. But still they themselves were to blame for their misfortunes, in allowing a woman to reign who madly desired it in her unreasonable love of power, and when her sons were in the prime of life. And so the queen, not knowing what to do consistent with her dignity, entrusted to them the guarding of the fortresses with the exception of Hyrcania, Alexandreion and Machaerus, where her most valuable possessions were. (A XIII, 399–417)

We recall that in *War,* Alexandra listened to the Pharisees "with too great deference," and they took advantage of her. The picture is unfavorable. They ran the government, but she paid. They wreaked terrible vengeance on their enemies, so many had to flee. Now we have Alexander Jannaeus, archenemy of the Pharisees, telling the queen to put the Pharisees in power! Everyone follows them. Therefore, if she can win their support, she can govern the country effectively. Josephus waxes lugubrious on this very point. No longer do the Pharisees take advantage of the woman's ingenuousness. Now they are essential for her exercise of power. Even Alexander Jannaeus himself would have had a better time of it had he won their support. He tells her, in essence, to "let them dishonor my corpse if necessary!" And above all, "Do anything they tell you." In place of a credulous queen we have a supine one. In place of conniving Pharisees we have powerful leaders of the whole nation. The Pharisees are won over, and they win over the masses—even eulogizing Jannaeus. What do the Pharisees do with their power? They teach the people to live in accordance with "the tradition of their fathers." John Hyrcanus' and Alexander Jannaeus' work is undone. Exiles are called back. Prisoners are set free. To be sure, the queen organized a professional army. Josephus adds that the Pharisees sought to avenge themselves upon their enemies. They killed one of them, and then more, and so the account of Aristobulus' protection of the Pharisees' enemies is included. Somehow, the Pharisees fell away from the account. The mass slaughter of *War,* in which the Pharisees killed anyone they wanted, is shaded into a mild persecution of the Pharisees' opposition.

In Herod's Court

The Pharisees now have a different, and more important, place in the account of Herod's reign. They have foresight. They seek to oppose Herod. No one now takes for granted that the Pharisees can be bribed. Their foresight, not their love of money, warned them that Herod's family was destined for a bad end (which everyone knew by A.D. 95). The Pharisees are accused of corrupting people at court, not of being corrupted. Some of them are put to death on that account:

> There was also a group of Jews priding itself on its adherence to ancestral custom and claiming to observe the laws of which the Deity approves, and by these men, called Pharisees, the women [of the court] were ruled. These men were

able to help the king greatly because of their foresight, and yet they were obviously intent upon combating and injuring him. At least when the whole Jewish people affirmed by an oath that it would be loyal to Caesar and to the king's government, these men, over six thousand in number, refused to take this oath, and when the king punished them with a fine, Pheroras' wife paid the fine for them. In return for her friendliness they foretold—for they were believed to have foreknowledge of things through God's appearance to them—that by God's decree Herod's throne would be taken from him, both from himself and his descendants, and the royal power would fall to her and Pheroras and to any children that they might have. These things, which did not remain unknown to Salome, were reported to the king, as was the news that the Pharisees had corrupted some of the people at court. And the king put to death those of the Pharisees who were most to blame and the eunuch Bagoas and a certain Karos, who was outstanding among his contemporaries for his surpassing beauty and was loved by the king. He also killed all those of his household who approved of what the Pharisee said. Now Bagoas had been carried away by their assurance that he would be called the father and benefactor of him who would some day be set over the people with the title of king, for all the power would belong to him and he would give Bagoas the ability to marry and to beget children of his own. (*A* XVII, 41–45)

Conclusion

The materials before us (except for the *Life*) have been given in chronological order. They illustrate the definitive judgment of Morton Smith:

to which group within the Jewish tradition was he [Josephus] loyal? Here a comparison of the *War* with the *Antiquities* is extremely informative. In the *War*, written shortly after the destruction of Jerusalem, Josephus still favors the group of which his family had been representative—the wealthy, pro-Roman section of the Priesthood. He represents them . . . as that group of the community which did all it could to keep the peace with Rome. In this effort he once mentions that they had the assistance of the chief Pharisees, but otherwise the Pharisees hardly figure on the scene. In this account of the reign of Salome-Alexandra he copies an abusive paragraph of Nicholas of Damascus, describing the Pharisees as hypocrites whom the queen's superstition enabled to achieve and abuse political power. In his account of the Jewish sects he gives most space to the Essenes. (Undoubtedly he was catering to the interests of Roman readers, with whom ascetic philosophers in out-of-the-way countries enjoyed a long popularity.) As for the others, he merely tags brief notices of the Pharisees and Sadducees onto the end of his survey. He says nothing of the Pharisees' having any influence with the people, and the only time he represents them as attempting to exert any influence (when they ally with the leading priests and other citizens of Jerusalem to prevent the outbreak of the war), they fail.

In the *Antiquities,* however, written twenty years later, the picture is quite different. Here, whenever Josephus discusses the Jewish sects, the Pharisees take first place, and every time he mentions them he emphasizes their popularity, which is so great, he says, that they can maintain opposition against any government. His treatment of the Salome-Alexandra incident is particularly il-luminating: he makes Alexander Janneus, Salome's husband and the lifelong en-emy of the Pharisees, deliver himself of a deathbed speech in which he blames all the troubles of his reign on the fact that he had opposed them and urges the queen to restore them to power because of their overwhelming influence with the people. She follows his advice, and the Pharisees cooperate to such extent that they actually persuade the people that Alexander was a good king and make them mourn his passing!

It is almost impossible not to see in such a rewriting of history a bid to the Roman government. That goverment must have been faced with the problem [after A.D. 70]: Which group of Jews shall we support? . . . To this question Josephus is volunteering an answer: The Pharisees, he says again and again, have by far the greatest influence with the people. Any government which secures their support is accepted; any government which alienates them has trouble. The Sadducees, it is true, have more following among the aristoc-racy . . . but they have no popular following at all, and even in the old days, when they were in power, they were forced by public opinion to follow the Phar-isees' orders. As for the other major parties, the Essenes are a philosophical curiosity, and the Zealots differ from the Pharisees only by being fanatically anti-Roman. So any Roman government which wants peace in Palestine had better support and secure the support of the Pharisees.

Josephus' discovery of these important political facts (which he ignored when writing the *Jewish War*) may have been due partly to a change in his per-sonal relationship with the Pharisees. Twenty years had now intervened since his trouble with Simeon ben Gamaliel, and Simeon was long dead. But the mere cessation of personal hostilities would hardly account for such pointed passages as Josephus added to the *Antiquities*. The more probable explanation is that in the meanwhile the Pharisees had become the leading candidate for Roman sup-port in Palestine and were already negotiating for it.[7]

It therefore seems that the time has come to stop describing the Pharisees as the "normative" sect of pre-A.D. 70 Palestinian Judaism. The sole source that explicitly claims they predominated turns out to be post-70 propaganda. The rabbinical traditions about the pre-70 Pharisees contain no such claim, though, to be sure, they take for granted that Pharisaic Judaism was identical with the Mosaic revelation of Sinai. The rabbis do allege that the Pharisees ran the Temple. But they tell no stories about how the Pharisees governed Pal-estine, or how the Maccabean or Roman regimes in Palestine had to rely upon Pharisees for help in controlling the populace. They attribute to pre-70 Phari-saic masters no laws about the administration of the country, no sayings about how the government should be organized, no indication that they believed, as did Josephus, that pre-70 times were marked by Pharisaic political ascen-dancy outside of the cult. The picture of the Gospels is of a sect devoted to commensality, whose dietary laws—careful tithing, ritual purity even at home, outside of the Temple precincts—were the main concern.

Smith, in my view, has placed into perspective the distorted view of the pan-Pharisaic, pan-rabbinic scholars who declare the Pharisaic viewpoint to be normative Judaism, and in a fundamentalist, uncritical spirit cite Josephus as proof of that proposition.

What, then, is to be learned about the historical Pharisees from Josephus? We obviously must discount all of his references to the influence and power of the Pharisees, for, as Smith points out, these constitute part of his highly tendentious case in behalf of the Yavnean rabbis, the post-70 Pharisees' heirs, and not data about the pre-70 ones.

The picture of the *War* contains two important elements. First, the Pharisees were a political party, deeply involved in the politics of the Hasmonaean dynasty. They were opponents of Alexander Jannaeus, but we do not know why, and they supported Alexandra Salome, who put them into power, but we do not know for what purpose.

In the first century A.D., individual Pharisees remained active in political life. Simeon ben Gamaliel and other Pharisees certainly took a leading role in the conduct of the war. But, strikingly, Josephus makes no reference to the sect as a party within the revolutionary councils, and one may fairly conclude that Simeon and others were members of the group, but not the group's representatives, no more than Judah the Pharisee represented the group in founding the Fourth Philosophy. The group itself probably was not an organized political force. Evidently, the end of the Pharisaic party comes with Aristobulus, who slaughtered many of them, and was sealed by Herod, who killed even more. From that point forward, so far as Josephus is concerned, the Pharisees no longer play a role in the politics and government of Jewish Palestine.

Second, the Pharisees also constituted a "philosophical school." Smith's observation[8] that Jews thought of groups in their society distinguished by peculiar theories and practices as different schools of the national philosophy, helps us understand the foundations of Pharisaic policy. As a political party, the Pharisees stood for a particular perspective within the national philosophy. They presumably claimed they ought to rule because they possessed the true and wise doctrine. The specific doctrines alluded to by Josephus, however, seem to me unrelated to the political aspirations of the group. Why people who believed in fate and in the immortality of the soul should rule, or would rule, differently from those who did not, and how such beliefs might shape the policies of the state are not obvious. But evidently what characterized the group—these *particular* beliefs—and what rendered their political aspirations something more than a grab for power presumably are inextricably related.

Josephus thus presents us with a party of philosophical politicians. They claim to have ancient traditions, but these are not described as having been orally transmitted, nor are they attributed to Moses at Sinai or claimed to be part of the Torah. They are excellent lawyers. They are distinguished from other groups by a few, relatively trivial philosophical differences. As a political party they function effectively for roughly the first fifty years of the first century B.C. While individuals thereafter are described as Pharisees, as a sect the group seems to end its political life with the advent of Herod and of Hillel.[9]

Notes

1. In my *Rabbinic Traditions about the Pharisees before 70* (Leiden, 1971; three volumes), I have analyzed the largest corpus of traditions on pre-70 Pharisaism. The New Testament traditions are thoroughly discussed, most recently, in Wolfgang Beilner, *Christus und die Pharisäer* (Vienna, 1959).

2. H. St. J. Thackeray, *Josephus, I: The Life, Against Apion* (Cambridge, Mass., 1926), pp. vii–xii. All references to Josephus' works are from the Loeb edition.

3. *V*, 21.

4. Elias Bickerman, *The Maccabees: An Account of Their History from the Beginnings to the Fall of the House of the Hasmoneans* (New York, 1947), p. 103.

5. See my *Life of Rabban Yohanan ben Zakkai* (Leiden, 1970²).

6. Solomon Zeitlin, *The Rise and Fall of the Judaean State*, I (Philadelphia, 1962), pp. 168–170.

7. Morton Smith, "Palestinian Judaism in the First Century," in Moshe Davis, ed., *Israel: Its Role in Civilization* (New York, 1956), pp. 75–76.

8. Smith, "Palestinian Judaism," pp. 79–81.

9. See my *From Politics to Piety: The Emergence of Pharisaic Judaism* (Englewood Cliffs, 1973).

13 The Conversion of the Royal House of Abiabene in Josephus and Rabbinic Sources

LAWRENCE H. SCHIFFMAN

a mong the material in the writings of Josephus which still requires a comprehensive study is that relating to Jewish law. Study of the Jewish legal traditions in Josephus must be based on an understanding of the close connection between the legal and historical material. Up until now, almost everyone who has dealt with Josephus as a historiographer has ignored questions of Jewish law; and those who sought to investigate his legal traditions have not paid attention to the main purpose of his works: the narration of the history of the Jews in antiquity. We shall attempt here to demonstrate the importance of legal matters for an understanding of Josephus' historical sources. At the same time it will be shown that it is necessary to clarify the provenance of these sources used by Josephus before employing them to reconstruct the history of Jewish law.

These principles may be illustrated by the story of the conversion of the House of Adiabene.[1] This narrative poses many questions concerning its own structure and has implications for the understanding of Jewish legal procedure during the period in which it is set. (1) From what source or sources did Josephus draw his knowledge regarding the House of Adiabene, particularly their conversion, and what is the perspective of that source? (2) What are the structural and literary characteristics of the narrative? (3) Is there a relationship between this source and the traditions preserved in rabbinic literature regarding this family? (4) How reliable is Josephus' source regarding this episode? (5) What conclusions can be drawn from this account regarding the history of proselytism at the end of the Second Temple period?

Josephus' Source

The passage before us is *A* XX, 17–96. The beginning of the passage (κατὰ τοῦτον δὲ τὸν καιρόν, "at this time") contains a typical device used by Josephus to move from one source to a second that supplies additional material. The second source in this instance refers us three times (XX, 48, 53, 96) to subjects not otherwise contained in the writings of Josephus as we have them, raising great doubts regarding the originality of the passage.[2] Despite the attempts of scholars to explain such inconsistencies, here and elsewhere in Josephus,[3] it is clear that this passage was copied by Josephus from another source together with cross-references appropriate only to that source. Josephus did little, if anything, to modify this passage to accord with his context, as can be seen from the fact that he did not even bother to delete the irrelevant cross-references.

Our episode about the House of Abiabene appears in the narrative after the Emperor Claudius decides in favor of the Jews against the procurator Fadus, permitting them to keep in their custody the vestments of the high priests and granting authority over the Temple to Herod of Chalcis (*A* XX, 6–16). Immediately after the account of the House of Adiabene, Josephus returns to the affairs of Fadus and recounts the story of Theudas (*A* XX, 97). Josephus, using his own chronological determination (a matter with which we shall not deal in this study[4]), decided that the conversion of Helena and Izates occurred during the procuratorship of Fadus (A.D. 44–45/46). The insertion of this episode in its entirety into the account of the procuratorship of Fadus shows that this passage was taken from another source and set within the framework of Josephus' narrative.

A. Schalit attempted to determine the source of Josephus' account of the House of Abiabene.[5] In his view, the account reached the hands of Josephus as part of a corpus that was originally composed in Aramaic and that had already been translated into Greek. Schalit maintained that our account originated as an official history of the dynasty composed by the court chronicler of Adiabene. This corpus also included the story of Asinaeus and Anilaeus (*A* XVIII, 310–370), which is both chronologically and geographically close to that of the House of Adiabene.[6]

Schalit explained the connection between the conversion and the political history of Abiabene in this narrative. The House of Adiabene desired to circulate this chronicle in order to prove that they were blessed from heaven as a result of their conversion, thereby appeasing their subjects who resented their having abandoned the local cult. According to Schalit, the author of the source included the details of Adiabene's political history in order to emphasize the untenable position of the kingdom, standing between Rome and Parthia, a situation in which the House of Adiabene survived only because of the divine favor bestowed upon it. The corpus reached Rome (or was sent there by Agrippa II), where Josephus encountered it and drew our episode from it.[7]

In addition, this composition underscored the righteousness of the House of Adiabene and their legitimacy as proselytes and, afterwards, as observant Jews. Despite the claims of certain scholars, the population of Adiabene did not convert.[8] Therefore, it appears that the target of this propaganda was the Jews—either the Jews of Nisibis (over whom Izates eventually came to rule) or the Jews of Palestine. The halakhic details of the account, with its emphasis on the circumcision of Izates, are provided as if the royal family wished to circulate among the Jews its certificate of conversion. To this second motive we shall return below.

Literary Analysis

We must now ask if the court historian who composed the account drew on other sources or if he composed it himself out of whole cloth. To answer this question we must undertake a literary analysis of the passage. It is possible to distinguish eight sections in the account.

1. The birth of Izates, his relationship to his brothers, and his marriage (XX, 17–23).

Josephus' source begins with a typical mythic story regarding a hero who is born under strange circumstances[9] and whose name presages his nature (XX, 17–19). Such stories are, in general, etiological. Afterward, our text emphasizes the hatred Izates' brothers bore toward him (XX, 20–22) in order to justify Izates' sending them as hostages to Rome and Parthia (XX, 37). Then Izates arrives at Charax Spasini.[10] There he marries Symmacho (Samakhos), the daughter of Abennerigus, king of Charax Spasini (XX, 22–23). In this section relating to Izates' stay in Charax Spasini, there is no mention, or even a hint, of the influence of Judaism upon the wives of the king or upon Izates (as is described in A XX, 34).

2. The return of Izates to Adiabene, the death of his father, and his coronation (XX, 24–33).

The story now describes the return of Izates to Adiabene during the last days of Monobazus I, his father.[11] Monobazus sends for his son and presents him with a district over which to rule. Here we encounter "haggadic" details such as the mention of Noah's ark, which was said to be found in the district of Izates (XX, 25). Monobazus dies, and the description of the coronation of Izates (XX, 26–33) follows. While there are definitely historical foundations here, there is also the literary expansion and embellishment typical of Greek historiography.

3. The conversion of Izates and his mother, Helena (XX, 34–48).

In Charax Spasini a Jewish merchant influences the wives of the king to worship according to the Jewish tradition. He later exerts his influence to convert Izates. Helena is likewise won over. Izates goes so far as to have himself circumcised over the objections of his mother. It appears that this section and the fourth section constitute a separate source since XX, 54 is a natural continuation of XX, 33. It is noteworthy that this section returns to the stay of Izates in Charax Spasini (XX, 23). This lack of chronological order raises doubts regarding the unity of the entire passage. A logical explanation for this discrepancy is that the author of the passage inserted the story of the conversion, a literary unit in and of itself, into his historiographic narrative. The motif of the righteous king (XX, 36–37) who cannot maintain his brothers as prisoners and therefore sends them away as hostages, an act justified earlier in the narrative, also appears here. Since the author of the episode had already supplied us with the background information (XX, 20–22), we can deduce that he composed his account with the story of the conversion at hand. This story is, furthermore, an imitation of the story of Joseph and his brothers in Genesis.[12]

4. Helena's journey to Jerusalem and her charitable deeds (XX, 49–53).

Helena travels to Jerusalem to worship at the Temple and discovers upon her arrival that the people are suffering from a famine. She orders provisions and informs Izates, who likewise sends relief. Helena's journey constitutes a direct continuation of the story of the conversion, since she wanted to fulfill the obligation of the proselyte and offer a sacrifice in the Temple. Izates' help during the famine in Palestine, certainly a historical fact, is described here in order to prove his adherence to the commandments and (perhaps even more important) the support of the House of Adiabene for the Jews of Palestine.

5. Izates' assistance to Artabanus and the acquisition of Nisibis (XX, 54–68).

Artabanus, deposed king of Parthia, journeys to meet Izates in order to ask him for help in regaining his throne. Izates greets him with deference and manages to restore him to his position (XX, 63). This section continues the motif of the righteous king. Izates appears as a major force in the Parthian Empire. His influence and good fortune are a result of his conversion. The story of the submission of Artabanus and the humility of Izates (XX, 56–61) is a legend that was intended to prove once again the righteousness and greatness of King Izates. A myth of this kind could spring up only among the supporters of Izates. Further, this story emphasizes the obligations of the Parthian royal family toward the Jewish kings of the Adiabenian dynasty. After he is restored to his throne, Artabanus presents Izates with privileges and the district of Nisibis (XX, 66–68) with its large Jewish population.[13] Now, for the first time, the Jewish king reigns over a Jewish population.

6. Izates' refusal to fight against Rome and his war against Vardanes (XX, 69–74).

The sixth section continues the political history of Izates. Vardanes, successor to Artabanus, king of Parthia, tries to enlist Izates in a war against the Romans. When he fails to convince Izates to join him, he turns his attack upon Izates, but God foils Vardanes' plans, and he is killed by the Parthians.[14] Here Izates appears as a wise man who recognizes well the military and political situation in his region (XX, 69–70). The author of the account mentions the presence of King Izates' five sons and his mother, Helena, in Palestine (XX, 71). On the one hand, Adiabene was a part of the Parthian Empire. On the other, the connections between the House of Adiabene and the Jews of Roman Palestine forced Izates to avoid a confrontation with Rome.

7. The rebellion of the nobles of Adiabene and Izates' wars against Abias and Vologeses (XX, 75–91).

The account now returns to the matter of the conversion, which definitely served as its literary basis. Here we learn that after Monobazus II, the king's brother, and his relatives had converted to Judaism (a short time after Izates, XX, 75), the nobles of Adiabene prepared to rebel against them. It is certain that only the royal family converted and that the populace and the nobles continued their ancestral cult. The nobles tried twice to overthrow their ruler, once with the help of Abias, the Arab sheik (XX, 77–80), and a second time with the help of Vologeses, king of Parthia (XX, 81–91). They failed both times. Täubler is certainly correct in asserting that biblical motifs appear here.[15] Again and again the author emphasizes that God saved King Izates from all his enemies (XX, 81, 89, 91). The prayer in XX, 90 served as the basis for Schalit's conclusion that the entire account had originally been composed in Aramaic.

8. The death of Izates, the crowning of Monobazus II, and the death of Helena (XX, 92–96).

From a literary pont of view, the death of Izates brings to a close the account that had started with his wondrous birth. It is possible to see mythical significance in the fact that the number of years that Izates reigned, as well as the number of his sons and the number of his daughters (XX, 92) was twenty-four (twice the number of Jacob's sons). Monobazus II continues the dynasty (XX, 93). Helena dies of sorrow (XX, 95), and she and Izates are buried near Jerusalem.

It is now possible to draw conclusions from the literary analysis just presented. Our account is, in fact, the life of Izates, beginning with his birth and ending with his death. We have observed the historical elements as well as the mythical tendencies of the source. We have also seen how the author used the story of the conversion (including the journey of Helena to Jerusalem), which previously existed as a separate literary unit, as the basis for this final composition. The author then combined it with the political history of Izates and the legends about him. The legitimacy of Izates' and his family's conversion is stressed to prove that they were blessed from heaven as a result of it.

The Tannaitic Sources

The conversion of this family and its righteousness appear as well in rabbinic literature. First we shall deal with references to the House of Adiabene in tannaitic sources. Afterward, we shall investigate the description of the conversion itself, which appears in the Midrash *Bereshith Rabbah*. It is not necessary to subject these sources to exhaustive examination, but only to understand them from a historical point of view and to compare them to Josephus' source. Tannaitic sources dealing with Helena the queen, Monobazus the king, and the House of Monobazus will be treated separately.

1. Helena the queen.

The journey of Helena to Jerusalem is mentioned in M. *Nazir* 3:6 in a story (*maʿaseh*) recounted in order to prove that she observed the Nazirite laws in accordance with the views of the House of Hillel. At the same time, we are told several other details: seven years before she left Adiabene, Helena took Nazirite vows to help her son in battle. When he was successful, she began her Nazirite period. (Apparently, there was no one in Adiabene to tell her that the Nazirite status cannot be observed outside of the land of Israel.) When she arrived in Palestine, the House of Hillel instructed her to continue her Nazirite observances for another seven years.

In order to fix the chronology of the House of Adiabene, scholars have assumed that the seven-year interval described in the Mishnah was the time between the battle in question and the famine described by Josephus (XX, 49). The Mishnah, however, assumes that Queen Helena left Adiabene after the battles in which her son, Izates, was involved, while Josephus relates that she left Adiabene before those battles. The two accounts are completely at variance regarding this issue. Thus, it is not methodologically sound to apply this seven-year interval of the Mishnah to the account of Josephus, which does not indicate any particular time interval. Therefore, the battles cannot be dated seven years before the famine, nor can the conversion be dated by means of this rabbinic source. Furthermore, it is appropriate to see in these two periods of Nazirite observance echoes of events involving the patriarch Jacob in the Book of Genesis. The significance of the number seven is clear.

Queen Helena is mentioned once again in T. *Sukkah* 1:1.[16] The discussion in this source concerns a difference of opinion between Rabbi Judah[17] and the Sages regarding the maximum height of a *sukkah* ("festival booth") [also in M. *Sukkah* 1:1]. The Tosefta relates that while the Sages limited the height of a *sukkah* to twenty cubits, Rabbi Judah permitted it to be higher. Rabbi Judah defends his position by telling a story (*ma'aseh*) about Queen Helena, who had a *sukkah*[18] higher than twenty cubits that was constantly being visited by *zeqenim* ("elders"),[19] none of whom criticized its height. The Sages replied that the *zeqenim* did not express disapproval of Queen Helena's *sukkah* since, as a woman, she was not obligated to fulfill this commandment, and so it was not mandatory that her *sukkah* be built according to the details of the law. Rabbi Judah counters that the *sukkah* was also built for and used by her seven sons (*she-hayu lah*, "which she had") who were *talmide ḥakhamim* ("students of the Sages"). Once again we learn of the close relationship between Helena and the Sages, as well as of her observance of the commandments, here the obligation to dwell in the *sukkah*.[20]

What is most interesting, however, is the mention of seven sons who were students of the Sages. Josephus' source speaks of the five sons of Izates whom he sent to learn Hebrew and to study Judaism in Palestine (XX, 71). Since these sons do not appear in the description of the journey of Helena (XX, 49–50), it seems that Izates sent them to join her after she had arrived in Jerusalem. The tannaitic Sages took these grandchildren as the children of Helena. The number seven seems to be a haggadic round number appearing here in place of the exact number known to the author of Josephus' source. Further proof of Helena's piety is added by M. *Yoma'* 3:10 and T. *Kippurim* (*Yoma'*) 2:3, wherein mention is made of the gold vessels donated by Helena to the Temple.[21]

2. Monobazus the king.

Monobazus the king appears in T. *Pe'ah* 4:18.[22] According to this *baraitha*, Monobazus squandered his fortune in the years of drought. "His brothers sent to him" (in the reading of the editio princeps, "said") their protest of his having squandered the state treasury. The language of this *baraitha* indicates its literary and haggadic character: the phrase "Monobazus [*munbaz*] squandered [*bizbez*] his treasury" is a play on words based on the name Monobazus. When his brothers protest using this play on words, Monobazus answers them with his own pun and claims: "My fathers stored up [*gnz*] below [on earth], but I have stored up above [in heaven]," a play on words based upon different letters of his name (*munbaz*). Behind this beautiful phrasing there are echoes of the charitable deeds of the House of Adiabene in Palestine in the times of famine (XX, 51–53).[23] It is also possible to detect here the opposition of the nobles of Adiabene to the conversion of the royal family (XX, 75). We also find once again the theme of the righteousness and piety of the members of this family.

In this case, however, Helena does not appear as the primary benefactor, as she does in the account of Josephus, and, whereas Josephus relates how Izates aided the inhabitants of Jerusalem, here we are told it was Monobazus.[24]

Either the formulators of this tradition did not know the personal name of Izates and referred to him by his father's name, using it as a dynastic title, or, from a chronological point of view, they thought that the famine occurred in the reign of Monobazus II, Izates' brother. In M. *Yomaʾ* 3:10 and T. *Kippurim* (*Yomaʾ*) 2:3, which describe the donations of Monobazus and Helena to the Temple (he donated golden handles for the Day of Atonement), it is stated explicitly that Helena was his mother. If so, some tannaim knew the relationship between them.

    3. The House of Monobazus.

    To the tannaim, the House of Monobazus (*beth munbaz*) was composed of the members of the family who remained in Palestine until the days of the Great Revolt.[25] T. *Megillah* 3(4):30[26] relates that the House of Monobazus placed the *mezuzah* on a pole and hung it behind the door at inns. Since the Tosefta describes this as a dangerous act which fulfills no commandment, it appears at first glance that the House of Monobazus observed a mistaken custom that was liable to bring harm to them. But it is possible to explain that the danger was only in times of religious persecution,[27] when the Jews wanted to conceal their *mezuzoth*. During the reign of the House of Monobazus, when there was no danger, members of the family followed this custom to maintain some remembrance of the commandment of *mezuzah*, even when they were not obligated to fulfill it in a temporary abode. The customs of the House of Monobazus are praised in a *baraitha* in B. *Niddah* 17a even though they apparently deviated from the normal practice.

    Whereas the entire account of the House of Adiabene in Josephus is actually the story of Izates, Izates himself does not appear in tannaitic sources. It is clear that Helena the queen, who dwelled in Jerusalem toward the end of her days, made the greatest impression on the tannaim. It is interesting, too, that Monobazus the king takes the place of Izates and appears to be more important. Even though it is possible to see in him Izates,[28] it appears that actually it was Monobazus II who contributed to the Temple after the death of Izates. Monobazus II later turned into the hero of the haggadah, and the help that Izates provided during the famine was attributed to him.

    All the tannaitic sources that we have examined deal with the contribution of the House of Adiabene to the land of Israel and the Temple. The members of the family appear always as exceptionally righteous. It is certain that these sources are concerned only with what occurred in Palestine and are acquainted with the family only from this perspective. There is no interest in the politics or history of Adiabene here, or even in the history of the family. On the contrary, these sources know nothing of all this.[29] It is most surprising that tannaitic sources do not mention anywhere the conversion of this family, even though we, in the footsteps of Schürer,[30] are accustomed to seeing them as the crowning glory of the proselytizing movement in the Second Temple period.

The Conversion of Izates and Monobazus II
in *Bereshith Rabbah*

Bereshith Rabbah 46:11 (pp. 467–468) describes the conversion of Izates and Monobazus II as follows:

> "You shall circumcise [*u-nemaltem*] the flesh of your foreskin" [Gen. 17:11]; like a sore [*ke-nomi*] it [the foreskin] is attached to the body. And it happened [*u-ma'aseh*] that Monobazus [*munbaz*] and Izates [*zoitos*], the sons of Ptolemy the King, were sitting and reading the Book of Genesis when they came to this verse, "You shall circumcise." One turned his face to the wall and began to cry, and the other [also] turned his face to the wall and began to cry. One went and circumcised himself, and the other circumcised himself. After [a few] days, they were sitting and reading the Book of Genesis, and when they reached the verse, "You shall circumcise," one said to his companion, "Woe to you, my brother." [31] He said, "Woe to you, my brother, and not to me." They revealed the matter one to another. When their mother became aware, she went and said to their father, "A sore (*nomi*) has developed on their flesh, and the physician has prescribed that they be circumcised." He [their father] said that they should be circumcised. How did the Holy One, blessed be He, repay him? Said Rabbi Pinchas: When he went forth to war, an ambush [32] was set for him, but an angel descended and saved him.

This story is part of the interpretation of the word *u-nemaltem*, "you shall circumcise," from Genesis 17:11. Since the *nif'al* form is anomalous, the Midrash seeks to explain its appearance by understanding *nemaltem* as *nomi* (νομή [33]) *maltem*, and the story (*ma'aseh*) illustrates this explanation. Since both the explanation and the haggadah are anonymous, we are unable to fix their dates. At the very least, it is clear that the explanation and the story were already before Rabbi Pinchas, a fifth-generation Palestinian amora, as a literary unit.

This haggadah speaks of two brothers, Munbaz and Zoitos, sons of Ptolemy the king. Scholars have determined that Munbaz (who appears before Zoitos) is Monobazus II, who ruled after Izates, and that Zoitos is Izates. [34] Most scholars explain that Ptolemy was a general name for kings in this period. [35] It is certainly true that this name can serve for the kings of Egypt, but definitely not for the kings of Syria, let alone of Adiabene. We may infer, then, that the formulator of the haggadah did not know that he was dealing with two princes of Adiabene when he wove it together. (In tannaitic sources Adiabene does not appear as the place of origin of Helena and Monobazus.) While Josephus' source knew the names of the two Jews who influenced the House of Adiabene to convert to Judaism, the formulator of this haggadah does not know anything about them. Even the name of their mother, who was known to the tannaim, does not appear in this Midrash.

According to the Midrash, both brothers were circumcised at the same time, and their mother was afraid after their circumcision, whereas according to Josephus' source, Izates was circumcised first. Afterward Monobazus II and the other relatives converted. Their mother feared before the circumcision of Izates. According to this Midrash the conversion occurred before the death of their father, whereas according to Josephus' source, they were converted after the death of their father. As a result of their father's decision that they should be circumcised, the Midrash rewards him with his deliverance from danger by an angel. In Josephus' source, this reward is granted to Izates and his descendants as a result of Izates' circumcision (XX, 48). As in Josephus' source (XX, 44–45), we find mention of the reading and studying of the Torah as preparation for conversion. However, in the Midrash Izates and Monobazus II read the portion dealing with circumcision, while Josephus does not specify which portion of the Torah Izates was reading, and Monobazus II is not mentioned at all in this connection.

From a literary point of view, this haggadah is constructed of pairs: two sons of Ptolemy were separately sitting and reading. Both of them turned their faces to the wall and cried. They both had themselves circumcised. Each said to the other, "Woe to you, my brother," thus revealing the matter one to another. The words *nomi* and *u-nemaltem* appear at the beginning of the exposition and at its end. Thus far we have a literary unit. The comment of Rabbi Pinchas that their father (Ptolemy), even though he did not understand the matter, received a reward for decreeing that his sons should be circumcised, is a later addition to the source.

The foregoing analysis demonstrates that in this haggadic narrative of Palestinian amoraic origin, the amoraim have already forgotten the names and the details. The circumcision of the two princes served merely as an example for the interpretation of a verse. All that can be concluded from this source is that haggadic remnants—including a number of accurate details—regarding the House of Adiabene were in existence in the academies of the Palestinian amoraim, and that these details served as the basis of this Midrash. We cannot know, unfortunately, what the source of these traditions is. There is no historical evidence here that both brothers were circumcised at the same time. There remains only a popular haggadah that was repeated in order to make a point unrelated to the preservation of historical fact.

Proselytism According to Josephus' Source

We shall return now to the details of the conversion that appear in Josephus' source. Izates learned about Judaism in Charax Spasini. There a Jewish merchant named Ananias visited with the wives of the king and taught them Judaism. Through them the merchant reached Izates. According to the author of the account, Ananias taught them "to worship God after the manner of the Jewish tradition" (XX, 34). The use here of ϑεὸν σέβειν shows that we are dealing not with proselytes converted according to Jewish law, but with God-fearers or semi-proselytes who are known to us from the Graeco-Roman world.[36] At the same time Helena, Izates' mother, "had likewise been instructed by another Jew and had been brought over to their laws" (XX, 35). The use of εἰς τοὺς ἐκείνων μετακεκομίσθαι νόμους is proof that Helena, according to Josephus' source, indeed did convert in accordance with Jewish law.[37]

After Izates had arrived home and had realized "that his mother was very much pleased with the Jewish religion, he was zealous to convert to it himself (XX, 38). Here the Greek uses καὶ αὐτὸς εἰς ἐκεῖνα μεταθέσθαι. This idiom, as we have already established in regard to Helena, denotes conversion in accordance with Jewish law. Since his mother was already a Jewess of unquestionable status, Izates also decided to become a full-fledged Jew. Immediately, he realized that to be "genuinely a Jew" (βεβαίως Ἰουδαῖος) he had to undergo circumcision. Both his mother and Ananias attempted to dissuade him from undergoing circumcision. The reasons they advanced were not halakhic but political. They feared the repercussions likely to result from the circumcision of the new king, for his subjects "would not tolerate the rule of a Jew over them" (XX, 39). They all knew that without undergoing circumcision Izates would not be a Jew.

Ananias also feared for his own life, a matter we can well understand in light of the later Roman enactments that forbade Jews from performing circumcision upon non-Jews.[38] Ananias suggested to Izates that he "worship God" (τὸ θεῖον σέβειν) without circumcision (XX, 41). The Greek terminology proves that he was referring to the non-halakhic status of the God-fearer or semi-proselyte. Ananias requested that Izates remain in this status (which he had already entered in Charax Spasini) and exempted him from full conversion, basing his argument on what the rabbis later called 'ones, constraint from the performance of a commandment. Ananias was not of the opinion that it was permissible to convert fully without circumcision. Rather, Ananias suggested to Izates that circumcision was much too dangerous for him and that he, therefore, should remain a semi-proselyte.

Here a second Jew, named Eleazar, enters the picture. According to our source, he came from Galilee and "had a reputation for being extremely strict when it came to the ancestral laws." He advised Izates to undergo circumcision. Eleazar, according to the author of the account, found Izates reading from the law of Moses and suggested to him that he read the passage relating to circumcision. Immediately, Izates (without even examining the passage) was circumcised. He informed his mother and Ananias of his deed. Although they were quite fearful of the consequences, God, nonetheless, preserved them and delivered them (XX, 43–48).

Helena, after the conversion of Izates, desired "to go to the city of Jerusalem and to worship at the Temple of God . . . and to make thank-offerings there" (XX, 49). It is probable that this first sacrifice of the queen was the proselyte's offering to which we shall return below. Only after this did Monobazus II, the king's brother, and several of his relatives convert. According to Josephus' source, they understood "that the king because of his pious worship of God had won the admiration of all men" and, therefore, decided "to abandon their ancestral religion and to adopt the practices of the Jews" (XX, 75). The Greek terminology used to express Izates' "pious worship of God" (πρὸς τὸν θεὸν εὐσέβειαν) raises the possibility that Monobazus and his relatives wanted only to be semi-proselytes and not undergo the conversion process according to Jewish law. On the other hand, the words ἔθεσι χρῆσθαι τοῖς 'Ιουδαίων (XX, 75), "to adopt the practices of the Jews," can mean only that they underwent the process of conversion according to Jewish law.[39]

The Process of Conversion at the End of the Second Temple Period

It is necessary to survey the requirements for conversion according to Jewish law at the end of the Second Temple period and to ask if the royal House of Adiabene fulfilled all of these requirements. Further, much can be learned about these requirements from our account as it appears in Josephus' source. According to tannaitic halakhah, there were four requirements for conversion: acceptance of the Torah, circumcision for males, immersion in a ritual bath (*miqweh*), and the offering of a sacrifice.[40]

1. The acceptance of the Torah.

According to the tannaim, the proselyte was required to accept the entire Torah.[41] For this reason he was to be taught some of the easier commandments and some of the more difficult ones before entering the community of Israel.[42] The first instance in which it is possible to establish this requirement with historical certainty is the conversion of the House of Adiabene. According to Josephus' source, Izates and Helena began the process of their conversion with the study of the Torah, but the author does not mention the study of the Torah in connection with Monobazus II. Here the source apparently depends upon the description of the conversion of Izates and leaves the reader to assume that Monobazus II and the other relatives followed the same procedure.[43]

2. Circumcision.

Circumcision was required of every Jew in biblical times.[44] It was the distinguishing sign of the Jew in the Graeco-Roman world.[45] Those who wished to attach themselves to the House of Israel without circumcision were the God-fearers or semi-proselytes. Some scholars have pointed to the tannaitic dispute regarding a proselyte who was circumcised but did not immerse and one who immersed but was not circumcised[46] and have attempted to prove that according to one view it was permissible to convert without circumcision.[47] These same scholars sought to find this dispute in the account of the House of Adiabene. In their view, Ananias believed that it was permissible to convert without circumcision, while Eleazar, the strict "Galilaean," did not agree. These scholars did not interpret the tannaitic dispute correctly. The question there was the determination of the decisive stage in the process of conversion. The tannaim wanted to know which requirement, circumcision or immersion, established definitively the status of the proselyte.[48] These scholars did not pay attention to the reports of Josephus regarding the Hasmonaeans and his stories of the marriages of the Herodian family, from which it is possible to prove that circumcision was unquestionably a requirement for conversion among all segments of the Jewish community.[49] As we have already shown, even Ananias agreed that circumcision was required, and he proposed to Izates the non-halakhic status of semi-proselyte only because of the risk involved in his full conversion.

3. Immersion in a ritual bath.

According to tannaitic halakhah, the proselyte is obligated to be immersed in a ritual bath (*miqweh*) as part of the conversion procedure.[50] This immersion was intended to purify the proselyte of his state of being a non-Jew and to initiate him into his new status. Since Christian baptism is an imitation of proselyte immersion as required by Jewish law, we can establish that immersion was a requirement for conversion to Judaism before the redaction of the books of the New Testament, that is, the latter part of the first century A.D.[51] An argument between the Houses of Hillel and Shammai regarding the details of proselyte immersion already indicates that this requirement was in force by their time.[52]

In Josephus' source there appears no mention of immersion. Since the author of the account certainly wanted to prove the legitimacy of the proselytes of the House of Adiabene, it can be assumed that if the royal family had indeed been immersed, he would not have failed to mention it. Therefore, it is probable that they did not undergo proselyte immersion in Adiabene. Perhaps this requirement, which appears to have been the last to be established in the history of the conversion procedure, had not yet taken root in the Diaspora. On the other hand, it is possible that immersion occurred only in connection with the offering of the sacrifice, for the proselyte had to purify himself in order to enter the Temple. If so, this immersion would not have been practiced outside the land of Israel. Helena would have immersed herself in Jerusalem, and the others would not have been obligated to immerse themselves so long as they remained in Adiabene.

4. Offering a sacrifice.

From tannaitic sources it can be established without a doubt that the obligation of a proselyte to offer a sacrifice was in force at the end of the Second

Temple period.[53] If, in fact, Helena's first sacrifice was that of the proselyte offering, then in her time this offering was required. According to one *baraitha*, soon after the destruction of the Temple proselytes were still setting aside money for their offerings, even though they were unable to offer them. Rabbi Yohanan ben Zakkai eliminated this custom.[54] We can assume that in the time of the Temple there were proselytes who were unable to offer their sacrifices but who were nonetheless accepted as Jews. In this way, it may be possible to explain why the sacrifices of Izates and Monobazus II are not mentioned in the account of the House of Adiabene.

In his presentation of the story of the conversion of Izates and his family, Josephus' source made every effort to prove to his reader that the Adiabenian rulers converted according to Jewish law—exactly as the Sages of the land of Israel required. They studied the Torah and accepted it upon themselves, and afterward they were circumcised. Helena also offered a sacrifice in Jerusalem. The members of this family entered the House of Israel in accordance with all the prescriptions of Jewish law.

Reliability of the Sources

The author of the account of the House of Adiabene preserved in the works of Josephus had a firm grasp of the history of Adiabene and its international relations. Despite his use of legendary sources, the author understood the chronology of the events as well as the process of conversion. He definitely knew the names of the dramatis personae, their place of origin, and the order of the events. Certainly the focus of his interest was on what happened in Adiabene, and his account revolves around this axis. With the exception of the legendary details that we have found in his narrative, he may be relied upon as a historical source.

On the other hand, the tannaitic sources were interested only in the actions of the Adiabenians in Palestine and in their righteousness. The tannaim do not know of Izates, and there is no mention of the conversion of the family. Almost all the details that appear in tannaitic sources can be attributed to sages of the haggadah who set their narrative against a historical backdrop. Even the amoraic source that deals with the circumcision of Monobazus II and Izates lacks knowledge of the characters and places.

There is no doubt that the testimony of Josephus' source must be preferred to that of the rabbinic sources regarding the House of Adiabene. Furthermore, we may not combine the Hebrew and Greek sources in our quest to clarify the history of Adiabene and its chronology. The rabbinic sources regarding this episode can be relied upon only when they do not appear haggadic and when they do not contradict the words of Josephus' source.

Conclusions

The author of the account of the House of Adiabene as it appears in Josephus' source meshed together two kinds of material. He began with a story about Izates' life, birth, conversion, and piety. He added to it a historical narrative about Izates' reign, which dealt with his foreign and domestic affairs and which described his successes as if they were the result of his conversion. All of this was done, as Schalit showed, to demonstrate to the population of Adiabene that no harm had come from the royal household's abandonment of the ancestral cult of Adiabene. This polemic was directed against a powerful group of nobles who attempted to convince the people to overthrow their rulers.

The author of the account also sought to prove that the House of Adiabene converted according to Jewish law and that they were entirely righteous. This second polemic was aimed at the Jews of Nisibis, who found themselves in the midst of the Adiabenian kingdom after Artabanus had ceded this region to his ally, Izates. These Jews must have been extremely dubious of the legitimacy of the Jewish status of the House of Adiabene, and the author of this official history attempted to allay their fears.

According to J. Neusner, one of the motivations behind the conversion of the House of Adiabene was the family's desire to rule a Jewish empire that would include the Jews of Palestine, Adiabene, and Babylonia. As the war drew near, the House of Adiabene thought, in Neusner's view, that the Jews of Palestine would accept its members as kings since they were legitimate proselytes.[55] If so, the emphasis in this official history on their legitimacy as converts was directed as well toward the Jews of Palestine, as was the description of the benevolence of the Adiabenians in the land of Israel.

But why did Josephus include this long account in his *Antiquities?* At first glance, two reasons might be cited. First, Josephus displays a marked tendency to copy anything from any source that is nominally relevant to his discourse. Second, Josephus endeavored to include in his *Antiquities* material pertaining to the history of nations that came into contact with the Jews. But here there were also more important reasons.

At the time of Helena and her son, Monobazus II, the members of the House of Adiabene constructed homes in Jerusalem[56] and sent their sons to study in the city. The princes of Adiabene continued to dwell in Jerusalem up until the Jewish War. They took part in the revolt on the side of the Jews and fought valiantly.[57] It is certain that during the revolt the Jews of Palestine looked to their brethren in Adiabene and the Parthian kingdom for help.[58] Although Parthia was afraid to fight against Rome, apparently she chose to look the other way when the kings of Adiabene aided the Jewish revolt surreptitiously.[59] At the end of the revolt, a number of Adiabenian princes remained among the Roman captives and were brought to Rome as hostages to assure the tranquility of Adiabene.[60] Josephus may have been personally acquainted with these members of the Adiabenian royal family.[61] Certainly there was great interest in the history of this family when Josephus wrote his *Antiquities*.

Furthermore, the account of the House of Adiabene served Josephus' apologetic aims. It is well known that in the Hellenistic period, one of the accusations that was most widely disseminated against the Jews was their alleged hatred of the non-Jews.[62] Josephus himself, in his polemic *Against Apion*, which he wrote after *Antiquities*, argues against the claim of the anti-Semite Apion, which was widespread in the Graeco-Roman world, that the Jews swore allegiance to "show no good will to a single alien, above all the Greeks."[63] In order to disprove this accusation, Josephus points to the proselytes, stating that "not one has ever said that he had heard the oath in question" (*Ap* II, 121–124). Josephus stresses again and again the acceptance of proselytes by the Jews with a "gracious" and "glad" welcome (*Ap* II, 210, 261).[64]

Against this background we may understand the importance of the account of the House of Adiabene to Josephus. This story was part of his polemic against Hellenistic anti-Semitism. Josephus took pride in the conversion of this family and sought to present them to his readers as a family of righteous proselytes who had been accepted by the Jews. Even before he composed his polemic, *Against Apion*, Josephus had encountered the claim that the Jews hated all others, and he sought to dispel it in his *Antiquities*. If so, the account of the House of Adiabene found its place in the *Antiquities* because it served Josephus' two purposes—historiography and apologetics.

Notes

1. For its location, see A. Neubauer, *La géographie du Talmud*, Paris, 1868, 374–375, N. Brüll, "Adiabene," *JJGL* 1 (1874), 58–75, and B. Eshel, *Yishuve Ha-Yehudim Be-Vavel Bi-Tequfat Ha-Talmud*, Jerusalem, 1979, 118. For a survey of the sources, see I. Gafni, "Giyyur Malekhe Ḥadyev [Adiabene] Le-ʾOr Ha-Sifrut Ha-Talmudit," *Niv Ha-Midrashiyah* (1970–1971), 209–212, and "Adiabene," *EJ* 2, 267–268. The Hebrew Union College–Jewish Institute of Religion doctoral dissertation on the Jews of Adiabene by David Barish was not yet available as this article went to press.

2. See the article of D. Schwartz, "ΚΑΤᾺ ΤΟῩΤΟΝ ΤῸΝ ΚΑΙΡΌΝ: Josephus' Source on Agrippa II," *JQR* 72 (1982), 241–268.

3. Cf. L. Feldman, *Josephus* 9, London and Cambridge, Mass., 1965, 414, 418–419, 439.

4. For the chronology of the episode, see Brüll (above, n. 1), 66–72, H. Graetz, "Zeit der Anwesenheit der Adiabenischen Königin Jerusalem und des Apostel Paulus," *MGWJ* 26 (1877), 241–255, J. Neusner, *A History of the Jews in Babylonia* 1, Leiden, 1956, 58–62.

5. A. Schalit, "Evidence of an Aramaic Source in Josephus' 'Antiquities of the Jews,'" *ASTI* 4 (1975), 163–188 and especially 178–181. E. Täubler, *Die Parthernachrichten bei*

Josephus, Berlin, 1904, 62–65, dealt with our story and claims that the source of the account was a "Missionsbericht" that had reached Josephus. In this way, Täubler explains the religious emphasis in Josephus' history of the House of Adiabene. He denies the possibility that Josephus drew the account from reports he had received orally from the Adiabenian princes who dwelled in Jerusalem or Rome. According to Täubler, the source was a kind of travelogue ("Reisebericht") of an itinerant Jewish missionary. The theory itself is apparently built (even though he does not indicate it) upon the model of the journeys of Paul. However, there is little evidence of missionary journeys of this kind among the Jews, although Matthew 23:15 does seem to refer to them. (Graetz [above, n. 4], 289–306, attempts to prove that the presence of Helena and her family in Jerusalem influenced Paul.)

6. Cf. Neusner (above, n. 4), 50–54.

7. Schalit (above, n. 5), 187 n. 49. Regarding the story of the two brothers, Schalit pends on the reading κτιλίων in order to prove that the source of the story was Aramaic. Even if we assume that this word is, indeed, part of the original text, and that it is Aramaic (*qeṭila*ʾ, i.e. *bar qeṭila*ʾ, "one deserving of death"), it is possible that the author composed his text in Greek but made use of a transliterated Aramaic expression. Regarding the account of the House of Adiabene, Schalit bases his claim of an Aramaic source on the presence of one phrase from Daniel 7:8f. in the prayer of Izates (XX, 90). This phrase is found in the reading of the editio princeps, but not in the manuscripts. Even if we assume that this phrase, in fact, belongs to Josephus' source, it is possible that it was inserted directly into a Greek text. In light of Schalit's article, these two narratives require a wide-ranging philological study based on unquestioned readings. A start toward such a study was made by N. G. Cohen, "Asinaeus and Anilaeus," *ASTI* 10 (1976), 30–37.

8. E.g. M. Stern, "The Jewish Diaspora," *The Jewish People in the First Century*, ed. S. Safrai, M. Stern, Assen, 1974, vol. 1, 170–178, G. Widengren, "Quelques rapports entre Juifs et iraniens à l'époque des Parthes," *Supplements to VT* 4 (1956), 200 n. 5; *A* XX, 75–76.

9. Cf. Täubler (above, n. 5), 63.

10. See Pauly-Wissowa, "Charax (10),"; Eshel (above, n. 1), 135–136, and S. A. Nodelman, "A Preliminary History of Characene," *Berytus* 13 (1959–1960), 83–120.

11. Täubler (above, n. 5), 63, saw here echoes of Gen. 27:1 and 47:29.

12. Thackeray, according to Feldman (above, n. 3), 399 note d.

13. See Neusner (above, n. 4), 43–49 and Neubauer (above, n. 1), 370.

14. On Gotarzes, who ruled after Vardanes' execution by the Parthians, see Tacitus, *Annals* 14:1, discussed in M. Stern, *GLAJJ* 2, Jerusalem, 1980, 73–74, and Feldman (above, n. 3), 427 note d.

15. Täubler (above, n. 5), 63 n. 3, calls attention to parallels between the story of the messenger of Vologeses who came to Izates and what is related about Hezekiah, king of Judah, in II Kings 18:3ff. and II Chronicles 32:1ff. In both cases the messengers attempted to convince the Jewish kings not to fight against the great empire. The messengers mentioned the greatness of their kings and blasphemed the God of Israel. Both Jewish kings prayed to God and were suddenly delivered when their enemies abandoned the battlefield.

16. Cf. S. Lieberman, *Tosefta*ʾ *Ki-Fshuṭah*, B. *Sukkah* 2b, P.T. *Sukkah* 1:1 (51d). The version of the Babylonian Talmud adds: "and furthermore, she did not do anything, except according to the view of the Sages." It is certain from the Babylonian *sugya*ʾ (B. *Sukkah* 2b) that this addition was already in the text by the time of the rabbis who formulated the anonymous *gemara*ʾ.

17. Rabbi Judah bar Ilai, a fourth-generation tanna. From M. *Nazir* 3:6 it is certain that Rabbi Judah already had before him the story (*ma* ʿ*aseh*) regarding the Nazirite status of Helena.

18. According to the manuscripts and medieval citations, we may conclude that the word *be-lod* ("in Lydda") in some texts is an addition and that almost certainly the *sukkah* was in

Jerusalem, where Helena made her home. (So Lieberman, who notes that the matter needs further investigation.) On the building of Helena's palace in Jerusalem, see below, n. 56.

19. Brüll (above, n. 1), 75 n. 16 explains the *zeqenim* of the Tosefta as being the *ziqne beth Hillel* ("the elders of the House of Hillel"), according to M. *Sukkah* 2:7.

20. Although women are exempt from the commandment of dwelling in the *sukkah* (M. *Sukkah* 2:8), Helena sought to fulfill it in accordance with the rule that women are permitted to perform positive commandments with time limitations (*she-ha-zeman gerama²*) if they wish.

21. Cf. B. *Yoma²* 37b and P. T. *Yoma²* 3:8 (41a).

22. Quoted in P. T. *Pe²ah* 1:1 (15b), and B. *Bava² Bathra²* 11a.

23. A. Schalit, "Helena," *EJ* 8, 288.

24. Cf. U. Rappaport, "Monobaz I and II," *EJ* 12, 258.

25. *BJ* II, 520, IV, 567, V, 474, VI, 356.

26. Quoted in B. *Menaḥoth* 32b.

27. Cf. Lieberman, *Tosefta² Ki-Fshuṭah*, to T. *Megillah* 3(4):30.

28. J. Klausner, *Historiyah shel Ha-Bayit Ha-Sheni*, Jerusalem, 1968, vol. 5, 46 n. 10.

29. This lack of knowledge led a number of sources in the Middle Ages to attribute Helena and Monobazus to the Herodian or Hasmonean dynasties. See Brüll (above, n. 1), 73f., n. 14.

30. E. Schürer, *Geschichte des jüdischen Volkes im Zeitalter Jesu Christi*, Leipzig, 1901, vol. 3, 169–172.

31. Equivalent to *²oy lekha ²aḥi*, as in MS. Rome.

32. Levy, s.v. *śyᶜh*, explains *śiᶜ ah shel pisṭon* as "eine Versammlung der Auflauerer" (so *ᶜArukh*), although in the entry *psṭwn* he translates "eine Schar Fussvolk" (so *Musaf Heᶜ Arukh*). There Levy derives "pisṭon" from πεζίτης or πεζόν (which appears in Liddell-Scott as πεζός), "infantry." *ᶜArukh*, s.v. *pśt*, follows Brüll (above, n. 1), 74, and translates "Abtrünnige," and derives the word "maybe from Greek ἀποστάται."

33. Levy, s.v. *nōmi*, translates, "fressendes Geschwür." It should be mentioned that the meaning of this word in Greek is "fodder," as is noted in *ᶜArukh*, s.v. *nm*. Our technical, medica. usage is attested in Liddell-Scott, definition 3b. In Latin the form *nome* appears, and, according to Lewis-Short, it is borrowed from the Greek, meaning "a corroding sore, eating ulcer." For example, Pliny uses *nome intestina*. Cf. also J. Preuss, *Biblical and Talmudic Medicine*, New York, London, 1978, 195.

34. Brüll (above, n. 1), 73, J. Derenbourg, *Essai sur l'histoire et la géographie de la Palestine*, Paris, 1867, 223–227, following Azariah dei Rossi, *Sefer Me²or ᶜEinayim* (Vilna, 1865–1866), 440.

35. Following dei Rossi (above, n. 34), 441. It is unlikely that the author of this tradition saw the story as being set in Egypt. It is even more unlikely that there is any connection with the Septuagint that might be suggested by the name Ptolemy (cf. B. *Megillah* 9a, *Bereshith Rabbah* 8:11).

36. Gafni (above, n. 1), 204f., already recognized this. On God-fearers, see L. H. Schiffman, "At the Crossroads: Tannaitic Perspectives on the Jewish-Christian Schism," *Jewish and Christian Self-Definition* 2, ed. E. P. Sanders, London, 1981, 137–138, and the literature cited there in n. 133 (p. 346). On this idiom, see Schürer (above, n. 30), 3, 174f. (and n. 70) and K. G. Kuhn, "προσήλυτος," *TDNT* 6, 741–744 (English ed.), Stern (above, n. 14), 2, 103–106, L. Feldman, "'Jewish Sympathizers' in Classical Literature and Inscriptions," *TAPA* 81 (1950), 200–208, R. Marcus, "The Sebomenoi in Josephus," *JSS* 14 (1952), 247–250, S. Pines, "The Iranian Name for Christians and the 'God Fearers,'" *PIASH* 2 (1968), 143–152.

37. Cf. εἰς τὰ Ἰουδαίων ἔθη τὸν βίον μετέβαλον in connection with Helena and Izates in *A* XX, 17 and εἰς ἐκεῖνα μεταθέσθαι in connection with Izates in section 38. The laws of the Jews are referred to in the writings of Josephus as ἔθος . . . Ἰουδαίοις (*BJ* II, 1); τὰ τῶν

'Ιουδαίων ἔθη (*BJ* VII, 50); ἔθος . . . οἱ 'Ιουδαῖοι (*A* I, 214, regarding the commandment of circumcision); and τοὺς 'Ιουδαίους ἔθους (*A* XV, 268). Regarding proselytism, cf. ἐς τὰ πάτρια τῶν 'Ιουδαίων ἔθη μεταβαλεῖσθαι (*A* XIII, 397); τὰ 'Ιουδαίων ἔθη μεταλαβοῦσιν (*A* XV, 255, cf. also 254); and ἐγγραφῆναι τοῖς τῶν 'Ιουδαίων ἔθεσι (*A* XVI, 225). Cf. also *A* XIV, 237, 240, XVI, 166, and Kuhn (above, n. 36), 732.

38. See E. M. Smallwood, "The Legislation of Hadrian and Antoninus Pius against Circumcision," *Latomus* 18 (1959), 334–347, and "Addendum," *Latomus* 20 (1961), 93–96.

39. See n. 28.

40. On the laws relating to proselytes, see Schiffman (above, n. 36), 122–139; Kuhn (above, n. 36), 736–740; D. Daube, "Conversion to Judaism and Early Christianity," *Ancient Jewish Law, Three Inaugural Lectures,* Leiden, 1981, 1–47, and L. H. Schiffman, *Who Was a Jew? Rabbinic and Halakhic Perspectives on the Jewish-Christian Schism,* New York, 1984.

41. Including the *diqduqe soferim,* "the subtleties of the scribes [rabbinic ordinances]." See T. *Demai* 2:5 and Schiffman (above, n. 36), 124f.

42. A baraitha in B. *Yevamoth* 47a–b, cf. Schiffman (above, n. 36), 123.

43. For the polemics of I. H. Weiss and Y. I. Halevy regarding the study of the Torah in Babylonia in this period, see Gafni (above, n. 1), 207f.

44. Gen. 13:23–27, Lev. 12:3, Josh. 5:2–9, and cf. J. Licht, "Milah," *Ensiqlopedia Miqra'it* 4, 896–898.

45. See Schiffman (above, n. 36), 126f., and Stern, *GLAJJ* 1, 169–170, 225, 300, 312, 315, 325, 356, 415, 436, 442–444, 525–526, 528. In *Antiquities,* I, 214, Josephus writes that the Jews were accustomed to circumcising "eight days later [after birth]," i.e. on the eighth day. Following the Septuagint to Esther 8:17, Josephus (*A* XI, 285) says that "many of the other nations also, from fear of the Jews, had themselves circumcised." In *Vita* 113 Josephus says regarding the two nobles of Trachonitis who defected to his side that "the Jews would have compelled them to be circumcised as a condition of residence among them." Josephus did not agree with this compulsion since "every one should worship God in accordance with the dictates of his own conscience and not under constraint." According to *War* II, 454, Metilius promised "to turn Jew, and even to be circumcised."

46. B. *Yevamoth* 46a, P. T. *Qiddushin* 3:12 (3:14, 64d) and Schiffman (above, n. 36), 134–136.

47. For bibliographic details, see B. J. Bamberger, *Proselytism in the Talmudic Period,* New York, 1968, 48, 58 nn. 44–47, and cf. Gafni (above, n. 1) 205–207.

48. Bamberger (above, n. 47), 51, and following him, Feldman (above, n. 3), 410f. note a.

49. For the Hasmoneans, cf. *A* XIII, 257 (the conversion of the Idumaeans) and 318 (the conversion of the Itureans). For the Herodian family, see *A* XVI, 225 ("When they asked Syllaeus to be initiated into the customs of the Jews," it was certainly circumcision that was intended); *A* XX, 139 ("Agrippa [II] gave his sister, Drusilla, to Azizus, king of Emesa, who had consented to be circumcised. Epiphanes, son of King Antiochus, had rejected marriage to Drusilla since he was not willing to convert to the Jewish religion." Certainly, the explanation of βουληθεὶς τὰ 'Ιουδαίων ἔθη μεταλαβεῖν here is περιτέμνεσθαι, "to be circumcised."); and *A* XX, 145 (Polemo, King of Cilicia, who married Berenice). Cf. Bamberger (above, n. 47), 19–24. For circumcision as a requirement for conversion, see a *baraitha* in B. *Yevamoth* 47a–b, M. *Pesaḥim* 8:8, T. *Pesaḥim* 7:14, and *Sifrei Bemidbar* 108 (ed. H. S. Horovitz, Leipzig, 1917, 112).

50. A *baraitha* in B. *Yevamoth* 47a–b, *Sifrei Bemidbar* 108 (ed. H. S. Horovitz, Leipzig, 1917, 112), and Schiffman (above, n. 36), 127f.

51. Cf. H. H. Rowley, "Jewish Proselyte Baptism and the Baptism of John," *HUCA* 15 (1940), 313–334.

52. M. *Pesaḥim* 8:8, and T. *Pesaḥim* 7:14. See also B. *Pesaḥim* 92a and Schiffman

(above, n. 36), 128–131. It is possible that this immersion is mentioned by Juvenal (ca. A.D. 60–130). See Stern, *GLAJJ* 2, 102–103, 107 n. It is explicitly referred to by Epictetus (ca. A.D. 50–130), on which see the comments of Stern, 1, 541–544.

53. M. *Kerithoth* 2:1. See Schiffman (above, n. 36), 131f., as well as *Sifrei Bemidbar* 108 (ed. H. S. Horovitz, Leipzig, 1917, 112). This requirement does not appear in the previously mentioned *baraitha* in B. *Yevamoth* 47a–b because it reflects the situation after the destruction of the Temple (Schiffman, 123).

54. B. *Kerithoth* 9a; B. *Rosh Ha-Shanah* 31b; *Gerim* 2:4; and cf. Schiffman (above, n. 36), 133.

55. Neusner (above, n. 4), 1, 62–67, and his article "The Conversion of Adiabene to Judaism," *JBL* 83 (1964), 60–66. Cf. also Widengren (above, n. 8), 200f.

56. The palace of Helena (*BJ* V, 253, VI, 355); the monument of Helena (*BJ* V, 55, 119, 147, and cf. *A* XX, 95, and M. Kohn, *Qivre Ha-Melakhim, Nefesh Malekhe Bet Ḥadayev*, Tel Aviv, 1946–1947); the "courthouse" of Monobazus (*BJ* V, 252 [on αὐλή, see Arndt-Gingrich]; it is certain from *BJ* V, 253, that this Monobazus is Monobazus II, the son of Helena); and the palace built by Grapte, a relative of Izates (*BJ* IV, 567).

57. *BJ* II, 520, V, 474–475.

58. *BJ* I, 5, II, 388, VI, 343.

59. Cf. A. Schalit, "Darkhe Hapoliṭiqah Ha-Mizraḥit shel Romi Mi-Niron ʿad Traianus," *Tarbiz* 7 (1935–1936), 159–180. Neusner (above, n. 4), 1, 65.

60. *BJ* VI, 356. It is possible that the brothers (ἀδελφοί) of Izates in this paragraph are his relatives (cf. Liddell-Scott) or even his compatriots (cf. Arndt-Gingrich).

61. In the introduction to *War*, Josephus (I, 6) includes the people of Adiabene among those who already knew about the *Jewish War* from his work, which had appeared in an earlier edition, most probably in Aramaic. On the history of the House of Monobazus and the Jews of Adiabene after the war, see Brüll (above, n. 1), 79–82 and notes. J. Neusner, "The Jews in Pagan Armenia," *JAOS* 84 (1964), 239–240, raises the possibility that the royal family of Adiabene migrated to Armenia during the reign of Trajan. J. Teixidor, "The Kingdom of Adiabene and Hatra," *Berytus* 17 (1967–1968), 1–9, attempts to prove that a statue that was found in Hatra, with the inscription "ṣlmʾ dy ʾtlw mlkʾ ntwnʾšryʾ / plḥ ʾlhʾ bryk ʾlhʾ dy" on it, is a statue of Izates, king of Adiabene, which was erected in Hatra at the end of the second century A.D.

62. I. Heinemann, "Ha-Yahaduth Be-ʿEyne Ha-ʿOlam Ha-ʿAtiq," *Zion* 4 (1938–1939), 283f.

63. *Ap* II, 121. Trans. Thackeray.

64. Cf. *Ap* II, 281–286.

3
christianity

14 The Works of Josephus and the Early Christian Church

HEINZ SCHRECKENBERG

t is apparent in the case of Josephus that an author's work and its impact are inseparable and that literary-sociological aspects must complete the purely literary-historical view. Indeed, the reception of Josephus' writings produces, among others, spiritual responses that arise more from the subjective bias or motivation of his readers than from the works themselves. This Jewish historian was for a long time paid little or no attention by his countrymen while, on the other hand, he was esteemed highly in Christian circles of the early church. In fact, Josephus placed a great abundance of information at the disposal of the young church's early developing historical, historical-theological, and apologetic interests. His works, created in the style of Greek historiography, offered (in *Jewish Antiquities*) a colorful recapitulation of the Old Testament, rich in detail and arranged with skill, and (in the *Jewish War*) the tragic fate of the city of Jerusalem, a shocking and moving drama that appeared to be the continuation and culmination of the reports of the New Testament in which, to be sure, the prophecies of misfortune regarding Jerusalem play an important part (Mark 13:2; Matt. 23:38, 24:2; Luke 19:40–44, 21:6, 20–24). Beyond these accounts one soon saw during this time of early Christianity that there was, throughout the works of Josephus, the mention of numerous persons, places, and occurrences that either were known from the New Testament or whose stories completed the biblical accounts. In all cases, the works of Josephus furnished background information for the Bible in a welcome and impressive manner. Due to this strong affinity between Josephus and the Bible, the Jewish historian's great future as a famous author in Christian circles was determined almost in advance. One may assume that the theologians of the early Christian church at first reached for the works of Josephus with hesitation and astonishment, then, as they read, with a greater and greater joy of discovery.[1]

I

The development of the early Christian church had already begun at the time of the New Testament; indeed, the New Testament reflects the first stages of its history. Hence, the relevance of our theme does not begin with the reception of Josephus by the church fathers but earlier, with the New Testament. In this connection, first and foremost, it is important to note that some parts of the New Testament, such as the Gospel of Luke, probably attained their final edited form only after A.D. 70; accordingly, one expects here and there, an echo of the Roman conquest of Jerusalem. This, indeed, occurs, and we have to realize this fact.[2] The prophecies of misfortune, which, in the mouth of Jesus of Nazareth, were at first meant eschatologically, obtained their historical color in part from flashbacks to the fall of Jerusalem, that is from *ex eventu* presentations. These prophecies became the point of departure for the later reception of Josephus. The affinity between the historical depiction by Josephus and the reports given in the New Testament were destined to become the crucial factor of reception and impact. Besides this affinity, there were numerous points of contact so apparent that modern theologians did not discover them at first—namely the reports by Josephus about Jesus (*A* XVIII, 63–64; XX, 200), John the Baptist (*A* XVIII, 116–119), and James, the brother of Jesus (*A* XX, 200–203).[3] In addition to these accounts about early Christianity, reports, for example, about the house of Herod,[4] the Jewish sects, and the death of Herod Agrippa (*A* XIX, 343f.; Acts 12:21–23) stimulated much interest among the church fathers.[5] The church fathers did not yet perceive the full extent of the areas of contact and anticipated only partially what the current scientific exegesis partly confirms and partly ascertains, namely, that there are almost surely structural and formal correspondences between the actions of Jesus of Nazareth and the actions of the prophets and miracle workers of the period of the New Testament described by Josephus. Note, for instance, the actions of Theudas (*A* XX, 97–99; Acts 5:36), Judah the Galilaean (*BJ* II, 118, 433, VII, 253; *A* XVIII, 4–10, 25, XX, 102; Acts 5:37), the Egyptian (*BJ* II, 261–263; *A* XX, 169–172; Acts 21:38), and the Samaritan who wished to lead his followers to Mount Gerizim (*A* XVIII, 85–89; possibly related to Luke 13:1). The connections perhaps help us to understand better the entrance and the messianic activities of Jesus.[6] As Jesus was a Galilaean, an investigation of the connotations of the concept "Galilaean" in Josephus can also help to disclose certain characteristics of Jesus of Nazareth.[7] The descriptions of the Zealots by Josephus and in relevant passages in the New Testament probably also illuminate each other.[8] Even as complex a subject as the friendship for Rome by the Jew Josephus may perhaps allow one to understand better some pertinent features of the New Testament.[9]

Because the publication of the works of Josephus (ca. A.D. 75–96) as well as the editing of the New Testament partially overlapped and in each case extended over a long period of time, an interaction of some sort between Josephus and the early Christian church of the first century is not to be discounted. In other words, the influence or dependence of one text upon the other is quite possible; and this problem presents itself, above all, in the case of parallel reports. It has often been assumed that Luke made use of Josephus.[10] On the other hand, P. Fornaro[11] has presented the view that Josephus, with his representations of the passing of Moses (A IV, 326) and of Enoch and Elijah (A I, 85; IX, 28), created an indirect polemic against the views of the early church about the death and resurrection of Jesus of Nazareth. P. W. Barnett[12] concludes, from the affinities between the reports of Josephus about the prophetic miracle workers of the first century and the figure of Jesus, that Josephus in his description was influenced by the Jesus tradition.

Neither Fornaro nor Barnett is convincing in his hypothesis. It is more likely that the New Testament authors and the historian wrote independently of each other.[13] To be sure, it is inevitable that the similarity in content between Josephus' report about the destruction of Jerusalem and the relevant assertions in the Gospel of Luke should lead us to draw conclusions regarding the dating of Luke.[14] One cannot contest the legitimacy of such attempts, though the results are not certain, partially because varying premises must be taken into account. However, investigations regarding coincidences of literary peculiarity, as, for instance, between Luke and Josephus, move on a relatively secure terrain; and this area of research will, in the future, prove to be fruitful.[15]

II

Since the work of Origen and of Eusebius of Caesarea, the judgment that Josephus is of incalculable value as source material forced its way increasingly into the Christian church,[16] so that eventually one hears of Josephus as "a kind of fifth gospel"[17] and as a "little Bible."[18] Certainly the extant works of the Jewish author were valued for the most diverse reasons as an authoritative source regarding Judaica of all kinds. The *Jewish War* dominated the tastes of the Christian reading public so much that, in the tradition of the early church regarding Josephus' works, the *Jewish War,* the earliest chronologically, was transmitted under the title *Halosis* (i.e. conquest [of Jerusalem in the year 70]) and placed in manuscripts after the *Jewish Antiquities.* In this way, Jewish history, as seen from a Christian point of view, ended chronologically in a catastrophe that took place as a result of the Jews' rejection of Jesus. Even B. Niese adheres to this order of the works in his major critical edition (Berlin, 1885–1895).

Origen was the first to make use of the Jewish historian with apologetic zeal. On the basis of a reinterpretation of suitable passages (A XVIII, 118–

119; XX, 200; cf. XVIII, 63–64), he develops an anti-Jewish interpretation of the fall of Jerusalem (*GCS* 2.96, 33f.; 40.22, 7f.), according to which the Jews lost their homeland and their Temple in the year 70 on account of their crimes and their rejection of Jesus.[19] Eusebius goes even further. In his case, the anti-Jewish apologetic attains a surpassing importance. The tragic fate of the Jews in the year 70 and afterwards, as described in detail by Josephus, becomes for him a historical proof of the truth of Christianity (*GCS* 9.6, 9–11; 9.118, 10–12; 9.170, 23–24; 9.172, 3–11; 9.196–198). He does not shrink from falsifying the report of Josephus (*GCS* 9.198, 5–12, regarding *BJ* VI, 425–428) and speaks about a collective *servitus Judaeorum* ("servitude of the Jews") since the year 70 (*GCS* 23.349, 17–19). This collective servitude of the Jews is an unhistoric, apologetically motivated assertion; for the Jews of the Roman Empire, while they suffered in the course of late antiquity various legal disadvantages, remained, even under Christian emperors, free citizens in principle, and their cult remained a *religio licita*.[20]

Quite similarly, the church father Jerome utilizes the reports of Josephus (*CChr* 73.49, 1–12; 75.55, 47ff.; 75.58, 155ff.; 75.85, 1042–1044; *CSEL* 54.333, 16ff.; 55.489, 24ff.; cf. 56.173, 22–175, 6).[21] It is characteristic of the Christian appropriation of Josephus that Jerome includes him in his Christian history of literature, *De Viris Illustribus* (*PL* 23, 629–631). This chapter (cols. 629–631) was often selected, moreover, in the Christian Latin tradition of Josephus, as a substitute for the *Vita* of Josephus, which is the one work of Josephus that was not translated into Latin in antiquity. For before the Western world became acquainted with Josephus' autobiography, preserved only in Greek and edited by Arlenius as the editio princeps of the Greek text (Basel, 1544), this was the only comprehensive information about the life of the Jewish historian. How much Jerome himself esteems him one may glean from the way in which he refers to him in connection with exegetic problems as if to a manual of high rank: "Read the history of Josephus" (*CChr* 77.16, 207; cf. 73.198, 1). Isidor of Pelusium (*PG* 76.1136) and Frechulf of Lisieux (*PL* 106.1139) refer to Josephus in a similar manner. An ambivalent posture of early Christianity toward Josephus becomes especially clear in *Hegesippus,* a Latin revision of the Greek *Jewish War* (*CSEL* 66) that originated about 370. The Christian translator praises, on the one hand, the valuable deposition of the truth-loving Jew whose testimonial in favor of Jesus (i.e. *A* XVIII, 63–64) actually ought to oblige his fellow believers to turn to the Christian belief; but, on the other hand, he reproaches Josephus for his hardness of heart (*duritia cordis*) and for his stubborn disbelief (*perfidia*) (*CSEL* 66.1, 164; cf. 66.1, 3).[22]

The example of the Venerable Bede allows one to recognize the extent of the Christian reception of Josephus in the early Middle Ages; for, as to

Josephus' value as a faithful bearer of biblical Hebrew tradition, Bede places him side by side with Origen, Jerome, and Augustine (*PL* 94.675). From that time on, the Jew Josephus often achieves almost the authority of a church father.

III

After our look at the significance of Josephus for some important authors of early Christianity, there are still some general aspects to be noted that are significant for the developing and forever more intensive relationship between the church and the Jewish historian. The foremost guiding theme and the dominant characteristic of the reception and appropriation of Josephus by Christian writers become apparent. From the third century on, the writings of Josephus, above all, the *Jewish War,* appeared to Christian theologians to be a commentary or a historic appendix to the New Testament, like the welcomed documentation of the *veritas christiana,* and to be evidence of the substitution of the disinherited Jewish people by God's new people, the Christians, in the history of salvation. Partially because of the reception of Josephus, a consciousness of the superiority of Christianity, based not only on theology, but also on history, developed.

The victory of the Romans over the rebellious Zealots in the year 70 was considered, in a certain sense, almost as a victory of Christianity over Judaism, as the *Vindicta Salvatoris* ("the Revenge of the Savior") and as God's punishment of the stubborn Jews for their misdeeds against the redeemer.[23] This was already present in a preliminary way, so to speak, in the description and the theology of Josephus, above all in the *Jewish War.* As especially H. Lindner[24] has shown, the historian introduces reflections about the history of salvation relative to the contrast of Rome with the Zealots (the Jews). This happens in such a way that there could easily result an anti-Jewish debate among the theologians of the early church as soon as the arguments were taken out of their context and were transplanted to the Christian realm of thought. Indeed, it lay only too close at hand to regard the lack of repentance on the part of the stubborn Zealots, who had been reprimanded by Josephus (*BJ* I, 10; V, 415, 417), as stage scenery for viewing Christian ways of thinking. The reader was probably scarcely aware of the distortion on the part of the Jewish author or took it into account because the color of historic authenticity borrowed from Josephus gave a great power of conviction to the new Christian picture of history. Thus, at least partially, a model of the later anti-Judaism of Christian theologians could develop out of the anti-Zealotism of Josephus. Josephus' friendliness for Rome, visible in this anti-Zealotism, leads the Jewish historian to the conclusion that God had turned away from his disloyal, sinful people for an indefinite time and stood now on the side of the Romans and, indeed, even wished that the Jews be subject to Rome.

It cannot come as a surprise that in this connection the events before the fall of Jerusalem in the year 70 (*BJ* VI, 288–309) play a certain role. These omens and miracles were snatched up with special eagerness by the Christian theologians since the time of the early church because their evidence seemed almost to be situated on the same plateau as the corresponding prophecies of destruction in the New Testament (i.e., Luke 19:40–44, 21:20–24). They are arranged dramatically in the work of Josephus and were, therefore, far more impressive than the parallel account in Tacitus. On the whole, Josephus awakened, especially with his *Jewish War,* the emotions of his Christian readers; indeed, his depiction of the destruction of Jerusalem was in individual scenes composed almost like a tragedy and, especially at certain climaxes of the story, was perceived in just this way by Christian readers.[25] They felt horror and fright in the face of the Jewish catastrophe; they felt, at the same time, on account of the frequently moralizing historical view of Josephus, a certain edification and satisfaction in stationing themselves on the side favored by God. Historical dependability mattered little in this; and, so, in the case of the Christian appropriation of the Jewish historian, distortions and misrepresentations appear that are not unimportant and that are motivated apologetically. For instance, the artificial coincidence of the timing of the crime (the crucifixion of Jesus) and of the punishment (the destruction of Jerusalem) on Passover,[26] which Eusebius contrives and which numerous later Christian authors copy, is startling. In fact, the fall of Jerusalem did not take place in spring but, on the contrary, in midsummer.

Several elements of the pre-Christian anti-Judaism probably entered into the early Christian church.[27] Josephus reports often about these matters; and so, possibly, elements of this hostility toward Jews could also become known to the early church through the reports of the Jewish author and intensify or confirm Christian prejudices that were already present. The church likewise learned from the manner in which Josephus carried on a discussion with the non-Jewish contemporary world and with non-Jewish Greek authors, above all, in *Against Apion.*[28] This, however, is yet to be investigated.

The strong attraction, even fascination, which the works of Josephus held for the early church has various causes. As a kind of exegetic textbook they made more understandable many details of the Old and New Testaments. They also filled gaps of reporting or offered complete information and confirmation for the increasingly historically interested Christian theologians. Josephus' reports were all the more desirable since they came, so to speak, from the side of the antagonist. The detailed reports, for example, about the family of Herod and the Jewish sects, in addition to his often dramatic style and his treatment of the Jewish tradition according to the rules of Greek historiography, met the interests and tendencies of early Christianity obligingly—though Josephus had not really intended that—and he partially advanced these interests. The already tendentious development of historical material in the *Jewish War* favored a Christian-apologetic interpretation of the year 70 as the end of the history of the Jewish people, whose remnants must live in perpetual servitude as an atonement for the crimes that they had committed.

Thus, Christian theologians utilized Josephus to account for an anti-Jewish interpretation of the history of salvation, in which the Jewish historian's real intentions were distorted. In sum, the reception of Josephus is of great importance for the intellectual history of the early Christian church. Current interests bring about a new formulation of problems, for instance the question concerning the similar and different ways of viewing biblical tradition in the New Testament and Josephus. Moreover, the history of the early reception of Josephus can continue to lead to new exegetic knowledge, when, even more than hitherto, Josephus, as well as Philo, is read as a commentary on the New Testament.

—Translated by Henry Regensteiner

Notes

1. First efforts in the interest of a literary and sociological investigation of the works of Josephus are found in Eva M. Sanford's "Propaganda and Censorship in the Transmission of Josephus," *TAPA* 66 (1935), 127–145. H. Schreckenberg continues this research in his *Die Flavius-Josephus-Tradition in Antike und Mittelalter*, Leiden, 1972; *Rezeptionsgeschichtliche und textkritische Untersuchungen zu Flavius Josephus*, Leiden, 1977; and, especially, "Josephus und die christliche Wirkungsgeschichte seines 'Bellum Judaicum,'" *ANRW* 2, pt. 21, sec. 2, ed. by W. Haase, Berlin, New York, 1984, pp. 1106–1217 (further bibliography given there). Comprehensive bibliographical information concerning Josephus can be found in L. H. Feldman, *Studies in Judaica: Scholarship on Philo and Josephus (1937–1962)*, New York, 1963; H. Schreckenberg, *Bibliographie zu Flavius Josephus*, Leiden, 1968 (supplementary volume, 1979); *Bibliographie zur jüdisch-hellenistischen und intertestamentarischen Literatur. 1900–1970*, ed. by G. Delling, Berlin, 1975² (pp. 80–94: "Josephus"); M. Mor and U. Rappaport, *Bibliography of Works on Jewish History in the Hellenistic and Roman Periods 1976–1980*, Jerusalem, 1982 (pp. 57–63: "Josephus Flavius"); L. H. Feldman, *Josephus and Modern Scholarship (1937–1980)*, Berlin, New York, 1984 (cf. *ANRW* 2, pt. 21, sec. 2, pp. 763–862). Good general information is given in *Josephus Flavius, Historian of Eretz-Israel in the Hellenistic-Roman Period: Collected Papers*, ed. by U. Rappaport, Jerusalem, 1982; and by T. Rajak, *Josephus: The Historian and His Society*, London, 1983.

2. Cf. H. Schreckenberg, "Flavius Josephus und die lukanischen Schriften," in *Wort in der Zeit: Neutestamentliche Studien, Festgabe für K. H. Rengstorf*, ed. by W. Haubeck and M. Bachmann, Leiden, 1980, pp. 179–209; Schreckenberg, *Die christlichen Adversus-Judaeos-Texte und ihr literarisches und historisches Umfeld (1.–11. Jh.)*, Frankfurt am Main, Bern, 1982, pp. 115–118.

3. The *Testimonium Flavianum* (*A* XVIII, 63–64), in view of its questionable authenticity, is in itself a difficult problem that cannot be discussed here in greater detail. Pertaining to it, though, see P. Bilde ("Josefus' beretning om Jesus," *DTT* 44 [1981], 99–135), who, like most of

his predecessors, expresses himself convincingly against the *Testimonium*'s authenticity; cf. Schreckenberg, *Die christlichen Adversus-Judaeos-Texte,* (above, n. 2) pp. 311, 383 and elsewhere. The *Testimonium* documents how far the early church's joy at discovery went: a fictitious text was introduced into the genuine Josephus tradition because it was thought that it must, indeed, have been present in the work of the Jewish historian. Recently A. Strobel has drawn attention to *A* XX, 200–203, in a noteworthy manner, in *Die Stunde der Wahrheit: Untersuchungen zum Strafverfahren gegen Jesus,* Tübingen, 1980 (pp. 31–36: "Josephus über die Hinrichtung des Jacobus"). Cf., in addition, D. Flusser, *Die letzten Tage Jesu in Jerusalem,* Stuttgart, 1982, pp. 155–163; and A. Feuillet, "Flavius Josèphe, témoin des origines chrétiennes, a-t-il parlé du Christ?," *E & V* 93 (1983), 532–539; moreover, T. Middendorp, "Het geheim van de Messias bij Josephus," *SK* 4 (1983), 41–58 (*A* XVIII, 63–64, is a later, Christian adaptation of an originally incidental observation); E. Nodet, "Jesus et Jean-Baptiste selon Josèphe," *RB* 92 (1985), 321–348, 497–524; a good description of this field of research is given by J. N. Birdsall, "The Continuing Enigma of Josephus' Testimony about Jesus," *BJRL* 67 (1985), 609–622.

    4. Cf. on this subject R. T. France, "Herod and the Children of Bethlehem," *NT* 21 (1979), 98–120; and C. Saulnier, "Hérode Antipas et Jean le Baptiste. Quelques remarques sur le confusions chronologiques des Flavius Josèphe," *RB* 91 (1984), 362–376.

    5. A discussion of the numerous thematic affinities is found in Schreckenberg, "Flavius Josephus und die lukanischen Schriften", above, n. 2.

    6. Cf. D. Hill, "Jesus and Josephus' 'Messianic Prophets,'" in *Text and Interpretation: Studies in the New Testament presented to M. Black,* Cambridge, 1979, pp. 143–154, and P. W. Barnett, "The Jewish Sign Prophets—A.D. 40–70—Their Intentions and Origins," *NTS* 27 (1981), 679–697. Also to be mentioned here is B. Noack, *Jesus Ananiassøn og Jesus fra Nasaret. En drøftelse af Josefus, Bellum Judaicum VI, 5, 3,* Copenhagen, 1975, concerning the strange figure of Jesus, son of Ananias (Chananja), *BJ* VI, 300–309. With regard to this Jesus, cf. Strobel, *Die Stunde der Wahrheit* (above, n. 3), pp. 24–25.

    7. On this point, see F. X. Malinowski, "Torah Tendencies in Galilean Judaism According to Flavius Josephus with Gospel Comparisons", *BTB* 10 (1980), 30–36; P. Bilde, "Galilaea og galilaerne på Jesu tid," *DTT* 43 (1980), 113–135; and J. R. Armenti, "On the Use of the Term 'Galileans' in the Writings of Josephus Flavius: A Brief Note," *JQR* 72 (1981–1982), 45–49. The fruitful discussion is carried forward by L. H. Feldman, "The Term 'Galileans' in Josephus," *JQR* 72 (1981–1982), 50–52; and by G. Jossa, "Chi sono i Galilei nella 'Vita' di Flavio Giuseppe?," *RiBi* 31 (1983), 329–339.

    8. Cf. W. Stenger, "Bemerkungen zum Begriff 'Räuber' im Neuen Testament und bei Flavius Josephus," *BK* 37 (1982), 89–97.

    9. B. J. Hubbard, "Luke, Josephus and Rome: A Comparative Approach to the Lukan 'Sitz im Leben,'" in *SBLSP,* 1979, I, ed. by P. J. Achtemeier, Missoula, Montana, 1979, pp. 59–68, pertaining to this relationship between Luke and Josephus. More problematical but, nevertheless, worthwhile, if weighed methodically, are literary and structural comparisons from the point of view of historical genre, for instance between the editorial technique of Luke and that of Josephus, as they are proposed by F. G. Downing, "Redaction Criticism: Josephus' 'Antiquities' and the Synoptic Gospels," *JSNT* 8 (1980), 46–65, and 9 (1980), 29–48. A cautious step in the same direction has been taken by M. Hengel, *Zur urchristlichen Geschichtsschreibung,* Stuttgart, 1979, pp. 36–39.

    10. See, above all, M. Krenkel (*Josephus und Lukas: Der schriftstellerische Einfluss des jüdischen Geschichts schreibers auf den christlichen nachgewiesen,* Leipzig, 1894) and his successors; cf. Schreckenberg, "Flavius Josephus und die lukanischen Schriften" (above, n. 2), p. 182. Most recently, F. Parente has expressed himself similarly (concerning Acts 21:38; *BJ* II, 261–263; and *A* XX, 160–166) in "L'episodio dell' Egiziano in Acta 21.38: Qualche osser-

vazione sulla possibile dipendenza degli Atti degli Apostoli da Flavio Giuseppe," *RIL* 112 (1978), 360–376.

11. P. Fornaro, "Il Cristianesimo oggetto di polemica indiretta in Flavio Giuseppe (Ant. Jud. IV 326)," *RSC* 27 (1979), pp. 431–446. Also A. Paul, "Flavius Josephus' 'Antiquities of the Jews': An Anti-Christian Manifesto," *NTS* 31 (1985), 473–480, tries to reveal some anti-Christian tendencies in Josephus. The results are not yet convincing, and the issue needs further discussion.

12. P. W. Barnett, "The Jewish Sign Prophets" (above, n. 6), pp. 679–697.

13. This is an important result of research in Schreckenberg, "Flavius Josephus und die lukanischen Schriften," above n. 2.

14. See, most recently, in this context, H. Staudinger, "Die Zerstörung Jerusalems bei Flavius Josephus und im Evangelium des Lukas: Ein Beitrag zur Frage der Datierung des Lukasevangeliums," *IDIBW* 19 (1981), 179–180. Staudinger's conclusion is that Luke wrote prior to the year 70.

15. Good beginnings for a literary-critical and stylistic comparative study between Luke and Josephus are to be found in the work of E. Plümacher, *Lukas als hellenistischer Schriftsteller: Studien zur Apostelgeschichte*, Göttingen, 1972, pp. 9–10, 62–63, 99–100; cf. also, e.g., A. Schlatter in the work of H. Schreckenberg, *Bibliographie zu Flavius Josephus* (supplementary volume), Leiden, 1979, p. 124. On the whole, comparative studies can help to understand better certain peculiarities in Luke as well as in Josephus. See, e.g., F. G. Downing, "Common Ground with Paganism in Luke and Josephus," *NTS* 28 (1982), 546–559.

16. See the pertinent documents of the church fathers in the work of Schreckenberg, *Die Flavius-Josephus-Tradition* (above, n. 1), pp. 70ff., and *Rezeptionsgeschichtliche und textkritische Untersuchungen* (above, n. 1), pp. 13ff. It was probably in the third century, in the period between Origen, who did not know it yet in the form in which we have it, and Eusebius, who cites it for the first time, that the *Testimonium Flavianum* (*A* XVIII, 63–64) was interpolated or forged.

17. T. Keim, *Aus dem Urchristentum*, vol. 1, Zürich, 1878 (in the chapter "Josephus im Neuen Testament," pp. 1–27), p. 1.

18. J. Berggren, *Bibel und Josephus über Jerusalem und das Heilige Grab*, Lund, 1862, p. xii; cf. Schreckenberg, "Flavius Josephus und die lukanischen Schriften" (above, n. 2), p. 179.

19. Concerning this, see Schreckenberg, *Die christlichen Adversus-Judaeos-Texte* (above, n. 2), p. 233; as to Eusebius, see there, pp. 266f.

20. Schreckenberg, *Die christlichen Adversus-Judaeos-Texte* (above, n. 2), index, p. 729. The apologetic procedure of Eusebius in his *Ecclesiastical History* is described correctly by E. Schwartz, *Griechische Geschichtsschreiber*, Leipzig, 1959², p. 538: "Der Gewährsmann ist bis zur Zerstörung Jerusalems fast ausschliesslich Josephus, in den durch geschickte Auswahl der Exzerpte Eusebius seinen Standpunkt hineinträgt." Cf. the equally cogent evaluation by R. M. Grant, *Eusebius as Church Historian*, Oxford, 1980, p. 111: "Whenever Eusebius is making statements about the theological-historical importance of the Jewish people in the first century, he relies on ideas already set forth first by Josephus and then by Origen"; and p. 39: "He frequently uses Josephus' accounts to confirm the historical truth of the scriptures." Cf. Grant, pp. 29ff., 100ff., 128ff., 147ff., and *idem*, "Eusebius, Josephus and the Fate of the Jews," *SBLSP*, 1979, II, ed. by P. J. Achtemeier, Missoula, Montana, 1979, pp. 69–86. M. Pavan ("La distruzione di Gerusalemme nella storiografia cristiana," *CS* 21 [1982], pp. 250–255) compares the pertinent report of Josephus with those of Christian theologians.

21. Cf. Schreckenberg, *Die christlichen Adversus-Judaeos-Texte* (above, n. 2), pp. 310f., 336ff., concerning *Hegesippus*.

22. Concerning *Hegesippus*, see A. A. Bell, "Classical and Christian Traditions in the Work of Pseudo-Hegesippus," *ISSQ* 33 (1980), 60–64.

23. In the course of Christian antiquity there develops, often in connection with the reception of Josephus, a Christian view of retaliation that culminates in the fiction and legend of the *vindicta*-genre, according to which Vespasian and Titus march into the Holy Land, almost as crusaders, on a mission of punishment and retribution. Concerning this, see Schreckenberg, *Die christlichen Adversus-Judaeos-Texte* (above, n. 2), pp. 463–465.

24. See H. Lindner, *Die Geschichtsauffassung des Flavius Josephus im Bellum Judaicum: Gleichzeitig ein Beitrag zur Quellenfrage*, Leiden, 1972. To be sure, Lindner goes, here and there, too far with his interpretations, no matter how obvious they are fundamentally. The same theme is treated with more reserve by P. Fornaro, *Flavio Giuseppe, Tacito e l'impero (Bellum Judaicum VI, 284–315; Historiae V 13)*, Turin, 1980. Fornaro contrasts Tacitus' anti-Judaism with the attitude of Josephus and interprets the latter's friendliness toward Rome in such a way that Josephus recognizes the superiority of the Romans as ordained by God and hopes for a future of Judaism, even without a temple, within the framework of the Roman Empire.

25. Cf., e.g., Basil the Great (*PG* 31, 324) concerning Mary's devouring of her child (*BJ* VI, 201–213): τοῦτο τὸ δρᾶμα ᾿Ιουδαϊκὴ ἐτραγῴδησεν ἱστορία, ἣν ᾿Ιώσηπος ἡμῖν ὁ σπουδαῖος συνεγράψατο. Cf. John Chrysostom (*PG* 58, 695): πᾶσαν ἐνίκησε τραγῳδίαν ἐκεῖνα τὰ δεινά. Furthermore, Isidor of Pelusium says (*PG* 78, 968) that the sorrowful fate of the Jews should serve the world as a tragic spectacle.

26. Cf. Eusebius, *GCS*, 9.198, 5–12, concerning *BJ* VI, 425–428: so that they might receive the appropriate punishment, the Jews had to be punished on exactly the same days (i.e., on the Passover holiday) during which they had let Jesus suffer.

27. Schreckenberg, *Die christlichen Adversus-Judaeos-Texte* (above, n. 2), p. 32.

28. Concerning this subject see C. Schäublin, "Josephus und die Griechen," *Hermes* 110 (1982), 316–341. Schäublin (p. 327) emphasizes correctly the biting criticism that Josephus has for the Greek religion and for the monstrosities of Greek mythology. Cf. p. 341: The quarrel between the Jews and the Greeks paves the way, in some respects, for the controversy between Christians and Greeks.

15 Origen and Josephus

WATARU MIZUGAKI

I

*t*he relationship between Origen (ca. 185–253/4), the greatest church father of the ancient Christian church prior to Augustine, and Josephus, the Jewish historian who was about 150 years senior to him, is one of paramount interest and significance. Although not the first to mention Josephus' name, Origen was the first to incorporate Josephus into Bible interpretation and Christian apologetics and thus the first to mention him substantially and meaningfully. His treatment of Josephus had a lasting influence on later generations. Origen's references to Josephus were not accidental or passing. Hence, it is necessary to analyze the extent of his knowledge of Josephus.

Among the ancients, Origen was almost legend for producing so many volumes that no one could possibly read them all. A majority of his works are devoted to the elucidation of the Bible. First in Alexandria and then in Caesarea in Palestine, he lectured freely on varied disciplines in the schools he conducted, in which he emphasized the exposition of the Bible as the center of education. His lectures were published as the *Commentaries,* and the practical and edifying preachings based on it were published as the *Homilies.* There are other Bible studies, which are extant as *Excerpts,* as well as his textual criticism, which resulted in the *Hexapla.* Despite the fact that a substantial number of his works on the Bible are missing, and many are extant only in Latin, it is evident that his studies covered almost all the books of the Bible. Among these are commentaries on the histories and the prophets in the Old Testament, and the gospels in the New Testament, which he might have clarified even further if he had made a more thorough study of Josephus.

The purport of Josephus' works was of an enlightening and apologetic order—to refute the prevalent slanders and accusations against the Jews as groundless by proving the honorable and noble lineage of the Jews. Likewise, there are works by Origen that were counterarguments against the anti-Christian criticisms. *Contra Celsum*, Origen's last masterpiece, was an apology intended to refute exhaustively Celsus' fierce and tenacious criticism against Christianity. It is only natural that there is a common denominator between the criticisms against the Jews and those against Christianity, which, from the very beginning, accepted the Old Testament as the Bible. It is, therefore, no wonder that the issues of and the arguments applied in anti-Semitic attacks were adapted to those against Christianity. In Origen's day, anti-Jewish criticism, and the issues and counterarguments employed against it, were incorporated in the criticism and defense of Christianity. All of these arguments and counterarguments became a heritage of certain *topoi* with consistent patterns. Thus, it is no surprise to find an apology for Christianity accompanying that of Judaism.[1] Consequently, there was ample possibility for Josephus' apology to become a case study for Christian apology. Viewed from a perspective that embraces the history of the apologies of Judaism and Christianity, Josephus and Origen may be treated together. Within this context, Origen's allusions to Josephus' works, which are found in his apology *Contra Celsum*, have a special significance.

Origen was not merely a man of letters or an educator who walked only between his study and school. Unlike Kant, who hardly ever left Königsberg, Origen was versed in world geography and traveled widely. He had great experience and knowledge of the Mediterranean world, having visited Rome, Arabia, Caesarea, Antioch, and Greece. Most of his journeys must have been for church purposes, but they certainly also provided him opportunities to acquire, with his strong curiosity and quickness of mind, considerable mastery of the language and knowledge of the history, geography and general customs of the lands he visited. These were the major sites of the founding and the development of Christianity. It is scarcely imaginable that, traveling through the lands where Peter and Paul had evangelized and where the blood of the martyrs was shed, he would not be reminded of these incidents. Moreover, Palestine, which Origen once visited and where he would spend many of his later years, was the site of the dramas of the Old Testament. It takes little imagination to think that Origen, who was always paying great attention to the Old Testament text, should recall its characters, places, and incidents in association with his actual experiences. This granted, it may also be said that if he were a reader of Josephus, he should have reflected on Josephus' vivid descriptions, along with those of the Old Testament.

Of course, Origen was by no means an empiricist in the modern sense of the word, but neither was he a Gnostic who, having absorbed himself in his speculation, drew elaborate allegorical interpretations. As is seen in his being accused of ignoring the historical aspect of the Bible, not only by the Jews and the Gnostics but also by those within his church, he was generally reputed to have slighted historic facts.[2] It is true that the so-called Alexandrian fathers, such as Clement of Alexandria and Origen, lacked interest in history in its strictly academic sense. Clement, as well as Origen, did not touch purely historic researches, such as the *Chronicles* by Julius Africanus, a friend of Origen.[3] The absence of Origen's commentary on Acts might be related to such a lack of historic interest.[4] Origen, however, did pay due attention to the vocabulary and historic meaning of the Bible. Even when such attention may not be apparent in his Bible commentaries, it should not be concluded that he shows a deficiency of historic interest. Rather, in his case, interest in historic facts is sublimated to the level of the eternal and the spiritual. It would be unreasonable to discount the relationship between him and Josephus the historian, inasmuch as Origen had actual experience and knowledge earned from travel and gave consideration to the historical meaning of the Bible.

Origen's stay in Rome is most significant when we examine his relationship with Josephus. According to Eusebius' *Church History,* Book 6, 14, 10–11, Origen sojourned in Rome for a while when Zephyrinus was bishop of the Roman Church.[5] Eusebius explains the purpose of this journey as Origen's desire "to see the most ancient churches of the Romans," citing Origen's own words. This very phrase demonstrates his interest in history. This interest was probably directed not only at the church in Rome. There were several libraries, founded by the emperors, in Rome at that time.[6] It is certain that at least one of them kept the works of Josephus, who published books under the auspices of the emperor in Rome. Although there is no evidence that Origen visited these libraries during his stay in Rome, it would be the logical place where he could have derived and deepened such knowledge, since he was acquainted with Josephus' works and even cited from them. On the other hand, Clement, who was active in Alexandria, merely testifies that there is a piece on Jewish history by Josephus (*Stromateis,* I 147, 2) and does not treat it substantially. Moreover, it is revealing that Origen possessed a considerable knowledge concerning Judaism through direct contacts with rabbis. The relationship between Origen and the Jews is elucidated by the research by N. R. M. de Lange and H. Bietenhard.[7]

Although these observations are based upon some speculations, they show that conditions existed for Origen to have a knowledge of Josephus, because of his background and interests, to a greater degree than the church fathers prior to or contemporary with him. Especially noteworthy is that, unlike those of other apologists, Origen's themes were closely related with the Bible (Old Testament) and the Jews.[8] In fact, Origen has a closer affinity with Josephus than do Justin, Irenaeus, Clement of Alexandria, Tertullian, and Hippolytus. Based upon these preliminary observations, this essay attempts to clarify Origen's attitude toward Josephus by analyzing the passages in which Origen refers to Josephus by name.

II

Let us first examine the nature of Origen's knowledge of Josephus. He cites Josephus by explicitly mentioning his name in eleven instances:

1. *Fragmenta et selecta in Psalmos*, LXXIII 5–6 (*PG* 12, 1529 D). Greek.
2. *Commentarii in Canticum Canticorum*, Lib. 2, Cant. 1, 5 (*GCS* 8, 116). Latin.
3. *Selecta et fragmenta in Ieremiam*, Nr. 14, Jer. 22, 24–26 (*GCS* 3, 204–205). Greek.
4. *Fragmenta in Lamentationes*, Nr. 105, Lam. 4, 10 (*GCS* 3, 273). Greek.
5. *Ibid.*, Nr. 109, Lam. 4, 14 (*GCS* 3, 274). Greek.
6. *Ibid.*, Nr. 115, Lam. 4, 19 (*GCS* 3, 275). Greek.
7. *Contra Celsum*, I 16 (*GCS* 1, 68). Greek.
8. *Ibid.*, I 47 (*GCS* 1, 97). Greek.
9. *Ibid.*, II 13 (*GCS* 1, 143). Greek.
10. *Ibid.*, IV 11 (*GCS* 1, 281). Greek.
11. *Commentarii in Matthaeum*, X 17 (*GCS* 10, 22). Greek.[9]

In view of the fact that a majority of Origen's works are extant only in Latin translation, it is quite peculiar that almost all of the references to Josephus (ten out of eleven) are in the original Greek, which is hardly accountable to pure chance. This is further reinforced by the fact that in *Fragmenta in Lamentationes* and *Contra Celsum*, comprising nearly two-thirds of all the references in Origen of Josephus' works, the citations are found in the Greek version. It must have been necessary for Origen to mention Josephus more frequently here than in other works. This will be analyzed extensively later.

Origen spells Josephus' name Ἰώσηπος. In some manuscripts, a different form, Ἰώσηππος, is also found. There are seven passages in which this spelling is used (1, 3, 4, 5, 6, 8, and 9). Φλαβίος Ἰώσηπος and Φλαύιος Ἰώσηπος appear in *Contra Celsum* (passages 7 and 10) and in *Commentarii in Matthaeum* (passage 11), which are his later works. This means that in *Contra Celsum*, both Ἰώσηπος and Φλαύιος Ἰώσηπος are employed. While Clement of Alexandria calls Josephus "Phlauios Iosepos the Jew" (*Stromateis*, I 147, 2), Origen simply writes "Iosepos" or "Phlauios Iosepos," without adding an explantory "the Jew" (ὁ Ἰουδαῖος).

Origen is thoroughly versed in Josephus' works. He knows the correct appellation Ἰουδαικὴ Ἀρχαιολογία for *Jewish Antiquities* (passages 8 and 11), and refers to it more simply as Ἀρχαιολογία (passage 3). He is aware that this work consists of twenty books (passage 11). In the Latin translation of *Commentarii in Canticum Canticorum* by Rufinus, there is a mention of the

Jewish Antiquities as "historia sua," but since this is by Rufinus, who makes considerably liberal translations, this can hardly be called the title of a book. The *Jewish War* is referred to as ἡ τῶν Ἱεροσολύμων ἅλωσις, (passage 1) or τὰ περὶ ἁλώσεως (passage 4) and τά ἁλώσεως (passage 5). These correspond to the title in the many manuscripts of this work. *Against Apion* is called "the work in two books concerning the antiquity of the Jews" (περὶ τῆς τῶν Ἰουδαίων ἀρχαιότη τος δύο βιβλία) or ἐν δυσίν instead of δύο βιβλία (passages 7 and 10). Origen, therefore, knew three works by Josephus but not his *Vita*.

When Origen refers to Josephus, he rarely gives the exact passage of his quote. For example, in *Selecta et fragmenta in Ieremiam* (passage 3) he writes, "Josephus [also says] so in the tenth book of *Jewish Antiquities*"; and in *Contra Celsum*, he states, "Josephus testifies in the eighteenth book of *Jewish Antiquities*" (passage 8). The original passages of the first quote are found in X, 82 and X, 97, in *Jewish Antiquities* and that of the second in XVIII, 116–119. Thus, Origen correctly acknowledges his references.

The terms he uses to introduce Josephus are "says" (λέγει; passage 7),[10] "writes" (γράφει; passage 9), "testifies" (μαρτυρεῖ; passage 8), "stated" (ἀναγράψαντα; passage 11), and "transmitted" (παρέδωκεν; passage 4), but the most significant is ἱστορεῖ. "Josephus records" (Ἰώσηπος ἱστορεῖ) is a formula that is found in passages 1, 5, and 6. In *Fragmenta et selecta in Psalmos* (passage 1) it is written that "all these were accomplished in the capture of Jerusalem—exactly as Josephus records in detail," in reference to the passage in Psalms 74:5 (Septuagint 73:6): "At the upper entrance they hacked the wooden trellis with axes." ἱστορεῖ is related to the historical approach of "recording all the incidents in detail" (καθένα διηγούμενος τῶν πεπραγμένων). In his *Fragmenta in Lamentationes* (passage 4), moreover, Origen writes that "Josephus accurately transmitted in *On the Capture*" (μετ' ἀκριβείας Ἰώσηππος ἐν τοῖς περὶ ἁλώσεως παρέδωκεν) that the women killed and ate their children, in reference to the passage in Lamentations 4:10. Furthermore, Origen appreciates Josephus by noting that he has "researched on the cause of the fall of Jerusalem and the destruction of the temple" (ζητῶν τὴν αἰτίαν τῆς τῶν Ἱεροσολύμων πτώσεως καὶ τῆς τοῦ ναοῦ καθαιρέσεως; passage 8) and concludes that Josephus is "not far from the truth" (οὐ μακρὰν τῆς ἀληθείας; passage 8) in concluding that the reason for the calamity was the assassination of James the Just by the Jews. Similarly, in *Commentarii in Matthaeum*, Origen states that Josephus cites the assassination of James the Just as the cause of the same calamity, "wishing to present the cause" (τὴν αἰτίαν παραστῆσαι βουλόμενον; passage 11).[11] It must be noted here that the phrases Origen uses to evaluate Josephus, such as "search for the cause," "accuracy," and "truth," are the ones used by the ancient Greek historians, such as Thucydides; and they became the fundamental terms used for historical studies. Therefore, it may be said that Origen esteems Josephus as a historian who explores the causes of incidents, makes correct judgments on the truth, and presents them accurately in detail.

Origen, however, rarely treats Josephus' accounts as such. Rather, he simply mentions that Josephus also states something about the matter he himself is dealing with and does not touch on the content itself (passages 1 and 3); or he encourages the readers who have more interest in the theme in question to refer to Josephus' text (passages 7 and 10); or he alludes to Josephus, merely adding a simple summary explanation (passages 6, 7, 8, and 9). It is in passages 2 and 11 that he draws on Josephus somewhat extensively. We would like to analyze passage 4, in which Origen interprets the Bible employing Josephus' account and terminology. As is seen above, Origen usually paraphrases Josephus' account. The fact that he suggests that his readers refer directly to Josephus in *Contra Celsum* shows that Josephus' works were well known and available. In other places, too, Origen's treatment of Josephus assumes a certain amount of knowledge about Josephus on the part of his readers and a situation in which Josephus' works are within easy reach.

This did not, however, mean that there was no necessity for him to introduce fully the works by Josephus. In *Lamentationes* (passage 5), Origen cites the *Jewish War* VI, 299–300. Origen says, "Josephus records as follows in *On the Capture:* The priests on entering the Temple by night, as their custom was in the discharge of their ministrations, reported that they were conscious, first of a commotion and after that of a voice as of a host, 'depart hence.'"
(νύκτωρ οἱ ἱερεῖς προσελθόντες εἰς τὸ ἱερόν, ὥσπερ αὐτοῖς ἔθος ἦν πρὸς τὰς λειτουργίας, πρῶτον μὲν κινήσεως ἔφασαν ἀντιλαμβάνεσθαι μετὰ δὲ ταῦτα φωνῆς ἀθρόας μεταβαίνωμεν ἐντευθεν.)

The discrepancies between Origen's and Josephus' texts (as in Loeb Classical Library) are as follow:

Origen	Josephus
1. προσελθόντες εἰς τὸ ἱερόν	παρελθόντες εἰς τὸ ἔνδον ἱερόν
2. ἔθος ἦν	ἔθος
3. ἀντιλαμβάνεσθαι	ἀντιλαβέσθαι καὶ κτύπου
4. μεταβαίνωμεν	μεταβαίνομεν

The second and fourth changes are negligible. Some manuscripts of Josephus read, as in Origen's case, μεταβαίνωμεν. The first and third show more significant changes—in both cases Origen makes minor cuts from Josephus' original text. As we shall see later, these cuts may have been done to suit his purpose. Nevertheless, the alterations are not so total as to change the whole as citations. Rather, Origen generally makes faithful citations. He neither summarizes Josephus' passages nor changes them to indirect speech;

he just quotes Josephus' texts as they are. This also serves as a proof that Origen was acquainted with Josephus' original texts.

The major purpose of Origen's references to Josephus is, by employing his detailed historical account, to endorse and fortify his own interpretation of the Bible. In *Selecta et fragmenta in Ieremiam* (passage 3), Origen deals with the incident where the Pharaoh Neco changes the name of Josiah's son Eliakim to Jehoiakim (2 Kings 23:34) and states that the Babylonian king exiled Jehoiakim, "as had been predicted by this prophet." He furthermore adds that "Josephus also [says so] in the tenth book of *Jewish Antiquities.*" This is an attempt at supporting the explanation given in the Bible by citing Josephus. The passage from *Lamentationes* is similar. Origen writes, "Josephus also refers [to this] by adding as follows" ("etiam Iosepum . . . facere mentionem addentem etiam hoc, quod"). The "also" (καὶ; *etiam*), too, reinforces the text.

The previous argument endorses the following statement by Harnack concerning citations of Josephus by Origen: "Origen, unlike Clemens and Tertullian, does not explicitly (or implicitly) cite a large quantity. He, rather, tries to avoid citation; it is only when necessary to prove a certain thing that he quotes. This is how he cites Josephus and Philo." [12]

III

The reference to Josephus in *Fragmenta in Lamentationes* is of primary interest. The third volume, pp. 235–278, of *Origenes Werke* in *GCS* contains 118 fragments edited by Klostermann. Although there are commentaries up to the fourth chapter of the Lamentations, none on the fifth chapter is extant. Since Eusebius mentions "those on Lamentations, of which there have come to us five tomes" (*Church History* 6, 24, 2), it must have been a greater work than what is left to us now. From this we may conclude that there were more references to Josephus than the three found among the 118 fragments. At any rate, in proportion to the remaining fragments, this chapter contains the highest frequency of references to Josephus among all of the extant works of Origen. In this respect, there are more references in it than in *Contra Celsum*, in which at least four explicit references are made. It is worthy of note that *Lamentationes*, which can be characterized as having the most references to Josephus among Origen's works, was written early in Origen's career as a writer. As Eusebius asserts in the previous passage (*Church History* 6, 24) that Origen states in the ninth volume of his commentary on Genesis that he has completed in Alexandria the first eight volumes of the same commentary, commentaries on Psalms 1 to 25, and *Fragmenta in Lamentationes* before working on this ninth volume, this commentary must have been finished by A.D. 232 at the latest. [13] Why was Lamentations treated at approximately the same time as Genesis and Psalms, which are significant and inspiring books, while the studies of Jeremiah, which is closely related to the Lamentations, were conducted much later?[14] Unfortunately this question is not answered.

Fragment 105 of *Fragmenta in Lamentationes* explains Lamentations 4:10. The Revised Standard Version reads, "The hands of compassionate women have boiled their own children; they became their food in the destruction of the daughter of my people." The word for "boiled" is ἥψησαν in the Septuagint. Here, Origen notes that "to burn" (τὸ ἥψαν) means "to burn and to roast" (τὸ ἀνάψαι καὶ ὀπτῆσαι) and states that this happened when the Romans besieged Jerusalem. Origen writes that in *On the Capture,* Josephus accurately relates the annihilation of the Jewish race, which is bewailed in Lamentations. Origen here refers the horrible events that accompanied the siege of the city (*BJ* VI, 199). Josephus details "an act . . . as horrible to relate as it is incredible to hear"—a woman named Maria escapes to Jerusalem and finding herself involved in the siege and being cornered into an extreme situation where she has nothing to eat, kills her own son from anger and hunger, and then "having roasted the body and devoured half of it, she covered up and stored the remainder." (*BJ* VI, 208). Josephus uses ὀπτήσασα for "to roast." This means that Origen explains the τὸ ἥψαν in the Lamentations by adding the concrete image of τὸ ὀπτῆσαι by Josephus. Thus, Origen juxtaposes the fall of Jerusalem to the Romans and the ancient fall of Jerusalem some six hundred years before by stressing the similarity of the two situations through the use of Josephus' report concerning a later age to interpret the incident of an earlier age.

Fragment 109 (passage 5 above) concerns Lamentations 4:14. The Revised Standard Version reads thus: "They wandered, blind, through the streets, so defiled with blood that none could touch their garments." But Origen, following the Septuagint, discusses this according to Symmachus' interpretation. The Septuagint reads, "Her [Jerusalem's] awakened ones staggered" (ἐσαλεύθησαν ἐγρήγοροι, αὐτῆς). Origen asserts that the "awakened ones" are, according to the Bible, the angels (ἄγγελοι), and that the laws of Moses were probably given through them. The angels were supposed to have stayed in the Temple of Jerusalem to do their duty, but they "withdrew shivering" (σαλευθέντες μετέστησαν). It is here that Origen quotes the *Jewish War* VI, 299–300, almost verbatim. The call, "Now, let us leave this place" (μετα-βαίνωμεν ἐνθεῦθεν), which is reported by Josephus as being heard by the priests, is associated with the departure of the angels. Origen clearly considers the strange voices in the Temple, which are one of the many omens prior to the fall of Jerusalem, as the angels' voices announcing their departure from the Temple. Therefore, Origen omits the phrase καὶ κτύπον in Josephus because the phrase right before it, "they were conscious, first of a commotion," is appropriate to the departure of the angels, but καὶ κτύπου is not. Origen believes that the escape of the angels decisively marks the Temple's and, eventually, the city's fall. It is by the same token that he, in his citation, alters Josephus' original text, "into the inner court of the Temple" (εἰς τὸ ἔνδον ἱερόν), to "into the Temple" (εἰς τὸ ἱερόν). Again, the fate of the Temple itself is significant. This is because to Origen, the elimination of the Temple is related to the coming of Jesus. Origen alludes to the Septuagint, Genesis 49:10, and interprets it as "the one who was awaited by all the nations" has arrived, and so "they departed" (ἐξέλιπον).

Both here and in fragment 105, Origen compares the incidents of A.D. 70 with those of Lamentations, which occurred in the sixth century B.C., and interprets them together. The basis for such a view is the theological interpretation that the angels' departure from the Temple is an omen of the fall of the Temple, and this fall is a necessity accompanying the arrival of the Christ within the framework of redemptive history. This is why Origen is strongly attracted by Josephus' detailed description of the destruction of the Temple. In *Selecta et fragmenta in Psalmos* (passage 1), Origen asserts that "all these were accomplished in the capture of Jerusalem. This is exactly so as Josephus reports it in detail." Origen's statement concerns the passage in the Septuagint, Psalms 73:6, that reads, "At the upper entrance they hacked the wooden trellis with axes." In his exegesis of this passage also, Origen refers to Josephus' description of the destruction of the Temple.

Fragment 115 of *Fragmenta in Lamentationes* says about Lamentations 4:19 that, "Josephus reports that even the mountains did not save those who were trying to escape." It is not certain to which passage of Josephus this refers but it is indeed a concise account of the fall of Jerusalem. Here, too, Origen overlaps the two occasions of Jerusalem's fall.

As we have noted, by citing and using Josephus to his own purpose, Origen interprets his historical account from his theological viewpoint and adapts it to his interpretation of the Bible. As in fragment 109 (passage 5) of *Fragmenta in Lamentationes*, when the subject of the destruction of the Temple is closely related to his theological interpretation, he cites a considerable amount from Josephus' work, modifying the passage to fit his interpretation. Origen, however, neither alters nor adds in his adaptation—he merely omits a few words. The fact that there are substantial allusions to Josephus in *Fragmenta in Lamentationes* proves that such historic incidents as the destruction of the Temple and fall of Jerusalem were significant to Origen's theology. As is seen in *Contra Celsum* (passages 7 and 10 above), it is when the subject is not related to the fall of Jerusalem that he suggests the reading of Josephus to interested readers. In this respect it may be concluded that the significance of Josephus to Origen was in his description of the capture of Jerusalem. As we have already discussed, the reason for Origen's allusion to Josephus in regard to the assassination of James the Just was that the incident was the cause of the fall of the holy city.

IV

Next, let us analyze Origen's references to Josephus that are mainly found in *Contra Celsum,* written from an apologetic viewpoint. We shall not consider the so-called *Testimonium Flavianum* because there is a long-standing train of arguments on it, and, in fact, there is an essay on it in this collection.

Celsus' *The True Doctrine* (ἀληθὴς λόγος) is an apology that praises "the ancient doctrine [of natural reason] that existed from the beginning," which many wise races, cities, and sages have abided by,[15] and, at the same time, criticizes Judaism—along with Christianity, a derivative of it—which is accused of having distorted and corrupted "the ancient doctrine." It is only natural that Origen's Christian apology, which argues against Celsus' Hellenistic apology, has a sophisticated procedure and structure. Origen has to criticize and rectify Celsus' understanding of the Jews and Judaism. He often refers to "Celsus' Jew" (ὁ παρὰ τῷ Κέλσῳ Ἰουδαῖος)[16] when he mentions the Jew whom Celsus describes. Moreover, when Celsus tries to eliminate Jewish elements in his argument and to ignore Jewish testimonies altogether, Origen has not only to point out such facts, but also to complement them by furnishing apposite Jewish testimonies that are missing. This is done from a Jewish apologetic point of view. But Origen cannot continue from the Jewish standpoint, for he has to make an apology for Christianity, which he does by criticizing the Jewish apology. Thus, he has to criticize as one "Celsus and his Jew, and all who have not believed in Jesus,"[17] which, after all, is nothing but Christian apology. Such weaving in of Jewish apology and Christian apology is the element that gives this book its complex structure. Origen's reference to Josephus in this book is embedded in this dual complication of apology for both Judaism and Christianity. This is, in fact, epitomized in the later *Testimonium Flavianum.*

Origen attacks Celsus by using Jewish apology. Accusing Celsus of omitting the Jews from the "most ancient and wise nations," he points out that evidence among the works of the Egyptians, Phoenicians, and Greeks proves the antiquity of the Jews; and he advises those who are interested to become acquainted with Josephus' two-volume work concerning the topic, for it might be superfluous to cite it. In this work, *Against Apion,* Origen explains that Josephus "produces a considerable collection of writers who testify to the antiquity of the Jews" (passage 7).

Likewise, in response to Celsus' claim that the Jews and the Christians mistakenly teach that conflagrations and floods occur within the cycles of the universe according to God's plan, Origen argues that Celsus, though possessing vast knowledge gained from scholarship, does not realize that Moses had existed long before those who preached such doctrines and suggests to those interested to refer to Josephus' "book in two volumes concerning the antiquity of the Jews" (passage 10).[18]

It is clear that when Origen insists on the antiquity of the Jews, he acknowledges and depends on Josephus as a provider of evidence. Origen perceives that Josephus' collection of Greek assertions provides him with effective arguments against Celsus. Thus, Josephus is highly appreciated.

Origen can depend totally on Josephus to argue for the antiquity of the Jewish race, but not to defend Christianity. On this account, Origen's attitude toward Josephus is one of qualified acceptance. An example of this may be found in his statement that "the same author, although he did not believe in Jesus as Christ [καίτοι γε ἀπιστῶν τῷ 'Ιησοῦ ὡς Χριστῷ], sought for the cause of the fall of Jerusalem and the destruction of the Temple" (passage 8). Origen makes this remark when he suggests that readers turn to *Jewish Antiquities* XVIII, 116–119, in his argument concerning John the Baptist. A similar example is found in *Commentarii in Matthaeum* (passage 11) in which Josephus, despite the fact that "he did not accept that our Jesus is the Christ" (τὸν 'Ιησοῦν ἡμῶν οὐ καταδεξάμενος εἶναι Χριστόν), is said to attest to the righteousness of James the Just. These two instances show that although Origen values Josephus' accounts, he is aware that they are not by a Christian, and, moreover, he must explicitly acknowledge this fact. Jewish apology, be it of incomparable value, has to be clearly defined and discriminated from Christian apology.

In order to distinguish Jewish apology from Christian apology, it is important for Origen to mention that Jewish apology is negative and insufficient, inasmuch as Josephus is not a Christian. Josephus' account must be reinterpreted from a Christian viewpoint. In *Contra Celsum* I, 47, Origen notes with favor that Josephus seeks the cause of the fall of Jerusalem and the destruction of the Temple in the assassination of James the Just but gravely adds that Josephus ought to have stated (δέον αὐτὸν εἰπεῖν) that the calamity happened because the Jews killed Christ. Here Origen interprets Paul's remark that James is "the Lord's brother" (Galatians 1:19) to be based upon the similarity in their beliefs on ethics and teaching rather than upon any real blood relationship. Thus, Origen views their deaths as synonymous: "If, therefore, he says that the destruction of Jerusalem happened because of James, would it not be more reasonable to say that this happened on account of Jesus the Christ?"

Origen reiterates this thought in *Contra Celsum* II, 13 (passage 9). "His [Vespasian's] son, Titus, captured Jerusalem, so Josephus writes, on account of James the Just, the brother of Jesus the so-called Christ, though in reality, it was on account of Jesus the Christ of God." Origen draws a contrast between "as Josephus writes" (ὡς μὲν Ἰώσηπος γράφει) and "as the truth shows" (ὡς δὲ ἡ ἀλήθεια παρίστησι), in which the latter is said to be "more reasonable" (εὐλογώτερον).

Origen does use Josephus' historical explanation of the fall of Jerusalem but expands it. Origen tries to find the real cause of the fall in Jesus Christ's death on the cross. Here Josephus' historical account is theologically interpreted. At this point, Origen's approach is by no means historical. He evaluates and employs Josephus' historical material within certain limitations. But even in this case Origen uses Josephus' historical material only for his theological purpose. To him, the fall of Jerusalem is an incident important within the framework of God's redemptive plan, which has to be related to Jesus' crucifixion. As we have seen, this applies also to *Fragmenta in Lamentationes*. Josephus' historical account, which has an apologetic trait, is incorporated by Origen in his history of theology, which has the identical trait. Such an attempt of Origen anticipates the "theology of history" that is vastly constructed by Augustine in *De civitate Dei*.

Notes

1. For Origen's Jewish apology, see H. Bietenhard, *Caesarea, Origenes und die Juden* (Stuttgart, 1974), pp. 53–60. I mention with gratitude that the English renditions of *Contra Celsum* cited in this essay are from *Origenes: Contra Celsum*, translated with an introduction and notes by H. Chadwick (Cambridge, 1965.)

2. Cf. O. Bardenhewer, *Geschichte der altkirchlichen Literatur* II (Darmstadt, 1962 [= Freiburg i. Br., 1914²]), p. 159.

3. Cf. *ibid.*, p. 27.

4. Only a small part of the commentaries on the Acts is, however, extant.

5. The actual date of his travel to Rome is disputed. Nautin presumes it to be around A.D. 215 and to have lasted for a few months. P. Nautin, *Origène. Sa vie et son œuvre* (Paris, 1977), p. 409.

6. Cf. the article "Bibliothekswesen" II (by E. Plümacher), *Theologische Realenzyklopädie* VI, pp. 413f.

7. N. R. M. de Lange, *Origen and the Jews*, (Cambridge, 1970); H. Bietenhard, *op. cit.*

8. Cf. H. Conzelmann, *Heiden-Juden-Christen* (*Beiträge zur Historischen Theologie* 62) (Tübingen, 1981), p. 319.

9. For an enumeration of passages from a different point of view, see pp. 73–76 of H. Schreckenberg, *Die Flavius-Josephus-Tradition in Antike und Mittelalter* (*Arbeiten zur Literatur und Geschichte des hellenistischen Judentums* 5) (Leiden, 1972), pp. 73–76. *Homiliae in Genesim* 17, 6, however, cannot be used because its authenticity is dubious.

10. "He says" (εἰπεῖν; φησί) is also used (passage 8).

11. Comments to the same effect are also found in *Contra Celsum* II 13 (passage 9).

12. "Origenes bringt nicht wie Clemens und Tertullian viele ausdrückliche (oder stillschweigende) Zitate; er vermeidet sie vielmehr und macht fast nur dort von ihren Gebrauch, wo er sie zum Beweise notig hat. Daher zitiert er Josephus und Philo." A. von Harnack, *Der kirchenge-*

schichtliche Ertrag der exegetischen Arbeiten des Origenes, Part 2, *TU* 42/4 (Leipzig, 1919), p. 50. But since Greek and Roman authors tend to avoid literal references because of their emphasis on the totality of their literary style, those of Origen may be considered to be following the traditional Judeo-Christian manner of references. Cf. W. Speyer, *Die literarische Fälschung in heidnischen und christlichen Altertum* (*Handbuch der Altertumswissenschaft*. Erste Abteilung, Zweiter Teil) (München, 1971), p. 173.

13. Nautin figures the dates between A.D. 222 and 229 (Nautin, *op. cit.*, 410).

14. Similarly, according to Nautin, between A.D. 239 and 242. (Nautin, *op. cit.*, 411).

15. *Contra Celsum*, I 14.

16. For example, *Contra Celsum*, I 56, 61, 67 *passim*.

17. *Contra Celsum*, I 56.

18. Parallels in Josephus are found in *Ap* I, 70ff.

16 The Testimonium Flavianum and the Martyrdom of James

ZVI BARAS

*t*he famous paragraph of Josephus (*A* XVIII, 63–64), known in the historical literature under the title *Testimonium Flavianum* because of its testimony on Jesus, is an ever-puzzling question and an inexhaustible source of scholarly research. The passage quoted below, along with its translation, is traditionally known as the "vulgate version" of the *Testimonium:*

Γίνεται δὲ κατὰ τοῦτον τὸν χρόνον Ἰησοῦς σοφὸς ἀνήρ, εἴγε ἄνδρα αὐτὸν λέγειν χρή. ἦν γὰρ παραδόξων ἔργων ποιητής, διδάσκαλος ἀνθρώπων τῶν ἡδονῇ τἀληθῆ δεχομένων καὶ πολλοὺς μὲν Ἰουδαίους, πολλοὺς δὲ καὶ τοῦ Ἑλληνικοῦ ἐπηγάγετο. ὁ χριστὸς οὗτος ἦν. καὶ αὐτὸν ἐνδείξει τῶν πρώτων ἀνδρῶν παρ' ἡμῖν σταυρῷ ἐπιτετιμηκότος Πιλάτου οὐκ ἐπαύσαντο οἱ τὸ πρῶτον ἀγαπήσαντες. ἐφάνη γὰρ αὐτοῖς τρίτην ἔχων ἡμέραν πάλιν ζῶν τῶν θείων προφητῶν ταῦτά τε καὶ ἄλλα μυρία περὶ αὐτοῦ θαυμάσια εἰρηκότων. εἰς ἔτι τε νῦν τῶν Χριστιανῶν ἀπὸ τοῦδε ὠνομασμένον οὐκ ἐπέλιπε τὸ φῦλον.

About this time there lived Jesus, a wise man, if indeed one ought to call him a man. For he was one who wrought surprising feats and was a teacher of such people as accept the truth gladly. He won over many Jews and many of the Greeks. He was the Messiah. When Pilate, upon hearing him accused by men of the highest standing among us, had condemned him to be crucified, those who had in the first place come to love [him] did not cease. On the third day he appeared to them restored to life. For the prophets of God had prophesied these and myriads of other marvelous [things] about him. And the tribe of the Christians, so called after him, has still up to now, not disappeared.[1]

This testimony acquired cardinal importance for the Christian church since it was first quoted by Eusebius of Caesarea (260–339) in his *History of the Church*.[2] Its importance lies in the fact that it was considered reliable evidence for Jesus' divine nature, passion, and messiahship. Such testimony coming from a Jewish historian, who wrote shortly after Jesus' time,[3] was thought to be convincing evidence for the discussions held between Jews and Christians in the early centuries of Christianity.[4] No wonder, therefore, that it was reproduced time and again and used intensively by Christian authors as decisive and solid proof for Jesus' messiahship.[5]

However, since the sixteenth century the authenticity of the *Testimonium* has become a controversial issue, ardently questioned or defended by scholars and students of both sides. This problem has produced over the years a vast literature with a variety of opinions and is still an intricate subject of recent scholarship.[6] The participants in the debate over the genuineness of the *Testimonium* are divided into three groups: those who accept its authenticity; those who reject it entirely as a forgery; and those who accept only parts of it as authentic and reject the rest for being a Christian interpolation. This paper will not discuss the arguments of those who accept the *Testimonium* dogmatically nor those who reject it completely. Both groups adhere to their own positions and try hard, by versatile argumentation, to convince the readers that theirs is the right cause. However, it seems that the third group has something more plausible to offer by accepting parts of the passage and rejecting others. Nevertheless, the attempt of such scholars to reconstruct the genuine passage of the *Testimonium,* commendable as it may be, is also an unresolvable matter. For until unquestionable proof is found, in the form of a manuscript containing the genuine version of Josephus' passage, no decisive answer can be given, and the entire matter remains in the domain of sheer speculation.

We, therefore, propose at this stage not to deal with the reconstruction of the text—such an attempt would undoubtedly drag us into a polemical discussion. Instead, we suggest to follow another path, which will help us to understand the *metamorphosis* which this passage underwent, to realize how, by whom, and on what grounds the vulgate version was altered.

First of all, it is imperative to draw attention to the contradiction of two primary and important sources—Eusebius and Origen. The vulgate version of Eusebius is clearly contradicted by the statement of Origen (185–254), the revered church father who preceded Eusebius at the school of Caesarea.[7] Origen, in his writings, twice criticizes Josephus for not having accepted Jesus as the messiah. The first occurs in his polemical book, *Contra Celsum* I, 47, which was intended to refute the attack on Christianity made by Celsus the pagan. Here Origen refers explicitly to Josephus: "The same author, although he did not believe in Jesus as Christ."[8] The second appears in his *Commentarii in Matthaeum* X, 17. Origen's commentary on this verse,[9] refers to the case of James, the brother of Jesus, who, according to Josephus (XX, 200), was handed over for trial to the Sanhedrin.[10] Here Origen repeats his discontent with Josephus' skeptical attitude toward Jesus' messiahship: "and wonderful it is that while he did not receive Jesus for Christ, he did nevertheless bear witness that James was so righteous a man." [11]

Such a clear contradiction cannot be pushed aside; one is therefore bound to conclude that the text of the *Testimonium* was tampered with—a conclusion corroborated also by modern scholarship. [12] Indeed, reserved and moderate tones concerning the messiahship of Jesus on the part of Josephus are discernible not only prior to the quotation by Eusebius; we find them later on as well. The Latin version of the *Testimonium* translated by Jerome (342–420) [13] is, indeed, very close to the vulgate version, except for the crucial phrase which reads: "He was believed to be the Messiah." [14]

Neutral and balanced tones, entirely different from those of the vulgate version, are also to be found in a tenth-century Arabic version, to which S. Pines has drawn attention. [15] This Arabic version, included by Agapius (also known as Mahboub of Menbidj), [16] a Syrian churchman and historian, in his *Universal History,* reads:

> At this time there *was* a wise man *who was called* Jesus. And *his conduct was good,* and [he] *was known to be virtuous.* And many people *from among* the Jews *and the other nations became his disciples.* Pilate condemned him to be crucified *and to die.* And *those who had become his disciples did* not abandon *his discipleship.* They *reported* that he had appeared to them *three days after his crucifixion and* that he *was* alive; *accordingly,* he was *perhaps* the Messiah concerning whom the prophets *have recounted* wonders. [17]

This variant is regarded as having escaped Christian censorship to a greater extent than the vulgate version. [18] Although it is not considered the genuine text of Josephus, it provides us with an example of another more moderate attempt at the Christianization of the original text, probably unfavorable to Christians, and one which may have been known to Origen and Jerome.

Moreover, even recent scholars, such as E. Bammel—who tend to accept the vulgate version as authentic with slight emendations [19]—agree that the main phrases of the extant text are too favorable and too Christian, and therefore incompatible with either Josephus' attitudes or with Origen's remarks. [20] The present form of the *Testimonium,* according to Bammel, displays the touch of a "reviser-editor," who altered the original text according to his own historical conceptions. [21]

From what has been said so far it is obvious that in the days of Origen (third century A.D.), the text of the *Testimonium* had not yet been subjected to Christian emendations and corrections, such as are found in the vulgate version quoted later by Eusebius. It seems that the passage seen by Origen had no derogatory references or, for that matter, ironic allusions; [22] otherwise we may be sure that they would have caused outspoken denunciation on the part of Origen. From his remarks we can deduce that the paragraph was probably neutral or contained information easily considered dubious or skeptical.[23] It is this very "neutral" version, unsatisfactory to Christians, that had been copy edited according to the editor's beliefs. This Christianized version gradually became the prevailing version, while the less assertive or skeptical version was overshadowed and completely ignored. How, then, had this passage undergone such a substantial alteration from a doubtful reference to Jesus' messiahship into an unequivocal assertion of it?

In order to understand the possible alterations made to the *Testimonium,* we propose to examine another account by Josephus—the account of the trial and death of James, brother of Jesus[24]—and observe closely the treatment it is given by Origen and Eusebius. Such an examination is suggested not only for the purpose of mere parallelism and comparison but also because the account mentions jointly the two founders of the early Christian community.[25] Moreover, Josephus' reference here to "Jesus called the Messiah" is considered authentic by most scholars, and its relevance to the *Testimonium* is therefore self-evident. To these considerations we may also add that both Origen and Eusebius held Josephus in high esteem mainly for being a historian who was contemporary with Jesus and a Jew whose testimony was regarded as very important.[26]

Let us first reproduce the passage of Josephus concerning the trial and death of James, in which he recounts that Ananus the Younger, the high priest, brought James, during the absence of the Roman procurator from Judea, to trial:

> Ananus thought that he had a favorable opportunity because Festus was dead and Albinus was still on the way. And so he convened the judges of the Sanhedrin and brought before them a man named James, the brother of Jesus who was called the Christ, and certain others. He accused them of having transgressed the law and delivered them up to be stoned. Those of the inhabitants of the city who were considered the most fair-minded and who were strict in observance of the law were offended at this.[27]

In the hands of Origen and Eusebius, this incident, defined as "the martyrdom of James," became, through Christian historiosophical interpretation, the main cause for the destruction of Jerusalem and of the Temple. Moreover, they went so far as to say that Josephus himself regarded this catastrophe as just punishment for the execution of James—a statement not supported by the text reproduced above or by any other extant version. But Origen did not stop here; he not only attributed to Josephus a statement unknown to us from any other source or version but also "corrected" Josephus' alleged statement in a way favorable to the Christian historiosophical point of view.

Let us observe these stages in Origen's writings and note carefully how Origen uses Josephus apropos the martyrdom of James. Origen mentions James' martyrdom three times in connection with the destruction of Jerusalem and the

Temple, and each time he introduces a small but meaningful addition. First, in his *Commentarii in Matthaeum* X, 17:

> This James was of so shining a character among the people, on account of his righteousness, that Flavius Josephus, when, in his twentieth book of the *Jewish Antiquities*, he had a mind to set down what was the cause why the people suffered such miseries, till the very holy house was demolished, said that these things befell them by the anger of God, on account of what they had dared to do to James, the brother of Jesus, who was called Christ; and wonderful it is that while he did not receive Jesus for Christ, he did nevertheless bear witness that James was so righteous a man. He says further that the people thought they had suffered these things for the sake of James.[28]

What strikes us immediately is the unanimous conclusion that places the blame for the destruction of the Temple on the execution of James. Yet Origen bothers to distinguish between Josephus' conclusion and that of the people. He directs us to *Antiquities* XX, where, indeed, the story of James is recounted; but when he refers to the people's same deduction, he fails to produce direct documentation and only says vaguely "further."

The second time Origen refers to the martyrdom of James and to the destruction of the Temple is in his polemical book *Contra Celsum* I, 47:

> For Josephus in the eighteenth book of the *Jewish Antiquities* bears witness that John was a baptist and promised purification to people who were baptized. The same author, although he did not believe in Jesus as Christ, sought for the cause of the fall of Jerusalem and the destruction of the Temple. He ought to have said that the plot against Jesus was the reason why these catastrophes came upon the people, because they had killed the prophesied Christ; however, although unconscious of it, he is not far from the truth when he says that these disasters befell the Jews to avenge James the Just, who was a brother of 'Jesus the so-called Christ,' since they had killed him who was a very righteous man. This is the James whom Paul, the true disciple of Jesus, says that he saw, describing him as the Lord's brother, not referring so much to their blood-relationship or common upbringing as to his moral life and understanding. If therefore he says that the destruction of Jerusalem happened because of James, would it not be more reasonable to say that this happened on account of Jesus the Christ?[29]

Here we find some new elements. Origen "corrects" Josephus' alleged conclusion, saying that Josephus should have assigned the blame for the destruction not on the execution of James the Just, but rather on the Jews' mistreatment of Jesus. The other element introduced here by Origen to strengthen his argumentation is the logical category of inference or deduction, twice repeated: "If therefore . . . , would it not be more reasonable?" A further point to note is that while Origen refers us to *Antiquities* XVIII, where the account about John the Baptist is given, he remains tacit as to where Josephus' so-called conclusion can be found.

The third time Origen refers to the same conclusion is also in *Contra Celsum* II, 13:

While Jerusalem was still standing and all the Jewish worship was going on in it, Jesus foretold what was to happen to it through the Romans. For surely they will not say that Jesus' own pupils and hearers handed down his teaching of the gospels without writing it down, and that they left their disciples without their reminiscences of Jesus in writing. In them it is written: 'And when you see Jerusalem compassed with armies, then know that her desolation is at hand.' At that time there were no armies at all round Jerusalem, compassing it about and surrounding and besieging it. The siege began when Nero was still emperor, and continued until the rule of Vespasian. His son, Titus, captured Jerusalem, so Josephus says, on account of James the Just, the brother of Jesus the so-called Christ, though in reality it was on account of Jesus the Christ of God.[30]

This stage, however, asserts as fact that the destruction of the Temple and Jerusalem "in reality was on account of Jesus." In order to make his historical deduction more plausible, Origen first refers to Luke 21:20, where Jesus foretold the destruction of Jerusalem, then he "corrects" Josephus' alleged conclusion as found in *Contra Celsum* I, 47. This interpretation—developed through the stages seen above and hardly unintentionally—culminated in Origen's concept of universal history, which was presented in *Contra Celsum* IV, 22. Here Origen states, this time without reference to James' martyrdom, that the destruction of Jerusalem was a just retribution for the mistreatment of Jesus.

But although Josephus' importance for Origen lay mainly in the fact that he was a contemporaneous historian ("a man who lived not long after John and Jesus"), Origen did not quote him directly; only in indirect speech (*oratio obliqua*) did Origen summarize Josephus' information. How, then, could Origen have arrived at such a conclusion, attributed by him to Josephus, and whence could he have found support? The lack of such a version in the extant text of Josephus has induced scholars to explain it in different ways. One is the assumption that Origen's version of James' martyrdom indeed appeared in Josephus' original text, but has not been preserved.[31] Such an assumption overlooks the question of why the *Testimonium* passage should have remained in Josephus' text, while the story of James' martyrdom—neither disdainful nor defamatory toward Christ—should have been excised from Josephus' writings.

The other generally accepted explanation is that Origen confused the accounts of James and John the Baptist in Josephus and Hegesippus and followed the latter, who associated James' martyrdom with the siege of Jerusalem. We reproduce here only the last few relevant lines of Hegesippus, as quoted at length by Eusebius: "Such was his martyrdom. He was buried on the spot, by the Sanctuary, and his headstone is still there by the Sanctuary. He has proved a true witness to Jews and Gentiles alike that Jesus is Christ. Immediately after this Vespasian began to besiege them." [32] Could Origen have confused the sources? Such negligence on the part of so meticulous a scholar is unacceptable. I have already pointed out elsewhere that it seems more likely that the sequential events (*hoc post hoc*) in Hegesippus—namely, James' martyrdom and the siege—became for Origen causal events (*hoc propter hoc*).[33]

In fact, I believe that we can now point to a specific place, or incident, in Josephus' own writings—unnoticed so far by scholars in this context—which led Origen to say that Josephus should have corrected his historical interpretation. I refer to *Antiquities* XI, 297–305, where the remarks of Josephus may have served Origen as guideposts in leading him in the direction he took. In this paragraph Josephus recounts the death of Jeshua (i.e. Jesus; this is another name for Christ) at the hand of his brother, Johanan (Joannes) the high priest. Josephus condemns the crime and says that God punished the Jews by enslaving them and by desecrating the Temple:

> Joannes had a brother named Jesus; and Bagoses, whose friend he was, promised to obtain the high priesthood for him. With this assurance, therefore, Jesus quarrelled with Joannes in the Temple and provoked his brother so far that in his anger he killed him. That Joannes should have committed so impious a deed against his brother while serving as priest was terrible enough, but the more terrible in that neither among Greeks nor barbarians had so savage and impious a deed ever been committed. The Deity, however, was not indifferent to it, and it was for this reason that the people were made slaves and the Temple was defiled by the Persians. Now, when Bagoses, the general of Artaxerxes, learned that . . . , he at once set upon the Jews . . . . This, then, being the pretext which he used, Bagoses made the Jews suffer seven years for the death of Jesus.[34]

This story contains many elements that are relevant to the Christian historical interpretation. For instance, here the high priest causes the death of Jesus, as it is in the case of Jesus Christ and his brother, James; the crime brings about God's retribution; and the punishment for Jeshua/Jesus' death comes shortly afterwards. Moreover, the paragraph offers clear causal argumentation ("and it was for this reason") for the miseries that befell the Jews: the terrible sin committed was followed by God's punishment. Even the kinds of retribution described in this chapter—the enslavement of the people and the desecration of the Temple—could very easily fit the Christian attitude; namely, that the punishment for the mistreatment of Jesus Christ was the overthrow and dispersion of the Jewish nation and the destruction of the Temple. Indeed, Origen says this in his *Contra Celsum* IV, 22:

> I challenge anyone to prove my statement untrue if I say that the entire Jewish nation was destroyed less than one whole generation later on account of these sufferings which they inflicted upon Jesus. For it was, I believe, forty-two years from the time when they crucified Jesus to the destruction of Jerusalem. . . . For they committed the most impious crime of all, when they conspired against the Savior of mankind, in the city where they performed to God the customary rites which were symbols of profound mysteries. Therefore, that city where Jesus suffered these indignities had to be utterly destroyed. The Jewish nation had to be overthrown, and God's invitation to blessedness transferred to others, I mean the Christians, to whom came the teaching about the simple and pure worship of God.[35]

It seems, therefore, that Josephus served Origen not so much for explicit documentation and direct quotation as for supporting his own Christian historiosophy.

Now we turn to Eusebius to observe the way he treated Josephus' account of James' martyrdom. But first we have to point out that Eusebius was Origen's successor at the school of Caesarea; he was not only acquainted with the works of Origen but also indebted to them.[36] Eusebius, like Origen, regarded Josephus as an important historian, contemporary with Jesus, worthy of being quoted many times and of having his reputation stressed among Jews and Romans alike.[37] It is, therefore, only natural that Eusebius grasped the full historical significance of Origen's observation that Josephus should have explained differently the disaster that befell the Jews. So seriously did he take Origen's suggestion that he tried his best to follow it in his own *History of the Church*.

Indeed, Chapter 23 of this book is devoted to the martyrdom of James. In it Eusebius quotes various sources to prove the far-reaching historical implication for Christianity and reveals he shared his master's opinion on that point. However, unlike Origen, who in indirect speech (*oratio obliqua*) stressed that Josephus allegedly recognized the causality between the killing of James and the destruction of Jerusalem, Eusebius quotes Josephus in direct speech (*oratio recta*), as can be seen from a comparison of the two quotations:

Origen, *Contra Celsum* I, 47: "[he says that] these disasters befell the Jews to avenge James the Just, who was a brother of Jesus the so-called Christ, since they had killed him who was a very righteous man" (Chadwick trans., p. 43).	Eusebius, *History of the Church*, II, 23, 20: "These things happened to the Jews in requital for James the Righteous, who was a brother of Jesus known as Christ, for though he was the most righteous of men, the Jews put him to death" (Williamson trans., p. 102).

The precise parallelism between the two texts has already been remarked by Chadwick, who proved that Eusebius quoted Origen's passage verbatim, but changed it to direct speech.[38]

It seems that only his dogmatic adherence to Origen's interpretation of history can explain Eusebius' departure from his custom of exact and attributive citation.[39] Eusebius' faithfulness to Origen's interpretation is made obvious by his insistent refrain—sometimes without any reference to James' martyrdom—that the crime against Jesus resulted in the destruction of Jerusalem and of the Temple.[40] In order to convince his readers, he, too, equates historical causality with sequential events,[41] and points to a series of calamities that befell Jerusalem—all occurring under the procuratorship of Pilate, during whose regime the crime against Jesus was committed:

Beside this, the same writer shows that in Jerusalem itself a great many other revolts broke out, making it clear that from then on the city and all Judea were in the grip of faction, war, and an endless succession of criminal plots, until the final hour overtook them—the siege under Vespasian. Such was the penalty laid upon the Jews by divine justice for their crimes against Christ.[42]

Loyalty to Origen is apparent in the way Eusebius applies Origen's recommendation of how Josephus should have explained the calamities of the Jewish nation. He subtly attributes such an explanation to Josephus himself, not by quoting him as one might have expected and as it was his custom, but by summing up: "His statements are confirmed by Josephus, who similarly points out that the calamities which overtook the whole nation began with the time of Pilate and the crimes against the Savior."[43]

We seem to have come full circle: it begins with Origen's "emendation" of Josephus' explanation for the Jewish catastrophe, through James' citation, allegedly from Josephus, but in fact deriving from Origen; then it continues with Eusebius' full application of Origen's proposal that events be given a Christian interpretation focused on the crucifixion by attempting to put into the mouth of Josephus the imputation that the Jews were punished because of their crime against Jesus.

The changes, for purposes of Christian historiosophy, proposed by Origen and carried out by Eusebius in the story of James' martyrdom, are therefore not without bearing on the *Testimonium* itself.[44] It seems plausible to assume that Eusebius treated the *Testimonium* in a way similar to what he had done with the story of James' martyrdom. He seems to have been concerned only with the need of the hour; being preoccupied more with the Christian historiosophy shared by Origen and himself, he probably overlooked or even ignored the contradicting tiny differences between his master and himself (especially regarding the *Testimonium* and the citation of James)—discrepancies that only meticulous research could reveal in due time.

Notes

1. L. H. Feldman's translation in Loeb Classical Library, *Josephus*, IX, London and Cambridge, Mass., 1965, p. 40.

2. See Eusebius, *Historia Ecclesiastica* in the edition of J. P. Migne, *PG*, vol. 20; critical edition by E. Schwartz in *GCS* I–II, Breslau, 1903–1908; English translation by: K. Lake and J. E. L. Oulton, I–II, London, 1927–1928, and lately by G. A. Williamson, Harmondsworth, 1965.

3. On this important point stressed both by Origen and Eusebius, see below.

4. In such a discussion held at the Sassanid court (*PG*, vol. 89, col. 1248), this testimony was referred to by the Christian contestant, who, among other things, said: "Josephus, your historian, who talked of Jesus, a righteous and good man, manifested by God's grace through signs and miracles, doer of many things." On this, see in particular A. B. Hulen, "The Dialogues

with the Jews as Source for the Early Jewish Arguments against Christianity," *JBL* 59 (1932), pp. 85f.

5. See H. Schreckenberg, *Die Flavius-Josephus-Tradition in Antike und Mittelalter,* Leiden, 1972, as listed in index, p. 199.

6. For a review of the recent scholarship on this subject, see Z. Baras, *"Testimonium Flavianum:* The State of Recent Scholarship," in *Society and Religion in the Second Temple Period* (World History of the Jewish People, vol. 8), M. Avi-Yonah and Z. Baras, eds., Jerusalem, 1977, pp. 303–313, 378–385. See also the recent bibliography on this subject in the vast compendium, with annotated entries, published by L. H. Feldman, *Josephus and Modern Scholarship (1937–1980),* Berlin, 1984, pp. 679–703, 957–958.

7. On Origen, his scholarly activity, and his relations with the Jews of Caesarea, see N. R. M. de Lange, *Origen and the Jews,* Cambridge, 1976.

8. Origen, *Contra Celsum,* translated by H. Chadwick, Cambridge, 1953, p. 43.

9. Matthew 10:17: "But beware of men: for they will deliver you to the councils, and they will scourge you in their synagogues."

10. It seems worthwhile to draw attention to the fact that in both instances Origen mentions jointly the personalities of Jesus and James, his brother—references that are not without consequences, as we shall see later on.

11. Translation of W. Whiston, *Josephus* (complete works), repr. Grand Rapids, 1974, p. 639.

12. See my article (above note 6), pp. 304–307.

13. Jerome, who ran the monastery he founded in Bethlehem (A.D. 386), translated into Latin several works by Origen and Eusebius.

14. Jerome, *De Viris Illustribus* XIII, in *PL* 23, col. 631.

15. See his study, *An Arabic Version of the Testimonium Flavianum and Its Implications,* Jerusalem, 1971.

16. Agapius (Mahboub) de Menbidj, *Kitab Al-'Unvan (Histoire Universelle)* in *Patrologia Orientalis,* A. Vasiliev, ed. and trans., VIII, 3, repr. Turnhout, 1971, pp. 399–457.

17. Translation by Pines, *op. cit.,* p. 70.

18. See Pines, *op. cit.,* pp. 57–64.

19. E. Bammel, "Zum Testimonium Flavianum (Jos. Ant. 18, 63–64)," *J-S,* Göttingen, 1974, pp. 9–22.

20. *Ibid.,* pp. 10–12.

21. *Ibid.,* p. 21.

22. I have already pointed out (see p. 306 of my article, above note 6) that Bammel's slight emendations attributing ironic tones to the *Testimonium* passage leaves us wondering why Josephus would first praise Jesus and then mock him. We are also hardly convinced by another attempt (A. A. Bell, "Josephus the Satirist? A Clue to the Original Form of the Testimonium Flavianum," *JQR* 67 [1976], pp. 16–22) to discern subtle and ironic overtones in Josephus' text. If the incident Bell refers to (on p. 19; the seduction of Paulina) is so transparent a parody of the Christian Annunciation, we wonder how it happened that it was dealt with only by Hegesippus and escaped the Christian censorship.

23. We should like to draw attention to another skeptical reference to Jesus' messiahship, which has gone unnoticed and without criticism. This reference, in a form very similar to that of Jerome's, was made by Hegesippus in connection with James' martyrdom. In it we read: "Some of them came to believe that Jesus was the Christ" (see Eusebius, *History of the Church,* trans. by G. A. Williamson, Harmondsworth, 1965, p. 120).

24. James, first elected bishop to the church of Jerusalem, had the reputation of being a saintly man and was identified by early Christian sources (Hegesippus, Clement of Alexandria, Origen, and Eusebius) as "James the Righteous" or "James the Just."

25. Both Jesus and James shared a common fate of trial, conviction, and death.

26. Origen (*Contra Celsum* I, 47) says that Josephus was "a man who lived not long after John and Jesus" (Chadwick's translation, p. 43), while Eusebius stresses the fact that Josephus was "a historian sprung from the Hebrews themselves [who] has furnished in his own writing an almost contemporary record of John the Baptist and our Savior" (*History of the Church*, Williamson's translation, p. 64).

27. Josephus, *Antiquities* XX, 200, L. H. Feldman's translation, Loeb Classical Library, IX, London, Cambridge, Mass., 1965, pp. 495–497.

28. W. Whiston's translation, p. 639.

29. Chadwick's translation, p. 43.

30. Chadwick's translation, p. 80.

31. This unacceptable assumption was brought forth by R. Girod in Origène, *Commentaire sur l'Evangile selon Matthieu*, R. Girod, editor and trans., I, Paris, 1970, pp. 114–116.

32. Eusebius, *The History of the Church*, II, 23, 17, Williamson's translation, p. 102.

33. See pp. 310–311 of my article, above note 6.

34. Josephus, *Antiquities* XI, 297–305, Loeb Classical Library, VI, pp. 457–461.

35. Chadwick's translation, pp. 198–199.

36. As contributor to the *Defense of Origen*, a work produced in collaboration with Pamphilius in order to prove Origen's orthodoxy, Eusebius must have had a thorough knowledge of Origen's ideas and writings. Indeed, Eusebius carefully collected the works of Origen and was proud to specify those he had in his possession. See his *History of the Church* VI, 36, 3, Williamson's translation, pp. 271–272, and Chadwick's note 2 in *Contra Celsum*, p. 43.

37. For the quotations of Origen and Eusebius regarding the contemporaneity of Josephus, see above note 26. See also Eusebius, *History of the Church*, III, 10, 1, Williamson's translation, p. 121.

38. See Origen, *Contra Celsum*, H. Chadwick, trans., p. 43, note 2.

39. For the story of James Eusebius quotes several sources, always with specific references; see, for example, Clement of Alexandria (*History of the Church*, II, 1, 1, Williamson's translation, p. 72); Hegesippus (II, 23, p. 99); and Josephus (II, 23, 17, p. 102). Only the alleged quotation of Josephus (II, 23, 17, p. 102), set among other quotations, is given without exact reference.

40. See, for example, in his *History of the Church*, II, 5, Williamson's translation, p. 79; II, 6, pp. 79–80; III, 11, p. 123.

41. Eusebius' own words are: "After the martyrdom of James and the capture of Jerusalem, which instantly followed" (Williamson's translation, p. 123).

42. Eusebius, *History of the Church*, II, 6, 3, Williamson's translation, p. 80.

43. *History of the Church*, II, 6, 3, Williamson's translation, p. 79.

44. We ought not to ignore the extent of Eusebius' efforts to convince his readers that the citations drawn from Josephus are not only relevant but also truthful. He does so through presenting a series of statements and by comparing Jesus' predictions about the Jews and Jerusalem with the accounts of Josephus: "Anyone who compared our Savior's words with the rest of the historian's account of the whole war could not fail to be astonished and to acknowledge as divine and utterly marvellous the foreknowledge revealed by our Savior's prediction" (Williamson's translation, p. 118). Moreover, in a paragraph dedicated entirely to Josephus, his works, and their value, Eusebius says explicitly: "In view of his general truthfulness, we may accept this" (*ibid.*, p. 121). Finally, Eusebius sums up this passage regarding Josephus by saying: "It would be appropriate to reproduce the words attached to the end of *Antiquities;* and so to confirm the testimony of the passages I have borrowed from him" (*ibid.*, p. 123). This statement on the part of Eusebius carries, in my opinion, significant weight in relation to the famous *Testimonium*.

17 Josephus and Pseudo-Hegesippus

ALBERT A. BELL, JR.

*a*fter the fourth century the *Jewish War* of Josephus was inaccessible
in its original form to Greekless western European readers.[1] It was
known only in a Latin translation variously attributed to Jerome,
Ambrose, or Rufinus.[2] This *De Bello Judaico* was a literal version in seven
books, done for the pragmatic purpose of making this important work available to those unable to consult the original.

Often confused with this translation was a five-book account of the destruction of Jerualem written in Latin by an anonymous Christian late in the
fourth century. Sometimes styled an "adaptation" of Josephus' work,[3] this history blends material from Josephus (both the *War* and the *Antiquities*) and
from other sources to create "substantially an independent book."[4] This study
will briefly introduce this author, known to modern scholars only as pseudo-
Hegesippus, and examine the relationship of his work to that of Josephus.[5]

The name Hegesippus is unfamiliar to most students of ancient or medieval
literature. The truly erudite may know it as the name of a minor Greek orator
of the third century B.C. Those familiar with the history of the early church
may recognize it as the name of a mid-second-century Christian author cited
several times by Eusebius.[6] This Hegesippus wrote a five-book "memoir" of
the church from apostolic times to the age of the Antonine emperors; only
those fragments quoted by Eusebius survive.

At some time between the fourth and early ninth centuries, however, the
name Hegesippus becomes associated with the five-book "adaptation" of
Josephus that is the subject of this study. The name Hegesippus was certainly
not chosen by the author. It appears in no citation before the mid-ninth century[7] and in no manuscript, except as an emendation, before the ninth century. The medieval writers who cite him seem to have thought they were using
the Hegesippus known to Eusebius. A number of manuscripts of the work
contain a gloss to the effect that "Ambrosius episcopus de graeco transtulit."[8]

This assumption is understandable, though entirely unwarranted. The coincidence of five books in each work and the apocryphal stories of the apostles in the opening chapters of pseudo-Hegesippus' third book, combined with his overarching Christian viewpoint, seem sufficient to explain the association with the earlier Hegesippus.

The author's identity and the title of his work were lost, along with the first few folios of the oldest manuscripts, Ambrosianus C 105 inf. and Cassellanus, both of which date from the early sixth century.[9] But a tenth-century Spanish manuscript, which is shown by a number of its readings to be a direct copy of Ambrosianus,[10] bears the title *De excidio Hierosolymitano*. This title, or some variation, appears in several other codices as well.[11] The editors of the *Patrologia Latina* (volume 15) used it, but V. Ussani, the most recent editor, preferred the noncommittal *Historiae libri v.*

Even though the author cannot be identified, some clues to his date and place of origin can be deduced. A reference to Antioch as the fourth city of the empire after the founding of Constantinople (*De excidio* 3.5, 2) establishes a definite *terminus post quem,* while a verbatim quotation by the French monk and bishop Eucherius sets the *terminus ante quem* in about 430.[12] The date can be narrowed to the last third of the fourth century. Virtually all scholars who have studied the matter agree that the references to *Britannia redacta* (2.9, 1; 5.15) indicate a date soon after 367, when Count Theodosius led an expedition to reassert Roman supremacy in the island.[13] The optimism of the two lengthy panegyrics on the might of Rome (2.9, 5.46) and the description of the barbarian tribes on the frontier (5.50) display no knowledge of the disaster at Adrianople and the Germanic incursions of the last two decades of the century, so that most scholars cite 378 as the *terminus ante quem.*[14]

One other clue may allow a more precise dating. To the best of my knowledge, no one has suggested a possible relationship between the emperor Julian's abortive attempt to rebuild the Temple at Jerusalem in 363 and the composition of pseudo-Hegesippus' work, the theme of which is that the destruction by Titus was the *supremum excidium* (5.2).[15] Even as late as 387 John Chrysostom could preach, in Antioch, a sermon (*Contra Judaeos* 5.11) laying great stress on the failure of Julian's effort. Apparently, the memory was still vivid some twenty-five years after the event. This, taken with the factors just mentioned, points inescapably to a date of about 370 for the composition of the *De excidio.*

A few suggestions have been made about the identity of the author. Ambrose of Milan is a popular candidate,[16] though the arguments are largely stylistic and not entirely convincing. H. Dudden says Ambrosian authorship has been questioned "without sufficient reason," but J. P. McCormick, after an extensive study, concludes that the evidence points "definitely away from Ambrosian authorship."[17]

Alternatives are few. The name of Nummius Aemilianus Dexter, a friend of Jerome and proconsul of Asia at the end of the fourth century, has been put forth.[18] But there is no evidence that Dexter ever saw Palestine or Syria; and the author of the *De excidio* displays a first-hand knowledge of those areas, adding to Josephus' description of various points of interest, especially the city of Antioch (cf. *De excidio* 1.41, 1; 3.5, 2).

Karl Mras, in his notes for Ussani's edition, diffidently suggests a certain Isaac the Jew, who is known from Jerome's writings to have been in Rome at the time the *De excidio* seems to have been written.[19] But Jerome says that Isaac "pretended that he believed in Christ," while he actually created dissension by dwelling on the discrepancies between the genealogies of Jesus in the Gospels of Matthew and Luke and in this way "perverted the faith of the simple."[20] The author of the *De excidio*, however, has just the opposite purpose; there is no hint of Isaac's contentiousness in the entire work. Furthermore, the few short tracts which are known to be Isaac's bear no stylistic resemblance to the *De excidio*.[21] There seems little likelihood that he could be the author.

In an earlier publication I raised the possibility that Evagrius of Antioch might be pseudo-Hegesippus.[22] That is, admittedly, a conjecture, but it is not unfounded. Evagrius is known to have been an intimate friend of Jerome (himself no mean translator and adaptor), was fluent in Greek and Latin (as attested by his loose translation of Athanasius' *Life of St. Antony*), and can be shown to have been in Italy in the late 360s and even to have been a friend of Ambrose.[23] Jerome had heard him read works on various subjects, many of which were not published in Jerome's lifetime.[24] In short, nothing that is known of Evagrius militates against his being pseudo-Hegesippus. Happily, it is not essential to know the identity of the author in order to examine the way he has adapted Josephus' *Jewish War* to his own purposes, and it is to that portion of the task to which we must now turn.

If pseudo-Hegesippus was not merely translating Josephus, what was he doing? He was writing history in the only way ancient historians knew how, by adapting an earlier work. Adaptation was the lifeblood of historiography in antiquity. Seneca says (*Epistulae* 79.6–7) that the writer who comes last to a subject has merely to select and rearrange from his predecessors' material in order to compose a new work. The younger Pliny (*Epistulae* 5.8) debated whether to write on modern history, which would require some research, or on an ancient subject, where the sources—that is, published works—were easily available.

Perhaps the best guideline for judging whether a historical work is a legitimate adaptation of an earlier author or a mere imitation is found in Josephus himself. "The industrious writer," he says, "is not one who merely remodels the scheme and arrangement of another's work, but one who uses fresh materials and makes the framework of the history his own" (*BJ* I, 15). Pseudo-Hegesippus can lay legitimate claim to having put his own imprint on the Josephan material that he uses. He has changed the theme of the work from the Jewish War to the destruction of Jerusalem and its significance, and he has omitted and adapted sections of the *War* or included material from various other sources as it relates to that theme. Unlike Ambrose, Hilary, and Marius Victorinus—contemporaries whom Jerome (*Epistulae* 84.7) criticizes for passing off their translations of Origen, Basil, and other Greek fathers as their own writings—pseudo-Hegesippus is no mere translator. We shall first examine his statement of his theme and then see how he has restructured Josephan material and incorporated other sources to create his own history.

Like the monographs of Sallust, whose influence on pseudo-Hegesippus' vocabulary and style is strong, the *De excidio* has a coherent, though more expansive, theme: the destruction of Jerusalem, its causes and implications. Josephus, pseudo-Hegesippus says, "wept over the disaster but did not understand its cause" (preface, 1). As early as 2.5, 2 he begins to foreshadow the climax of the work: "exitium genti temploque maturatum excidium"; similarly, in 2.6, 2: "ultimum excidium praeparabatur." Neither statement has a parallel in Josephus.

The use of *excidium* in both passages is more than coincidental. The word appears at least forty-nine times in the *De excidio*. In five cases it applies to an individual or a town other than Jerusalem, but in every other case it refers to Jerusalem, the Temple, or the Jews. It occurs three times in Book 1, eight times in Book 2, six times in Book 3, and four times in Book 4. But in Book 5, where pseudo-Hegesippus exercises his greatest independence from Josephus, *excidium* appears twenty-eight times.

This conception of his theme as different from Josephus' determines what Josephan material pseudo-Hegesippus uses or omits. Some passages that are intrinsically interesting and pertinent to a history of the Jewish War (e.g., the digressions on the three Jewish "sects" [*BJ* II, 119–166] and on the organization of the Roman army [*BJ* III, 70–109]) are extraneous to pseudo-Hegesippus' theme and are omitted without even a passing summary. Other passages, particularly military maneuvers, are condensed to the point of obscurity.

Pseudo-Hegesippus makes it obvious from his opening words that he regards himself as a historian, not a translator, and shows what his attitude toward Josephus will be. Since this passage is unfamiliar it will be worthwhile to include it here (in my own translation):

> 1) I have composed a historical version of the four books of Kingdoms that are contained in Holy Scripture, down to the captivity of the Jews, the destruction of the Wall, and the Babylonian triumph. A prophetic sermon has also treated briefly the brave deeds of the Maccabees. The rest of the story, down to

the burning and looting of the Temple by Titus Caesar, has been told by Josephus, an outstanding historian, if only he had paid as much attention to religion and truth as he did to the investigation of facts and moderation in writing. For he shows himself to be sympathetic to Jewish faithlessness even in the very things he sets forth about their punishment. Although he deserted them in a military sense, he did not wholly forsake their sacrileges. He bemoaned the catastrophe which befell them, but he did not understand the cause of it.

2) Therefore, not relying on a wealth of intellect but on the application of my faith, I have felt the need to proceed a little further in the history of the Jews beyond the chronological limits of Holy Scripture so that, like those who look for a rose among thorns, we may dig out from among the savage deeds of wicked men (which were paid for with a price worthy of their wickedness) some lesson about reverence for the sacred law or about the marvel of the divine order of things. To the heirs, albeit evil ones, these were a pretext in adversity or a source of pride in prosperous times. At the same time it will be made clear to the whole world that—and this is an indication of the depravity of the race—they brought their misfortunes on themselves. In the first place, they turned the Romans' attention on themselves when the Romans were involved in other matters and encouraged them to become aware of their kingdom, when they would have been better off had the Romans ignored them. They who were not going to remain loyal asked for friendship; although outmanned, they broke the peace; and finally they started a war, when their only hope was in their walls and not in their strength.

3) And so that no one will think I have undertaken a useless task, or one of no value to the Christian faith, let us consider the whole race of the Hebrews embodied in its leaders, so that it may be perfectly clear whether the succession of his generation "from the thighs of Judah" has ever been closed or whether it has truly failed in the line of princes but continues in him "to whom all things remain entrusted" and who is himself "the hope of the Gentiles." From this point then I shall begin.

There is nothing in this to indicate that the writer perceives himself to be translating a Greek work for the convenience of a Latin-reading audience.[25] He thinks of himself as some of the manuscripts designate him: a *historiographus*. The only reference to Josephus points out the inadequacies of his account. Pseudo-Hegesippus intends his work as a corrective and as the last volume in a comprehensive "History of the Jews," the rest of which is lost. But it is a history written "to prove something, not to tell a story," if we may paraphrase Quintilian. He wants to show that God has abandoned the Jews in favor of the Christian church. The war between A.D. 66 and 70 was, in his view, God's effort to destroy the Jews.

This difference of theme can be seen in a comparison of pseudo-Hegesippus' version of Cestius' siege of Jerusalem in November of 66 (*De excidio* 2.15, 5) with Josephus' account (*BJ* II, 539). Cestius withdrew from the siege for reasons that are unclear. Had he only maintained his position a little longer, Josephus says, the city would have fallen and the Jews would not have had to undergo the ordeal of the lengthy war. "But God, I suppose, because of those miscreants, had already turned away even from His sanctuary and ordained that that day should not see the end of the war."

Pseudo-Hegesippus keeps to the general sense of the passage but attributes a much harsher motive to God: "The will of God delayed the imminent end of the war until the ruin could involve much—almost all—of the Jewish race. God expected, I think, that the enormity of their crimes would increase until, by the heaping up of impiety, it would equal the measure of his supreme punishment." These different interpretations of God's rejection of the Jews exemplify the basic differences in theme between Josephus and pseudo-Hegesippus. Josephus depicts God as punishing misdeeds; pseudo-Hegesippus sees him as deliberately setting out to destroy the Jewish race.

Such a harsh interpretation of the divine activity is without an exact parallel in Christian literature before this time. The early fathers display a considerable range in their attitudes toward the Jews.[26] Justin Martyr is quite moderate in his dialogue with Trypho.[27] Minucius Felix (*Octavius* 33.4) says the Jews deserved what befell them, but lays their ruin to willful disobedience after they had been warned of the consequences. Most of the patristic attacks on the Jews arise from charges of deicide.[28] Ambrose and John Chrysostom are probably the harshest of all the fathers in their anti-Judaism, and it is significant that they are contemporaries of pseudo-Hegesippus, and perhaps were even known to him personally. Even Ambrose and Chrysostom, however, do not seem to have thought of God as taking the initiative in destroying the Jews, though Chrysostom preached a series of strongly anti-Jewish sermons about 386–387, which one scholar described with considerable restraint as having "un caractère offensif."[29]

Pseudo-Hegesippus bluntly restates his theme at various points in his history. In 2.3, 3 he repeats his purpose in writing the *De excidio:* "It is my intention to reveal the reasons why the Jews cut themselves off from the Roman Empire and hastened their own destruction." In 2.12, 1 he says that the Jews "paid the penalty for their crimes, because after they had crucified Jesus they persecuted his disciples." He is perhaps most explicit in 5.32, where he speaks of the Jews' *perfidias mentes* and says that they stained themselves by crucifying Jesus: "this is he whose death is the destruction of the Jews."

By developing his own theme pseudo-Hegesippus fulfills one of Josephus' criteria for the industrious writer: he has made "the framework of the history his own." But Josephus says the industrious writer should do more than merely "remodel the scheme and arrangement of another's work." Hence we must examine pseudo-Hegesippus' treatment of Josephan material and note where he also relies on other sources.

We have already seen that pseudo-Hegesippus' prologue is entirely his own composition; Josephus' prologue is cast aside in its entirety. The Latin writer's treatment of Josephus in the first few pages of the *De excidio* further demonstrates his intention to compose his own interpretation of events, not simply to translate Josephus. He omits or radically condenses most of Josephus' opening discussion (*BJ* I, 31ff.) of the struggle between Antiochus IV (Epiphanes) and Ptolemy VI and the dissension among the Jewish nobility. It quickly becomes evident that he has a Latin version of I Maccabees in his mind, if not open before him.[30] When Josephus refers to Antiochus as Ἀντίοχος ὁ κληθεὶς Ἐπιφανής (*BJ* I, 19, 31), with no mention of his father, it would not have been unusual for Hegesippus simply to have transliterated the Greek into "Epiphanes," as he does when he mentions "Antiochus cui nomen Aspondius" (*De excidio* 1.1, 9), which corresponds almost literally to Josephus' Ἀντίοχος ὁ κληθεὶς Ἀσπένδιος (*BJ* I, 65). But pseudo-Hegesippus goes to his other source and writes, "Antiochus cui nomen Illustris, Antiochi regis filius," a virtual quotation of I Maccabees 1.11.

Summarizing *War* I, 31–35, in one brief paragraph, pseudo-Hegesippus comes to the story of the revolt begun by the priest Mattathias and his five sons. Here he departs from Josephus and relies on, even copies from, I Maccabees. Josephus gives the priest's name as Matthias and records that he killed one of Antiochus' officers, a man named Bacchides. (But in *A* XII, 265–270 the priest is called Mattathias and the officer Apelles.) Pseudo-Hegesippus, like I Maccabees, calls the priest Mattathias and leaves the officer anonymous. Pseudo-Hegesippus and I Maccabees also mention that Mattathias killed a fellow Jew who was sacrificing in accordance with Antiochus' edict; Josephus knows nothing of this. Another striking verbal parallel with I Maccabees occurs when pseudo-Hegesippus mentions (1.1, 2) that a group of Hasidim joined with Mattathias' band ("congregata manu atque Asidaeis in societatem adscitis"). In I Maccabees, 2.42, the passage reads "congregata est ad eos synagoga Asideorum." Josephus makes no mention of the Hasidim in either of his works. Nor does Josephus record that Mattathias was the first to fight on the Sabbath, as I Maccabees, 2.41, and pseudo-Hegesippus (1.2) both do.

The rest of pseudo-Hegesippus' account of the Maccabean wars is only a summary, hardly more than annalistic. The exploits of the four older sons of Mattathias are covered in only twelve lines of printed text, compared to some seventy-three in the *War* (I, 38–49). The only one of Mattathias' sons who receives more than a passing reference is the last to rule, Simon (*De excidio* 1.1, 5; cf. *BJ* I, 50–54). His death has a certain moralistic interest, because he is characterized as "probatus" and yet is assassinated while carousing at a banquet given by his son-in-law Ptolemy. Josephus says specifically that Ptolemy killed Simon in the banquet hall and sent men to arrest his sons. Pseudo-Hegesippus, following I Maccabees, 16.16, says that two of Simon's sons were slain at the banquet while the third, John Hyrcanus I, eluded Ptolemy's soldiers. Pseudo-Hegesippus and I Maccabees also concur in describing Simon as drunk, which Josephus nowhere alleges.

It should be clear by now that pseudo-Hegesippus is consciously selecting material from two sources, and preferring another source to Josephus. He follows this pattern throughout the *De excidio,* though he is somewhat limited by the fact that his subject was not a popular one among Roman writers. Limitations of space do not allow us to make a full examination of his technique, but one more example might serve to emphasize the point.

In *De excidio* 4.18 pseudo-Hegesippus describes the Dead Sea in terms that do not rely solely on Josephus; and, in fact, he discounts Josephus' information, displaying an interesting combination of critical acumen and credulity at this point. First he says that the story is told (in *BJ* IV, 476ff.) that the lake changes color three times a day, but he refuses to believe this, since it is a common property of bodies of water to change color as the angle of the sun's rays changes; this is nothing new or miraculous. But he then goes on to accept as *certum* the story that the bitumen which collects on the lake's surface shrinks from a cloth stained by a woman's menstrual flow, as Tacitus, Pliny, and Josephus all recount.

The vocabulary of this passage owes much to Tacitus (*Hist.* 5.6). Compare the following phrases, neither of which is paralleled in Josephus, with their Tacitean models:

Pseudo-Hegesippus: "denique neque pisces neque adsuetas aquis et laetas mergendi usu patitur."
Tacitus: "neque piscis aut suetas aquis volucris patitur."

Pseudo-Hegesippus: "atro liquore."
Tacitus: "ater suapte natura liquor."

Other non-Josephan material incorporated into the work includes passages from Suetonius, Livy, Lucan, and Christian Apocryphal material, including one of the earliest extant versions of the *quo vadis* story (*De excidio* 3.2). It should be evident, then, that pseudo-Hegesippus has conformed to Josephus' criterion of using "fresh material."

He has also adapted Josephus' *War* according to a very deliberate scheme. For the first three books he follows Josephus' general chronological and geographical framework, although he ends Book 2 at a more appropriate point than that at which Josephus ends his second book. Book 3 presents a particular problem to someone adapting Josephus' work because it is almost exclusively concerned with military operations in Galilee in the early days of the war, especially with Josephus' role in the defense of Jotapata.[31] Much of what pseudo-Hegesippus omits is military material and Josephus' self-serving accounts of his own actions and speeches.

In *War* III, 340–355, for example, which is the dramatic climax of the book, Josephus urges a group of his comrades not to commit suicide in the face of the Roman conquest of the town, but to surrender. He tells them that God has revealed to him in a dream that he is delivering the Jews into the Romans' hands. "I go," he concludes, "not as a traitor, but as God's minister." But he fails to persuade the others, and they compel him to join them in a suicide pact, each one happy, he modestly admits (III, 390), "in the assurance that his general was forthwith to share his fate; for sweeter to them than life was the thought of death with Josephus." Such nonsense forms no part of pseudo-Hegesippus' purpose and he omits it (*De excidio* 3.18, 1–2).

Early in Book 4 pseudo-Hegesippus signals the beginning of a new division of the work in an introductory section that has no counterpart in Josephus. Up to this point, he says, he has been surveying what was taking place in the other towns of Palestine. Now he is ready to focus on Jerusalem: "sed iam tempus est ut quae Hierosolymis gesta sunt adoriamur" (4.5). After alerting the reader to the beginning of this last act, as it were, of the drama, pseudo-Hegesippus makes all the action and actors flow toward Jerusalem. First, Josephus' nemesis, John of Gischala, flees from Galilee to Jerusalem. There he stirs up others who had come from various parts of Palestine and "quasi in sentinam confluxerant." (The echo of Sallust's *Catilina* 37.5 is unmistakable.) The effect is disastrous for Jerusalem: "hoc enim illi urbi maioris causa excidii fuit" (4.6, 2).

The last two books also focus on a smaller period of time, barely more than a year. Josephus, on the other hand, spends his fourth book describing Vespasian's advance toward Jerualem, Books 5 and 6 relating the siege and capture of the city, and Book 7 surveying the last stage of the war during the years A.D. 70 to 73. Pseudo-Hegesippus' structure is not necessarily better or worse; it is simply determined by his different purpose. This ability to correlate purpose and structure, to conceive a theme, and then arrange material so that it illustrates that theme without doing violence to historical reality is a primary qualification of a historian.

The fifth book is pseudo-Hegesippus' most original composition. Since it comprehends three of Josephus' books without being longer than any of the other books of the *De excidio,* it obviously omits a great deal. In it, as Ussani says, "l'intento apologetico sopraffa e travolge l'intento storico con larghi e appassionati sviluppi omiletici e oratorii."[32] This tendency is evident in the very structure of the book. Early in his fifth book Josephus laments briefly the fate awaiting Jerusalem (*BJ* V, 19). Pseudo-Hegesippus takes this theme (which is, after all, his main theme) and builds an elaborate threnody (*De excidio*

5.2, 1), which takes up six pages in Ussani's text. Although presented in the author's own persona, it does the work of a major speech at the beginning of the book, while Eleazar's exhortation to the Jews at Masada (inserted merely as a rhetorical flourish) balances it at the end of the book by restating the main points of the threnody: God's abandonment of the Jews and the justness of their punishment. The threnody serves as an overview of what is about to happen and allows pseudo-Hegesippus to include some horrific passages about the suffering of those besieged in Jerusalem. It also enables him to incorporate and summarize much of what Josephus tells in narrative form, like a messenger in a Greek tragedy reporting on all the mayhem that takes place offstage.

The *excidium* theme becomes a death knell in Book 5. In *War* V, 59–65 Josephus tells how Titus escaped injury when attacked by surprise while reconnoitering the Jews' positions. He reflects that "the hazards of war and the perils of princes are under God's care." Pseudo-Hegesippus is less vague. In *De excidio* 5.4, 1, he claims that Titus escaped unharmed "quod ad excidium urbis illius vir tantus reservaretur." His concern with this theme leads him to make a minor but noteworthy change in *War* V, 299, where Josephus says that the Jews dubbed the Romans' largest battering ram Νικῶν, "from its victory over all obstacles." Pseudo-Hegesippus (*De excidio* 5.11, 2) says they called it *excisorem urbium*.

In addition to the threnody and Eleazar's speech, other speeches also play pivotal structural roles in this book. Josephus is given a long speech in 5.15–16, emphasizing the futility of further resistance without God's help against the Romans, whom he shows to be invincible. The speech of the priest Matthias before his execution by the leader of a rival faction is particularly significant since it has no parallel in Josephus. It sums up the attitude which pseudo-Hegesippus thinks the Jews should have, namely that they have brought their troubles upon themselves and deserve their punishment. Matthias, who is probably a representative of the nation in pseudo-Hegesippus' mind,[33] accepts his fate as just recompense for his own part in the factionalism (*merui, fateor*). The Romans, he says, offer peace and have no intention of destroying the Temple, but the Jewish factions are fighting one another harder than they are fighting the enemy and setting fire to their own holy place (5.22). The same theme is emphasized again in the speeches which Titus and Josephus make in 5.31; and, as if that were not enough, it is restated even more forcefully in 5.32 in the author's own Christian persona. The city has been captured before, he editorializes, but will not be again; this is the *supremum excidium*.

After recounting the destruction of the city (5.49), probably using a portion of Tacitus' *Histories* that is now lost, pseudo-Hegesippus sums up almost at random a few events which took place between A.D. 70 and 73, giving the most attention to the pogrom against the Jews at Antioch (5.51). The author's interest in this incident, out of all the material in this section of Josephus, might best be understood by assuming that he had some connection with that city, as suggested earlier. The last two sections of Book 5 are concerned with Masada and Eleazar's speech there. The book as a whole is, therefore, highly rhetorical, with little of Josephus' narrative preserved.

It should be clear by now that pseudo-Hegesippus has done more than merely "Christianize" or "Latinize" Josephus' history of the Jewish War by translating it and inserting disjointed Christian material. He has actually restructured it around his own theme so that it reflects his viewpoint and his prejudices. His success in differentiating himself from Josephus is apparent when Alvarus of Cordova, a late ninth-century Jew turned Christian, in his dispute with Bodonus, a former priest converted to Judaism, promises to quote, "nihil tibi ex Egesippi verbis, sed ex Iosippi vestri doctoris" (*Epistulae* 16.10). At the end of that century Notker Balbulus recommends that "Iosephi vero Iudaici historias et Hegesippi nostri legendas" (*De interpretatione divinarum scripturarum* 12).

In the tradition of classical historiography pseudo-Hegesippus has composed elaborate speeches and, unlike Eusebius, quotes no documents or inscriptions, nor does he name his sources. He has handled Josephus' work with the freedom that any ancient historian enjoyed in treating the work of a predecessor. He may not have created a first-rate piece of historical writing, but he has crafted "one of the more careful products of the late period." [34]

Notes

1. H. Marti, *Übersetzer der Augustin-Zeit. Interpretation von Selbstzeugnissen* (Munich: Fink, 1975), pp. 1–25. Cf. also J. T. Muckle, "Greek Works Translated Directly into Latin before 1300. Part I: Before 1000," *MS* 4 (1942), 33–42.

2. Cassiodorus, *Institutiones divinarum et humanarum litterarum* 1.17. Jerome denies translating anything by Josephus (*Epistulae* 71.5), and no such work appears in Gennadius' catalogue of Rufinus' works (*De viris illustribus* 17). There is nothing to support or disprove Ambrose's role in the translation.

3. G. Bardenhewer, *Geschichte der altkirchlichen Literatur* (Freiburg: Herder, 1913), vol. 3, p. 554. Muckle (above, n. 1), 38 says "it can hardly be called a translation."

4. E. M. Sanford, "Propaganda and Censorship in the Transmission of Josephus," *TAPA* 66 (1935), 133.

5. The text, the title of which is uncertain, is available in two critical editions, one by C. F. Weber and J. Caesar (*Hegesippus qui dicitur sive Egesippus De bello judaico ope codicis Cassellani recognitus* [Marburg: Elwert, 1864]), the other by V. Ussani (*Hegesippi qui dicitur Historiae libri v* [*CSEL* 66, part 1; Vienna: Hoelder-Pichler-Tempsky, 1932]). K. Mras wrote notes and compiled indexes for Ussani's edition (*CSEL* 66, part 2, 1960).

6. *Historia ecclesiastica* 2.23, 3.20, 3.32, 4.8, 4.11, 4.22.

7. Hincmar of Rheims is the first known author to cite by name a passage *in Hegesippi historia* (*De regis persona et regio ministerio* 32).

8. V. Ussani, "Su le fortune medievali dell'Egesippo," *RPARA* 9 (1933), 115–116.

9. E. A. Lowe, *Codices Latini Antiquiores*, 3.44, 8.1139.

10. Mras (above, n. 5), p. xiii.

11. Laon 403 (twelfth century) and 403b (ninth century); Saint-Omer 700 (twelfth century); Troyes 287 (twelfth century).

12. *De situ Hierosolimitanae urbis atque ipsius Iudaeae Epistula ad Faustum presbyterum.*

13. Cf. Ammianus Marcellinus 27.8, 5–10.

14. See Mras (above, n. 5), pp. xxxi–xxxii. As early as the mid-eighteenth century, J. A. Fabricius had reached this conclusion in his *Bibliotheca Latina mediae et infimae aetatis* (2nd ed.; Florence: Baracchi, 1858), vol. 3, pp. 183–184.

15. Ammianus Marcellinus 23.1, 1–3, provides a contemporary account; cf. Rufinus *Historia ecclesiastica* 10.37–39. Also see S. P. Brock, "The Rebuilding of the Temple under Julian: A New Source," *PEQ* 108 (1976), 103–107.

16. William of Malmesbury was the first to note stylistic resemblances between Ambrose and pseudo-Hegesippus (*Gesta regum Anglorum* 4.358). Bardenhewer (above, n. 3) called the work a "jugendarbeit" of Ambrose (*Geschichte*, vol. 3, p. 505). Ussani (above, n. 8) thought Ambrose wrote the *De excidio* in 370 but that it was not published until 398 ("Sue le fortune," p. 107). Also arguing in favor of Ambrosian authorship are G. Landgraf ("Die Hegesippus-Frage," *ALL* 12 [1902], 465–472) and A. Lumpe ("Zum Hegesipp-Problem," *BF* 3 [1968] 165–167).

17. H. Dudden, *St. Ambrose: His Life and Times* (Oxford: Clarendon, 1935), vol. 2, p. 703. J. P. McCormick, *A Study of the "Nominal Syntax" and of Indirect Discourse in Hegesippus* (Washington: Catholic University Press, 1935), p. 212. Mras also doubted Ambrosian authorship ("Die Hegesippus-Frage," *AOAW* 95 [1958], 143–153).

18. G. Morin, "L'Opuscule perdu du soi-disant Hegesippe sur les Macchabées," *RBén* 31 (1914–1919), 90–91.

19. *CSEL* 66, part 2, p. xxxiii.

20. *Commentarii in Epistulam ad Titum* 3.9.

21. Gennadius (*De scriptoribus ecclesiasticis* 26) criticizes Isaac's tracts for their "very obscure reasoning and convoluted style." The tracts, on the Trinity, were edited by A. Hoste in the *CCL*, vol. 9, pp. 331–348.

22. "The Blending of Classical and Christian Traditions in the Work of pseudo-Hegesippus," *ISSQ* 33 (1980), 60–64.

23. For Evagrius' friendship with Jerome, cf. *Epistulae* 3.3 and 5.3, where Evagrius is "carissimus mihi." He is also described in the warmest terms in *Vita Malchi* 1. Jerome lived in Evagrius' home in the early 370s; and J. N. D. Kelly pictures Evagrius at that time as "trying his hand as an original author" (*Jerome: His Life, Writings, and Controversies* [London: Duckworth, 1975], p. 66). For Evagrius' friendship with Ambrose, see *Epistulae* 8.76, 56.

24. *De viris illustribus* 125.

25. By contrast, Jerome's translation of Eusebius' *Chronicon* begins with a two-paragraph discussion of the problems of translating from Greek to Latin. He admits that everything in the work from the time of Abraham to the Trojan War is "pura Graeca translatio." From the Trojan War to Constantine's day, however, "I have added a number of things which I have carefully excerpted from Suetonius and other famous historians." And yet Jerome and all subsequent writers regarded the work as a translation and nothing else.

26. G. B. Ladner, "Aspects of Patristic Anti-Judaism," *Viator* 2 (1971), 355–363.

27. A. L. Williams, *Adversus Judaeos* (Cambridge University Press, 1935), pp. 31–42.

28. F. G. Bratton, *The Crime of Christendom: The Theological Sources of Anti-Semitism* (Boston: Beacon Press, 1969), p. 79.

29. M. Simon, "La polemique anti-juive de s. Jean Chrysostome et la mouvement judaisant d'Antioche," *AIPHOS* 4 (1936), 411.

30. A Latin text of I Maccabees was certainly in circulation as early as A.D. 200. The Vulgate text is actually a barely revised version of this earlier translation. Cf. F. M. Abel, *Les livres des Macchabées* (Paris: Gabalda, 1949), pp. lv–lvii, and O. de Bruyne, *Les anciennes traductions latines des Macchabées* (Anecdota Maredsolana IV; Maredsous, 1932), pp. 11–14.

31. Josephus complicates the problem by giving a quite different version of his activities in his *Vita*.

32. Ussani (above, n. 8), p. 108.

33. This may be what he meant when he said he wanted to consider the Jewish nation "per principes ductum" (preface, 3).

34. McCormick (above, n. 17), p. 212.

18 Josephus in Byzantium

STEVEN BOWMAN

B yzantine civilization was the heir of both Graeco-Roman and Jewish
traditions. Byzantines of various ethnic backgrounds reinterpreted
these two rich legacies through a Christian prism to produce a vibrant
and multifaceted society and culture that successfully adapted to changing historical circumstances for over a millennium.[1] Thus while Byzantines saw
themselves as the perpetuators of antiquity, they functioned and created within
a medieval state whose numerous traditions are still evidenced in the many
lands they influenced.

Byzantium saw her models in the golden past. Ancient Rome provided
the concept of empire and the historical experience to sustain Byzantine rule
both militarily and diplomatically throughout the ages. Greece supplied a rich
cultural and literary legacy. The Bible provided the outline for God's plan: the
Hebrew Scriptures supplied the framework (especially during the period of
the monarchy), and the New Testament contributed the rationale that this brief
historical continuum between creation and the messianic redemption was toler-
able only if man lived in a state of salvation, that is, as an Orthodox Christian.[2]

What was the place of the writings of Josephus Flavius, the historian and
apologist of one strand of the double helix of Byzantine tradition, the history
of the Jews? What is the relationship of Josephus to the other first-century
historians? We shall deal with these two themes first and then examine the way
that Byzantine authors made use of Josephus' works.

Josephus provided two important supports to the foundation of Byzantine
identity. Josephus was an independent witness to the sacred history of the Jews
that was recorded in the biblical text. His histories (or "archaeologies," as he

The author thanks Professors Louis H. Feldman and Alexander Kazhdan for their
comments.

called them, paralleling Dionysius of Halicarnassus' *Roman Antiquities*) both confirmed and amplified the biblical story. And, moreover, his later books filled in the gap between the closing of the Hebrew Scriptures and the period covered by the New Testament. As with the efforts of most ancient chroniclers and historians, his works were recognized as authentic and, therefore, authoritative.[3]

Still, there were other recorders of the history of the Jews: Hellenistic Jewish historians such as Eupolemus and Demetrius, the Syrian Nicholas of Damascus, and Justus of Tiberias, to note but a few. How is it that only Josephus was preserved in toto in Byzantium while the works of the others must be salvaged from the florilegia that proliferate in Byzantine literature?[4]

One answer to this question is that of all first-century authors outside of the New Testament texts, only Josephus unequivocally mentions Jesus of Nazareth, the Christ of the Gentiles. Despite scholarly debate over the extent of interpolation in *Antiquities* XVIII, 63–64, by later Christian (and even anti-Christian authors), it is most probable that some nucleus of the Jesus narrative (inoffensive to later Christians) was put into the text by Josephus himself. Thus Josephus becomes in Byzantine literature the major extrabiblical witness for the existence of a savior upon whom an entire civilization was predicated.[5]

Josephus attained a central place in Byzantine literature for the Christians because he was an independent source for the history of the Jews from creation to the reign of Domitian. Though he was the primary nonbiblical witness to the existence of the Byzantine Christ, Byzantines did not find it necessary to prove the historicity of Christ. Josephus, too, was to have an important place in the identity of Byzantine Jews, albeit only from the tenth century onward.

In this short essay we shall not be able to explore all of the ramifications of Josephus' influence in Byzantine literature. A large number of articles in this volume deal with themes that are at their base Byzantine. We shall therefore only outline those areas that are chronologically Byzantine and treat in detail some of the specifics whose long-term effects are not eminently clear in these specialized essays.[6]

The role of Eusebius is pivotal in the canonization of Josephus as a source for Christian historical identity. Eusebius, bishop of Caesarea, was the contemporary biographer of Constantine, the founder of Constantinople and today conventionally recognized as the first of the Christian Roman emperors (even though he did not convert until the eve of his death and then as an Arian). Eusebius created the basic framework for subsequent Christian world histories. To him Josephus was an authentic eyewitness to the period of Jesus' career, as well as an independent Jewish source to ancient history.[7] Eusebius was convinced of his veracity and of his authenticity in validating the truth of

Scripture. In his *Ecclesiastical History* and in his two theological works, *Praeparatio Evangelica* and *Demonstratio Evangelica,* Eusebius quoted extensively from Josephus' *Antiquities* and *Jewish War.*[8] Eusebius' works became the major vehicle through which the Josephan corpus was transmitted to Byzantine chronographers for the next nine centuries. A most important scholarly question is the extent to which Eusebius and his colleagues edited the works of Josephus in light of their theological predilections.[9]

In the sixth century, a major chronography was assembled by Ioannes Malalas of Antioch. While his interest was centered on his own city in Syria, he provides considerable data on the period of the Second Commonwealth and on the impact of the Jews of Israel upon events in Syria in the first century. Only some of this material comes from Josephus or from a source common to both, especially in regard to his description of Antioch and its buildings. He cites Josephus directly as his source for Jesus, his crucifixion, and the subsequent fate of the Jews (Malalas, X, 14, 247–248). According to Rivka Duker-Fishman, Malalas used florilegia rather than the actual texts of Josephus, and this accounts for his variant readings.[10]

In the *Chronikon Paschale,* written about 630, an anonymous author draws his citations of Josephus primarily from the works of Eusebius. While he is more concerned with the history of the early church, in particular the Josephan evidence for the life of Jesus, he also cites Josephus for the death of John the Baptist, the register of high priests from Ananias to Caiaphas, the heirs of Herod, the assassination of James (Jacob) the brother of Jesus, and the meaning of the word Pascha ($\dot{v}\pi\varepsilon\rho\beta\alpha\sigma\dot{\iota}\alpha$). The author, too, cites the chronographia of Malalas, as well as Eusebius, along with such sources contemporary to his theme as the New Testament and Philo.[11]

George the Synkellos was a monk in late eighth-century Palestine and Constantinople. His chronicle provided the basic synchronism of Graeco-Roman and Judeo-Christian history for subsequent generations of chronographers. In addition, he preserves notices from the works of many lost authors of ancient history and chronology.[12] Among the many sources used by this monk are excerpts from Josephus which he seems to have derived via Eusebius, in particular the passages describing the voice that prophesied in the Temple, the destruction of the Second Temple and the captivity of the Jews, Herod's heirs, the assassination of James (Jacob) the brother of Jesus, and the career of John the Baptist. These are the traditional Christian elements that appeared earlier in Eusebius and in later chroniclers, such as Malalas and the *Chronikon Paschale.* The important passages from the *Testimonium Flavianum* do not appear in his chronicle, however.[13] Important extracts from Josephus appear in the chronicle of the monk George Harmatolos, which influenced later Russian chronographers and the author of the Slavonic Josephus.[14]

Some of the non-Josephan material incorporated by George the Synkellos is of special interest since it leads us back to the first century. The *terminus ad quem* of his chronicle may come from one of his major sources, the five books of chronology of Sextus Julius Africanus. George's chronicle extends from creation to A.D. 284, which date would seem to be the upper limit of Africanus' life, since the latter was apparently born in the early years of the third century. Africanus was also a Jerusalemite and a Christian, as recorded by Eusebius, the fourth-century Christian historian from Caesarea in Palestine. His proximity to the source of Christian tradition allowed him a unique access to local material, some of it no doubt oral, but also to any surviving fragments of the prolific literature of the late Hellenistic period.[15]

Africanus was very much interested in establishing the date of Jesus' birth and of reconciling the problems stemming from the different gospel genealogies. For the first he was fortunate enough to have either a copy of, or excerpts from, the chronological and genealogical work of the first-century Galilean historian and chronographer Justus ben Pistus of Tiberias, interesting segments of whose chronicles he anonymously preserves.

Justus ben Pistus has not fared well over the past two millennia. A contemporary of Josephus, he penned a Galilean version of the war with Rome that apparently was sufficiently at odds with Josephus' apologetic work that it evoked a stinging attack from the Roman sycophant in his *Vita*. This first-century rivalry, however, has been dealt with by a number of authors.[16] We are more concerned with the fate of Justus' work or works in the succeeding Byzantine period, in particular in the writings of ninth-century authors.

The learned patriarch Photius (about 820 to 891) notes in his *Bibliotheca,* or *Myriobiblion,* that he had read a chronicle of Justus of Tiberias, the title of which he designates as ἡ ἐπιγραφὴ Ἰούστου Τιβεριέως Ἰουδαίων βασιλέων τῶν ἐν τοῖς στέμμασιν.[17] This chronicle, no longer extant, contained a historical survey of the Jews from Moses to Agrippa, that is, from the first leader of the Jews to their last king. Was this an independent political history? Or was it a synchronic study in the tradition of Hellenistic Jewish historiography? Or was it a preface to Justus' war memoirs? We have no way of knowing the thesis of the work. All we can say at this point is that Justus attacked Josephus for misrepresenting the war in Galilee. Clearly, then, there was more than a little polemic in the chronicle. Photius, too, indicates that much of the material was worthless (πεπλασμένην τὰ πλεῖστά φασι τυγχάνειν), especially Justus' remarks on the war with Rome and the capture of Jerusalem.[18]

Now, why was Photius so negative in his appraisal of Justus that he refused to cite from his chronicle? Aside from the hypothesis that he had not actually read the chronicle[19] (and this problem can only be solved within the framework of the entire *Bibliotheca*), two remarks may shed some light on this exclusion. Photius was very much aware of style; early in his career he had taught literature and rhetoric in the imperial school at Constantinople.

Indeed, he remarks on style and language throughout the *Bibliotheca,* his valuable literary digest with its important summaries and comments on the books he had read.[20] Josephus, in particular, is singled out by Photius for the purity, eloquence, and clarity of his exposition.[21] Justus, on the other hand, wrote very concisely, skipping over most of the important points (e.g., Christ): Ἔστι δὲ τὴν φράσιν συντομώτατός τε καὶ τὰ πλεῖστα τῶν ἀναγκαιοτάτων παρατρέχων. Photius also had a copy of Josephus' *Vita* which attacked Justus as a liar and a cheat.[22] No doubt this prejudiced his reading of Justus.

Even more to the patriarch's disdain was Justus' disregard of the (to Photius) most important aspect of Jewish history in the first century: the birth of Christ, the events surrounding his career, and all the miracles he performed. It is, therefore, to his career as a Christian master of rhetoric, who, in addition, was prejudiced by his reliance upon Josephus, that we owe Photius' condemnation of Justus and his work. No further copies of the chronicle were made, and the one available to Photius was later lost, its fate unknown.

But the *ipsissima verba* of Justus are not unknown. Indeed, fragments not only survived buried in the plethora of Byzantine chronographical studies, but also, according to one modern scholar, became the very base of the pyramid that constitutes Byzantine chronography. The work of George the Synkellos (ninth century) is acknowledged as the linchpin of Byzantine chronography.[23] In turn, he incorporates the work of the third-century Jerusalemite Sextus Julius Africanus, as preserved by the fourth-century Christian Eusebius of Caesarea. Justus is considered by several scholars to be the basis for Africanus' system.[24]

Thus, ironically, while Justus was ignored by Byzantine historians and literary scholars, his contribution to biblical chronology was preserved by the monastic tradition that was concerned primarily with synchronism and chronology.[25] Justus' literary style—the very attribute Photius criticized as at least an affectation of the patriarch scholar—was subordinated to Justus' more interesting chronological data as excerpted by several early church fathers.[26] Eusebius, who is perhaps most responsible for the ultimate reputation of Josephus among later Christian scholars, is also, therefore, a primary link in the survival of Justus of Tiberias, albeit anonymously. Though Justus' name was eclipsed by the subsequent reputation of his contemporary rival, his chronological structure not only survived but also had an important impact via George the Synkellos in the ninth-century and later Byzantine perception of ancient chronography. Despite recent studies devoted to Justus, a monograph study of his work set against his contemporary background and its impact upon future generations of biblical chronographers is a desideratum.[27]

The reputation and works of Nicolaus of Damascus fared somewhat better in Byzantium than those of Justus. For a number of reasons the literary career of Nicolaus of Damascus is apposite to our inquiry. Despite his provenance from an upper-class Hellenized family in Damascus, Nicolaus became the court historian of Herod and subsequently wrote a universal history that included an official and detailed, if not sycophantic or apologetic, study of Jewish history, capped by a panegyric of Herod himself. Nicolaus apparently provided the major source of information, followed by Josephus, for the second and first centuries B.C. Further, the fragments of Nicolaus that survive outnumber by far the combined total of all of the Hellenistic Jewish historians who preceded him.[28]

The largest number of Nicolaus' fragments are found in the *Excerpta Historica* compiled under the direction of the Byzantine Emperor Constantine VII Porphyrogenitus (d. 959).[29] These fragments include a summary of books one through seven (out of a total of 144 books) of his universal history and Nicolaus' autobiography. Apparently, Nicolaus was a source for other parts of the *Excerpta Historica* that have not survived.[30] These lost sections may have given us further information on the structure, scope, and content of the later books of his universal history. Enough, however, has survived to indicate the Byzantine interest in and possible attitude toward Nicolaus.[31]

In all the surviving fragments of Nicolaus of Damascus we find no reference to his material on Jewish history. Photius, for example, was interested in his *Collection of Remarkable Customs*.[32] Constantine was concerned with the geographical data on the Peloponnesus and with Nicolaus' material on the history of Assyria, Babylonia and Medea, Hellas, Lydia, the cities of the Peloponnesus, the rise of Persia, and the early history of Rome.[33] Constantine, too, although there is no evidence for it, may have used Nicolaus' *Vita Augusti* as a model for his encomium of his father, Basil.[34]

Since it appears that much, if not all, of the 144 books of Nicolaus' history and his other works were extant in the tenth century, why, we may ask, was the Jewish component of Nicolaus' work ignored? Was Josephus' reputation so established that the Jewish history of Nicolaus suffered the same fate as that of Justus of Tiberias? The question is difficult to answer since we cannot impute to Byzantine scholars the same tradition of source criticism as that of modern historians nor the latter's interests in matters of historiography. Rather, it seems that these ancient scrolls were considered encyclopedias to be mined for their contemporary interest and value.[35]

This suggestion does not answer our first question: why was Nicolaus' Jewish material ignored? It may well be that Josephus was considered the ultimate authority for biblical history during the Byzantine period. Inasmuch as Eusebius gave to Josephus' collected works his imprimatur, the surviving rivals a priori would have had to take second place. Also, in the case of Nicolaus, whatever value he must have had for the reconstruction of Jewish history (of the intertestamental period), in the eyes of the later Byzantine authors he had already been excerpted by Josephus, whether by acknowledged citation or by inclusion in his general treatment.[36] Therefore, Nicolaus' works languished in the imperial library until the great historical project undertaken by Constantine resurrected them. The fate of Josephus, however, was quite the opposite.

The medieval career of the writings attributed to Josephus is impressive in the works' ubiquity.[37] Of all the Hellenistic literature to have survived (certainly that of the Jewish authors), Josephus' writings were undoubtedly the most widespread, and correspondingly, quite influential. Josephus, after all, presented a connected history of the world from creation to his own day, thus providing in an expanded secular fashion a parallel to the sacred traditions recorded in the holy books of the three religious civilizations of the medieval world.

A number of translators had a hand in making the works of Josephus, or parts of them, available to their respective peoples. Cassiodorus provided the basis for a number of Christianized versions for the Latin-speaking West. In the Greek-speaking orbit, Greek, Hebrew, and Slavonic versions provided mutually exclusive and independent extrabiblical source material for internal denominational and sectarian consumption.[38]

The Greek-speaking population was familiar with the lengthy Greek version of Josephus. The long scrolls were piously copied and epitomized by countless generations of chronographers and historians of the Second Commonwealth period.[39] Photius, for example, in his *Bibliotheca,* summarizes the *Jewish War* (no. 47), of which he read the seven books, and later he comments on the twenty books of the *Antiquities* (no. 76). Apparently, the latter manuscript had appended to it a copy of the *Vita.* As late, too, as the fifteenth century, echoes of Josephus might be found in the poetic collection of Old Testament material attributed to Georgios Choumnos.[40] Indeed, a study of the extant manuscript tradition of the entire Josephan corpus, alongside the excerpts available in the vast literature of the Byzantine period, would shed considerable insight on the influence of this first-century Jewish writer among Byzantine scholars.[41] Such a study would center on the role of the prolific Eusebius of Caesarea as a key transmitter of the Josephan corpus.

The availability of Josephus to Byzantine writers can be partially ascertained from the number of extant manuscripts and from citations of his works. Schreckenberg, in his valuable summary of this material, has counted the following manuscripts: one from the ninth or tenth century, one perhaps from the tenth century, three dated between the tenth and eleventh centuries, nine from the eleventh century, four dated between the eleventh and twelfth centuries, and four from the twelfth century. Two are dated between the twelfth and thirteenth centuries, seven from the thirteenth, and two more from between the thirteenth and fourteenth centuries. The bulk of the manuscripts are from the fourteenth to the sixteenth century: thirty-one (fourteenth), seven (fourteenth to fifteenth), ten (fifteenth to sixteenth), nine (sixteenth), while six others are seventeenth-century copies. Of the more than 120 extant Greek manuscripts, then, thirty-three are anterior to the fourteenth century, with two-thirds of these from the period of the Comnenoi; more than half are from the Palaeologan period and less than 20 percent are from the period after the fall of Constantinople.[42] If nothing else, this catalogue shows the popularity of Josephus, at least in the last three centuries of Byzantium.

Another control over the text of Josephus comes from the tenth-century *Excerpta Historica* of Constantine VII. Josephus scholars have compiled a concordance of the excerpts found in that encyclopedia; it designates some 119 citations from the *Jewish War, Antiquities,* and the *Vita.*[43] An analysis of these passages indicates that the tenth-century investigators were primarily interested in Josephus' comments on the virtues and evils inherent in government, a not-surprising observation given the theme of one section of the *Excerpta Historica,* the Greek title of which is περὶ ἀρετῆς καὶ κακίας.[44] Josephus' observations and comments are a mine for such a Deuteronomic theme. We may profitably examine to what extent these excerpts were viewed by the emperor as applicable to his own time in general and to the vicissitudes of his career in particular.[45]

Some understanding of the underlying themes of the *Excerpta Historica* may be gleaned from the use to which Josephus' comments were put by the compilers of the encyclopedia. The name of one section in Greek is clearly derived from the passage in Josephus which deals with his condemnation of the Zealots: πολλὰ δ᾽ αὐτοῖς περὶ ἀρετῆς καὶ κακίας προεθέσπισαν, ἃ παραβάντες οἱ ζηλωταὶ καὶ τῆς κατὰ τῆς πατρίδος προφητείας τέλους ἠξίωσαν.[46] The following passage strongly suggests one background against which Constantine Porphyrogenitus (or his editors) saw the problems of his own period: ἦν γὰρ δή τις παλαιὸς λόγος ἀνδρῶν ἔνθα τότε τὴν πόλιν ἁλώσεσθαι καὶ καταφλεχθήσεσθαι τὰ ἅγια, ὅταν πολέμου νόμῳ στάσις ἐγκατασκήψῃ καὶ χεῖρες οἰκεῖαι προμιάνωσι τὸ τοῦ θεοῦ ἅγιον τέμενος οἷς οὐκ ἀπιστήσαντες οἱ ζηλωταὶ διακόνους ἑαυτοὺς ἐπέδοσαν.[47]

Who might these contemporary Zealots be, who by their defilement of the sanctuary and their civil strife might bring about the capture of the holy city of Constantinople? What we have here may very well be a reflection of Constantine's hostility toward the Lekapenoi who, led by Romanos Lekapenos, the admiral of the imperial fleet, had seized the throne of the empire in 919 from the young Constantine (he was fifteen at the time) and had established his sons as Constantine's co-emperors along with the illegitimate son of the Emperor Leo's fourth (and hence illegal) marriage. The supplanting (at least to Constantine) of the reigning Macedonian house by the upstart Lekapenos must have continued to shock and anger the quiet scholar until the deposition of Romanos in 944 and his sons soon after. Would Constantine not find a parallel to their deeds in the evils that befell the Second Commonwealth period as recorded in the works of Josephus: the usurpation of the purple (a pun on the name Porphyrogenitus), a scandalous and immature patriarch (or high priest) in the form of Romanos' youngest son, who preferred racing horses to celebrating mass, and the ruin of great and noble men? Would not the prophecy be fulfilled in Constantine's own time unless some basic changes were made in the policies of his unwelcome co-emperors or, better yet, unless the legitimate Macedonian rulers were restored?[48]

The self-identification of Byzantines with the course of Israel's history, both biblical and intertestamental, lends credence to the suggestion that Constantine read Josephus as a blueprint for his own time.[49] This may be seen as much from the excerpts of Josephus that were used as from the material that was excluded. Generally, the excerpts deal with good and evil rulers. Some of the leaders mentioned by Josephus, however, are conspicuous by their absence, such as Jezebel, Nebuchadnezzar, and Antiochus IV. A number of excerpts emphasize the theme of the wicked sons of a leader who cause his dynasty to be destroyed. Others stress the evils of civil strife (stasis), which weakens the resolve of a people to resist the common enemy.[50] And several suggest that loyalty to a reigning monarch will be rewarded by sustenance and protection.[51] It would be difficult to argue how many of the passages from Josephus in the Excerpta Historica were chosen on the basis of their relevance to Constantine's own situation as a co-emperor in a gilded cage—we simply do not know the criteria for selection used in this particular section of the encyclopedia. Still, there may have been an overt or, at least, a covert reason for the selections that were made. It may be argued that Constantine saw some contemporary relevance to the oracle cited by Josephus in the passage immediately following the one from which Constantine derived the title for this section of the encyclopedia.

Characteristic of this anthologizing of Josephus, although not done with the same motive, is the anonymous "De obsidione toleranda," more than half of which consists of examples drawn verbatim from Polybius, Josephus, and Arrian; this text, dealing with how to resist a siege, may have relied upon another florilegium that survives only in fragments.[52] Another example of this anthologizing of Josephus is the passage about Moses' Ethiopian war in the tenth-century anonymous Palaea Historica, which is derived from Josephus, A II, 238–253.[53]

While the study and use of Josephus was endemic in Byzantine tradition throughout the period of the empire, it was during the tenth and eleventh centuries that new uses of the texts were made by both Jews and Christians. The question of an orthodox and connected view of biblical history was solved by the works of Josephus. The works of his contemporaries were used mainly to solve certain chronological questions and were allowed to languish in the library collections where they were ultimately lost when these great repositories of ancient literature were destroyed. The works of Nicolaus of Damascus, on the other hand, were epitomized for their value in providing a quasi-authoritative universal history. Among the Jews we find an interest in chronology that more likely reflects an intellectual rather than an eschatological orientation.[54] The *War* of Josephus, on the other hand, was rewritten in Hebrew, the so-called *Josippon,* and in the process its Latin source was de-Christianized. Indeed, the view of the Second Commonwealth period in *Josippon* is quite different from the traditional rabbinic attitude that emphasizes its Pharisaic antecedents, except that *Josippon's* condemnation of the Zealots and other fighting groups is parallel to that of the rabbis. *Josippon,* however, at the same time that it condemns the internecine fighting, is quite proud of Jewish valor against the Romans. The author also displays a favorable attitude toward Josephus. His attitude toward Titus, however, was decidedly in the Josephan tradition and the opposite of that of the rabbis. He portrays him as a noble Roman, heartsick at the destruction of a great temple and of its city at the hands of rebels and malcontents.[55]

An expanded study of the present essay may divide the influence of Josephus upon the plethora of Byzantine authors among the following categories: the problem of the so-called *Testimonium Flavianum* or Josephus' witness to Jesus; his example as literary stylist and historiographer; and his influence on developing ethnic groups as an authentic witness to their newly attained identity as the Christian heirs of Israel. A number of writers overlap several of these categories; yet a systematic survey of all of Byzantine literature will show that Josephus' multifaceted influence in the three major areas (the *Testimonium* is quite a separate problem in this respect) is much more than would be apparent were we to restrict our inquiry to direct citations.

Schreckenberg lists nearly fifty Byzantine authors and works that rely directly or indirectly upon Josephus for their citations of Second Commonwealth Jewish history. Research is currently proceeding on a number of these authors and their use of Josephus.[56] There is much work to be done in this respect, since the process of selection and adaptation of the citation differs among many of these works. Two examples from post tenth-century authors may indicate further lines of research.

Ioannes Zonaras wrote his historical *Epitome* in the twelfth century. Both in his choice of structure and in his reliance upon Josephus, Zonaras is most unique among Byzantine chroniclers. His first volume is the history of the Jews from creation to the rebellion against Rome (including the only full account of the Maccabees and Herod in later Byzantine literature), which is based primarily on Josephus, with supplements from other sources. Zonaras judiciously edits Josephus to present a straightforward historical account and excludes much of the supplementary literary, philosophical, and documentary material found in Josephus, and as well the theological reflections of earlier epitomizers of Josephus' Jewish history. He does not synchronize Jewish and pagan history as do his predecessors, but rather he follows Josephus' example of treating the history of the Jews and of the Romans separately.[57]

Nicetas Choniates, who died shortly after 1210, wrote a valuable history covering events in Byzantium from 1118 to 1206. Its historical import for the twelfth century is unmatched, while its literary quality reflects a solid familiarity with ancient stylists. For our purposes the latter is apposite. It has been shown that Nicetas' description of the fall of Didymoteichon to the Latins in 1206 is modeled on Josephus' account of the fall of Jotapata to the Romans. His literary borrowings were clear enough to an educated Byzantine reader, and thus the implication that the fall of Didymoteichon had the same import as the fall of Jotapata was emphasized.[58]

These two twelfth-century authors, the chronicler Ioannes Zonaras and the historian Nicetas Choniates, reflect a constructive and unique use of Josephus as a source for their historiographic style, which goes beyond that of the traditional epitomizing chronicler. The latter more often than not excerpted directly from Josephus where appropriate and adjusted the original (or the version before him) to meet the historical or theological purposes of his narrative. In the works of the two aforementioned authors, Josephus' actual structure of historical presentation and literary influence can be educed through a comparison with the original. Herein, given the plethora of Byzantine authors, lies a vast and fruitful area for further research.

Another area of potential research is the extent to which Josephus' description of the fall of Jerusalem influenced the historiographers of the fall of Constantinople in 1453. We know that the lamentation ascribed to Jeremiah was cited directly and indirectly by Greek, Latin, Armenian, and Hebrew recorders of that event as a striking biblical prototype of that tragedy.[59] To what extent Josephus served as a model for the historians of the *Halosis,* as his description of Jotapata did for Nicetas Choniates, has yet to be determined.[60]

Byzantium provided the vehicle through which the Slavic-speaking peoples to the north became acquainted with Josephus. The translation of the Slavonic version of Josephus into German and French at the beginning of this century has engendered a lively scholarly debate that has not yet seen its resolution. Scholarly opinions concerning the Slavonic version revolve around the questions of date and authenticity. Do we indeed have a first-century document in Slavonic translation? Is it based upon the Aramaic original of Josephus, with interpolations by subsequent gnostic or sectarian Christians? Or do we, in fact, possess a medieval forgery? These questions reflect the concerns of the scholars during the period between the two world wars.[61] Since then the medieval history of Byzantium and Eastern Europe has come into its own with an established discipline of scholarship.[62] We may, therefore, cease to look at every source that mentions a first century document as a medieval forgery and begin to judge such material on its own merit, namely as a manifestation of the intellectual development of these medieval societies.[63] The Slavonic Josephus should therefore be removed from the scholarly problems of the first century and seen rather against the background of Macedonia in the tenth and eleventh centuries.[64]

This is not the place to argue the questions involved in the Slavonic Josephus.[65] What is important to emphasize is that the famous passage in Book XVIII of Josephus' *Antiquities,* the so-called *Testimonium Flavianum,* which provides the *only* contemporary historical and extratestamental notice of Jesus (outside of the short allusions to James [Jacob] in *A* XX, 200–203),[66] necessitated a Slavonic interpretation or (more accurately) reinterpretation of the Christian interpolations of the original Greek text of Josephus.[67] The Slavonic version actually increases and intensifies the Christian element. Josephus, then, as a witness to the origins of Christianity by virtue of his having mentioned, however obliquely, its founder, became a necessary part of the ninth- and tenth-century Byzantine scene and the successive cultures it introduced to its world view.[68]

The Slavs, who only a century or two before had threatened to inundate and destroy the Byzantine civilization in Greece, were successfully "Graecized" through their acceptance of the Greek language and Orthodox Christianity.[69] Through this twin process they became Greek. Their ethnic cousins to the north were absorbed in another way. The missionary work of Cyril and Methodius in the ninth century, in particular the creation of an alphabet to render the Slavic language, gave to these tribes the possibility of an ancient history and a central niche in the family of man in *their own language.*[70] Henceforth, they, too, would compete as equals in the continued unfolding of God's plan for the world as outlined in the Scriptures or Josephus.

This seems a more appropriate line of research in which to pursue the problems involved in the Slavonic Josephus, namely to illuminate the proper background against which to study the text and its tradition and to examine the identity of its translators, along with the theological motivation behind the project. Such an investigation might show the Slavonic Josephus to be a theologically motivated piece of counterpropaganda to offset the imperial and orthodox image of a Christian Byzantine penetration among the northern Slavs. The work of Josephus, after all, was the optimal vehicle of ancient literature into which to interpolate such material.[71] The Greek prototype of the *War* used for the Slavonic version appears to be a twelfth- or thirteenth-century version into which a number of anti-Latin interpolations were inserted. This reflects the understandable hostility of the Comnenian period with its anti-Lombard basis or of the Nicaean court of the Lascarids, whose metropolis—

Constantinople—was occupied by the villains of the Fourth Crusade. As such, the story has indirect value for our understanding of how the Josephan corpus could be put to use for contemporary propaganda purposes.[72]

The career of Josephus among his co-religionists in Byzantium is somewhat different. Whether he was known to the Jews in Greek or only in Latin has yet to be resolved; the lack of any source material for the former is the most limiting factor in any investigation of this question despite some indirect evidence (for example, a Hebrew translation of Pseudo-Callisthenes' Alexander Romance). We may surmise, however, that Greek-speaking Jews should have been aware of the Josephan material either directly from Josephus or through Christian epitomizers. In either case they have left us no literary remains to hazard an opinion. The Hebrew Josephus is another story.

In the mid-tenth century southern Italy was still an integral part of the Byzantine world. There the interplay of three cultures produced a lively cultural and intellectual environment, of which the medical school at Salerno is perhaps a better-known later manifestation. With respect to the Jewish inhabitants of the area, the career of Shabbetai Donnolo, one of the first physicians of medieval Europe and a prolific writer and thinker, has long been known. Several important historical sources, too, stem from this area, in particular a Hebrew version of Josephus and an interesting chronology of kings and emperors, both of which come from the mid-tenth century, and the eleventh-century family history of Aḥima'az ben Paltiel and the chronicles of Yeraḥme'el, which includes most of *Josippon*. We should also note in passing important recent research that has identified a number of southern Italian liturgical poets and their influence on the development of the synagogal poetry of Ashkenazi or central European Jewry.[73]

In the very midst of this cultural renaissance an anonymous southern-Italian Jew produced a Hebrew version of Josephus for the benefit of his co-religionists. This Hebrew version served as a source of unparalleled authority for the Jews (in several versions) throughout the medieval period, and even to the present day, in certain circles for the history of the Second Commonwealth. It was also cited as an authority by the Christians (who knew, however, only its Latin predecessors until the sixteenth century, when the Hebrew version was translated into Latin for the first time) in their dialogues and polemics. The great fourteenth-century Muslim historian, Ibn Khaldun, used a Judeo-Arabic version of *Josippon* (perhaps an eleventh-century translation), which he found in Egypt, as his source for the Second Commonwealth period. The extant and nonextant manuscript tradition is so rich that it is not completely possible at this stage of research to ascertain the mutual influence of the various Josephan works upon each other.[74] The date of the Hebrew version of Josephus is 953. The author's sources have been identified as the Latin version of Josephus known by the name of *Hegesippus* (from the Latinized form of Josephus), as well as a manuscript (now lost) which consisted of sixteen (out of the twenty) books of the *Antiquities* and perhaps *Contra Apionem*. The author also knew the twenty-four books of the Jewish Bible in Hebrew and Latin, as well as, especially, I and II Maccabees (in Latin) and a number of medieval chronicles that supplied him with background on the origins of the peoples whom he includes in his table of nations and with information on the history of Rome.

The methodology of the author of the Hebrew version is harmonious with his intellectual environment; however, he does differ from his contemporaries in a number of ways. In his approach to his material, the historian had to deal with a complex of historical, legendary, and religious elements, some of which he reproduced uncritically, while from others he removed obvious Christian interpolations. The author in one place describes his methodology: "I excerpted facts from the book of Joseph ben Gorion [Flavius Josephus] and from the books of other authors who wrote about the deeds of our ancestors, and I collected them in one treatise." But the author did not merely excerpt and translate: he also on occasion commented on the historical meaning of his sources, to which he was faithful and which he was also careful to present in a literary form that did them justice.

In his treatment of the subject—the history of the Jews from the destruction of the First Temple through the destruction of the Second—the author does not indicate any intellectual reliance on the general medieval Jewish tendency to emphasize *Kiddush ha-Shem* ("Sanctification of the Name"), that is, martyrdom.[75] The only passages where martyrdom is treated are reproduced directly from his Latin source, the fourth-century version of Josephus (known as *Hegesippus*) written by a Jewish convert to Christianity. Nor is there any indication that his historiological approach was influenced by the eschatological framework of the Four Kingdoms outlined in the Book of Daniel and accepted by all medieval chronographers. Moreover, he was well aware of the Byzantine Empire within which he lived and understood that it was the direct heir of the Roman Empire, which flourished in the period about which he was writing. Thus, he made legitimate, albeit anachronistic, use of contemporary Byzantine practices to flesh out the picture of Rome in her earlier days.[76]

The author of *Josippon*, as argued by David Flusser, is the only medieval author who restricts himself to an interpretation of the distant past based on a rationalist and independent approach to the sources available to him; that is, he does not introduce direct contemporary notices to make his work "relevant." It is not before the nineteenth century that we find another Jewish historian with the same method. Interestingly enough, the author's modern-day successors often come to the same conclusion as their medieval predecessor.

The author's treatment of the Hasidim, Pharisees, and Sadducees, for example, reads like a number of twentieth-century interpretations and stands up better than most.[77]

Thus our author has approached his task in a modern critical manner and has utilized a methodology that in many respects is superior to a number of the latter-day investigators of the Second Commonwealth period. At the same time his approach to the past reflects the historiographical outlook of the mid-tenth-century Byzantine world. While written for Jews, it has few rabbinic citations and is thus less "Jewishly" structured; rather, it parallels the historical approach of his Christian colleagues.

The later career of *Josippon* in Byzantium is not without interest in this respect. It was known to the twelfth-century Karaite Jewish encyclopedist Judah Hadassi, who listed it in an important citation. In the mid-fourteenth century, a young scholarly bibliophile, Judah ibn Moskoni of Ochrida, embarked on a "postdoctoral" research project that entailed extensive travel throughout the Mediterranean world in order to collect all the extant manuscripts of the Spanish-Jewish polymath Abraham ibn Ezra as a preparation for his own supercommentary upon the latter's biblical commentary. During the course of his travels he ran across several manuscripts, some complete, others mutilated, of *Josippon*. His reaction to this material is worthy of note: after he spent some time wandering about copying and purchasing manuscripts for his projects, he ran across this book by accident "and I read in it, and its words were like honey in my mouth." For a number of reasons this book was of value to its discoverer: it afforded insights into the history of empires that had failed, insights that were of interest to intelligent scholars for their contemporary application; it was also valuable to the Jews for the story it told of the destruction of the Temple and the loss of their city. It, moreover, had a special message for the Jews, namely that God had lengthened the days of the exile because of the manifold sins of the Jews, and that this had prevented their repatriation to the Land of Israel. Its historical value, too, was obvious; the book, after all, was written by a Jew who saw the Temple when it was still standing. His descriptions, therefore, were to be trusted as accurate, especially since they antedated the material in traditional rabbinic sources, namely, the Mishnah and Talmud.[78]

What the author had discovered, therefore, was a Jewish history to replace or, at least, to stand alongside the traditional accounts contained in rabbinic literature. Since the latter was ahistorical,[79] it could not contradict the eyewitness account of a participant in the tragic events of the first century. In a historically minded civilization, such as was Byzantium, the discovery of a valid historical account of the first century was a tremendous event for the young scholar. (We should emphasize that Judah ibn Moskoni of Ochrida antedated by only two generations the Latin Renaissance scholars who discovered their intellectual origins through the purchase and transfer of Greek manuscripts to the West.) His excitement was such that he put aside for the moment his current research project and avidly collected whatever supplemental information was available in the communities that he visited. The result was that he edited four or five manuscripts to produce an edition of *Josippon* that was the basis for the first printed edition of the work by Tam ibn Yahya in Constantinople in the early sixteenth century. That edition, with minor changes, has remained the most popular edition among Orthodox Jews until the present day.[80]

The ubiquity of the writings of Josephus in Byzantine literature, both in Greek from the fourth century and in Hebrew from the tenth century, until the end of that civilization is based on two factors. Josephus provided a semisacred history of the world from creation to his own day that was accepted as authentic by subsequent authors. Also, he preserved data of correlative value in citations from other authors or in the form of subsidiary information on non-Jewish matters.[81] In other words, from the standpoint of a chronicler of the ancient world or a historian who foresaw the world of the Byzantines, the works of Josephus enjoyed the reputation and authority of an ancient encyclopedia whose contents and style were a major influence on the Byzantine perception of its own past. Moreover, his works were capable of those interpolations that could express the contemporary biases of his successive epitomizers. In sum, rather than disparaging Byzantine authors for their lack of originality in their reliance on Josephus, we can turn to the words R. D. Hicks applied to Diogenes Laertes and his contemporary writers of biography: "Originality comes out in selection and arrangement rather than in research. The materials are in the main the same, but the structure varies with the fashion of the day." [82]

Notes

1. In one of his last contributions to our understanding of Byzantine history and society, John Teall suggested a parallel with early modern state-building as a key to understanding Byzantium's later history ("The Problem of Byzantine Decline: Towards a New Paradigm," in *First Annual Byzantine Studies Conference, Abstracts of Papers* [Cleveland, 1975], pp. 40f.). For the Byzantines themselves the situation was precisely the opposite: see Alexander Kazhdan and Anthony Cutler, "Continuity and Discontinuity in Byzantine History," *Byzantion* 52 (1982), pp. 429–478. Also cf. Steven Bowman, "Another Medieval Heritage: The Jews of Byzantium," *Forum* 36 (1979), pp. 131–141.

2. The basic work, although in many areas out of date, is K. Krumbacher, *Geschichte der byzantinischen Literatur von Justinian bis zum Ende des oströmischen Reiches (527–1453)* (2nd ed., Munich, 1897); a new edition of the ecclesiastical authors is in H. G. Beck, *Kirche und theologische Literatur im byzantinischen Reich* (Munich, 1959); the basic reference work for Byzantine historians is G. Moravcik, *Byzantinoturcica* (2nd ed., Berlin, 1958) vol. 1. See Steven Bowman, *The Jews of Byzantium, 1204–1453* (University, Ala., 1985), Chapter 1, for further discussion and references, and below, n. 49.

3. The basic research has been conveniently collected by H. Schreckenberg, *Die Flavius-Josephus-Tradition in Antike und Mittelalter* (Leiden, 1972) and *Rezeptionsgeschichtliche und Textkritische Untersuchungen zu Flavius Josephus* (Leiden, 1977); for supplements, see notes below. See now Louis H. Feldman, *Josephus and Modern Scholarship (1937–1980)* (Berlin, New York, 1984), pp. 856f.

4. On these authors, cf. Ben Zion Wacholder, *Eupolemus: A Study of Judaeo-Greek Literature* (New York, Jerusalem, 1974), and his earlier monograph, *Nicolaus of Damascus* (Berkeley, Los Angeles, 1962), especially pp. 8f.

5. On the *Testimonium Flavianum*, see the bibliography cited below in notes 66 and 67. To these one must add the thorough investigation of Shlomo Pines, *An Arabic Version of the Testimonium Flavianum and Its Implications* (Jerusalem, 1971), and among Byzantine chroniclers, Rivka Duker-Fishman, "The Second Temple Period in Byzantine Chronicles," *Byzantion* 47 (1977), n. 26 and text.

6. We shall confine our dates to the history of Constantinople as the capital of the Roman Empire from 330 to 1453, since the Byzantines never formally recognized the division of the Roman Empire.

7. *Historia Ecclesiastica*, Book II, X, 10. For Josephus' influence on Eusebius, see André Pelletier, ed., *Flavius Josèphe: Guerre des Juifs, Livre I* (Paris, 1975), who argues that Eusebius' variants are the result of his own emendations. See also Robert M. Grant, "Eusebius, Josephus and the Fate of the Jews," *SBLSP*, vol. 2, edited by Paul J. Achtemeier (Missoula, Montana, 1979), pp. 69–86, who attempts to identify Eusebius' sources in order to explain the confusion between his *Chronicle* and *Ecclesiastical History*.

8. Schreckenberg, *Flavius-Josephus-Tradition* (above, n. 3), pp. 79ff.

9. H. Gelzer, *Sextus Julius Africanus und die Byzantinische Chronographie* (Leipzig, 1884, 1888; repr. New York, 1967); A. A. Mosshammer, *The Chronicle of Eusebius and Greek Chronographic Tradition* (Lewisburg, London, 1979); Rivka Duker-Fishman, "The Works of Josephus as a Source for Byzantine Chronicles" [Hebrew], in *Josephus Flavius: Historian of Eretz-Israel in the Hellenistic-Roman Period, Collected Papers*, edited by Uriel Rappaport (Jerusalem, 1982), pp. 140f.

10. Duker-Fishman, "Second Temple Period" (above, n. 5), pp. 141–146; Duker-Fishman, "Works of Josephus," (above, n. 9), pp. 142–144. Cf. E. Bickerman, "Les Maccabées de Malalas," *Byzantion* 21 (1951), pp. 63–84; and G. Downey, *A History of Antioch in Syria from Seleucus to the Arab Conquest* (Princeton, 1961), pp. 193ff. and pp. 37–40 for the sources of Malalas.

11. Duker-Fishman, "Second Temple Period," (above, n. 5), *passim*, and "Works of Josephus," (above, n. 9), pp. 145f.

12. The chronicle was edited by G. Dindorf, *Ekloge Chronographias*, Vols. 1, 2 (*CSHB*, Bonn, 1829) and by A. A. Mosshammer (Leipzig, 1984); the basic study of George the Synkellos' sources is in Gelzer, *Sextus Julius Africanus*, pp. 176–249; cf., in general, R. Laqueur, "Synkellos," in *RE* 45, pp. 1388–1410; and more recently G. L. Huxley, "On the Erudition of George the Synkellos," *PRIA* 81, c., no. 6 (Dublin, 1981), pp. 207–217. Cf. also Cyril Mango, "Who Wrote the Chronicle of Theophanes?" *Zbornik Radova. Recueil des Travaux de l'institut d'études byzantines*, 18 (1978), pp. 9–17. Mango's argument that George the Synkellos is the primary compiler of the *Chronicle* attributed to Theophanes, if accepted, would enhance considerably our appreciation of this late eighth-century polymath.

13. Duker-Fishman, "Works of Josephus" (above, n. 9), pp. 146–148.

14. See below and Francis I. Anderson, "The Diet of John the Baptist," *Abr-Nahrein* 3 (1961–1962), pp. 60–74.

15. The classic study is Gelzer, *Sextus Julius Africanus*. A separate edition of the frag-

ments of Africanus is in Migne, *PG* 10, 63–94, with translation and commentary by A. Cleveland Coxe in *The Anti-Nicene Fathers*, vol. 6 (New York, 1925), pp. 123–140.

16. See now Tessa Rajak, "Justus of Tiberius," *CQ*, n.s. 23 (1973), pp. 148–168, and Yaron Dan, "Josephus Flavius and Justus of Tiberias" [Hebrew], in *Josephus Flavius, Historian of Eretz-Israel*, pp. 57–78. Older studies include H. Luther, *Josephus und Justus of Tiberias* (Halle, 1910); R. Laqueur, *Der Historiker Flavius Josephus* (Giessen, 1920); A. Schalit, "Josephus und Justus," *Klio* 26 (1933), pp. 67–95; F. Ruhl, "Justus von Tiberias," *RhM* 71 (1916), pp. 289–308; T. Frankfort, "La date de l'autobiographie de Flavius Josèphe et des oeuvres de Justus de Tibériade," *RBPH* 39 (1961), pp. 52–58; and the summary in Wacholder, *Eupolemus*, pp. 298ff. See also Shaye J. D. Cohen, *Josephus in Galilee and Rome: His Vita and Development as a Historian* (Leiden, 1979); Hans Drexler, "Untersuchungen zu Josephus und zur Geschichte des jüdischen Aufstandes 66–70," *Klio* 19 (1925), pp. 277–312; and F. Jacoby, "Iustus," in *RE* 10, pp. 1341–1346.

17. *Bibliotheca*, no. 33.

18. Dan, "Josephus Flavius and Justus of Tiberias" (above, n. 16), pp. 60f. and *passim*, accepts that originally there were two books of Justus: a *History* of the Jewish War and a *Chronicle* of Jewish leaders from Moses to Agrippa. Some time between the second and the ninth centuries the two came to form one continuous piece, with the *Chronicle* serving as a prolegomenon to the *History*. E. Schürer, *The History of the Jewish People in the Age of Jesus Christ*, edited by G. Vermes and F. Millar, vol. 1 (Edinburgh, 1973), pp. 35f., gives cogent reasons for separating the two works. Also, the existence of a third work, *Commentarioli de scripturis*, is noted in the comments of Jerome (*De viris illustribus* 14), which is otherwise unattested (Schürer, p. 35). Cf. discussion by Wacholder, *Eupolemus* (above, n. 4), pp. 298–306, and below, n. 26.

19. Rajak is the latest to suggest that Photius did not actually read the chronicle but rather relied on some notes and the comments of Josephus in his *Vita* ("Justus of Tiberias," [above, n. 16] pp. 358ff.).

20. On the *Bibliotheca*, see now Warren Treadgold, *The Nature of the 'Bibliotheca' of Photius* (Washington, D.C., 1980), and for Photius' career, pp. 2f.

21. Bibliotheca, no. 47: Ἔστι δὲ αὐτῷ τὸ σύνταγμα ἐν λόγοις ἑπτά. Καθαρὸς τὴν φράσιν καὶ ἀξίωμα λόγου μετὰ εὐκρινείας καὶ ἡδονῆς δεινὸς ἐκφῆναι, πιθανός τε ταῖς δημηγορίαις, καὶ ἐπίχαρις, κἄν ἐπὶ τἀναντία ὁ καιρὸς καλῇ χρήσασθαι τῷ λόγῳ, δεξιὸς καὶ γόνιμος ἐνθυμημάτων ἐφ' ἑκατέρᾳ, καὶ γνωμολογικὸς δὲ ὡς εἴ τις ἄλλος, καὶ πάθη τῷ λόγῳ παραστῆσαι ἱκανώτατος, καὶ ἐγεῖραι πάθος καὶ πραῦναι δοκιμώτατος. H. St. John Thackeray, *Josephus, the Man and the Historian* (New York, 1929; repr. 1967), p. 104, supports this opinion for the *War*; cf. also Josephus, *Against Apion* I, 50. Theodore Metochites in the fourteenth century wrote an essay on Josephus in which he praises his style (*Miscellanea philosophica et historica*, edited by Ch. Müller [Leipzig, 1821; repr. Amsterdam, 1966], chapter 15).

22. Cf. comments by Josephus in his *Vita* (Loeb ed.), I, 336–367.

23. Cf. remarks by Wacholder, *Eupolemus* (above, n. 4), p. 203, and the note there.

24. In the *Bibliotheca*, Africanus (no. 34) follows directly after Justus (no. 33). Although Photius does not mention it, his copy of Africanus may have alluded to Africanus' use of Justus' works, which fact was forgotten by Photius when he put together his notes and wrote his *Bibliotheca*.

25. Wacholder, *Eupolemus* (above, n. 4), pp. 303ff.

26. *Ibid.*, p. 305 n. 189, cites Jerome, *De viris illustribus* 14, on Justus as the author of Bible commentaries. Wacholder is inclined to accept this notice. See above, n. 18.

27. Diogenes Laertius cites an anecdote from Justus about Plato in which Plato is shouted down by the judges in Socrates' trial (*Lives of the Philosophers*, edited and translated by R. O. Hicks [Loeb Classical Library, 1925], vol. 2, p. 41): φησιν Ἰοῦστος ὁ Τιβεριεὺς ἐν τῷ Στέμ-

μᾱτι. The title should not be translated as "The Wreath," as Hicks has done; rather, the word refers to Justus' chronography. This is one indication that Justus included more than the bare chronography that Photius ascribes to him; cf. Schürer, *History of the Jewish People*, 1, p. 37n.

28. The basic study is by Wacholder, *Nicolaus of Damascus* (Berkeley, Los Angeles, 1962).

29. Edited by K. de Boor, et al. (Berlin, 1903–1910) and reproduced by F. Jacoby, *FGrHist* (Berlin, 1926), vol. 2, no. 90, pp. 324–430. On the *Excerpta Historica* in general, see Paul Lemerle, *Le premier humanisme byzantin. Notes et remarques sur enseignement et culture à Byzance des origines au Xe siècle* (Paris, 1971), pp. 280–288, and G. L. Huxley, "The Scholarship of Constantine Porphyrogenitus," *PRIA* 80, c (1980), pp. 29–40.

30. Lemerle, *Le premier humanisme*, estimates that we possess only one thirty-fifth of this massive project. Nicolaus appears in several of the extant sections. Cf. Wacholder, *Nicolaus* (above, n. 28), index s.v.

31. Cf. Wacholder, *Nicolaus*, pp. 8f., and 65f.

32. *Bibliotheca*, no. 189.

33. Wacholder, *Nicolaus*, pp. 8f.

34. *Ibid.*, p. 9; see R. J. H. Jenkins, "The Classical Background of the *Scriptores post Theophanem*," *DOP* 8 (1958), pp. 11–30, and Alphonse Dain, "La transmission des textes littéraires de Photius à Constantin Porphyrogénète," *DOP* 8 (1958), pp. 31–47. Professor Igor Ševčenko of Harvard University is preparing an edition and translation of the *Vita Basili*.

35. Such is the clearly stated methodology of the project; cf. the translation of one prologue in Lemerle, *Le premier humanisme* (above, n. 29), pp. 281f.

36. This perhaps explains the anomaly of Josephus' harsh treatment of the Hasmoneans. Nicolaus, as a supporter of Herod, cast them in a derogatory light; Josephus, on the other hand, was a descendant of high priests and, on his mother's side, from the Hasmoneans.

37. Schreckenberg, *Flavius-Josephus-Tradition* (above, n. 3), pp. 48–51, cites 133 Greek and 230 Latin manuscripts (p. 59).

38. Cf. Schreckenberg, *Rezeptionsgeschichtliche* (above, n. 3), and below. On the problem of the four Septuagint manuscripts (dated between the tenth and fourteenth centuries) that contain the so-called Lucianic texts, which are very close to the Josephan text and thus a good control for their antiquity as a separate tradition, see Thackeray, *Josephus* (above, n. 21), pp. 83ff.

39. Cf. Duker-Fishman, "Second Temple Period" (above, n. 5).

40. Georgios Choumnos, *Old Testament Legends from a Greek Poem on Genesis and Exodus*, edited and translated by F. H. Marshall (Cambridge, 1925).

41. See preliminary work by Schreckenberg, *Flavius-Josephus-Tradition* and *Rezeptionsgeschichtliche* (above, n. 3). One corrective to the latter (p. 26): Thaddaios Pelusiotes did not write a polemic work against the Jews in 1265. It is actually a sixteenth-century forgery from the hand of Constantine Paleocappa based upon the fourteenth-century polemic against the Jews by Matthew Blastares. On the latter, see my *Jews of Byzantium* (above, n. 2), pp. 30f. and 34n.

42. Schreckenberg, *Flavius-Josephus-Tradition* (above, n. 2), pp. 13–51.

43. *Ibid.*, pp. 124–127, based on the preface to the Bonn edition.

44. See above, n. 29. The phrase ἀρετῆς γὰρ καὶ κακίας ἐσμὲν αὐτοκράτορες is used by Theophylact Simocatta, an Egyptian scholar of the early seventh century, apparently also derived from Josephus. Cf. *Theophylacti Simocattae Quaestiones Physicas et epistolas*, edited by J. Boissonade (Paris, 1835), epistola 40.

45. For a preliminary discussion, cf. S. Bowman, "The Study of Josephus in the 10th Century: Christian and Jewish Approaches to Antiquity," in *Abstracts of the Ninth Annual Conference of Byzantine Studies* held at Duke University (November, 1983), pp. 1–2.

46. *Excerpta Historica*, p. 102; the citation from *BJ* IV, 387, has the following variants from the Loeb edition of Josephus: δ'οὗτοι, τῆς προφητείαν.

47. *Excerpta Historica*, p. 102; *BJ* IV, 388, has the following variant readings: ἐνϑέων [variant, ἔνϑα], καταφλέξεσϑαι τὸ ἁγιώτατον νόμῳ πολέμου, στάσις ἐὰν κατασκήψῃ, τὸ τοῦ ϑεοῦ [ἅγιον omitted] τέμενος, αὐτούς.

48. For the Byzantine background, see George Ostrogorsky, *History of the Byzantine State*, translated by J. Hussey (Oxford, 1968), pp. 261ff.; Steven Runciman, *The Emperor Romanus Lecapenus and His Reign* (Cambridge, 1963); Arnold Toynbee, *Constantine Porphyrogenitus and His World* (London, 1979); and Huxley, "Scholarship of Constantine Porphyrogenitus" (above, n. 29).

Thackeray in his Loeb commentary (*ad locum*) cites the *Sybilline Oracle*, IV, 117ff. as a *vaticinium post eventum* for this tradition. There were, however, a large number of such oracles in the Byzantine libraries, a number of which were collected by the contemporary author of the tenth-century Byzantine Jewish apocalypse, *Ḥazzon Daniel*; cf. Reuben Bonfils, "The Vision of Daniel as a Historical and Literary Document" [Hebrew], *Zion* 44 (1979) = *Yitzhak F. Baer Memorial Volume* (Jerusalem, 1980), pp. 111–147, xv–xvi (English abstract) and an English summary in S. Bowman, "Recent Hebrew Scholarship on Byzantium," *BSEB* 12 (1986). Any one of these could have provided a pseudepigraphic source for this tradition.

The influence of the Sybilline Oracles on medieval Greek scholars is a subject beyond the limits of this essay, yet their survival is worth noting here in light of the proposed centrality of the oracle cited in the encyclopedia of Constantine VII and because, as we suggest, it was so important to Constantine's anti-Lekapenan theme. Cf. also Paul Alexander, "Medieval Apocalypses as Historical Sources," *AHR* 73 (1968), pp. 997–1018 (repr., London, 1978); his earlier *The Oracle of Baalbek: The Tiburtine Sibyl in Greek Dress* (Washington, 1967), with comments by David Flusser in "An Early Jewish-Christian Document in the Tiburtine Sibyl," *Paganisme, Judaisme, Christianisme—Mélanges offerts à Marcel Simon* (Paris, 1978), pp. 153–183, and supplementary bibliography in Bonfils, "The Vision of Daniel."

49. Cf. John Wortley, "Israel and Byzantium: A Case of Socio-religious Acculturation," *Traditions in Contact and Change: Selected Proceedings of the XIVth Congress of the International Association for the History of Religions* (Waterloo, Ontario, 1983), pp. 361–376, and literature cited. Also cf. S. Alexander, "Heraclius, Byzantine Imperial Ideology and the David Plates," *Speculum* 52 (1977), pp. 217–237.

Cf. Theodore Synkellos, "Homilia de bello Avarica," edited by Leo Sternbach, *Analecta Avarica* (Cracow, 1900), pp. 309f., for reference to Jeremiah's and Josephus' witness to the conquest of Jerusalem as an analogue to the siege of Constantinople in the reign of Heraclius. See, too, the discussion in Alexander, "Heraclius," pp. 222f. One of the latest authors to rewrite Josephus in this vein was Nikephoros Kallistos Xanthopoulos, an early fourteenth-century hymnographer and church poet who has left us a short survey of the historical sections of the Old Testament in iambic verse and a versified synopsis of Jewish history whose post-Maccabean section is derived from Josephus; cf. Beck, *Kirche und theologische Literatur* (above, n. 2), p. 705, and Günter Genz, *Die Kirchengeschichte des Nicephorus Callistus Xanthopulus und ihre Quellen Nachgelassene Untersuchungen* (Berlin, 1966).

50. *Excerpta Historica*, II, 1, 47 (=A VI, 33–34, 261) notes that evil sons can come from a good father and vice versa, and reports the fulfillment of Eli's prophecy that his house (the priesthood of Nob) would be destroyed because of the iniquity of his two sons. *Excerpta Historica*, II, 1, 45 (=A V, 338ff.) shows the evils of a commoner become king, namely, Saul (*Excerpta Historica, ibid.*, 47ff. = A VI, 262ff.), and relates Jeroboam's usurpation (*Excerpta Historica*, I, 63–65 = A VIII, 265–274).

51. Cf. treatment of Herod (ultimately based on Nicolaus of Damascus) in *Excerpta Historica*, I, 2, 366–368 = A XV, 187–201ff.

52. Hilda van den Berg, *Anonymous de obsidione toleranda* (Leiden, 1947) is the critical edition; cf. A. Dain, "Memorandum inédit sur la défense des places," *REG* 53 (1940),

pp. 123–136, who edits the Greek fragments with a French translation of a tenth-century work that may have been the source of *De obsidione toleranda*; the fragments follow *BJ* III, 258–264.

53. Text published by A. Vassiliev, *Anecdota Graeco-Byzantina* (Moscow, 1893) and commented upon by David Flusser, "Palaea Historica: An Unknown Source of Biblical Legends," *SH* 22 (1971), pp. 48–79.

54. The earlier rabbinic chronologies, namely, *Seder Olam Rabba* and *Zuta*, and the letter of the Gaon Sherira were primarily concerned with rabbinic chronology, sometimes for apologetic reasons but also for background reference.

55. David Flusser, ed., *The Josippon (Josephus Gorionides)*, vol. 1 (Jerusalem, 1978), pp. 410ff., 416ff.

56. See below, n. 58, and the forthcoming dissertation of Rivka Duker-Fishman at the Hebrew University of Jerusalem.

57. Ioannes Zonaras, *Epitome*, I–III, edited by M. Pinder (Bonn, 1841–1844); see Duker-Fishman, "The Second Temple Period" (above, n. 5), pp. 151ff.

A sixteenth-century Jewish historian from Spain (one of the exiles of 1492 writing in Italy) follows a similar though considerably modified pattern in his treatment of the two world empires of his time; cf. Joseph ha-Kohen, *Divre ha-Yamim le-Malkhe Ṣarfat u-beit Otoman* ("Chronicles of the Kings of France and the Ottomans") (Sabbioneta, 1554; Amsterdam, 1744); cf. *EJ*, vol. 10, 241f. Even his name—Joseph the Priest—recalls his first-century predecessor.

58. I wish to thank Professor Alexander Kazhdan of Dumbarton Oaks for pointing out this parallel to me. His study has appeared in *GRBS* 24 (1983), 375–376. The basic study is by T. Uspensky, *Vizantijskij pisatel, Nikita Akominat iz Chon* ("A Byzantine Writer, Nicetas Acominatus, of Chonae") (St. Petersburg, 1874). The Greek text was edited by I. Bekker, *Nicetae Choniatae, Historia* (Bonn, 1835), cf. pp. 809ff. and reedited by A. Van Dieten (*CFHB* 11; Berlin, New York, 1975) in two volumes, cf. pp. 624ff. The German translation is by Franz Grabler in *Byzantinische Geschichtsschreiber*, 3 vols. (Graz, 1958), I, pp. 192f. The English translation is by Harry Magoulias, *O City of Byzantium, Annals of Niketas Choniates* (Detroit, 1984), pp. 346f.

Tzetzes, too, included Josephus among his prolific prose readings; cf. J. E. Sandys, *A History of Classical Scholarship*, (reprint N.Y., 1958), vol. 1, p. 419.

59. The literature on the subject is noted in chapter five of Bowman, *Jews of Byzantium* (above, n. 2); cf. also A. E. Vacalopoulos, *Origins of the Greek Nation: The Byzantine Period, 1204–1461* (New Brunswick, 1970), pp. 198–205 and notes.

60. English translations of all the major Greek recorders of the fall of Constantinople are included in the following: J. R. Melville Jones, tr., *The Siege of Constantinople 1453: Seven Contemporary Accounts* (Amsterdam, 1972) and Marios Phillippides, tr., *The Fall of the Byzantine Empire: A Chronicle of George Sphrantzes 1401–1477* (Amherst, 1980).

61. Cf. H. Schreckenberg, *Bibliographie zu Flavius Josephus* (London, 1968). Robert Eisler popularized the Slavonic Josephus to western scholars through his *The Messiah Jesus and John the Baptist—According to Flavius Josephus' Recently Discovered 'Capture of Jerusalem' and Other Jewish and Christian Sources* (abridged ed., London, New York, 1931) and his ponderous two-volume ΙΗΣΟΥΣ ΒΑΣΙΛΕΥΣ ΟΥ ΒΑΣΙΛΕΥΣΑΣ: *Die messianische Unabhängigkeitsbewegung vom Auftreten Johannes des Täufers bis zum Untergang Jakobus des Gerechten nach der neuerschlossenen Eroberung von Jerusalem des Flavius Josephus und den Christlichen Quellen* (Heidelberg, 1929–1930). He was challenged, among others, by the inimitable Solomon Zeitlin in his *Josephus on Jesus with Particular Reference to the Slavonic Josephus and the Hebrew Josippon* (Philadelphia, 1931). Eisler and Zeitlin carried on a lively debate in the pages of the *Jewish Quarterly Review* throughout 1930 and 1931. Other criticisms are cited in Schreckenberg's *Bibliographie*. A more dispassionate overview is provided in J. M. Creed, "The Slavonic Version of Josephus' History of the Jewish War," *HThR* 25 (1932), pp. 277–319.

62. Cf. *Cambridge Mediaeval History*, (Cambridge, 1966), vol. 4, parts 1–2; D. Obolensky, *The Byzantine Commonwealth, Eastern Europe, 500–1453* (London, 1971); C. Diehl's *Byzantium: Greatness and Decline* (New Brunswick, 1957), with introduction and bibliographic essay by Peter Charanis, and the subsequent volumes in the Rutgers Byzantine Series; and the comprehensive annual bibliography in *Byzantinische Zeitschrift*.

63. Cf. comments by Rivka Duker-Fishman in her "Second Temple Period" (above, n. 5) and E. M. Jeffries, "The Attitude of Byzantine Chroniclers toward Ancient History," *Byzantion* 49 (1979), pp. 199–238.

64. Jeffries, "Attitude of Byzantine Chroniclers," (above, n. 63) pp. 235f.; M. Spinka, tr., *Chronicle of John Malalas* (Books VIII through XXVIII, translated from the Church Slavonic) (Chicago, 1940), introduction.

65. Cf. Eisler and his critics cited in Schreckenberg, *Bibliographie*. For a linguistic study of the old Russian translation of Josephus, cf. Alfons Höcherl, *Zur Übersetzungstechnik des altrussischen "Jüdischen Krieges" des Josephus Flavius* ("Slavistische Beiträge," 46, München, 1970). Cf. S. W. Baron, *A Social and Religious History of the Jews* (2nd ed., New York, 1958), vol. 2, p. 379n. For an updated bibliography, cf. Louis H. Feldman, *Scholarship on Philo and Josephus (1937–1962)* (New York, 1963), pp. 28b–30a; and his *Josephus and Modern Scholarship* (above, n. 3), pp. 48–56.

66. Tacitus (*Annals* XV, 44) refers to Christus as having been put to death at the hands of Pontius Pilate. Suetonius (*Claudius* 25) states that the Emperor Claudius banished from Rome the Jews who made continuous tumult at the instigation of Chrestus; whether this Chrestus is the Jesus of Christianity has been subject to debate. There are several references to Jesus in the Talmud, cf. *EJ*, vol. 10, p. 15; others were expurgated by Jews or censored by Christians during the later Middle Ages. On the *Testimonium*, cf. Thackeray, *Josephus* (above, n. 21), pp. 136ff., for commentary; for texts and bibliography, cf. Josephus, *A*, vol. IX, pp. 48ff. and appendix K (Loeb ed.). See now Louis H. Feldman, "The *Testimonium Flavianum*: The State of the Question," in Robert F. Berkey and Sarah A. Edwards, eds., *Christological Perspectives: Essays in Honor of Harvey K. McArthur* (New York, 1982), pp. 179–199, 283–293.

67. Cf. Feldman's notes to Eisler's fanciful restoration of the "original" text in his edition of *Antiquities*, IX, *ad locum*.

68. See A. C. Bouquet, "References to Josephus in the *Bibliotheca* of Photius," *JTS* 36 (1935), pp. 289–293.

69. On the Slavs, cf. Constantine VII Porphyrogenitus, *De Administrando Imperii*, translated and edited by G. Moravcik and R. Jenkins, 2 vols. in 3 (Budapest, 1949; London, 1962), chapters 30, 49, *passim*. The term "Graecized" was introduced by Peter Charanis to describe Basil I's attempts to incorporate the Slavs into Byzantine society. A description of the four stages of this process can be seen in Shephatiah's dealings with Basil as related in *The Chronicle of Ahimaaz*, edited and translated by M. Salzman (New York, 1924); cf. Joshua Starr, *The Jews in the Byzantine Empire, 641–1204* (Athens, 1939), pp. 127–135.

70. Cyril's introduction of the Hebrew letter "shin" to represent the sounds "sh" and "shch" has been attributed to the Jewish community in Cherson (Crimea), where Cyril purportedly learned Hebrew. Cf. F. Dvornik, *Les légendes de Constantin et de Méthode vues de Byzance* (Prague, 1933) and his *Byzantine Missions among the Slavs, S. S. Constantine—Cyril and Methodius* (New Brunswick, 1970).

71. Eisler develops one interesting theory (among the many discredited by his contemporaries, yet worthy of being reexamined in light of the past fifty years of scholarship that has illuminated the history of Byzantium and its influence on neighboring lands) that Josephus was used both by the church in power to justify its historical and theological interpretation of the origins of Christianity and by opponents to the organized church, i.e., heretics, outlaws (*hairetikoi*), and non-Orthodox churches, to develop their respective identities, which were a priori anti-

thetical to the establishment. If his specifics are open to question, these particular theses may be reflective of just that kind of historical development. Josephus was so respected as an authority since the days of Eusebius that arguments pro and con could easily be defended by adroit interpretations and excisions from the test. Thus, Josephus could become in the hands of apologists even more of a tool for self-justification than the Bible itself, whose text was frozen by the accuracy of the Hebrew transmission and the authority of the New Testament canonization backed by imperial edict. The subject remains open for further study in all of its ramifications with the necessity to provide a critical commentary or refutation to Eisler's prodigious effort. Such a task is beyond the limits of the present summary, however.

72. Cf. remarks by Jeffries on the emphasized Slavonic view in the Slavic translation of the Byzantine chronicle of Constantine Manasses, "Attitude of Byzantine Chroniclers" (above, n. 63), pp. 235f.

73. A monograph on the Jews of Byzantine Italy from the ninth to the eleventh centuries is a desideratum. For preliminary studies, cf. Bowman, "Another Medieval Heritage" (above, n. 1); Andrew Sharf, *Byzantine Jewry from Justinian to the Fourth Crusade* (New York, 1971); and Suessman Muntner, *R. Shabtai Donnolo (913–985)* [Hebrew] (Jerusalem, 1949). *The Chronicles of Jerahmeel,* translated by M. Gaster (London, 1899; repr. New York, 1971), with an introduction by Haim Schwarzbaum, excerpts most of *Josippon.* Cf. D. Flusser, *The Josippon,* vol. 2 (Jerusalem, 1980), pp. 6f.

74. Cf. S. Bowman, "A Tenth-Century Byzantine Jewish Historian," *BSEB* 10 (1984), pp. 133-136, with the bibliography cited there. The following paragraphs summarize Flusser's main findings.

75. Yitzhak Baer, "Sepher Yosipon ha-ʿIvri" [Hebrew], in *Sepher Ben Zion Dinaburg* (Jerusalem, 1948–1949), pp. 178–205, recognizes two opposing trends running through *Josippon:* one to submit to the Romans and the other to suffer martyrdom. Shlomo Simonsohn, in his afterword to *Violence and Defence in the Jewish Experience,* edited by S. W. Baron and George W. Wise (Philadelphia, 1977), pp. 337–343, compares the attitude toward martyrdom in Eleazar ben Jair's speech in Josephus (*BJ* VII, 323–336) and in *Josippon.* On the tradition in general, cf. *Holy War and Martyrology* (lectures delivered at the eleventh convention of the Historical Society of Israel in March 1966) (Jerusalem, 1967) [Hebrew].

76. A parallel can be found in a late Midrash, *Kisse ve-ippodromin shel Shlomo hamelekh,* edited by A. Jellinek, in *Beth Hamidrash* (Leipzig, 1853; repr., Jerusalem, 1967), vol. 2, pp. 83–86; cf. Sharf, *Byzantine Jewry* (above, n. 73), pp. 23f. and 38f. (notes), and *JE,* vol. 11, p. 442, for summary. Constantine Porphyrogenitus emphasized his biblical prototype, Solomon; cf. Huxley, "Scholarship of Constantine Porphyrogenitus" (above, n. 29), pp. 37ff.

77. Cf. David Flusser, "The Author of *Sefer Josippon* as Historian" [Hebrew], in *Mekomam shel Toldoth ʿAm-Yisrael be-misgereth Toldoth he-ʿAmim* (lectures delivered at the sixteenth convention of the Historical Society of Israel) (Jerusalem, 1972–1973), pp. 203–226; reprinted in D. Flusser, ed., *Josippon. The Original version MS Jerusalem 8°41280 and Supplements* (Jerusalem, 1978: Texts and Studies for students "KUNTRESIM" Project, No. 49), pp. 28–51.

78. At least the Alexander interpolation (*Eshkol Ha-kofer,* Gozlow, 1836, 24b); cf. Flusser, *The Josippon,* vol. 2 (above, n. 55), p. 50. On Judah ibn Moskoni and his edition of the *Josippon,* cf. Flusser, *ibid.,* pp. 42ff. For the correct name, cf. Bowman, *Jews of Byzantium* (above, n. 2), index s.v.

79. On the rabbinic approach to the past, cf. Y. H. Yerushalmi, *Zakhor: Jewish History and Jewish Memory* (Seattle, London, 1983), chapter 2. Yerushalmi, in this excellent survey of group memory among the Jews, neglects the historiographical traditions of Byzantine Jewry.

80. Such is the tenor of the "Orthodox" edition of *Josippon* published by Hayyim Hominer [Hebrew] (4th ed., Jerusalem, 1977–1978), with an introduction by Rabbi Abraham Wertheimer.

Judah ibn Moskoni's preface is published there, pp. 34–40, which is discussed and partially translated in Bowman, *Jews of Byzantium* (above, n. 2), pp. 134–137. Flusser discusses his manuscripts and methodology in his edition of *Josippon* (above, n. 55). Flusser's critical edition is about one-third shorter than Hominer's popular edition, which relies upon the edition of Judah ibn Moskoni, with its interpolations of later material.

81. The mention of Kinnamos in the Byzantine epic poem *Diogenes Akritas*, according to H. Grégoire, derives from a "self-proclaimed king in Persia during the reign of Artabanes III." The story is mentioned by Josephus (*A* XX, 63–65) in the context of the latter's comments on Izates, the Jewish king of Adiabene. As Josephus is a unique literary source about Kinnamos, the latter's exploits apparently became part of the oral tradition of upper Mesopotamia during the Persian and Arab periods and eventually reached the assembler of the tenth-century Byzantine epic (Henri Grégoire, "Digénis, notes complémentaires," *Byzantion* 7 (1932), p. 320 (repr., London, 1975); cf. Grégoire, *Ho Digenēs Akritas: Hē Byzantinē Epopoiia stēn historia kai stēn Poiēsē* ("Digenis Akritas: The Byzantine Epic in History and Poetry") (New York, 1942), pp. 310f., and John Mavrogordato, ed. and tr. *Digenes Akritas* (Oxford, 1956), who attempts to tone down Grégoire's reference. (See also H. G. Beck, *Geschichte der byzantinischen Volksliteratur* [München, 1971], p. 86, who rejects Grégoire's thesis regarding Kinnamos. There are, however, several classical and biblical allusions in the poem.) See now Michael Jeffreys, "Digenis Akritas and Commagene," *Svenska Forskningsinstitutet i Istanbul Meddelanden* 3 (Stockholm, 1978; repr., London, 1983), pp. 5–28, which does not mention Josephus, however.

On the other hand Cosmas Indicopleustes (*Topographie Chrétienne*, I–III, edited and translated by Wanda Wolska-Conus [Paris, 1968–1973]), finds in Josephus a cache of ancient authors (more than 12 citations in Book XII, primarily from the latter's *Contra Apionem*). Thus, too, there are more than two hundred citations from Josephus in the tenth-century Byzantine lexicon called *Suda*, 5 vols. (Leipzig, 1923–1938). Cf. also *Ioannes Zonarae Lexicon*, edited by I. Tittman, 2 vols (Leipzig, 1808), s.v.

82. Diogenes Laertes, *Lives of Eminent Philosophers*, ed. by R. D. Hicks (Loeb ed.), vol. 1, introduction, xv.

19 Josippon, *a Medieval Hebrew Version of Josephus*

DAVID FLUSSER

t he rebirth of Hebrew literature in Europe occurred in the ninth and
tenth centuries after Christ. This is approximately the same period in
which Japanese literature flourished. The most important centers of
Hebrew literature were then in Greece and in southern Italy. Since the Jews
there had connections with their non-Jewish environment, they were able to
read such books as were current among their Greek and Italian neighbors. Hebrew literature was revitalized and a new self-awareness came into existence
among the Jewish people. The Jews began to be interested in their ancient
achievements. They studied and commented on the Old Testament and the rabbinic literature of antiquity. At the same time they discovered that the Christian
churches had preserved, in Greek and Latin, numerous Jewish works, which
were composed after the New Testament period and which had been lost to the
Jews themselves. These Jewish books were easily accessible and were included
in the bibles of the Greek and Latin churches but were not incorporated into the
Hebrew Old Testament. Such books are today known by the name Apocrypha
(the hidden books). They belong to the canon of the Catholic church, but are
absent from the Protestant canon, which returned to the Hebrew Old Testament.

The so-called Apocrypha include, among others, the first two books of
Maccabees, describing the heroic wars of the Jews against pagan oppression
in the second century B.C., the Books of Tobit and Judith and other historical,
or pseudohistorical, books and also sapiential literature. When the Jews of
Europe began to write in Hebrew again, they recognized the value of such
books for their own historical past. Because only a small part of the Jewish
intelligentsia knew Greek or Latin, some of these intellectuals felt that it was
their duty to translate the most important Apocryphal works into Hebrew, in
order to pass these treasures of ancient Jewish literature on to those Jews who
did not know Greek or Latin. Much of the Apocrypha was translated into Hebrew during the Middle Ages. But the most important source for Jewish

postbiblical history, the historical writings of Josephus Flavius, was not contained in the Apocrypha. The need for this history was felt by a Hebrew author from southern Italy, who wrote in the year A.D. 953. He employed a classical biblical Hebrew style and retold Jewish history during the time of the Second Temple using the writings of Josephus Flavius as his main source. This Hebrew book is named *Josippon* and is also known as *Josephus Gorionides* in Latin.[1]

The book was badly needed by the Jews. It supplied additional information about Jewish and world history from the return of the Jews from the Babylonian exile to the destruction of the Temple in A.D. 70 and the subsequent conquest of Masada by the Romans (A.D. 74). *Josippon* was very useful to the Jews for the interpretation of the later books of the Old Testament, such as the Book of Esther, the Books of Ezra and Nehemiah, and the Book of Daniel. The medieval Jewish commentators of these books found *Josippon* to be a great help. The same is true concerning those who were occupied with commenting on the Talmud (which is the main rabbinic text), because the Talmud contains passages about the Second Temple period. It is no wonder that *Josippon* became widely known to the Jews of many countries in a very short time. The book was already translated into Arabic in the eleventh century, and the Arabic translation of *Josippon* was then translated into Ethiopian.[2]

From the sixteenth century on, the book was translated from printed editions into Judeo-German, Judeo-Spanish, Latin, German, English, Czech, and Polish. Until modern times very few Jews had direct access to the Old Testament Apocrypha or to the works of Josephus Flavius, and so *Josippon* became a favorite historical and literary reference among the Jews.[3] In addition, the authority of the book became immense, because it was commonly thought to have been written by Josephus Flavius himself, who lived during the period of the Second Temple. This belief caught hold some decades after *Josippon* was written[4] and persisted until the time of modern scholarship. It was only natural for Christians who knew about the existence of the Hebrew book to assume that *Josippon* was written by Josephus himself. Thus, the book became very important, because they believed that *Josippon* furnished further authentic information about Jewish history in the time of Jesus and his first followers. Christian scholars even wanted to know if there was any mention of Christ himself. The false assumption that *Josippon* had been written by Josephus, a witness to the events of the intertestamental period and to the beginnings of Christianity, was the main reason why the book was translated into so many European languages.

Until my own critical edition of *Josippon* from ancient manuscripts was prepared,[5] the real purpose of the book could not be discovered, because *Josippon* was known to modern scholarship only through its first two printed editions, which are later versions and are not based upon the original text of the book. The older printed edition was published in Mantua in Italy about

1480. It is based on a carelessly restyled and, at times, even abbreviated manuscript of the original version. In this edition Josephus appears as a dramatis persona, but all reference to him as an author has been omitted. The other edition was published in Constantinople in 1510. This edition is based upon a Hebrew manuscript which stems from an expanded and revised version of *Josippon* written not later than A.D. 1160. Its author restyled the book and added fictitious elements, although he himself was not lacking in Jewish or in secular knowledge. The most famous among the passages to be found in the expanded version of Josippon is a fictitious description of the crowning of Vespasian in Rome. This narrative had been influenced by the crowning of emperors during the Middle Ages.[6]

As we have already said, *Josippon* was commonly ascribed to Josephus, though no such claims are made in the original text of the book. This mistaken ascription of the Hebrew book to Josephus became explicit in the expanded version of *Josippon,* which was composed in the first half of the twelfth century.[7] The reviser evidently knew from Josephus that before writing the Greek book about the Jewish war Josephus had already composed an account about it in his own language, which had not survived (*BJ* I, 3). So the author of the expanded, later version of *Josippon* not only changed the book into a pseudepigraphon, in which Josephus speaks about himself and about the purpose of his work in the first person, but also pretends that his book is the lost original that Josephus wrote for the Jews, different from the extant *Jewish War* of Josephus, which was written for the Romans.

Before dealing with the original version of *Josippon* and its connection with the writings of Josephus, it is necessary to explain the Hebrew name "Josippon" and to show why in *Josippon* the Jewish historian Josephus is named Joseph the son of Gorion (or Gurion), although the name of Josephus' father was in reality Matthias. The Hebrew author was misled by the so-called *Hegesippus,* a rewritten Latin Josephus, which was one of his main sources. In this Latin book, Josephus' father is never named; but its author, following Josephus, names Josephus the son of Gorion in the first place among the Jewish leaders of the war (*Hegesippus* III, 3, 27). The Hebrew medieval author identified this man with Josephus the historian. Thus, Josephus is always named Joseph ben (the son of) Gorion (or, in a more correct Hebrew form, ben Gurion) in the Hebrew book.[8] Therefore, in Latin translations the book *Josippon* is named *Josephus Gorionides*. Otherwise, the Hebrew Josephus is commonly named *Josippon:* this is the Judeo-Greek form for Josephus.[9] The name crept into the later manuscripts and redactions of the book but did not appear in the original text. The Hebrew version of Josephus was named the book of *Josippon* because its main source was Josephus' writings and because very early it was wrongly thought that its author was Josephus. The Judeo-Greek form betrays that the book was written in the vicinity of a Greek-speaking public, and Greek was then the official language of the Byzantine Empire. The first readers of the book of *Josippon* were Byzantine Jews.

Until the age of modern critical scholarship, both Jews and non-Jews had believed that the book of *Josippon* was written by Josephus. From the sixteenth century on, scholars appeared who were able to show that the Hebrew book could not have been written by Josephus.[10] They claimed that the book contains names of medieval towns and nations, and they had discovered that its author had used the Latin translation of Josephus. Until the manuscripts of *Josippon* had been studied, it had been impossible to discover that the book's author had no intention of ascribing the book to another. We have already seen that the common opinion that *Josippon* was written by Josephus himself was incorporated into one of the printed editions and that in the other, lesser-known, printed edition the authorship of *Josippon* is completely unclear. Thus, the scholars who did not read the manuscripts of *Josippon* thought that its author pretended to be Josephus. Rationalistic scholarship came, therefore, to the conclusion that *Josippon* was a kind of falsification. Later on, from the nineteenth century until the new critical edition of the book, both Jewish and non-Jewish scholars developed a psychological understanding for the fictitious ascription of *Josippon* to Josephus because they thought that such a procedure was characteristic of the general spirit of the Middle Ages.

Now, as can be seen from the manuscripts, the medieval author of *Josippon* did not pretend to be Josephus, but only quotes Josephus (or, according to his language, Joseph ben Gurion) as his main source. All his allusions to Josephus are to real passages of his writings or to the later Latin version of Josephus, commonly named *Hegesippus*,[11] and the author of *Josippon* was not alone in attributing this work to Josephus. Moreover, the Hebrew author of *Josippon* speaks about himself in the first person. He writes, for instance: "Joseph ben Gurion [i.e. Josephus] the priest is the head of the writers of all the books which were written, except the twenty-four holy books [i.e. the books of the Old Testament] and except the books of Wisdom which Solomon the king of Israel wrote, and [the writings of] the sages of Israel. And I have collected stories from the book of Joseph ben Gurion and from the books of other authors who recorded the deeds of our ancestors, and I compiled them in one scroll."[12] The "books of other authors" are the Apocrypha, contained in the Latin Bible (the so-called Vulgate), but the author of *Josippon* rightly stresses that his main source was Josephus' writings.

Thus, in the original version of the book the author speaks clearly about himself, about his sources, and about the purpose of his book. In the extant manuscripts, the author speaks openly about himself, but his name does not appear in them. It is possible that the name was eliminated in the manuscripts because their writers accepted the common opinion that *Josippon* was the work of Josephus and therefore mistook the real name of the author for a scribe's name. Another possibility is that the medieval Hebrew author did not include his name in the book. If the second possibility is correct, then it was easy to ascribe an anonymous book to Josephus because the author, quoting Josephus, introduces the quotations with the opening words: "So says Joseph ben Gurion in his book." This might have been understood as Josephus speaking about the book of *Josippon* itself.

In any case, it is easy to understand why the real date of the composition of *Josippon* is preserved in only one manuscript. The recorded time when *Josippon* was written was easily deleted, because such a late period contradicted the supposed authorship of Josephus. Thus, the date of the composition of *Josippon* was preserved only by a fortunate coincidence. The real author himself explains the situation:[13] "And we have written and translated from the book, namely from the book of Joseph ben Gurion the priest in the year 885 after the Destruction." Since it was customary then to reckon the destruction of the Temple of Jerusalem by the Romans from the year A.D. 68, it follows that the Hebrew book was composed in A.D. 953.

This date is independently and fully confirmed by other indications contained in *Josippon*. Like many other Christian and Jewish medieval historical books, *Josippon* begins with the opening of human history, which was seen in the division of nations after the Flood. The author begins his book with the list of the sons of Japheth, the son of Noah, in the Book of Genesis (10:2–5) and identifies their descendants with the nations and with their locations during his time. He rightly states that the location of the Russians was Kiev (which was then the territory of their duke); he does not see the Russians ("Russi") as Slavs, who are treated separately, but names the Russians together with two other Teutonic tribes. He is right, because the "Russi" were Teutons from Scandinavia and they established their power in Kiev at the beginning of the tenth century. According to the same first chapter of *Josippon*, the Hungarians are settled on the great river Danube. The Hungarians entered their new homeland on the river Danube about A.D. 895–96. Thus, it is clear that the book of *Josippon* was not written earlier than A.D. 900. He also mentions that the city of Tarsus (in Asia Minor) was conquered by the Moslems and that the Byzantines were struggling with the Moslems, who were in Tarsus.[14] Inasmuch as Tarsus was not reconquered by the Byzantines until the year 965, the book of *Josippon* must have been written before this date; and in connection with the Russians and Hungarians, it reflects the geographical situation after A.D. 900. If so, the above-mentioned datae of the composition of *Josippon*, namely, A.D. 953, is genuine, because this year is between the years 900 and 965.

In his introduction of his book, the author of *Josippon* very probably adapted the geographical situation of his day to an earlier medieval list of Japheth's descendants, which he had taken from an unknown source. After this first chapter he recounts the history of ancient Italy and the founding of Rome.

This chapter is also dependent on unknown nonhistorical sources from the early Middle Ages. Then the author passes on to the period of the Second Temple. The book ends with the fall of Masada, like Hegesippus' Latin paraphrase of Josephus' *Jewish War*.[15]

Besides the Apocrypha of the Old Testament and the writings of Josephus and their Latin paraphrase *Hegesippus,* the Hebrew author of *Josippon* occasionally used early medieval Latin historical sources in order to fill in the gaps within the stream of his narrative. These sources were written at the beginning of the Middle Ages, were of inferior quality, and sometimes contained fantastic stories. These sources themselves are not preserved, but we are able to interpret them with the help of similar writings that do exist. *Josippon* also used a later elaboration of the *Chronicle* by the Latin church father Jerome. His story about the violent death of the Persian king Cyrus is indirectly derived from Orosius (fifth century A.D.), who himself is dependent on the Greek historian Herodotus. Jerome's description of the wars between Hannibal from Carthage and the Romans is taken from an unknown source that stems from Titus Livy. It is impossible to discover the precise source of *Josippon*'s narrative about the life and death of Julius Caesar. According to *Josippon,* Caesar was extracted from his mother's womb by a caesarean section; "caesarean" is a popular etiological etymology, as if this kind of operation received this name because the famous Julius Caesar was born in this way. This legend was very popular in the Middle Ages, and *Josippon*'s wording of it is very similar to that of the Byzantine author Johannes Malalas (491–578).[16] An extreme specimen of early medieval fantasy is the history of Italy and foundation of Rome, which follows the first chapter of *Josippon:* distorted mythology and biblical reminiscences are combined with echoes of Roman wars, as described by the Roman poet Virgil, the wars with Carthage, and the war with the Teutonic Vandals in the time of the emperor Justinian. All three of these wars are compressed into this report of the history of one family! Also, it is clear here that the author of *Josippon* is dependent on an early medieval source, or other sources of the same kind.[17] With the exception of such passages that originate from early medieval pseudohistorical sources, the Hebrew author of *Josippon* is an excellent historian with a sound judgment who is a realist in connection with historical developments. It seems that he incorporated the dubious early medieval sources in his narrative in order to inform the reader about important events that had not found a place in his main sources.[18]

It should be stressed that the author of *Josippon* was not able to read the works of Josephus in their original Greek language, as he did not know Greek and had to rely on a Latin translation. Both Josephus and the Apocrypha of the Old Testament were available to him in Latin. His knowledge of Latin enabled him to use pseudohistorical treatises from the early medieval period, the Apocrypha of the Latin Old Testament, and the Latin Josephus. To be more precise, the author constantly had two books on his desk: the Latin Bible and the (Latin) "book of Joseph ben Gurion," i.e. Josephus.

As to the Apocrypha in Latin, the author of *Josippon* is dependent on the two first books of Maccabees, which he combines in order to create a clear picture of the events.[19] When writing about the contest of the three young men in which the biblical Zerubbabel was victorious, he used the Apocryphal I Esdras (3–4). When he wrote about how Daniel demonstrated the truth of Jewish monotheism by showing that the Babylonian god Bel does not eat and by killing a holy dragon, *Josippon* is dependent on the noncanonical additions to the biblical Book of Daniel. The story of Esther and Mordecai is recounted according to the Apocryphal additions to the biblical Book of Esther. The author also used for Esther's prayer, as an additional source, the prayer of Asenath as it appeared in one of the Latin translations of the Greek Jewish romance *Joseph and Asenath*.[20]

As to the copy of Josephus that was on the author's desk, it contained sixteen of the twenty books of the *Antiquities* and the so-called *Hegesippus*, which was made up mainly of Josephus' *Jewish War*. The author of *Josippon* mentions also Josephus' apology, *Against Apion*, but if he read it, he had no occasion to use it for his historical book. It seems that he also knew Josephus' *Jewish War* (in Latin translation), but this is by no means completely certain. If, indeed, he really read the original *Jewish War*, he only occasionally referred to it. He certainly did not use it as his main source, because he wrongly believed that the *Hegesippus* was also written by Josephus, and, thus, he was sure that he did not need Josephus' other book that dealt with the same subject. It is sure that he did not know the last four books of Josephus' *Jewish Antiquities*. There are two events about which he speaks that are narrated in the eighteenth book of the *Antiquities*, namely the persecution of the Jews in the time of the mad Roman emperor Gaius Caligula and his subsequent violent death. He could not have found these stories in his manuscript of Josephus. Caligula's death in *Josippon* is narrated in the same ahistorical and inaccurate way as the other strange stories taken from the other early medieval sources. The author of *Josippon* has taken this story from one of these sources and not from the eighteenth book of the *Jewish Antiquities*.

Four Latin manuscripts survive[21] that contain sixteen books of the *Jewish Antiquities* and the *Hegesippus*, like the manuscript used by the author of *Josippon*. All these manuscripts were written in Italy, where the author of *Josippon* lived. Thus, the combination of the sixteen books of *Antiquities* with *Hegesippus* evidently originates in Italy. As to the *Hegesippus* itself,[22] the author of this book is unknown. He was surely a Jew who became Christian.[23] He had written his book about A.D. 375.[24] *Hegesippus* is one of the main sources of *Josippon;* though the author of *Josippon* believed, as others did, that *Hegesippus* was written by Josephus, he recognized that it contained Christian passages and evidently thought that these were later interpolations, and so he did not use these typically Christian passages for his book.

Hegesippus is mainly a paraphrase of the *Jewish War* of Josephus, but its author also used the *Jewish Antiquities*. The author of *Hegesippus* starts his book with the Maccabean revolt, but he begins to speak more explicitly about Jewish history during the last years of the king Herod. On the other hand, the last event reported in the sixteenth book of the *Antiquities* is the execution of the two sons of Herod. Hence, the man who created the type of Latin manuscripts, of which four survive and one of which was *Josippon*'s author's main source, decided that it would be superfluous to repeat what is written in Books XVII–XX of the *Antiquities* because these events were already narrated by the author of *Hegesippus*. Therefore, he copied only the first sixteen books of the *Jewish Antiquities* and then followed them with *Hegesippus*. No doubt a manuscript of this type was on the desk of the Hebrew author of *Josippon*, together with the Latin Bible.

We have already found that the book of *Josippon* was written in the year A.D. 953 by a Jew who wrote in Hebrew and knew Latin and whose aim was to teach such Jews as did not know Latin their own history from the return from the Babylonian exile to the fall of Masada in A.D. 74. We have suggested that his main Latin source was written by an Italian scribe. Our research has confirmed the assumption that the author of *Josippon* was an Italian Jew. This can be seen, in particular, from the Italian spelling and grammatical forms of Latin proper names. It is also clear that he lived in southern Italy. He knew from his own experience some places in southern Italy, among others, the town of Venosa, where the famous Roman poet Horace was born and where a flourishing Jewish community was located.[25] Moreover, he knows that the inhabitants of Naples always collect oil that has seeped to the surface of the sea from subterranean levels between Naples and the new site of Sorrento.[26] *Josippon* contains other indications that the author knew southern Italy.

The reference to Naples is possibly important. Sergius, the duke of Naples (840–864), had dedicated three manuscripts of Josephus to the library of the bishopric there. More important is the fact that John III, the duke of Naples (928–969), had commanded that a manuscript of Josephus be written in memory of his wife, Theodora, who died about the year 951.[27] Thus, this manuscript of Josephus was written very shortly before the author of *Josippon* composed his work (in A.D. 953). We have already seen that the Hebrew author writes about the inhabitants of Naples from his own day. Thus, it is possible that he himself lived in Naples. He knew Latin, which was then not commonly known among Jews, and his book betrays some medical interests. It is possible that the author of *Josippon* was a doctor who served the duke of Naples; and after seeing the duke's manuscript of Josephus, he decided to communicate his newly acquired knowledge about the ancient history of his people to his Jewish compatriots.

A part of southern Italy was then under the direct sway of the Byzantine Empire; other parts there depended on the Byzantine Empire indirectly; the duke of Naples was, for example, dependent on the emperor of Constantinople. The Roman Empire in the West, renewed by Charlemagne (A.D. 800), was then in complete decline (it was renewed by Otto the Great only in A.D. 962). Thus, in the days when the author of *Josippon* lived, the only heir to ancient Rome was the Byzantine Empire. This was a period in which Byzantine art and letters flourished. Though the author of *Josippon* did not know Greek, he was impressed by the Byzantine culture and civilization in southern Italy. No wonder that when he described the ancient Roman institutions of Josephus' day, he interpreted them in the light of the parallel institutions of the Byzantine Empire, which was the continuation of ancient Rome.

Southern Italy was then probably the most important center of Hebrew poetry and Jewish learning in Europe.[28] It was also one of the places where the Hebrew language was revived. Around the tenth century (in which *Josippon* was written), tombstone inscriptions there were being composed in Hebrew and not in Latin or Greek, as they had been previously. Precious manuscripts of ancient rabbinic literature were copied, and the rabbinic learning of southern Italy deeply influenced Jewish culture in the rest of Europe. The author of *Josippon* is one of the outstanding witnesses of Italian Jewish achievements. On the other hand, the author is not typical of his Jewish cultural environment. Though his history is a classical Hebrew book, written more or less in biblical Hebrew, its author was far more at home in the Latin culture of the non-Jewish world than in the world of the rabbinic learning of his Jewish compatriots. His knowledge of Talmudic literature was comparatively poor; and when he knew of a Talmudic parallel to the events which he described, he preferred citing Josephus to citing the pertinent text from the Talmudic literature. His position toward the historical function of the Pharisees, the ancestors of rabbinism, is critical. He likes the force and prowess of the Sadduccees and the piety of the Essenes, whom he identifies with the Hassidaeans of the early Maccabean period. It seems that this independent evaluation of the various groups in ancient Judaism is influenced by the early feudal European world. In any case, the author of *Josippon* was not a full member of the rabbinic Judaism of his time and of his homeland. He was surely not one of the well-known rabbinic scholars of his day, and this explains why his name was so quickly forgotten and why his book could be so easily ascribed to Josephus, his primary source.

From the aspect of Hebrew and world literature, *Josippon* is a classical work, both in its content and in its literary achievements; and there can hardly be found in contemporary European literature a historical book with such out-standing qualities. One of the exceptional qualities of the author of *Josippon* is his critical approach to his sources, which is based upon a realistic under-standing of the forces operating in human history. He knows of the antago-nism among various groups within human society and adequately describes the struggle for power and refers to both the passions of his heroes and the intrigues among the various antagonists. These observations and his view-point are surely influenced by the non-Jewish political and social order in his environment. Although like most medieval writers he exaggerates the num-bers of soldiers and the descriptions of military struggles, he knows the battles as an eyewitness and has admiration for prowess and for fair play in combat. His realistic world view makes the author of *Josippon* an excellent historian. He is a believing Jew but does not show a special feeling for the deeper sides of religion or theology. He admires the greatness and splendor of the ancient period of Jewish history, which he describes. He sees the present dispersion of the Jews as a catastrophe. Therefore, he follows Josephus in opposing the Zealots and considers the war of the Jews against the Romans as an unneces-sary and disastrous conflict. As has already been noted, he is a gifted histo-rian, who is aware of his responsibilities and endowed with excellent histori-cal insight. His narrative is filled with national pride and is written in an excellent Hebrew biblical style. As a writer, he is an uncommonly good artist who is able not only to master the information which he learned from his sources but also to write a work that is mostly well composed. He has a natu-ral gift to describe dramatic situations. All these qualities became clearly pa-tent only after the original text became known by my edition, which is based on old manuscripts.

The author of *Josippon* writes about John the Baptist in his book, follow-ing Hegesippus' account, but does not speak about Jesus. Two manuscripts of *Josippon* contain a strange interpolation about Jesus and the beginnings of Christianity[29] that has no historical value and is written in a spirit that is un-friendly toward Christianity, like some other Jewish notices about Christianity from the Middle Ages, a time when the Jews endured the persecutions imple-mented by the medieval Catholic church. The interpolation in the two manu-scripts of *Josippon* about Jesus and his followers puts Jesus in the time of the emperor Gaius Caligula!

Some manuscripts and the first two editions of *Josippon* contain another interpolation. The content of this addition treats the history of Alexander the Great from the time of his father's death and also contains a chronicle of the history from Alexander to Jesus' birth.[30] This small booklet is also preserved in an independent Hebrew manuscript from Parma. The small work was also probably written in southern Italy and was directly translated from Greek. The first part is an abridged version of the Alexander Romance, ascribed to

Callisthenes, and the second part is a Hebrew translation from an unknown Byzantine Greek chronicle. This part contains some new historical information, which enlarges our knowledge of antiquity.

Notes

1. The scholarly, critical edition was recently published in two volumes: *The Josippon (Josephus Gorionides)*, edited with an introduction, commentary, and notes by David Flusser, I (Jerusalem 1978); II (Jerusalem 1980) (in Hebrew). A facsimile of the best manuscript of the book has been published with an introduction by David Flusser and entitled *Josippon, the Original Version, MS Jerusalem 8°41280 and Supplements* (Jerusalem 1978). See also D. Flusser, "Josippon," *Encyclopaedia Judaica* X (Jerusalem 1971), pp. 296–298; and D. Flusser, "Der lateinische Josephus und der hebräische Josippon," *J-S*, pp. 122–132.

2. The Ethiopian translation was edited by Murad Kamil, *Des Josef Ben Gorion (Josippon) Geschichte der Juden (Zēna Aïhūd)* (New York 1938). A complete critical edition of the Arabic version is badly needed. It was used by, among others, the famous Arabic historian Ibn Khaldūn (1332–1406). See W. J. Fischel, "Ibn Khaldūn and Josippon," *Homenaje a Millás-Vallicrosa* I (Barcelona 1954), pp. 587–598. About the Arabic translation of *Josippon*, see also J. Wellhausen, *Der arabische Josippus* (Berlin 1897), and S. Pines, *Studies in Christianity and in Judaeo-Christianity: Jerusalem Studies in Arabic and Islam* (Jerusalem 1985), pp. 745–761.

3. It was even recommended by the rabbinic authorities that the pertinent passages of the book should be read on the memorial days of the rededication of the Temple of Jerusalem by Judas Maccabaeus and of the destruction of the Second Temple by the Romans. The passage in *Josippon*, which followed the apocryphal additions to the Book of Esther, was read by the Jews on the commemorative day of Esther.

4. The first known witness for the belief that *Josippon* was written by Josephus himself was the Spanish, Arabic, and Islamic scholar Ibn Hazm (994–1064). See my edition of *Josippon*, II, pp. 11–12, and the Spanish translation of Ibn Hazm by Miguel Asim Palacios, II, pp. 211–212. This Islamic scholar, like later Christian scholars, was interested to know how the beginnings of Christianity are reflected in *Josippon*. Ibn Hazm was mistaken when he said that Jesus is mentioned in *Josippon*, but he was correct when he said that there is a passage about John the Baptist. See now the study of Pines, above, end of note 2.

5. See above, n. 1.

6. The text about the coronation of the Roman emperor was printed in my edition, I, pp. 447–453, and it was analyzed in II, pp. 32–42. See also Percy E. Schramm, *Kaiser, Könige und Päpste* III (Stuttgart 1969), pp. 360–368: "Die Schilderung der Krönung eines römischen Kaisers aus dem hebräischen Geschichtswerk des Josippon."

7. The 1510 Constantinople edition of the rewritten *Josippon* is very rare. It was reprinted in Venice in 1540. This was the source of almost all other printed editions of *Josippon*. The Venice edition was reprinted by H. Hominer, with an introduction by A. J. Wertheimer (Jerusalem 1962).

8. As he told me himself, David Ben-Gurion, the late prime minister of Israel, whose original name was Gruen, took his name from this. It shows how popular *Josippon* is even today.

9. See my edition, II, pp. 69–71.

10. The first and the greatest of these scholars was Joseph Scaliger (1540–1609). See my edition, II, pp. 71–74.

11. The name "Hegesippus" is a later corruption of the original name "Josippus." See L. Traube, "Zum lateinischen Josephus," *RhM* 39 (1884), pp. 477–478, reprinted in *Vorlesungen und Abhandlungen von Ludwig Traube* III (München 1920), pp. 82–83.

12. See my edition, I, pp. 176–177, and II, pp. 76–84.

13. For a discussion of the evidence as to the date of *Josippon,* see my article "The Author of the Book of Josippon: His Personality and His Age" (in Hebrew), *Zion* XVIII (1953), pp. 109–126.

14. See the precise wording and the notes in my edition, I, pp. 6–7, and II, pp. 80–81.

15. Josephus' *Jewish War* does not end with the fall of Masada (VII, 406) but contains descriptions of other events that follow the fall of Masada (until VII, 455).

16. Since the author of *Josippon* did not know Greek, it is certain that the words of Malalas, whose book was written in Greek, were incorporated into *Josippon*'s Latin source (or sources) about Julius Caesar.

17. Similar products of early medieval fantasy are treated, e.g., in Arturo Graf, *Roma nella memoria del Medio Evo* (Torino 1923).

18. It is interesting that when reproducing his dubious sources, the Hebrew author writes in a slightly different, more poetical style. Does this show that he did not trust his sources of this kind?

19. It is even probable that the author of *Josippon* produced a Hebrew translation of the two books of Maccabees before he wrote his book. A fragment of this composition has been preserved in a Hebrew medieval manuscript. See my edition, II, p. 132 n. 399. The Hebrew text itself was published by D. Chwolson in *Sammelband kleiner Handschriften* VII (Berlin 1896–1897), pp. 3–74.

20. See my edition, vol. 1, chapter 9, lines 57–84, pp. 51–52. See my Hebrew study in *Dappim, Research in Literature* II (Haifa 1985), p. 78.

21. See D. Flusser, "Der lateinische Josephus und der hebräische Josippon" (above, n. 1), pp. 127–130.

22. The critical edition of *Hegesippus* was published by V. Ussani in *Corpus Scriptorum Ecclesiasticorum Latinorum* (Vienna 1932, reprinted, New York 1960). The second volume appeared in the same collection, LXVI (Vienna 1960); it contains an introduction by K. Mras and indexes.

23. This was shown by K. Mras, *op. cit.,* pp. xxxiii–xxxvii. The same thing happened to the author of *Hegesippus* that happened to the author of *Josippon;* although he did not identify himself as Josephus, his work was later attributed to Josephus.

24. For a treatment of this Latin paraphrase of the *Jewish War,* see E. Schürer, *The History of the Jewish People in the Age of Jesus Christ (175 B.C.–A.D. 135),* ed. by G. Vermes and F. Millar, I (Edinburgh, 1973), pp. 58–60.

25. The author of *Josippon* writes about Venosa (my edition, I, p. 93): "Venusia, a town which is situated between the mountains and the plain." This geographical description betrays the author's first-hand knowledge. About Venosa, see Attilio Milano, "Venosa," *EJ* XVI (Jerusalem 1971), p. 102.

26. See my edition, I, p. 18, and the notes there.

27. For further details, see my "Der lateinische Josephus und der hebräische Josippon" (above, n. 1), pp. 129–130.

28. See Attilio Milano, "Italy," *EJ* IX (Jerusalem 1971), pp. 1119–1120.

29. The text forms an appendix in my edition, I, pp. 439–442. See also II, pp. 54–60, 252 n. 680.

30. The annotated text is published in my edition, I, pp. 461–491; see also II, pp. 216–248.

20 The Illustration of Josephus' Manuscripts

GUY N. DEUTSCH

Flavius Josephus' influence on Christian civilization is apparent in the works of art inspired by his writings. As an integral part of that civilization, this influence is difficult to define with precision. The subject of this discussion will be the gradual evolution of an established set of themes, which were utilized to illustrate and adorn Josephus' works. Our study, based on the analysis of forty-five manuscripts in twenty-two libraries,[1] will bear upon the manuscripts of the *Jewish Antiquities* and *The Jewish War*, from the oldest known specimens to those done just before the introduction of printing in the sixteenth century. We shall attempt to follow the evolution of illustration from the earliest drawings until the appearance of wood or copperplate engravings in the first printed editions. The chief patterns, selected in accordance with the frequency of their recurrence in the various manuscripts, will be examined in relation to their symbolic value. As authentic contemporary documents, the manuscripts represent an important source of information on the cultural atmosphere in which Josephus was read.

Let us first recall Josephus' position in relation to the Bible. It is known that, to the Christian world, the Scriptures were never within easy reach. As a rule, Christian readers found the Hebrew original wrapped in mystery, while its various translations were not accepted without difficulty.[2] The biblical text is often obscure and unfathomable without the help of exegesis. Josephus' works were modeled on classical writings and were intended for the benefit of the same audience. Around the fourth century, when the Greek original became incomprehensible to the larger public in Western Christendom, it was adapted in Latin, into which it was actually translated two centuries later.[3] Josephus recounted clearly and entertainingly the chief incidents of biblical history, which he supplemented with a history of the Jews down to the destruction of Jerusalem by Titus in A.D. 70. This he inserted within the corresponding context of Roman history. As in classical writings, Josephus made major events dependent on a host of great figures whom he magnified into heroes, while flavoring his narrative with a wealth of spicy details. He provided the Christian reader with a comprehensive picture of the adventure of the Jewish people, from its coming into being in the time of Abraham until what could be termed the end of its national existence, approximately forty years after the crucifixion of Jesus. Whereas Josephus attributed this tragic fate to the sins committed by the Jews, Christians deemed it as punishment for the sin of condemning Jesus to the cross. Thus, Josephus confirmed the assumption of theologians, according to whom Jews had been succeeded by Gentiles in the divine favor.

It is, therefore, hardly surprising that Josephus should have been regarded at one time as a Jewish prophet and his works as part of the biblical canon. The total lack of reference to the life and death of Jesus in the chapter of the *Antiquities* corresponding to his times was remedied at a very early date. Thus, paradoxically, Josephus became the authentically Jewish and unwitting witness to the veracity of the Gospels.[4] We shall examine how the illustrations reflect the ambiguous nature of this indefinable, albeit venerable, personality and his works, which represent the touchstone of the Christian theological structure. However, the illustrations through the centuries indicate an increasingly objective historical perspective, which was subsequently to rank Josephus among the great authors of antiquity.

The Chronology of the Illustration of Josephus' Works

The existence of Josephus' earliest illustrated manuscripts is attested by evidence that dates from the first centuries of our era.[5] Whether they were illustrated during the lifetime of the author or to what purpose is not known. In order to ascertain their origins, the two chief requirements of the genre must be taken into account. These were: a public for whose benefit the illustrations were specially designed, and a model to which artists could refer. The attitude of the Jewish public to Josephus' works written in Greek scarcely justified their illustration. Nor did Latin Christendom constitute an audience for these illustrations before the earliest translations into Latin, around the sixth century. The two above-mentioned requirements were to be found in Oriental Christendom, in centers such as Antioch or Edessa, where Hellenistic civilization converged with Jewish ideological creation. The lack of illustrated Oriental manuscripts of Josephus to date is probably due to the iconoclastic wave which swept the Byzantine and Moslem world around the eighth century. Against a background reminiscent of the revival of the plastic arts brought about in the West by an influx, almost totally unknown today, of Greek manuscripts salvaged from Byzantium after its investment by the Turks in 1453, illustrated Oriental manuscripts showing signs of Hellenistic, Sassanid, or other influence must have found their way to and around Europe at the time of the iconoclasm. The first signs of this influence were felt in the chief centers of Western culture in the Carolingian era. At Gerona, details extracted from the illustration of Josephus' works interfere with other texts, while a portrait of Josephus at Micy, near Orléans, is copied on the flyleaf of a Latin version of the *Antiquities,* together with the Greek letters which identified it in the original text. However, his barbaric appearance and the strangeness of his dress point to a Sassanid origin.[6]

The chief patterns of the illustration of Josephus were determined as early as the eleventh century, as evidenced by the three surviving manuscripts of the period.[7] Despite Oriental influence, still prevalent on the busts of heroes depicted in the margins of the text, the tradition of the portrait of the author writing or dedicating his book, as well as the programmatic representation adorning the first page of text, was already established. In addition, most of the heroes' portraits recurred regularly among later illustrations of Josephus' writings.

In the twelfth century, the period of the Crusades gave rise to an abundance of illustrated texts of Josephus' works. Their novelty lay both in theme and technique. The pictures, to which large blobs of color were added with the brush, were joined to the initial letters. The latter, broken up into several parts to suit the purposes of ornamentation, sometimes assumed monstrous proportions. In them can perhaps be detected an attempt to bridge the gap between the literal message and the pictorial language by a new form of synthetic pictogram. This impression is confirmed by the grotesque figures which frequently illustrate the complex interlacements of illuminated initials.[8]

The scenes depict, with carefully calculated simplicity intended to facilitate reading, some significant incident recounted at the beginning of the illustrated book. Unfortunately, the meaning they imply is seldom that of the author or of the inner logic of the text. Furthermore, the lack of explanatory captions makes their interpretation a very delicate matter. These illustrations usually represent, in a schematic and hardly differentiated manner indicative of an allegorical and edifying intention, two small figures confronting or complementing one another. The scenes were executed by skilled artists in large monasteries for the benefit of the monks, in order to answer the intellectual or moral preoccupations of the community. A wealth of information on the spiritual atmosphere of these monasteries would be available if these pictorial representations could be deciphered with any degree of certainty. For example, a mysterious parallel between the struggle of Jacob and Esau for the birthright and the confrontation of two saints of the church, John and Paul, is evidenced by inscriptions at the level of Book II of the *Antiquities* in two of the most ancient illustrated manuscripts, and is further corroborated by corresponding illustrations in later versions.[9]

The thirteenth century was characterized by the growing ascendancy of cities, which were to become the leading cultural centers of the period. The book, open wide on the lectern in the monastery's chapel or refectory, was designed for the religious edification of a homogeneous community. Due to changes in urban conditions, authors and bookmakers were confronted with new demands. The new public was as wide as it was varied. Most readers came from the middle class, motivated by its incipient individualism and ambition to assert itself. Prevalent was the law of supply and demand.[10] Scarcely any illustrated manuscripts of Josephus from the thirteenth and fourteenth centuries have survived to date: this seems to indicate that Josephus' histories no longer suited the cultural climate of the period.

This new reading public, which had formerly favored the emergence of the Chanson de Geste, likewise stimulated the creation of popularizing literary works. Clerics, quick to adapt to new conditions, undertook the rewriting and editing of the fundamental works of Christianity in order to render them more palatable to the masses. From the end of the twelfth century, particularly in France, there appeared gigantic compilations in which innumerable incidents with unexpected developments were recounted, with special emphasis on narrative tone. These books dealt indiscriminately with the history of the world and nature, the Jewish people and the Gospels, the lives of the saints, and the miracles of the Virgin Mary. Although they were originally composed in Latin, the language of scholarship, they were soon followed by translations into various vernacular dialects.[11] Thus, these works enjoyed a diffusion which would be difficult to imagine today and which enabled the masses to familiarize themselves with the bulk of Josephus' works. Although these books were partly illustrated, the analysis of their iconographic content is outside the scope of this study.

Previously stylized forms, on being reproduced for the purpose of executing manuscripts for the middle classes, now lost their original significance and took on naive shapes. Artists no longer sought to convey a message through illustration: the search was for pictorial patterns that would give the book an attractive appearance. To this end, artists used any illustrated material available: illustrated manuscripts from various periods, bearing upon various topics, scenes of everyday life, "grand" painting,[12] as well as theatrical performances. The account of the capture of Jerusalem by Titus, of primary importance as regards Christian dogma, had long been dramatized and performed inside a church or on its square.

The dramatization of the chief incidents of *The Jewish War* can be inferred by extrapolation from the periodic recurrence of a literary theme entitled "The Revenge of Our Lord." A Latin Apocryphal gospel, probably from the ninth century, bears a similar title (*Vindicta Salvatoris*). A twelfth century poem in Old French develops the same theme. The fifteenth century witnessed the appearance of at least two texts in dialogue form, which described the plot of a mystery play bearing the same name. A common characteristic of all these texts is that their volume steadily increased with time. New borrowings from various sources, as well as rather vulgar witticisms, were added. The basic framework of all these narratives was the story of the siege and destruction of Jerusalem by Titus, with the somewhat fanciful participation of a Jewish captain, Josephus. According to contemporary documents, the "Revenge" was performed in several French towns as counterpart to the "Passion" play.[13] Such a spectacular and colorful production must have had a vivid effect on the popular imagination, and its impact can easily be detected in later illustrations of Josephus. Since no other indexes are available, we must content ourselves with the dramatic elements which illustrated Josephus' books, especially in the fifteenth century.

Thus, when Josephus' texts grew back into public favor in the fifteenth century, the social environment and climate in which Josephus was read were markedly different. This is considerably felt in the symbols and style of the illustrations. Form was emphasized to the detriment of content. Instead of clarifying the hidden meaning of the text, illustration now tended to represent its literal meaning in a concrete, dramatic, and attractive manner. Pictures now diverged from the initial letter into a frame carefully drawn with a ruler, within a specially reserved space, distinct from the text on the parchment. It became a small, autonomous painting known as the frontispiece, which reproduced the action with the background, atmosphere, and problems of a stage production. This new, realistic, and illusionistic genre developed within the space of one generation. The three-dimensional representation technique was mastered more quickly than actual historical sense. As a framework to the action described the illustrator did depict his own environment. Moreover, he did not attempt to dissociate himself from his predecessors' moralizing intentions. The result was a composite picture, often admirably realistic, but no less suggestive of deep, implied meanings and anachronisms. Another consequence of the new urban conditions in the fifteenth century was the role of the artist in relation to his work. To his credit was the achievement of a harmonious balance among the elements composing the frontispiece. It must be emphasized that, as at the present time, works of high quality were few and far between.

The market for these books was great. Both the aristocracy and middle class read extensively and had prestige manuscripts made to order. The initiative of providing the larger public with literary works of high standard and in accessible form had been taken by the French royalty since the end of the fourteenth century. Charles V had had Josephus' works translated into French, along with those of other classical authors. Henceforth, Josephus ranked among the great historians of antiquity: it is known that history was considered to be moralizing and edifying.[14] However, the public did not forget that Josephus was a Jew who recounted biblical history. Confusion no longer reigned between Josephus and the Scriptures, but between Christianity and classical antiquity. Most Humanists, in their profound devotion, saw latent elements of Christianity in all the great philosophical movements and in the cultural achievements of Hellenistic civilization, which their admiration placed together in harmonious juxtaposition. Genius, considered to be a spark of divine spirit, could not germinate in the midst of falsehood. Everything was embraced in one simple truth, which pervaded all times and places.[15] Thus, the Temple of Jerusalem was represented as a Gothic cathedral on whose portal the statue of Moses with his horns and tablets of the law replaced that of Christ. And the Romans, sporting feathers and carrying the rapiers of contemporary lansquenets, aimed culverins and rock-hurling bombards at the walls of Jerusalem.[16] Josephus was indeed the link connecting the Bible and the classical age to Christianity.

Whenever possible, fifteenth century artists must have taken the illustrations of the ancient manuscripts for their models. Otherwise, when there was no model available and the customer required mass-produced miniatures (up to two hundred in a single book, e.g. in manuscripts 405 and 406 in the French collection of the Paris Bibliothèque nationale), it became necessary to invent. There were many spectacular scenes that could fit more than one historical text: for example, a royal entrance or coronation scene and representations of battles or funerals. Pictures copied from the Bible led to inconsistencies, such as the inclusion of a scene depicting the worshiping of the golden calf, which Josephus had deliberately omitted from his narrative.[17] This is further proof of the intellectual ecumenism of the day, in which truth was universally diffused and all component elements were harmonized into one unlimited whole. In such a perspective, Josephus, the Scriptures, and classical antiquity were all derived from one and the same essence.

Toward the end of the fifteenth century, when the manuscript gave way to the printed book, illustration assumed the characteristics of industrial production: the same clichés were used for various kinds of works and circulated from publisher to publisher. The few artists who created new illustrations for book publishers had to comply with their publishers' demands in quantity and time. Thus, Bible clichés were used for the *Jewish Antiquities* and Latin historical text clichés for *The Jewish War*. The same images recurred time and again in different contexts of the same edition. These hastily and coarsely engraved illustrations enjoyed the widest diffusion and influence. Although no study on the subject enables us to judge their impact on the history of painting and sculpture, our own observations of the work of Poussin, done in the seventeenth century, indicate that such influence must have existed and that it calls for more ample research.[18]

Analysis of the Chief Patterns

Through Josephus and the manner in which he was portrayed, the main developmental trends, which have just been touched upon, converged in a series of pictorial representations. Through the centuries, the portrait of Josephus was the most frequently recurring image in the manuscripts of the *Jewish Antiquities* and *The Jewish War*. It was, as we have seen, the first-known illustration of these texts. Josephus reappears in engravings of printed editions, but in a different context: he is portrayed as an actor rather than as an author. In order to follow the evolution of Josephus' portrait in his works, we must first attempt to understand the complexities of this multifaceted figure—author, Jew, witness, wise man, doctor, and rebel warrior—as he cast himself in the incidents of *The Jewish War*. The attire given Josephus and the scenery provided tell us how the portrait is oriented. In the earliest representation, Josephus assumes the martial bearing of the military commander, with his helmet and great staff.[19] Other military attributes were later conferred upon him, especially in the depictions of his encounter with the two Roman emperors, Vespasian, the father, and Titus, the son. This warlike attitude was the predominant feature of fifteenth-century portraits of Josephus. To distinguish him from the Roman soldiers that surround him, he is depicted as dark-skinned, shaggy and hairy, and often clad in gilded armor and riding a white steed. The front of his war helmet has a nose-shield similar to that worn by the Saracens.[20]

Josephus' meeting with the two emperors, father and son, was remembered as the capital event in his career. This was true for him personally, but it was also considered to be a symbolic turning point from a national and cultural standpoint. Vespasian and Titus were confronted by the rebel son of Israel, who had fallen into captivity and been subjected to the law of the victor. It appears from the illustrations that this scene conjured up, in the artists' perspectives, the long-awaited conversion of the Jewish people to the new faith, since Vespasian and Titus were always shown together and this encounter was also the theme of the most ancient dedicatory scenes. In this depiction, Josephus presents his book to the two crowned and enthroned emperors.[21] However, as an author offering his works to his two patrons, Josephus in this scene appears without his military trappings.

The custom of placing the presumed portrait of the author at the beginning of the book apparently goes back to antiquity. Oriental Christendom borrowed from it in depicting the four Evangelists in the act of composing their book. Western Christendom took over this pattern to extend it to authors of biblical works, including Josephus. In an eleventh-century Latin manuscript at Brussels (II 1179, fol. 1vo.), Josephus is seated on the median bar of the initial "H"; with his right hand he dips a pen into an inkwell while in his left hand he holds an eraser with which he supports a book on a lectern. In a twelfth-century manuscript at Cambridge, Josephus, curly-haired and bearded, is standing under a triple-arched portico while dictating his text to a scribe named Samuel. To indicate the essential part of the text being dictated, the artist has placed in Josephus' hands a roll on which the words "Fuit autem iisdem diebus . . ." can be read. This is the opening sentence of the *Testimonium Flavianum,* the interpolated passage in which Josephus is made to testify to the life of Jesus. This device enables us to tell in which capacity Josephus ranked among sacred writers.[22]

By the fifteenth century, the author's portrait had become a common stereotype, which appeared at the beginning of all of Josephus' illustrated works. In Italy, Josephus still figured, in the initial letter, as a town councillor or magistrate (Lat. 5060, Bibliothèque nationale, Paris), or as an Oriental magus wearing a conical hat with a wide and curving brim (Lat. 5051, *ibid.*). The frontispieces of contemporary French manuscripts represent the interior of a Humanist's cell; seated on a wooden and high-backed chair, Josephus is perusing a book and dictating its text to one or several scribes (French 11, 405 and 6446, Bibliothèque nationale, Paris; 5082, Arsenal, Paris).[23] The latest extant illustrated manuscript of Josephus in French, dating from the sixteenth century, significantly portrays the author as a handsome young man clad in a long robe, with one hand holding his book to his chest while the other carries an impressive sword. He is standing in the middle of a large and sumptuous cell, strewn with war instruments on the left and books on the right (Lat. 1581, Mazarine, Paris). Thus, the old Jewish ideal of the Midrash,[24] revived by the Humanists, was focused on Josephus himself. The ambiguity of his personality, in which two apparently incompatible worlds were able to coexist, is what seems to have caused his immense popularity through the ages.

The author's portrait usually adorned the initial letter of the Prologue. The actual text began with an illustration that was meant to embody the quintessence of the book. Most of Josephus' manuscripts began with the *Jewish Antiquities,* which was followed by *The Jewish War.* Josephus did not shrink from opening his text with the words "In the beginning," literally copied from the Book of Genesis and later taken up by the Gospel of John. These words naturally caught the attention of the artists responsible for decorating the manuscripts and intrigued the exegetes who attempted to unravel their hidden meaning. Since nothing is known of any illustrated Greek manuscripts of Josephus, the origin of the practice of linking together, in monogram form, the two letters "IN" of the Latin phrase *In principio* (i.e., "In the beginning") cannot be determined. We know of approximately fifteen manuscripts, comprising copies of the Bible, Gospels, and Josephus' *Antiquities* and ranging from the ninth to the eleventh centuries, that are decorated with the two capital letters "IN" linked together, with the "I" serving as a median axis to the "N." The letter "I," standing alone, or the monogram "IN" were used as starting points for complicated iconographic projects which could not have been initiated by the artist responsible for their execution; in them can be detected the clever speculations of a scholar.

The most common themes used in the monograms were based upon reflections of a philosophical or theological nature concerning the governing principle of the universe. The basic sketch of the monogram was exploited and enriched by means of medallions and small figures, sometimes together with explanatory captions. The four elements represented in their numerical relationships, the six days of the Creation, references to the Fall and to the need for salvation, or typological parallels between various biblical incidents and the crucifixion of Jesus can be found in the monograms. In the vast majority of cases, these themes were developed and framed within the single initial "I," which was excessively lengthened and enlarged for that purpose. One twelfth-century illuminator went so far as to represent Christ standing in place of the vertical letter "I," a bold personification of the monogram (Lat. 5047, fol. 2, Bibliothèque nationale, Paris).[25]

This carefully elaborated structure collapsed and became obsolete when the letter "I" ceased to be used as the vertical support. When all books were translated into the vernacular, conditions had changed and artists no longer sought to derive mysterious meanings from the shapes of letters. As was remarked above, illustrations became isolated frontispieces, which, in the fifteenth century, maintained a remarkable uniformity among Josephus' works. As a rule, they depicted the creation of the world, with emphasis on a particularly little-known episode, the marriage of Adam and Eve, which symbolized the fulfillment of creation. Man and woman were represented naked, on either side of the Creator, with their hands joined in His, under the watchful eyes of the animals surrounding them. The origin of this story, which is found neither in the Bible nor in Josephus' works, is doubtful. The earliest mention of marriage in relation to Adam and Eve appears in the rabbinical Midrash. Through some mysterious channel, it must have reached the authors of popular works, who had been paraphrasing the Bible since the end of the twelfth century. Within the context of the fifteenth century, the popularity of this theme may be explained symbolically and mystically: this first sacrament of the Church may indeed have referred to the marriage of Jesus and the Virgin Mary. This concept is corroborated by various sources.[26]

Adam and Eve were but the first of a long succession of figures whose stories were told by Josephus and who had been portrayed in illustrations since the most ancient of times. Thanks to Josephus, they gained a celebrity and popularity that would be difficult to understand today. We have seen the fate reserved for Josephus and his two patrons, Vespasian and Titus; we have touched upon the parallel between Jacob and Esau and John and Paul. We shall now give a brief summary of the iconography of several figures, chosen specially to show how enlightening illustration can be in revealing the historical atmosphere that no other contemporary document illuminates.

The first figure to be discussed is Jesus. As has already been explained, his appearance in Josephus' texts was contrived by means of interpolation. However, illustrations show to what extent his presence was real in the perspective of Josephus' medieval readers. The short paragraph of the *Testimonium Flavianum* appeared only in Book XVIII of the *Antiquities,* but Christ was represented, sometimes unexpectedly, in many of the manuscripts of Josephus. As the basic element of the initial miniature to the text, Christ was usually linked with the words *In principio.* The initial "I" of a twelfth-century manuscript originally from Zwiefalten, Germany (Hist. fol. 418, Stuttgart regional library), ends at bottom with a crucifixion scene placed upon the heads of Adam and Eve. On either side of the initial are rows of small biblical figures supposed to foreshadow the crucifixion: Adam, Eve, and the serpent; Noah and the dove in the Ark; Abraham's sacrificial ram; the Brazen Serpent; and the widow of Sarepta.[27] In the interpolated text relating to Jesus, in Book XVIII, several illustrators have painted either a cross, a crucifixion, or Christ enthroned (Lat. 5047, Lat. 5049, French 6446, Bibliothèque nationale, Paris). A thirteenth-century Burgundian artist, deliberately ignoring the text he was supposed to decorate, illuminated the initials of the last five books of *The Jewish War* with scenes taken from the Passion (Manuscript 534, Pierpont Morgan Library, New York).

Since Josephus was "mobilized" by the church for its own needs, it was natural that his works should be brought into direct relationship with Christological illustrations. The picture of Cyrus, king of Persia, appears in Book XI of the *Antiquities,* the one that relates his history, in twelve or thirteen manuscripts ranging from the eleventh to the sixteenth centuries. Cyrus' appearance in the manuscripts, while many heroes in the *Antiquities* are not depicted, is because Cyrus was surrounded by an aura of popularity. This is corroborated by certain ancient texts: Cyrus was the hero of numerous legends, which originated in his country and were subsequently transmitted to the West by Greek historians of antiquity, to be kept alive all through the Middle Ages.[28] Some of the biblical figures cast by Josephus, such as Saul, David, Solomon, and the Queen of Sheba, owed their celebrity to the vicissitudes of their destinies and to the typological interpretations given to them by Christian theologians. However, several secondary figures bear the name of Jesus, and so they deserved a portrait: thus Joshua, whose Latin name is Jesus Nave, and a victim of the Zealots whose murder was recounted in Book V of *The Jewish War* and whose name was also Jesus, appear in illustrations. It seems that the trio made up of King Herod, his wife Mary (Mariamne), and his brother Joseph, the latter two suspected of fornication, must have conjured up certain associations in the reader's mind and perpetuated their memory. However, this was especially true of the extraordinary destiny of Jehoshaphat, an obscure Judean king who appears in the succession of heroes' portraits, in approximately ten manuscripts from the eleventh to the sixteenth centuries. His name is no doubt associated with eschatological traditions connected with the Valley of Jehoshaphat in Jerusalem, a place of pilgrimage already mentioned by the prophets.[29]

This study of the heroes who constitute both the framework and the attraction in Josephus' works cannot be concluded without a word about King Herod. A fascinating figure in the text, he enjoyed a special relationship to the Christian public through the stories of John the Baptist and the Massacre of the Innocents. His career in the theater, from its liturgical beginnings to the present, was unparalleled. As a cruel tyrant plagued by disease and misfortune, he was variously represented as executing his beloved wife on the strength of a foul machination, immersed in his bath, writhing in agony, or attempting to cut his throat with a knife.[30] Once again, it needs to be stated that the relationship between printed illustration and the theatrical stage remains to be defined.

Next to the heroes portrayed by Josephus in his works, a number of scenes described by him engraved themselves on the readers' imaginations and have become the most important pictorial representations of the whole narrative. Most of the scenes were unfolded at the beginning of the books, and the illustrators played an important part in fixing them in the readers' memories. This was true of the various stages of the creation of the world in Book I and of the tragic fate of the young Amalekite, at the beginning of Book VII, who tells David that he helped Saul kill himself and pays David homage with Saul's crown and armband. Likewise, the rebuilding of the Temple by order of Cyrus was frequently depicted at the beginning of Book XI, and the attempt on the life of the Roman Emperor Gaius Caligula in Book XIX. Other scenes, represented in *The Jewish War,* were depictions of Vespasian being instructed by Nero to repress the revolt in Book III and of Titus laying siege to Jerusalem in Book V or Book VI.[31]

Another scene from *The Jewish War* was taken out of context and enhanced by means of illustration, because of the profound horror it inspired. In Book VI, section 201, in modern editions, Josephus tells the story of Mary of Bethezob. Caught in the siege of Jerusalem and driven by hunger, she decides to slaughter her son, cook, and eat him. According to the text, Titus himself was horrified to learn of this incident and increased his efforts to capture the city and end the suffering. To the Christians this rapidly became Mary's sacrifice, with all the connotations which can be derived from the name. It condensed, in a striking form, the relationship between the pitiful mother and the over-possessive one, between the sacrifice on the cross and the Eucharist, and between Christianity and Judaism, considered to be the wicked stepmother. For a long time, this episode was regarded as the supreme symbol of horror and used as evidence of the cruelty of the world before Christ. It appeared in the apocryphal Gospel mentioned above, "The Revenge of Our Lord," and in medieval written and dramatic literature. It was represented on the stage and described on the pages of manuscripts and remained engraved on what could be called the collective memory as the Great Taboo, at once close and repulsive, a symbol of the tortured soul of Western man.[32] Thus, Josephus secured his place deep in modern man's subconscious, long after he had ceased to play the part of witness or biblical prophet at the crossroads of three civilizations.

Notes

1. This whole study, entitled *Iconographie de l'Illustration de Flavius Josèphe au temps de Jean Fouquet,* has been published under the editorship of Professor Dr. K. H. Rengstorf (*Arbeiten zur Literatur und Geschichte des Hellenistischen Judentums,* 12; Leiden: Brill, 1986). We wish to thank the editor and his collaborator, Professor Dr. Heinz Schreckenberg, for their kindness and cooperation.

2. On this subject, see *The Cambridge History of the Bible,* G. W. H. Lampe, ed., 3 vols., Cambridge, 1963–1970, and especially Raphael Loewe, "The Medieval History of the Latin Vulgate," vol. 2, pp. 102–154.

3. See Franz Blatt, *The Latin Josephus,* Aarhus, 1958, pp. 17–24.

4. For the bibliography on this section, see pp. 13ff. and 18ff. of our above-mentioned work, to which we shall henceforth refer as *Iconographie.*

5. *Iconographie,* pp. 30ff.

6. G. N. Deutsch, "Un portrait de Josèphe dans un manuscrit occidental du IXᵉ siècle," *Revue de l'art* 53, 1981, pp. 53–55.

7. One of them is in the Bibliothèque nationale, Paris, Lat. 5058; another in the Brussels Royal Library, II 1179; the third, manuscript 29 in the Chartres Municipal Library, was seriously damaged during World War II. It is described by Yves Delaporte, *Les Manuscrits enluminés de la Bibliothèque de Chartres,* Chartres, 1929; *Iconographie,* pp. 32ff., figs. 2, 3, 5.

8. See Jürgen Gutbrod, *Die Initiale in Handschriften des 8. bis 13. Jahrhunderts,* Stuttgart, 1965; *Iconographie,* pp. 34ff.

9. Codex 50 of Bern Bürgerbibliothek, fol. 2; 29 of Chartres, fol. 9vo. (Delaporte, *op. cit.,* p. 12); and Lat. 8959 of the Paris Bibliothèque nationale, fol. 9 (*Iconographie,* pp. 76–77, fig. 7).

10. On this development, see e.g. Georges Duby, *Le Temps des cathédrales, L'art et la société, 980–1420,* Paris, 1976, pp. 223ff.

11. Erwin Panofsky, in *Renaissance and Renascences in Western Art,* London, 1960, pp. 68ff., explains this phenomenon.

12. Millard Meiss, *French Painting in the Time of Jean de Berry, the Late 14th Century and the Patronage of the Duke,* 2 vols., London, 1967, pp. 7–17.

13. G. N. Deutsch, "Déicide et Vengeance," *Archives juives* 16, 1980, No. 4, pp. 69–73.

14. E. M. Sanford, "The Study of Ancient History in the Middle Ages," *JHI* 5, 1944, pp. 21–43.

15. This idea was developed by Erwin Panofsky, *op. cit.,* pp. 82ff.

16. *Iconographie,* pp. 117ff. and 174, figs. 62, 131, 137, 140.

17. Represented in the Lat. ms. 6446, Bibliothèque nationale, Paris, fol. 47 (*Iconographie*, p. 11, fig. 39).

18. G. N. Deutsch, "Légendes midrachiques dans la peinture de Nicolas Poussin," *JJA* 9, 1982, pp. 47–53.

19. See above, note 6.

20. *Iconographie*, p. 63, figs. 127, 147.

21. *Iconographie*, pp. 61–62, figs. 2, 3.

22. *Iconographie*, pp. 59–61, figs. 5, 6.

23. *Iconographie*, ibid., figs. 14–20.

24. "R. Eliezer says: 'The book and the sword came down together,'" *Midrash Sifrei*, 40. The illustration here referred to is reproduced on the cover of David Flusser's *Josephus Flavius*, Tel Aviv, 1985.

25. Harry Bober, "In principio, Creation before Time," *Essays in Honor of Erwin Panofsky*, ed. by Millard Meiss, New York, 1961, pp. 13–28; Johannes Zahlten, *Creatio mundi, Darstellung der sechs Schöpfungstage und naturwissenschaftliches Weltbild im Mittelalter*, Stuttgart, 1979, pp. 54–58; *Iconographie*, pp. 66–68, figs. 21, 24.

26. Adelheid Heimann, "Die Hochzeit von Adam und Eva in Paradies," *Wallraf-Richartz Jahrbuch* 37, 1975, pp. 11–40; *Iconographie*, pp. 70–74, figs. 26–29.

27. Karl Löffler, *Schwäbische Buchmalerei in Romanischer Zeit*, Augsburg, 1928, p. 65, pl. 39. *Iconographie*, p. 69.

28. *Iconographie*, pp. 135–137; figs. 75–81.

29. *Iconographie*, pp. 96, 102–104, 107–122, 123–125, 155, 175, figs. 8, 12, 50, 51, 53, 54, 56–63, 95, 96.

30. Abraham Schalit, *König Herodes*, Berlin, 1969; *Iconographie*, pp. 153–155, figs. 96–105.

31. *Iconographie*, figs. 125–127, 133, 134, 137, 140, 147.

32. G. N. Deutsch, "The Myth of Mary of Bethezob," *Zemanim* 4, nr. 16, Autumn 1984, pp. 20–28 [in Hebrew]. See also *Iconographie*, pp. 179–182, figs. 1, 143–147.

21 Martin Luther and Flavius Josephus

BETSY HALPERN AMARU

n the enormous compendium that constitutes Martin Luther's writings—from lectures to sermons, from biblical commentaries to expository writings—Josephus is directly mentioned and/or cited as a source reference only twenty-one times. In spite of this sparsity, the direct references confirm that Luther used Josephus' works and suggest that the use might well have been more extensive than acknowledged by the reformer.[1]

That Luther was familiar with Josephus' works is not particularly notable. In the sixteenth century there was great interest in Josephus, and printed editions of his works in Latin were available by 1470.[2] Indeed, interest in the writings of the first-century Jewish historian had long been a tradition in Christian scholarship. His works had been respected and widely used not only by the church fathers but also by subsequent medieval church historians and scholars. They valued Josephus as "most historical," cited him as an authoritative source on geography, history, chronology, and etymology, and at times even used his writings to buttress their theologies.[3]

In many ways Luther was not unlike his Catholic predecessors. He occasionally used Josephus as a source in support of his own analysis of a Hebrew term. More often, he turned to Josephus for details with which to enhance the historical setting of his biblical commentaries or to support his theological interpretation of a text. Finally, Luther attacked certain aspects of the character portraits Josephus had drawn of biblical figures. In this study I shall examine each of these types of references to and uses of Josephus' works. In addition, I shall explore some areas where the historian is not mentioned by name but may possibly have been used as a source.

In the area of etymology, neither Josephus nor Luther was particularly expert.[4] Consequently—perhaps fortunately—Luther uses only two direct citations from Josephus for etymological purposes. Both of these instances relate to the Hebrew word אדם, which Josephus tells us "signifies 'red' " and is the name given to the first man because he was made "from the red earth kneaded together; for such is the color of true virgin soil" (*A* I, 34). Luther uses this bit of information twice, once in order to discuss the nature of man in terms of the three Hebrew words איש, אנוש, and אדם ("Lectures on Hebrews," XXIX, 128–129), and again in his discussion of Esau as אדמוני ("Lectures on Genesis," IV, 369). The citation is essentially correct. But in each case there is a slight exaggeration of Josephus' words, a liberal paraphrasing, which we shall find quite common in Luther's use of Josephus. At times such paraphrasing leads the reformer into significant distortions. In the present context, however, it involves only the slight change from "the color of true virgin soil" to "virgin earth in its unspoiled and true nature" in one case (XXIX, 128–129) and to "red earth which Pliny and Josephus maintain is the best" in the other (IV, 369). The slight change is intentional and lends support to Luther's theological purpose.

The whole matter of Esau's name, an issue upon which Luther dwells extensively, raises the possibility of yet another etymological use of Josephus. This one is not credited and may have come to Luther through a secondary source. While Luther cites Josephus to explain the biblical description of the infant Esau as אדמוני, Josephus himself ignores the matter of "redness" in describing Esau at birth. Instead he stresses (*A* I, 258) the hairiness of the newborn and derives the name Esau from "esauron." [5] The "redness" description arises only in the context of the story of the reddish pottage, in which Josephus elaborates on the biblical association of Esau with *Adom* ("red") by telling us that the older twin "was jestingly nicknamed by his youthful comrades 'Adom' . . . and that was how he called the country; the more dignified name of Idumaea it owes to the Greeks" (*A* II, 3). With Esau's third name, Seir, Josephus returns to the "hairiness" theme, noting that Esau "so names the place after his own shaggy hair" (*A* I, 336).

Luther makes much of the redness as well as the hairiness of the baby Esau, interpreting the characteristics as bad signs misinterpreted by the child's parents, who then inappropriately name him "doer of all things." [6] But when he comes to the pottage story, he summarizes the derivations of Esau's three names in a manner that could indicate a certain confused use of Josephus:

> Esau has three names. Esau is his own name, which he received at birth or at his circumcision. His surname is Edom from the red pottage. His third name is Seir
> . . . He got the name Seir either from the mountain on which he lived—previously it was called Seir—or from his shagginess, because he was red and hairy; perhaps even the region he occupied was rough and wild. Hence the Idumean nation is called the nation of Seir, from Esau, who occupied Mount Seir. ("Lectures On Genesis," IV, 394)

Thus, while Luther avoids Josephus' derivation of the name Esau from "esauron," like Josephus, he does relate the name Seir to Esau's hairiness.[7] Moreover, in both expositions the names of Esau are somehow then related to the term "Idumaea."[8]

Luther's second major use of Josephus' works—for historical detail in elaborating on and interpreting biblical narratives—is closely related to the break the reformer made from traditional exegetical technique, a break rooted in Luther's revolutionary attitude toward the historicity of the Hebrew Scriptures.

Traditional Christian exegesis viewed the Hebrew Scriptures and the Old Covenant basically as a prefiguration of the New Covenant that would be established through Christ. The truly significant (or spiritual) content of the Old (unlike the New) was not clearly spelled out in the biblical text. Rather, it was buried and hidden in the language of ritual and law and could be uncovered only by removing the words from the husks of their literal contexts through an elaborately developed tradition of allegorical interpretation. Consequently, in the reading of the Hebrew Scriptures no real significance was attributed to historical Israel before the Christ event. Jewish history *qua* history was essentially irrelevant within the Christian scheme of salvation.

Luther's exposition of biblical text diverged from this traditional method of exegesis in two major areas: he disagreed with the stress on allegorical method and with the negation of history that the allegorical approach to the Hebrew Scriptures implied.[9] Luther started with the basic premise that the history of Israel contained more than allegorical allusions to a future event. Rather, the Hebrew Scriptures related a true history of God and of Christ. They narrated God's promises of saving grace and man's responses, as they were recorded in the real experiences of historical personalities. The approach did not, however, involve any legitimization of the Jews as a lasting people of God. They had, indeed, once been His people, covenanted through promises. But their ultimate infidelity resulted in their rejection and replacement by a new Israel. In spite of this rejection, Jewish history remained significant to the "New Israel" because it contained within it the "hidden church," the believers who could and would maintain their faith in God's promises. This hidden, true church ("the faithful synagogue")[10] was composed of real biblical Jewish characters who, as models of faithfulness, were, in fact, spiritual Christians in terms of their belief in the promise of Christ.

Luther's approach brought a certain unity to the narratives of the two Testaments. With Luther, both Testaments involved the steps of one Christ in history, through the challenge of the conditional promise in the Old and the gift of fulfillment in the New.[11] Moreover, both "spoke" to the contemporary believer directly because each evidenced the tribulations of the true church in its battle against the false, a battle which Luther saw as ongoing in his own quarrel with the papists. This "speaking" was no longer dependent upon allegory in order to be understood; on the contrary, "before all else the historical sense must be dug out," and the Scriptures must be read as history.[12]

Luther's view of the Hebrew Scriptures as history effected a certain sense of historicity and a respect for the works of historians. But Luther's sense of history was not that of modern scientific study. For the reformer, history in any form remained essentially a form of theology: "histories are nothing else than a demonstration, recollection, and sign of divine action and judgment, how He upholds, rules, obstructs, prospers, punishes, and honors the world and especially men, each according to his just desert, evil or good" ("Preface to Galeatius Capella's History," XXXIV, 275). Nothing takes place in time that does not reflect the activity of God. There can be no history without God either as subject or author. Where God is the subject, as in the history of Israel, His activity is open and direct. Through His Word, He creates faith and offers grace ("Lectures on Deuteronomy," IX, 33). This type of divine activity, however, is only one side of the historical picture. More often, God's power in history is masked, making it possible for man to have some sense of significance in his own story. Yet God is always the actor, and man His tool. At His appointed times He effects the rise and fall of nations, kingdoms, and rulers as manifestations of divine wrath and judgment.[13] World history may appear to be without meaning or purpose, but, in fact, to the understanding eye, it reflects the hand of God. What the ancients called "Fortuna" was, in fact, that hidden hand punishing God's "enemies through other enemies: the Jews through the Romans, the Romans through the Goths and Wends. He will find someone to ruin both the Turk and the pope" ("Lectures on Psalms," XIII, 258).

Each form of history—that of the Gentiles as well as that of the Jews—teaches that "everything happens by the ordinance of God" ("Notes on Ecclesiastes," XV, 103). In one case the learning is direct. In the other, human talent, luck, or fortune may be credited, but to the eyes of the faithful, God's hand is clearly visible.[14]

For Luther history and theology are so intertwined that he can deal with neither without reference to the other. Consequently, Luther's exegetical works are filled with references to classical historians whom he lauds as promoters of law and order, as "the most useful people," and as "the best teachers."[15] Decrying the neglect of "poets and historians" in his own education, he urges the teaching of histories "in whatever language they are to be had."[16]

It is in this context that Luther uses the writings of Josephus for the decorative details that support his presentation of the Scriptures as a historical narrative. This Josephan material is presented in asides and frequently involves bits of historical and geographical miscellanea, which are not always essential to the text. Three of the six direct examples of this appear in Luther's "Lectures on Genesis."

In dealing with Abraham's altar building at Shechem (Gen. 12:7), Luther uses Josephus in order to "update" the characters and locale of the story. He tells us that the Shechemites (whom he identifies with the Samaritans) got permission from Alexander to build a "splendid temple on Mount Gerizim" because Abraham had built an altar on Mount Moreh" ("Lectures on Genesis," II, 285). The detail is entirely gratuitous; indeed, it is even confusing, for it associates the altar built after the Akedah (Gen. 22:14) with an earlier one. As for the Josephan source, Luther leaves little doubt that he has consulted the historian directly, for he notes that the information is to be found in "the eighth chapter of his second volume" (A XI, 322–324). The citation is correct, but like many of Luther's references to Josephus, it is not at all in the historian's context.[17]

In a second gratuitous aside, Luther moves by his own logic from שאול (Gen. 42:38) to גיא שמז and cites Josephus as a backup to Jerome's description of Gethsemane as having "wonderfully delightful gardens" ("Lectures on Genesis," VII, 308).[18] Josephus is cited again as "the authority" in an effort to verify the Scriptural text against the Greek historians. Here the issue involves the building of Babylon and its famous gardens, which the Greeks attributed to Queen Semiramis rather than to King Nebuchadnezzar (Dan. 4:30). With the short note, "Josephus writes about this," Luther "proves" the biblical text ("Lectures on Minor Prophets," XIX, 215). Here book and chapter are not specified, but the content and context of Luther's remarks are so similar to those in Josephus that there can be little doubt of direct reference to the historian.[19]

In this matter of Babylon, Luther uses Josephus without mentioning that Josephus had acknowledged the Babylonian historian Berosus as his own source. In another reference to Josephus, Luther not only again ignores the accreditation to Berosus but also distorts the citation in such a way as to cast doubt upon Josephus' credibility as a historical witness: "Josephus has some rather amazing statements about the mountains of Armenia. He records that remnants of the ark were found there in his time. But I suppose that nobody will consider me a heretic if I doubt his reliability in some instances" ("Lectures on Genesis," II, 108). Perhaps the result of a mistranslation, the attack is unjustified, for Josephus clearly sets the story in the far earlier era of Berosus: "Berosus[20] the Chaldaean . . . in his description of the events of the flood writes somewhere as follows: 'It is said, moreover, that a portion of the vessel still survives in Armenia on the mountain of the Cordyaeans, and that persons carry off pieces of the bitumen, which they use as talismans'" (A I, 93).

This is not the only time that Luther questions the judgment of the historian. When he comes to describe Herod's building of the Temple, he notes that

Josephus described Herod's Temple as "equal or superior to the Temple of Solomon in splendor." However, as much as he "would like to believe the history books," this is impossible, for the remodelled building would be lacking "the items mentioned from that sublime, old holy place" ("On the Jews and Their Lies," XLVII, 224). The critique of Josephus here would seem to be in response to a passage in *The Jewish War*.[21] But for that context, Luther's paraphrase is somewhat exaggerated. I would suggest that what Luther really objects to in Josephus is the relatively sympathetic portrait of Herod, whom Luther considers "an impious enemy of God" (XLVII, 224).[22]

In spite of his posture as a "critical" user of historical sources, Luther does not always use Josephus with a discerning eye. In his search for an identity to the city of "No-Amon" in Nahum 3:8 (which Luther calls "Alexandria of the peoples"), he turns again to Josephus (*A* II, 249–250) and pulls his geographic detail out of the context of an outrageously romantic legend of an Egyptian attack on Ethiopia led by Moses ("Lectures on Nahum," XVIII, 310).

It is not possible to enumerate or to specify with any certainty the passages where Luther uses Josephus for historical detail without crediting the source. There are, however, several passages where Luther's use of Josephus can be posited at least hypothetically through Nicholas de Lyra.[23] One such example involves Luther's identification of the rivers in the Garden of Eden story. Like Josephus (*A* I, 13) and in contrast to other extant Midrashim, Luther identifies Havilah as India, the Pishon River as the Ganges, and the Gihon as the Nile ("Lectures on Genesis," I, 97).[24] The same identification appears in Lyra's commentary, and it is quite plausible that Luther drew his information from there, if not directly from *Antiquities*.[25]

Again, in relating the story of Dinah going out "to see the daughters of the land" (Gen. 34:1), Luther adds the little detail that her venture was motivated by a desire to see how the girls of the region were "decked out" ("Lectures on Genesis," VI, 192). Similarly, Josephus tells us that she went "into the city to see the finery of the women of the country" (*A* I, 337). Although the language is not identical, the bit of unnecessary detail is the same; and a link is provided in Lyra, who cites Josephus on this passage.[26]

Much more difficult to establish are the passages where Lyra does not serve as a potential connection. For example, both Josephus and Luther relate that when Jacob buried the strange gods and earrings taken as booty from the Shechemites (Gen. 35:2–4), he also buried the *teraphim* that Rachel had stolen from her father (*A* I, 342, and "Lectures on Genesis," VI, 237). Again the unnecessary detail rather than similarity in language suggests the possibility of a connection between Luther and Josephus.[27] There are a number of such examples: Eliezer requiring ten camels when he traveled to the home of Laban because they were needed to carry "the garments and the finery of the women" ("Lectures on Genesis," IV, 259), as compared to Josephus' note that Eliezer requested lodging because he was "the bearer of women's apparel of great price" (*A* I, 250); Laban ceasing in his search for the *teraphim* because he thought, "My daughter would not hold my religion in such slight esteem" ("Lectures on Genesis," VI, 60), as compared to Josephus' Laban "never suspecting that his daughter in that condition would approach the images" (*A* I, 322).

The trivial quality of the material, combined with the fact that Luther directly cites Josephus on other occasions, adds to the possibility that the historian was also used in these cases. But without any other connecting link, the differences in language and style make it difficult to do more than hypothesize.

Luther did not use material from Josephus solely for historical adornment. His desire to establish the historicity of the biblical text also extended to the realm of theology. Indeed, of all the credited citations of Josephus, those used for theological purposes are the most numerous. They occur most frequently in Luther's commentaries on prophetic material. As with the decorative citations, Josephus is used as a historical source, this time to root theology in a historical context.

In five of the credited references, Josephus is cited as evidence of the fulfillment of the predictions of the prophet Zechariah. The first of these involves the puzzling opening of chapter nine: "In the land of Hadrach and in Damascus shall be His resting place. For the Lord is the eye of man and all the tribes of Israel. And Hamath also shall border therein; Tyre and Sidon; for she is very wise" (9:1–2). Luther admits that the text is obscure and has been variously interpreted. To his understanding the prophet is predicting a great destruction that will precede the conversion of the peoples of Palestine and its surrounding neighbors. Citing Josephus (and the Book of Maccabees),[28] he affirms that the prophecy has been fulfilled through the destruction of Tyre and Sidon and by the perpetual conflict that plagued the area after the death of Alexander.[29]

When he comes to Zechariah 8:20, a prophecy of the coming of many peoples to Jerusalem to "entreat the favor of God," Luther again turns to Josephus for evidence of fulfillment: "And all that was fulfilled, and so Josephus writes that many kings and princes and also others bestowed great honors on the Temple in Jerusalem" ("Lectures on Zechariah," XX, 280).[30] In Josephus' writings there is no single clear statement of such a reception to the Temple. But in various places he does mention gifts sent by foreign monarchs.[31] These references are wide-ranging in time span (from Cyrus to Ptolemy Philadelphus) and are not clearly applicable to Luther's understanding of Zechariah's prophecy. But, as previously noted, it is not unusual for Luther to use Josephus' material rather loosely.

In two other passages regarding the fulfillment of the prophecies of

Zechariah, Josephus is cited (again in general fashion), but now the context is God's withdrawal from and rejection of the Jews:

> we read in Josephus that horrible sects and rebellions arose among the Jewish people shortly before the birth of Christ . . . Herod first of all fulfilled the prophecy of the above verse (11:7) by treating the Jews terribly with his sword. But the factions of the Pharisees treated them even more terribly with their tongues and their teachings; and the Jews fared as though they no longer had a God who would regard them. ("Lectures on Zechariah," XX, 314)[32]

Luther's use of Josephus for theological purposes does not always involve general references. In his interpretation of Isaiah 34:3 ("Their slain shall be cast out") as a description of the horrors of the Roman siege of Jerusalem, Luther cites Josephus on the stench of the uninterred corpses ("Lectures on Isaiah," XVI, 293).[33] And in the anti-Semitic tract "On the Jews and Their Lies," (XLVII, 233), Josephus is Luther's source for the number of men slain in the Jewish rebellion against Rome.[34]

For Luther, as for Josephus, the fate of the Jews in this conflict is a foregone conclusion. Whereas Josephus argues that point from a military realism at one time (*BJ* II, 345ff.), from "Fortuna" at another (*BJ* V, 367), and from a theological perspective at a third (*BJ* V, 378–401, and VI, 267–270), for Luther the issue is always theological and christological. True both to traditional Christianity and to his own concept of Jewish history as the visible working of God, Luther argues that the Romans were God's agents, punishing the Jews for their "delusions regarding their false Christ and their persecution of the true Christ" ("On the Jews and Their Lies," XLVII, 233). Except for his christological context, Luther comes extremely close to Josephus' own venture into theology. It is surprising that the closest Luther comes to acknowledgment of Josephus' theological perspective is in the general statement that "the historians write that Jerusalem was captured by a special divine command from God" ("Lectures on Isaiah," XVI, 187). Although Luther never mentions Josephus directly in this context, he shares with him the belief that God controls history and moves His favor from nation to nation. They also share a sense of themselves as possessors of the special gift of being able to use their exegetical skills to interpret the present, and, in Josephus' case, to predict future historical events. Neither is so arrogant as to call himself a "prophet." But on at least one occasion Josephus comes close to seeing himself as a Jeremiah (*BJ* V, 391–393); and, in his correspondence, Luther compares himself with that prophet as well as with Isaiah.[35]

In three additional references Luther uses Josephus to support other aspects of his theology. One involves his interpretation of Daniel's apocalyptic calendar, in which the reformer cites Josephus against "rabbinic lies" regarding a three-year truce between the Judean state and Rome prior to the year A.D. 70.[36] In another text, Josephus' description of the bronze gates of the

Temple (*BJ* V, 201) becomes the basis for a spiritual (as opposed to literal) understanding of Psalm 74:6 ("Lectures on Psalms," X, 441).

A last instance of direct reference to Josephus for theological purposes appears in the context of a discussion of inward as opposed to outward circumcision. Luther notes that Josephus, like all the Jews (referred to as "they" in the text), maintained that "the actual deed, not the intention," is culpable ("Lectures on Romans," XXV, 24). Although the historical content of Josephus is inaccurately cited by Luther, his statement of Josephus' "Jewish" theology is correct.[37]

Unacknowledged references to Josephus' writings in the context of the exposition of Luther's theology are even more difficult to verify than the examples suggested in regard to historical detail for its own sake. Given the plethora of sources available to Luther, it is perhaps wise to limit suggestions of such usage to a few examples where the historical content in Luther is very similar to that of Josephus. One such text involves a subject of interest to both writers: the human predisposition to misinterpret God's signs as positive when in fact they are "against us." In his discussion of the misinterpretation of Esau's appearance at birth ("Lectures on Genesis," IV, 374–375), Luther goes on to describe the incident of the massive gate to the Temple opening of its own accord, an incident which the Jews misread as a sign of God's presence and blessings. The story is also related in Tacitus' *Histories* (V, 13, 1). But in Josephus (*BJ* VI, 290–295), as in Luther, it is not only set in the context of a discussion of premonitory signs, but also is interpreted in terms of the withdrawal of divine protection.

Another possible use of Josephus involves the words of comfort Luther puts into the mouth of Philo when he and his fellows are frustrated at their meeting with Gaius Caligula: "Well, then, dear brethren, do not be afraid, but take heart; just because human help fails us, God's help will surely be with us" ("Preface to the Wisdom of Solomon," XXV, 342). In Josephus' rendition of the meeting, the words are paraphrased, but the sense is essentially the same.[38]

Luther's historical portraits are not always in agreement with those of Josephus.[39] Indeed, in the matter of three biblical portraits, Luther cites Josephus in order to refute him. In all three cases—Cain, Abraham, and Saul—the objection to the historian's portrait is rooted in Luther's theological perspective.

The biblical narrative tells very little about the character of Cain before the act of fratricide. He is called "Cain" because at birth his mother exclaimed, "I have gotten a man of God" (Gen. 4:1);[40] and when he grows older, he becomes a "tiller of the ground." In his rendition of this narrative, Josephus picks up the etymological play on קנה/קין but significantly alters the connotation of the name by taking it out of the context of Eve's joyous words. Instead Josephus states: "The first was called Cain, whose name being interpreted means 'acquisition'" (*A* I, 52). Immediately thereafter, Josephus, like the Genesis text, describes the different pursuits of the brothers, but for Josephus, occupation reflects personality. Abel has "respect for justice," pays "heed to virtue," and leads "the life of a shepherd." Cain, on the other hand, is "thoroughly depraved," has "an eye only to gain" (a second play on his name), and is "the first to think of ploughing the soil" (*A* I, 53).

Having thus set forth the contrasting character types, Josephus describes their respective offerings: "milk and the firstlings of his flocks" from Abel and "fruits of the tilled earth and of the trees" from Cain.[41] A final play on קנה connects Cain's name to his offering and, in contrast to Genesis, clearly explains the basis of God's rejection of the older son: "God . . . is honored by things that grow spontaneously and in accordance with natural law and not by the products forced from nature by the ingenuity of grasping man" (*A* I, 54). Thus prepared, we come with a Cain oddly flawed by his given name to the scene of the fratricide.

Luther's Cain is christologically portrayed and reflects none of this. At his birth, his mother rejoices in her acquisition of a son who she believes is the savior spoken of in God's promise of a Christ.[42] Cain's defect lies not in a tragic nominal flaw, but in his parent's indulgence of him as the first born. Like Haran, Ishmael, Esau, *and* the nation of Israel, Cain abuses the gift of primogeniture and becomes overly proud and confident of his place as the first born.[43] It is for reasons of self-conceit and lack of faith that Cain and his offering are rejected, not for any fault in the material of the offering.

For Luther the issue is the old one of faith and works. In his "Lectures on Genesis" he associates the interpretation of the rejection of Cain as a rejection of a poor offering with the Jewish "folly" of stressing works (I, 251).[44] And when he confronts Josephus' portrait of Cain, he deals with it only in terms of that "works" fallacy: "what Josephus thought up about the poor fruits that Cain offered is nonsense" ("Lectures on the First Epistle of St. John," XXX, 94).

The attack is skimpy and poor. It reflects little sense of Josephus' flawed Cain. Luther's interest in making his theological point distorts his reading of Josephus, and he reduces the portrait of Cain to the Jewish folly. In dealing with Abraham, however, Luther directly confronts Josephus' Hellenized portrait.

Josephus presents Abraham in the garb of a natural philosopher and statesman.[45] The revolutionary "discovery" of God in Chaldea is the product of his observation of the irregularities of natural phenomena. "Determined to reform and change the ideas universally current concerning God" (*A* I, 155), he comes into direct conflict with the idolatrous Chaldeans and consequently emigrates to Canaan.[46] The subsequent migration to Egypt is attributed not only to the famine in Canaan but also to an elaborately described desire to study theology with Egyptian priests. Intellectual curiosity and philosophic objectivity motivate the first patriarch who, "if he found their doctrine more excellent than his own," would "conform to it."[47] Once in Egypt, he moderates quarrels between rival schools of thought and, through his gift of persuasion, convinces the Egyptians of the truth of his own position. Ultimately gaining their confidence and admiration, he introduces them to knowledge of arithmetic and astronomy.

Luther's portrait contrasts in every respect with that of Josephus. In place of the revolutionary philosopher, he sets a "captive slave" of Satan, an idolator in Chaldea. Totally unworthy of praise, the Chaldean Abraham is simply the human clay which the power of God forms into a "new human being" who is then ready to submit to the first command ("Lectures on Genesis," II, 247).

When he comes to the migration to Egypt, Luther follows the biblical stress on famine, but adds two aspects to the narrative. He describes the famine and exile as tests of faith,[48] and he transfers to the Canaan context the native hostility Josephus had cited as a reason for the departure from Babylon. In Egypt, Luther has Abraham doing what Luther himself would have done, preaching the Word of God. It is in this context that he takes issue with the Abraham of Josephus: "The Jews prattle that while Sarah was living at court Abraham taught the Egyptians astronomy: and Josephus goes to great lengths to show that the Jews surpassed all the other nations in their knowledge of the mathematical sciences and governmental affairs" ("Lectures on Genesis," II, 305).[49] The historian's error is not a matter of inaccurate information. Abraham "did not neglect the study of nature"; like all "eminent" men, he contemplated "the outstanding works of God" (II, 306). But, in his emphasis on Abraham's intellect, as opposed to his spiritual gift, Josephus, according to Luther, loses sight of the real significance of the patriarch. It is to present a model of faith, a "missionary of the Word," that Moses recorded the story of the patriarch in Egypt; and "whether Abraham instructed the Egyptians concerning these sciences or whether . . . he himself learned these matters from the Egyptians, is of no importance" (II, 305).

The ultimate clash between the historian and the theologian comes in their portraits of Saul whom each presents in exaggerated archetype.[50] Developed biographically and in historical context, the Josephan Saul is a "grand, heroic, and tragic figure" who embodies all the classical Hellenistic virtues.[51] Biblical narratives that portray him otherwise are interpreted so as to moderate, if not explain away, the monarch's behavior. Saul's extreme jealousy of David hence is described as the effect of medical and psychological disorders (A VI, 166, 250, 258). His disobedience of the command to kill the king of Amalek is motivated by human compassion as well as the "beauty of his enemy" (A VI, 138, 144). The murder of the priests of Nob brings Josephus to the flaw that dooms his hero. Saul becomes the "signal example" (VI, 268) of the transformation of character effected by the acquisition of power. As long as men "are of private and humble station," they are "kindly and moderate," piously aware that God "is present in all that happens in life." But when power is attained, these wonderful virtues are replaced by "audacity, recklessness," and "contempt for things human and divine" (A VI, 262–266).

The notion of man's predilection for vainglorious self-esteem and the statement that God "is present in all that happens in life" could as well appear in Luther's writings. But they would never appear in the context of a portrait of Saul. Much as Josephus' Saul embodies the cardinal virtues, for Luther, Saul is the embodiment of every cardinal sin. Luther did not lecture directly on the text of I Samuel; and hence, his remarks on Saul do not appear in a biographical, historical context. Instead, scattered throughout all his writings are references to Saul as the model for every form of spiritual vice: arrogant self-love, false humility, diabolical cunning, work righteousness, and feigned repentance. There is barely a biblical villain to whom Saul is not compared at one time or another. In sending David to fight the Philistines, he is likened to Judah advising his brothers not to kill Joseph and to the Jews who would not enter the praetorium in fear that they be regarded as authors of unjust murder ("Lectures on Genesis," VI, 385). His court is as corrupt as that of Ahab and Jezebel ("Lectures on Psalms," XIII, 183), and his counsel as bad as that of Ahithophel against David and the Jews against Christ ("Lectures on Psalms," X, 28). Like Adam and Eve, the Jews, the pope, and the Turks, he arrogantly sets up his own standards of righteousness and excuses himself when he sins ("Lectures on Psalms," X, 31; "Lectures on the Gospel of St. John," XXII, 405). His repentance is always false and superficial, for like Esau, Laban, and Pharaoh, he is really concerned only with personal disgrace and a bad reputation ("Lectures on Genesis," III, 39; V, 152; VI, 42–43; "Catholic Epistles," XXX, 231; and "Whether Soldiers Too Can Be Saved," XLVI, 131). In spite of his obsession with sacrifices, Saul, like Judas and the "work righteous Jews," stands permanently outside of grace ("Lectures on Zechariah," XX, 137; "Lectures on Romans," XXV, 408; and "Brief Confession Concerning the Holy Sacrament," XXXVIII, 312).

In these multiple allusions to Saul as the personification of sinfulness, Luther refers twice to Josephus' portrait—once indirectly and once directly. The indirect reference appears in a discussion of the importance of obedience without question or argument. In contrast to Abraham, Saul questions God's command when his "reason is offended by its senselessness, and he supposes that it can be dispensed with on the ground that mercy is more pleasing to God than tyranny" ("Lectures on Genesis," III, 172). In a later direct attack upon Josephus for his portrayal of a Saul moved by compassion, Luther makes it clear that he is quite aware of the apologetic goal behind the historian's treatment: "Josephus, who in other respects was a great man, in his zeal for his nation, nevertheless, tells the most disgraceful lies in his histories contrary to Holy Scripture, as, for example, when he makes a hero and a holy man out of Saul" ("Lectures on Genesis," VI, 213).

It is not surprising that in Luther's portraits of biblical characters he turns to Josephus only for negative contrasts.[52] Each portrait reflects its writer's approach to the Hebrew Scriptures. For Josephus this involves setting characters in a "Greek light." For Luther, the perspective must reflect his Christian theology. To a certain extent each must rework the biblical text. Josephus, the Hellenized Jew, must work through the theology inherent in the biblical narrative, and reconstruct it so as to paint a picture attractive to his Roman readers. And Luther, given his attitude toward Hebrew Scriptures as history, must adopt a historian's stance only to reinterpret that history then from his own theological viewpoint.

The surprising element in Luther's use of Josephus lies not in his attacks on Josephus' approach, but in the fact that in every case those attacks are distinguished in quality and tone from the aspersions Luther is so quick to cast upon Jewish interpretations of the Scriptures.[53] Luther does acknowledge the Jewishness of the historian; but he never makes it the focal point of his attack, as he does repeatedly with Lyra's "Rabbi Solomon." To Luther, Josephus always remains the historian, who at worst may err in judgment. He is never the Jew whose faithlessness negates even the possibility of such judgment.

Notes

1. In their notes the editors of the Fortress/Concordia English edition of Luther's *Works* suggest many areas where Luther's comments are supported by Josephus.

2. For the popularity of Josephus, see Peter Burke, "A Survey of the Popularity of Ancient Historians (1450–1700)," *H&T* V (1966), 135–152.

3. See Eva Sanford, "Propaganda and Censorship in the Transmission of Josephus," *TAPA* LXVI (1935), 127–145.

4. In regard to one of Josephus' word analyses, H. St. J. Thackeray, editor of the Loeb edition of *Antiquities*, notes, "Josephus is weak in philology, and it is idle to discuss his text and meaning" (Josephus, *The Jewish Antiquities*, tr. H. St. J. Thackeray, Loeb Classical Library [Cambridge, Mass., 1934] I, 258). All citations of Josephus, hereafter inserted directly into the text, are from the Loeb edition.

On Luther's limited knowledge of Hebrew, see Louis I. Newman, *Jewish Influences On Christian Reform Movements* (New York, 1925) and Jerome Friedman, *The Most Ancient Testimony: Sixteenth Century Christian Hebraica in the Age of Nostalgia* (Athens, Ohio, 1983). Luther was ambivalent about the usefulness of Hebrew as an exegetical tool. While he very frequently approached textual questions from the perspective of the linguistic analysis of Hebrew words, he complained that Hebrew grammar obscured and corrupted the true meaning of the text. He theoretically resolved the issue by insisting that knowledge of Hebrew was beneficial to exegesis of Hebrew Scriptures only when the New Testament intervened as a spiritual mediator. See Martin Luther, *Works*, gen. eds., Helmut T. Lehman and Jaroslav Pelikan (Philadelphia and St. Louis, 1955–1972), IV, 351; VII, 216, 285; VIII, 141–142 for expressions of this attitude. All citations from Luther, hereafter directly inserted into the text, are from this edition.

5. It is in this context that Thackeray makes the deprecatory comment cited in note 4.

6. A play on the name "Esau" through the Hebrew root עשׂה.

7. In midrashic literature the association of Seir, "the hairy one," with Esau occurs elsewhere only in *Midrash HaGadol* I, 395–396.

8. Admittedly, this is done in different contexts; Josephus in relation to Edom; Luther, in relation to Seir. The use of Josephus here might well be through secondary sources.

9. For extensive studies of Luther's exegetical technique and concept of history in Scripture, see Heinrich Bornkamm, *Luther and the Old Testament* (Philadelphia, 1969); Jaroslav Pelikan, *Luther the Expositor* (St. Louis, 1959); James Samuel Preus, *From Shadow to Promise* (Cambridge, Mass., 1969); and especially John A. Headley, *Luther's View of Church History* (New Haven and London, 1963).

10. On the development of Luther's notion of "faithful synagogue," see Preus, *op. cit.*

11. See Bornkamm, *op. cit.*, 254.

12. "Lectures on Genesis," VI, 125. See also I, 19; VI, 134; X, 4; XVI, 136–137.

13. "Notes on Ecclesiastes," XV, 71. See Headley *op. cit.*, 2–19.

14. "Whether Soldiers Too Can Be Saved," XLVI, 124; and "Lectures On Psalms," XIII, 199.

15. He particularly mentions Herodotus, Varro, Livy, and Suetonius. For examples, see "Lectures on Genesis," I, 280, 345; VI, 106, 157, 244, 261, 331; VII, 39ff., 65; and "Lectures on Deuteronomy," IX, 195–196. Luther's praise for the historian's craft is in "Preface to Galeatius Capella's History," XXXIV, 276.

16. "To the Councilmen of All the Cities of Germany that They Establish and Maintain Christian Schools," XLV, 370, 378.

17. It is probable that Luther took the detail that Abraham had built an altar on Mount Moriah from Josephus (*A* I, 224). In Josephus the issue of the Samaritan temple is connected with the relationship between the Jews and the Greeks in the person of Alexander. See Shaye J. D. Cohen, "Alexander the Great and Jaddus the High Priest According to Josephus," *AJSR* VII–VIII (1982–1983), 41–68.

18. The reference to Jerome is to "Liber de nominibus Hebraicis," *PL* XXIII, 885–886. I have been unable to find the description Luther attributes to Josephus.

19. Josephus' comments on the origins of Babylon are presented in the context of a citation from the Chaldean historian Berosus, who censured the Greek historians for "their deluded belief that Babylon was founded by the Assyrian Semiramis." He goes on to explain that Nebuchadnezzar built the elaborate gardens "because his wife . . . had a passion for mountain surroundings" (*Ap* I, 139–141). Luther mentions both the Greek attribution to Queen Semiramis and the matter of Nebuchadnezzar's wife.

20. Josephus (*A* XX, 25) does, to be sure, mention that the remains of Noah's ark are to be seen in his own day; but he gives the locale as Carron, which is apparently not in Armenia but in Babylonia.

21. Josephus mentions Herod's Temple in both the *War* and the *Antiquities*. In the former he describes the enlargement of the building to "a magnificence never surpassed" (I, 401). In the latter he puts an elaborate speech into Herod's mouth in which the monarch explains that due to the "necessity and subjection of that earlier time," the temple of Haggai lacked the height of Solomon's Temple. The new building would rectify that lack as an "act of piety," a means of thanking "God for this kingdom" (XV, 385).

22. The passage in *Antiquities* does not exemplify the more critical portrait that Shaye Cohen sees reflected in Josephus' later work. See Shaye J. D. Cohen, *Josephus in Galilee and Rome* (Leiden, 1979), 234ff.

23. See Luther's comments on his sources and the editorial notes in XVI, 269; XLVII, 130.

24. For discussion of the Midrashim on the identification of the rivers, see Louis Ginzberg, *The Legends of the Jews* (Philadelphia, 1968), V, 91–92; Thomas W. Franxman, *Genesis and the Jewish Antiquities of Flavius Josephus* (Rome, 1979), 52–53; and Salomo Rappaport, *Agada und Exegese bei Flavius Josephus* (Vienna, 1930), 77–78.

25. Nicolas de Lyra, *Biblia sacra cum glossis, interlineari, et Ordinaria, Nicolai Lyrani postilla, ac moralitatibus, Burgensis, additionibus, & Thoringi Replices etc.* (Venice, 1588), I, Genesis 2:12, section 1.

26. See Lyra on Genesis 34:1.

27. The other known source for the story is the Book of Jubilees (31:2). It was not available to Luther in the sixteenth century, but possibly could have been cited in an earlier source.

28. "See the histories of the Maccabees and Josephus" ("Lectures on Zechariah," XX, 90).

29. In Josephus, *A* XII, 1–11, 129ff.

30. Luther repeats the same prophecy, again citing Josephus in XX, 87.

31. *A* XI, 136–137 mentions gifts sent by King Cyrus and later by Alexander the Great. In *A* XII, 40 he mentions the gifts sent to the high priest of the Temple in Jerusalem by Ptolemy Philadelphus on the occasion of the latter's proposal that the Pentateuch be translated into Greek (the Septuagint).

32. See also XX, 119–120. The description of Herod's oppressive reign could come from *A* XVII, 304–314 or from *BJ* II, 84–89. The sectarian emphasis could involve an anti-Pharisaic interpretation of material from *BJ* II, 111–168 and *A* XVII, 339; XVIII, 14.

33. The reference is to *BJ* V, 514–515, 518–519.

34. See *BJ* VI, 420.

35. Bornkamm, *op. cit.*, 28–29. On Josephus' self-image as a prophet see Joseph Blenkensopp, "Prophecy and Priesthood in Josephus," *JJS* XXV (1974), 239–262.

36. "Read Josephus and the history books and you will learn that the Romans slew many thousands of Jews a long time before, and that there was no peace up to the time when they were constrained to destroy Jerusalem and the country" ("On the Jews and Their Lies," XLVII, 251).

37. Luther notes that Josephus had criticized the historian Polybius for saying that Antiochus was punished by God for wanting to destroy Jerusalem. In fact, Josephus took issue with Polybius' statement that Antiochus had died because he intended to plunder the Temple of Diana. See *A*, XII, 358.

38. "Philo, having thus been treated with contumely, left the room, saying to the Jews who accompanied him that they should be of good courage, for Gaius' wrath was a matter of words, but in fact he was not enlisting God against himself" (*A* XVIII, 260).

39. For example, note their differences in regard to Herod, cited previously in this essay. See also their differences in regard to Pompey, "Lectures on Habakuk," XIX, 206, as compared to *A*, XIV, 71–72.

40. The name Cain is a play on קניתי in the sentence: ותאמר קניתי איש את ה'.

41. In Genesis, Abel's offering is described as "the firstlings of his flock and the fat thereof." Josephus reads "milk" instead of "fat" for חלב. Cain's offering in Genesis is "of the fruit of the ground."

42. According to Luther, after the Fall Adam and Eve became model Christians who properly understood Genesis 3:15 as a christological promise. Hence, Luther plays on the verb קנה to mean "acquiring salvation."

43. Unlike Josephus, Luther considers the occupation of Cain higher than that of Abel. The former followed in the footsteps of his father as a farmer, an occupation which Luther associates with government. See "Lectures on Genesis," I, 346.

44. The association may well have been reinforced by Lyra's paraphrase of Rashi on Genesis 4:3.

45. Rabbinic aggada also embellishes the biblical picture of Abraham. For extensive comparisons between the rabbinic approach and that of Josephus, see Louis H. Feldman, "Abraham the Greek Philosopher," *TAPA* XCIX (1968), 143–156. For pseudepigraphal and other Hellenistic portraits, see Samuel Sandmel, *Philo's Place in Judaism: A Study of Conceptions of Abraham in Jewish Literature* (Cincinnati, 1956).

46. The motive is original with Josephus. See Franxman, *op. cit.*, 143.

47. *A* I, 161.

48. Rashi, citing *Pirke d'Rabbi Eliezer* (26), makes the same comment.

49. Lyra (Genesis 12:16, section h) cites Josephus as his source for the information that Abraham taught astronomy to the Egyptians.

50. Louis Feldman points out that Josephus devotes three times as many lines to his encomium of Saul as to that of Moses ("Josephus' Portrait of Saul," *HUCA* LIII (1982), 52. Luther refers to Saul's evil character more than sixty times in his various writings.

51. *Ibid.*, 56.

52. It is theoretically possible that Luther used Josephus for part of his description of the Akedah scene. He, like Josephus, gives Isaac's age as twenty-five (instead of the traditional thirty-seven). He also uses the Greek historiographical technique of inserting fictitious speeches into the mouths of the main characters. See "Lectures on Genesis," IV, 111–113. Luther also shares with Josephus an unscriptural stress on Joseph's concern for the welfare of Benjamin and Jacob. See "Lectures on Genesis," VII, 99, 225, 230, 236, 241, 257, 263–264, 358, and *A* II, 88, 124.

53. In "Lectures on Genesis" alone, he fulminates against Jewish exegesis and exegetics on more than forty occasions. He uses such adjectives as "worthless and silly," "obscure and corrupt," "carnal and bloodthirsty," and "perverse and pernicious." On Luther and Jewish exegetics, see A. Agee, "Luther and the Rabbis," *JQR* LVIII (1976–1978), 63–68.

Index of References to Josephus

Antiquitates Judaicae

V.548: 209n
VI.7: 209n
VI.37: 244
VI.47: 238, 241
VI.63: 245
VI.176: 244
VI.186–87: 102
VI.187: 113n
VI.199: 332
VI.201–13: 324n
VI.220ff.: 231
VI.250: 244
VI.252: 242
VI.267: 243
VI.267–70: 418
VI.268: 244
VI.283–87: 230
VI.285: 226, 227, 250, 251
VI.285f.: 230
VI.286: 227
VI.287f.: 228
VI.288: 222, 227, 231
VI.288–310: 246, 255n
VI.289: 47
VI.290: 232
VI.290–95: 419
VI.291: 231–32
VI.292–93: 232
VI.298–99: 232
VI.299–300: 232, 242, 330, 333
VI.300–306: 233
VI.300–309: 231
VI.303: 247
VI.309: 233
VI.311: 247
VI.312: 247
VI.314: 248
VI.356: 51
VI.399: 244
VI.420: 640
VI.425–28: 318
VI.433–34: 86
VI.438: 243
VII.1: 24
VII.32–34: 104
VII.72: 238
VII.89: 112
VII.98: 209n
VII.108f.: 241, 249
VII.185: 240

VII.203: 244
VII.260–64: 87
VII.262: 28, 95, 103
VII.262–74: 54
VII.271: 55
VII.318: 242
VI.320: 103
VI.321: 105
VII.323: 98
VII.327: 103
VII.330: 98
VII.331f.: 242
VII.332–33: 104
VII.337: 105
VII.337–40: 98
VII.342: 106
VII.343–44: 98
VII.346: 239
VII.351–57: 27, 250
VII.355: 27
VII.387: 98, 111n
VI.389: 98, 102
VII.390: 102
VII.393: 104, 105
VII.397: 103, 105
VII.405: 27, 105
VII.406: 28, 105
VII.418: 98
VII.419: 113n
VII.437: 95
VII.437f.: 226, 251
VII.440: 230
VII.451–53: 104
XI.23: 232

Contra Apionem
I.2–3: 195
I.12: 136
I.31: 38
I.35: 176n
I.45–46: 94n
I.48: 186
I.50: 135
I.54: 134, 198, 199
I.163–65: 249
I.167: 133
I.179: 250
I.200–204: 42
I.201–4: 246

Vita

Index

Abbahu, Rabbi, 48
Abraham, 34, 36, 157, 158, 159, 160; and
charge of misanthropy, 142–43; defense of deceits by, 144–45; descendants of, 147–48, 163, 178n; and
diminished role of God, 145; hospitality of, 140–41; as ideal statesman,
138–39, 420–21; science of, 139;
Luther on, 421; as man of faith, 146,
160–61; and marriage of Isaac,
161–62; as merciful figure, 142; military role of, 139–40; as national hero,
137–38; noble birth of, 138; as Stoic
ideal, 30–32; treatment of Pharaoh,
142, 148–49
Adam and Eve, in illustrated manuscripts,
406
Adiabene, conversion of House of: acceptance of Torah in, 304; circumcision
in, 301–2, 303, 304–5; dwelling in
sukkah and, 298–99; immersion in,
305; Josephus' interest in, 51–52,
307–8; Josephus' sources on, 294–
95, 306; literary analysis of Josephus'
episode on, 295–98; motivation for,
53, 307; sacrificial offering in, 305–6;
in Tannaitic sources, 52–53,
298–300, 306; and theme of righteousness, 296, 299, 300
Africanus, Sextus Julius, 365, 366
Against Apion. See Contra Apionem
Agapius (Mahoub of Menbid), 58, 340

Agrippa I, 30, 118, 120, 247; memorandum
of and to Gaius, 122–23, 125–26
Agrippa II, 26, 75–76, 81, 83, 89, 90, 92,
240
Akiva, Rabbi, 48
Alexander Polyhistor, 136, 140, 148, 153n,
180
Alexander the Great, 262
Alexandra Salome, Queen. *See* Salome Al-
exandra, Queen
Alexandria: embassy to Caligula from,
116, 118–19; Jewish community or-
ganization in, 117; Jewish rights in,
116–17, 118–19; Josephus in, 29;
riots against Jews in, 115, 116,
117–18
Alvarus of Cordova, 359
Amaru, Betsy Halpern, 63, 64, 65
Ambrose of Milan, 350, 354
Ambrosianus, 350
Amram, dream of, 35
Ananias, 302, 303, 305
Ananus, 56, 105, 110
Angels: departure of from Temple, 332; ref-
erences in Josephus to, 240
Antiochus, King of Commagene, 74
Antiochus Epiphanes, 265, 355, 425n
Antipater, 247, 249, 253, 277
Antiquitates Judaicae (Josephus), 25, 29,
77, 102, 116, 120, 135, 136, 151,
176n, 182, 226, 274–75, 315, 392;
cited by Origen, 329, 331, 335; illus-

trated manuscripts of, 403, 404, 407; Jewish law in, 198–207; Pharisees in, 49–50, 274, 280–89, 290; Samaritans in, 258–63, 265–68, 270. *See also* Adiabene, conversion of House of; Biblical narratives; Matriarchs (biblical); *Testimonium Flavianum*

Anti-Semitism: and Alexandrian riots, 117–18; ass worship slander in, 188–89, 196n; atheism slander in, 192–93; dietary law slanders in, 191; in early Church, 24, 53–54, 58–59, 318, 319–20, 354; Egyptian origins slander in, 182; human sacrifice slander in, 140, 144; leprosy slander in, 183–84, 186, 190–91; misanthropy slander in, 140, 143, 193–94, 308; refutation by Josephus of, 31, 32–33, 35, 137, 139, 140–41, 142–43, 144–45, 149, 181–82, 183–84, 185, 188–89, 191–95, 308, 325–26

Apion, 37, 118, 137, 140, 149, 181, 182, 183, 188, 192, 194

Apocrypha, 386, 392

Apollodorus, 36

Apollonius Molon, 138, 139, 180, 183, 192, 194

Apollonius of Tyana, 221

Appian, 109

Apuleius, 47

Archelaus, 50

Aristides, Aelius, 76

Aristobulus, son of Salome Alexandra, 277, 278, 287–88, 291

Aristophanes, 209n

Aristotle, 250

Artabanus, King of Parthia, 296

Artapanus, 34, 35, 36, 44, 139, 196n

Ass worship slander, 188–89, 196n

Astrology, 47

Attridge, Harold W., 137, 179n

Augustine, 57

Augustus, Emperor, 125

Babylon, gardens of, 415

Baer, Yitzhak F., 209n

Bailey, James, 32

Bammel, E., 340, 347n

Bannus, 275, 281

Baras, Zvi, 55

Bar Kochba rebellion, 54

Barnett, P. W., 317

Basil I, 383n

Bede, Venerable, 318

Bell, Albert A., 58, 347

Bellum Judaicum (Josephus), 24, 72–78, 102, 120, 169, 176n, 226, 274–75, 315, 330, 332, 392; adaptation by pseudo-Hegesippus, 352–53, 355–58; cited by Origen, 330, 332; date of, 72; illustrated manuscripts of, 401–2, 403, 404, 407, 408; influence on Christianity, 54, 317, 319, 321; Josephus' reliability in, 24; Latin translation of, 349; mistranslations of, 105; Pharisees in, 277–80, 289, 291; Roman sources for, 71–72; Samaritans in, 258, 268–71; suicide themes in, 102–4. *See also* Jewish War; Masada narrative

Berenice, 99

Berossus, 136, 415

Betz, Otto, 43, 44

Biblical narratives in Josephus, 398–99; alterations and modifications of, 35–37, 133–35, 136–50, 157–68, 170–75, 182–90; descriptive geography in, 31; diminished role of God in, 145–46; God's providence in, 44–45; and Greek sources, 136; Hellenized portraits in, 30–34, 136–37, 150, 155, 168–69; historical approach to, 43, 150; human dimension in, 34; Jewish law in, 198–207; for Jewish and non-Jewish audience, 134–35, 136, 168–69; refutation of anti-Semitism in, 31, 33, 34–35, 137, 139, 140, 142–43, 144, 149, 181–82, 183, 185–86, 188–89, 190–95; romantic motifs in, 34, 148–50, 166–67, 169–70. *See also* Matriarchs (biblical); Miracles; Signs; *specific names*

Bickerman, E. J., 277

Bietenhard, H., 327

Bilde, Per, 56, 321n

Birdsall, J. Neville, 56

Blasphemy, Jewish law on, 192–93

Herod (*cont.*)
Pharisees, 288–89, 291; temple of,
424n
Herodotus, 36, 43, 62, 108, 142
Hicks, R. D., 377, 380n
Hillel, 282–83
Historia Ecclesiastica (Eusebius). *See History of the Church* (Eusebius)
Historiae libri v. (Pseudo-Hegesippus), 350
History of the Church (Eusebius), 57, 58, 327
Holladay, Carl H., 137
Homer, 135–36
Honi (Onias), 220
Human sacrifice slander, 140, 144
Hypothetica (Philo), 29
Hyrcanus, John, 50, 52, 246, 266, 267, 287; and Pharisees, 277, 283–86

Illustrated manuscripts of Josephus: author's portrait in, 400, 404–5; chronology of, 399–403; Herod in, 62, 408; heroes' portraits in, 407–8; Jesus in, 407; marriage of Adam and Eve in, 406; monogram form in, 405–6; narrative scenes in, 63, 408–9
Immersion, as requirement for conversion, 305
In Flaccum (Philo), 114, 116, 117–18
Iphigenia in Aulis (Euripides), 144, 146
Isaac: birth of, 160; birth of progeny to, 163; sacrifice of, 146–47, 160–61; search for wife for, 149–50, 161–62
Isaac the Jew, 351
Isaiah, 239
Isbili, Yom Tob, 207
Ishmael (son of Abraham), 143, 160
Ishmael, Rabbi, 48
Isidor of Pelusium, 318
Isocrates, 139
Izates, 51, 52; conversion of, 295–96, 301–2, 303; political history of, 297; as righteous king, 296

Jacob, 34, 416; agreement with Laban, 165–66, 169; competition between wives of, 167, 168; and Esau, 63, 163–64; return to Hebron, 168
Jacobs, I., 111n
James the Just (brother of Jesus), martyr-

dom of, 55, 56, 316; Eusebius on, 345–46; Josephus on, 341, 343, 344; Origen on, 329, 335, 339, 341–44
Jannaeus, Alexander, 277–78, 383, 290
Jehoiada, 48–49
Jehoshaphat, heroic portrait of, 408
Jericho: fall of walls of, 229; purification of well at, 221, 253–54
Jerome, 58, 59, 134, 318–19, 340, 351, 352, 360n, 391, 415
Jerusalem: fall of, 320, 329, 332, 343, 358 (*see also* Temple, destruction of); House of Adiabene in, 296, 299, 306; Pilate in, 126–27; siege of, 331–32, 345–46, 353–54, 358, 408, 418
Jesus, 26, 47, 207n, 222, 227, 316, 335, 395; destruction of Temple as retribution for death of, 53, 55, 59, 64–65, 318, 319–20, 336, 341–46, 354; in illustrated manuscripts, 407; in Slavonic Josephus, 61; testimony of Josephus about (*see Testimonium Flavianum*)
Jesus son of Ananus, 232–33
Jewish Antiquities. See Antiquitates Judaicae
Jewish law in Josephus: on blasphemy, 192–93; on conversion, 52 (*see also* Adiabene, conversion of House of); dietary laws, 191–92; on hating evil and evildoers, 205–6; Josephus' disagreement with, 38–40; Josephus' knowledge of, 199; on quarrels with resulting injury, 200–203; reasons for inclusion of, 40; reformulation of, 40–42; survey of, 37–39; on withholding wages, 203–5, 206–7
Jewish War: Adiabenians in, 51–52, 307–8; fall of Jerusalem in, 320, 329, 332, 343, 358; false prophets in, 227; Justus of Tiberias on, 82–85; lack of God's intervention and, 218; revolt of Tiberias in, 85–86, 88–91; role of Titus in, 72–73, 74; role of Vespasian in, 73–74, 357; siege of Jerusalem in, 353, 408, 418; siege of Jotapata in, 82, 102, 242, 269, 356–57, 372. *See also* Masada narrative; Rome; Temple, destruction of
Jewish War, The. See Bellum Judaicum

Sadducees, 49–50, 276, 279, 280, 282–83, 284, 290
Sallust, 352
Salome Alexandra, Queen, 32, 50, 277–78, 280, 286–88, 290
Samaritans: defined, 258; designated Sidonians, 266; diaspora community of, 263–65; false prophet of, 48, 229–30, 251, 316; and Hyrcanus, 267; and Jewish community, 261, 263, 268, 271; Josephus' attitude toward, 47–49, 260, 262, 263–64, 268, 269–70, 271–72; Josephus' sources on, 259, 263; links with Judaism, 47–48, 265, 270; and Persians, 49, 261; in rebellion against Antiochus Epiphanes, 265; and rebuilding of Temple, 260–61; religious character of, 257–58; and resistance to Roman rule, 267–69; schism of, 260, 271; temple on Mount Gerizim of, 262, 264, 265, 266, 424n
Samson, 33, 43
Sanders, E. P., 270
Sarah, 157, 169; alteration of biblical details on, 170–71; beauty of, 157–58; death of, 161; and divine messengers, 160; favorable features of, 172; and Hagar, 159, 160; Pharaoh's passion for, 32–33, 34, 142, 148–49, 158, 169–70, 178n. See also Matriarchs (biblical)
Satan, 255n
Saul, 65, 421–23
Schalit, A., 87, 88–89, 205n, 294, 307, 308n, 309n
Schäublin, C., 324n
Schiffman, Lawrence, 51
Schreckenberg, Heinz, 53–54, 151n, 274, 368, 371
Schürer, E., 300
Schwartz, Daniel, 29, 51
Schwartz, Seth, 28
Sejanus, 127
Selecta et fragmenta in Ieremiam (Origen), 329, 331
Seneca, 97, 102, 195, 351
Septuagint, 30, 46, 58, 97, 133, 134, 223, 254, 332, 380n

Severus, Sulpicius, 73
Sicarii, 48, 95; characterized, 28, 96, 105, 106; suicide of, 28, 97–98, 100, 103–4, 105, 109–10
Signs: characteristics of, 224; in claims of false prophets, 226–27, 228–30, 250–51; vs epiphany, 223–24; faith in, 225; of freedom, 227–28; to Moses, 223–24; as portents, 231–33, 246
Silva, Flavius, 28
Simeon ben Gamaliel, 48, 50, 86, 276, 291
Simeon ben Shetah, 285
Simocatta, Theophylact, 380n
Slaves, law on killing, 201
Slavonic Josephus, 61, 372–73
Smallwood, E. Mary, 28–29
Smith, Morton, 45, 47, 274, 275, 289–91
Socrates, 27, 97, 98
Solomon, 44, 47, 220, 241, 253
Sophocles, 32, 136, 138, 149, 151, 153n
Stern, Menahem, 24, 180
Stoicism, 30–32, 44, 96, 99, 100, 101, 102, 138–39, 141, 147
Strabo, 62, 66n, 136, 180, 196n
Strobel, A., 322n
Suetonius, 99, 124, 383n
Suicide: amor mortis in, 103, 109, 113n; collective, 107–9; patterns of reporting in Josephus, 102–4; in Plato's Phaedo, 97–98, 100; retributive, 104, 110; of Sicarii, 28, 97–98, 100, 103–4, 105, 109–10; Stoic approval of, 96, 100, 102
Sukkah (festival booth), 298–99
Sutcliffe, E. F., 205
Sybilline Oracles, 381n

Tacitus, 30, 31, 52, 63, 73, 76, 77, 181, 191, 195, 231, 324n, 356, 358, 383n, 419
Talmud, 25, 28, 44, 45, 57, 76–77, 387. See also Jewish law in Josephus
Täubler, E., 308–9n
Temple: contribution of Adiabene to, 296, 299, 300, 304; described by Josephus, 42; Gaius's attack on, 30, 115, 120–65; in illustrated manuscripts, 403; rebuilding of, 261–62, 350, 408;

Temple (*cont.*)
supernatural power of the Place of,
242–43; tax for, 125
Temple, destruction of: cosmic speculation
of, 244; demonic impulse in setting
fire to, 242; Origen on, 329, 332–33,
341–43; portents of, 231–33, 246,
332–33, 419; prophecy of, 216, 218,
227, 247; reliability of Josephus on,
24–25; as retribution, 53, 55, 59, 65,
318, 319–21, 329, 332, 335–36,
341–46, 354, 358; role of Titus in,
72–73
Ten Commandments, 188
Testimonium Flavianum, 24, 53, 54, 61,
63, 65, 215, 321–22n, 334, 371,
373, 405; alterations to, 340–41, 346;
Arabic version of, 58, 340; authenticity of, 55–57, 252, 339–41, 348n;
influence on Christianity, 338–39,
363; Josephus' motive in, 58, 252;
Vulgate version of, 338, 340
Thackeray, Henry St. John, 28, 104–5,
136, 151n, 177n, 201, 379n,
423n
Thallus, 180
Theon, 137
Theudas, 228, 251, 316
Thucydides, 43, 136, 138, 150, 151n,
153n
Tiberias, revolt of, 85–86, 88–92
Tiberius, 127, 247
Titus, 65, 71, 72, 74, 77, 105, 230–31,
358, 371; and Berenice, 99; and de-
struction of Temple, 72–73; and
Gischala, 73; in illustrated manu-
scripts, 404, 408; merciful attitude of,
77, 100
Toachians, mass suicide of, 108
Trogus, Pompeius. *See* Pompeius Trogus
True Doctrine, The (Celsus), 334
Tyche, 244

Ussani, V., 350, 357

Van Unnik, W. C., 176n, 245
Vardanes, 297
Vespasian, 24, 65, 71, 72, 90, 221,
237–38, 242, 246; attack upon Samaritans by, 269; conspiracies against,
99; divine retribution upon, 104; in illustrated manuscripts, 404, 408; and
overthrow of Antiochus, King of
Commagene, 74; treatment of Jews by,
73–74
Vita (Josephus), 72, 88, 176n, 318; John of
Gischala in, 86; Pharisees in,
275–76, 280; rivalry with Justus of
Tiberias in, 81–82, 85, 91–92, 366

Wages, Jewish law on withholding, 203–5,
206–7
Weil, M., 192
Weitzmann, Kurt, 62
Weyl, Heinrich, 201
Whiston, William, 61
Witch of Endor, 247
Women: in Hellenistic period, 177n;
Josephus' view of, 32, 154, 155–57,
175–76. *See also* Matriarchs (bibli-
cal); *specific names*

Xanthians, mass suicide of, 108, 109
Xanthopoulos, Nikephoros Kallistos, 381n
Xenophon, 108, 138

Yadin, Yigael, 27, 95, 106
Yahweh, 237, 245, 254, 255n
Yavetz, Zvi, 100
Yohanan ben Zakkai, Rabbi, 306

Zealots, 48, 54, 112n, 319, 369
Zechariah, 417–18
Zeitlin, Solomon, 285, 382n
Zonaras, Ionnas, 371